American Premium Guide to

# KNIVES & RAZORS

## Identification and Value Guide, 6th Edition

JIM SARGENT

©2004 Jim Sargent
Published by

kp books
An imprint of F+W Publications, Inc.

700 East State Street • Iola, WI 54990-0001
715-445-2214 • 888-457-2873

Our toll-free number to place an order or obtain
a free catalog is (800) 258-0929.

All rights reserved. No portion of this publication may be reproduced or transmitted in
any form or by any means, electronic or mechanical, including photocopy, recording, or any
information storage and retrieval system, without permission in writing from the publisher,
except by a reviewer who may quote brief passages in a critical article or review to be printed in
a magazine or newspaper, or electronically transmitted on radio, television, or the Internet.

Library of Congress Catalog Number: 2004093885

ISBN: 0-87349-825-9

Designed by Kara Grundman
Edited by Dan Brownell

**Printed in the United States of America**

# The Pocket Knife

Every man needs a good knife,
    not just for himself,
    but also to assist others.
There is no greater value
    for a knife
    than to be carried by a father.
His imprint makes it part of himself,
    the wooden handles soaks oils
    from his hand.
The blades of steel
    will sometimes pierce him,
    and draw his blood.
Placed just out of reach on the dresser,
    with all other items of treasure,
    treasure because they are from his pockets.
Over time, sharing knowledge and experience
    in the gentleman's art
    and appreciation of a good knife.
Thrills of boyhood in a moment's handling,
    dreams of manhood,
    one day it will be mine.

By Stanley F. Smart
1/26/95

# Contents

Preface ............................................................................................................................. 5
Acknowledgments ........................................................................................................... 6
Around the Shows ........................................................................................................... 7
Alliance of Local Knife Clubs ........................................................................................ 11
Introduction ................................................................................................................... 17
    Caring for Your Knives ............................................................................................ 17
    What to Collect ....................................................................................................... 18
    Knives as Investments ............................................................................................ 18
    Finding Pocketknives ............................................................................................. 18
    Condition ................................................................................................................ 18
    Restoration ............................................................................................................. 19
    Counterfeiting ........................................................................................................ 19
General Knife Reference Information ........................................................................... 20
    Handle Materials and Descriptions ....................................................................... 20
    Glossary ................................................................................................................. 21
    Pattern Names ....................................................................................................... 22
    Pocket Knife and Sheath Knife Parts .................................................................... 23
    Blade Styles ........................................................................................................... 24
    Common Abbreviations ......................................................................................... 25
Case Knife History ......................................................................................................... 26
Case Knife Reference Information ................................................................................ 31
    Numbering System ................................................................................................ 31
    Numbers and Letters of Handle Materials ............................................................ 31
    Blade Types ........................................................................................................... 31
    Miscellaneous Abbreviations ................................................................................. 31
    New Grind Blades .................................................................................................. 32
    Trappers ................................................................................................................. 33
    Case Stampings ..................................................................................................... 34
Vintage Case Knives ..................................................................................................... 42
    Case Brothers Cutlery Company (1896-1915) ..................................................... 43
    W. R. Case & Son Cutlery Company (1902-1903) ............................................... 70
    W. R. Case & Son's Cutlery Company (1903-1905) ............................................ 76
    W. R. Case & Sons Cutlery Company (1905-1914) ............................................. 82
    The Bradford Era (1914-1919) ............................................................................. 120
    Case Family (1900-1920) ..................................................................................... 146
    Case Memorabilia and Miscellaneous .................................................................. 157
Case Knives Tested (1920-1971) ................................................................................. 159
Case Price Charts for Stag Sets, Individual Stags, and Miscellaneous ...................... 238
Case Fixed Blade Hunting Knives ................................................................................ 240
Little Valley Knife Association/Crandall Cutlery Company ........................................... 271
The Continuing Hawbaker Saga ................................................................................... 329
Queen / Schatt & Morgan Cutlery ................................................................................. 333
Remington ..................................................................................................................... 417

# Preface

Since the last publication of this guide in 1999, enormous change has taken place. Every aspect of our lives has been impacted by changes that no one could possibly have anticipated in 1999. These include the way we communicate by means of e-mail and cell phone. It includes the way we travel as a result of the tragedy of September 11. In turn, each of these has had an equally enormous impact on the way we pursue our hobby or business of collecting, buying, and selling cutlery.

Another tremendous impact has been the world of cyberspace or the Internet. At any one time, online auction sites list about 50,000 knives. One site, Theo's Favorites, has links to over 3,000 sites of knife collectors, manufacturers, custom makers, museums, clubs, and associations that span every country. This has allowed many more people to take up the hobby. It has allowed individuals to be exposed and to gain exposure to aspects of knife collecting that were just not available five years ago.

In spite of all this change, some things have not changed. This includes the many rare and antique pocketknives that so many of us collect. The prices have certainly changed, and we have found many previously undiscovered patterns and handle materials. The custom makers and cutlery companies have continued to produce more interesting patterns in many new materials. Some have reproduced the past, and I find that refreshing.

This guide has changed in ways we think will assist you in you efforts to collect knives. In considering my approach to this guide, there were several things I wished to bring to the collector. First and foremost was to have the most realistic values available; next was to photograph as many knives as possible and to have them so distinct that the reader could see the smallest details. Last, but certainly not least, was to produce a guide for the novice as well as the expert knife collector.

The reader will also see that an emphasis was placed on older knives such as Case vintage knives, as well as Tested XX through 10 Dot (1970); anything after that usually carries the suggested retail price.

A lot of old knives out there still haven't been discovered or just haven't been brought forward. Hopefully we can encourage the folks who possess those Remington Bullets and other rarities to join us in the camaraderie of knife collecting.

This sixth edition now includes a completely revised section on vintage Case knives. We have included more than 700 new photos of Case pocket and sheath knives. These sections are now in chronological order and pattern number sets up each era. There are also 300 new Queen and Schatt & Morgan photos.

The prices quoted in this book are as accurate as possible in reflecting current market value. Keep in mind that the prices are a guide, not hard fact. Prices will vary depending on many factors including economic trends, collector interests, rarity, location, condition, exceptional handles, cash prices, trades, popularity of patterns and, most importantly, the buyers' willingness to pay the requested price.

Comparisons of knife lists, knife-show prices, dealer inquiries, auction sites, and discussions with numerous collectors were the basis of the prices arrived at in this book. Obviously, prices will vary from those quoted. Dealers will generally pay 60 to 70 percent of the prices quoted when purchasing knives. The older and more rare knives may bring a higher percentage, while the more common or recent production knives may bring a lower percentage. Pricing vintage Case knives is quite subjective and difficult. We have, however, listed prices according to the general formula explained at the beginning of the vintage Case section on page **42**. While a great deal of debate exists among experts regarding vintage knife values, we believe our formula is the most accurate one available and that our prices give the best possible general estimate of the value of these knives.

Every possible effort was made to make this book the most complete and accurate one ever published on pocketknives. It was a true labor of love and as always took more effort than we expected. I appreciate the many letters and conversations that led to the vast new material, patterns, variations, photos, historical notes, and information in this new volume. Most importantly, I appreciate the effort of so many of my fellow collectors.

**Jim Sargent**

# Acknowledgments

I worked very hard on the sixth edition to make it the best one yet. I could not have accomplished this task without the knowledge and expertise of the following people who helped with each phase of the book. No one individual has the capacity or time to be an expert in all the categories listed.

Without the historical value of the companies listed, and the actual photos, the book would be incomplete at best. Without the knowledge of the collectors involved in this endeavor, it would have been hard to gather this much information. To those of you who worked so hard on my behalf, I hope the finished product meets with your approval.

Special thanks to **Bob Wurzelbacher** for the update of the Case family and the photos of his vintage knife collection.

Special thanks to **Brad Wood** and **Tony Clemmons** for allowing us to photograph their Case sheath knife collection and furnishing all the descriptions. Thank you **Joe Raymond** for the color photos of your knife/axe combinations and sheath knives.

Also, the following allowed their collections to be photographed, and we are indebted to them: **G. A. Miller, John Osborne, M. D. Wells, Ralph Scruton,** and **John O'Kain**.

Thanks to **Richard White** for the photos he provided for the color section.

Thanks to **Tony Foster** for his research, expert knowledge of Case cutlery, and for exchanging his thoughts with me. Thanks also to **Jim Parker** for the Case "New Grind" section.

Thanks to **Ralph Scruton** for the update of the Case Hawbaker section.

Special thanks to **Bob Crandall** for the entire section on Crandall knives and razors. That also includes the section on Little Valley Knife Association (LVKA) knives and razors.

Thanks to **Jim Pitblado, Hollis Large, Gail Miller**, and **Bill Wright** for their work on updating the Remington section, with photos from Jim Pitblado, bullet knives from Hollis Large, totem pole color photos from Gail Miller, and sheath knife photos from Bill Wright.

Special thanks to **Fred** and **Linda Fisher, David Clark, Howard Drake, Mike Sullivan,** and **David Krauss**, for a complete revision of the Queen knife section. Thanks to **David Clark** for photos of his Schatt & Morgan knife collection. The seven of us spent two days in Ohio revising this section.

Thanks to **David Krauss** for the short history of Queen Cutlery. Other contributors are **Gerald Witcher** for photos, **Elmer Kirkland** for sheath knife photos, **Joe Chance** for photos, and **Billy Burns** for photos and information on 47 and 75 patterns.

The following also provided photos and we are deeply grateful to them: **J. L. Johnson III, G. A. Miller, Gary Darling, Shelby Lowery, Russ Haehl, M. D. Wells, Jean Sargent, Marlyn Kepner, Dave Fitzgerald, Wayne Robertson, Herbert Aycock, John Petzel, Ron Burton, Mark Nagle, Gurney Davis,** and **Dave Dempsey.**

Thanks to **Mark Zalesky** for providing the listings under the Alliance of Local Knife Clubs.

Special thanks to **Lisa Foster**, (who has been with our company and family for many years), for her hard work in pulling the pictures together for me.

Special thanks to **Jean Sargent** who has traveled every mile with me and assisted in every way needed.

Without the interest and knowledge of the people listed above and the many others involved with the world of cutlery, it would be impossible for any one person to author a book of credibility. A very special thanks to all for their assistance and expertise.

**Jim Sargent**

## We Need Your Help

Should you find a knife you think should be included in our next book, please send a 4" x 6" matte photograph, along with the pattern number (if there is one), handle material, length (closed), and stamping to Jim Sargent, 449 Lane Drive, Florence, AL 35360.

# Around the Shows

John Martin and Joe Chance chat at one of the knife shows. Do you have a clue as to who's the "good" guy? (Hint: Joe is wearing the white hat.)

**Tommy and Perry**

**NKCA Show
Wilmington, Ohio**

*Joe and Mark*

*Steve*

*Chris and Nichelle*

*Don and Millie*

*John*

*Clarence and Lisa*
*NKCA*

*Bruce*

*Ben and Chris*
*Hydrick and Reba*

**Mark**
**Knife World**

**Bill and Faye**

**P.J., Jean, and Gail**

**Imogene, Willis, Dan, and Joe**

**Dan and Sandy**

**Del and Joy**

**James and Betty**

# Alliance of Local Knife Clubs

Membership in the Alliance of Local Knife Clubs is free; just send the name, address and phone number of your club representative to Mark D. Zalesky, c/o Knife World Publications, P.O. Box 3395, Knoxville, TN 37927, or e-mail knifepub@knifeworld.com.

If you would like to start a local club, contact the Alliance of Local Knife Clubs for a free starter package: 4499 Muddy Ford Road, Georgetown, KY 40324-9280.

If your club is inadvertently omitted or is a newly formed club, please notify the author and it will be included in future editions. Jim Sargent, 449 Lane Drive, Florence, AL 35360.

American Bladesmith Society was established to preserve and promote the art of bladesmithing and to educate collectors and the public on the qualities of the forged blade. For more information, contact ABS, 176 Brentwood Lane, Madison, AL 35758.

American Knife Throwers Alliance is looking for members to help preserve and promote the sport of knife throwing. Call 843-928-3624 or write 4976 Seewee Road, Awendaw, SC 29429.

Australasian Knife Collectors Club was established in 1990 for knife collectors, makers, users, and historians. The AKC promotes Australian knife culture, caters to collectors, encourages custom knifemakers, and maintains the largest register of Australian knifemakers. International members welcome. For information, write to Keith Spencer, PO Box 1025, Morley, WA 6943, Australia, or visit AKC's Web site at www.akc.iinet.net.au.

Buck Collectors Club, Inc. is an international organization of knife enthusiasts interested in collecting knives produced by the H. H. Buck family and Buck Knives, Inc. For more information, contact Joe Houser, 110 New Kent Drive, Goode, VA 24556, or jhouser@buckknives.com.

Camillus Collectors Club is an international organization of knife enthusiasts who are interested in Camillus knives. Membership includes a quarterly newsletter featuring knife articles, classified ads, club merchandise, and support for Camillus collectors. Annual dues are $12 per year or $100 for a lifetime membership. Contact Rick Roney or Tom Williams at collectorsclub@camillusknives.com. Camillus Collectors Club, 54 Main Street, Camillus, NY 13031. Phone 315-672-8111, ext. 287 or visit www.camillusknives.com.

Case Collectors Club. Founded in 1981, the Case Collectors Club is an international organization that promotes the collecting of W. R. Case & Sons Cutlery Company's knives. The club offers Lifetime ($100) and Regular ($12) memberships and the option of sponsoring free Junior members 16 and under. Membership benefits include exclusive knife offering and promotions, The Case Collector quarterly magazine, free tours of the manufacturing plant, a copy of the annual Case Product Catalog, coverage of the bi-annual Zippo/Case Swap Meet and more. Call 1-800-523-6350 or visit the web site at www.wrcase.com.

Case Classics Club. Founded in 2000, devoted to all Case Classic collectors and anyone interested in the 36 patterns of the "Case Classics Knives" marketed by Blue Grass Cutlery between 1989 and 1997. Log on to caseclassics club.com and see never before published information, photos, and the history surrounding the prototypes, displays, and low run special classics. Membership is $15 a year.

KA-BAR Collectors Club is a company sponsored club dedicated to the collecting of KA-BAR knives. For more information write KA-BAR Knives, PO Box 688, 200 Homer Street, Olean, NY 14760 or call 716-372-5952 or visit www.ka-bar.com.

The Knifemakers' Guild. Current officers are President Alfred Pendray; Vice President Melvin Pardue; and Secretary/Treasurer Steven Johnson. Directors are Eugene Shadley, Steve Jernigan, Wayne Hensley, and Warren Osborne. Contact Knifemakers Guild, PO Box 5, Manti, UT 84642, or visit knifemakersguild.com

Miniature Knifemakers' Society is made up of collectors, makers, dealers, and others interested in miniature knives and other edged tools/weapons. It is the largest organization in the world in regards to miniature knives, their manufacture, availability, and styles etc. Dues are $20 in the U.S. and $25 outside the U.S. For information, write Terry Kranning, 548 W. Wyeth, Pocatello, ID 83204, or e-mail: terrykranning@juno.com.

National Knife Collectors Association is the world's largest organization of its kind, founded to support and promote knife collecting in all its branches. Yearly membership is $28. For more information, write NKCA, PO Box 21070, Chattanooga, TN 37424, or call 423-892-5007, or e-mail nkca@aol.com

North Carolina Custom Knifemaker's Guild was formed to meet the needs of a growing body of custom knifemakers in the southeastern United States. Membership $50, Collector membership $25, Students $10. NCCKG c/o Tony Kelly, 348 Bell Road, Kinston, NC 28504. Web site: www.ncknifeguild.org.

Queen Cutlery Collectors, Inc. The formation of "Queen Cutlery Collectors, Inc." has been announced. Annual memberships are available at this time. Contact Queen Cutlery Collectors, Inc., PO Box 109, Titusville, PA 16354.

Randall Knife Society of America has been formed with the approval of Randall Made Knives, Orlando,

Florida, and currently has over 1,700 members. Members receive quarterly newsletters on old and new knives, military Randalls, Randall history, and the latest shop news, with a classified ad free to members and a chance to get to know your fellow Randall collectors. Send $20 yearly dues to The Randall Knife Society of America, PO Box 539, Roseland, FL 32957.

Victorinox Swiss Army Knife Collectors Society dedicated to furthering knowledge of and interest in Victorinox brand Swiss Army Knives. Approved by Victorinox, currently listing members in the U.S.A. and foreign countries, providing a source for the "Original" Swiss Army knives and their history. Membership information: TOVSAKCS, PO Box 145, Cochrane, WI 54622, or e-mail tovsakcs@mwt.net.

## Canada

Associated Blade Collectors meets once a month at the ABC Restaurant at 9 a.m. on Saturday, #101 15373 Fraser Hwy., Surrey, BC, Canada. Contact Bob Patrick at 816 Peace Portal Dr., Blaine, WA 98230, or bob@knivesonnet.com, or www.knivesonnet.com.

## Arizona

Arizona Knife Collectors Association meets the fourth Tuesday of each month at 7 p.m. at the Disabled American Veterans Hall, 1510 N. 79th Street, Scottsdale, Arizona. Dues are $15 per year. Web site is www.arizonaknifecollectors.com. For more information, contact Mike Mooney, 19432 E. Cloud Rd., Queen Creek, AZ 85242, or e-mail president@arizonaknifecollectors.com.

## Arkansas

Arkansas Knifemakers Association holds randomly scheduled meetings and educational shop visits, and sponsors the Annual Arkansas Custom Knife Show in Little Rock and annual Hammer-In. Dues are $25 per calendar year. Chuck Ward, President 501-778-4329, Lloyd Peterson, Vice President 501-893-0000, David Etchieson, Secretary/Treasurer 501-513-1019. Visit our Web site at www.ar-knife-assn.com.

## California

Bay Area Knife Collectors Association meets the second Thursday of each month at 7:30 p.m. at the Newark Recreation & Community Center, 35501 Cedar Blvd, Newark CA. Dues are $25 per year. Membership is open to anyone with a sincere interest in knife collecting. Contact BAKCA Membership, PO Box 2787, Dublin CA 94568, visit www.bakca.org, or e-mail knfman@pacbell.net.

The Northern California Knife Collectors Association Between BAKCA and OKCA. Free, open to all responsible blade enthusiasts. Meets first Wednesday of the month at 7 p.m., in the Big Oak Plaza, Leasing Office, 2472 W. 3rd St. at Fulton Rd., Santa Rosa. For additional information, visit www.nckca.com, or email news@nckca.com.

Southern California Blades Knife Collectors Club meets the first Tuesday of each month at 7:30 p.m. at the Crystal Park Hotel & Casino, 123 East Artesia, Compton, CA 90220. Dues are $15 for an individual or $20 for a family for one year. Contact the club at PO Box 1140, Lomita, CA 90717, visit our Web site at www.scblades.com, or contact Lowell Shelhart at 310-530-8412.

## Colorado

Rocky Mountain Blade Collectors Club meets at 6:30 p.m. on the second Friday of each month at the Best Western Denver Central Hotel, 200 W. 48th Ave., Denver, Colorado. Dues are $20 per year. Membership is open to all interested in knife collecting. For information, write RMBC, PO Box 324, Westminster, CO 80036, or call Mike Moss at 303-680-0408 or Mark Miller at 303-280-3816.

## Florida

Fort Myers Knife Club meets the first Tuesday night of each month at the Perkins Restaurant on Palm Beach Blvd. (SR80). Exit 141 off I-75 and go west 1.3 miles. Starts at 6:30 p.m. Come early and have dinner. For information, contact the club at PO Box 706, St. James City, FL 33956 or rsmegal@earthlink.net.

South West Florida Knife Collectors Club meets the fourth Tuesday of each month at 7 p.m. at Leverocks Restaurant, 5981 Fruitville Road, Sarasota, Florida. For more information, visit www.KnifeCollector.net or e-mail: KnifeCollector@SimplySarasota.com.

Florida Knife Collectors Association, Inc. meets the first Tuesday of every month at Indian River Civic Center, Titusville, Florida. For information, contact the club at PO Box 6405, Titusville, FL 32782.

Gold Coast Knife Club meets the third Thursday of the month at 7 p.m. at the Embassy Suites Hotel, 1100 SE 17th Street, Ft. Lauderdale. Information: Alan Weinstein 954-747-1851, or e-mail TLViking@aol.com.

Riverland Knife Club meets first Thursday of the month at 7:30 p.m. at St. Johns Church Hall, 4 miles North of Dunnellon, Florida, on Highway 41. Dues $10. For information, call 352-489-5027 Tuesday to Friday 10 a.m. to 4 p.m.

Gator Cutlery Club meets every third Tuesday of the month at 7 p.m. at Shelby's Restaurant, 110 E. Reynolds Street, Plant City, Florida. Dues $10 adult. For more information, contact Dan Piergallini at 813-967-1471 (days) or at 813-754-3908 (evenings).

## Georgia

Chattahoochee Cutlery Club celebrating its thirty-first anniversary, meets the fourth Monday of each month at 7:30 p.m. at the Georgia Power Tucker Operating Headquarters Building, classroom, 1697 Montreal Circle, Tucker, Georgia. Dues $25 a year. Swap meet at 6:30 p.m. before meeting. Also, newsletter, annual club knife, and more. For information, write CCC, PO Box 1301, Snellville, GA 30078, or phone President H. S. Wardell at 770-786-9323.

Flint River Knife Club, Inc. meets at 7 p.m. the first Tuesday night during most months of the year at the First Baptist Church of Jonesboro in classroom #116 on the ground floor. Our club sponsors an annual knife show, a monthly newsletter, an annual club knife, Christmas dinner, and two knife-making workshops each year. Dues are $15 per year and $6 for each dependent family member. Contact June or Rade Hawkins at 110 Buckeye Rd., Fayetteville, GA 30214, or call 770-964-1177.

Three Rivers Knife Club meets the second Tuesday of each month at 6:30 p.m. at the Landmark Restaurant, 2740 Martha Berry Hwy. NE., Rome, Georgia. We offer to our members an annual club knife (a 207 Case mini trapper with different handle material each year). For more information, contact Jimmy Green, 783 NE Jones Mill Road, Rome, GA 30165, or call 706-234-2540 (nights).

## Illinois

American Edge Collectors Association. Dues $25. Renewal dues $20. Monthly meetings and knife show held at the Glen Maker Post #1160, American Legion, 10739 S. Ridgeland Ave., Chicago Ridge, Illinois, every third Sunday except for the annual Pavilion Show in September. Contact AECA, c/o Louie Jamison, 24755 Hickory Court, Crete, IL 60417, or call 708-868-7784 or 708-672-8838.

Bunker Hill Knife Club meets the first Sunday of each month at 4 p.m. at Franks Uptown Cafe, 116 N. Washington, Bunker Hill, Illinois. Dues $10. A short business meeting follows our trading session. Come and see us; we welcome visitors and new members. For more information, call Dale Rice at 618-377-8050 or W. H. LeClaire at 618-278-4558.

## Indiana

Greater Evansville Knife Club meets at Weinbach's Cafeteria the second Monday of the month at 6 p.m. President Bill Brummett; Vice President Tom Whitten; Secretary/Treasurer Tim Shehorn. For information, contact John Wells, Sergeant at Arms, PO Box 7, Newburgh, IN 47629, or e-mail wellsjd53@msn.com.

Indiana Knife Collectors meets second Wednesday of each month at the Local 663 Union Hall, 29th and Madison Avenue, Anderson, Indiana from 6 to 9 p.m. Free admission. Free tables. For more information, contact Ed Etchason 317-835-7487, or write PO Box 101, Fountaintown, IN 46130-0101.

## Iowa

The Hawkeye Knife Collectors Club holds one-day shows in January, April, July, and October. Dues $10 regular; $15 family. A newsletter precedes each show. For show dates and further information, call Hawkeye Knife Collectors at 515-266-0910, or e-mail tck0910@aol.com.

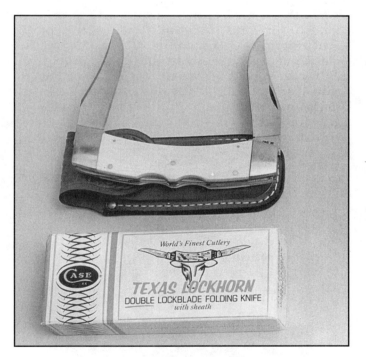

## Kansas

Kansas Knife Collectors Association meets the first Wednesday of each month at 7 p.m. at 3219 West Central, Wichita, Kansas. Dues are $15 per year. Annual club knife, club patches, and business cards are available. For information on club, contact Bill Davis 316-838-0540 or Gene Ritthaler 316-943-4438, or write KKCA, PO Box 1125, Wichita, KS 67201.

## Kentucky

Central Kentucky Knife Club meets the second Monday each month at Continental Inn, 801 New Circle Rd., Lexington, Kentucky. Swap & Sell starts at 6 p.m., meeting at 7:30 p.m. Visitors welcome. Dues $10 for adults; $5 under 17. Monthly program, annual club knife. For further information, contact CKKC, PO Box 55049, Lexington, KY 40555.

Kentucky Cutlery Association meets the second Monday each month at Executive West Hotel on Freedom Way at the Fairgrounds entrance at 7 p.m. Club dues are $10 per year and $5 for youth and other family members. Contact club at 7248 Briscoe Vista Way, Louisville, KY 40228, or call 502-239-3480.

## Maryland

Chesapeake Bay Knife Club meets the second Monday of each month at 7:30 p.m. at the Rosedale Federal Savings & Loan, 9616 Belair Rd., Perry Hall, Maryland. A show, sell, and trade is held at each meeting. Dues are $15 per year, and membership includes the opportunity to purchase special club knives and special edition club offerings. Visit www.knifeshows.com/clubs/cbkc.

## Michigan

Wolverine Knife Collectors Club, PO Box 52, Belleville, MI 48112, meets the first Saturday of each month at the Clubhouse of the Belleville Manor Trailer Park on 8701 Belleville Road, just north of I-94, Belleville, Michigan. Business meeting at 9:30 a.m., with a knife swap beginning at 10:30 a.m. Dues are $15 per year. Contact Patrick Donovan at 586-786-5549 (evenings).

Mid-Michigan Knife Collectors meet the first Thursday of the month (except June, July, and August) at 7 p.m. at Anschutz Cafe, Breckenridge, Michigan. Call Bill McMall, President, at 989-642-5750, or Don Burns, Treasurer, at 989-842-5214.

Marble Plus Knife Club, PO Box 228, Gladstone, MI 49837. Established 3/93, meets the first Tuesday each month at 7:00 p.m. in the Rapid River Lions Club, Rapid River, Michigan. Limited edition products available to members. Membership $25 first year, $15 thereafter. For more information, call Jim Decremer, President, at 906-474-6774 (evenings) or Bob Schmeling, historian and secretary, at 906-786-5186. Write directly to the club for membership applications.

## Minnesota

North Star Blade Collectors. Since 1982, this has been a club for any type of cutlery collector. We meet at 12:30 p.m. on the third Saturday of each month at the Creekside Community Center, 98th & Penn Avenue South, Bloomington, Minnesota. A club knife is made for us each year by Queen Cutlery. Annual dues are $15 and include a newsletter. Everyone is welcome to join and/or attend our meetings. See Web site at www.knifecorner.com/nsbc/.

## Missouri

Gateway Area Knife Club promotes knife collecting and knifemaking through its 150+ membership. Meetings are held in Carpenter's Union Hall, 1401 Hampton, St. Louis, Missouri, second Thursday each month, from 6 p.m. to 9 p.m. Contact Paul Swirck at 314-241-6006, or fax 314-241-6169, or email swirck@yahoo.com.

Show Me Club. This is the newest, fastest growing knife club in Missouri. Meets second Monday of each month at Living Waters Church, 1351 Parkway Rd., St. Clair, Missouri, at 6:30 p.m. Yearly dues are $10; under age 18, $5. For more details, call Secretary/Treasurer Phyllis Briggs at 636-583-6840 or President Fred Rohrs at 636-583-1453, or write 6 Lindsey Drive, Union, MO 63084, or email briggs@fidnet.com.

## Montana

Montana Knifemakers Association meets every other month at 14440 Harpers Bridge Road, in Missoula, Montana. Dues are $25 per year. Annual knife show and newsletter six times per year. For more information, contact Darlene Weinand at 406-543-0845, or Bob Crowder at 406-827-4754.

## New England

Northeast Cutlery Collectors Association Regional club, all interests with 400 current members. Dues $15 January to December. $150 Life. Annual two-day show, plus five smaller shows each year (details in show calendar). Annual knife and bimonthly newsletter. For information, contact Joe Hughes, 28 Hosmer St. #1, Marlboro, MA 01752 or call 508-485-0035.

New England Custom Knife Association committed to the preservation and awareness of custom knifemaking, and collecting and preserving the fine art and craftsmanship of such tools. George Rebello, President; Dan Gray, Vice President. See Web site at www.knivesby.com/necka.html.

## New York

Empire Knife Club of N.Y.C. meets every second Wednesday of each month at 7:30 p.m. at American Legion Post 1130, E. 92nd Street, Brooklyn, NY. Each meeting is followed by a swap and sell. Dues are $20 per year. For information, contact Jan Muchnikoff at 718-763-0391.

## North Carolina

Bechtler Mint Knife Club meets at 7 p.m. the first Monday night of each month at the R-S Middle School Cafeteria at Rutherfordton, North Carolina. Dues are $10 annually per member and includes a monthly newsletter. Call 864-489-1469, or write PO Box 771 and 2, Rutherfordton, NC 28139. Visitors and new members are welcome.

N.C. Custom Knifemaker's Guild Membership fee $50 per year. Collector membership fee $25; Student membership $10. Contact Tony Kelly, 348 Bell Road, Kinston, NC 28504, or visit www.ncknifeguild.org.

Tar Heel Cutlery Club meets at 7:30 p.m. on the fourth Tuesday of each month at Miller Park Recreation Center, 400 Leisure Lane, Winston-Salem, North Carolina. A swap meet is held before each meeting. Annual dues are $10, which entitles members to purchase an annual club knife and free admission to our yearly knife show. Contact George Manuel, 3682 Bowens Rd., Tobaccoville, NC 27030 or 336-924-6876.

## North Dakota

Northern Plains Knife Collectors Association is dedicated to the enjoyment of our hobby. Members from around the Northern Plains are welcome and dues are $15 per year. Members will receive six newsletters per year, the association will meet on a quarterly basis, and an annual show and convention is in the planning stage. Write NPKCA, PO Box 42, Mott, ND 58646. Call Director Mark Resner at 701-824-4128 (evenings), or e-mail casev42@hotmail.com.

## Ohio

Fort City Knife Collectors Club meets the first Tuesday of each month at the Norwood Masonic Temple, 2020 Hopkins Avenue, Norwood, Ohio. Dues are $5 per year, due in January. Contact FCKC, 8325 State Route 128, Cleves, OH 45002.

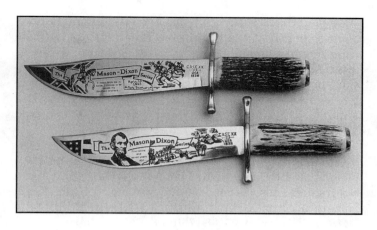

Johnny Appleseed Knife Collectors meet at 6 p.m. the third Tuesday of each month at Burton Park, Sunset Boulevard, off Lexington Avenue in Mansfield, Ohio. Dues $10 per year, which includes a quarterly newsletter. Yearly club knife available. For more information, contact Jerry Grega, 2215 Haywood Dr. R-10, Mansfield, OH 44903 or call 419-756-5024.

National Pike Knife Club meets the second Sunday of every month at the Belmont County Fairground in St. Clairsville, Ohio, in the Ruritan Building from 3 p.m. to 6 p.m. For more information, contact the club at 34841 Hendrysburg Road, Barnesville, OH 43713, or call Jerry at 740-758-5727 or Bob at 740-757-2540.

Western Reserve Cutlery Association Founded in 1977, the club meets on the second Tuesday of each month at 7 p.m. at the Glen Daniels Community Center, Doylestown, Ohio. Following a short business session, a program or activity follows, which revolves around the meeting's monthly theme. Membership dues are $15 annually. For information, write WRCA, PO Box 355, Dover, OH 44622, or see club Web site at http://wrca-oh.com.

## Oregon

Oregon Knife Collectors meets the second Thursday of each month in the Eugene area for a knife share and dinner meeting. Annual 470 table world class show. December winter mini show. Outstanding newsletter. "The OKCA is happily involved in anything that goes Cut." Write OKCA, PO Box 2091, Eugene, OR 97402, or call 541-484-5564. Web site www.oregonknifeclub.org.

## Pennsylvania

Allegheny Mountain Knife Collectors Association meets the second Sunday of each month at 2 p.m. at the Hunker Community Building, Hunker, Pennsylvania. Dues are $10; under age 18, $5, due by May 1 of each year. The club issues a quarterly newsletter, The Mountain Echo. The AMKCA has its own knife shield, a black bear in an oval shield in nickel silver, which is used on each club knife. Contact Allegheny Mt. Knife Collectors Assoc., PO Box 23, Hunker, PA 15639 or contact Secretary Ruth Trout at 724-925-2713.

Mason Dixon Knife Club meets on the second Sunday of each month at the State Line Ruritan Club in State Line, Pennsylvania. Doors open at 10 a.m.; business meeting starts at 1 p.m. Yearly activities include a club-sponsored show in the spring, swap meets and brag meets, guest speakers and a banquet. Dues are $12 annually. For information, write PO Box 66, Toms Brook, VA 22660, or call 540-436-9425.

Eastern Pennsylvania Knife Collectors Association meets monthly on the third Sunday for a meeting/swap meet/show from 10 a.m. to 3 p.m. at the Belfast Edelman Sportsman Association, 474 Sportsman Club Road, Nazareth, Pennsylvania. Contact Ed Petro at 610-965-9248, Bill Odor at 610-847-4600, or Tom Iobst at 610-965-8074. Annual knife show is the third Saturday in March. Visit our Web site at knifeclub.org.

## South Carolina

Palmetto Cutlery Club meets the first Tuesday of each month at the Greer Recreation Center, Greer, South Carolina at 7 p.m. Dues are $20 per year; $10 per year for the second member of the family at the same address. For information, contact the club at PO Box 1356, Greer, SC 29652, or call Gene Ravan at 864-325-3212 or 877-0303, or visit our Web site at www.palmettocutleryclub.org, or e-mail us at info@palmettocutleryclub.org.

## Tennessee

Memphis Knife Collectors Club meets the first Thursday of every month at 7 p.m. in the Beale St. Room of Days Inn Motel, Stage and Austin Peay Hwy. Membership open to all. For information, contact Wayne Koons at 901-476-3834 or A.B. Haines at 901-754-2089.

Williamson County Knife Club meets the first Monday of every month, at the Middle Tennessee Electric Building meeting room, 2156 Edward Curd Lane, Franklin, Tennessee (1/2 mile north of the Williamson Medical Center) at 6:30 p.m. Dues are $10 yearly, payable in January. For more information, write Williamson County Club, PO Box 681061, Franklin, TN 37068.

Soddy Daisy Knife Collectors Association meets the first Thursday of every month at the Soddy Daisy Community Center on Depot Street, Soddy Daisy, Tennessee. Visitors are welcome. Membership dues are $10 a year ($5 for under 18). Members are eligible for annual club knife and monthly newsletter. For more information, contact Harold Wilkey at 423-899-0287, or write PO Box 1224, Soddy Daisy, TN 37379, or visit www.wooden-box.com/sdkca, or e-mail sdkca@woodenbox.com.

## Texas

Central Texas Knife Collectors Association meets the first Saturday of each month at BBQ restaurants in Georgetown, Salado, and Belton, Texas. Membership dues: none. Show chairman: Chris Carlson, 108 Johnson Cove, Hutto, TX 78634. Club newsletter: Mark Nagle, 309 Highland Oaks Dr., Harker Heights, TX 76548.

Permian Basin Knife Club. For more information, write 4309 Roosevelt, Midland, TX 79703, or call Fred Nolley at 915-694-1209, or e-mail wfnolley@grandecom.net.

## Virginia

Shenandoah Valley Knife Collectors meets the third Tuesday of each month at the Izaak Walton League Barn in Harrisonburg, Virginia. Membership dues $10. Annual club sponsored knife show in April. For information, write SVKC, PO Box 843, Harrisonburg, VA 22803. Call 540-574-4511.

Northern Virginia Knife Collectors meets at 8 p.m. on the third Thursday of each month at 105 N. Maple Street, Falls Church, Virginia. Annual dues are $20 and life membership is $150. Yearly club knife available to members. For more information, write to PO Box 2754, Sterling, VA 20167, or call Gene White at 703-924-3686.

Old Dominion Knife Collectors Association meets the first Thursday of every month at 7 p.m. at the Bedford Library in Bedford, Virginia. Annual dues $10. Contact John Riddle, 224 Lake Ridge Circle, Troutville, VA 24175.

## Washington

Northwest Knife Collectors meets the first Thursday of every month at 6 p.m. at Elmer's Restaurant at 7427 S. Hosmer St., Tacoma, Washington. Dues are $20 per year; $5 for additional family members at same address. Contact us at NWKC, 10602 NE 60th Street, Kirkland, WA 98023, or call Don Hanham at 425-827-1644, or e-mail dhanham@earthlink.net.

## Wisconsin

Badger Knife Club meets quarterly on Sundays. Annual dues are $5, which includes a quarterly newsletter. All meetings are held at 7 p.m. at the Milwaukee County Council, Boy Scouts of America Building located at 330 So. 84th Street, Milwaukee, Wisconsin. Call Bob Schrap at 414-479-9765, or write PO Box 511, Elm Grove, WI 53122, or e-mail badgerknifeclub@aol.com.

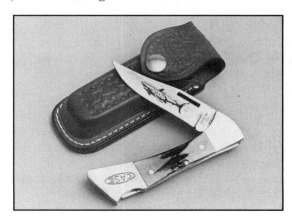

# Introduction

A crude cutting tool, or knife, was probably one of the first tools used by primitive man. From the first moment he used a sharp rock to crack a pterodactyl egg, man has never stopped looking for ways to improve on the knife. In reality, it has not been man's search for a better mousetrap that helped shape society, but rather his search for a better knife.

Some 175,000 years ago, give or take a century, man dropped down out of the trees, stood on his own two feet, picked up a sharp stone, and went out to search for dinner. He moved to a cave for warmth and protection. Then he discovered fire.

The discovery of fire, followed by the innovation of cooked foods, created a need for more refined tools (knives). To coin a phrase, "Necessity is the mother of invention" and so, the flint knife was born. Flint was easier to work than stone, and man found he could shape it to fashion a more efficient tool. He also found that by heating this tool in a fire, it became tougher and more durable.

During this period, the tribal or family unit was coming into its own. Man had begun to settle down. He had his cave and his fire; he hunted food and prepared it with his greatly improved knife. Yet, instinctively he knew things had just begun.

Metal was the next great step toward a more durable and pliable resource with which to ease his daily chores. With the introduction of iron around 3,000 BC, man had truly reached a "golden age" that would revolutionize his life.

Once iron was a routine part of the toolmaker's materials, steel was not far away. Steel was truly the one material that revolutionized our lives. The steel industry, as we know it today, which is actually the basis for all modern industry, came about because of man's search for the "better knife."

By the fourteenth century, advances in the steel industry, and therefore in the cutlery industry, caused a great deal of romance and fantasy to spring up around certain forges. The techniques of some steel makers were cloaked in more secrecy than surrounded the invention of the atom bomb. Mythology speaks of King Arthur's Excalibur, the singing sword, and it tells of Balmung, the knife Siegfried used to split the anvil with one stroke.

Metals were forged in India too. Laminating high carbon steel with milder steel in layers produced Damascus weapons. This process is still in use today.

During the early Christian era, production of the dagger, or sheath knife, was a forge's major product. The dagger was not just a form of protection, but a utensil important to good table manners.

By the fifteenth century, England emerged as the center for fine steel and cutlery. London, Hallamshire, and Sheffield were known then, as they are today, for skill in the cutler's art. The cutlery guilds began here and formed the basic models for our present day trade unions.

## Caring for Your Knives

Rust is as old as iron, and finding a cure for rust is like finding a cure for the common cold. Some precautions should be taken so your collection of knives will not diminish in value.

## Cleaning

Use a soft, all-cotton cloth or chamois to clean your knives. Then apply a coat of Simichrome Polish and wipe it off. A protective film will remain on the entire knife. A number of collectors are using a wax called "Renaissance." It has very little grit and does not leave any white film around edges and cracks. Never use Vaseline because it allows moisture to seep beneath its coat and cause rust. It is a good idea to check your knives often for possible trouble spots.

## Storage and Handling

The most recommended method of storing knives is in vinyl rolls with a cloth interior. The rolls also provide a convenient way to transport knives. Leather rolls have a small amount of tanning acid in them, which can cause rust. If possible, leave your knives unrolled during storage; this allows air movement and reduces moisture.

Display cases with felt interiors are another way to store knives and also allow a collection to be exhibited easily. Some collectors use elastic bands to attach their knives to the display, while others use wire. Elastic makes it easier to slip knives in and out for closer inspection, while wires must be cut and replaced each time.

A Plexiglas top will also cut down on dust and possible theft.

Transporting your knives from cold to warmth will cause condensation, resulting in rust. In other words, don't leave your collection in your car trunk overnight during cold weather and then bring it into a show the next day without expecting some condensation. Keep your knives at a constant temperature or at least within a few degrees at all times.

Caution:
Celluloid is made from a petroleum base and emits fumes. The fumes will cause rust, so keep celluloid knives stored separately.

Direct sunlight can fade almost anything. Knife handles are fragile, especially bone, stag, and pearl, so don't toss them around carelessly, and **don't drop them.** Broken or cracked handles reduce value.

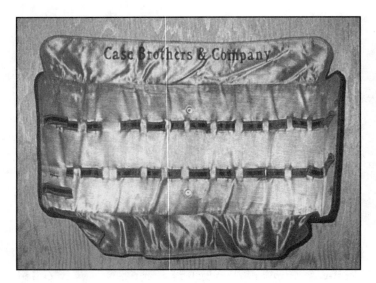

## What to Collect

Some people collect everything, as long as it is of excellent quality and brand. Then there are other schools of thought such as collecting within the following categories:

Patterns: trappers, peanuts, gunstocks, etc.
Handle Materials: goldstone, pearl, Rogers bone, etc.
Manufacturers: Case, Queen, Schrade-Walden, etc.
Specialties: advertising knives

Beginners should make a decision before investing a lot of money in a collection.

## Knives as Investments

Knife enthusiasts can be divided into two groups: knife dealers and knife collectors. It's very important to know the difference and to choose your direction before jumping in with both feet. Some people are both, but they know when to turn their hat around when it comes to dealing. So, if your main interest is turning a profit in knife marketing, you should learn a few things that affect prices.

**General economic conditions:** When times are bad, individuals and dealers are willing to take less than they would during the previous "good times" in order to get some badly needed cash. As a dealer, this may be the best time to pick up collections at a depressed price, but you also know that your own inventory isn't selling at the previous higher prices. If you have the staying power, your purchases at this time can reap benefits when times are better.

**Sudden increase in numbers of knives available:** Sometimes large collections are broken up and introduced back into the knife market. For instance a company may announce that it will no longer produce knives with a certain handle material. This drives up the price of knives with that particular handle material; however, several years later you may find that the company that stopped producing with that material is going to release another several thousand limited editions with this material, which will tend to level off prices. There have been warehouse discoveries of large numbers of certain patterns, with these being dumped into the market. You can imagine what that does to prices. Remember, not all knives continually go up in value. In short, playing the knife market is like playing the stock market; keep up with current trends by keeping your ears open and by reading newsletters and monthly knife publications.

Then there are investors who just enjoy their collection, and the price is inconsequential if a certain Peanut will finally fill out that treasured display. The collection is then thought of as part of the family and no one thinks of selling a child, right?

## Finding Pocketknives

Long gone are the days of wandering the back roads in search of general stores and hardware stores in order to relieve owners of outdated and overburdened knife displays. One reason that the once-fertile hunting grounds are a thing of the past is that these merchants discovered that they already had a decent start on their own collections. Another reason is that as knife collecting grew in popularity, it didn't take long for the collectors to clean these sources out. And still another reason is that so many of these popular gathering places have been pushed aside by more modern convenience stores, discount stores, and malls. Don't be disheartened though; excellent sources are still available for collectors.

Join a nearby club and become a student of knives. Get your hands on as many knife publications as possible and learn. (Many knife clubs have swap meets.) Attend knife shows. These are excellent places to find knives, and the prices are usually very reasonable because of the competitiveness of the dealers. Several other sources are antique shows, flea markets, estate auctions, and dealers' direct mail lists.

Also, don't forget the dark, cluttered corners of attics, barns, garages, and workshops. One never knows what lurks in the bottom of those tattered old cardboard boxes.

## Condition

**Mint:** Never been carried or sharpened, straight from the factory and sometimes in the original box.

**Excellent:** Handles are in good shape, blades still close with a snap and show only slight wear.

**Very Good:** Blades show approximately 25 percent wear, and handles are in good condition; although one blade may snap weakly, blades have not been repaired or changed, and stamp can still be seen clearly with the naked eye.

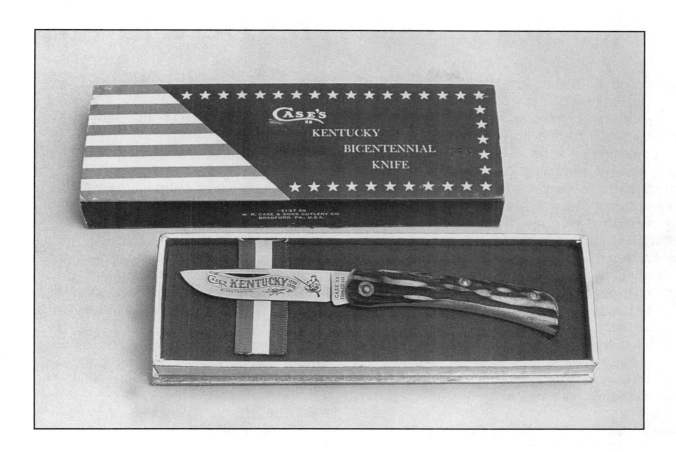

**Fair:** Blades show 50 percent wear, blade closing is mushy, handles are cracked or replaced, blades are repaired or changed, stamp is weak.

**Poor:** These are used mostly as parts knives and have well worn or broken blades, handles are broken or completely missing, stamp is barely visible, if at all.

## Restoration

There is absolutely nothing wrong with restoring a knife by using original parts that are available. Most of the time it makes a knife even more desirable than one in worn condition.

We can draw a parallel here with the restorations of antique and classic automobiles. When one of these is restored with original parts you can be sure it is more valuable, so don't worry about whether a knife has been restored. Of course, if you find an old knife and you're positive it is in original mint condition and it's still in the original box, you are better off.

## Counterfeiting

Counterfeit: "Something made to imitate another thing with the intent to defraud."

In 1999, Gerald Witcher made an enormous contribution to knife collecting by publishing a book about counterfeiting. We highly recommend you purchase this masterpiece from the NKCA or from Knife World. As prices increase, the darker side of human nature emerges. Unscrupulous people alter less valuable knives to look like genuine rare ones. Why not add two dots and make an 8 dot 6488 into a 10 dot 6488? Why not shave off the tang stamp of a USA knife and make it a XX knife? For that matter, why not shave off a XX tang stamp and make it a Tested knife?

The only safeguard for the collector is knowledge. Witcher displays various examples of genuine and fake items: a good stamp next to a bad stamp, a good blade versus a bad blade, a good frame versus a bad frame, a good shield versus a bad shield, good handles versus bad handles, and the list goes on and on. This is not a sit down and read it in one night type of book. This is something that will become your bible.

He explains the history of companies through tang stamps. He also provides individual knife critiques for the following manufacturers: Case, Eagle, Eye Brand, John Primble, KA-BAR, Napanoch, New York Knife, Queen, Remington, Winchester, Shapleigh Hardware, Russell, and Bowie.

If you deal in knives that cost more than $100, this book is one of the best investments you can make.

# Handle Materials and Descriptions

**Appaloosa:** brown and light colored spots (smooth bone)
**Black Bone:** smooth bone dyed black
**Birdseye:** not a handle material, but refers to large rivets on handle
**Bone:** shin bone of cattle
**Bone Stag:** same as bone with different jigging
**Brass:** brass metal
**Brown Bone:** dyed bone
**Buffalo Horn:** can be horn from any animal
**Burnt Orange:** brownish orange delrin
**Buttermilk:** two-color cream celluloid
**Candy Stripe:** red-and-white stripe celluloid
**Celluloid:** man-made material (translucent appearance)
**Christmas Tree:** celluloid of mingled red, green, and black
**Cocobolo:** hard wood
**Composition:** man-made material, dull (solid appearance)
**Cracked Ice:** off-color white (appearance of frosted window)
**Delrin:** man-made plastic, petro base
**Ebony:** ebony wood
**Engine-Turned Silver:** metal with uniform knurl lines
**Genuine Pearl:** mother-of-pearl shell
**Genuine Stag:** antlers of deer
**Gold:** self-explanatory, 14K, 12K, 10K, and plated
**Goldstone:** gold glitter celluloid
**Green Bone:** bone dyed shades of green
**High Art:** photos under clear celluloid
**Horn:** horn from various animals
**Imitation Ivory:** composition resembling ivory
**Imitation Onyx:** yellowish marble appearance
**Imitation Pearl:** man-made white composition
**Ivory:** animal tusk
**Jigged Bone:** machine-notched bone
**Laminated Wood:** layers of wood pressed together
**Marine Pearl:** imitation pearl
**Mother-of-Pearl:** same as genuine pearl
**Mottled:** mingled colors
**Multi-Color:** many colors in stripes or mingled, composition

**Nickel Silver:** self-explanatory, also known as German silver
**Pakkawood:** man-made, pressed-wood appearance
**Peachseed:** jigging on bone appears pitted like a peach seed
**Pyralin:** man-made, petro base such as celluloids
**Pyremite:** same as pyralin
**Red Bone:** bone dyed various shades of red
**Red Stag:** stag dyed various shades of red
**Redwood:** wood from redwood tree
**Rogers Bone:** bone processed by the Rogers Co.; dark to brilliant red, also green, brown; heavier than most bones
**Early Rogers:** brown tan or yellow color
**Late Rogers:** reddish brown to bright red
**Rough Black:** man-made plastic "PLASTAG"- 1940
**Saw Cut:** bone or composition; has been sawn and left marks
**Scales:** anything used as handle materials
**Second-Cut Stag:** pieces of stag with little or no character or with grooves that have been specially jigged and dyed to give the material a stronger stag appearance
**Slick Black:** man-made composition
**Smoked Pearl:** dark bluish-gray in either genuine pearl or imitation pearl
**Smooth Bone:** self-explanatory
**Stag:** same as genuine stag
**Staglon:** imitation stag
**Stained Bone:** dyed bone
**Stainless Steel:** self-explanatory
**Sterling Silver:** self-explanatory
**Tortoise:** actual tortoise shell; illegal to use now
**Tortoise (celluloid):** imitation of actual tortoise shell
**Walnut:** wood of walnut tree
**Waterfall:** translucent material that resembles a waterfall as knife is rotated
**Winterbottom Bone:** bone processed by Winterbottom Co.
**Wire:** knife frames made from #9 wire
**Wood:** various woods, such as walnut, ebony, redwood, maple, etc.

# Glossary

**Bail (shackle):** a metal ring attached to the bolster so the knife can be placed on a key ring or tied to a belt

**Drilled:** a hole drilled in bolster in order to put a lanyard through

**Jigging:** machine notching

**Lanyard:** cord or line (usually braided)

**Pull:** thumbnail groove on blade for opening (regular pull or long pull)

**Rockwell Hardness Test:** an analysis performed by pressing a diamond cone into metal; the deeper the penetration, the softer the metal

**Scale:** another term for man-made handle materials

**Serrated:** saw-toothed edge

**Shackle:** see bail

**Shadow:** no bolsters

**Springer:** spring operated (switchblade)

**Zipper:** a switchblade with square release button set into handle

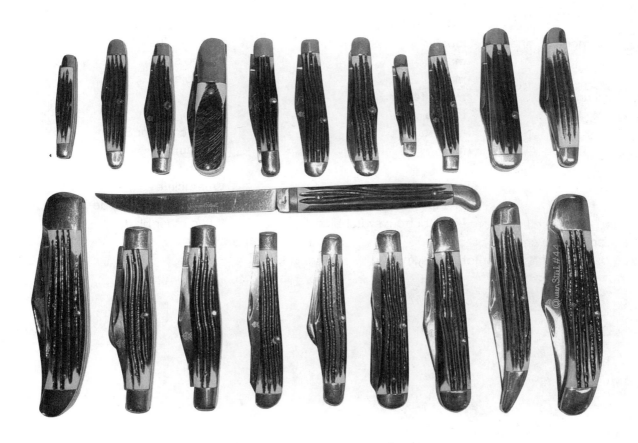

# Pattern Names

- baby copperhead
- banana
- bark loosener
- Barlow
- bartender
- birdseye (large rivets on handles)
- boss
- bowtie
- budding knife
- buffalo
- bulldog
- butterbean
- canoe
- carpenter whittler
- cattle
- cheetah
- cigar
- citrus: melon tester
- citrus peeler
- Coke bottle (small, medium, and large)
- congress
- copperhead (small and large)
- cotton sampler
- Daddy Barlow
- doctor's (phys.)
- dogleg jack
- dog groomer
- easy opener
- electrician's knife
- elephant's toe (also sunfish or rope knife)
- equal end
- fish scaler
- fisherman's knife
- fishtail
- florist's knife
- folding hunter
- grafting
- greenskeeper's knife
- gunboat
- gunstock
- half hawkbill
- half whittler
- hammerhead
- hawkbill
- hobo
- humpback
- jack
- leg
- lineman's knife
- lobster
- maize
- mako
- melon tester
- moose
- muskrat
- navy
- office
- one-arm man
- peanut
- press button: switchblade
- pruner
- rigger's knife
- rope
- Scout
- seahorse whittler
- senator
- serpentine
- shark's tooth
- shroud cutter (paratrooper's)
- sidewinder
- sleeveboard
- sod buster
- sowbelly
- stabber
- stockman
- sunfish (also elephant toe, toenail)
- swell center
- swell-end jack
- teardrop
- Texas jack
- Texas toothpick
- timberscribe
- Toledo scale
- toothpick
- trapper
- tuxedo
- utility-camp or Scout
- Vietnam
- whaler
- Wharncliffe
- whittler (master blade folds between two other blades)

General Knife Reference Information 23

# Pocket Knife and Sheath Knife Parts

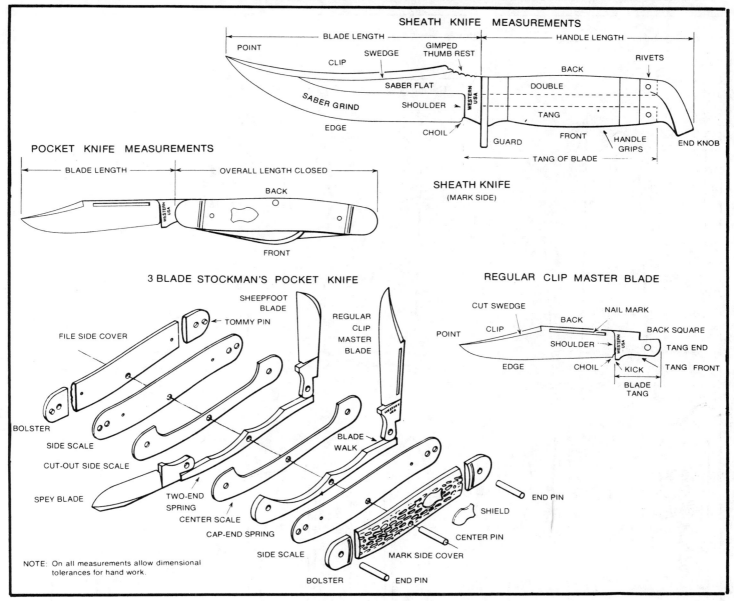

## Blade Styles

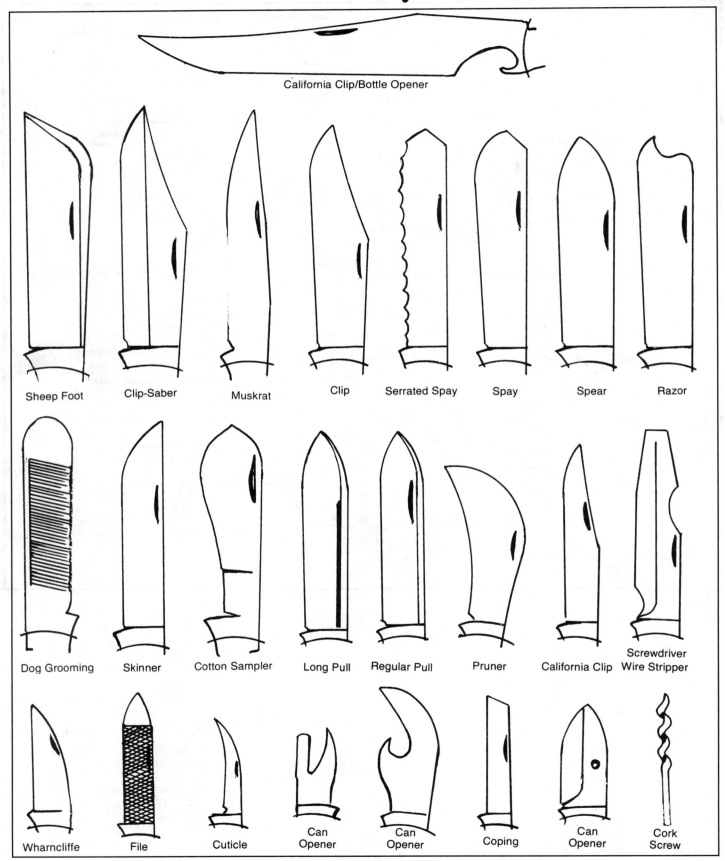

# General Knife Reference Information

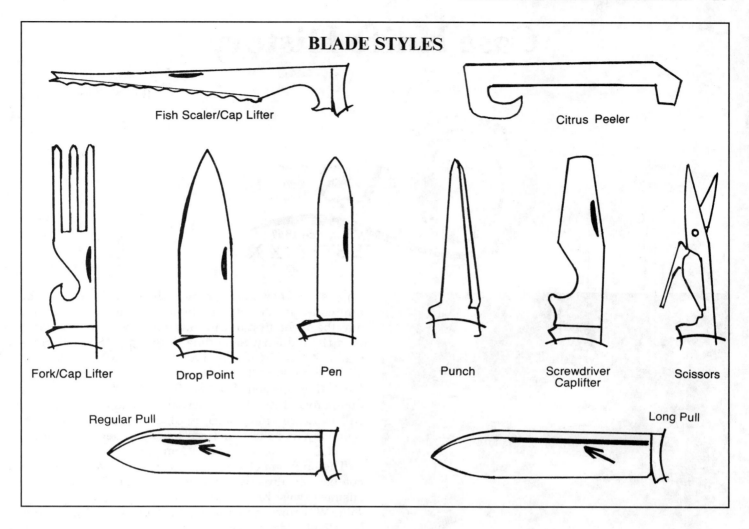

## BLADE STYLES

# Common Abbreviations

| | |
|---|---|
| **1/2** ............ master blade is clip blade | **P** ............... pen blade |
| **3/4** ............ front of the blade flat; rear saber | **PU** ............. punch blade |
| **B** ............... budding | **R** ............... bail in handle (shackle) |
| **B&G** .......... budding and grafting | **RAZ** .......... razor blade (one-arm man) |
| **EO** ............ easy opener | **S** ............... sterling silver |
| **F** ............... file | **SAB** .......... saber blade |
| **I** ................ iron | **SCI** ............ scissors |
| **J** ............... long spey blade | **SH** ............. sheepfoot blade |
| **K** ............... corkscrew | **SHAC** ........ shackle (bail) |
| **L** ............... lock back | **SHAD** ........ no bolsters |
| **LP** ............. long pull | **SP** ............. spey blade |
| **LR** ............. electrician's knife | **SSP** ........... stainless steel, polished blade edge |
| **M** .............. metal | **SS** ............. stainless steel |
| **NS** ............ nickel silver | **T** ............... tip bolsters |
| **P** ............... pakkawood | |

# Case Knife History

By Bob Wurzelbacher

*Bob Wurzelbacher*

The Case family's interest in the cutlery business goes well beyond the present facilities located in Bradford, Pennsylvania. It all started back in the late 1800s, with six of the nine children of Job Russell Case and Deborah Milks Case: Theresa, Emma, Jean, John, Andrew, and William Russell (better known as W. R.). Job Russell Case was never involved with the cutlery business. He was a horse trader, farmer, and freighter. It was these six children who first introduced the cutlery business into the Case family.

It is not known for sure how the Case family became interested in the cutlery business, but Theresa may have been the first of the children to become associated with the industry. Sometime in the late 1800s, Theresa married J. B. F. Champlin, who was a cutlery salesman at the time. The Champlins had a son and later, around 1882, they formed J. B. F. Champlin & Sons Cutlery Company in Little Valley, N.Y. About four years later, and still in Little Valley, J. B. F. Champlin & Sons Cutlery Company and the four Case brothers mentioned above joined Cattaraugus Cutlery Company.

The only one of the six children mentioned who did not become directly involved with the family cutlery business was Emma. However, Emma Case married John W. Brown and their son, Wallace, and grandson, Dansforth Brown, were connected with Union Cutlery and later KA-BAR.

While on the topic of companies related to the Case family, there is another one that should be mentioned. Jean Case had a daughter, Addie May, who married William Burrell and had a son, Dean. Dean later went on to form Burrell Cutlery Co. in Ellicottville, N.Y.

W. R. Case had three children: Debbie, J. Russell, and Theresa. Debbie and J. Russell went to work for Cattaraugus Cutlery Company. Theresa married Herbert Crandall, founder of Crandall Cutlery Company, which was located in Bradford, Pennsylvania, around the turn of the century.

While at Cattaraugus Cutlery, Debbie married H. N. Platts, son of Charles W. Platts, who emigrated from England in the 1860s. Charles Platts learned the cutlery business in Sheffield, England, and after coming to this country traveled through New England before coming to New York State. H. N. Platts, with his wife Debbie and the rest of the Platts family, formed C. Platts & Sons Cutlery Company in 1896. This company was first located in Gowanda, New York, but later moved to Eldred, Pennsylvania. During the same time (1896), Jean, John, and Andrew Case left Cattaraugus Cutlery Company and formed Case Brothers Cutlery Co., also located in Little

Valley. It is reported that when Case Brothers Cutlery Co. first began, it purchased its knives from C. Platts & Sons Cutlery Co. in Gowanda. This would account for the "Case Brothers and Co. Gowanda NY" found on some older Case knives. Soon after the Case brothers formed their own company, J. Russell Case (son of W. R.) left Cattaraugus Cutlery Co. and joined his uncles as a salesman for Case Brothers Cutlery Co.

Around 1902, J. Russell left Case Brothers Cutlery Co. and, backed by his father, formed W. R. Case & Son Cutlery Co. in Little Valley. J. Russell used a photograph of himself and his father and grandfather on all company literature and advertising. This gave the new company a three-generation image that helped the company to compete with the larger, more established, businesses of the day.

After a couple of years of prosperous business, W. R. Case & Son Cutlery outgrew its rented facilities in Little Valley and moved to Bradford, Pennsylvania, in 1903. After it moved to Bradford, the company merged with C. Platts & Sons Cutlery Co. and became W. R. Case & Son's Cutlery Co., which was incorporated in 1903. Around 1904, H. N. Platts left W. R. Case & Sons and moved to Colorado.

After H. N. Platts left, Crandall Cutlery Co. joined W. R. Case & Sons. Herbert Crandall, Theresa Case's husband, was W. R. Case's son-in-law, so they were still keeping it in the family.

It was around 1914 that W. R. Case acquired the equipment and trademark from Case Brothers in Little Valley. A few years earlier, Case Brothers was destroyed by fire. Even though the company rebuilt in Springville, New York, it never recovered the status it once had. It was also at this time that Case Brothers Cutlery Co. ceased to exist. Therefore, W. R. Case & Sons was able to produce its knives with the famous "XX" trademark.

After Case Brothers went out of business in Little Valley, Jean Case formed Jean Case Cutlery Company in Kane, Pennsylvania. This company was in business for several years before selling out to the Hollingsworth family.

W. R. Case & Sons Cutlery Co. was first located on Bank Street in Bradford. Under the leadership of J. Russell Case, the company continued to prosper and finally outgrew its facilities. In 1929, Case moved to its location on Russell Boulevard. The coincidence of the Case Company move and the stock market crash still prompts quips and chuckles today.

Even though the Depression that started in 1929 brought despair and ruination to many companies, W. R. Case & Sons survived. It did so by staying with its commitment to produce a quality knife, yet at a price the average man could afford. These were the years of the 10-, 15-, and 25-cent knife. These prices were actually incorporated into the tang stamping. When the country finally started to pull itself out of the Depression, W. R. Case & Sons acquired the equipment to produce household cutlery and, in 1936, patented Concave Ground Household Knives. It was also in 1936 that Case bought the Genco Company, manufacturers of straight razors. Also around this time, Adolph Hitler was beginning to mount his offenses on Eastern Europe. By the early 1940s, Case's reputation for quality had grown tremendously—to the extent the U.S. government came directly to the company to manufacture fighting and survival knives for the military without putting the project up for competitive bidding.

In May 1944, W. R. Case & Sons Cutlery Co. and E. W. Smiley of Sturgis, Michigan purchased the Schaaf and Good Company, manufacturers of scissors and shears. From this purchase, they formed Case-Smiley Corporation, located in Fremont, Ohio. In 1949, Smiley sold his interest to Case, and the company changed its name to Case Shear Corporation. In 1952, Case Shear Corp. leased a new factory building in Nashville, Arkansas. By 1953, Case Shear Corp. moved to Nashville, and the Fremont plant was sold. After several years, Case Shear Corp. purchased the building and remains there today.

In 1952, Case set up a corporation in Nashville named Case-Nashville. It took a lease on a modest building and began manufacturing Case pocketknives. This corporation continued producing pocketknives until 1975 when the pocketknife plant was built in Bradford. At the end of 1975, Case-Nashville Corp. was absorbed and became part of the W. R. Case & Sons Cutlery Co.

In 1941, representatives of Wear-ever pots and pans, a subsidiary of Alcoa, approached W. R. Case & Sons to discuss having it produce a nine-piece cutlery set under the Wear-ever brand. The sets were to be sold to housewives at demonstration dinners in conjunction with Wear-ever pots and pans. The proposal was agreed on and soon after, Case received an order for 40,000 sets. This operation had just begun when the attack on Pearl Harbor occurred, and within weeks it had to be abandoned to permit rapidly increasing production for the war effort.

In 1945, shortly after the war, Wear-ever and Case met to review the proposal. The fact that the original sets had sold so readily and that the demand for Case's own products was rapidly increasing indicated that Case did not have enough manufacturing capacity. After reviewing several alternatives, Case and Alcoa decided to form a separate corporation, in 1948, for the production of these sets. After reviewing several locations, Olean, N.Y. was selected as the site for the new company, named Alcas Cutlery, a combination of the names Alcoa and Case. Case sold its interest in the company in 1972. However, Alcas still operates today, subcontracting for other manufacturers.

The year 1948 was a busy one for Case. It was then that J. Russell Case and John O'Kain were approached by the minister of trade and industry in Nova Scotia, Canada. The minister proposed that Case try to salvage a cutlery company in Pictou, Nova Scotia. That same day, Mr. O'Kain was told to accompany the minister back to Nova Scotia and set up a new company called W. R. Case & Sons of Canada Ltd.

An inspection of the plant was a disaster, revealing that most of the equipment was antiquated and outmoded. However, Case decided to give it a go. Unfortunately, the company was short lived. Aside from the facilities, Case was faced with another problem. Lobster fishing was a big business in that area and for three months out of the year, employees expected to go out on the lobster boats. Consequently, it was decided to return the plant to the province and dissolve the corporation.

When J. Russell Case died in 1953, he was succeeded by O'Kain, who had joined the company in 1940. His wife, Rhea, was J. Russell's niece. Previous to her marriage to O'Kain, Rhea was married to Harold Osborne, a salesman for Case until his death.

In 1972, John O'Kain retired and W. R. Case & Sons Cutlery Co. was purchased by American Brands Inc. It was also in 1972 that J. Russell Osborne, great nephew of J. Russell Case and Rhea O'Kain's son, became operating head of the company.

Through the years, Case's reputation for quality continued to grow. By the early 1970s, the demand for Case products grew to such proportions that the company was only able to fill a fraction of its orders. With American Brands as its new parent company, Case was able to expand to meet this demand. In 1975, a new pocketknife manufacturing facility was built in South Bradford on Owens Way and all pocketknife operations were relocated there. It was also in 1975 that J. Russell Osborne died. Upon his untimely death, R. N. Farquharson, V.P. sales, assumed leadership of the company, a position he held until his retirement in 1981.

## Chronology

The "Case" name has been a standard bearer in the cutlery industry for more than 90 years. Although many cutlery-related businesses carry the "Case" name, Case Brothers and W. R. Case & Sons are the pivotal corporation and all others seem to revolve around them. A popular misconception among collectors of both knives and razors is that "Case Brothers" was the parent company of W. R. Case & Sons. In truth, they were two competing cutlery manufacturers, and for periods of time, unfriendly rivals.

## Case Brothers Cutlery Co.

**1881-86:** John D. Case Co., Little Valley, New York. John D. Case awarded patent for his butterfly razor on February, 8, 1881.

**1886-87:** Jean, John, and Andrew Case were involved with Cattaraugus Cutlery Co., Little Valley, New York.

**1890-1900:** Case Bros., Wholesalers of Cutlery, Spring Green, Colorado.

**1896:** John, Jean, and Andrew Case form Case Brothers Cutlery Co. in Little Valley, New York (jobbers).

**1900:** Case Brothers Cutlery Co. incorporated in Little Valley, New York (manufacturing company).

**1901:** Elliot and Dean Case leave Case Brothers to form Standard Knife Co., Little Valley, New York.

**1902:** J. Russell Case leaves Case Brothers.

**1903:** Standard Knife Company goes out of business.

**1907:** Case Brothers open a second factory in Kane, Pennsylvania.

**1909:** Andrew J. Case leaves Case Brothers to join Union Cutlery Co.

Case Brothers purchases the Smethport Cutlery Company in Smethport, Pennsylvania. Case Brothers, Kane, Pennsylvania, reorganized under the name Kane Cutlery Co.

Smethport factory burns to the ground in June, 1909.

**1910-11:** Case Brothers build new factory in Warren, Pennsylvania to replace Smethport works.

**1912:** Case Brothers Cutlery Co., Little Valley, New York, burns to the ground. On March 27, 1912, Case Brothers Cutlery Co. reaches an agreement to rebuild in Springville, New York.

**1913:** Case Brothers, Springville, New York, goes into operation.

**1914:** In late 1914, Case Brothers Cutlery Co., unable to recover from two devastating fires (Smethport, Pennsylvania, and Little Valley, New York) goes out of business. On October 21, 1914, Case Brothers Cutlery Co. sells its trademark "Tested XX" to W. R. Case & Sons.

## W. R. Case & Sons

**1900:** Little Valley Knife Association incorporated in Little Valley, New York (H. Crandall, jobber).

**1902:** In January 1902, J. Russell Case forms W. R. Case & Son Cutlery Company, in Little Valley, New York (jobber).

**1903:** December 31, 1903, H. N. Platts reaches an agreement to merge with W. R. Case & Son, as W. R. Case & Son's. This was after Harvey Platts purchased his brothers share of C. Platts Sons Cutlery Co., Elred, Pennsylvania.

**1905:** On February 5, 1905, the company applies for and receives its operating charter from the State of Pennsylvania. They move the business to Bank Street in Bradford, Pennsylvania.

**1905:** Crandall Cutlery Co. is incorporated as a manufacturing company in Bradford, Pennsylvania (formerly Little Valley Knife Association).

**1907-09:** Platts Brothers Cutlery Co., Andover, New York (in operation for less than two years).

**1911:** H. N. Platts leaves W. R. Case & Sons to form Western States Cutlery Co., Boulder, Colorado. The actual separation of the two companies took several years to complete (1911-1914).

**1912:** W. R. Case & Sons acquire Crandall Cutlery Co. of Bradford, Pennsylvania.

**1914:** W. R. Case & Sons acquire "Tested XX" trademark from Case Brothers Cutlery Co.

**1915:** W. R. Case & Sons first use "Tested XX" trademark. During this period (1914-20), W. R. Case & Sons reorganize its entire product line because of World War I and the departure of H. N. Platts.

**1917:** Start of United States participation in World War I.

**1920:** W. R. Case & Sons "Tested XX" line is in full production.

Case introduces a second, less expensive line under the Standard Knife Co., Bradford, Pennsylvania, mark.

**1923:** W. R. Case ends use of Standard Knife mark.

**1926:** Kinfolks incorporated in Little Valley, New York (Kinfolks razors are manufactured by W. R. Case & Sons).

**1936:** W. R. Case & Sons acquire razor stocks and trademark of Genco Corporation.

**1940:** W. R. Case changes its line stamping to "Case XX" (full implementation is delayed for several years due to World War II).

**1941:** Start of the United States' participation in World War II.

**1942:** Although Case had been reducing razor production since the mid-1930s, W. R. Case effectively ends razor production in January 1942 (relying on existing stocks and razors acquired from Genco) and begins tooling up for the war effort.

**1945:** World War II ends.

**1955:** Case introduces a new line of razors to replace exhausted stocks (marked "Made in USA by Case") (approx. 1955-60) Kinfolks Incorporated, Little Valley, New York, goes out of business.

**1962:** W. R. Case manufactures the genuine mother-of-pearl "CASE ACE" as mementos for its officers and salesmen; W. R. Case & Sons formally ends 57 years of straight razor production.

**1965:** W. R. Case changes product line marking to "Case XX USA."

**1970:** Case changes product line marking to the dot system.

**1972:** W. R. Case & Sons is sold to American Brands Inc.

**1980:** Case changes product line marking to lightning SS with dots system.

**1988:** American Brands sells W. R. Case & Sons to James F. Parker, Chattanooga, Tennessee.

**1990:** W. R. Case & Sons is sold to River Associates, Inc., of Chattanooga, Tennessee.

**1990:** Case changes product line markings to W. R. Case & Sons, Bradford USA, PA, and the year.

**1993:** W. R. Case & Sons is sold to Zippo Mfg. Co. of Bradford, Pennsylvania.

**1993:** W. R. Case & Sons change the product marking to a long tail C, USA, with dots underneath.

*Case Cutlery Works, Bradford, Pennsylvania*

*Case Bros. Cutlery Works, Springville, New York*

## Case: American Made

Knife collecting is perhaps the fastest-growing hobby in America. It provides plenty of enjoyment, as well as being an excellent investment for the future.

Of the thousands of knives collected, and the undisputed manufacturing behind them, the W. R. Case & Sons Cutlery Company has more dedicated followers than any other company. Case continues to produce fine quality cutlery items today.

In my opinion, a carefully assembled collection of selected Case knives will continue to grow in value year after year. Many Case knives that sold for $100 a year or two ago have doubled or tripled in value. The demand for older knives is very strong. I felt that collectors needed a realistic price guide to judge the current value of their knives. This guide contains carefully researched prices that reflect the current market and scarcity of many Case knife patterns.

Knife collecting is a very personal hobby in which each individual can select a specialty. Some Case collectors search for certain patterns, such as trappers, whittlers, canoes, muskrats, peanuts, folding hunters, etc. Others collect certain handle materials such as stag, bone, pearl, yellow, rough black, green bone, etc. Many collect certain blade stampings such as Case Tested, Case XX, Case XX USA, Case XX USA 10 Dots, etc. And, of course, certain collectors want any knife as long as it has a Case marking. Regardless of your desires for a Case specialty, you'll find willing buyers, sellers, and traders at any knife show.

I have endeavored to give each knife a fair market price for the knife in 100 percent mint condition.

If your preference is for used knives, you'll have to use your own judgment as to a fair value. As a general rule, used knives bring between 25 percent to 50 percent of this book's value. Make no mistake about it: used knives can have considerable value, but for a sound investment, it is more desirable to collect only mint Case knives. Knives that have exceptionally beautiful handles in bone and stag will bring a premium price that is usually $5 to $20 more than the book price.

Remember to take excellent care of your collection, as you are the curator during your lifetime for future generations to enjoy. Moisture and fingerprints are the prime villains to avoid. Check your collection periodically and keep your knives in a dry location. Make a concerted effort to wipe your knives at least once a month. You can very quickly have a sizable amount of money invested in your collection and just as quickly lose money if you allow your knives to deteriorate from lack of care and maintenance.

Beyond the shadow of a doubt, the best way to learn about Case knives is to attend as many knife shows as possible. Most dealers and collectors are very patient about explaining the many variations and subtleties that make some knives rarer than others. The more knives you examine, the more familiar you will become with them. This experience will also make it easier to spot counterfeits or altered knives. If you are just starting out, take the time to mostly look and talk, rather than buy. Don't start out hoping to collect every Case knife, as it would be virtually impossible. Set your goals at a more realistic level such as one particular pattern, a certain type of handle or one particular blade stamping. A collection with a theme or direction will be easier to sell than one that is simply a conglomeration of everything.

Above all, when you reach the point where you are purchasing knives costing hundreds of dollars, make sure that you buy only from reputable dealers who will stand behind the authenticity of the knife. Beware of a bargain because it is likely an attempt to cheat you. As in any hobby, there are always those unscrupulous few who will make a fast dollar in any way they can. Many counterfeiters are so good that only an expert can tell their knives are fakes. Simply be as careful as you can and familiarize yourself with Case manufacturing methods and details.

In any event, get your feet wet at a knife show. Look, ask questions, read books and articles, become a Case knife collector, and join thousands of us who enjoy this great hobby. It is advisable to join the National Knife Collectors Association, as well as any of the many local and individual knife clubs throughout the country. The Case company runs a Case Collectors Club for those of us who will collect nothing else. Its newsletter contains valuable information about both new and old Case knives.

# Case Numbering System

First digit denotes the handle material.
Second digit tells the number of blades.
Last two digits are the factory pattern numbers.
An "O" at the first or the third digit indicates a variation in that particular knife; for example, 06263S.S. or 62048SP.

## Number and Letters of Case Handle Material

| | | | |
|---|---|---|---|
| 1 | walnut | B | waterfall |
| 2 | black composition (slick black) | BM | brown mottled |
| 3 | yellow composition | GM | green mottled |
| 4 | white composition | GS | goldstone celluloid |
| 5 | genuine stag, second-cut stag, red stag | HA | high art |
| | | IV | ivory |
| 6 | bone, green bone, red bone, delrin, laminated wood, rough black Rogers bone | P | variety of celluloid colors |
| | | R | candy stripe or glitter stripe |
| | | RM | red mottled or Christmas tree |
| 7 | tortoise, imitation tortoise, curly maple (1970s) | SG | smooth green bone |
| | | SR | smooth rose bone |
| 8 | genuine pearl | SS | stainless steel |
| 9 | imitation pearl (cracked ice) | W | wire |
| A | Appaloosa | | |

## Case Blade Types

| | | | |
|---|---|---|---|
| 1/2 | master blade is clip style | L | locks open |
| 3/4 | front of blade is flat, rear is saber | LP | long pull |
| B&G | budding and grafting blade | PEN | pen blade |
| C | crown (C61050) | PU | punch blade |
| CC | concave ground | RAZ | razor (one-arm-man blade) |
| DG | dog grooming | SAB | saber ground |
| EO | easy open | SCIS or SC | scissors |
| F | file blade | SER | serrated edge |
| FK | fork | SH | sheepfoot blade |
| I | iron | SH | sheepfoot master blade |
| J | long spey or spear blade in rear | SKW | skate wrench |
| K | cap lifter or bartender's knife | SP | spey blade |
| K | cork screw | | |

## Miscellaneous Abbreviations

| | | | |
|---|---|---|---|
| BOLS | bolsters | SHAD | no bolster or S |
| DR | bolsters drilled | SSP | stainless blades and springs with polished blade edge |
| R | bail in handle | | |
| SB | spring blade | T | tip bolsters |

# New Grind Blades

Case decided in 1983 that it would modify the shape of its blades on a number of patterns. These blades would have a shoulder ground in an arc instead of straight (see drawing at right). The intent was to produce a blade that would be stronger, easier to clean, and appear sleek in design. This concept only lasted for three years until the company reverted to straight grinds. Jim Parker studied numerous boards and talked to many collectors to determine the following list of patterns for the years 1983, 1984, and 1985. If you find additional patterns please notify us.

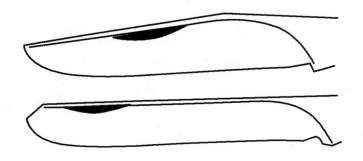

| Pattern | Price | Pattern | Price |
| --- | --- | --- | --- |
| 61048 | $25 | 6254 Bone | $150 |
| Dura Lock I | $20 | 06263 SSP Delrin | $25 |
| Dura Lock II | $20 | 6275 SP Bone | $110 |
| Dura Lock III | $20 | 6292 Bone | $80 |
| Dura Lock IV | $15 | 62109X Bone | $70 |
| Pro Lock I | $20 | 52131 Second-Cut Stag | $150 |
| Pro Lock II | $20 | 52131 Second-Stag Engraved Bolsters | $180 |
| Pro Lock III | $20 | 62131 Bone | $150 |
| Pro Lock IV | $15 | Muskrat Second-Cut Stag | $200 |
| 6207 Bone | $45 | Muskrat Second-Cut Stag Engraved Bolsters | $225 |
| 5220 Second-Cut Stag 1983 | $125 | Muskrat Bone | $150 |
| 5220 Second-Cut Stag Engraved Bolster | $150 | 6308 Bone Two Small Blades (transition) | $125 |
| 5225-1/2 Second-Cut Stag | $125 | 6308 Bone All Three Blades | $125 |
| 52032 Second-Cut Stag | $90 | 3318 | $45 |
| 62032 Bone | $55 | 5318HP Second-Cut Stag No Etch | $150 |
| 62033 Delrin | $30 | 6318HP Bone | $90 |
| 92033 | $25 | 6318SSP Bone (rare) | $150 |
| 62042 Delrin | $20 | 53032 Second-Cut Stag No Etch | $120 |
| 92042 | $25 | 63032 Bone | $85 |
| 6244 Delrin | $25 | 6344 Delrin | $30 |
| 62048 SP Delrin | $25 | 6347HP Bone | $120 |
| 62048 SSP Delrin | $30 | 6347HP SS Bone (rare) | $150 |
| 6249 Second Blade Spey | $150 | 6375 Bone | $200 |
| 6249 Bone | $150 | 5383 Second-Cut Stag | $190 |
| 3250 Gold Etch (1 of 600) | $250 | 5383 Second-Cut Stag Engraved Bolsters | $225 |
| 3254 | $80 | 5380 Second-Cut Stag | $275 |
| 5254 Second-Cut Stag No Etch | $175 | 5380 Second-Cut Stag Engraved Bolsters | $325 |
| 5254 Second-Cut Stag Etch | $175 | 63087 Delrin | $50 |
| 5254 Second-Cut Stag Engraved | $195 | 3392 | $85 |
| 6254 SSP Very Rare | $225 | 6392 Bone | $120 |

# Trappers

Collectors of trappers are familiar with the terms first model and Tested frame. In the same vein are terms such as regular and muskrat blade. All of these are transitions just like the Bulldog 1st model and the Texas Jack A blade, which have been presented in the preceding pages.

The photo to the right illustrates some of the early changes. The bottom knife is the earliest frame, which had very long handle material and very short bolsters (you are looking at the backs of these knives). The center knife is a later "Tested XX" knife, which has slightly shorter handle material. It is the 1st model knife. The top knife is a regular XX knife. You can see it has an even shorter handle material and longer bolsters.

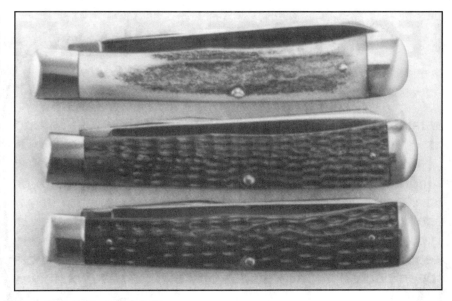

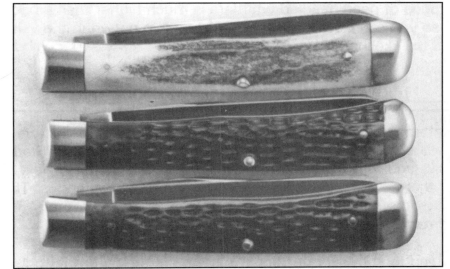

On trappers from the USA era (1965-69), you find a different type of 1st model. As illustrated in the photo to the left, the 1st model blade has the words "Tested XX Stainless" etched on the blade. The regular knife has the words "Tested XX Razor Edge" etched on the blade. In addition to the trapper, five other USA knives were etched, as was the trapper. These include 6347 SSP HP, 61048 SSP, 62048 SSP, 06263 SSP, 6318 SSP HP.

In addition to these changes, some trappers had muskrat primary blades. As illustrated in photo on the right, the top knife has a muskrat blade.

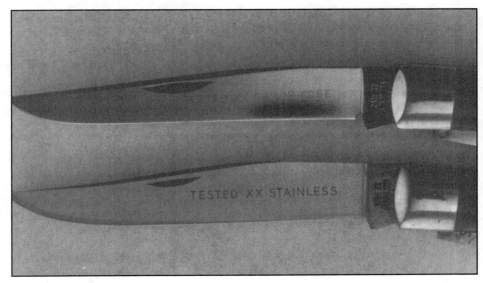

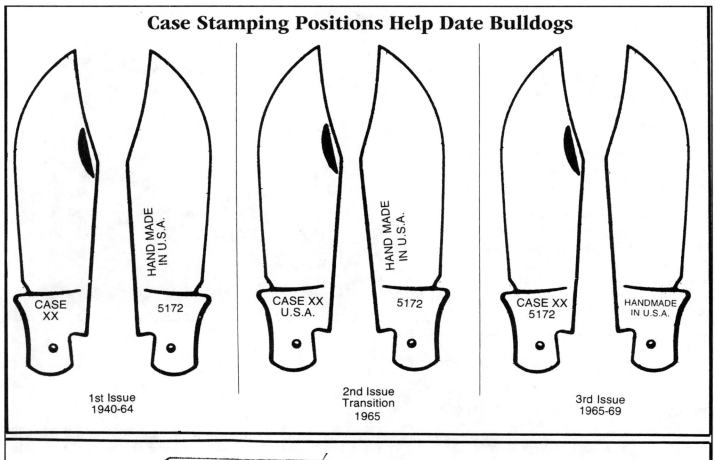

**Case Stamping Positions Help Date Bulldogs**

1st Issue 1940-64

2nd Issue Transition 1965

3rd Issue 1965-69

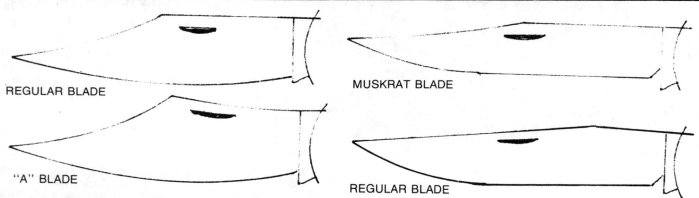

REGULAR BLADE
"A" BLADE
MUSKRAT BLADE
REGULAR BLADE

Between 1962 and 1965 Case changed the master blade of their XX99½ pattern to a smaller design. The "A" blade is the older and larger of the two and is more valuable.

Between 1963 and 1967 both the Muskrat and the regular blade was used in the trapper. The narrower Muskrat blade is more valuable.

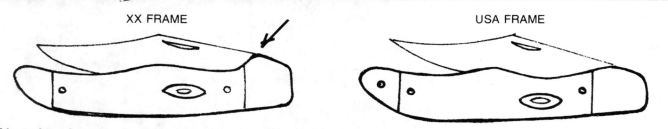

XX FRAME

USA FRAME

1965 brought a change in the Folding Hunter. The XX frame has a larger front bolster that has a more pronounced curve where it joins the handle on top. The XX frame was last used in 1964 and the lower bolster was drilled for a lanyard in only the 1964 knife. The USA frame took over in 1965 and the drilling for a lanyard is standard. In the mid-80s, Case stopped drilling again.

# CASE STAMPINGS

Used until 1920

Used until 1920

**CASE'S BRADFORD**
Used until 1920

**W.R. CASE & SONS CUTLERY CO BRADFORD, PA**
Used until 1915

**CASE & SONS BRADFORD PA**
Used until 1903-1904

**CASE XX**
Used until 1920

**CASE BRADFORD PA.**
Used until 1920

**STANDARD KNIFE CO**
1920-23

TESTED XX
1920-40

1920-40

1920-40

TESTED XX
1920-40

25¢
1935-40

**CASE XX METAL STAMPINGS LT.D.**
1942-45

1947-52

**CASE'S TESTED XX**
1940-50

1940-64

**CASE XX STAINLESS**
1950-64

**CASE XX U.S.A.**
1965-69

**CASE XX STAINLESS U.S.A.**
1965-69

**CASE XX U.S.A.**
· · · · · · · · · ·
1970-79

**CASE XX STAINLESS U.S.A.**
· · · · · · · · · ·
1970-79

**CASE XX**
· · · · · · · · · ·
**U.S.A.**
Used from 1980
(Lightning S)

**CASE XX**
**SS**
· · · · · ·   · · · ·
**U.S.A.**
Used from 1980
(Lightening S Stainless)

**CASE XX BRADFORD, PA.**
19 USA 91

CASE XX
U.S.A.
· · · · · · ·
1993

**EXPLANATION OF CASE "DOT" SYSTEM**

In 1970 Case began stamping the tang with 10 Dots underneath the U.S.A. and for each year thereafter, a dot was eliminated until 1979 had only 1 Dot. In 1980 they went back to 10 Dots but with the "lightning S". The Dots are between "Case XX and U.S.A." Again, a Dot is omitted for each new year.   * Beware of Case 75¢ & 1.00 knives, never made.

W.R. CASE & SONS CUTLERY CO.
ALGONGUIN
BRADFORD, PA. U.S.A.
(Clippers Stamp)

CASE BROS. & CO.
GOWANDA N.Y.

Ca. 1896

L. V. KNIFE ASSN.
LITTLE VALLEY
N.Y.
1900

CASE MFG. CO.
LITTLE VALLEY
N.Y.

circa early 1900's

W R CASE
&
SONS
MADE IN USA

1905-1914

W R CASE
&
SONS
MADE IN U.S.A.
1905-1914

W.R. CASE & SONS
GERMANY
1900-1915

W. R. CASE
& SON
BRADFORD PA
1902-1903

W.R. CASE
& SON
LITTLE VALLEY
N.Y.
1902-1903

W R CASE & SON
CUTLERY
CO
1902-1903

C. PLATTS & SONS
ELDRED, PA.
1904

J. D. CASE
CO.
KANE, PA
c. 1905-1910

CASE
KANE, PA.
1907-1909

KANE CUTLERY
CO.
KANE, PA
1907-1909

KANE CUTLERY
CO.
1909

W R CASE & SON
Little Valley, NY
1902-1903

CASE BROS.
CUT.
CO.
1912

W R CASE
& SONS
BRADFORD, PA

1916-1920
Military Stamp Used WWI

CASE
XX

1920-1946

# Case Stampings

## Case Stamping Positions Help Date Bulldogs

Between 1962 and 1965 Case changed the master blade of its XX991/2 pattern to a smaller design. The "A" blade is the older and larger of the two and is more valuable.

Between 1963 and 1967 both the muskrat and the regular blade were used in the trapper. The narrower muskrat blade is more valuable.

1965 brought a change in the folding hunter. The XX frame has a larger front bolster that has a more pronounced curve where it joins the handle on top. The XX frame was last used in 1964 and the lower bolster was drilled for a lanyard only in the 1964 knife. The USA frame took over in 1965, and the drilling for a lanyard was standard. In the mid-80s, Case stopped drilling the lanyard holes again.

## Explanation of Case "Dot" System

In 1970, Case began stamping the tang with 10 dots underneath the U.S.A. For each year thereafter, a dot was eliminated until 1979, when knives were stamped with only 1 dot. In 1980, Case went back to 10 dots but with the "lightning S." The dots are between "Case XX and U.S.A." Again, a dot is omitted for each new year.

Beware of Case knives stamped 75 cents or $1.00. Case never made these knives in the vintage era.

## Case Stampings

```
W.R. CASE & SONS
   CUTLERY CO.          FRONT
   BRADFORD, PA.


  GS197 SOLINGEN        BACK
     GERMANY
```

**1989.** This stamp can be found on four different knife patterns, 1,000 of which were made in four different handle materials. These knives were made on contract for Jim Parker in 1989. These knives can easily be identified by looking on the rear side of the tang. You will find the pattern number and the words, "Solingen, Germany."

```
    CASE
BRADFORD, PA.
19  USA  90
```

**1990-1996.** In 1990, Jim Parker first introduced an exclusive line of knives called "Case Classics." These knives were authorized under a licensing agreement with Case. Blue Grass Cutlery actually arranged for most of these knives to be manufactured on contract. However, four of the patterns were made by Case. They were the 54 trapper pattern, the 94 gunboat pattern, the four-bladed 88 congress pattern, and the two-bladed 52100 saddlehorn pattern. Each of these knives has the date stamped on the tang. This is the "Case Bradford" version. Smoky Mountain Knife Works had a special agreement to continue production of the Case Classics 6340 pattern during 1997 through 1999.

```
    CASE
19  XX  94
```

**c. 1993-1996.** This is the "Case XX" Case Classics stamping.

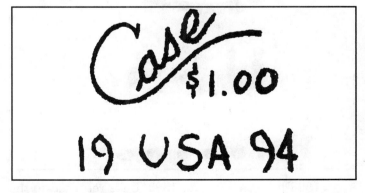

**c. 1994 ONLY** This is the "Case $1.00" version. (Case Classics).

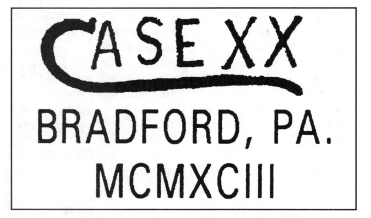

**c. 1990-1993.** For the first four years (1990-93), Case stamped its knives this way. Each year, the two numbers on the right were changed.

**c. 1993.** This stamp uses Roman numerals to indicate the year the knife was made. This stamp was used on special-order knives for two or three years.

**c. 1993-present.** In late 1993, Case returned to the dot dating system, removing one dot each year. This knife is a six-dot; thus, it was made in 1994. A few patterns may have been stamped with this stamp as early as 1990.

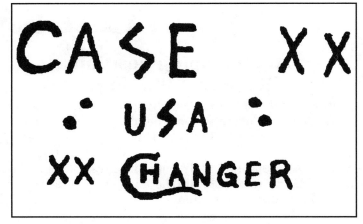

**1996-present.** This stamp is used today for the "Changer" series, which has a handle with interchangeable blades.

**1997-present.** This is the current stamp used for patterns with lock-back blades like 51225LSS. When the Copperlock (51549LSS) was introduced in 1997, Case made what was termed a "mistake." The initial stamp was made to indicate a lock-back blade, which it has. However, the intent was to have the standard stamp on this knife. So the first blades were used and now the standard stamp will be used on blades put in the Copperlock produced in the future. This is just one example of the many variations that have occurred throughout Case's history. Several years from now, one version of the Copperlock stamp will be worth more than the other, depending on how many of each were made.

**c. 1948-1952.** In 1948, W. R. Case & Sons, at the request of the Canadian government, purchased the Pictou Cutlery Company in Pictou, Nova Scotia. Case changed the name to R. Case & Sons Ltd.

**CASE XX**
**METAL STAMPINGS**
**LT.D.**

**c. 1948-1952.** This is another version of the stamp. Both are difficult to find in the U.S.

**CASE XX**
**U.S.A.**

**c. 1965-1969.** Many "USA"-era knives can be found in mint condition today.

**CASE**
**TESTED XX**

**c. 1920-1940.** This stamp is similar to the previous one, but the "E" turns outward on the far right side.

**CASE**
**PAT.**
**9-21-26**

**c. 1920s.** This stamp is on a wire knife that was patented by another manufacturer and was probably made on contract.

**c. 1920-1940.** This stamp is sometimes called a "circus" stamp. Note the box-like "C." It was not commonly used, but a few patterns have been seen with this stamp.

**CASE**     **CASE**
**STAINLESS**    **XX**
               **TESTED**
**U.S.**

**c. 1916-1920.** I have only seen this stamp on one pattern. It is a two-bladed goldstone senator pattern. It has a unique "S" shield for stainless. The back of the master blade also has a "U.S." stamped on it. All but one of the half-dozen or so I have seen have both blades broken about halfway up. This probably means they were some type of contract knives that were returned and never sold.

**c. 1932-1940.** This stamp is generally on large folding hunters and Coke-bottle patterns. This is a very rare version. Most have "TESTED XX" under the word "Case."

# CASE

**c. 1932-1940.** This stamp is also used on larger knives in most situations. This knife is a switchblade. There are similar stamps, but note the bottom of the "C." This is where the difference is.

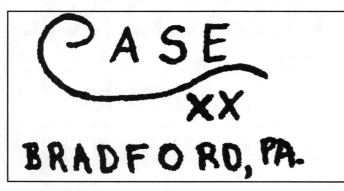

**c. 1930s.** This is a stamp found only on scissors.

# PRIMBLE BELKNAP

**c. 1930s.** Case made this contract knife for Primble. It is a C61050 pattern with green bone handles. They also made the 6265, the 5347, and the 6254 that we know of. Each has a pattern number unique to Primble.

# CUTSURE

**c. 1920s.** CUTSURE was a brand name used by Kruse & Bahlmann Hardware Company, in business from 1894-1962. Case made some of its patterns on contract. This particular knife is a 6214 pattern with green bone handles.

# WHITE HOUSE

**c. 1920s.** White House was a brand used by McWhorter-Weaver Hardware in Nashville, TN in the early '20s. Case made many of its knives on contract. This stamp is on a celluloid-handled Barlow.

# WINCHESTER -TRADE MARK- MADE IN U.S.A.

**c. 1920s.** Winchester contracted with Case in the late '20s to manufacture a one- and two-bladed 91 pattern (large sleeveboard). These knives have green bone handles.

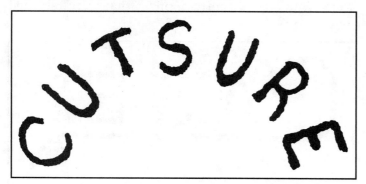

**c. 1915-1940.** Case made many knives for Clauss in Freemont, Ohio. They generally have green bone handles and are identical to Case knives except for the shield, tang stamp, and unique pattern numbers that are usually stamped on the back of the master blade tang.

## Case Stampings

**c. 1925-1948.** This stamp is frequently found on fixed-blade knives, as well as on pocketknives.

**c. 1925-1948.** This is another version, which has the word "Incorporated" instead of "U.S.A."

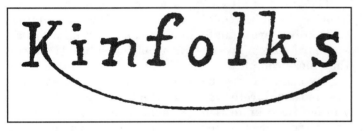

**c. 1925-1948.** Here you see a slightly different version, which has neither "Incorporated nor "U.S.A." under "Kinfolks."

**STANDARD KNIFE CO 2**

**c. 1925-1948.** A few of the Standard stamps have the number "2" under the words "Knife Co." No documentation exists to explain this variation. However, it is a much rarer version of the stamp.

**STANDARD KNIFE CO.**

**ca. 1925-1948.** This version of the stamp has all the words in a straight line and is less common than the two-line version.

**STANDARD**

**ca. 1925-1948.** Some fixed-blade knives are stamped with the single word "STANDARD." Generally STANDARD knives were made to be a less expensive line than Case knives. The shields are slick, but if you take the shield off a STANDARD knife, it will usually have CASE on the reverse side. It was not uncommon to simply reverse CASE shields for the STANDARD brand.

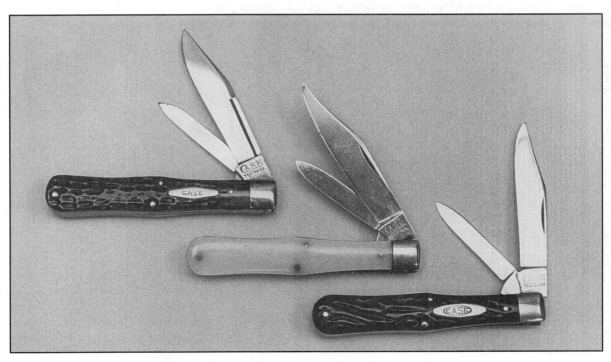

# Vintage Case Knives

By Bob Wurzelbacher

Any one who attempts to collect vintage Case knives immediately discovers that surprisingly there are an enormous number of patterns, blade configurations, and handle materials. The also discover very early in this pursuit that there are several very distinct eras and companies that are commonly associated with the vintage era. These would include:

Case Brothers (1896-1915)
W. R. Case & Son (1902-1903)
W. R. Case & Son's (1903-1905)
W. R. Case & Sons (1905-1914)
The Bradford Era (1914-1919)
Case Family (1900-1920)
Case Memorabilia and Miscellaneous

They will also discover, unfortunately that very little documentation is available as to what patterns, blade configurations, and handle materials these companies offered to the public. To complicate the matter, a number of contract knives were produced when these companies began. We do have some early catalogs that provide information about specific knives and the options that were available to customers. A number of individuals have over time provided photographs and listings from catalogs. There is however no complete listing of the knives produced by any of these companies.

The following chapters are designed to provide some perspective on how the individual companies fit into the history of what is generically referred to as the Case company. We will do this by providing a photograph of individual knives by company, pattern, and handle material. These photographs will be from museums and collections. This is a journey, and we need you to be a part of it. If you have a knife in your collection that is not shown here, please send us a photo anda description. We will try to include your submission in the next edition.

## Pricing

Pricing knives from these eras is difficult because very few of these knives are offered on the market. In addition, knives from these eras are rarely mint. Even unsharpened ones are rare, since these knives were meant to be used, not collected as museum pieces.

In general, we determined the price by starting with the Tested knife price and adding ten percent for each earlier period, then subtracting ten percent for each condition from mint. In each transaction, however, the price will be determined by the condition, the rarity of the knife, the level of desirability, and finally, the availability of funds to buy the knife.

The value of all vintage Case knives are listed with a price for mint condition. While almost no vintage Case knives are actually in mint condition, mint gives a standard starting point for estimating value. The factor that most complicates this issue is that vintage Case knives cannot easily be placed in a condition category. The most accurate way to evaluate the condition of a vintage Case knife is to personally examine it and let your experience and knowledge guide you to a judgment. Even then, a great deal of variation can exist among experts as to a vintage knife's value. Nevertheless, this system, even with its limitations, provides at least a ballpark guide to vintage Case knife values.

Have an inspiring journey!

# Case Brothers Cutlery Company (1896-1915)

By Bob Wurzelbacher

After a short time (1896-1897), the four Case brothers left the Cattaraugus Cutlery Company. W. R. Case pursued his interest in farming. The other three brothers—Jean, John D., and Andrew—opened their own cutlery jobbing business called Case Brothers & Co. Their knives were produced under contract by C. Platts & Sons in Gowanda, New York. Knives with this mark are extremely rare.

In February 1900, they incorporated as Case Brothers Cutlery Company, Little Valley, New York. At that time, they opened their own factory in Little Valley and began making their own knives. This was a very successful operation and the business grew rapidly. At one time, the Case Brothers catalog amounted to 94 pages. A second pocketknife plant was established in Kane, Pennsylvania. It was at this time that Andrew Case sold his interest in the operation. The plant in Kane closed after a short period of operation.

Case family members were often hired. Two of these individuals were Elliot and Dean Case, sons of Jean Case. They set out on their own and started a cutlery jobbing business using the name Standard Knife Company, Little Valley, New York. The firm suffered an abrupt end when Elliot died in 1903 after being stricken with typhoid fever upon his return to Little Valley from a sales trip. Knives with the Standard (Little Valley) stamp are rare and duplicate Case Brothers patterns. Typically, collectors put Standard knives in the same group titled Case Family.

On February 10, 1912, the Case Brothers factory in Little Valley was completely destroyed by fire. After reviewing offers from 140 towns, the brothers decided to build a new plant in Springville, New York.

The financial burden of the Little Valley loss, however, combined with a downturn in sales was so significant that Case Brothers declared bankruptcy in May 1915. The new plant, equipment parts, and inventory were sold at auction.

Knives with the Springville stamp are also very rare, and appropriately valued by collectors.

*Sampler, CASE BROTHERS, wood, LITTLE VALLEY NY, TESTED XX, rare, $600.*

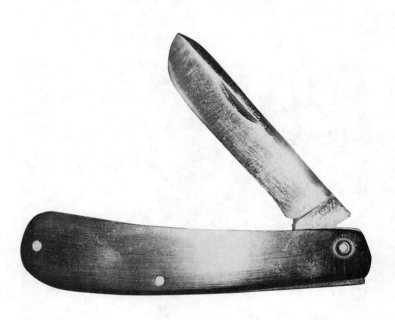

*2104, CASE BROTHERS, budding knife, cocoa, Little Valley, 3-1/2", $400.*

*Pricing Note: The value of Case vintage knives is subjective, but a good rule of thumb is to start with the Tested knife price and add ten percent for each earlier period, then subtract ten percent for each condition from mint. This is the formula we used to price vintage Case knives in this book.*

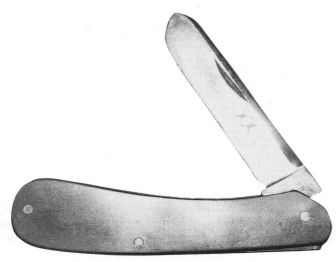

**2104, CASE BROTHERS, budding knife, cocoa, SPRINGVILLE, 3-1/2", $600.**

**5111-1/2 L LP, CASE BROTHERS, flat blade, stag, no guard, SPRINGVILLE, 4-3/8", $3,000.**

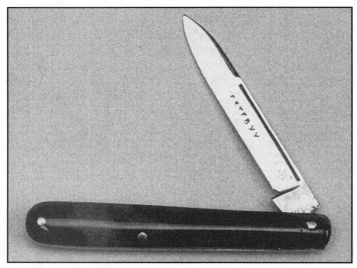

**71006, CASE BROTHERS, tortoise, SHAD, 2-1/2", $350.**

**5111-1/2 L, CASE BROTHERS, flat blade, stag, LITTLE VALLEY, 4-3/8", $500.**

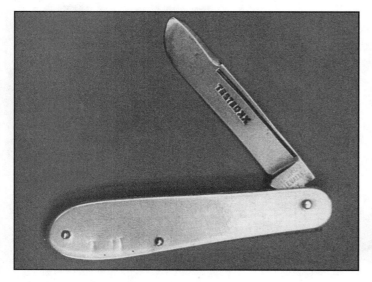

**M110, CASE BROTHERS, spey blade, metal, 3-1/8", $275.**

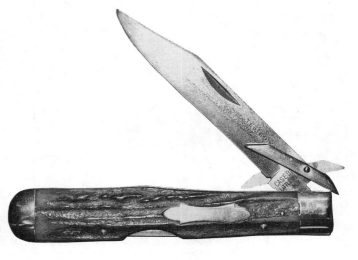

**5111-1/2 L SAB, CASE BROTHERS, stag, guards, 4-3/8", $3,000.**

Vintage Case - Case Bros. 45

*6111-1/2 L SAB, CASE BROTHERS, saber, bone, SPRINGVILLE, probably Utica, 4-3/8", $4,500.*

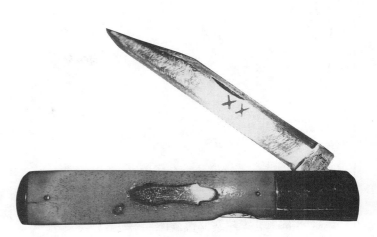

*6111-1/2 L, CASE BROTHERS, bone, SPRINGVILLE, 4-7/16", $1,500.*

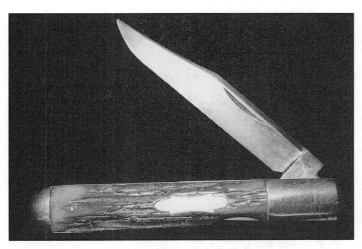

*6111-1/2 L SAB, CASE BROTHERS, bone, LITTLE VALLEY, etch (??COM & SMITH), 4-3/8", $3,000.*

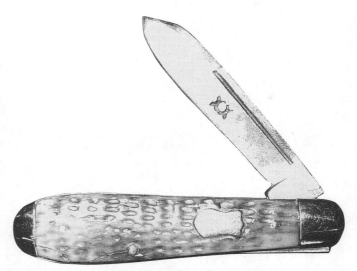

*6116 LP, CASE BROTHERS, Bradford frame, green bone, SPRINGVILLE, 2-9/16", $450.*

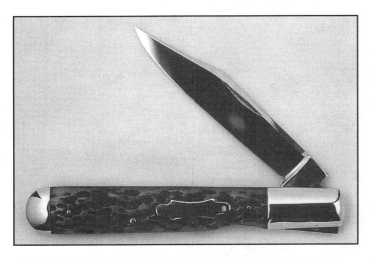

*6111-1/2 L, CASE BROTHERS, bone, LITTLE VALLEY, 4-7/16", $3,000.*

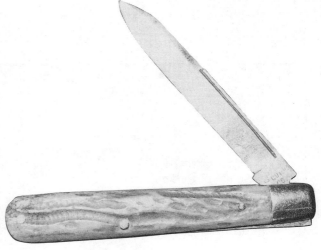

*6116 LP, CASE BROTHERS, bone, etch THE PEOPLE TRUST CO, 1-9/16", $600.*

*Pricing Note: The value of Case vintage knives is subjective, but a good rule of thumb is to start with the Tested knife price and add ten percent for each earlier period, then subtract ten percent for each condition from mint. This is the formula we used to price vintage Case knives in this book.*

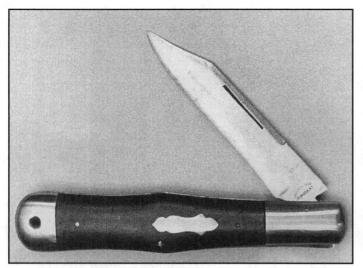

*C21050, CASE BROTHERS, large Coke, ebony, bail hole, Gowanda, rare, 5-5/16", $3,000.*

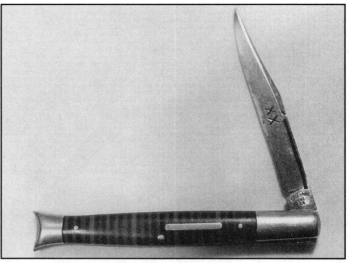

*P1051, CASE BROTHERS, fishtail, striped celluloid, Cut Co., 3-7/8", $750.*

*C61050 SAB, CASE BROTHERS, large Coke, bone, bail hole, 5-1/4", $2,500.*

*CASE BROTHERS, 61051 LP, fishtail, bone, guards, SPRINGVILLE, 3-13/16", $2,000.*

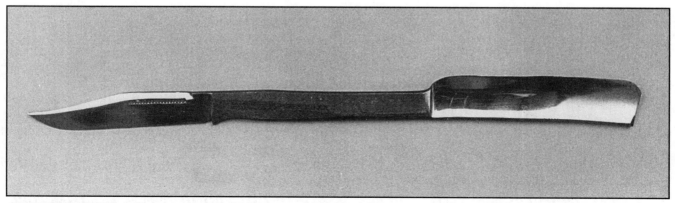

*CASE BROTHERS, unknown, metal, knife/razor, 9-1/4", $400.*

Vintage Case - Case Bros. 47

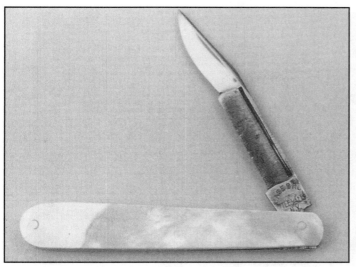

*unknown, CASE BROTHERS, cuticle file, pearl, 2-5/8", $750.*

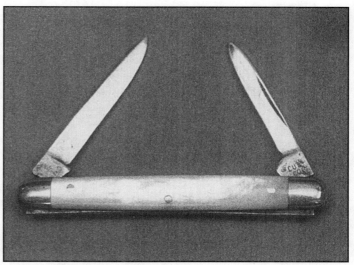

*8201, CASE BROTHERS, pearl, Cut Co., 2-11/16", $400.*

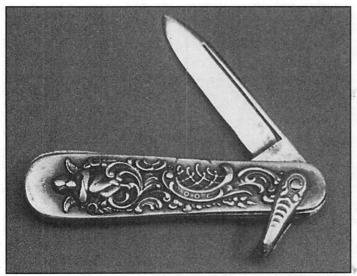

*unknown, CASE BROTHERS, sterling, figural w/bail, Cut Co., 3-1/16", $500.*

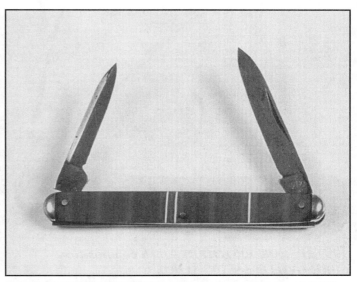

*R201, CASE BROTHERS, candy stripe, Cut Co, 2-3/4", $400.*

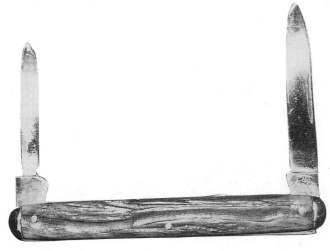

*6201, CASE BROTHERS, bone, tip bolsters, CUTLERY CO., 2-11/16", $500.*

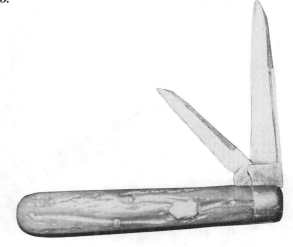

*6202 LP, CASE BROTHERS, bone, no lower bolster, 3-5/16", $250.*

Pricing Note: The value of Case vintage knives is subjective, but a good rule of thumb is to start with the Tested knife price and add ten percent for each earlier period, then subtract ten percent for each condition from mint. This is the formula we used to price vintage Case knives in this book.

**6202-1/2, CASE BROTHERS,** bone, no lower bolster, 3-5/16", $350.

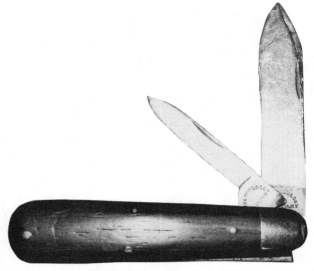

**1205 LP, CASE BROTHERS,** wood, GOWANDA, Bros & Co, very rare, 3-3/8", $1,000.

**1204 LP, CASE BROTHERS,** black composition, SPRINGVILLE, 3-9/16", $1,000.

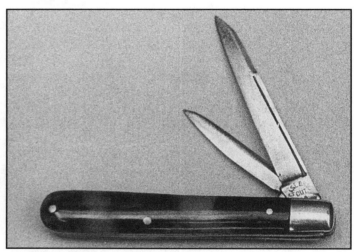

**7206, CASE BROTHERS,** tortoise, also pearl, 2-5/8", $400.

**6204 LP, CASE BROTHERS,** bone, Little Valley, 3-9/16", $900.

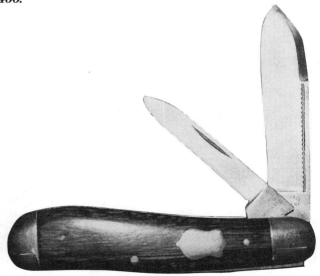

**1207 LP, CASE BROTHERS,** wood, GOWANDA, BROS & CO, very rare, 3-3/4", $1,000.

Vintage Case - Case Bros. 49

**6207 LP**, CASE BROTHERS, *bone, Little Valley, 3-3/4"*, $350.

**5212 LP**, CASE BROTHERS, *stag, flat bolsters, 3-5/16"*, $450.

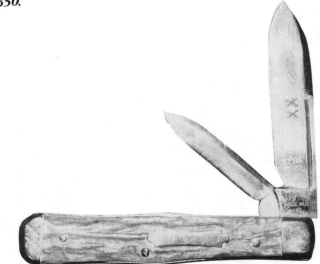

**5208 LP**, CASE BROTHERS, *stag, flat coffin, 3-1/2"*, $1,000.

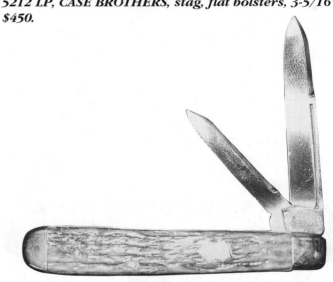

**6212 LP**, CASE BROTHERS, *bone, flat bolsters, 3-5/16"*, $400.

**6208 LP**, CASE BROTHERS, *bone, Little Valley, match striker, coffin XX, Cut Co, 3-1/2"*, $1,500.

**6212 LP**, CASE BROTHERS, *Rogers, flat bolsters, 3-5/16"*, $450.

*Pricing Note: The value of Case vintage knives is subjective, but a good rule of thumb is to start with the Tested knife price and add ten percent for each earlier period, then subtract ten percent for each condition from mint. This is the formula we used to price vintage Case knives in this book.*

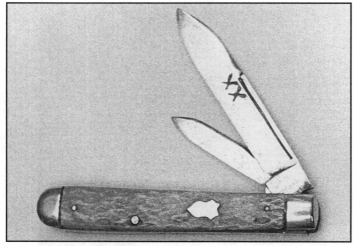

*6214 LP, CASE BROTHERS, bone, etch Cline Hardware Co., 3-3/8", $450.*

*6216 LP, CASE BROTHERS, file w/cuticle, bone, SPRINGVILLE, 3-3/8", $800.*

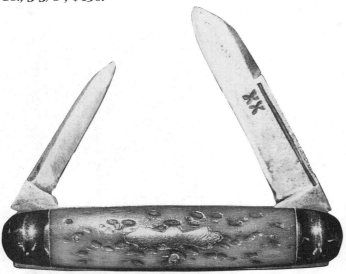

*6230 LP, CASE BROTHERS, Rogers, pinched bolsters, 3-3/8", $450.*

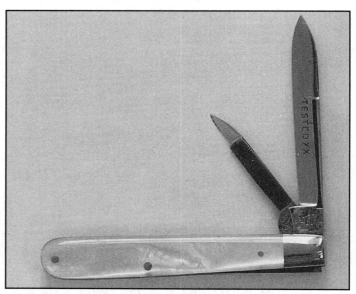

*8216 LP, CASE BROTHERS, file w/cuticle, pearl, Cut Co., 2-1/2", $450.*

*6230 LP, CASE BROTHERS, bone, pinched bolsters, 3-3/8", $450.*

*CASE BROTHERS, 62019, bone, SPRINGVILLE, 4-1/8", $1,500.*

Vintage Case - Case Bros. 51

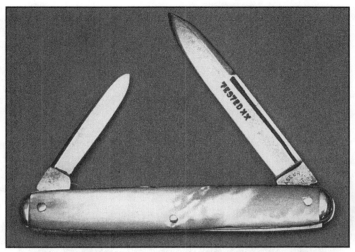

8221, CASE BROTHERS, pearl, tip bolsters, not shown, 4220, white composition, 3-3/8", $500.

6222 LP, CASE BROTHERS, bone, Little Valley, 3-5/16", $350.

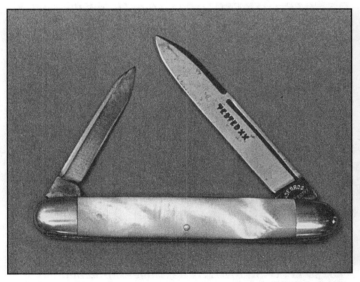

8220, Case Brothers, not a peanut, pearl, 3-3/8", $500.

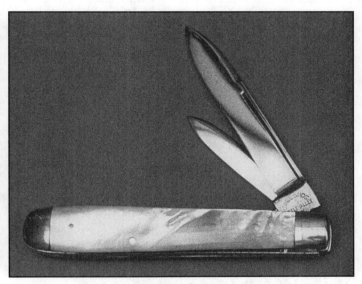

8222 LP, CASE BROTHERS, pearl, 3-1/4", $500.

6221 LP, CASE BROTHERS, bone, Little Valley, tip bolsters, 3-3/8", $300.

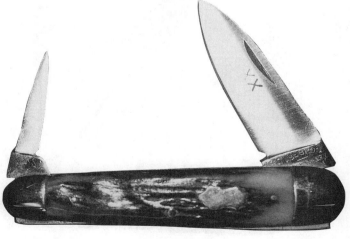

5223, CASE BROTHERS, stag, LITTLE VALLEY, 3-9/16", $1,050.

*Pricing Note: The value of Case vintage knives is subjective, but a good rule of thumb is to start with the Tested knife price and add ten percent for each earlier period, then subtract ten percent for each condition from mint. This is the formula we used to price vintage Case knives in this book.*

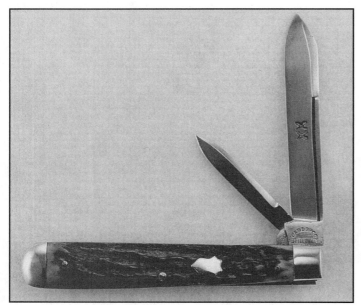

*5223, Case Brothers, stag, Little Valley, 3-5/8", $800.*

*O.5230 LP, CASE BROTHERS, stag, Little Valley, 3-3/8", $1,000.*

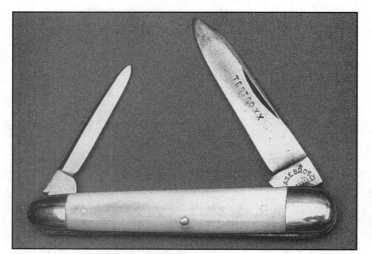

*82027, CASE BROTHERS, pearl, 2-7/8", $450.*

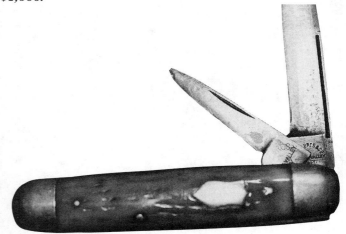

*O.6230 LP, CASE BROTHERS, Rogers, pinched bolsters, 3-3/8", $300.*

*6229LP, CASE BROTHERS, big teardrop, bone, 3-5/8", $1,000.*

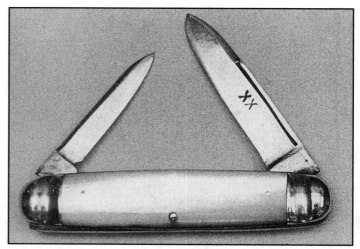

*O.8230 LP, CASE BROTHERS, pearl, pinched bolsters, 3-3/8", $450.*

Vintage Case - Case Bros.   53

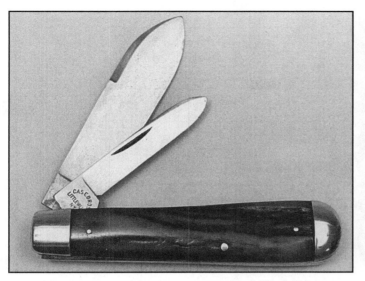

**5231 LP, CASE BROTHERS, LP stag, 3-3/4", $600.**

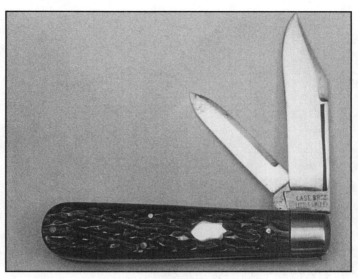

**62031-1/2 LP, CASE BROTHERS, bone, 3-3/4", $375.**

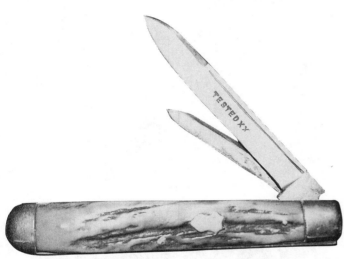

**5231 LP, CASE BROTHERS, slim versus normal, stag, 3-3/4", $600.**

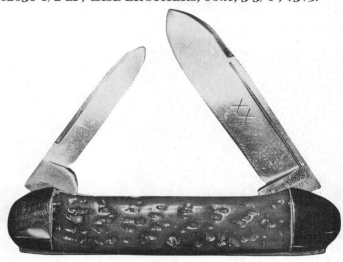

**62131 LP, CASE BROTHERS, canoe, Rogers, SPRINGVILLE 3-5/8", $2,500.**

**12031 LP, CASE BROTHERS, wood, 3-3/4", $300.**

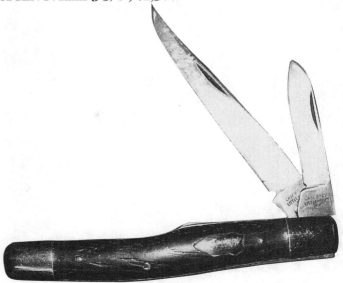

**1232, CASE BROTHERS, gunstock, wood, Little Valley, 3-5/8", $500.**

*Pricing Note: The value of Case vintage knives is subjective, but a good rule of thumb is to start with the Tested knife price and add ten percent for each earlier period, then subtract ten percent for each condition from mint. This is the formula we used to price vintage Case knives in this book.*

**5233 LP, CASE BROTHERS, stag, Little Valley, 4-1/8", $1,000.**

**O.5245 LP, CASE BROTHERS, stag, Little Valley, 3-5/8", $700.**

**6233 LP, CASE BROTHERS, Rogers, Little Valley, 4-1/8", $850.**

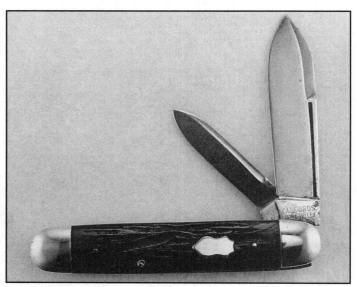

**6245 LP, CASE BROTHERS, bone, Little Valley, 3-5/8", $600.**

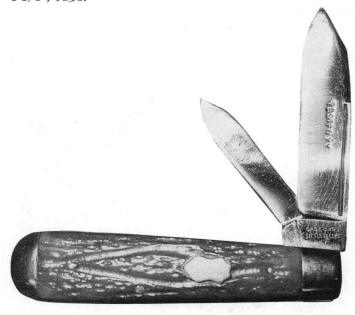

**6235 LP, CASE BROTHERS, bone, Little Valley, 3-1/2", $750.**

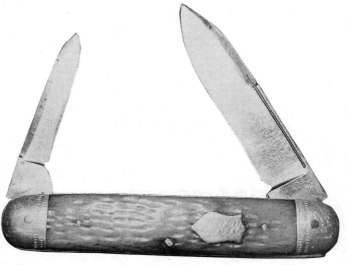

**O.6245 LP, CASE BROTHERS, bone, aluminum bolsters & spacer, Little Valley, 3-5/8", $1,000.**

Vintage Case - Case Bros.  55

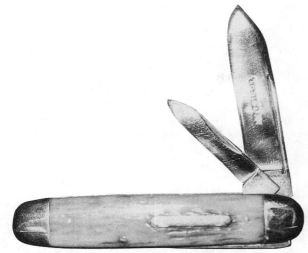

**6246 LP**, *CASE BROTHERS, bone, Little Valley, 3-5/8", $500.*

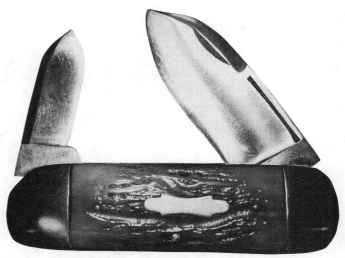

**6250**, *CASE BROTHERS, toenail, Rogers, double pull, 3-7/8", $3,500.*

**O.6246**, *CASE BROTHERS, bone, Little Valley, 3-5/8", $500.*

**6250**, *CASE BROTHERS, toenail, bone, double pull, 3-7/8", $3,500.*

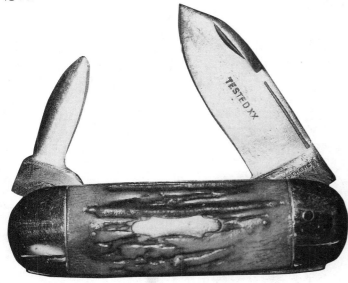

**5250**, *CASE BROTHERS, toenail, stag, double pull, 3-7/8", $3,500.*

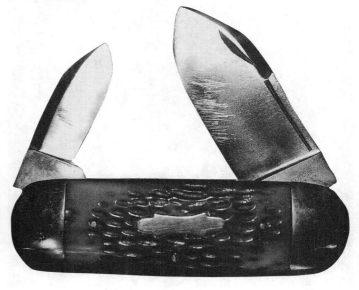

**6250**, *CASE BROTHERS, toenail, Rogers, double pull, 3-7/8", $3,500.*

*Pricing Note: The value of Case vintage knives is subjective, but a good rule of thumb is to start with the Tested knife price and add ten percent for each earlier period, then subtract ten percent for each condition from mint. This is the formula we used to price vintage Case knives in this book.*

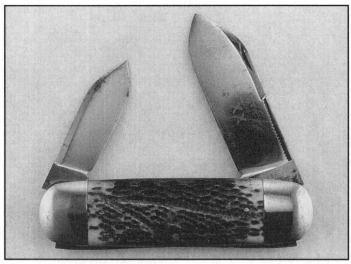

*6250, CASE BROTHERS, toenail, Rogers, etch TESTED XX, 4-5/8", $4,500.*

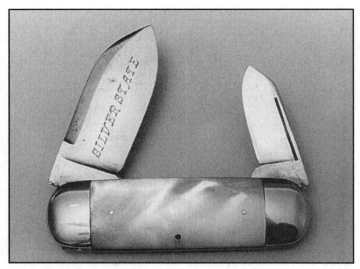

*8250, CASE BROTHERS, toenail, pearl, double pull, etch SILVER STATES, 4", $4,000.*

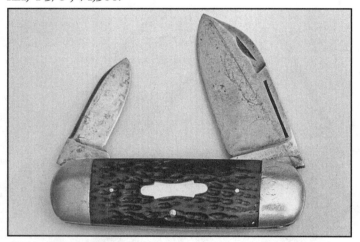

*6250, CASE BROTHERS, toenail, Rogers, regular pull, BRADFORD PA., 4", $2,000.*

*6251, CASE BROTHERS, toenail, bone, double pull, match striker, 4-3/16", $3,500.*

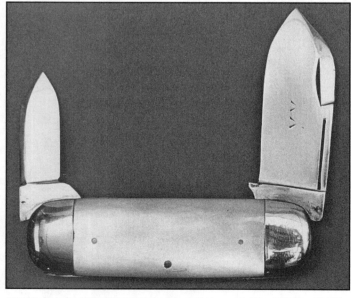

*8250, CASE BROTHERS, toenail, pearl, double pull, 4", $3,250.*

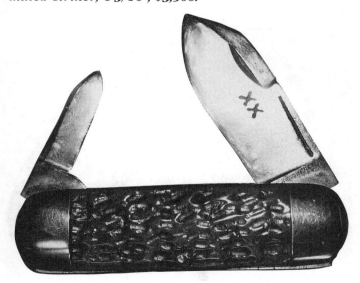

*6251, CASE BROTHERS, toenail, bone, double pull, small blade long pull, 4-3/16", $3,500.*

Vintage Case - Case Bros. 57

**6254, CASE BROTHERS, Wharncliffe, bone, Springville NY, 3-1/8", $1,000.**

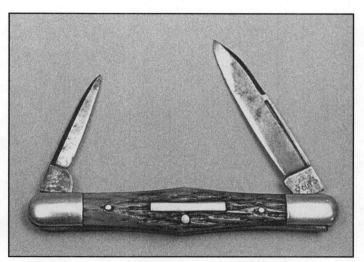

**62056 LP, CASE BROTHERS, swell center, bone 3", $600.**

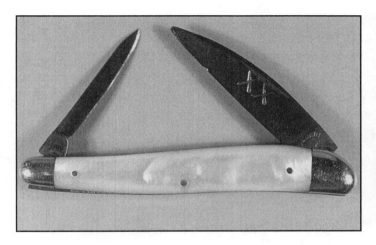

**8254, CASE BROTHERS, Wharncliffe, pearl, 3-1/8", $1,000.**

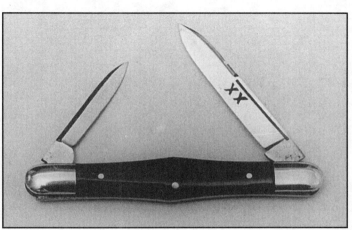

**72056 LP, CASE BROTHERS, swell center, tortoise, 3", $600.**

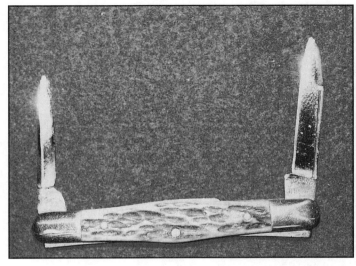

**62056 LP, CASE BROTHERS, Rogers, second blade, CUT CO, 2-15/16", $600.**

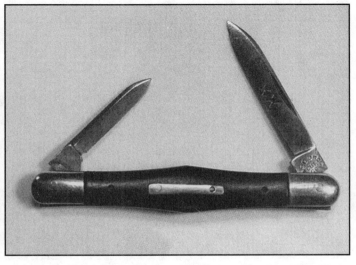

**2258, CASE BROTHERS, swell center, ebony, CUT CO, 2-7/8", $300.**

*Pricing Note: The value of Case vintage knives is subjective, but a good rule of thumb is to start with the Tested knife price and add ten percent for each earlier period, then subtract ten percent for each condition from mint. This is the formula we used to price vintage Case knives in this book.*

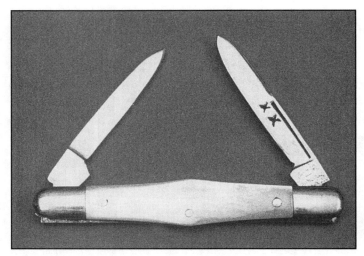

*8258, Case Brothers, swell center, pearl, Springville, 2-7/8", $750.*

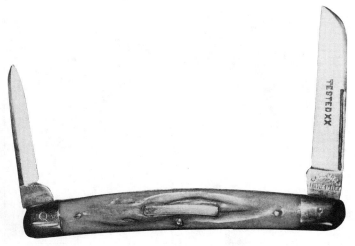

*6268 LP, CASE BROTHERS, congress, bone, second blade, CUT CO, 3-5/16", $2,000.*

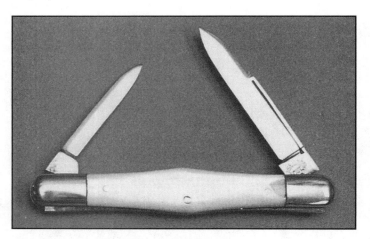

*82058, CASE BROTHERS, swell center, pearl, 2-7/8", $600.*

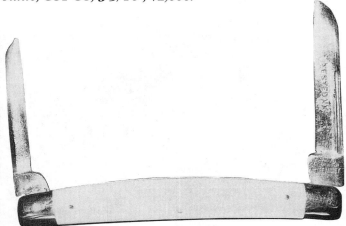

*8268 LP, CASE BROTHERS, congress, pearl, CUT CO, 3-5/16", $2,500.*

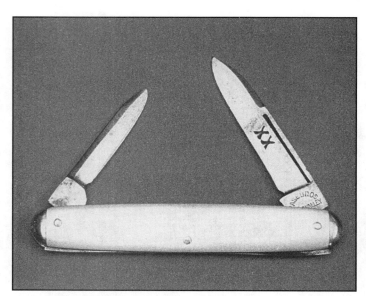

*8264, CASE BROTHERS, pearl, tip bolsters, 3-1/8", $450.*

*5270 LP, CASE BROTHERS, stag, Springville, CASE BROS, 3-3/4", $750.*

Vintage Case - Case Bros. 59

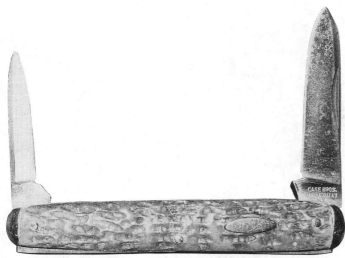

6272, CASE BROTHERS, bone, tip bolsters, LITTLE VALLEY, 3", $450.

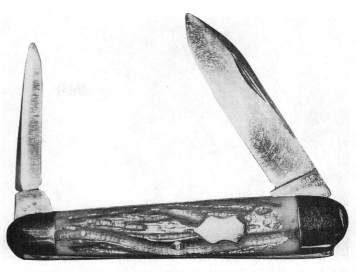

6278, CASE BROTHERS, sleeveboard, bone, 3-5/16", $500.

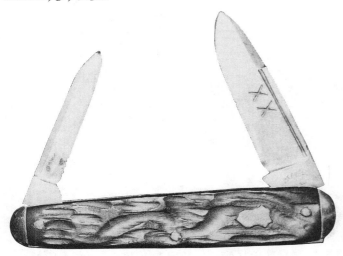

2278 LP, CASE BROTHERS, wood, tip bolsters, SPRINGVILLE, 3-5/16", $750.

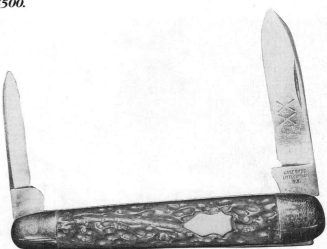

6278, CASE BROTHERS, sleeveboard, bone, 3-5/16", $500.

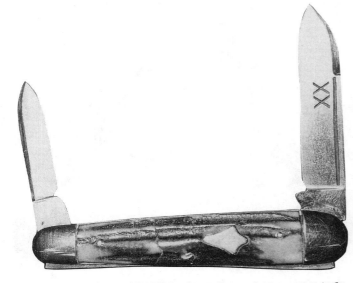

5278 LP, CASE BROTHERS, sleeveboard, stag, 3-5/16", $500.

6278 LP, CASE BROTHERS, sleeveboard, bone, 3-5/8", $500.

*Pricing Note: The value of Case vintage knives is subjective, but a good rule of thumb is to start with the Tested knife price and add ten percent for each earlier period, then subtract ten percent for each condition from mint. This is the formula we used to price vintage Case knives in this book.*

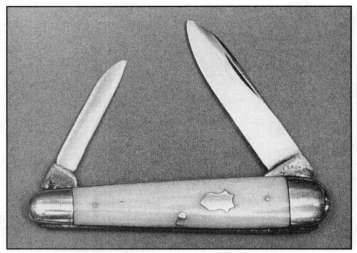

*6278, CASE BROTHERS, sleeveboard, white bone, 3-5/8", $450.*

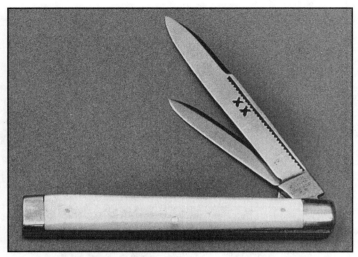

*8285, CASE BROTHERS, doctor's, match striker, pearl, Cutlery Co., 3-3/4", $1,000.*

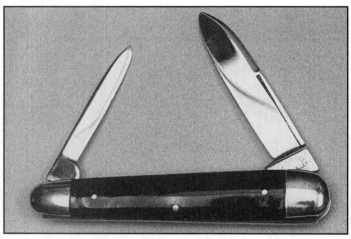

*7278 LP, CASE BROTHERS, sleeveboard, tortoise, 3-5/8", $550.*

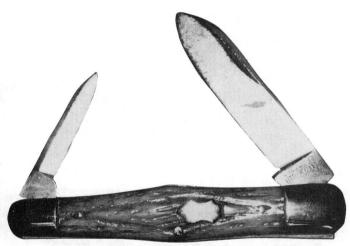

*6292, CASE BROTHERS, half whittler, bone, Little Valley, 3-3/4", $500.*

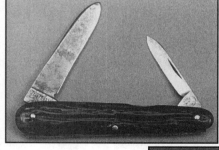

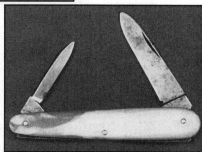

*82079 and 62079, CASE BROTHERS, sleeveboard (sales samples), bone and pearl, 3-1/4", $400.*

*6293 J LP, CASE BROTHERS, match striker, bone, Little Valley, 3-7/8", $850.*

## Vintage Case - Case Bros.　61

O.6294 LP, CASE BROTHERS, big cigar, bone, 4-1/4", $2,000.

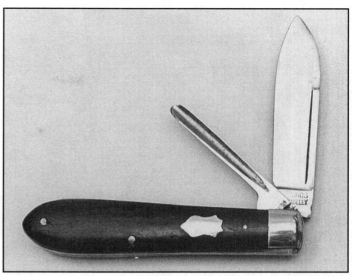

unknown, CASE BROTHERS, 2-blade jack w/punch, long pull, ebony, $300.

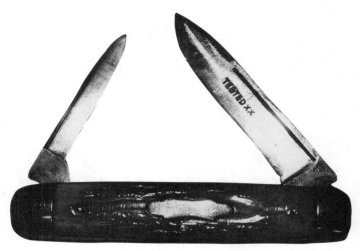

O.6294 LP, CASE BROTHERS, bone, Little Valley, 4-1/4", $2,000.

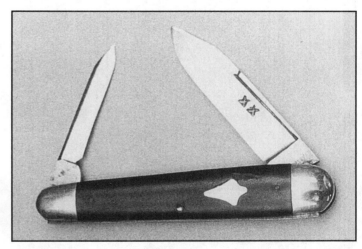

unknown, CASE BROTHERS, 2-blade sleeveboard, long pull, composition, 3-3/8", $500.

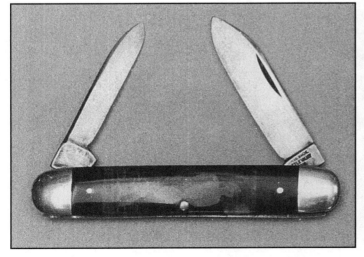

unknown, CASE BROTHERS, high art naughty lady, regular pull, celluloid, 3-3/8", $550.

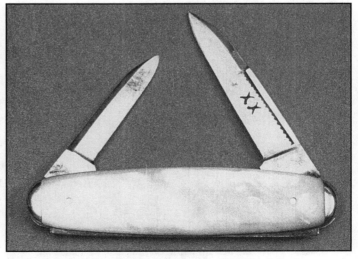

unknown, CASE BROTHERS, pearl, tip bolsters, Springville, 3", $450.

*Pricing Note: The value of Case vintage knives is subjective, but a good rule of thumb is to start with the Tested knife price and add ten percent for each earlier period, then subtract ten percent for each condition from mint. This is the formula we used to price vintage Case knives in this book.*

*unknown, CASE BROTHERS, 2-blade SHAD, pearl, regular pull, Cut. Co., 3", $375.*

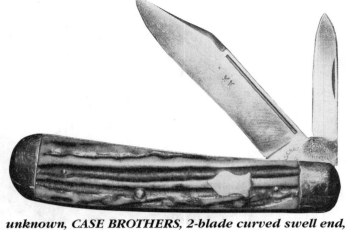

*unknown, CASE BROTHERS, 2-blade curved swell end, stag, 4-1/4", $500.*

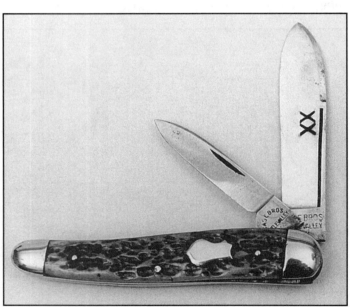

*unknown, CASE BROTHERS, 2-blade, bone, long pull, 3-3/8", $475.*

*unknown, CASE BROTHERS, 2-blade, similar to a 54 pattern or 55, 56, bone, 3-3/8", $475.*

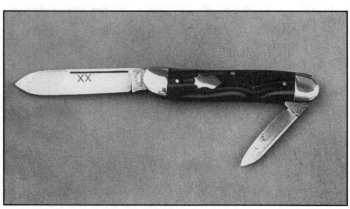

*unknown, CASE BROTHERS, 2-blade dogleg, celluloid, long pull, Springville, 3-1/2", $750.*

*unknown, CASE BROTHERS, similar to 85 pattern, Rogers, LITTLE VALLEY, 3-11/16", $450.*

Vintage Case - Case Bros.

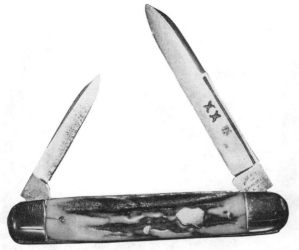

*unknown, CASE BROTHERS, 2-blade equal end, stag, SPRINGVILLE, NY, 3-7/16", $1,000.*

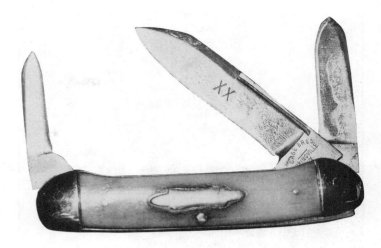

*53131 LP, CASE BROTHERS, canoe, stag, SPRINGVILLE, 3-5/8", $5,000.*

*unknown, CASE BROTHERS, 2 blade jack, long pull, match striker, bone, 4-9/16", $750.*

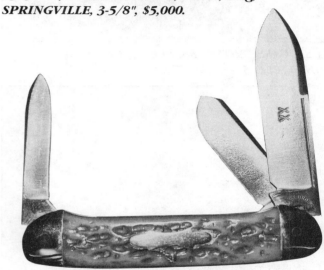

*63131 LP, CASE BROTHERS, canoe, Rogers, Little Valley, 3-11/16", $3,500.*

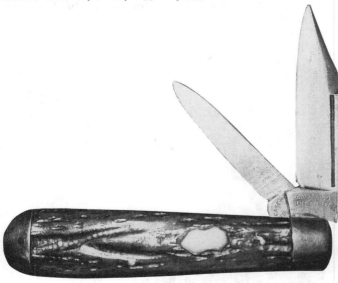

*unknown, CASE BROTHERS, 2 blade jack, long pull, bone, 3-1/2", $450.*

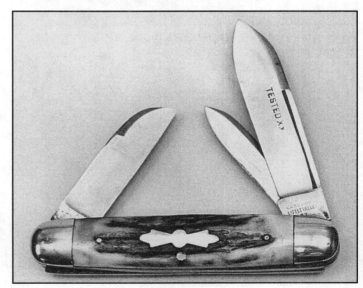

*5345-1/2 LP, CASE BROTHERS, stag, medium cattle, 3-1/2", $1,200.*

Pricing Note: *The value of Case vintage knives is subjective, but a good rule of thumb is to start with the Tested knife price and add ten percent for each earlier period, then subtract ten percent for each condition from mint. This is the formula we used to price vintage Case knives in this book.*

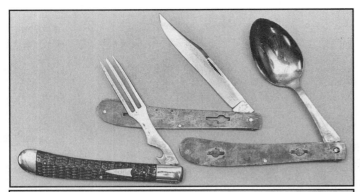

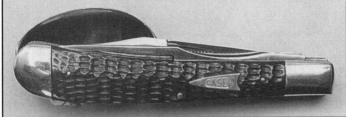

**6351 SP, CASE BROTHERS,** *bobo, green bone,* SPRINGVILLE, *5-1/4", $3,250.*

**6346 LP, CASE BROTHERS,** *whittler, Rogers, 3 backspring, 3-5/8", $600.*

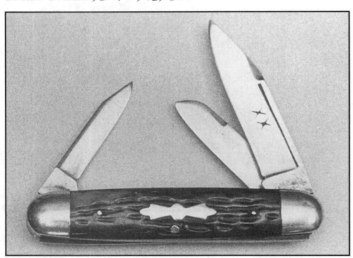

**6345-1/2 LP, CASE BROTHERS,** *bone,* SPRINGVILLE, *3-1/2", $1,500.*

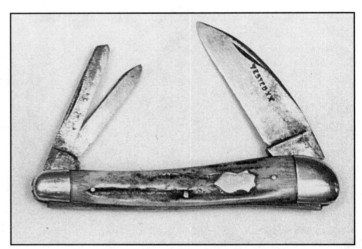

**5355 LP, CASE BROTHERS,** *Wharncliffe, whittler, stag,* CUT CO, *3-3/4", $1,500.*

**5346-1/2 LP, CASE BROTHERS,** *whittler, stag, 3 backspring, 3-5/8", $600.*

**6356 SAB LP, CASE BROTHERS,** *match striker, bone, Little Valley, 3-3/4", $1,500.*

Vintage Case - Case Bros.  65

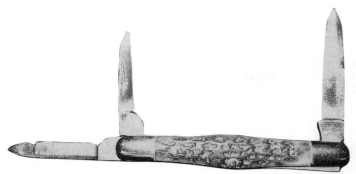

**63058 LP, CASE BROTHERS,** slender whittler, file w/cuticle, bone, W. R. Case, 2-7/8", $600.

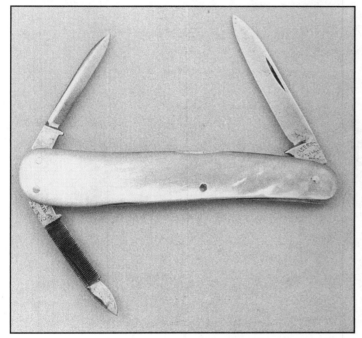

**8363, CASE BROTHERS,** 3-blade lobster, file, pearl, 3-1/4", $525.

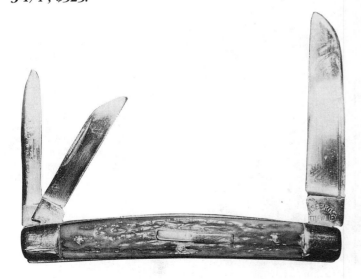

**5368 LP, CASE BROTHERS,** congress whittler, stag, 3-5/16", $3,000.

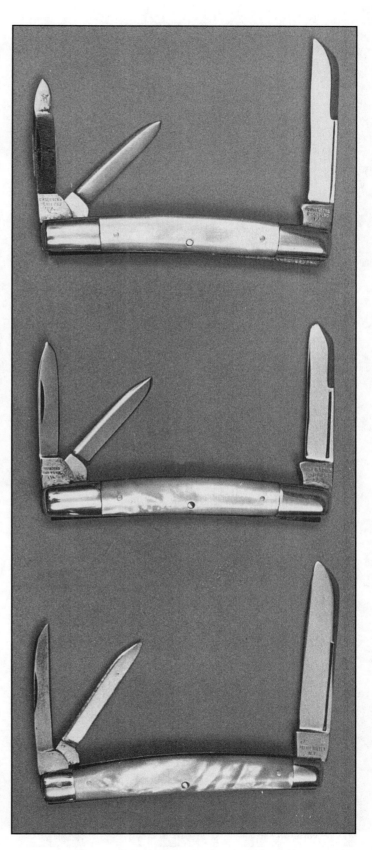

**8368 LP, CASE BROTHERS,** congress whittlers, pearl, 3-5/16", $4,000.

*Pricing Note: The value of Case vintage knives is subjective, but a good rule of thumb is to start with the Tested knife price and add ten percent for each earlier period, then subtract ten percent for each condition from mint. This is the formula we used to price vintage Case knives in this book.*

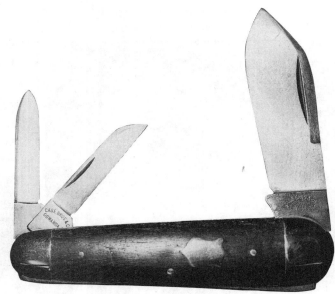

1370, CASE BROTHERS, wood, GOWANDA BROS & CO, very rare, 3-9/16", $2,000.

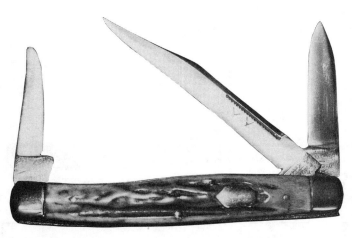

5375 LP, CASE BROTHERS, stag, SPRINGVILLE, 3-15/16", $1,500.

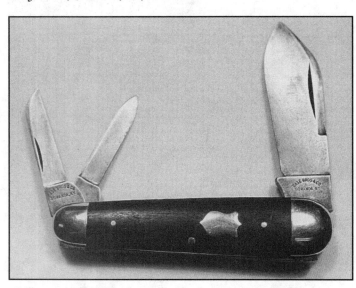

6370, CASE BROTHERS, 3-blade whittler, ebony, GOWANDA, 3-5/8", $2,000.

6375 LP, CASE BROTHERS, bone, 4-1/4", $2,500.

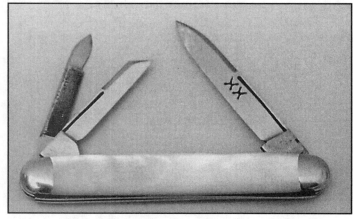

8371, CASE BROTHERS, 3-blade whittler, pearl, 3-1/2", $1,200.

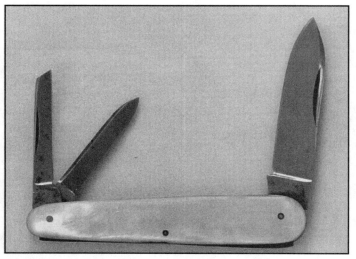

8377, CASE BROTHERS, whittler, pearl, SHAD, 3-3/8", $750.

Vintage Case - Case Bros.   67

6378 F, CASE BROTHERS, file w/cuticle, bone, Cut Co., 3-5/16", $1,000.

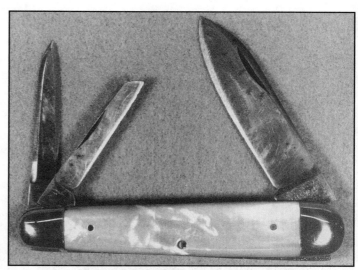

unknown, CASE BROTHERS, 3-blade whittler, pearl, Little Valley, 3-3/8", $900.

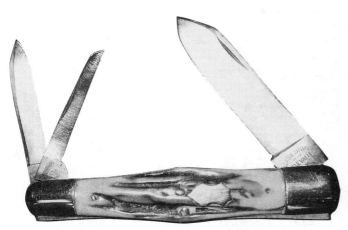

5392, CASE BROTHERS, stag, Little Valley, 3-3/4", $1,500.

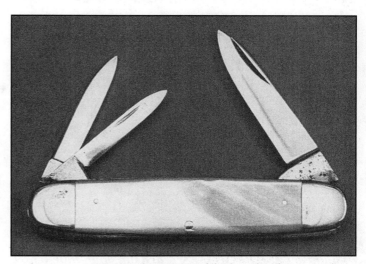

unknown, CASE BROTHERS, 3-blade whittler, regular pull, pearl, flat bolsters, 3-1/4", $750.

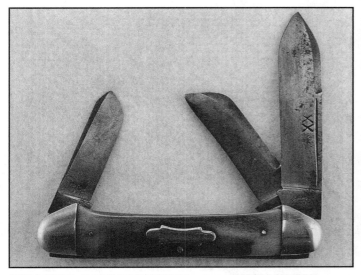

5394 X LP, CASE BROTHERS, stag, SPRINGVILLE, 4-1/4", $5,000.

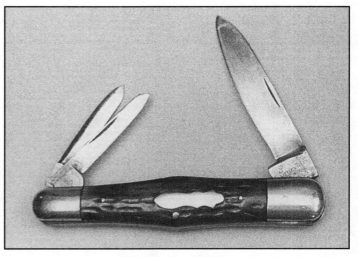

unknown, CASE BROTHERS, 3-blade whittler, regular pull, swell center, bone, 3-3/4", $900.

*Pricing Note: The value of Case vintage knives is subjective, but a good rule of thumb is to start with the Tested knife price and add ten percent for each earlier period, then subtract ten percent for each condition from mint. This is the formula we used to price vintage Case knives in this book.*

*unknown, CASE BROTHERS, 3-blade whittler, horn, 3-1/4", $600.*

*5427 F LP, CASE BROTHERS, congress, file w/cuticle, stag, flat square bolsters, 3-1/4", $1,500.*

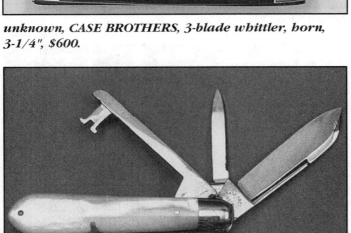

*unknown, CASE BROTHERS, teardrop, long pull, pearl, skeleton key, 3-3/8, $1,200.*

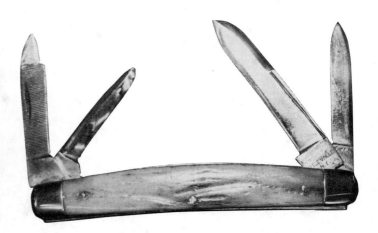

*54052 LP, CASE BROTHERS, congress, stag, 3-3/4", $4,000.*

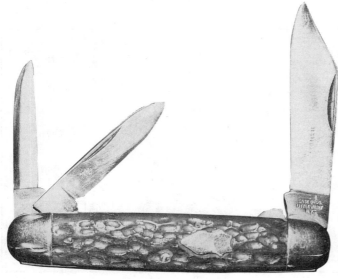

*unknown, CASE BROTHERS, 3-blade whittler, regular pull, bone, 3-1/2", $1,000.*

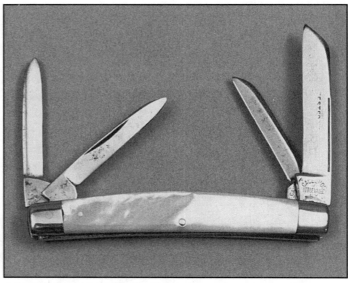

*84052 LP, CASE BROTHERS, congress, pearl, 3-3/4", $5,000.*

Vintage Case - Case Bros. 69

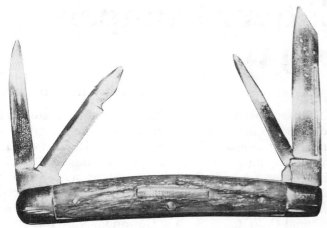

**5468 LP, CASE BROTHERS,** *congress, stag, CUT CO, 3-5/16", $2,000.*

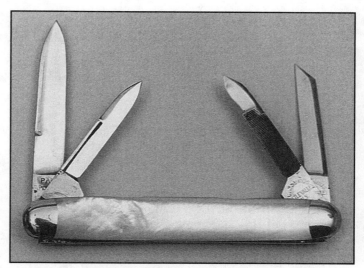

**8471 LP, CASE BROTHERS,** *equal end, pearl, 3-3/8", $2,000.*

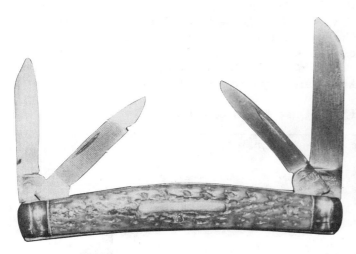

**6468, CASE BROTHERS,** *congress, file w/cuticle, bone, pinched bolsters, 3-5/16", $2,000.*

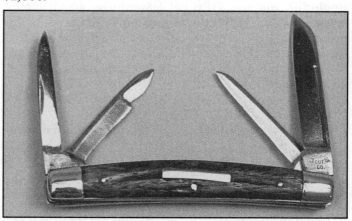

**unknown, CASE BROTHERS,** *congress 4 blade, stag, 3-1/4", $3,500.*

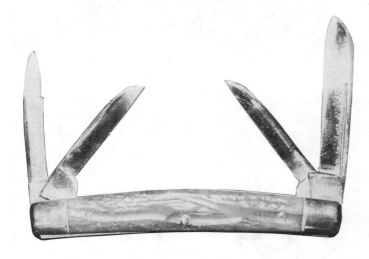

**6468 LP, CASE BROTHERS,** *congress, bone, 3-5/16", $2,000.*

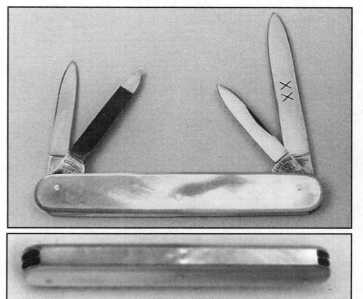

**unknown, CASE BROTHERS,** *4 blade, pearl, SHAD, covered backsprings, 3-3/8", $2,000.*

*Pricing Note: The value of Case vintage knives is subjective, but a good rule of thumb is to start with the Tested knife price and add ten percent for each earlier period, then subtract ten percent for each condition from mint. This is the formula we used to price vintage Case knives in this book.*

# W. R. Case & Son Cutlery Company (1902-1903)

By Bob Wurzelbacher

The W. R. Case & Sons Cutlery Company, as it is known today, has its roots in the frustration, anger, and enthusiasm of a 24-year-old by the name of J. Russell Case in 1902.

J. Russell Case was a salesman for his uncles who owned the Case Brothers Cutlery Company. The origins and demise of this company are recorded in a previous chapter. It must have been a career filled with excitement, despair, frustration, and the thrill of traveling across the country selling pocketknives. I am sure the accounts of any one of these trips from New York to Nebraska would fill volumes. J. Russell must have been a terrific salesman, and his cut was probably higher than his uncles'. After one of his trips, his uncles advised him that they were going to reduce his commissions and profit. Understandably, J. Russell told them to take their wagon and shove it.

J. Russell went to his father, W. Russell Case, and asked him to provide the financial backing to start his own jobbing company. He formed the W. R. Case & Son Cutlery Company (notice that "Son" is singular), Little Valley, New York. J. Russell contracted with various companies to produce his knives, but many were produced by the Napanoch Cutlery Company of Napanoch, New York, and C. Platts & Sons of Gowanda, New York, and Elred, Pennsylvania.

J. Russell built a small plant on Bank Street in Bradford, Pennsylvania. The tang stamp for this period reflects the full company name, W. R. Case & SON Bradford PA. Some tangs, however, bear the stamp W. R. Case & Son, Little Valley NY, or W. R. Case & Son Cutlery Co., with no city reference. These are probably contract knives.

This period lasted only two years and, as such, "Son" knives are very rare and collectible.

**Except as noted, All knives in this era are stamped W. R. Case & Son Bradford PA.**

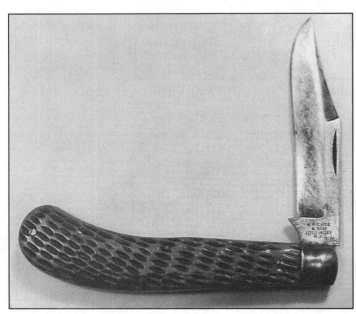

6100, W. R. CASE & SON, picked bone, 4-5/8", $2,000.

6151L SAB, W. R. CASE & SON, bone, 5-3/8", $1,500.

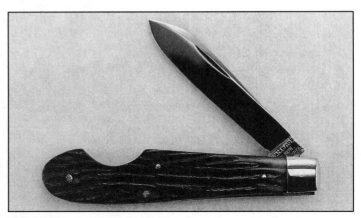

61028, W. R. CASE & SON, easy opener, red Winterbottom, 3-1/2", $750.

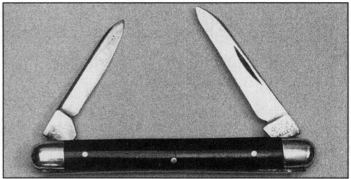

1201, W. R. CASE & SON, wood, Little Valley, 2-5/8", $450.

Case & Son 71

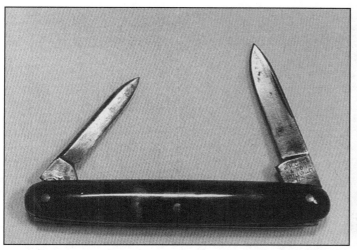

**72001, W. R. CASE & SON, tortoise, SHAD, 2-5/8", $600.**

**O.6230, W. R. CASE & SON, bone, 3-1/4", $500.**

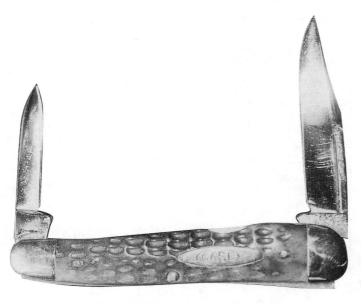

**6221, W. R. CASE & SON, green, 3-1/4", $600.**

**6241, W. R. CASE & SON, red Winterbottom, 3-1/2", $900.**

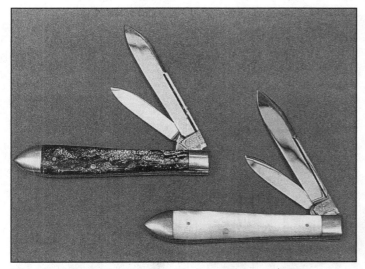

**Top: RM2028, Tested XX, Christmas tree, $550.
Bottom: 82028, W. R. CASE & SON, teardrop, pearl, 2-7/8", $600.**

**6246, W. R. CASE & SON, bone, 3-9/16", $900.**

*Pricing Note: The value of Case vintage knives is subjective, but a good rule of thumb is to start with the Tested knife price and add ten percent for each earlier period, then subtract ten percent for each condition from mint. This is the formula we used to price vintage Case knives in this book.*

*6250, W. R. CASE & SON, bone, 4-1/4", $5,000.*

*6250, W. R. CASE & SON, bone, 4-3/8", $5,000.*

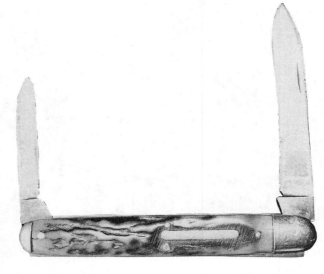
*52064, W. R. CASE & SON, stag, 3-1/2", $600.*

*6250, W. R. CASE & SON, bone, 4-1/4", $5,000.*

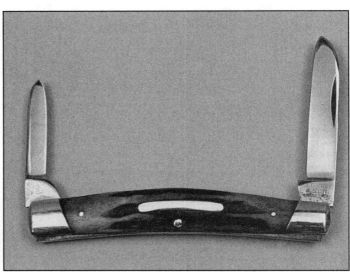
*52068, W. R. CASE & SON, congress, stag, 3-11/16", $1,000.*

*42057, W. R. CASE & SON, office, white composition, 3-3/8", $450.*

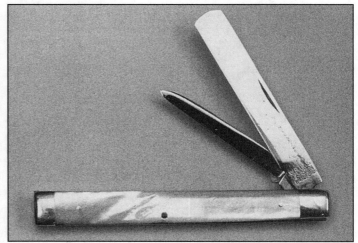
*8280, W. R. CASE & SON, doctor's spatula, pearl, 3-5/8", $1,500.*

Case & Son 73

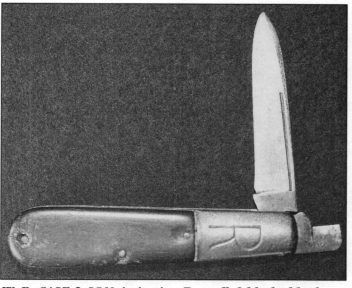

*W. R. CASE & SON, imitation Russell, 2 blade, black plastic, 3-3/8", $100.*

*unknown, W. R. CASE & SON, 2-blade jack, bone, 3-1/2", $600.*

*unknown, W. R. CASE & SON, 2 blade, bone, 3-1/2", $750.*

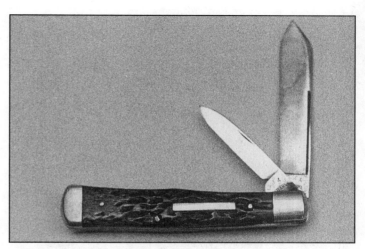

*unknown, W. R. CASE & SON, 2-blade jack, bone, 3-1/16", $750.*

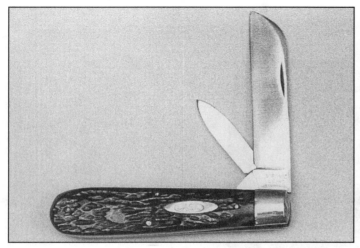

*unknown, W. R. CASE & SON, 2-blade jack, bone, 3-3/8", $600.*

*unknown, W. R. CASE & SON, 2-blade, waterfall, $900.*

Pricing Note: The value of Case vintage knives is subjective, but a good rule of thumb is to start with the Tested knife price and add ten percent for each earlier period, then subtract ten percent for each condition from mint. This is the formula we used to price vintage Case knives in this book.

*63109, W. R. CASE & SON, file, Rogers, 3-3/8", $1,000.*

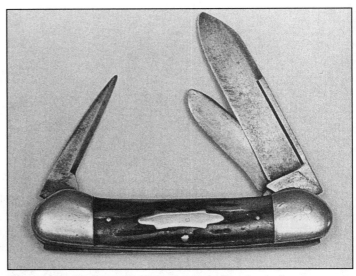

*53131, W. R. CASE & SON, long pull w/punch, stag, 3-3/4", $2,500.*

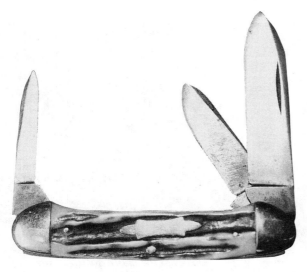

*53131, W. R. CASE & SON, regular pull w/pen, stag, 3-3/4", $3,000.*

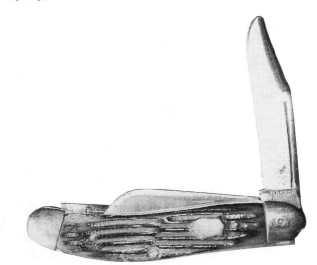

*6339, W. R. CASE & SON, sowbelly, red Winterbottom, 3-13/16", $4,500.*

*6339, W. R. CASE & SON, sowbelly, brown Winterbottom, 3-13/16", $4,500.*

Case & Son 75

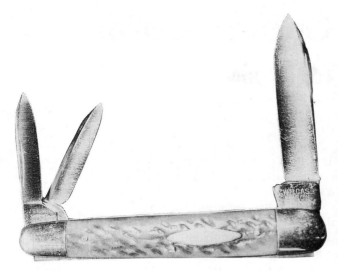

6378, W. R. CASE & SON, bone, 3-3/8", $750.

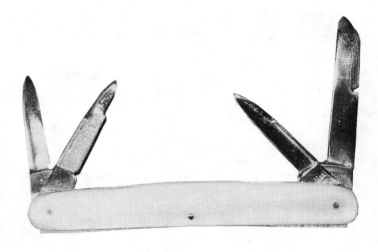

8438, W. R. CASE & SON, congress, pearl, 3-5/8", $3,000.

6393, W. R. CASE & SON, red Winterbottom, 3-7/8", $3,000.

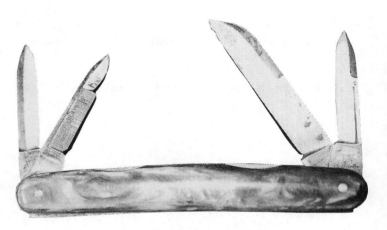

P438, W. R. CASE & SON, congress, pyremite, 3-5/8", $3,000.

unknown, W. R. CASE & SON, 3 blade, bone, 4", $1,000.

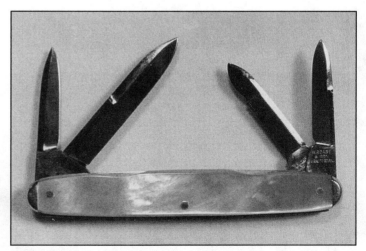

8460, W. R. CASE & SON, tip bolsters, pearl, 2-7/8", $900.

*Pricing Note: The value of Case vintage knives is subjective, but a good rule of thumb is to start with the Tested knife price and add ten percent for each earlier period, then subtract ten percent for each condition from mint. This is the formula we used to price vintage Case knives in this book.*

# W. R. Case & Son's Cutlery Company (1903-1905)

By Bob Wurzelbacher

J. Russell's sister Debbie was married to Harvey N. Platts, who not only supplied J. Russell's pocketknives, but also traveled with J. Russell on many of his trips. Harvey would sell Platt's knives down one side of the street and Russell would sell Case knives down the other. They decided to join forces with H. N. buying his brothers out of the Elred, Pennsylvania, plant business and moving the operation to Bradford, Pennsylvania.

On December 31, 1903, they decided to drop the Platt's name and form a new company called The W. R. Case & Son's Cutlery Company. (Note the addition of an apostrophe). They decided to build permanent headquarters on Bank Street in Bradford, Pennsylvania.

Harvey N. Platts, age 39, was in charge of all manufacturing, while J. Russell, age 27, was in charge of sales.

Like many grinders of that time, H. N. Platts was afflicted with grinder's consumption. In August 1911, he sold his portion of the company to J. Russell and moved his family to Boulder, Colorado. It was here that he formed the Western States Cutlery and Manufacturing Company.

The tang stamps during this era do not reflect the full company name. Rather, the normal tang stamp is CASE & SONS, Bradford PA. Since this era only existed two years at best, these knives are also very rare and collectible.

**All knives in this era have Case & Sons Bradford Pa. tang stamps.**

*61050L, CASE & SON'S, large Coke, bone, 5-1/2", $600.*

*6216, CASE & SON'S, bone, 3-5/8", $750.*

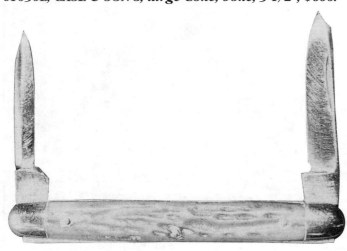

*6201, CASE & SON'S, bone, 2-7/16", $500.*

*6223, CASE & SON'S, bone, coffin bolster, 3-1/2", $1,000.*

Case & Son's 77

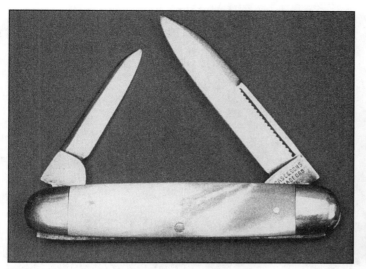

**O.8230, CASE & SON'S, pearl, 3-1/2", $600.**

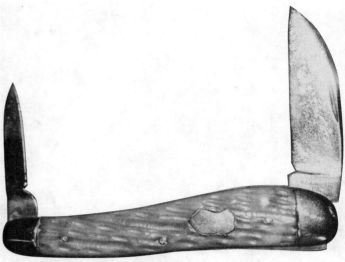

**6273, CASE & SON'S, bone, 3-3/4", $1,200.**

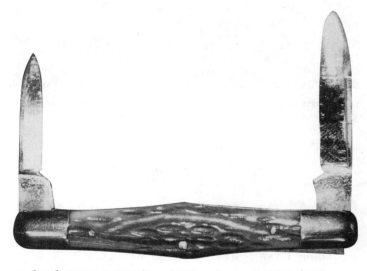

**O.6256, CASE & SON'S, whittler, bone, 2-7/8", $450.**

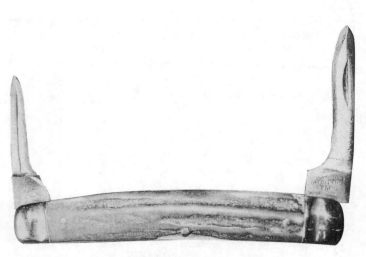

**52089, CASE & SON'S, congress, stag, 3-3/4", $500.**

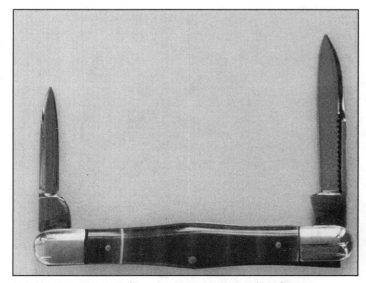

**R258, CASE & SON'S, candy stripe, 2-7/8", $750.**

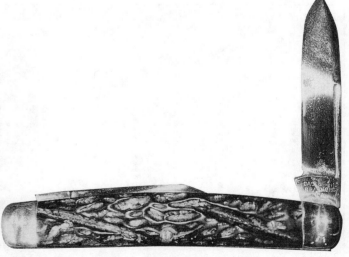

**62089, CASE & SON'S, congress, rough black, 3-3/4", $3,000.**

*Pricing Note: The value of Case vintage knives is subjective, but a good rule of thumb is to start with the Tested knife price and add ten percent for each earlier period, then subtract ten percent for each condition from mint. This is the formula we used to price vintage Case knives in this book.*

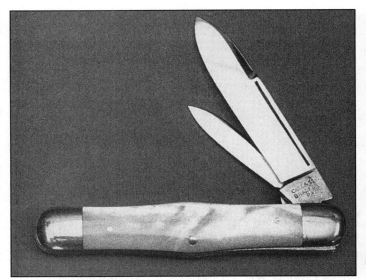

*unknown, CASE & SON'S, 2-blade jack, pearl, 3-3/8", $650.*

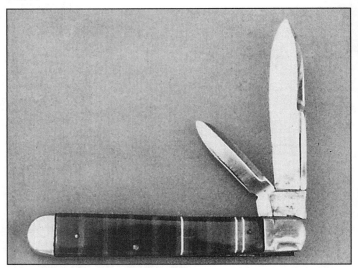

*unknown, CASE & SON'S, 2-blade jack, candy stripe, 3-3/8", $600.*

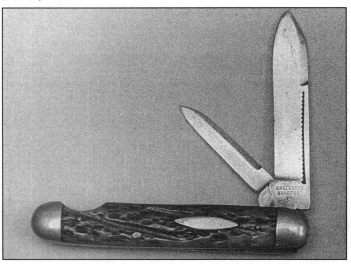

*unknown, CASE & SON'S, 2-blade jack, bone, 3-3/8", $550.*

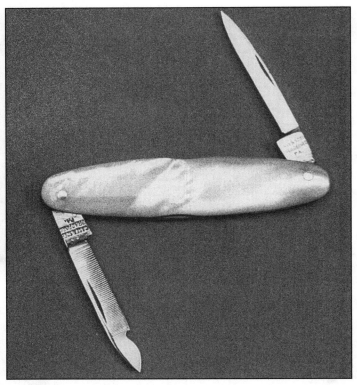

*unknown, CASE & SON'S, 2-blade lobster, pearl, 2-3/8", $550.*

*unknown, CASE & SON'S, 2-blade jack, stag, 3", $450.*

*unknown, CASE & SON'S, 2-blade similar to 48, stag, 3-7/8", $900.*

Case & Son's 79

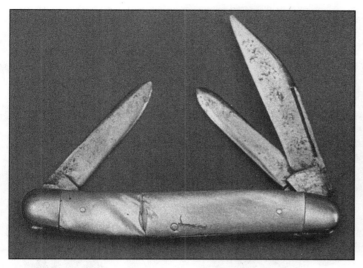

*8347 LP, CASE & SON'S, pearl, 3-15/16", $1,000.*

*8368, CASE & SON'S, congress, pearl, 3-5/16", $2,000.*

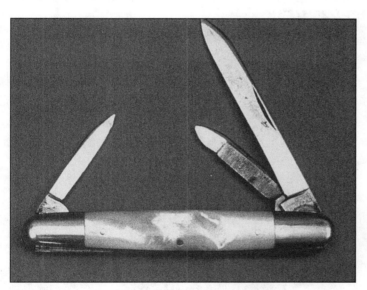

*83063, CASE & SON'S, pearl, 3-1/4", $650.*

*6370, CASE & SON'S, bone, 3-9/16", $2,000.*

*5374, CASE & SON'S, whittler, cut/file, stag, 4-1/16", $3,500.*

*unknown, CASE & SON'S, 3-blade similar to 95, bone, 4-1/4", $2,500.*

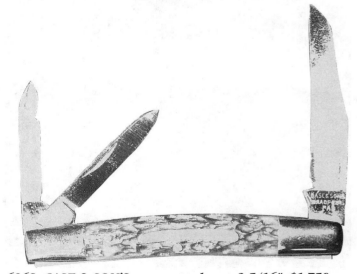

*6368, CASE & SON'S, congress, bone, 3-5/16", $1,750.*

Pricing Note: The value of Case vintage knives is subjective, but a good rule of thumb is to start with the Tested knife price and add ten percent for each earlier period, then subtract ten percent for each condition from mint. This is the formula we used to price vintage Case knives in this book.

*5375, CASE & SON'S, stag, 4-1/4", $5,000.*

*unknown, CASE & SON'S, 3-blade similar to 55, Rogers, 3-1/2", $1,750.*

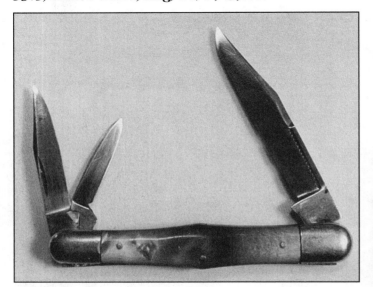

*RM383, CASE & SON'S, gold swirl, 3-1/2", $1,000.*

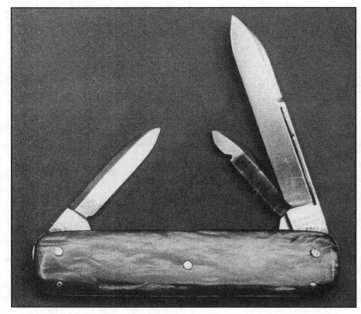

*unknown, CASE & SON'S, 3-blade cut/file, pyremite, 3-1/16", $500.*

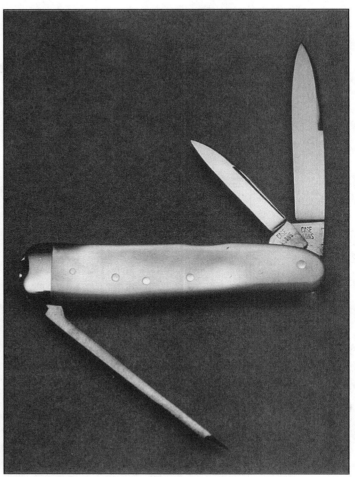

*unknown, CASE & SON'S, 3-blade clipper, pearl, 2-7/8", $1,000.*

Case & Son's 81

*Y4062, CASE & SON'S, corkscrew, red celluloid, 3-1/4", $450.*

*CASE & SON'S, 4-blade lobster, Rogers, 3-5/16", $525.*

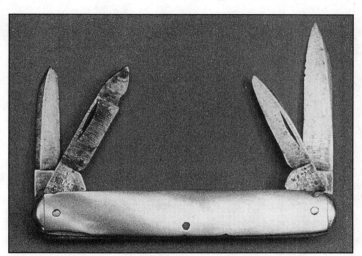

*8464F, CASE & SON'S, file, pearl, 3-1/8", $600.*

*unknown, CASE & SON'S, blade, corkscrew, stag, 3-1/2", $750.*

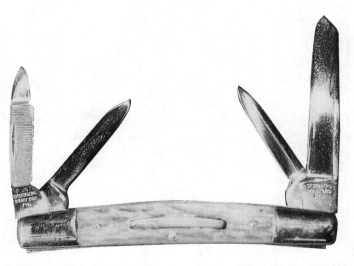

*6468, CASE & SON'S, congress, bone, 3-5/16", $2,500.*

Pricing Note: The value of Case vintage knives is subjective, but a good rule of thumb is to start with the Tested knife price and add ten percent for each earlier period, then subtract ten percent for each condition from mint. This is the formula we used to price vintage Case knives in this book.

# W. R. Case & Sons Cutlery Company (1905-1914)

By Bob Wurzelbacher

The departure of Harvey N. Platts for Colorado left J. Russell Case as the singular head of the W. R. Case & Sons Cutlery Company. (Note the absence of the apostrophe). This company name was reflected on the tang stamp of all knives produced until 1914. In addition, the city of Bradford PA was also noted on the tang stamp.

It was at this time that the Crandall Cutlery Company joined the W. R. Case Cutlery Company. Herbert Crandall, Theresa Case's husband, was a son-in-law, so they were keeping the business in the family.

It was a successful period, but one about which very little documentation is available. What is apparent is that an enormous number of patterns, handle materials and blade configurations were produced in response to the needs of the customers.

You will note that in some cases the tang stamp includes the words "made in the USA." This had to occur during World War I.

In general, the availability of knives has provided the means to establish a more stable pricing environment for knives in this era. My experience is that as with previous eras, the condition of knives is very good or excellent.

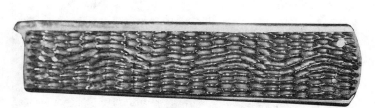

*6001, W. R. CASE & SONS, tri-fold, green bone, 4-5/8", $1,500.*

*2104 LP, W. R. CASE & SONS, cocoa, 3-5/8", $450.*

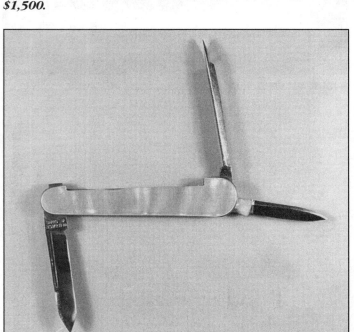

*OP101, W. R. CASE & SONS, lobster, opal pearl, $400.*

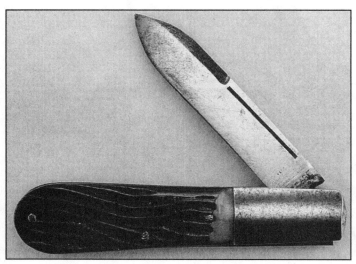

*61009-3/4 LP, W. R. CASE & SONS, front flat, back saber, brown Winterbottom, 3-3/8", $1,400.*

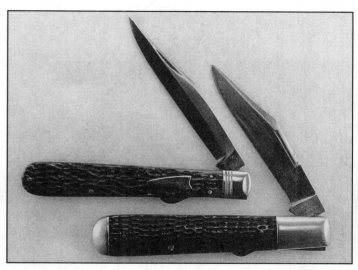

*61011, W. R. CASE & SONS, hawkbill, Rogers, 4-3/8",
$325.*

*6111-1/2L, W. R. CASE & SONS, bone, grooved bolsters,
4-1/2", $2,500.*

*6111 LP, W. R. CASE & SONS, Rogers, 4-1/2", $2,000.*

*6111-1/2 LP, W. R. CASE & SONS, Rogers, 4-1/2",
$2,500.*

*6111-1/2L LP, W. R. CASE & SONS, bone, "Made in
USA," contract challenge, 4-1/2", $2,500.*

*R111-1/2 LP, W. R. CASE & SONS, candy stripe, 4-7/16",
$2,500.*

*Pricing Note: The value of Case vintage knives is subjective, but a good rule of thumb is to start with the Tested knife price and add ten percent for each earlier period, then subtract ten percent for each condition from mint. This is the formula we used to price vintage Case knives in this book.*

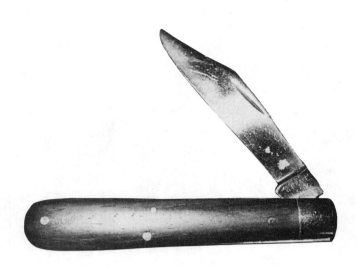

*1113, W. R. CASE & SONS, wood, 3-3/8", $350.*

*6149, W. R. CASE & SONS, rare 1-blade copperhead, Rogers, 3-15/16", $1,800.*

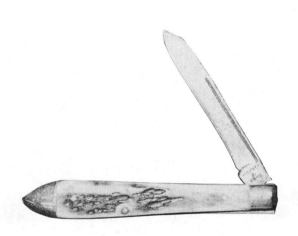

*61028 LP, W. R. CASE & SONS, teardrop, Rogers, 2-7/8", $800.*

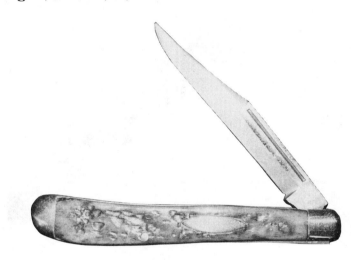

*61049SAB LP, W. R. CASE & SONS, Rogers, 5", $1,200.*

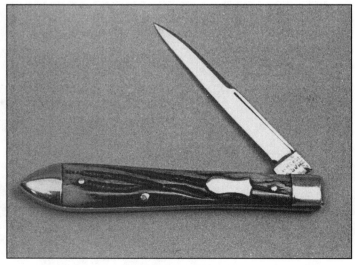

*61028 LP, W. R. CASE & SONS, teardrop, brown Winterbottom, 2-7/8", $800.*

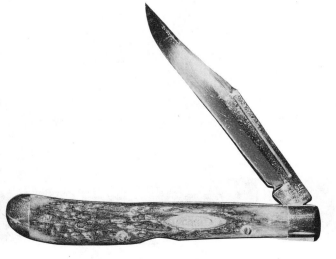

*61049L SAB LP, W. R. CASE & SONS, Rogers, 5", $1,200.*

Case & Sons 85

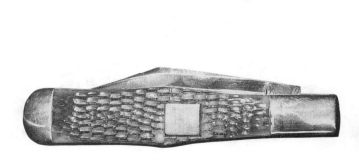

61050L, W. R. CASE & SONS, Coke switchblade, bone, 5", $7,500.

C61050, W. R. CASE & SONS, large Coke, Rogers, 5-1/8", $1,500.

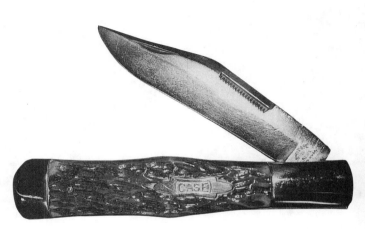

C61050 SAB, W. R. CASE & SONS, Coke, double pull, bone, MADE IN USA, match striker, 5", $1,300.

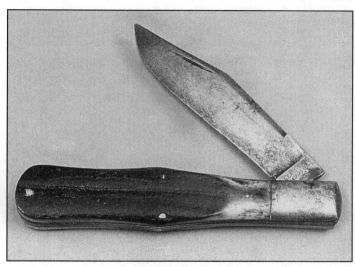

51050 LP, W. R. CASE & SONS, large Coke, slab stag, 5-1/8", $1,300.

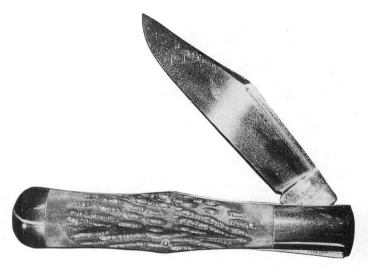

61050 LP, W. R. CASE & SONS, small frame Coke, bone, 5", $2,000.

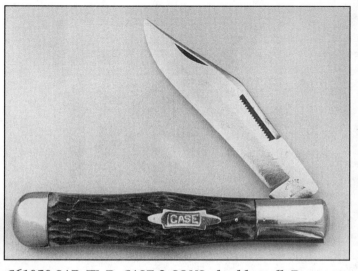

C61050 SAB, W. R. CASE & SONS, double pull, Rogers, match striker, Made in USA, 5-1/4", $1,500.

*Pricing Note: The value of Case vintage knives is subjective, but a good rule of thumb is to start with the Tested knife price and add ten percent for each earlier period, then subtract ten percent for each condition from mint. This is the formula we used to price vintage Case knives in this book.*

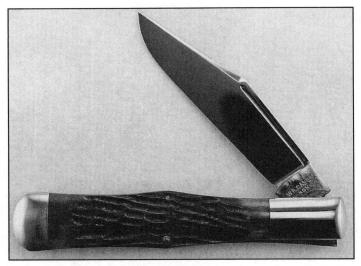

**610050**, W. R. CASE & SONS, large Coke, bone, no lower bolster, 5-1/8", $1,300.

**6151L SAB**, W. R. CASE & SONS, bone, match striker, 5-3/16", $1,500.

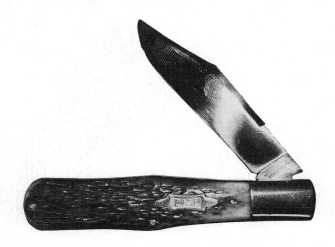

**610050**, W. R. CASE & SONS, large Coke, Rogers, no lower bolster, 5-1/4", $1,000.

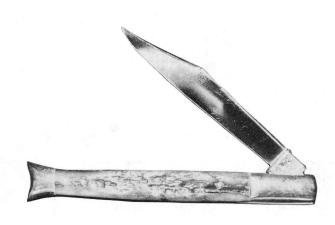

**61051 LP**, W. R. CASE & SONS, fishtail, Rogers, no guard, 3-7/8", $900.

**6151L SAB**, W. R. CASE & SONS, bone, CUTLERY CO, 3-7/8", $1,500.

**61051 LP**, W. R. CASE & SONS, Rogers, fishtail guards, 3-3/4", $1,200.

Case & Sons 87

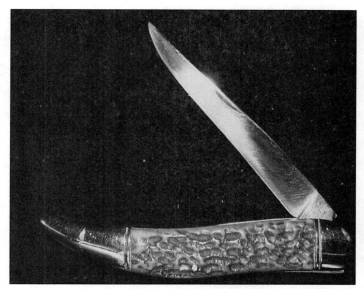

**61093**, *W. R. CASE & SONS, Rogers, MADE IN USA, 4-1/4", $850.*

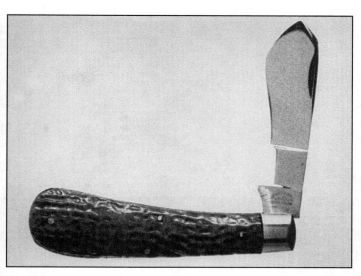

*unknown, W. R. CASE & SONS, cotton sampler, green bone, $400.*

**6195 LP**, *W. R. CASE & SONS, Rogers, very rare, 4-1/4", $1,000.*

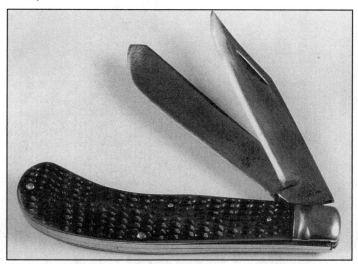

**62100**, *W. R. CASE & SONS, saddlehorn, green bone, 4-5/8", $2,200.*

**61095 SAB**, *W. R. CASE & SONS, toothpick, Rogers, 3-1/4", $850.*

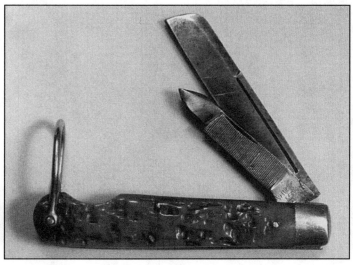

**6202SH R, F, LP**, *W. R. CASE & SONS, Military WW I, Rogers, MADE IN USA, bail, 3-1/4", $450.*

*Pricing Note: The value of Case vintage knives is subjective, but a good rule of thumb is to start with the Tested knife price and add ten percent for each earlier period, then subtract ten percent for each condition from mint. This is the formula we used to price vintage Case knives in this book.*

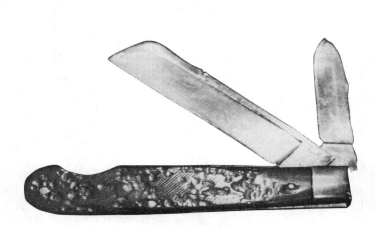

**6202 LP, W. R. CASE & SONS, Rogers, no MADE IN USA, no bail, 3-1/4", $450.**

**6204 LP, W. R. CASE & SONS, Rogers, 3-5/8", $600.**

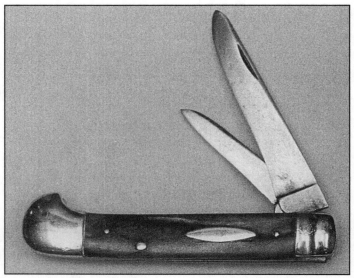

**5203, W. R. CASE & SONS, half canoe, stag, pinched bolster, 3-5/8", $1,000.**

**6206, W. R. CASE & SONS, tadpole, Rogers, 2-5/8", $550.**

**6203, W. R. CASE & SONS, half canoe, Rogers, pinched bolster, 3-5/8", $1,200.**

**7206 LP, W. R. CASE & SONS, tadpole, tortoise, 2-9/16", $650.**

Case & Sons 89

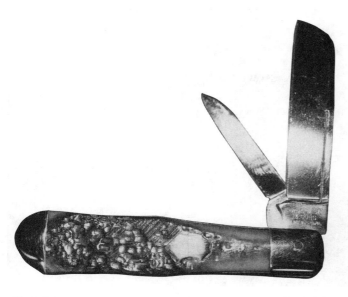

**6208 LP**, W. R. CASE & SONS, *medium Coke, Rogers, 3-13/16", $750.*

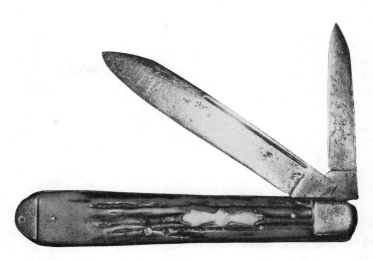

**52010 LP**, W. R. CASE & SONS, *similar to 019 pattern, stag, flat bolsters, 4-1/4", $1,500.*

**6210**, W. R. CASE & SONS, *medium teardrop, Rogers, 3-1/8", $500.*

**62010 LP**, W. R. CASE & SONS, *similar to 019 pattern, Rogers, flat bolsters, 4-1/4", $1,500.*

**62210**, W. R. CASE & SONS, *double switchblade, Rogers, 2-5/8", $2,200.*

**6211-1/2 LP**, W. R. CASE & SONS, *Rogers, 4-1/2", $2,500.*

*Pricing Note: The value of Case vintage knives is subjective, but a good rule of thumb is to start with the Tested knife price and add ten percent for each earlier period, then subtract ten percent for each condition from mint. This is the formula we used to price vintage Case knives in this book.*

*6211-1/2 LP, W. R. CASE & SONS, green bone, 4-1/2", $2,500.*

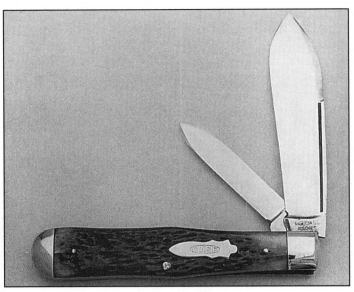

*6213 LP, W. R. CASE & SONS, Rogers, 3-15/16", $2,400.*

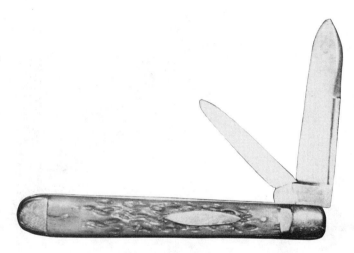

*6212 LP, W. R. CASE & SONS, Rogers, flat bolsters, pinched, 3-3/8", $475.*

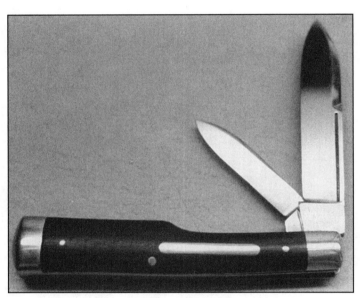

*1215 LP, W. R. CASE & SONS, gunstock, walnut, 3", $1,500.*

*6212 LP, W. R. CASE & SONS, red Winterbottom, flat bolsters, pinched, 3-3/8", $475.*

*6215 LP, W. R. CASE & SONS, gunstock, Rogers, 3", $2,200.*

Case & Sons 91

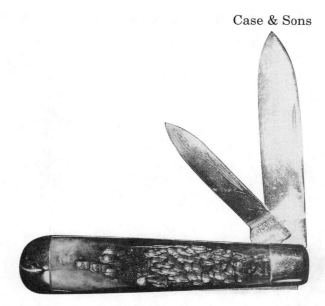

**6216**, W. R. CASE & SONS, Rogers, 3-1/2", $500.

**62016**, W. R. CASE & SONS, 2-blade jack, Rogers, 3-1/2", $500.

**6216S**, W. R. CASE & SONS, sheepfoot main, bone, 3-1/2", $550.

**62019**, W. R. CASE & SONS, Rogers, 4-1/2", $2,000.

**6216-1/2**, W. R. Case & Sons, 2-blade jack, Rogers, "Made in USA", 3-1/2", $600.

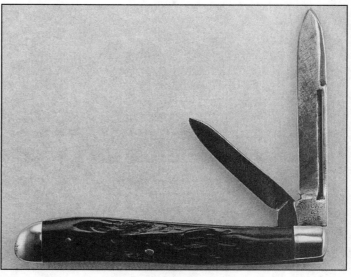

**6220 LP**, W. R. CASE & SONS, peanut, Rogers, 2-3/4", $600.

*Pricing Note: The value of Case vintage knives is subjective, but a good rule of thumb is to start with the Tested knife price and add ten percent for each earlier period, then subtract ten percent for each condition from mint. This is the formula we used to price vintage Case knives in this book.*

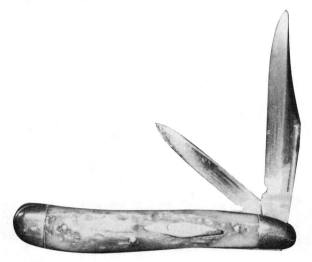

**6220SAB, W. R. CASE & SONS, peanut, Rogers, 2-3/4", $750.**

**62020-1/2, W. R. CASE & SONS, Rogers, 3-3/8", $800.**

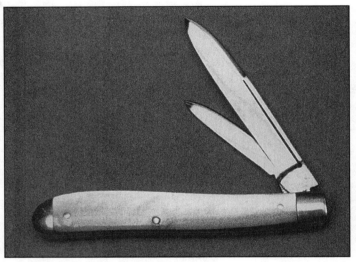

**8220 LP, W. R. CASE & SONS, peanut, pearl, 2-3/4", $750.**

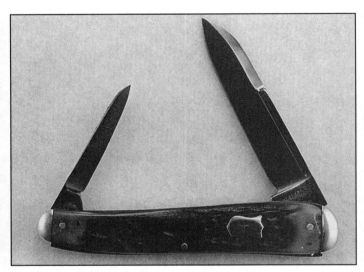

**6221 LP, W. R. CASE & SONS, bone, 3-1/4", $750.**

**62020, W. R. CASE & SONS, Rogers, 3-3/8", $800.**

**6222 LP, W. R. CASE & SONS, doctor's knife, bone, 3-1/4", $1,800.**

*6223 LP, W. R. CASE & SONS, small Coke, Rogers, coffin/pinched bolsters, 3-9/16", $1,500.*

*6225-1/2 LP, W. R. CASE & SONS, small Coke, Rogers, 3", $650.*

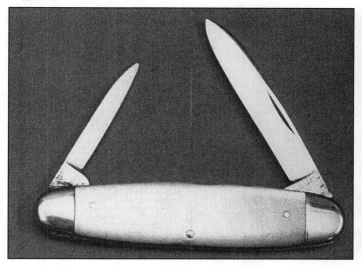

*8224, W. R. CASE & SONS, pearl, 3", $450.*

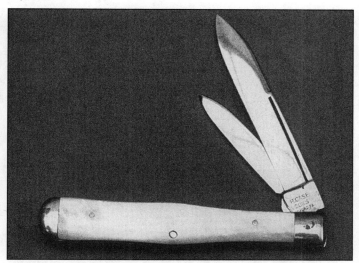

*8225 LP, W. R. CASE & SONS, small Coke, pearl, 3", $850.*

*6225 LP, W. R. CASE & SONS, small Coke, Rogers, 3", $650.*

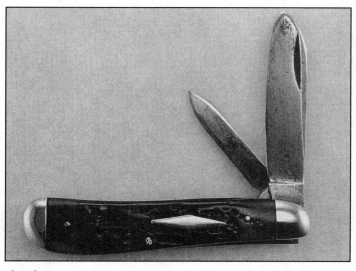

*6226, W. R. CASE & SONS, big peanut, Rogers, 3", $800.*

*Pricing Note: The value of Case vintage knives is subjective, but a good rule of thumb is to start with the Tested knife price and add ten percent for each earlier period, then subtract ten percent for each condition from mint. This is the formula we used to price vintage Case knives in this book.*

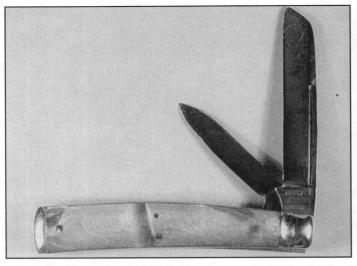

*P2026 LP, W. R. CASE & SONS, green celluloid, pinched bolsters, 3", $1,800.*

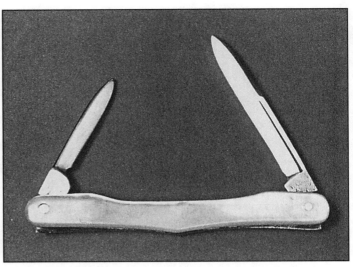

*8227 LP, W. R. CASE & SONS, congress, pearl, 3", $750.*

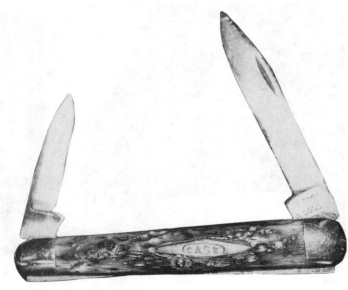

*62027, W. R. CASE & SONS, Rogers, 2-3/4", $350.*

*6228 LP, W. R. CASE & SONS, Rogers, 3-5/8", $600.*

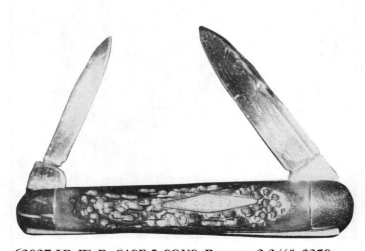

*62027 LP, W. R. CASE & SONS, Rogers, 2-3/4", $350.*

*6228PU LP, W. R. CASE & SONS, Rogers, flat punch, 3-5/8", $900.*

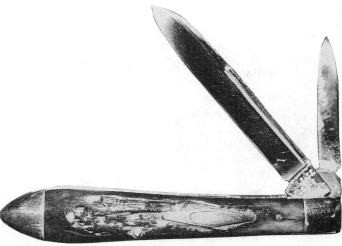

**62028 LP**, W. R. CASE & SONS, Rogers, 2-7/8", $750.

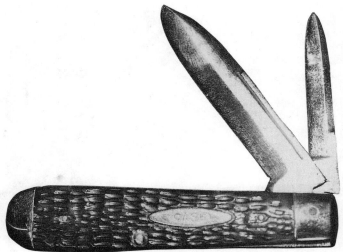

**6231 LP SAB**, W. R. CASE & SONS, green, CUT CO, second blade CASE & SON, 3-3/4", $950.

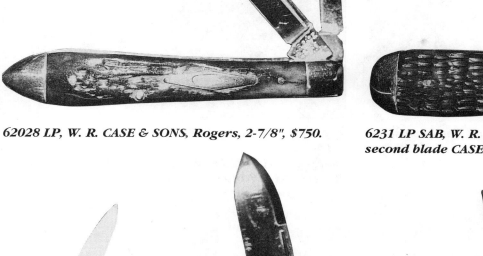

**O.6230 LP**, W. R. CASE & SONS, sample, front brown Winterbottom, rear Rogers, 3-3/4", $900.

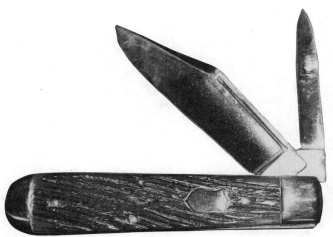

**6231-1/2 LP**, W. R. CASE & SONS, red Winterbottom, iron bolsters, 3-3/4", $900.

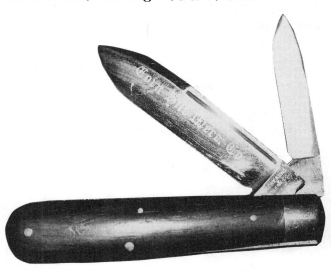

**12130 LP**, W. R. CASE & SONS, wood, etch main blade, 3-5/16", $300.

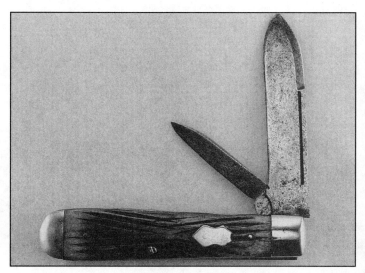

**6231-3/4 LP**, W. R. CASE & SONS, front flat, back saber, brown Winterbottom, 3-3/4", $750.

*Pricing Note: The value of Case vintage knives is subjective, but a good rule of thumb is to start with the Tested knife price and add ten percent for each earlier period, then subtract ten percent for each condition from mint. This is the formula we used to price vintage Case knives in this book.*

*6231-3/4 LP, W. R. CASE & SONS, front flat, back saber, Rogers, 3-3/4", $900.*

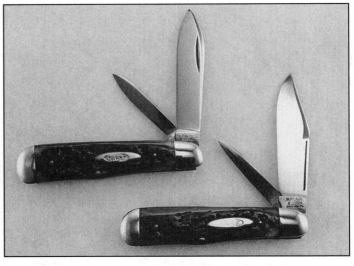

*Top: 62035, W. R. CASE & SONS, humpback, Rogers, 3-1/4", $800.*
*Bottom: 62035-1/2 LP, W. R. CASE & SONS, humpback, Rogers, 3-1/4", $800.*

*6235-1/2, W. R. CASE & SONS, Rogers, MADE IN USA, 3-1/2", $700.*

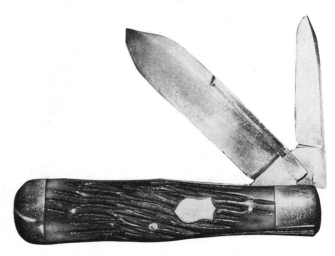

*6237 LP, W. R. CASE & SONS, medium Coke, red Winterbottom, rare, 3-1/2", $1,500.*

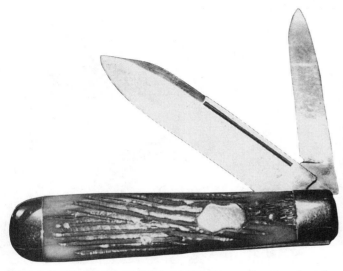

*6235-3/4 LP, W. R. CASE & SONS, front flat, back saber, brown Winterbottom, 3-1/2", $900.*

*6237 LP, W. R. CASE & SONS, medium Coke, Rogers, rare, 3-1/2", $1,500.*

**6237-1/2 LP**, W. R. CASE & SONS, medium Coke, brown Winterbottom, rare, 3-1/2", $1,500.

**6242**, W. R. CASE & SONS, Bros 6204 frame, Rogers, 3-5/8", $700.

**6239 LP**, W. R. CASE & SONS, sowbelly, Rogers, 3-13/16", $1,200.

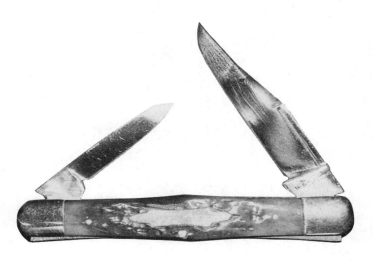

**O.6242-1/2 LP**, W. R. CASE & SONS, swell center, Rogers, 3-7/16", $700.

**GS2039**, W. R. CASE & SONS, sowbelly, green celluloid, 3-5/8", $1,000.

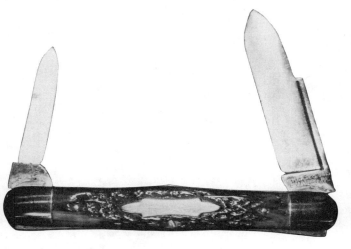

**O.6242 LP**, W. R. CASE & SONS, swell center, Rogers, 3-1/2", $750.

*Pricing Note: The value of Case vintage knives is subjective, but a good rule of thumb is to start with the Tested knife price and add ten percent for each earlier period, then subtract ten percent for each condition from mint. This is the formula we used to price vintage Case knives in this book.*

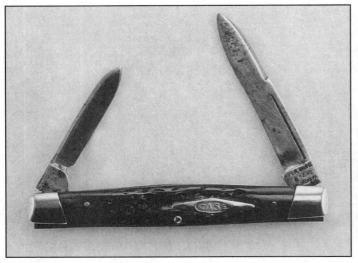

**62042 LP, W. R. CASE & SONS,** small stockman, Rogers, slant bolsters, 2-7/8", $500.

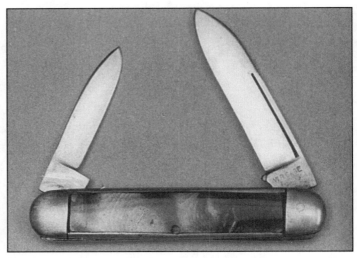

**GS245 LP, W. R. CASE & SONS,** small cigar, pyremite, 3-5/8", $700.

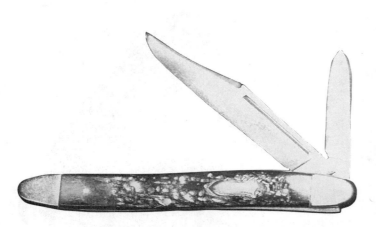

**6244 LP, W. R. CASE & SONS,** serpentine, Rogers, round flat bolsters, 3-1/8", $500.

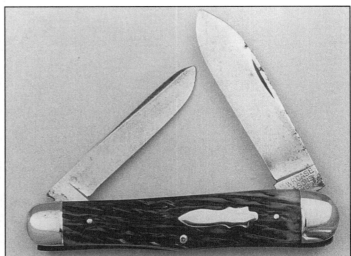

**6246, W. R. CASE & SONS,** swell-center jack, bone, 3-5/8", $650.

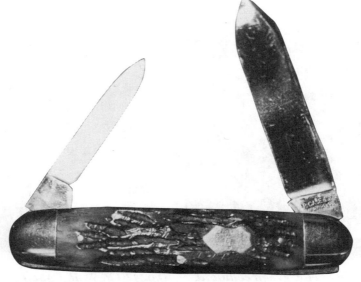

**O.5245 LP, W. R. CASE & SONS,** small cigar, stag, 3-5/8", $600.

Case & Sons 99

G2046 LP, W. R. CASE & SONS, congress, pyremite, 4-1/4", $2,500.

6250, W. R. CASE & SONS, sunfish, double pull, bone, Platts contract, Cut Co., 4-1/4", $5,000.

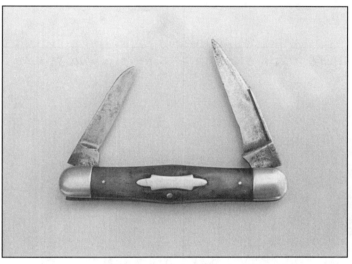

06246, W. R. Case & SONS, congress, bone, 4-1/4", $450.

6250, W. R. CASE & SONS, regular pull, bone, w/match striker, 4-1/8", $4,000.

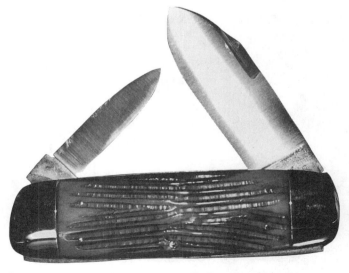

6250, W. R. CASE & SONS, sunfish, Winterbottom, 4-1/4", $5,000.

6251, W. R. CASE & SONS, double pull, bone, Platts contract, CUT CO., 5-1/4", $5,000.

*Pricing Note: The value of Case vintage knives is subjective, but a good rule of thumb is to start with the Tested knife price and add ten percent for each earlier period, then subtract ten percent for each condition from mint. This is the formula we used to price vintage Case knives in this book.*

6251SAB, W. R. CASE & SONS, hobo, Rogers, 5-3/8", $1,500.

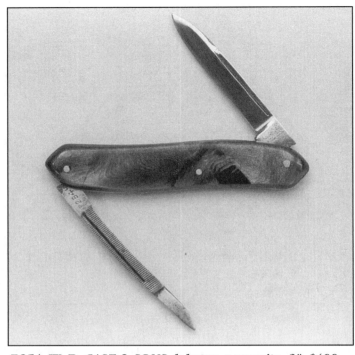

P254, W. R. CASE & SONS, lobster, pyremite, 3", $400.

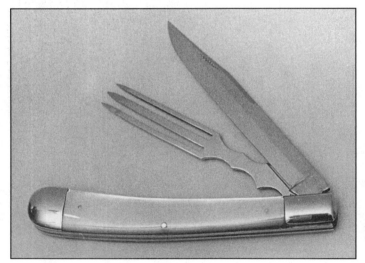

8251 SAB, W. R. CASE & SONS, hobo, pearl, 5-3/8", $2,500.

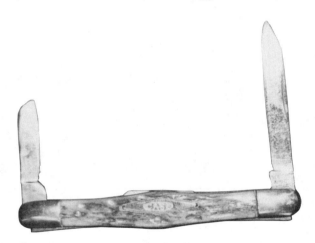

62056, W. R. CASE & SONS, swell center, Rogers, 2-7/8", $500.

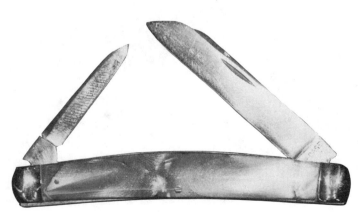

P2052, W. R. CASE & SONS, congress, pyremite, pinched bolsters, 3-1/2", $950.

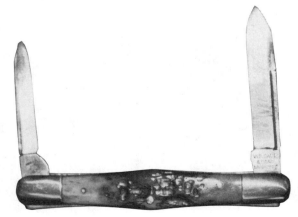

62056 LP, W. R. CASE & SONS, swell center, Rogers, 2-7/8", $500.

# Case & Sons

42057, W. R. CASE & SONS, *office knife, white composition, Made in USA, 3-5/16", $250.*

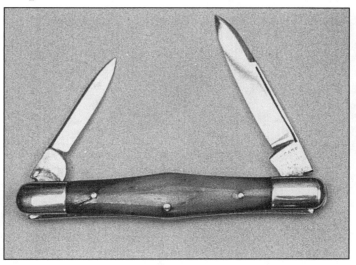

6258 LP, W. R. CASE & SONS, *swell center, bone, Little Valley, rare, 2-7/8", $650.*

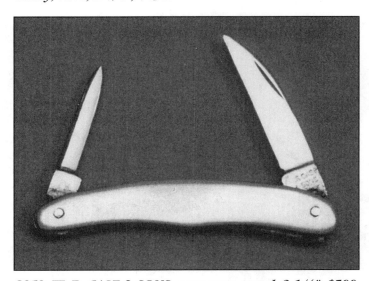

8259, W. R. CASE & SONS, *congress, pearl, 2-1/4", $500.*

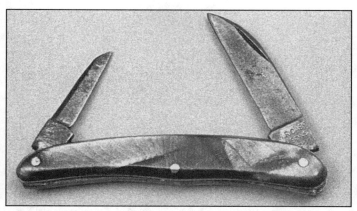

P259, W. R. CASE & SONS, *congress, pyremite green, 2-1/4", $650.*

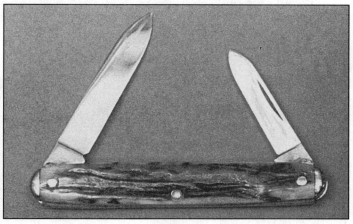

5260T, W. R. CASE & SONS, *stag, tip bolsters, 3-7/16", $500.*

6261R, W. R. CASE & SONS, *watch fob w/bail, bone, 2-1/4", $450.*

*Pricing Note: The value of Case vintage knives is subjective, but a good rule of thumb is to start with the Tested knife price and add ten percent for each earlier period, then subtract ten percent for each condition from mint. This is the formula we used to price vintage Case knives in this book.*

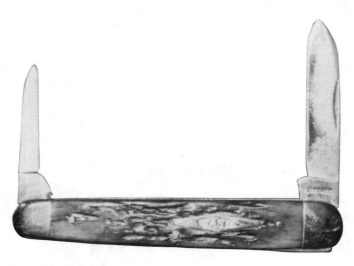

*62063, W. R. CASE & SONS, sleeveboard, Rogers, 3", $450.*

*O.6267 LP, W. R. CASE & SONS, swell center, bone, 3-1/4", $500.*

*82063 LP, W. R. CASE & SONS, sleeveboard, abalone, SHAD, 3", $350.*

*6267 LP, W. R. CASE & SONS, swell center, Rogers, 3-1/4", $500.*

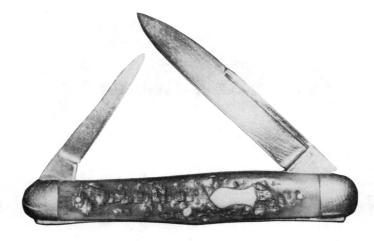

*6265 LP, W. R. CASE & SONS, similar to 08 pattern, Rogers, very rare, 3-1/4", $1,500.*

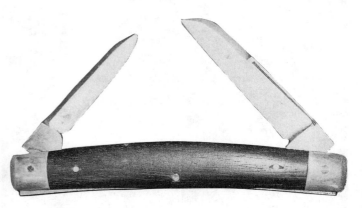

*1268 LP, W. R. CASE & SONS, congress, wood, aluminum bolsters, CUT CO, 3-5/16", $750.*

Case & Sons 103

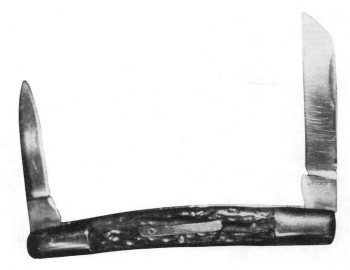

*6268, W. R. CASE & SONS, congress, bone, long bolsters, 3-5/16", $950.*

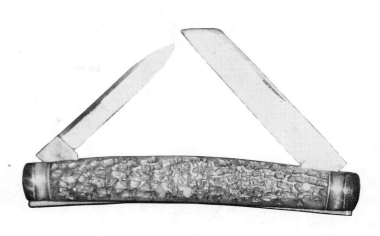

*6269, W. R. CASE & SONS, congress, bone, iron pinched bolsters, Cutlery Co., 3-5/16", $500.*

*8268 LP, W. R. CASE & SONS, congress, pearl, 3-5/16", $1,200.*

*6269, W. R. CASE & SONS, congress, bone, Cutlery Co., 3-1/16", $500.*

*62068, W. R. CASE & SONS, congress, Rogers, slant bolsters, 3-11/16", $1,200.*

*8269, W. R. CASE & SONS, congress, pearl, pinched bolsters, 3-1/16", $750.*

*Pricing Note: The value of Case vintage knives is subjective, but a good rule of thumb is to start with the Tested knife price and add ten percent for each earlier period, then subtract ten percent for each condition from mint. This is the formula we used to price vintage Case knives in this book.*

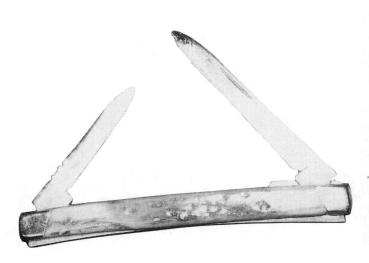

*62069, W. R. CASE & SONS, congress, Rogers, slant bolsters, 3-1/16", $1,200.*

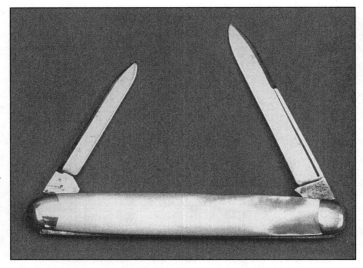

*8271 LP, W. R. CASE & SONS, pearl, 3-1/4", $500.*

*G2069, W. R. CASE & SONS, congress, pyremite, copper, slant bolsters, 3-1/2", $1,200.*

*62074-1/2, W. R. CASE & SONS, serpentine, Rogers, 3-1/2", $400.*

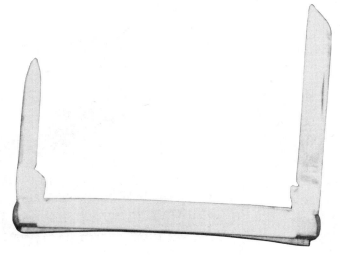

*82069, W. R. CASE & SONS, congress, pearl, slant flat bolsters, 2-13/16", $1,200.*

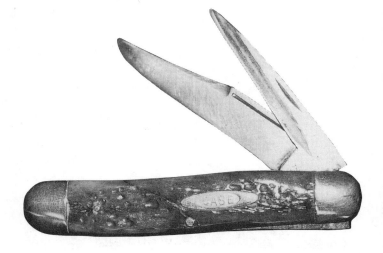

*620741/2 LP PU, W. R. CASE & SONS, serpentine, Rogers, w/punch, 4-1/4", $475.*

Case & Sons 105

6275LP P, W. R. CASE & SONS, large stockman pen, red Rogers, 4-1/4", $1,500.

6275LP S, W. R. CASE & SONS, moose, long spey, red Winterbottom, 4-5/16", $1,500.

6275LP P, W. R. CASE & SONS, large stockman pen, Rogers, match striker, Cutlery, rare, 4-1/4", $1,750.

6276-1/2, W. R. CASE & SONS, sleeveboard, Rogers, flat bolsters, 3-5/8", $650.

6275LP S, W. R. CASE & SONS, moose, long spey, Rogers, 4-1/4", $1,500.

62076, W. R. CASE & SONS, large sleeveboard, bone, Schatt & Morgan contract, 4", $750.

*Pricing Note: The value of Case vintage knives is subjective, but a good rule of thumb is to start with the Tested knife price and add ten percent for each earlier period, then subtract ten percent for each condition from mint. This is the formula we used to price vintage Case knives in this book.*

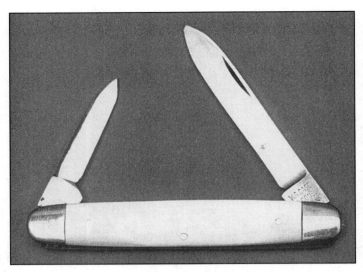

8279, W. R. CASE & SONS, equal end pen, pearl, 3-1/8", $450.

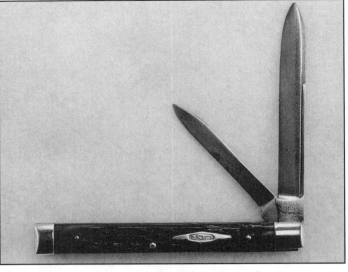

6280 LP, W. R. CASE & SONS, slim doctor's, Rogers, upside-down shield, 3-11/16", $1,200.

62079, W. R. CASE & SONS, sleeveboard pen, front brown Rogers, back red Rogers, 3-5/8", $350.

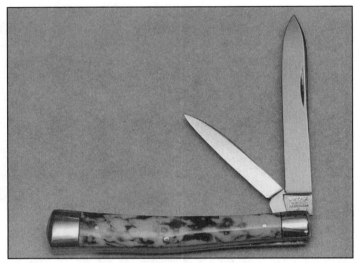

M281, W. R. CASE & SONS, bowed doctor's knife, butter & molasses, 3-3/4", $1,200.

62079-1/2, W. R. CASE & SONS, sleeveboard pen, Rogers, flat bolsters, 3-5/8", $350.

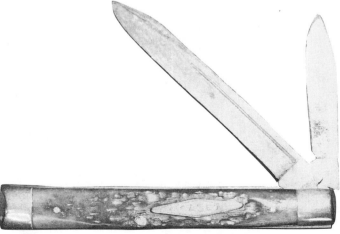

6282 LP, W. R. CASE & SONS, doctor's knife, green bone, 2-7/8", $750.

Case & Sons 107

*6282 LP, W. R. CASE & SONS, doctor's knife, bone, 2-7/8", $750.*

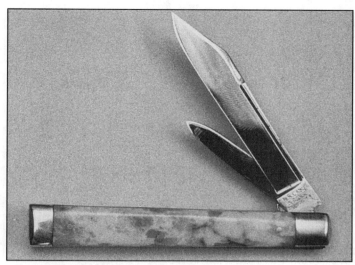

*M2086 LP, W. R. CASE & SONS, doctor's knife, linoleum, 2-7/8", $950.*

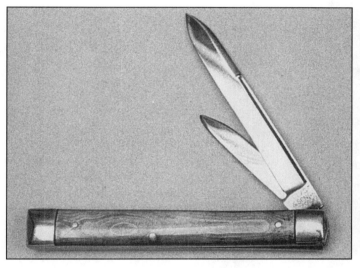

*BC283 LP, W. R. CASE & SONS, doctor's knife, green pyremite, 2-7/8", $900.*

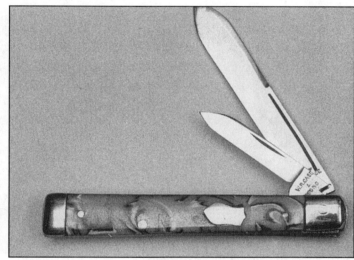

*BM2086 LP, W. R. CASE & SONS, doctor's knife, pyralin, 2-7/8", $950.*

*6283, W. R. CASE & SONS, half whittler, Rogers, rare, 3-1/2", $2,500.*

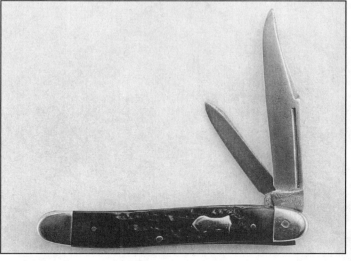

*6287, W. R. CASE & SONS, serpentine, Rogers, 3-1/8", $450.*

*Pricing Note: The value of Case vintage knives is subjective, but a good rule of thumb is to start with the Tested knife price and add ten percent for each earlier period, then subtract ten percent for each condition from mint. This is the formula we used to price vintage Case knives in this book.*

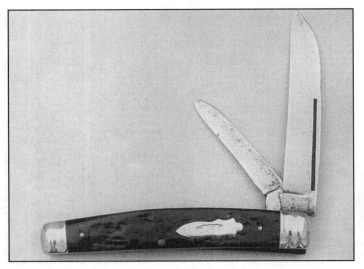

**6289 LP, W. R. CASE & SONS,** *congress, Rogers, pinched bolsters, 3-3/4", $3,500.*

**O.6294, W. R. CASE & SONS,** *large cigar, unstained bone, 4-1/4", $3,000.*

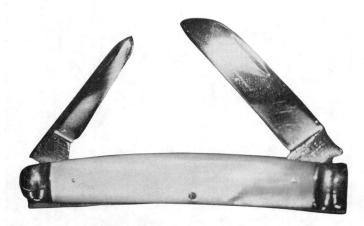

**82089, W. R. CASE & SONS,** *congress, green pearl, pinched bolsters, 3-3/4", $4,000.*

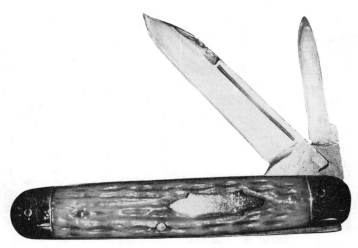

**6294 LP, W. R. CASE & SONS,** *large cigar, bone, 4-1/4", $3,000.*

**5294J LP, W. R. CASE & SONS,** *large cigar, stag, Penn. (Bank St. plant), circa 1920, 4-1/4", $3,000.*

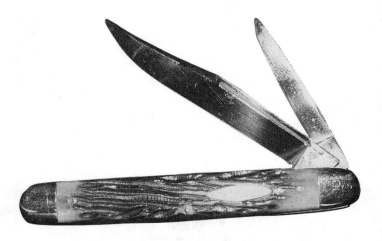

**6295 LP, W. R. CASE & SONS,** *long slender jack, brown Winterbottom, contract?, very rare, 4-1/4", $2,500.*

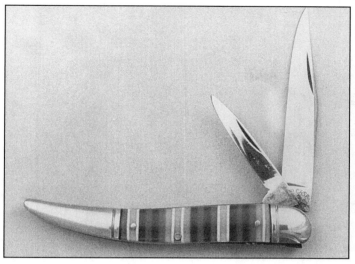

*R2096, W. R. CASE & SONS, toothpick, candy stripe, 3-1/4", $450.*

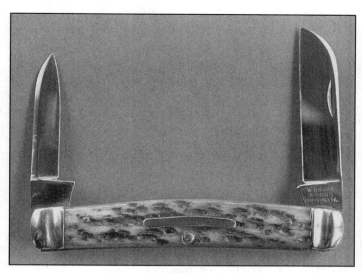

*unknown, W. R. CASE & SONS, similar to o68, congress, green bone, pinched bolsters, 3-3/4", $1,200.*

*unknown, W. R. CASE & SONS, green pyremite, slant bolsters, 3-3/8", $450.*

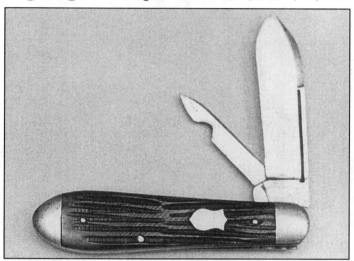

*unknown, W. R. CASE & SONS, teardrop, Winterbottom, easy opener, 3-1/2", $750.*

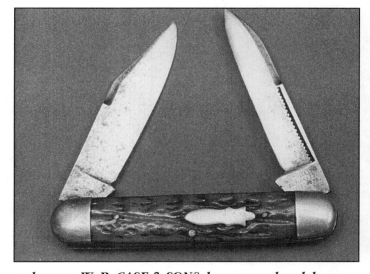

*unknown, W. R. CASE & SONS, large equal end, bone, J type, 3-11/16", $2,000.*

*unknown, W. R. CASE & SONS, metal, figural (Royal Order of Red Men), 3-1/4", $400.*

**Pricing Note:** *The value of Case vintage knives is subjective, but a good rule of thumb is to start with the Tested knife price and add ten percent for each earlier period, then subtract ten percent for each condition from mint. This is the formula we used to price vintage Case knives in this book.*

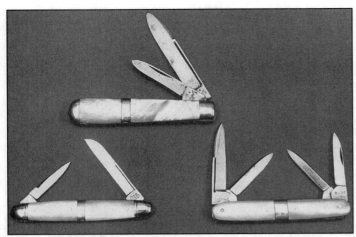

*Top: unknown, W. R. CASE & SONS, split pearl jack, pearl, 3-1/4", $425.*
*Bottom left: unknown, Tested XX, pearl, 3-1/8", $400.*
*Bottom right: unknown, CASE BRADFORD, pearl, 3", $575.*

*6307, W. R. CASE & SONS, bone, whittler, 3-1/4", $900.*

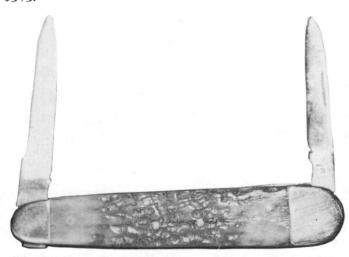

*unknown, W. R. CASE & SONS, small sleeveboard, Rogers, flat bolsters, 2", $1,000.*

*6321 LP, W. R. CASE & SONS, Rogers, whittler, 3-1/4", $950.*

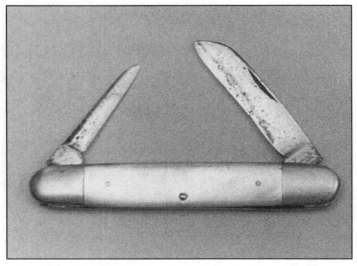

*unknown, W. R. CASE & SONS, 2-blade equal end, pearl, 3-3/8", $350.*

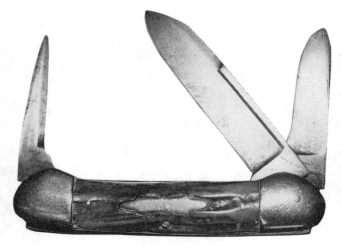

*53131P LP, W. R. CASE & SONS, stag, canoe w/punch, 3-5/8", $3,000.*

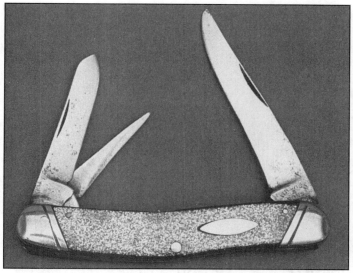

GS3038, W. R. CASE & SONS, goldstone, slant bolsters, 3-1/2", $600.

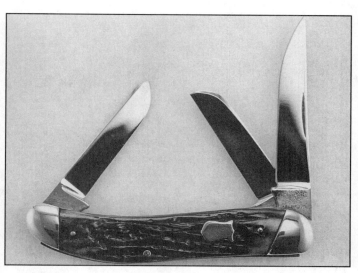

63039, W. R. CASE & SONS, small sowbelly, brown Winterbottom, slant bolsters, 3-7/16", $3,500.

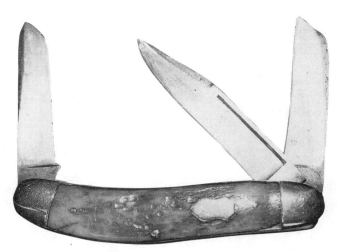

6339 LP, W. R. CASE & SONS, sowbelly, Rogers, 3-3/4", $3,500.

6342P LP, W. R. CASE & SONS, swell center, Rogers, 3-1/2", $750.

6339, W. R. CASE & SONS, sowbelly, brown Winterbottom, grooved bolsters, 3-3/4", $3,500.

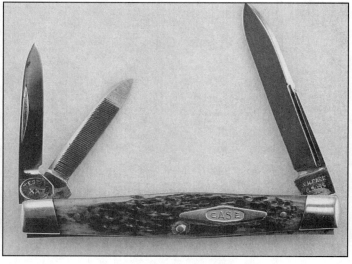

63042F LP, W. R. CASE & SONS, small stockman whittler, Rogers, slant bolsters, file, 2-15/16", $1,500.

Pricing Note: The value of Case vintage knives is subjective, but a good rule of thumb is to start with the Tested knife price and add ten percent for each earlier period, then subtract ten percent for each condition from mint. This is the formula we used to price vintage Case knives in this book.

**5343 LP**, W. R. CASE & SONS, *big serpentine whittler, stag, 3-3/4", $3,500.*

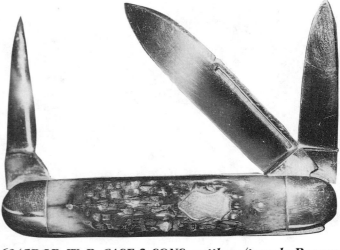

**6345P LP**, W. R. CASE & SONS, *cattle w/punch, Rogers, 3-5/8", $850.*

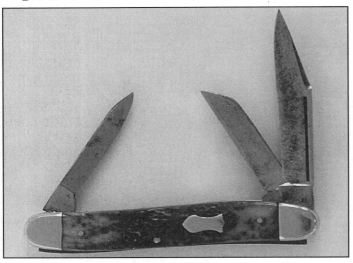

**6344 LP**, W. R. CASE & SONS, *Rogers, flat bolsters, 3-1/2", $450.*

**63045**, W. R. CASE & SONS, *tool knife, saber pen, bone, 3-5/8", $1,500.*

**6345 LP**, W. R. CASE & SONS, *cattle, Rogers, 3-5/8", $750.*

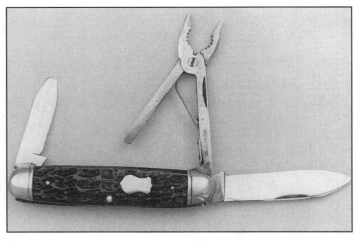

**63045**, W. R. CASE & SONS, *tool knife, screwdriver pen blade, bone, 3-5/8", $1,500.*

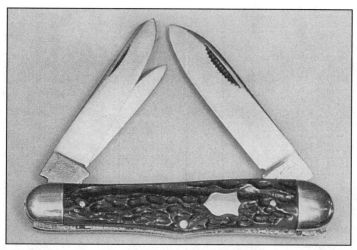

6346, W. R. CASE & SONS, 3-backspring whittler w/long spey, bone, 3-5/8", $3,500.

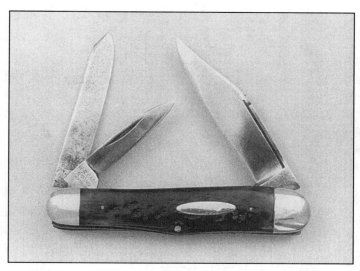

6346-1/2 LP, W. R. CASE & SONS, 3-backspring whittler w/long spey, Rogers, 3-5/8", $3,500.

6346, W. R. CASE & SONS, 3-backspring whittler, bone, match striker, 3-5/8", $3,500.

63046 LP, W. R. CASE & SONS, congress, humpbottom, Rogers, 3-5/8", $2,000.

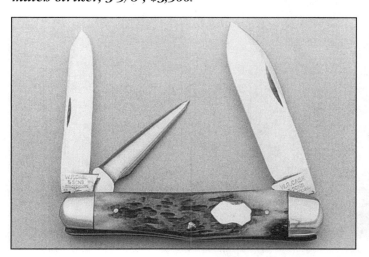

6346P, W. R. CASE & SONS, 3-backspring whittler w/punch, Rogers, 3-5/8", $3,500.

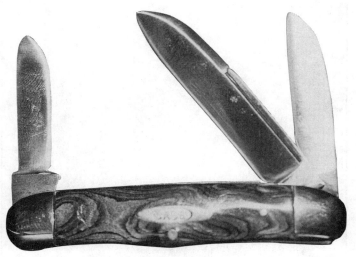

G3046, W. R. CASE & SONS, congress, humpbottom, silver pyremite, 3-5/8", $2,000.

*Pricing Note: The value of Case vintage knives is subjective, but a good rule of thumb is to start with the Tested knife price and add ten percent for each earlier period, then subtract ten percent for each condition from mint. This is the formula we used to price vintage Case knives in this book.*

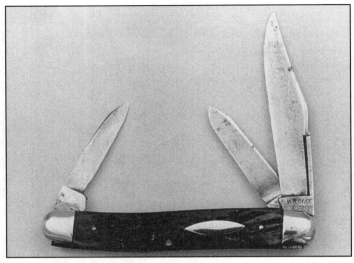

*6347 LP, W. R. CASE & SONS, stockman, Rogers, 3-7/8", $1,500.*

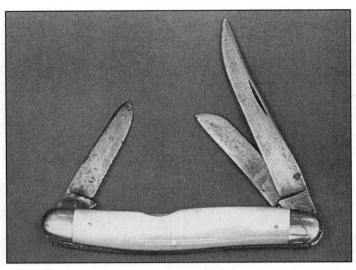

*83047, W. R. CASE & SONS, stockman, pearl, 4", $1,000.*

*6347X, W. R. CASE & SONS, stockman w/left pull, Rogers, 3-7/8", $1,500.*

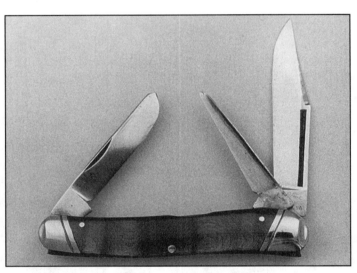

*P348 LP, W. R. CASE & SONS, pyremite, slant pinched bolsters, Made in USA, 3-7/8", $900.*

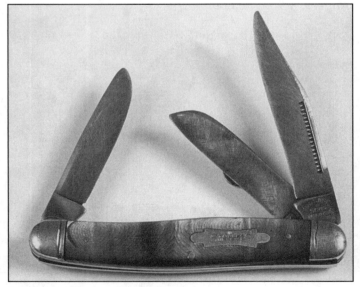

*G347 LP, W. R. CASE & SONS, stockman, green pyremite, Made in USA, stainless, 3-7/8", $1,000.*

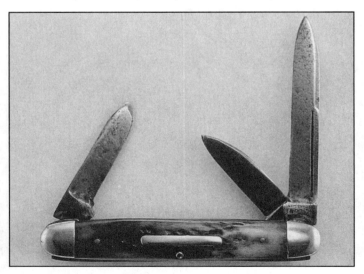

*6353 LP, W. R. CASE & SONS, small pen, Rogers, 3-1/4", $375.*

Case & Sons 115

6356, W. R. CASE & SONS, swell center, not whittler, Rogers, 3-1/8", $950.

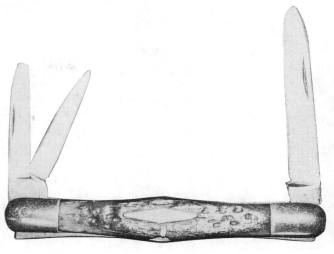

63067, W. R. CASE & SONS, long slender swell center whittler, Rogers, 3-1/4", $750.

63056F, W. R. CASE & SONS, small swell center whittler w/file & cuticle, Rogers, 3-9/16", $950.

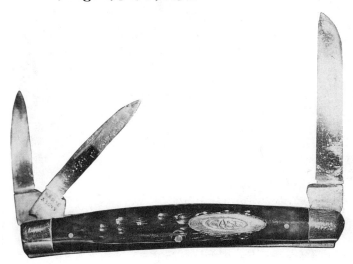

6368, W. R. CASE & SONS, congress whittler, red bone, 3", $4,250.

6363, W. R. CASE & SONS, pen, Winterbottom, 3-1/16", $750.

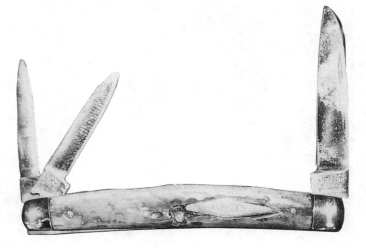

6369, W. R. CASE & SONS, congress whittler Rogers, pinched bolsters, 3-5/16", $3,750.

Pricing Note: The value of Case vintage knives is subjective, but a good rule of thumb is to start with the Tested knife price and add ten percent for each earlier period, then subtract ten percent for each condition from mint. This is the formula we used to price vintage Case knives in this book.

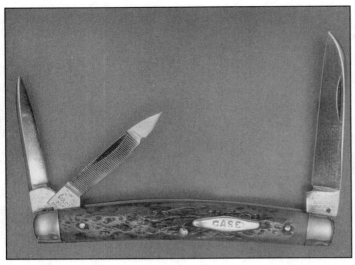

**6369, W. R. CASE & SONS,** *congress whittler, Rogers, file, 3-5/16", $3,750.*

**5374, W. R. CASE & SONS,** *big swell-center whittler, stag, pinched bolsters, 4", $3,000.*

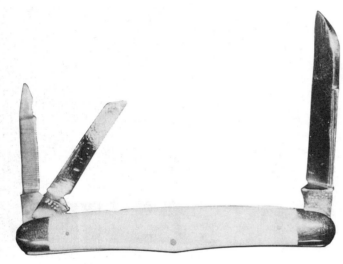

**8370 LP, W. R. CASE & SONS,** *humpback whittler, pearl, file/cuticle, HUDDLESTON, 4", $1,000.*

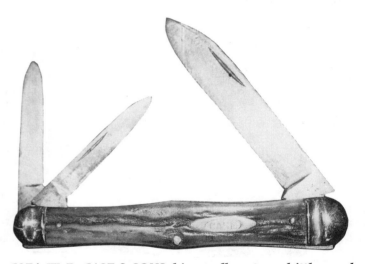

**5374, W. R. CASE & SONS,** *big swell-center whittler, red stag, pinched bolsters, 4", $3,500.*

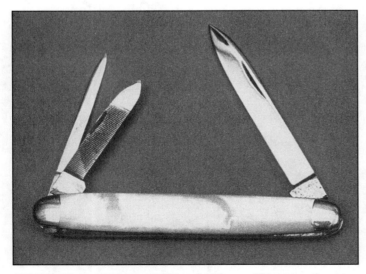

**8371F, W. R. CASE & SONS,** *whittler w/file, pearl, 3-1/4", $1,500.*

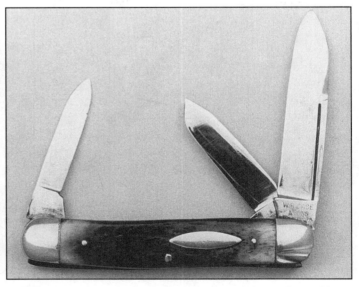

**63074 LP, W. R. CASE & SONS,** *Rogers, 4", $2,000.*

Case & Sons 117

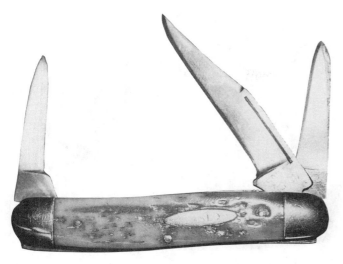

63074-1/2 LP, W. R. CASE & SONS, Rogers, 4", $2,000.

6383SAB LP, W. R. CASE & SONS, balloon center whittler, bone, 3-11/16", $2,000.

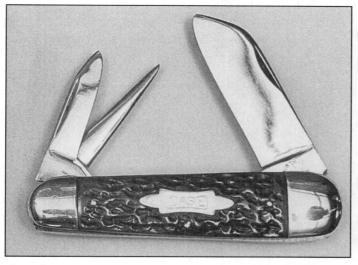

63076, W. R. CASE & SONS, big sleeveboard whittler, punch, green bone, Made in USA, 4", $3,000.

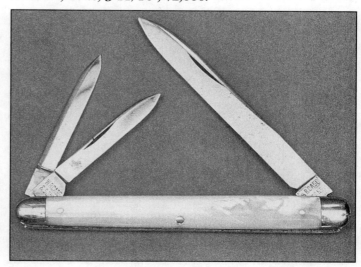

8385, W. R. CASE & SONS, long slender whittler, pearl, 3-5/8", $900.

63079, W. R. CASE & SONS, whittler, bone, 3-5/16", $850.

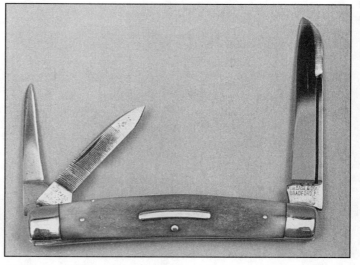

5388 LP, W. R. CASE & SONS, congress whittler, stag, center shield, 4-1/8", $7,500.

*Pricing Note: The value of Case vintage knives is subjective, but a good rule of thumb is to start with the Tested knife price and add ten percent for each earlier period, then subtract ten percent for each condition from mint. This is the formula we used to price vintage Case knives in this book.*

**6388 LP, W. R. CASE & SONS,** *congress whittler, Rogers, center shield, SONS/SON, 4-1/8", $7,500.*

**6393P LP, W. R. CASE & SONS,** *Rogers, punch, Made in USA, 3-7/8", $3,500.*

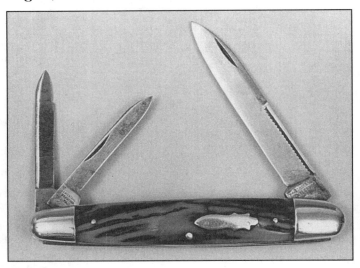

**5391F LP, W. R. CASE & SONS,** *whittler, double pull, cuticle file, stag, 4-1/2", $4,500.*

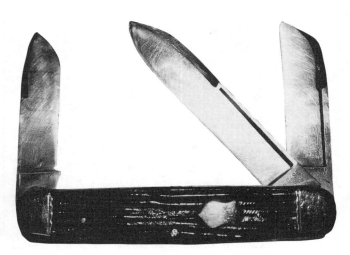

**6394 LP, W. R. CASE & SONS,** *big cigar, red Winterbottom, flat/grooved bolsters, 4-3/16", $5,000.*

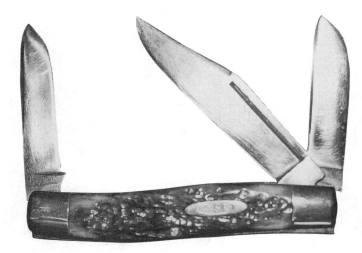

**6393 LP, W. R. CASE & SONS,** *Rogers, 3-7/8", $3,500.*

**unknown, W. R. CASE & SONS,** *3-backspring whittler, bone, tip bolsters & cuticle file, 3-3/8", $900.*

Case & Sons 119

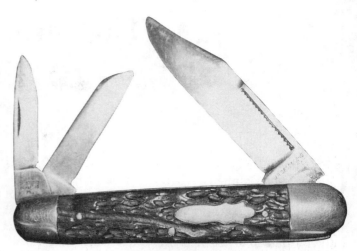
*unknown, W. R. CASE & SONS, 3-blade sleeveboard whittler, bone, 2-3/4", $850.*

*unknown, W. R. CASE & SONS, 3-blade stockman, long pull, bone, 3-7/8", $800.*

*unknown, W. R. CASE & SONS, 3-blade cloisonné w/ scissor & file, metal, 2-13/16", $500.*

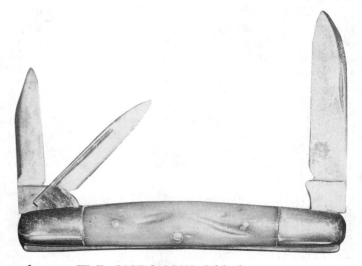
*unknown, W. R. CASE & SONS, 3-blade congress whittler, Rogers, long bolsters, $4,000.*

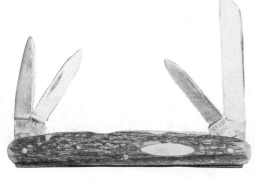
*5438, W. R. CASE & SONS, congress, red stag, 3-5/8", $3,000.*

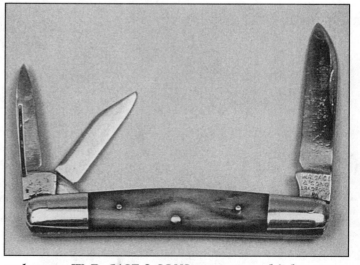
*unknown, W. R. CASE & SONS, congress whittler, stag, long bolsters, 3", $2,500.*

*Pricing Note: The value of Case vintage knives is subjective, but a good rule of thumb is to start with the Tested knife price and add ten percent for each earlier period, then subtract ten percent for each condition from mint. This is the formula we used to price vintage Case knives in this book.*

# The Bradford Era (1914-1919)

By Bob Wurzelbacher

Can you imagine the excitement at the W. R. Case & Sons Company, when they heard that the Case Brothers Cutlery Company was going to go out of business? As background, the Case Brothers lost their Little Valley, New York knife works to fire in 1912 and this had followed a fire at their Smedport works. They rebuilt in Springville, New York, but the financial burden was too great for them to continue operations. Their dilemma is fully explained in the section on the Case Brothers Cutlery Company.

It suffices to say that the knife business was going to change. First and foremost, there would be equipment, parts, and finished inventory for sale. Most importantly, however, in hindsight, was the fact that the copyright to the statement "CASE TESTED XX" was going to be for sale. This statement was as important to the knife business as 99 and 44/100 percent pure was to Ivory Soap and Procter and Gamble. People didn't remember the name Ivory or Procter and Gamble, but they did remember the soap that floats and that is how they asked for it, when they went to the general or grocery store. The same was true for knives; people asked for the knives that were Double X Tested. What this actually meant to them and what it stood for were one and the same thing. In the blade making process, blades were hardened with heat. When a blade was first hardened, an X was marked on the side of the box. Then it was hardened a second time and another X was put on the box. They were then tested for hardness and the box was marked TESTED XX. The Case Brothers knew the advertising value of this statement and put it on almost every knife they made in one way or another. Oftentimes, it was put right on the face of the main blade as a deep XX. Sometimes it was put on as TESTED XX, and often on the rear of the main tang as XX pattern number or TESTED XX. To the buyer, it meant the blade was hardened and would hold an edge.

J. Russell Case knew the value of the statement. After all, he was a salesman for the Case Brothers Cutlery Company, and he sold that value. He immediately started changing his tang stamps, catalogs, and advertisements to reflect the change. This was the beginning of what we call the CASE BRADFORD era that lasted from 1914 to 1919. First and foremost, he changed the tang stamp to CASE BRADFORD PA (two lines), from the W. R. Case & Sons Bradford PA tang stamp. Almost every knife did reflect the pattern number of the knife and, in some way or form, reflected the statement CASE TESTED XX. In the early part of the period, the words appeared on the rear of the tang of the main blade. In the latter part of the period, and the most common form were the words CASE TESTED XX inside a circle on one of the secondary blades. In one case, I have a knife that has the circle TESTED XX on both of the blades without the customary Case Bradford tang stamp.

It wasn't until 1919 that the change was made to the running C, or the Tested era, as it is called. But that's another story for another day and another chapter.

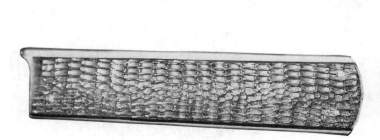

**6001, CASE BRADFORD, tri-fold, green bone, 4-3/4", $1,350.**

**61000 SAB, CASE BRADFORD, green bone, saddlehorn, pinched bolster, 4-1/2", $1,550.**

Bradford 121

**61005**, CASE BRADFORD, Rogers, bolster stamped CASE'S Tested, 3-3/8", $925.

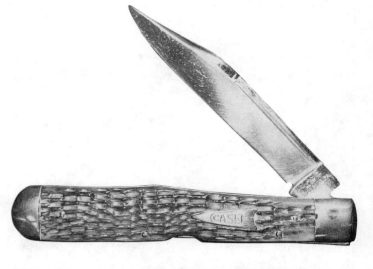

**6111-1/2 LP**, CASE BRADFORD, green bone, flat blade, lock, no guard, 4-3/8", $2,400.

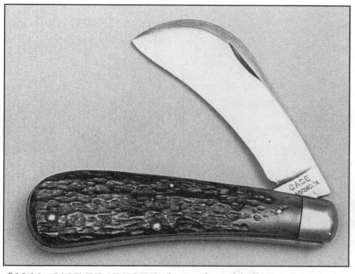

**61011**, CASE BRADFORD, large hawkbill, Rogers, 4", $360.

**6111-1/2 LP**, CASE BRADFORD, green bone, flat blade, no lock, 4-3/8", $1,800.

**6111-1/2 LP**, CASE BRADFORD, bone, flat blade, no lock, 4-3/8", $1,800.

**61048 LP**, CASE BRADFORD, green bone, 4-1/8", $650.

*Pricing Note: The value of Case vintage knives is subjective, but a good rule of thumb is to start with the Tested knife price and add ten percent for each earlier period, then subtract ten percent for each condition from mint. This is the formula we used to price vintage Case knives in this book.*

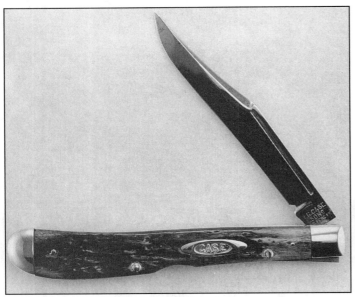

61049L, CASE BRADFORD, Rogers, 4-1/8", $1,550.

6151 L SAB, CASE BRADFORD, green bone, lock, 5-1/4", $1,650.

61050L, CASE BRADFORD, switchblade zipper, green bone, 5-7/16", $7,500.

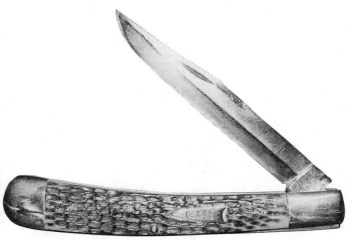

6151 SAB, CASE BRADFORD, green bone, no lock, 5-1/4", $1,350.

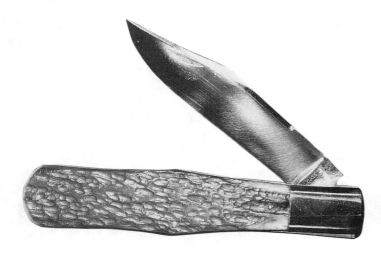

61050, CASE BRADFORD, large Coke, Rogers, no lower bolster, iron, 5-7/16", $1,200.

61051 LP, CASE BRADFORD, bone, fishtail, guard, 3-7/8", $1,000.

**6165, CASE BRADFORD,** *folding hunter, green bone,* 5-1/4", $1,350.

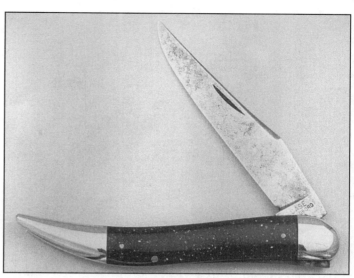

**GS1094, CASE BRADFORD,** *toothpick, goldstone,* 4-1/4", $600.

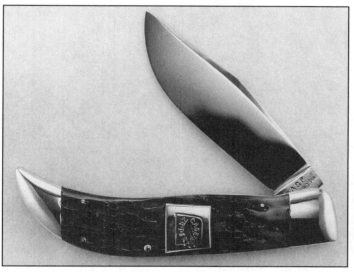

**6172 L, CASE BRADFORD,** *zipper switch, green bone,* ZIPPER *on switch,* 5-1/2", $9,500.

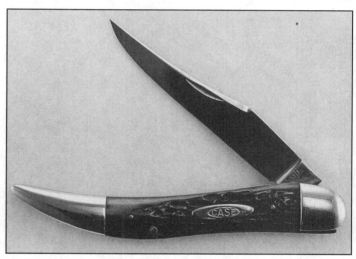

**61094, CASE BRADFORD,** *medium toothpick, Rogers,* 4-3/16", $900.

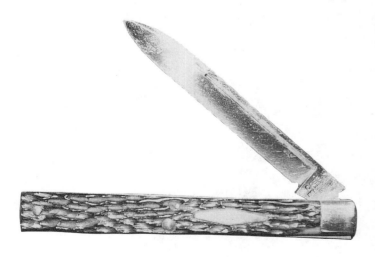

**6185 LP, CASE BRADFORD,** *doctor's knife, green bone,* 3-3/4", $1,000.

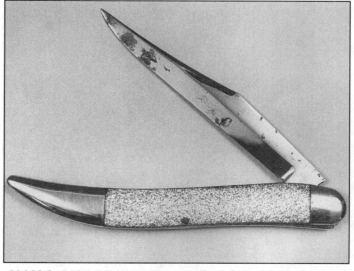

**GS1095, CASE BRADFORD,** *toothpick, goldstone,* 5", $650.

*Pricing Note: The value of Case vintage knives is subjective, but a good rule of thumb is to start with the Tested knife price and add ten percent for each earlier period, then subtract ten percent for each condition from mint. This is the formula we used to price vintage Case knives in this book.*

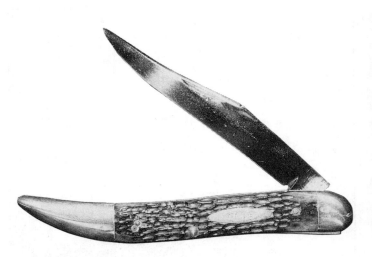

**61095 SAB, CASE BRADFORD,** *toothpick, green bone, 5", $1,000.*

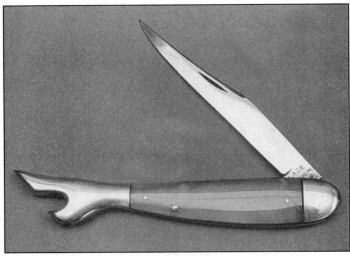

**B1097SAB, CASE BRADFORD,** *large leg knife, waterfall, 5", $775.*

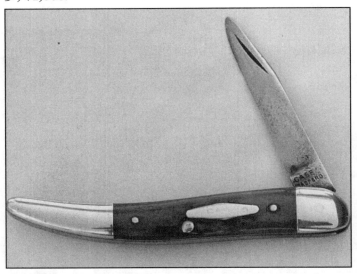

**61096, CASE BRADFORD,** *small toothpick, green bone, 3-1/8", $900.*

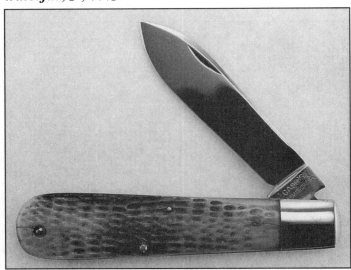

**6199, CASE BRADFORD,** *Texas jack, green bone, no lower bolster, 4", $650.*

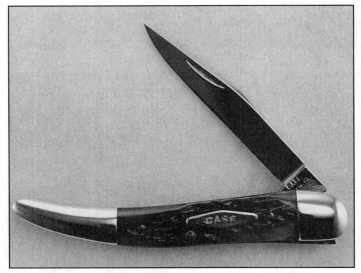

**61096, CASE BRADFORD,** *small toothpick, Rogers, 3-1/8", $900.*

**unknown, CASE BRADFORD,** *cam operated auto, cracked ice, 2-3/4", $350.*

**6202-1/2, CASE BRADFORD,** pattern #XX 6202-1/2, green bone, 3-3/8", $350.

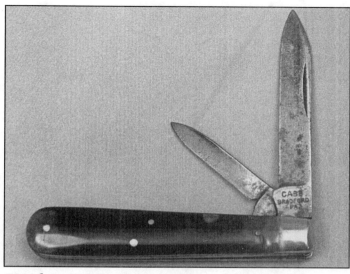

**72006, CASE BRADFORD,** tortoise, 2-5/8", $400.

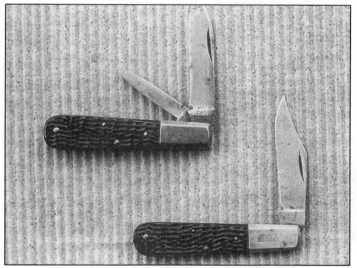

Top: **6205, CASE BRADFORD,** Barlow spear, green bone, 3-3/8", $1,350.
Bottom: **6205-1/2, CASE BRADFORD,** Barlow clip, green bone, 3-3/8", $1,750.

**62100 SAB, CASE BRADFORD,** saddlehorn, transition to Tested, green bone, 4-5/8", $2,450.

**6205R LP, CASE BRADFORD,** Barlow razor, green bone, no lower, fluted upper bolster, 3-3/4", $1,350.

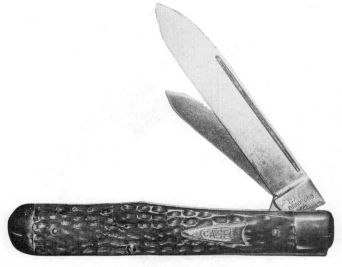

**6211 LP, CASE BRADFORD,** green bone, 4-7/16", $2,450.

*Pricing Note: The value of Case vintage knives is subjective, but a good rule of thumb is to start with the Tested knife price and add ten percent for each earlier period, then subtract ten percent for each condition from mint. This is the formula we used to price vintage Case knives in this book.*

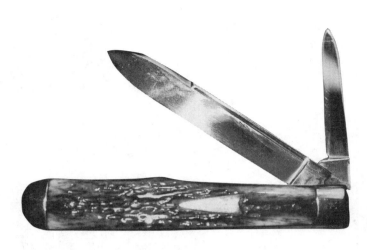

**6211 LP, CASE BRADFORD, Rogers, 4-7/16", $2,450.**

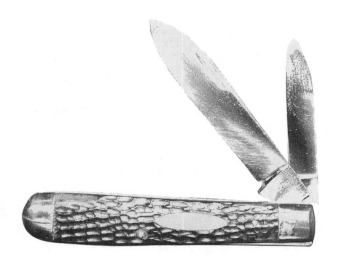

**6214, CASE BRADFORD, green bone, 3-3/8", $350.**

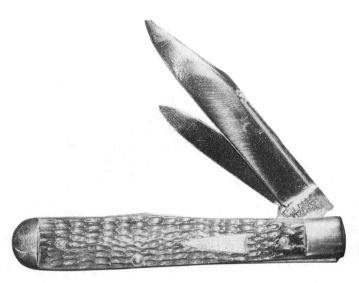

**6211-1/2 LP, CASE BRADFORD, green bone, 4-7/16", $2,450.**

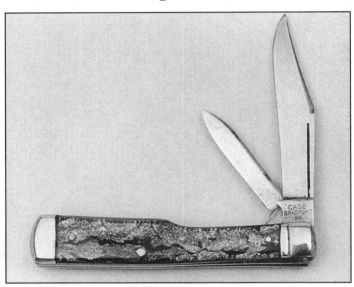

**RM6215, CASE BRADFORD, gunstock, Christmas yellow, 3", $2,450.**

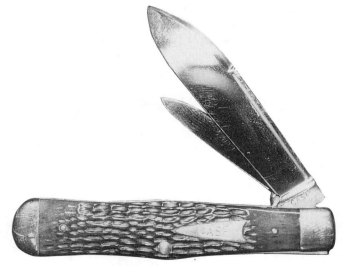

**6213 LP, CASE BRADFORD, large Coke, green bone, 3-7/8", $2,450.**

**6216 I, CASE BRADFORD, green bone, rare I stamp (iron), 3-7/16", $375.**

*6219 LP, CASE BRADFORD, green bone, 3-1/8", $900.*

*62019 LP, CASE BRADFORD, larger 6219, green bone, 4-1/8", $2,400.*

*62019 LP, CASE BRADFORD, larger 6219, Rogers, 4-1/8", $2,400.*

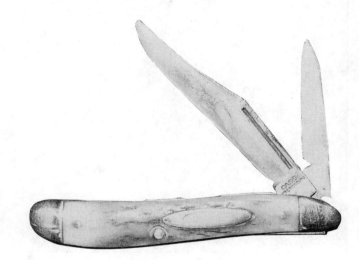

*5220 SAB LP, CASE BRADFORD, peanut, stag, 2-3/4", $825.*

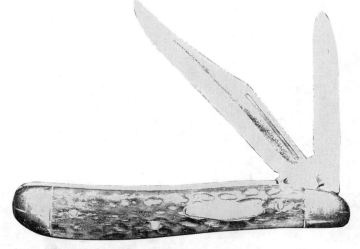

*6220 SAB LP, CASE BRADFORD, peanut, green bone, 2-3/4", $825.*

*Pricing Note: The value of Case vintage knives is subjective, but a good rule of thumb is to start with the Tested knife price and add ten percent for each earlier period, then subtract ten percent for each condition from mint. This is the formula we used to price vintage Case knives in this book.*

**62020, CASE BRADFORD**, Rogers, pinched bolsters, 3-1/4", $350.

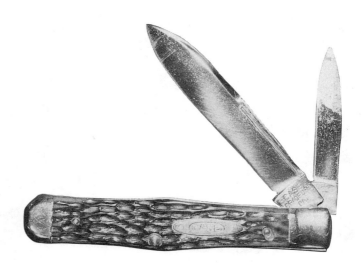

**6223 LP, CASE BRADFORD**, medium Coke, green bone, coffin/fluted bolster, 3-1/2", $1,550.

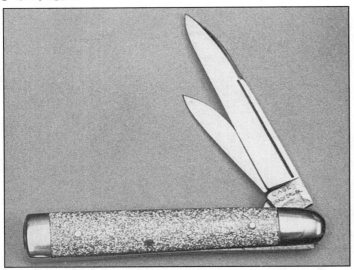

**GS2222, CASE BRADFORD**, doctor's knife, goldstone, 3-3/8", $2,000.

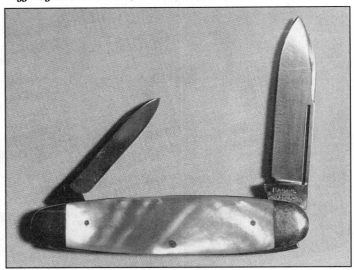

**8224, CASE BRADFORD**, pearl, 3-1/16", $500.

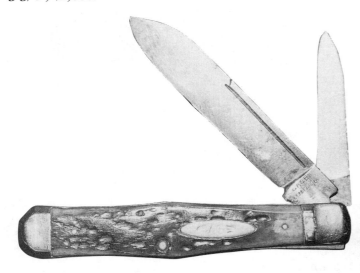

**6223 LP, CASE BRADFORD**, medium Coke, Rogers, coffin/fluted bolster, 3-1/2", $1,550.

**6225 LP, CASE BRADFORD**, small Coke, green bone, 3", $725.

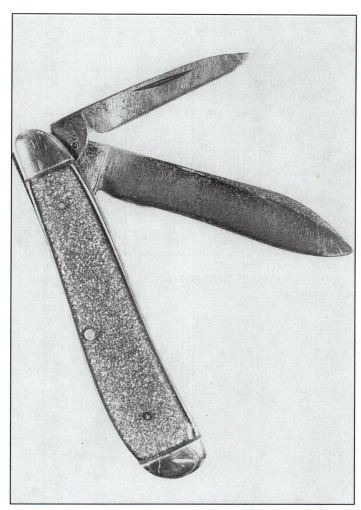

GS226, CASE BRADFORD, large peanut, goldstone, 3", $725.

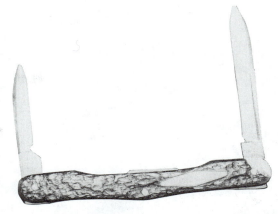

6227 LP, CASE BRADFORD, double reverse gunstock, Rogers, upside-down shield, 3", $750.

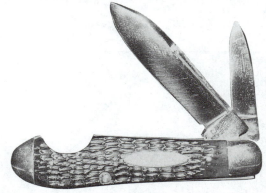

6228 EO LP, CASE BRADFORD, teardrop, green bone, EO, 3-9/16", $675.

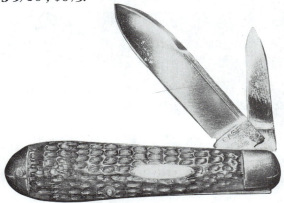

6228 LP, CASE BRADFORD, teardrop, green bone, 3-9/16", $600.

62025-1/2, CASE BRADFORD, small Coke, green bone, no lower bolster, 3", $725.

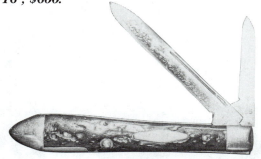

62028 LP, CASE BRADFORD, baby teardrop, green bone, 2-7/8", $775.

*Pricing Note: The value of Case vintage knives is subjective, but a good rule of thumb is to start with the Tested knife price and add ten percent for each earlier period, then subtract ten percent for each condition from mint. This is the formula we used to price vintage Case knives in this book.*

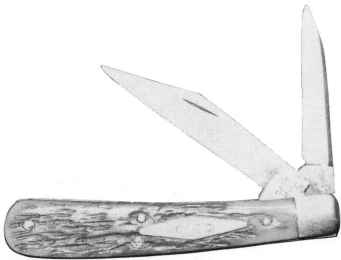

6229-1/2, CASE BRADFORD, Rogers, 2-1/2", $375.

O.6230-1/2 LP, CASE BRADFORD, small cigar, Rogers, 3-1/4", $600.

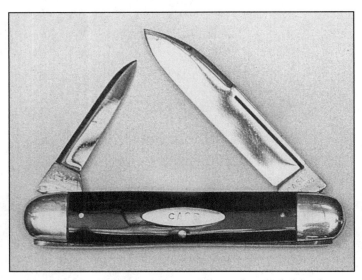

O.2230, CASE BRADFORD, small cattle, slick black, 3-1/4", $275.

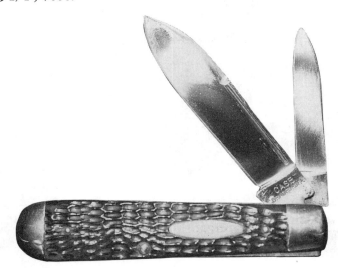

6231 LP, CASE BRADFORD, 2-blade jack, green bone, 3-9/16", $550.

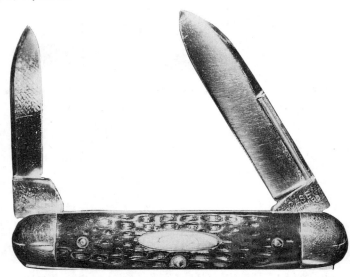

O.6230 LP, CASE BRADFORD, small cigar, green bone, 3-1/4", $600.

6233 LP, CASE BRADFORD, small stockman, green bone, 2-5/8", $425.

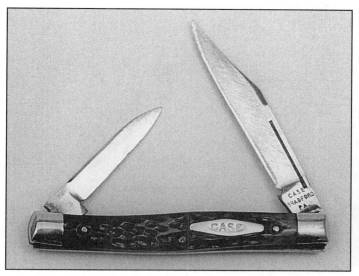

**6233 LP, CASE BRADFORD,** small stockman, Rogers, 2-5/8", $425.

**6237 LP, CASE BRADFORD,** medium Coke, green bone, 3-1/2", $1,500.

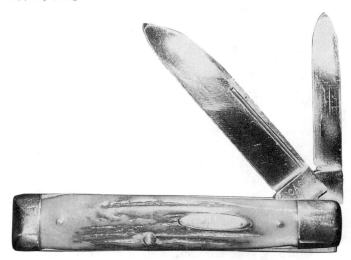

**6234 LP, CASE BRADFORD,** heavy doctor's knife, Rogers, 3-5/8", $1,750.

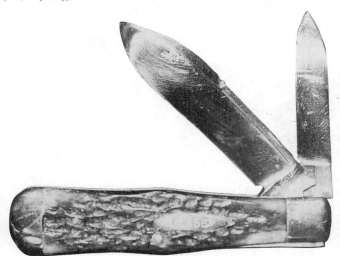

**6237 LP, CASE BRADFORD,** medium Coke, Rogers, 3-1/2", $1,500.

**42035-1/2 LP, CASE BRADFORD,** white composition, 3-1/4", $450.

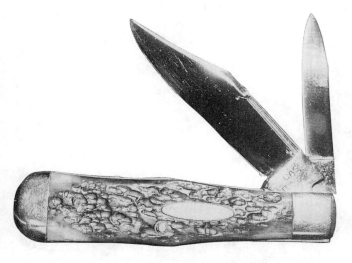

**6237-1/2 LP, CASE BRADFORD,** medium Coke, Rogers, 3-1/2", $1,500.

*Pricing Note: The value of Case vintage knives is subjective, but a good rule of thumb is to start with the Tested knife price and add ten percent for each earlier period, then subtract ten percent for each condition from mint. This is the formula we used to price vintage Case knives in this book.*

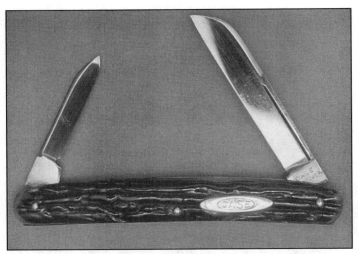

**6238, CASE BRADFORD,** congress, Rogers, 3-5/8", $1,750.

**6241 LP, CASE BRADFORD,** Rogers, 3-1/2", $725.

**6238, CASE BRADFORD,** bumpback congress, green bone, tip bolsters, 3-5/8", $1,750.

**6242, CASE BRADFORD,** similar to peanut, green bone, no lower bolster, 2-13/16", $775.

**62039, CASE BRADFORD,** small sowbelly, Rogers, 3-7/16", $1,200.

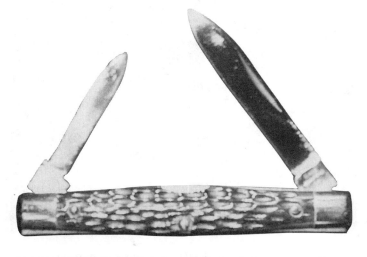

**62042, CASE BRADFORD,** small stockman, green bone, 2-15/16", $250.

Bradford 133

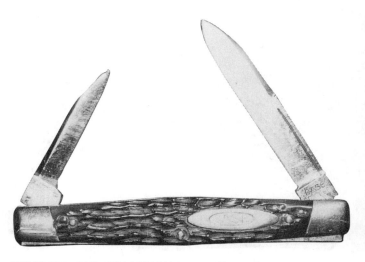

62042 LP, CASE BRADFORD, small stockman, green bone, 2-15/16", $275.

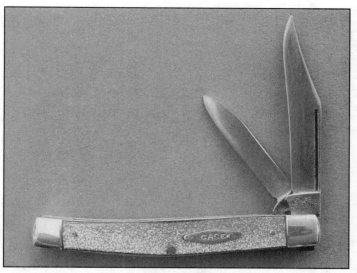

GS244 LP, CASE BRADFORD, goldstone, 3-1/4", $400.

82042 LP, CASE BRADFORD, pearl, stainless in oval, slant bolsters, 3", $350.

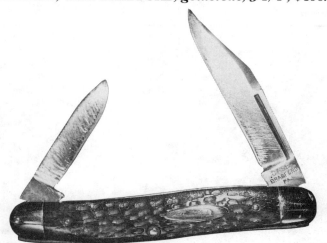

O.6247 S, CASE BRADFORD, stockman w/spey stamp (S), green bone, 3-7/8", $925.

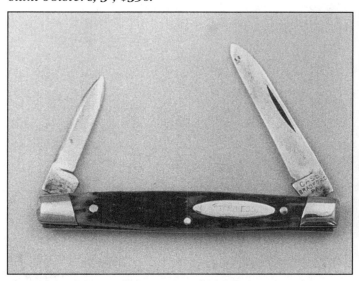

62042, CASE BRADFORD, small stockman, Rogers, slant bolsters, STAINLESS shield, 2-15/16", $300.

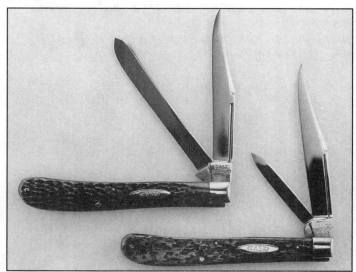

Top: 62048SP LP, CASE BRADFORD, spey, green bone, 4-1/8", $1,000.
Bottom: 62048P LP, CASE BRADFORD, pen, Rogers, 4-1/8", $1,000.

*Pricing Note: The value of Case vintage knives is subjective, but a good rule of thumb is to start with the Tested knife price and add ten percent for each earlier period, then subtract ten percent for each condition from mint. This is the formula we used to price vintage Case knives in this book.*

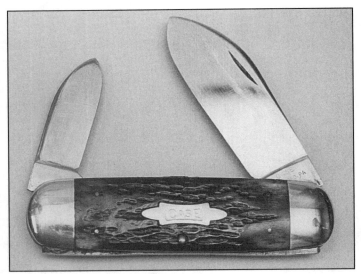

6250, CASE BRADFORD, toenail, Rogers, 4-3/8", $2,500.

O.6256 LP, CASE BRADFORD, swell center, Rogers, 2-7/8", $900.

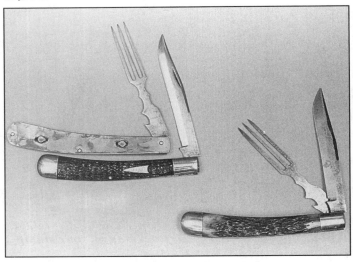

Top: 6251 SAB, CASE BRADFORD, hobo, green bone, 5-5/16", $1,650.
Bottom: 6251, CASE BRADFORD, hobo, Rogers, 5-5/16", $1,650.

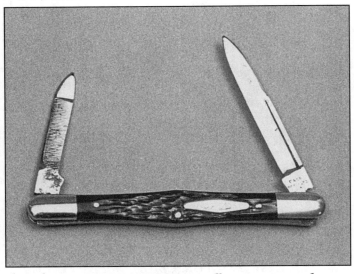

62056 LP, CASE BRADFORD, swell center, green bone, 3", $400.

62053 LP, CASE BRADFORD, equal end, green bone, 2-3/4", $175.

8258, CASE BRADFORD, congress, pearl, 3-7/16", $900.

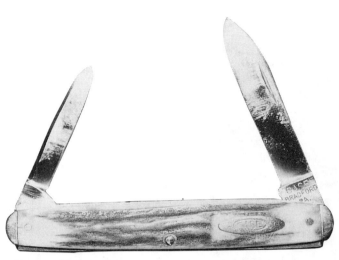

**5260, CASE BRADFORD,** pen, red stag, tip bolsters, 3-3/8", $450.

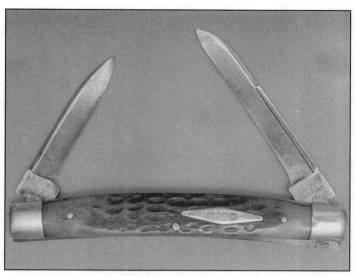

**6268 LP, CASE BRADFORD,** congress, green bone, 3-5/16", $925.

**O.6263 LP, CASE BRADFORD,** Rogers, 3-1/8", $275.

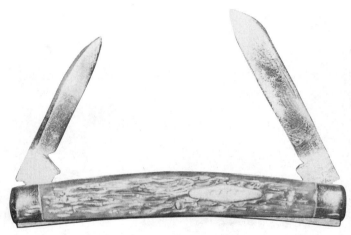

**6269, CASE BRADFORD,** congress, Rogers, pinched bolsters, 3", $600.

**O.6263 LP, CASE BRADFORD,** green bone, 3-1/8", $250.

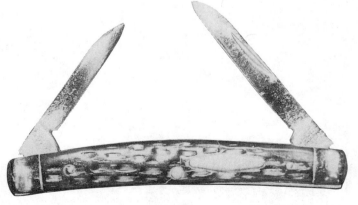

**6269, CASE BRADFORD,** congress, green bone, pinched bolsters, 3", $550.

*Pricing Note: The value of Case vintage knives is subjective, but a good rule of thumb is to start with the Tested knife price and add ten percent for each earlier period, then subtract ten percent for each condition from mint. This is the formula we used to price vintage Case knives in this book.*

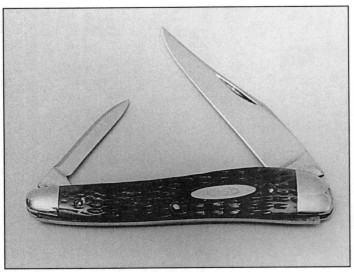

**6273, CASE BRADFORD,** *similar to 06221-1/2, green bone, 3-3/4", $1,350.*

**6280 LP, CASE BRADFORD,** *doctor's knife, green bone, 3-3/4", $1,350.*

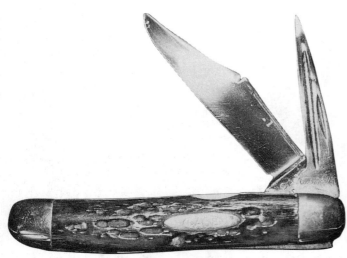

**62074-1/2 P LP, CASE BRADFORD,** *Rogers, flat punch in front, 3-7/16", $450.*

**6281, CASE BRADFORD,** *bowed doctor's knife w/ upside-down shield, Rogers, rare, 3-3/4", $1,350.*

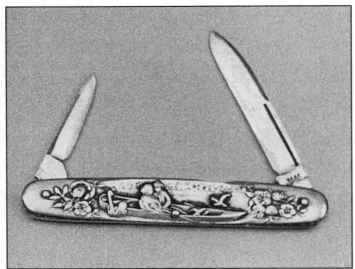

**M279, CASE BRADFORD,** *figural, metal, 3-1/8", $250.*

**6282 LP, CASE BRADFORD,** *doctor's, green bone, 2-7/8", $825.*

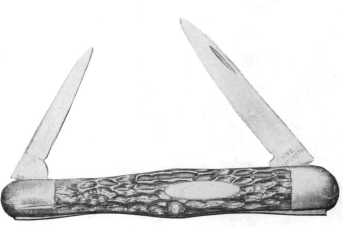

**6283, CASE BRADFORD,** *balloon center, half whittler, green bone, 3-9/16", $1,200.*

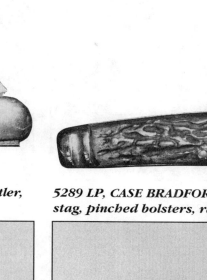

**5289 LP, CASE BRADFORD,** *congress sleeveboard, stag, pinched bolsters, rare, 3-3/4", $4,000.*

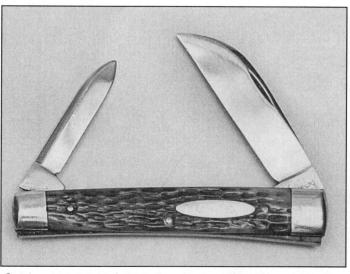

**6284, CASE BRADFORD,** *congress, green bone, 3-1/8", $3,500.*

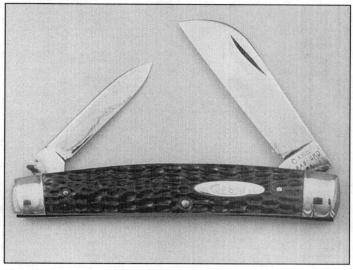

**62089, CASE BRADFORD,** *congress sleeveboard, green bone, pinched bolsters, rare, 3-3/4", $4,000.*

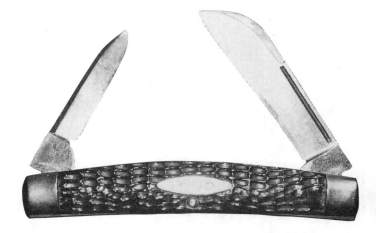

**6288 LP, CASE BRADFORD,** *congress, green bone, pinched bolsters, center shield, 4-1/8", $3,750.*

**6293 LP, CASE BRADFORD,** *large stockman, Rogers, 3-7/8", $600.*

*Pricing Note: The value of Case vintage knives is subjective, but a good rule of thumb is to start with the Tested knife price and add ten percent for each earlier period, then subtract ten percent for each condition from mint. This is the formula we used to price vintage Case knives in this book.*

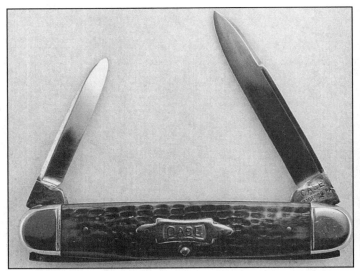

**O.6294 LP, CASE BRADFORD,** big cigar, green bone, flat grooved bolsters, 4-1/4", $2,200.

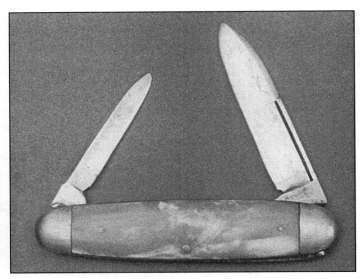

**unknown, CASE BRADFORD,** cracked ice, 3", $450.

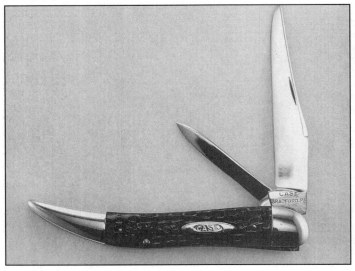

**62094, CASE BRADFORD,** medium toothpick, green bone, 4-1/4", $875.

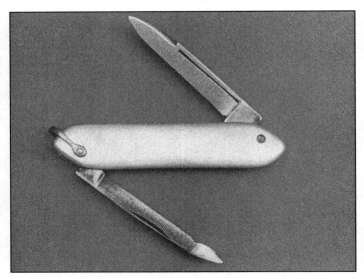

**unknown, CASE BRADFORD,** 2-blade lobster, pearl, 2-1/2", $250.

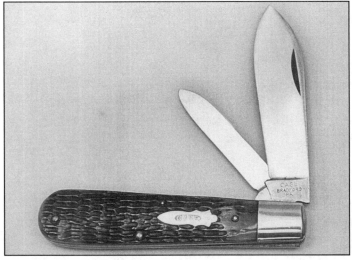

**62099, CASE BRADFORD,** Texas jack, green bone, no lower bolster, 4-1/8", $725.

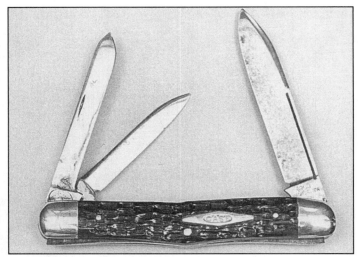

**63109 LP, CASE BRADFORD,** whittler, green bone, 3 backsprings, 3-3/8", $1,550.

*63109 LP, CASE BRADFORD, whittler, green bone, 3 backsprings w/flat punch, 3-3/8", $1,550.*

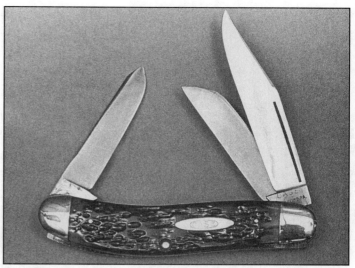

*6339 LP, CASE BRADFORD, sowbelly, Rogers, 3-3/4", $3,500.*

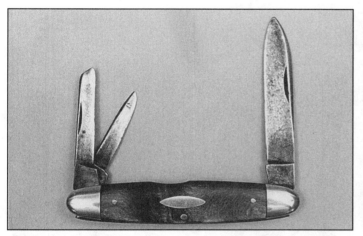

*P3024, CASE BRADFORD, whittler, equal end, green pyremite, 3-1/4", $750.*

*63042F LP, CASE BRADFORD, whittler, Rogers, file, slant bolsters, 2-7/8", $925.*

*GS344LP, CASE BRADFORD, goldstone, 3-1/4", $675.*

*Pricing Note: The value of Case vintage knives is subjective, but a good rule of thumb is to start with the Tested knife price and add ten percent for each earlier period, then subtract ten percent for each condition from mint. This is the formula we used to price vintage Case knives in this book.*

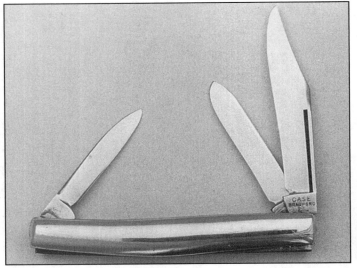

**M344 LP, CASE BRADFORD,** stockman, metal, 3-1/4", $350.

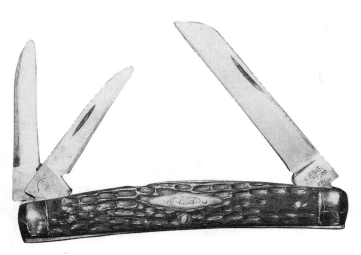

**63052, CASE BRADFORD,** whittler, green bone, center shield, pinched bolsters, 3-1/2", $4,000.

**6345-1/2 LP, CASE BRADFORD,** medium cigar, green bone, 3-5/8", $725.

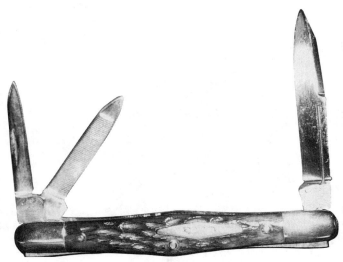

**63056F LP, CASE BRADFORD,** swell-center whittler, green bone, 3", $900.

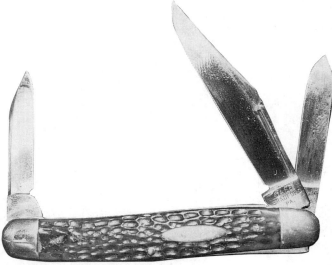

**6347PE LP, CASE BRADFORD,** stockman w/spey, pen, green bone, 3-7/8", $1,100.

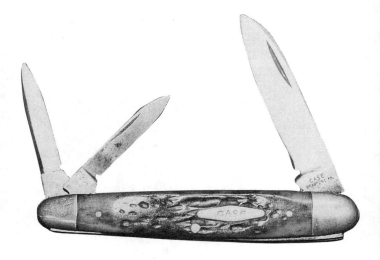

**63063, CASE BRADFORD,** whittler, Rogers, 3-1/8", $900.

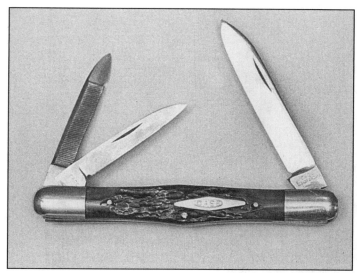

**63067F, CASE BRADFORD**, *swell-center whittler, file, Rogers, 3-7/16", $1,325.*

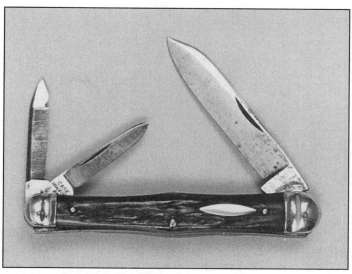

**5374F, CASE BRADFORD**, *whittler, file, stag, rare, 4-1/2", $2,500.*

**6368F, CASE BRADFORD**, *congress, whittler, green bone, 3-5/16", $4,750.*

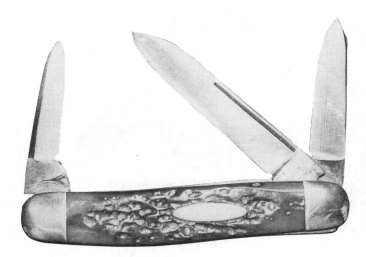

**63074 LP, CASE BRADFORD**, *Rogers, 3-7/16", $925.*

**6370F LP, CASE BRADFORD**, *congress, whittler w/ Wharncliffe green bone, cuticle file, splinter picker, 3-1/8", $1,100.*

**63079-1/2 LP, CASE BRADFORD**, *sleeveboard whittler, green bone, 3-5/16", $900.*

*Pricing Note: The value of Case vintage knives is subjective, but a good rule of thumb is to start with the Tested knife price and add ten percent for each earlier period, then subtract ten percent for each condition from mint. This is the formula we used to price vintage Case knives in this book.*

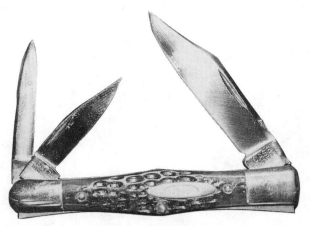

**6383, CASE BRADFORD**, balloon-center whittler, green bone, 3-3/8", $1,500.

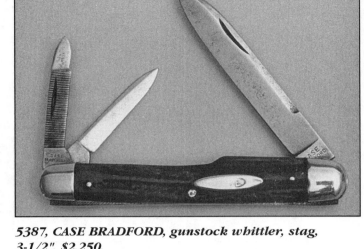

**5387, CASE BRADFORD**, gunstock whittler, stag, 3-1/2", $2,250.

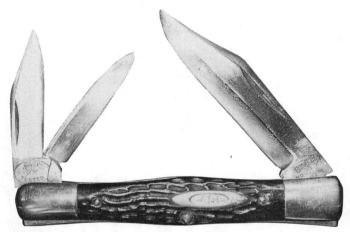

**6383SAB, CASE BRADFORD**, balloon-center whittler, saber, green bone, 3-3/8", $1,800.

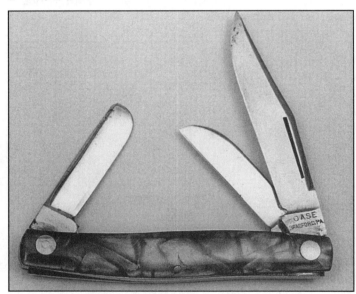

**P3092 LP, CASE BRADFORD**, stockman, green pyremite, 3-7/8", $650.

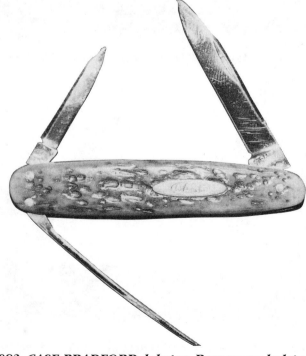

**63083, CASE BRADFORD**, lobster, Rogers, no bolsters, 3-3/16", $500.

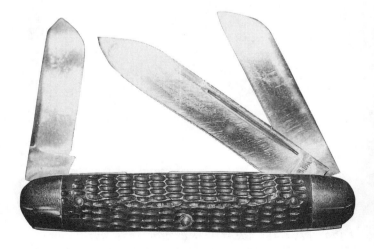

**6394 LP, CASE BRADFORD**, large cigar, green bone, 4-1/4", $5,000.

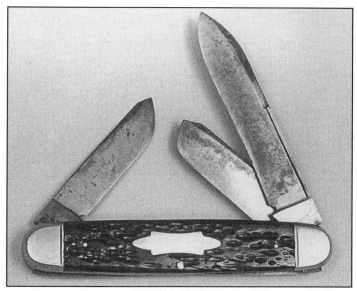

**6394 LP, CASE BRADFORD, large cigar, Rogers, flat grooved bolsters, 4-3/16", $5,000.**

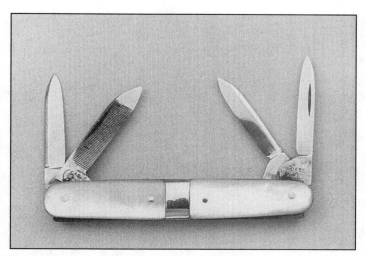

**8407F, CASE BRADFORD, pearl, 3", $1,200.**

**6394 LP, CASE BRADFORD, large cigar, Rogers, flat grooved bolsters, 4-1/4", $5,000.**

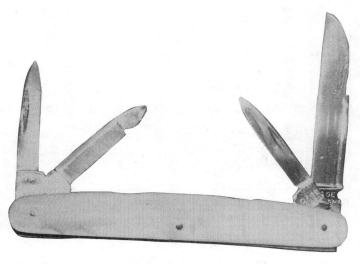

**8438, CASE BRADFORD, congress, file, cuticle, pearl, (WRC), 3-9/16", $4,500.**

**5395 LP, CASE BRADFORD, slim jack, stag, very rare, 4-1/4", $2,000.**

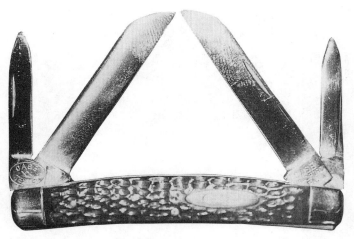

**64052, CASE BRADFORD, congress, double sheepfoot, green bone, 3-1/2", $4,500.**

*Pricing Note: The value of Case vintage knives is subjective, but a good rule of thumb is to start with the Tested knife price and add ten percent for each earlier period, then subtract ten percent for each condition from mint. This is the formula we used to price vintage Case knives in this book.*

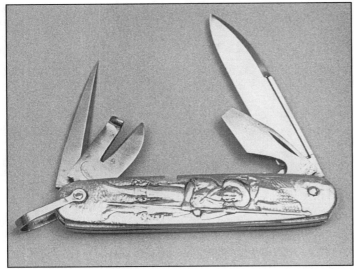

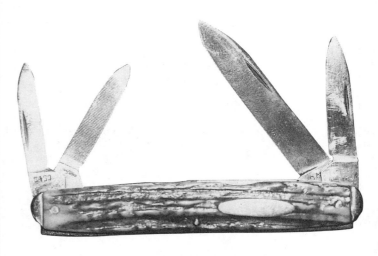

**5460, CASE BRADFORD,** *stag, tip bolster, 3-3/8", $775.*

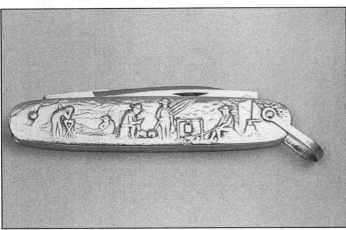

**M445 LP, CASE BRADFORD,** *figural camp knife, Boy Scouts, nickel silver, 3-3/4", $1,250.*

**6470 LP, CASE BRADFORD,** *congress, green bone, etch John Wanamacher, 3-1/8", $1,200.*

**64052, CASE BRADFORD,** *congress, green bone, BRAD/TESTED, 3-1/2", $4,500.*

**6488 LP, CASE BRADFORD,** *congress, Rogers, center shield, pinched, 2 liners, 4-1/8", $8,000.*

*6488 LP, CASE BRADFORD, congress, green bone, cuticle file, pinched, center shield, dual liners, 4-1/8", $10,000.*

*6490R, CASE BRADFORD, Scout Jr., punch, green bone, W ring, CASE SCOUT JR. shield, 3-5/16", $750.*

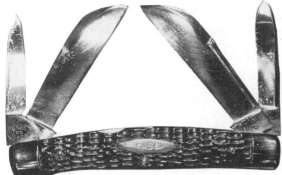

*6488 LP, CASE BRADFORD, congress, green bone, cuticle file, pinched, center shield, 4-1/8", $8,000.*

*6488 LP, CASE BRADFORD, congress, 2 sheepfoots, green bone, center shield, 4-1/8", $8,000.*

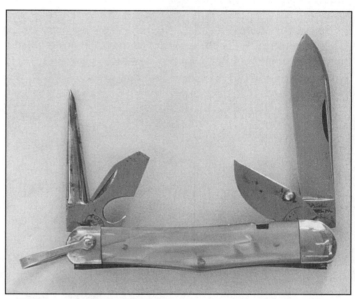

*9490R, CASE BRADFORD, utility, French pearl, 3-3/8", $450.*

*6488 LP, CASE BRADFORD, congress, 2 sheepfoots, Rogers, center shield, pinched bolsters, 4-1/8", $8,000.*

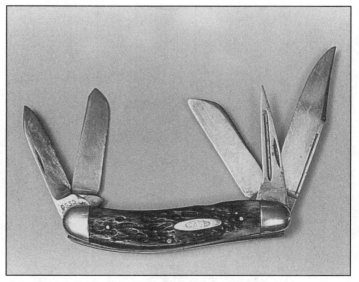

*6539, CASE BRADFORD, large sowbelly, Rogers, rare, 3-13/16", $12,000.*

*Pricing Note: The value of Case vintage knives is subjective, but a good rule of thumb is to start with the Tested knife price and add ten percent for each earlier period, then subtract ten percent for each condition from mint. This is the formula we used to price vintage Case knives in this book.*

# Case Family (1900-1920)

By Bob Wurzelbacher

Case family members were involved in a number of cutlery enterprises that did not bear the Case name. In some cases, this involved a contracting arrangement such as with Clauss Cutlery or Primble Belknap Hardware. The items provided by W. R. Case & Sons are exact duplicates of the Case pattern and handle materials. The only difference is the name on the tang stamp.

In other cases, related firms provided knives to Case companies, such as the Eldred, Pennsylvania, manufacturer C. Platts & Sons, which provided W. R. Case & Son with its knives when it started in 1902. The next year Harvey Platts bought out his brothers and with J. Russell Case merged their firms. Elliot and Dean Case left Case Brothers and formed the Standard Knife Company in 1901. It went out of business two years later. It was resurrected in the 1920s as the Standard Knife Co. In 1909, Case Brothers of Kane, Pennsylvania, was reorganized under the name Kane Cutlery Co. The Little Valley Knife Association became the Crandall Cutlery Company and was later purchased by the W. R. Case & Sons Company. John D. Case, previously of the Case Brothers, formed a company called J. D. Case & Sons Cutlery.

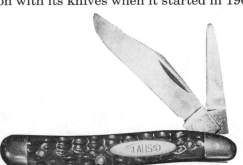

*CLAUSS, 059, similar to 6220, green bone, 3-1/4", $600.*

*CLAUSS, 55, green bone, 3-15/16", $1,000.*

*CLAUSS, 42, similar to 62035-1/2, green bone, 3-13/16", $900.*

*CLAUSS, 66, similar to 6237, green bone, 3-13/16", $1,500.*

*CLAUSS, 39, similar to 62028, green bone, 3-1/8", $775.*

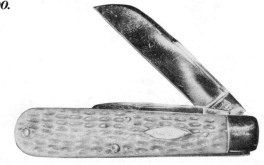

*CLAUSS, 70, similar to 62031, green bone, 3-1/2", $550.*

Case Family 147

*CLAUSS, 65, similar to 6228-1/2, green bone, 3-1/8", $600.*

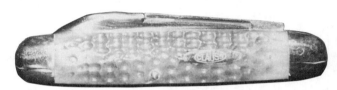

*CLAUSS, 63, similar to 6294, green bone, 4-1/4", $2,200.*

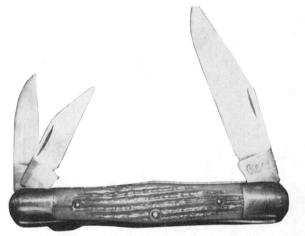

*CLAUSS, 33, similar to 6383, Winterbottom, 3-9/16", $2,000.*

*CLAUSS, 30, similar to 6345-1/2, Winterbottom, 3-19/32", $775.*

*CLAUSS, similar to 6452, green bone, 3-3/4", $1,000.*

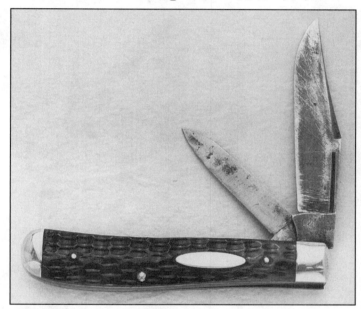

*CLAUSS, similar to 6207LP, green bone, 3-1/2", $1,000.*

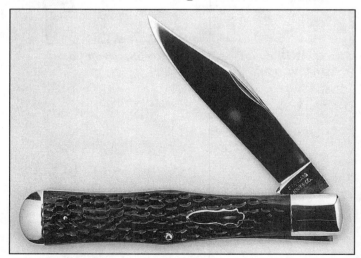

*STANDARD, Coke, similar to 050, green bone, 5-1/4", $1,200.*

*Pricing Note: The value of Case vintage knives is subjective, but a good rule of thumb is to start with the Tested knife price and add ten percent for each earlier period, then subtract ten percent for each condition from mint. This is the formula we used to price vintage Case knives in this book.*

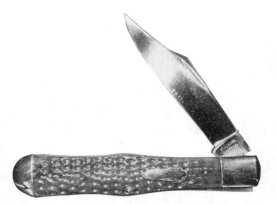

*STANDARD, Coke, similar to 050, green bone, 5-1/8", $1,200.*

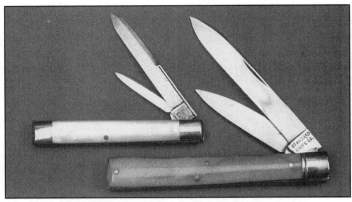

*Top: STANDARD, doctor's, pearl, 2-7/8", $1,200.*
*Bottom: STANDARD, doctor's, waterfall, 2-7/8", $1,200.*

*STANDARD, EO, similar to 028, bone, 3-5/16", $650.*

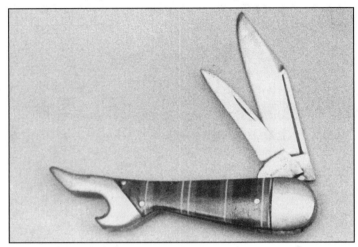

*STANDARD, leg, similar to 097, candy stripe, 3-1/4", $500.*

*STANDARD, congress, similar to 68, green bone, 3-5/16", $1,050.*

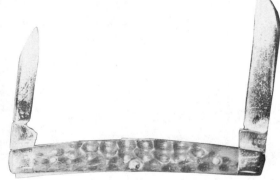

*STANDARD, congress, similar to 69, green bone, 3", $550.*

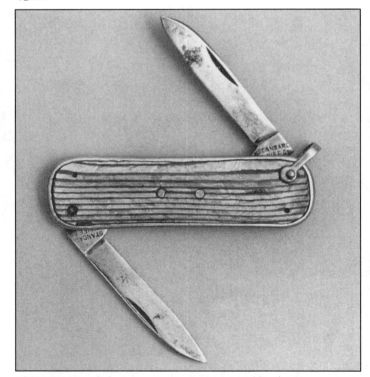

*STANDARD, lobster, green stripe, 2-1/4", $150.*

Case Family 149

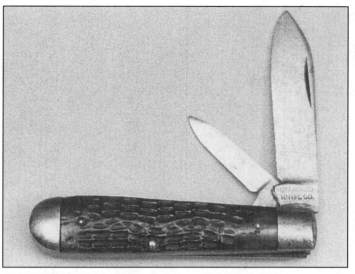

*STANDARD, 2-blade jack, bone, 3-1/2", $475.*

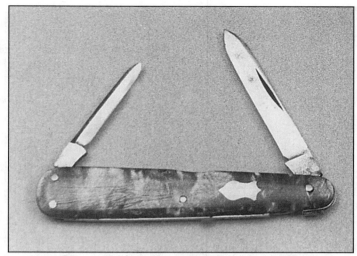

*CASE MFG, similar to 081, pyremite, 3-1/8", $250.*

*CASE MFG, 2-blade jack, bone, 4-1/2", $1,100.*

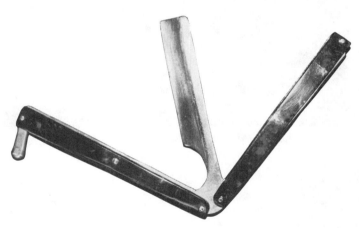

*CASE MFG, travel razor, tortoise, 3-3/8", $1,500.*

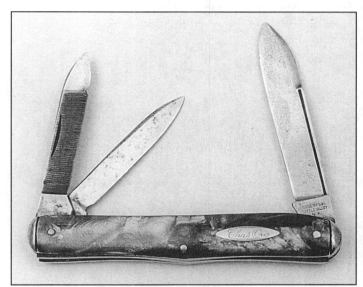

*CASE MFG, similar to B3109, pyremite, 3-5/8", $1,100.*

*R. CASE, bone, 2-3/8", $350.*

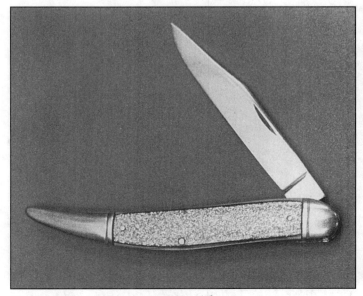

*CASE MFG, goldstone, 4-3/8", $600.*

*Pricing Note: The value of Case vintage knives is subjective, but a good rule of thumb is to start with the Tested knife price and add ten percent for each earlier period, then subtract ten percent for each condition from mint. This is the formula we used to price vintage Case knives in this book.*

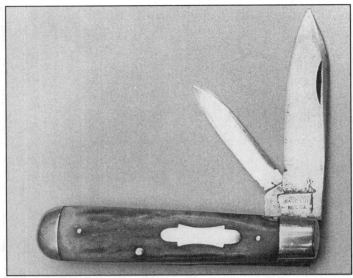
CASE MFG, similar to 5231, stag, 3-3/4", $550.

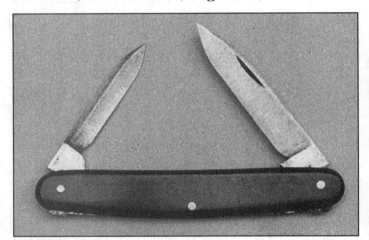
CASE MFG, Warren P., red plastic, 3", $350.

CASE MFG, Little Valley, shield "ChasOur", gold swirl, 3-3/8", $900.

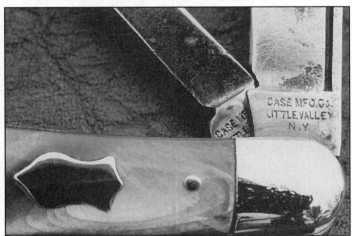
CASE MFG, similar to P2026, pyremite, 3", $700.

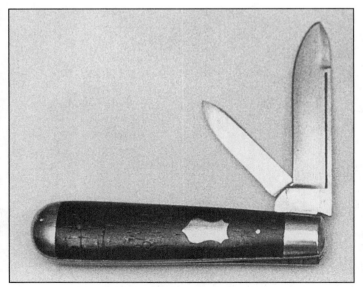
R. Case & Son, Little Valley, wood, 3-3/8", $275.

Case Family 151

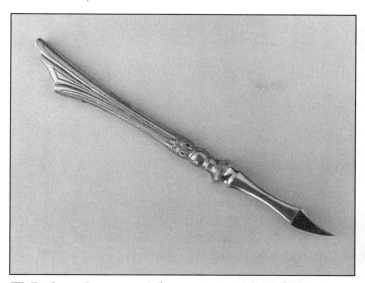

*W. R. Case Germany, ink eraser, metal, 5", $75.*

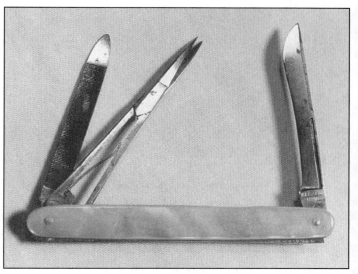

*W. R. Case & Sons Germany, 3-blade w/file, scissors, gold pearl, 2-7/8", $300.*

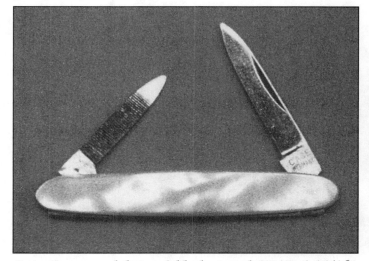

*Case Germany, lobster, 2-blade, pearl, SHAD, 1-15/16", $350.*

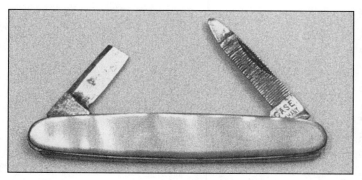

*Case Germany, 2-blade miniature, pearl, SHAD, 1-7/8", $100.*

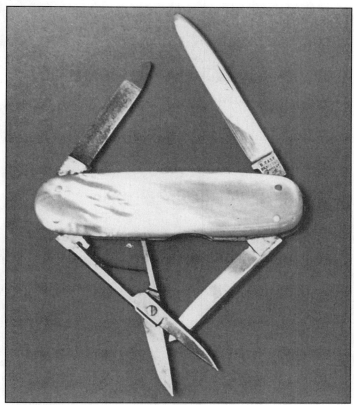

*R. Case Bradford Germany, lobster w/file, scissors, pearl, SHAD 2-7/8", $350.*

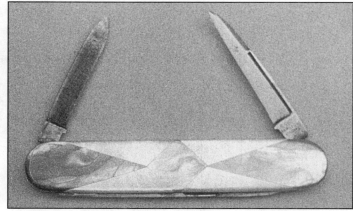

*R. Case Bradford Germany, 2-blade, pearl abalone, SHAD, 3", $350.*

*Pricing Note: The value of Case vintage knives is subjective, but a good rule of thumb is to start with the Tested knife price and add ten percent for each earlier period, then subtract ten percent for each condition from mint. This is the formula we used to price vintage Case knives in this book.*

LITTLE VALLEY, similar to 6235, Winterbottom, 3-1/2", $550.

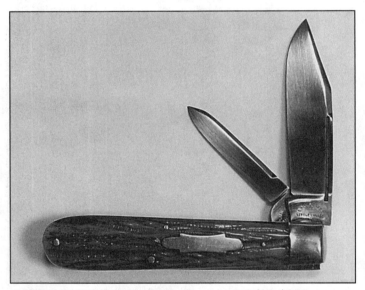

LITTLE VALLEY, 2-blade jack, stag, 3-3/4", $350.

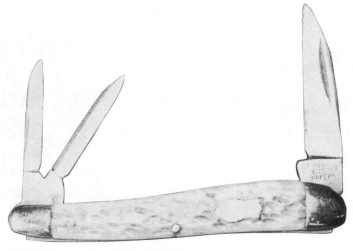

KANE, bone, 2-5/16", $1,500.

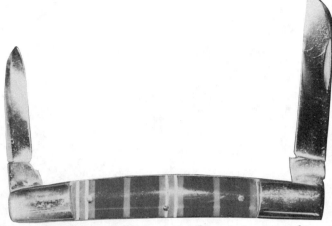

KANE, congress, similar to R 268, candy, 3-5/16", $1,000.

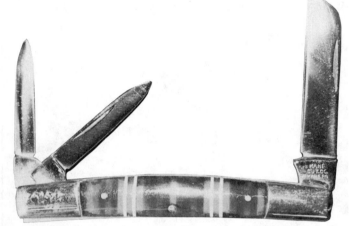

KANE, congress whittler, similar to R 368, candy, 3-5/16", $3,500.

KANE Cut. Co., congress, similar to 6488, bone, 4-1/8", $6,000.

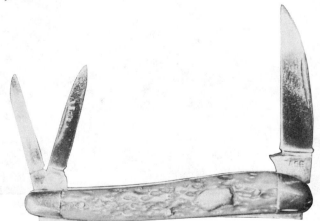

CASE, Kane, Pa., similar to 354, bone, 3", $1,500.

Case Family 153

**CASE-KANE, whittler, similar to 354, Rogers, 3", $900.**

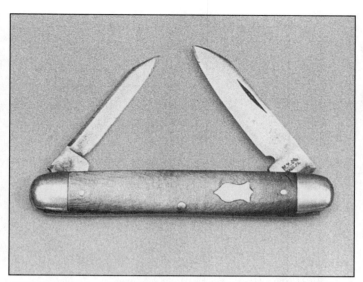

**KANE Cut. Co., 2-blade equal end, pyremite, 3-5/16", $325.**

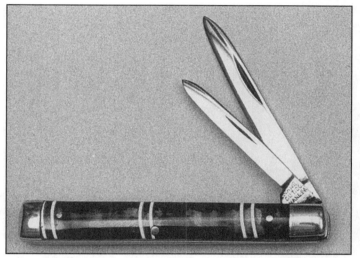

**KANE Cut. Co., doctor's, similar to R2082, candy stripe, 2-7/8", $700.**

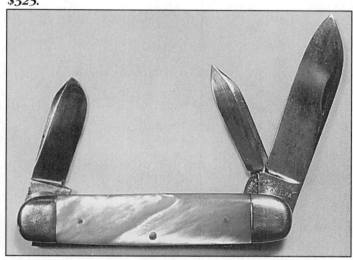

**KANE Cut. Co., 3-blade, pearl, 3-5/8", $650.**

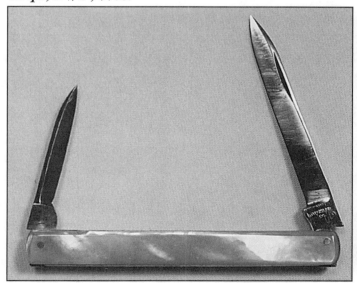

**KANE Cut Co., 2-blade, pearl, SHAD, 3", $300.**

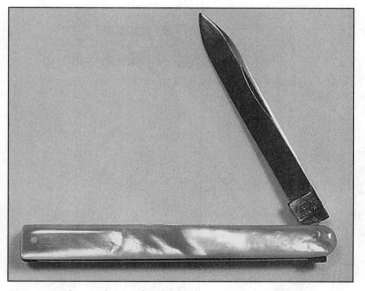

**Kane Cutlery, doctor's, 1 blade, pearl, 3", $850.**

*Pricing Note: The value of Case vintage knives is subjective, but a good rule of thumb is to start with the Tested knife price and add ten percent for each earlier period, then subtract ten percent for each condition from mint. This is the formula we used to price vintage Case knives in this book.*

*J. CASE, 6100SAB, Jaxon Case, bone, 4-5/8", $1,400.*

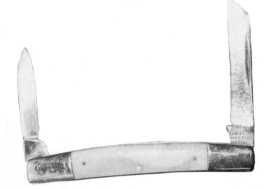

*J. D. C., B268, congress, waterfall, 3-5/16", $1,000.*

*J. D. C., cigar, similar to 6294-1/2 J, bone, 4-1/4", $4,500.*

*J. D. C., canoe w/punch, bone, 3-3/4", $3,500.*

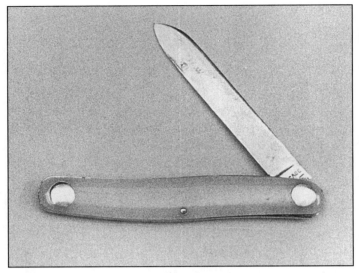

*J. D. Case, birdseye, 1 blade, yellow pyremite, 3-5/8", $250.*

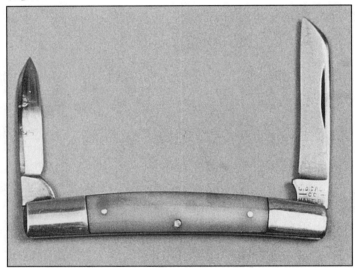

*J. D. Case, similar to B269, waterfall, 3", $1,000.*

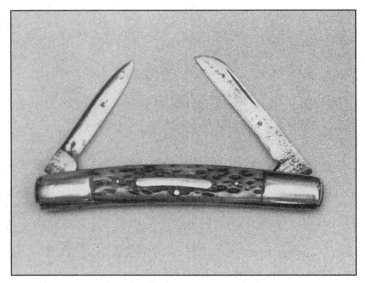

*J. D. Case, similar to 6268, bone, 3-5/16", $750.*

Case Family 155

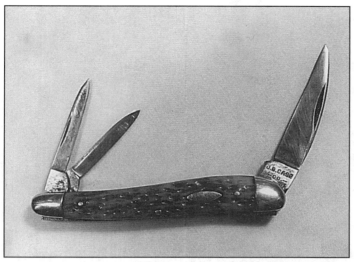

*J. D. Case, similar to 6355, Rogers, 3-1/2", $1,500.*

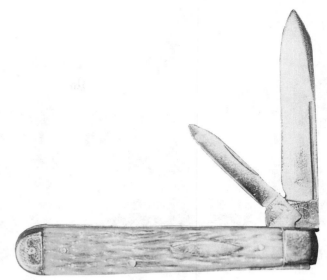

*PLATTS, 2-blade jack, bone, 3-5/16", $750.*

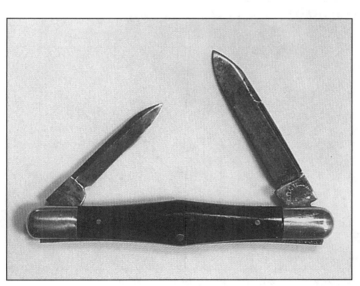

*PLATTS, similar to 2258, 2-blade, black celluloid, 2-7/8", $350.*

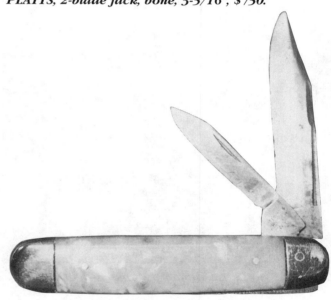

*PLATTS, 2-blade, saber, celluloid, 3-1/4", $300.*

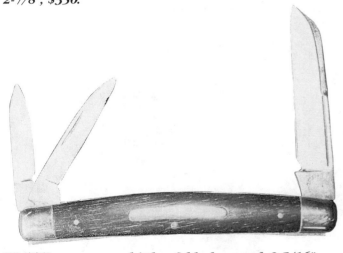

*PLATTS, congress whittler, 3-blade, wood, 3-5/16", $1,000.*

*PRIMBLE BELKNAP HDWRE, 7385, similar to 5347, red stag, 3-7/8", $600.*

*Pricing Note: The value of Case vintage knives is subjective, but a good rule of thumb is to start with the Tested knife price and add ten percent for each earlier period, then subtract ten percent for each condition from mint. This is the formula we used to price vintage Case knives in this book.*

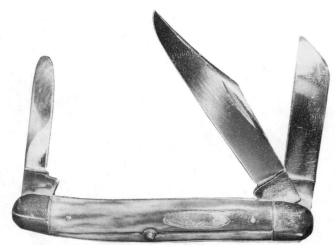

**PRIMBLE BELKNAP HDWRE,** 7007, similar to 5265, flat, red stag, 5-1/4", $900.

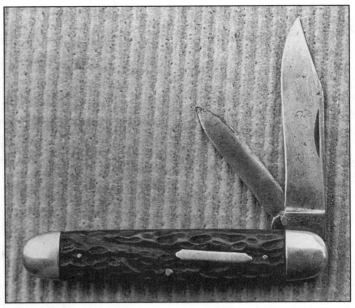

**CRANDALL,** 2-blade cigar, clip, brown bone, 4-1/8", $2,000.

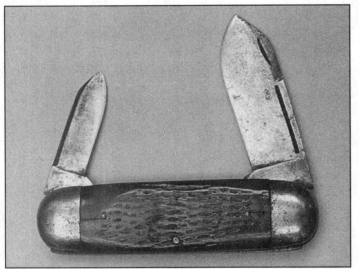

**CRANDALL,** sunfish, double pull, bone, 4-1/4", $1,200.

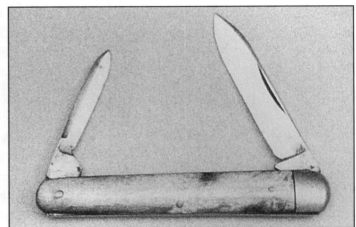

**CRANDALL,** equal end, 2-blade, celluloid, 2-13/16", $250.

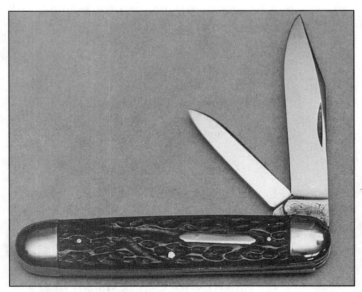

**CRANDALL,** 2-blade cigar, spear, brown bone, 4-1/8", $2,000.

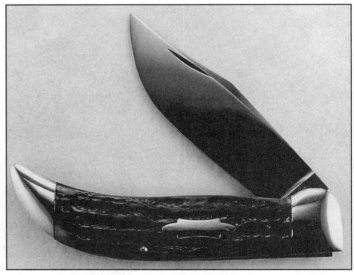

Kinfolks, similar to 6172, green bone, 5-1/2", $3,000.

# Case Memorabilia and Miscellaneous

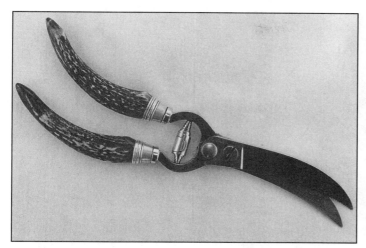

*Poultry shears, 1905-14, W. R. Case & Sons, stag, 10-1/2", $300.*

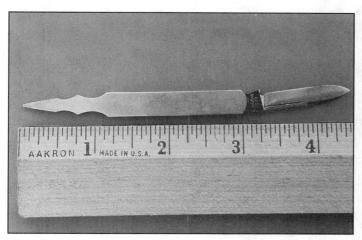

*One blade file & tweezers, 1915-19, Case Bradford, very rare, $400.*

*Case knife box w/ W. R. Case button, 1905-1914, $250.*

*Case pistol, 1900-14, Case Brothers, $5,000.*

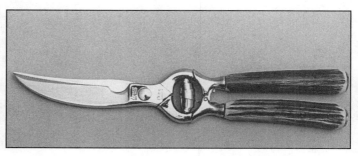

*Game shears, 1920-40, Case Tested XX, stag handles, $250.*

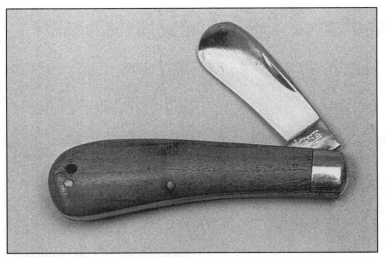

*Maize, Case Tested XX, 1 blade, walnut handle, 4", $225.*

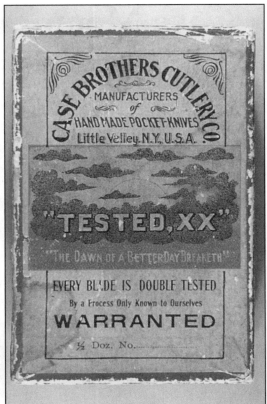

*Case Brothers box, w/Little Valley, NY, marking, $150.*

*Case knife box for sheath knife w/Job Case button, $250.*

*Display knife, approx. 500 made (note size in relation to quarter), $1,500.*

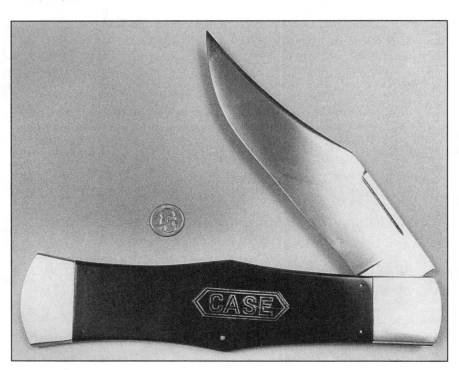

# Case Knives Tested (1920-1971)

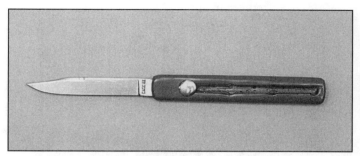

*M100, red cracked ice, 3-1/4", XX, $130.*

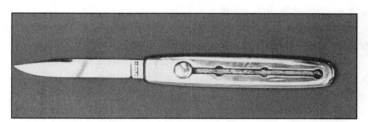

*M100, all metal, 3-1/4", XX, $110.*

**B100**, 1920-40, Tested XX, imitation onyx ................. 160
**RM100**, 1920-40, Tested XX, Christmas tree ............. 250
**G100**, 1920-40, Tested XX, celluloid .......................... 160
**M100**, 1920-40, Tested XX, metal, 3-1/4" .................. 130
**M100**, 1920-40, Tested XX, blue celluloid, 3-1/4" ....... 175
**M100**, 1920-40, Tested XX, cracked ice, 3-1/4" .......... 160
**M100**, 1920-40, Tested XX, green bone, 3-1/4" ........... 300
**M100**, 1940-64 XX, gold, 3-1/4" ................................. 175
**P100**, 1910-40, Tested XX, asst. celluloid, ................. 175
**M101R**, 1920-40, Tested XX, metal, 2-7/8" ................ 125

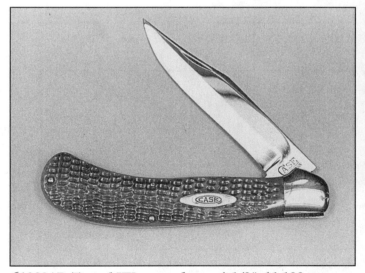

*6100SAB, Tested XX, green bone, 4-1/2", $1,100.*
**3100**, 1920-40, Tested XX, yellow composition, 4-1/2" ................................................................ 800

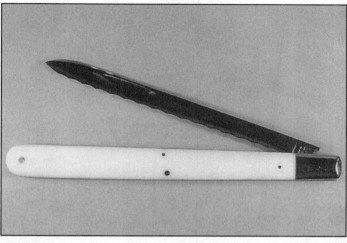

*4100SS, 1965-1969, U.S.A., white composition, serrated edge, 5-1/2", $750.*

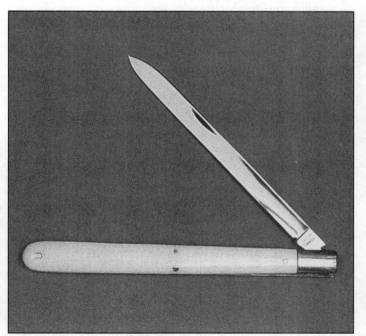

*4100SS, XX, melon tester or citrus, white composition, 5-1/2", $225. Has both small stamp & large stamp, $225 each.*
**4100SS**, 1965-69, USA, white composition, 5-1/2" ..... 150
**4100SS**, 1970, 10 Dot, white composition, 5-1/2" ....... 175
**4100SS**, 1970, 10 Dot, white composition, serrated edge, rare, 5-1/2" ................................................... 750

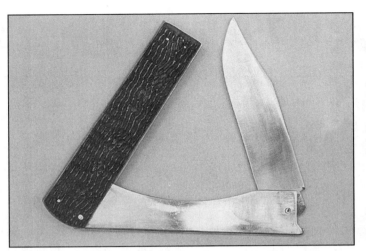

***6001**, green bone, W. R. Case & Sons, Bradford, PA, 4-3/4", $1,000. Not shown: W. R. Case & Sons, (same knife in Rogers bone, $1,100).*
***GS001**, W. R. Case & Sons, (same knife, w/goldstone handles, $1,000.)*
**6102 SH EO**, sheepfoot, easy opener, green bone, 3-5/8" ............................................................................ **300**
**5103SP**, 1920-40, Tested XX, budding knife, stag, 3-1/4" ............................................................................ **750**
**2103SP**, 1920-40, Tested XX, slick black, 3-1/4" ........ **400**
**3103SP**, 1920-40, Tested XX, yellow composition, 3-1/4" ............................................................................ **400**
**7103SP**, Tested XX, tortoise, 3-1/4" ............................ **700**
**8103SP**, Tested XX, pearl, 3-1/4" ................................ **800**
**4103B&G**, 1920-40, Tested XX, white composition, 3-1/4" ............................................................................ **325**
**6103B&G**, 1920-40, Tested XX, green bone, 3-1/4" .... **700**
**6104B**, 1920-40, Tested XX, green bone, 3-3/8" ......... **550**
**6104B**, 1940-55, XX, bone, 3-3/8" ............................... **400**
**61005**, 1920-40, Tested XX, green bone, bolsters stamped, 3-3/8" ............................................................ **650**

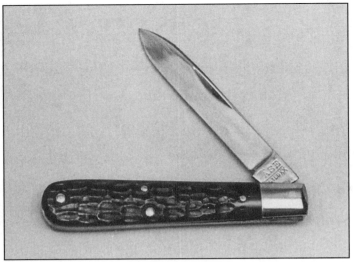

**6106**, 1920-40, Tested XX, green bone, 2-5/8", $300.
**6106**, 1920-40, Tested XX, green bone, 25-cent knife, 2-5/8" ............................................................................ **800**
**7106**, 1920-40, Tested XX, tortoise shell, 2-5/8" ........ **300**

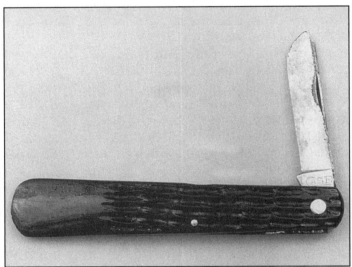

***6109**, CASE TESTED XX, bud, all bone, 4", $550.*

***Top: 61005-1/2**, 1920-40, Tested XX, green bone, bolsters stamped, 3-1/8", $650.*
***Bottom: 61005**, 1915-20, Case Bradford, Pa., Rogers bone, bolster stamped, 3-3/8", $700.*

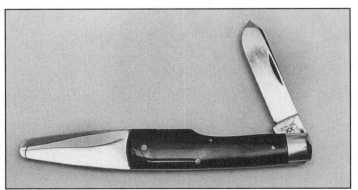

***2109B**, XX, gunstock, budding knife, slick black, 3-1/4", $140.*
**2109B**, 1920-40, Tested XX, slick black, 3-1/4" .......... **200**
**2109B**, 1965-69, USA, slick black, 3-1/4" ................... **150**

# Case Knives Tested (1920-1971)    161

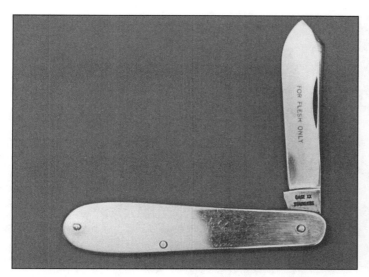

***M110, XX, all metal, spey blade, stainless, 3-1/8", $125.***
**M110**, 1920-40, Tested XX, metal spey, 3-1/8", .......... 160
**6110SP**, 1920-40, Tested XX, spey or budding knife, bone, 3-1/8", ...................................................................... 250

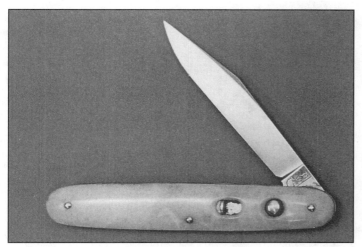

***91210-1/2, Tested XX, switchblade, onyx, 3-3/8", $800.***
**91210-1/2**, 1920-40, Tested XX, cracked ice, 3-3/8"... 800
**11011**, 1920-40, Tested XX, walnut, 4" ....................... 125

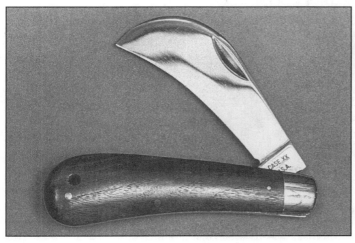

***11011, 1965-69, USA, hawkbill, walnut, 4", $50.***

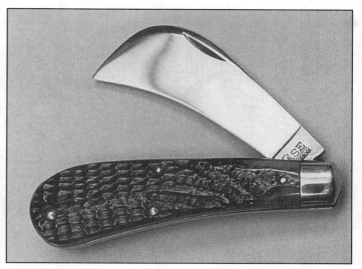

***61011, 1920-40, Case Tested XX, hawkbill, Rogers bone, 4", $300.***
**61011**, 1920-40, Tested XX, green bone, 4"................ 300
**11011**, 1940-64, XX, walnut, 4" ..................................... 60
**61011**, 1940-55, XX, green bone, 4"............................ 225
**61011**, 1940-64, XX, red bone, 4"................................ 175
**61011**, 1940-55, XX, laminated wood......................... 125
**61011**, 1940-64, XX, bone stag ................................... 150
**61011**, 1965-69, USA, laminated wood....................... 55
**61011**, 1965-69, USA, bone stag................................. 200
**11011**, 1970, 10 Dot, walnut......................................... 60

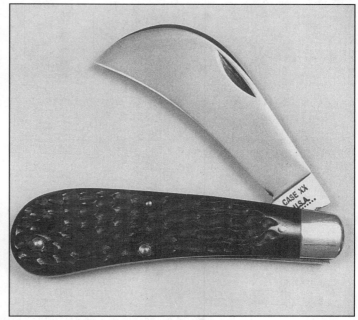

***61011, 1970, 10 Dot, laminated wood, $60.***
**P1211-1/2**, 1920-40, Tested XX, switchblade, mottled composition, 4" ......................................................... 1,000
**31211-1/2**, 1920-40, Tested XX, switchblade, yellow composition, 4" ......................................................... 1,000
**3111-1/2**, 1920-40, Tested XX, yellow composition, rare............................................................................. 1,000

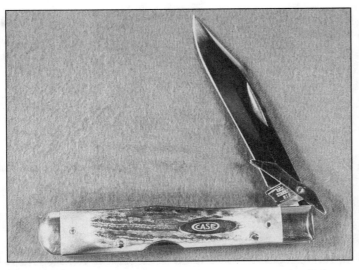

*5111-1/2L, 1970, 10 Dot, genuine stag, rare, 4-7/16", $3,000.*

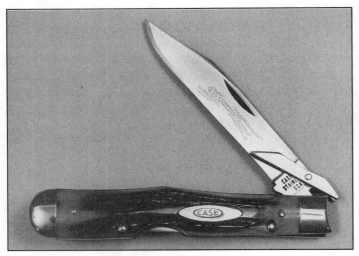

*5111-1/2 LSSP, 9 Dot, large or small stamp, cheetah, lockback, genuine stag, 4-7/16", $500.*

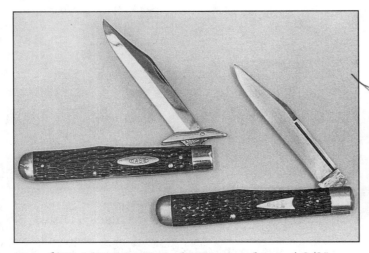

*Top: 6111-1/2L SAB, Tested XX, green bone, 4-3/8", $1,700.*
*Bottom: 6111-1/2, Case's Bradford, Pa., flat, long pull, green bone, 4-3/8", $2,000.*

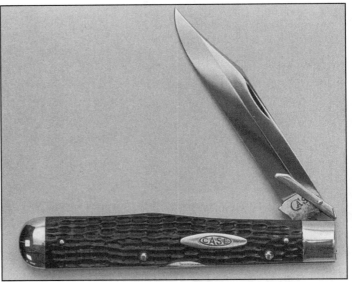

*6111-1/2, Tested XX, script Case, missing Tested XX, green bone, rare, 4-3/8", $2,000.*

| | | |
|---|---|---|
| 6111-1/2L, 1920-40, Tested XX, green bone, 4-3/8" | | 1,600 |
| 6111-1/2LP, 1920-40, Tested XX, green bone | | 1,500 |
| 6111-1/2, 1940-55, XX, green bone | | 1,200 |
| 6111-1/2L, 1940-55, XX, green bone | | 1,500 |
| 6111-1/2L, 1940-55, XX, red bone | | 750 |
| 6111-1/2L, 1940-64, XX, bone | | 550 |
| 61111-1/2L, 1965-69, USA, bone | | 750 |

Extra 1 was factory error.

6111-1/2L, 1965-69, USA, bone .................. 300
6111-1/2L, 1970, 10 Dot, bone .................. 300

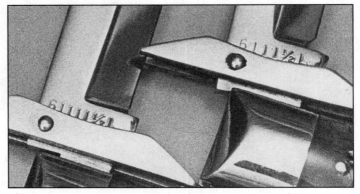

*6111-1/2, w/error: knife shows an extra 1. $750.*

Case Knives Tested (1920-1971) 163

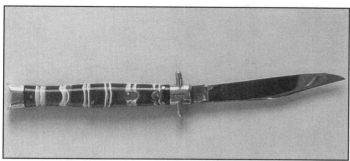

*R1212-1/2, 1920-40, Tested XX, switchblade, candy stripe, 4", $2,000. Not shown: 31212-1/2, 1920-40, Tested XX, yellow composition, 4", $1,500.*

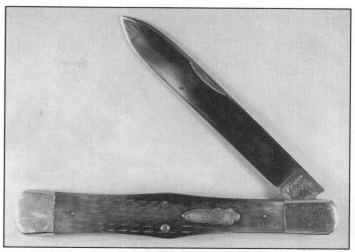

*61213, 1920-40, Tested XX, green bone, 5-3/8", $1,000.*

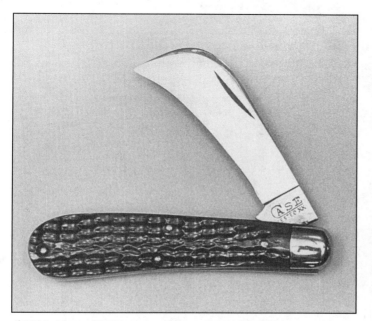

*61013, Tested XX, green bone, 3-9/16", $400.*

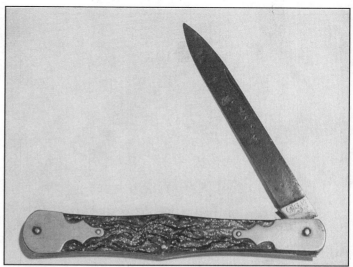

*RM1213, Tested XX, 5-3/8", Christmas yellow, barn door hinge, $1,500.*
31213, Tested XX, saber, yellow composition, 5-3/8". **650**
31213, 1920-40, Tested XX, spear, yellow composition, 5-3/8" ............................................................. **650**

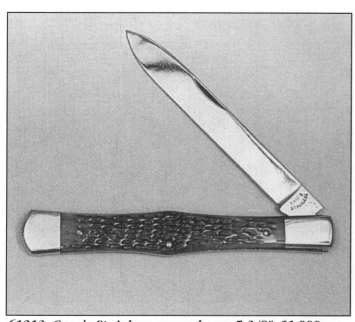

*61213, Case's Stainless, green bone, 5-3/8", $1,000.*

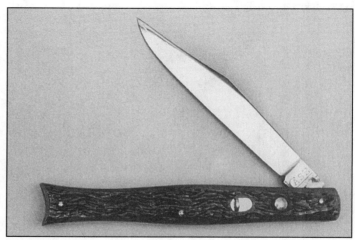

*61213-1/2, Tested XX, switchblade, Rogers bone, 4", $2,000.*

**61214-1/2, Tested XX, switchblade, brown bone, 4",
$2,500.**

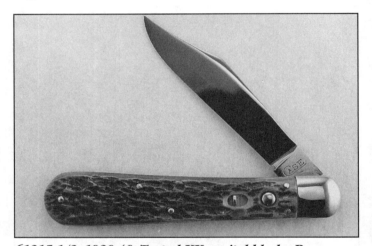

**61215-1/2, 1920-40, Tested XX, switchblade, Rogers bone, 5", $2,500.**
**51215-1/2F**, 1920-40, Tested XX, switchblade, stag, 5" .................................................................. **3,500**
**51215-1/2G**, 1920-40, Tested XX, switchblade, stag, 5" .................................................................. **3,500**
**6116**, 1920-40, Tested XX, spear, green bone, 3-3/8". **250**
**6116SH**, 1920-40, Tested XX, green bone, 3-3/8" ....... **300**

**6116, Case, Tested XX, green bone, 3-1/2", $225.**

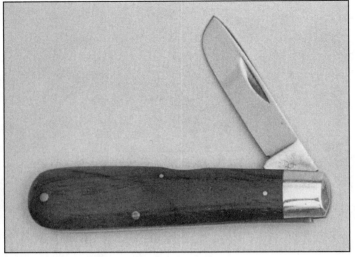

**1116SP, XX, walnut, 3-1/2", $110.**
**1116SP**, 1965-69, USA, bud, walnut, 3-1/2" ................. **65**
**1116SP**, 1970, 10 Dot, bud, walnut, 3-1/2" .................. **55**

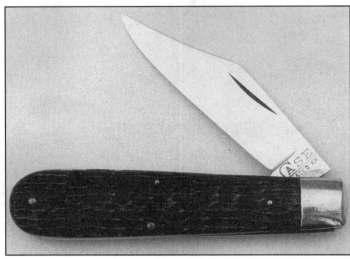

**6116-1/2, Tested XX, green bone, 3-3/8", $150.**

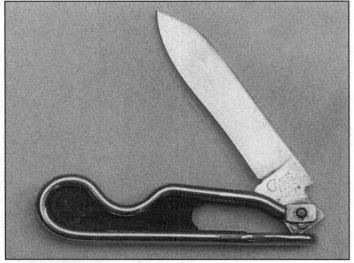

**W1216, Case Tested, Pat. 9/21/26, metal wire, 3-1/4", $200.**

Case Knives Tested (1920-1971) 165

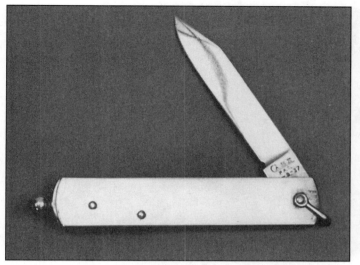

*M1217, Tested XX, all metal, 2-7/8", $400. Made for Case by Schrade (contract late 1930s).*
M1218K, 1920-40, Tested XX, metal, 3"..................... **150**

*31024-1/2, XX, yellow, 3", $90.*
31024-1/2, Tested XX, flat yellow, 3".......................... **150**
3124, 1920-40, Tested XX, yellow composition, 3"..... **150**
6124, 1920-40, Tested XX, green bone, 3"................... **225**
3124-1/2, 1920-40, Tested XX, yellow composition, 3"
................................................................................ **150**
6124-1/2, 1920-40, Tested XX, green bone, 3" ........... **225**
61024, 1920-40, Tested XX, green bone, 3"................ **225**
31024, 1920-40, Tested XX, yellow composition, 3"... **150**

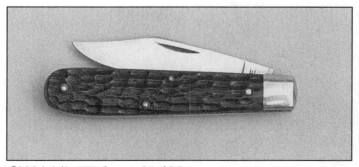

*61024-1/2, XX, bone, 3", $85.*
61024-1/2, XX, red bone, 3" ......................................... **100**
61024-1/2, 1965-69, USA, bone, 3"............................... **75**

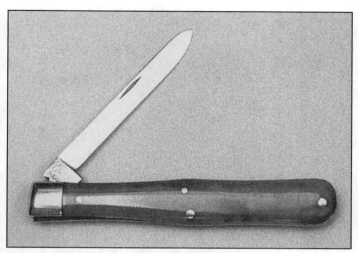

*B1025, Tested XX, waterfall, 3", $350.*

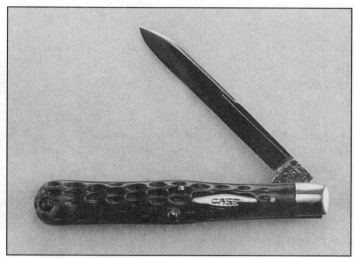

*61025, Tested XX, 1920-40, green bone, 3", $375.*
7129-1/2, 1920-40, Tested XX, tortoise shell ............. **250**

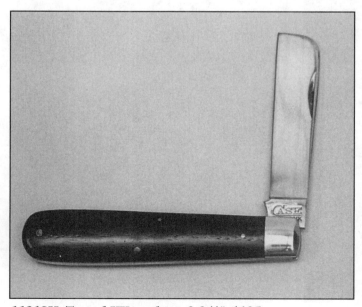

*1131SH, Tested XX, walnut, 3-3/4", $125.*

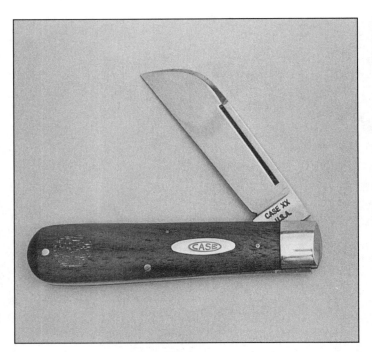

***11031SH, USA, walnut, long pull, 3-3/4", $40.***
**1131EOSH**, 1920-40, Tested XX, walnut, 3-1/16" ...... **150**
**11031SH**, 1920-40, Tested XX, walnut, 3-1/16" ......... **125**
**11031SH**, 1920-40, Tested XX, concave ground blade, walnut, 3-1/16" .............................................................. **175**
**11031SH**, 1940-64, XX, walnut, 3-1/16" ....................... **55**
**11031SH**, 1940-64, XX, concave ground blade, walnut, 3-1/16" ................................................................................ **75**
**11031SH**, 1970, 10 Dot, walnut, 3-1/16" ...................... **45**

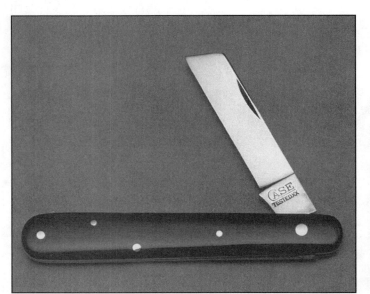

***2136, Tested XX, black composition, 4-1/8", $200.***
**2136B**, 1940-55, XX, slick black, 4-1/8" ....................... **160**
**2137**, 10 Dot, 1970, black composition, 3-5/8" ............. **45**
**G137**, green delrin, 3-1/2" ............................................. **45**
**P137**, pakkawood, 3-1/2" .............................................. **45**
**5137**, stag, carbon, 3-1/2" ............................................. **55**

***2138, USA, black composition, 4-5/8", $35.***
**2138**, 1970, 10 Dot, black composition, 5-5/8" ............. **40**
**2138SS**, 1970, 10 Dot, black composition, 5-5/8" ......... **40**
**2138LSS**, 1970, 10 Dot, black composition, 5-5/8" ...... **100**

***1139, Case XX, walnut banana knife, 4-1/4", $185.***
**1139**, 1920-40, Tested XX, walnut, 4-1/4" .................. **185**
**6143**, 1940-45, Tested XX, red fiberloid, rare ............ **350**
**6143**, 1920-40, Tested XX, brown bone, 5" ................. **300**
**6143**, 1920-40, Tested XX, green bone, 5" .................. **350**
**6143**, 1940-55, XX, green bone, 5" .............................. **275**
**6143**, 1970, 10 Dot, jigged bone, rare, 5" .................... **250**

***6143, XX, Daddy Barlow, slick black, 5", $150.***
**6143**, 1940-64, XX, red bone, 5" .................................. **125**
**6143**, 1940-64, XX, bone, 5" ........................................ **100**
**6143**, 1965-69, USA, bone, 5" ....................................... **90**
**6143**, 1970, 10 Dot, bone, 5" ......................................... **90**

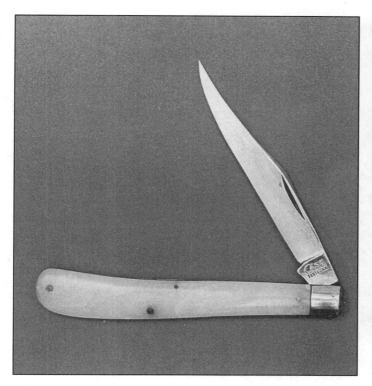

***91048, Tested XX, imitation onyx, 4-1/8", $400.***
**RM1048**, 1920-40, Tested XX, Christmas tree, 4-1/8"
.................................................................................. **450**
**GS1048**, 1920-40, Tested XX, goldstone, 4-1/8".......... **400**
**R1048**, 1920-40, Tested XX, candy stripe, 4-1/8"....... **400**
**31048**, 1940-64, Tested XX, flat yellow, 4-1/8".......... **125**
**61048**, 1920-40, Tested XX, green bone, 4-1/8".......... **400**
**61048**, 1920-40, Tested XX, Rogers bone, 4-1/8"........ **450**
**61048**, 1940-55, XX, green bone, 4-1/8" ..................... **300**
**61048**, 1940-64, XX, red bone, 4-1/8" ......................... **175**
**61048**, 1940-64, XX, bone, 4-1/8"................................ **125**
**61048**, 1940-64, XX, late Rogers bone, 4-1/8" ............ **250**
**31048**, 1940-64, XX, yellow composition, 4-1/8" ........ **110**
**31048**, 1965-69, USA, yellow composition, 4-1/8" ....... **75**
**61048**, 1965-69, USA, delrin, 4-1/8"............................. **35**
**61048**, 1965-69, USA, bone, 4-1/8" .............................. **75**
**61048SSP**, 1965-69, USA, stainless, polished blade, bone, 4-1/8" ....................................................................... **110**
**61048SSP**, 1965-69, USA, stainless, polished edge, delrin, 4-1/8" ........................................................................ **40**
**61048SSP**, 1965-69, USA, blade etched "Tested XX Stainless" (1st mod.), bone stag, 4-1/8" ..................... **150**
**61048SSP**, 1965-69, USA bone stag, 4-1/8" .................. **90**
**31048**, 1970, 10 Dot, yellow composition, 4-1/8" ......... **75**
**61048**, 1970, 10 Dot, delrin, 4-1/8"............................... **45**
**61048SSP**, 1970, 10 Dot, stainless, polished edge, delrin, 4-1/8" .................................................................................. **50**

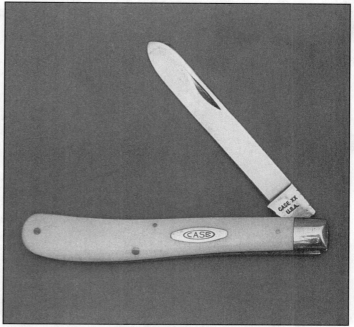

***31048SP, USA, yellow, 4-1/8", $75.***
**31048SP**, 1940-64, XX, flat yellow, 4-1/8"................... **125**
**31048SP**, 1940-64, XX, yellow composition, 4-1/8" .... **125**

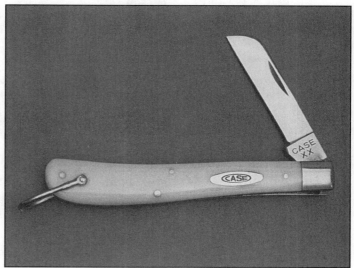

***31048SH-R, XX, florist knife, yellow, 4-1/8", $150.***
**61048SP**, 1940-55, XX, green bone, 4-1/8" ................. **350**
**61048SP**, 1940-64, XX, bone, 4-1/8"............................ **125**
**61048SP**, 1940-64, XX, red bone, 4-1/8" ..................... **150**
**61048SP**, 1940-64, XX, late Rogers bone, 4-1/8" ........ **250**
**61048SP**, 1965-69, USA, delrin, 4-1/8"......................... **50**
**61048SP**, 1965-69, USA, bone, 4-1/8" ........................ **150**
**31048SP**, 1970, 10 Dot, yellow composition, 4-1/8" ..... **90**
**61048SP**, 1970, 10 Dot, delrin, 4-1/8"........................... **50**
**61049**, 1920-40, Tested XX, green bone, 4-1/16"..... **1,000**
**61049L**, 1920-40, Tested XX, Rogers bone, 4-1/16". **1,500**
**R1049**, 1920-40, Tested XX, candy stripe, 4-1/16".. **1,000**
**R1049L**, 1920-30, Tested XX, candy stripe, 4-1/16" **1,200**

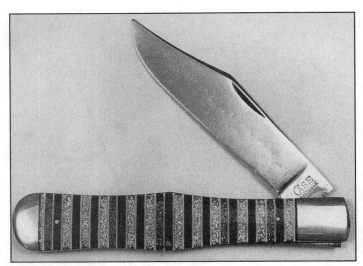

*R10050, Tested XX, glitter stripe, 5-1/4", $1,200.*

*PB91050F, Tested XX, push-out, onyx, 5-3/8", $750.*

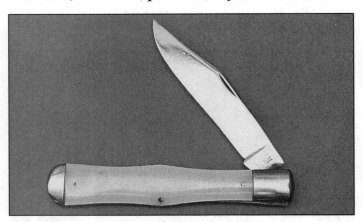

*310050, Tested XX, yellow, 5-1/8", $500.*

GS10050, Tested XX, goldstone, 5-1/8" .................... **1,000**
910050, Tested XX, cracked ice French pearl, 5-1/8"
................................................................................ **650**

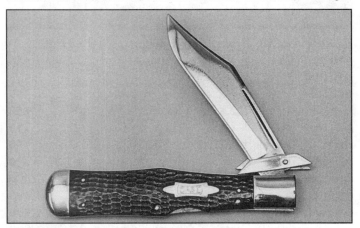

*C61050L, SAB, LP, Tested XX, green bone, 5-1/4", $3,000.*

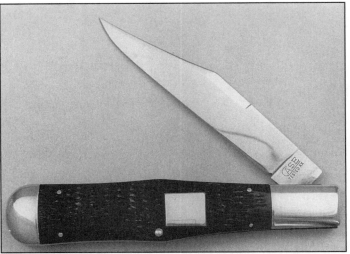

*Switchblade "zipper release." The knife shown is 61050L, 1920-40, Tested XX, flat blade, bone, 5-1/8", $7,500. Not shown: 61050L, 1920-40, Tested XX, green bone, no lower bolster, rare, 5-1/8", $7,500.*

RM1050SAB, 1920-40, Tested XX, Christmas tree, 5-1/8" ............................................................................ **1,200**
RM1050, 1920-40, Tested XX, flat blade, Christmas tree, 5-1/8" ............................................................... **1,200**
HA1050, 1920-40, high art, 5-1/8" .......................... **1,200**
PB31050, 1920-40, Tested XX ..................................... **700**
PB31050F, 1920-40, Tested XX, yellow celluloid ....... **800**
C31050SAB, 1920-40, Tested XX, yellow composition
................................................................................ **700**
C31050, 1920-40, Tested XX, flat ground, yellow composition, 5-1/8" ...................................................... **700**
C51050SAB, 1920-40, Tested XX, stag, 5-1/8" ......... **1,200**
61050, 1920-40, Tested XX, flat blade, green bone, 5-1/8" ........................................................................... **950**
610050, 1920-40, Tested XX, flat blade, green bone, 5-1/8" ........................................................................... **850**
710050, 1920-40, Tested XX, flat blade, tortoise, 5-1/8" ........................................................................... **850**
C91050SAB, 1920-30, Tested XX, French pearl, rare handle, 5-1/8" .............................................................. **900**
C91050SAB, 1920-40, Tested XX, onyx, 5-1/8" .......... **850**
C91050, 1920-40, Tested XX, flat blade, cracked ice, 5-1/8" ........................................................................... **850**
C61050SAB, 1940-55, XX, green bone, Coke bottle, 5-1/8" ........................................................................... **700**
C61050SAB, 1940-64, XX, Coke bottle, wood, 5-1/8"
................................................................................ **175**
C61050SAB, 1940-64, XX, Coke bottle, bone, 5-1/8"
................................................................................ **275**

# Case Knives Tested (1920-1971)

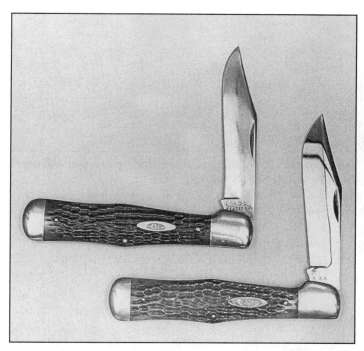

Top: C61050, SAB, Tested XX, green bone, 5-3/8", $800.
Bottom: C61050, SAB, XX, red bone, 5-3/8", $550.

C61050SAB, 1965-69, USA, Coke bottle, wood, 5-1/8" ............................................................................ 90
C61050SAB, 1965-69, USA bone, 5-1/8" ............ 400
C61050SAB, 1970, 10 Dot, Coke bottle, wood, 5-1/8"... 90

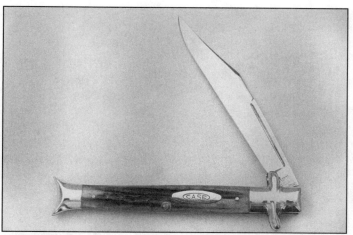

51051 LP, Case Tested XX, bow tie, second-cut stag, rare, 3-7/8", $900.

| | | |
|---|---|---|
| RM1051, 1920-40, Tested XX, Christmas tree | | 750 |
| GS1051, 1920-40, Tested XX, goldstone | | 650 |
| R1051, Tested XX, candy stripe | | 650 |
| 81051, Tested XX, pearl | | 800 |
| 31051, 1920-40, Tested XX, yellow celluloid | | 600 |
| R1051L, 1920-40, Tested XX, candy stripe | | 1,000 |

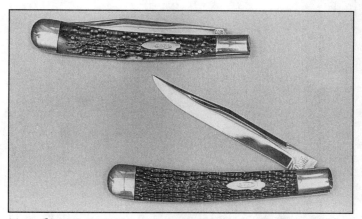

Top: 6151 L SAB, Tested XX, green bone, 5-1/4", $1,200.
Bottom: 6151 SAB, Tested XX, green bone, 5-1/4", $1000.

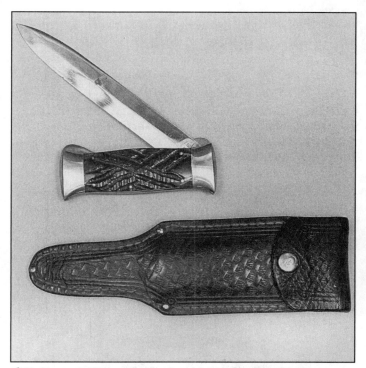

651, Tested XX, green bone w/sheath, $1,200. Not shown: 551, Tested XX, stag w/sheath, $1,200.

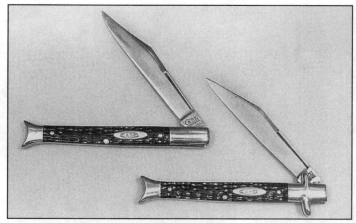

Top: 61051 LP, Tested XX, green bone, 3-7/8", $800.
Bottom: 61051 LP, Tested XX, green bone w/guard, 3-7/8", $800.

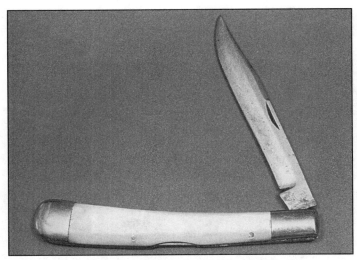

*8151L SAB, Tested XX, pearl, 5-1/4", $1,800.*

| | |
|---|---:|
| **8151SAB**, Tested XX, pearl, 5-1/4" | 1,500 |
| **9151SAB**, 1920-40, Tested XX, cracked ice | 750 |
| **9151LSAB**, 1920-40, Tested XX, imitation onyx | 900 |
| **3151SAB**, 1920-40, Tested XX, yellow | 600 |

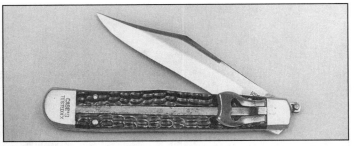

*6161L, SAB, Tested XX, switchblade, green bone, hinge-type release, 4-3/8", $3,000.*
**5161L SAB**, 1920-40, Tested XX, switchblade, genuine stag, 4-3/8", 3,000.

| | |
|---|---:|
| **5161L**, 1920-40, Tested XX, switchblade, flat blade, genuine stag, 4-3/8" | 3,000 |
| **RM165**, 1920-40, Tested XX, Christmas tree, 5-1/2" | 1,600 |
| **GS165**, 1920-40, Tested XX, goldstone, 5-1/2" | 1,500 |
| **3165SAB**, 1920-40, Tested XX, yellow composition | 600 |
| **5165SAB**, 1920-40, Tested XX, genuine stag | 800 |
| **5165**, 1920-40, Tested XX, flat blade, genuine stag | 900 |
| **5165**, 1920-40, Tested XX, flat blade, second-cut stag | 1,200 |

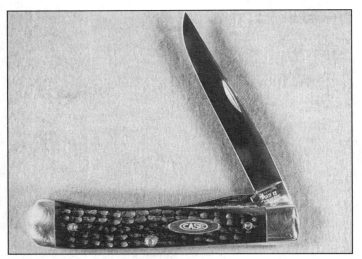

*6154LSS, USA, muskrat blade, (proto model), rare, $600.*

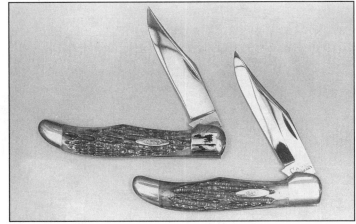

*Top: 6165, Tested XX, flat blade, second-cut bone, 5-1/4", $1,000.*
*Bottom: 6165SAB, Tested XX, second-cut bone, 5-1/4", $900.*

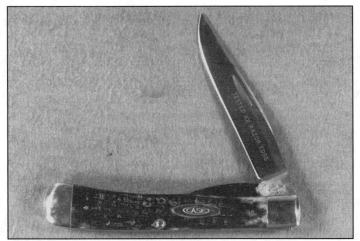

*6154LSSP, USA, glazed finish, second model, blade etched, brass liner lock (proto model), $600.*

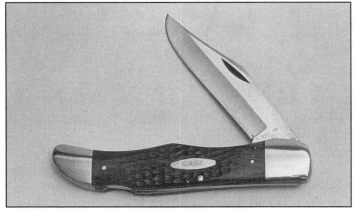

*6165LSAB SSP, 3 Dot, wood, 5-3/4", $55.*

Case Knives Tested (1920-1971) 171

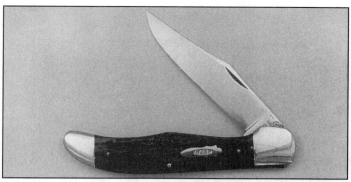

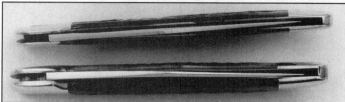

*6165, flat blade, green bone, bottom photo shows thinness of knife bolsters compared to another 6165SAB Tested XX, which is considered rare; thin bolster, 5-1/4", $1,250.*

**6165SAB**, 1920-40, Tested XX, green bone ................. **800**
**6165**, 1920-40, Tested XX, flat blade, green bone ...... **900**
**6165SAB**, 1940 Tested XX, rough black ..................... **700**
**5165**, 1920-40, Case XX Tested, master blade, flat ground, stag, bomb shield ............................................ **900**
**5165SAB**, 1920-40, Case XX Tested, stag .................. **800**
**6165**, 1920-40, Case XX Tested, master blade, flat ground, green bone, bomb shield ............................... **900**
**6165SAB**, 1920-40, Case XX, Tested, green bone ....... **800**
**6165SAB**, 1920-40, Case XX, Tested, rough black ..... **600**
**3165**, 1920-40, Case XX, Tested, yellow composition **600**
**6165SAB**, 1965-66, XX, laminated wood ..................... **175**
**6165SAB**, 1950-65, XX, small pattern number, bone. **300**
**6165SAB**, 1950-65, XX, large pattern number, bone . **300**
**6165**, 1940-60, XX, master blade, flat ground, red bone ................................................................................. **650**
**6165SAB**, 1950-65, XX, bone, worm groove ................ **450**
**6165**, 1940-55, XX, green bone .................................... **800**
**6165SAB**, 1940-49, XX, rough black ........................... **450**
**5165SAB**, 1949-65, XX, stag, low pull, not drilled for lanyard .............................................................................. **450**
**5165SAB**, 1949-65, XX, stag, low pull ........................ **400**
**5165SAB**, 1949-56, XX, stag, high pull ...................... **450**
**5165**, 1949-55, XX, master blade, flat ground, stag .. **700**
**6165SABDR**, 1965-70, U.S.A., small pattern number, laminated wood ................................................................ **90**
**6165SABDR**, 1965-70, U.S.A., large pattern number, laminated wood ................................................................ **90**
**6165SAB**, 1965-66, U.S.A., XX frame, laminated wood, not drilled for lanyard ..................................................... **125**
**6165SABDR**, 1965-1966, U.S.A., XX frame, laminated wood ................................................................................ **125**
**6165SABDR**, 1970-71, 10 Dot, laminated wood ........... **90**

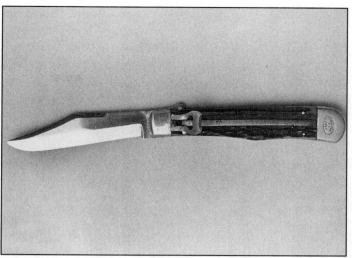

*5171L, Tested XX, switchblade, stag, bolster stamped, 5-3/8", $3,000.*

**5171L**, 1920-40, Tested XX, genuine stag, lower bolster not stamped, 5-1/2" ....................................................... **3,500**
**6171L**, 1920-40, Tested XX, green bone, lower bolster not stamped, 5-1/2" ....................................................... **4,000**
**6171L**, 1920-40, Tested XX, green bone, lower-bolster stamped, 5-1/2" .............................................................. **4,000**

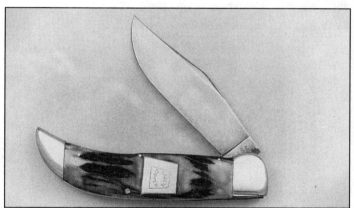

*5172, Case's zipper, clasp switchblade, 5-1/2", $9,000.*

**6172**, Case's zipper, clasp switchblade, green bone, 5-1/2" ................................................................................ **9,000**
**6172**, Case's zipper, clasp switchblade, red stag, 5-1/2" ................................................................................ **9,000**

*5172, USA Bulldog, engraved bolsters, probably a prototype, $350.*

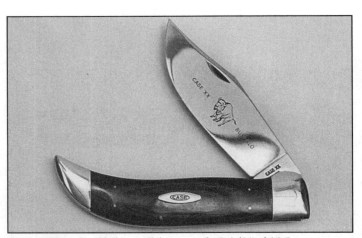

**P172, USA, buffalo, pakkawood, 5-1/2", $125.**
MB172, 1920-40, Tested XX, mottled brown, 5-1/2" ........................................................................... **2,000**
RM172, 1920-40, Tested XX, Christmas tree, 5-1/2" ........................................................................... **2,500**
2172, 1920-40, Tested XX, slick black, 5-1/2" ......... **1,200**
3172, 1920-40, Tested XX, yellow composition, 5-1/2" ........................................................................... **1,500**
GS172, 1920-40, Tested XX, goldstone, 5-1/2" ......... **2,500**
P172, pakkawood, 5-1/2", 1970, 10 Dot was not made. There were a few 1980 10 Dots.
Dots were on top of tang backside............................... **125**

**5172, 1965-69, USA, stag, 5-1/2", $350.**
5172, 1920-40, Tested XX, genuine stag, 5-1/2" ...... **3,000**
5172XX, 1940-64, genuine stag, 5-1/2" ..................... **350**

**6172, Tested XX, green bone, 5-1/2", $2,800.**
5172, 1965, USA, stag, 5-1/2", transition stamp & pattern number on same side of blade **400**
5172, 1965, USA, stag (plain), 5-1/2", no handmade stamp, rare ............................................................... **600**

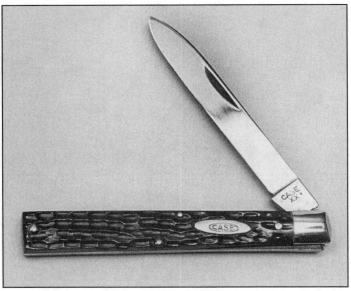

**6185, XX, doctor's knife, bone, 3-3/4", $175.**

**Top: 6185, 1920-40, Tested XX, physician's knife, green bone, 3-3/4", $600.**
**Bottom: 6185LP, Tested XX, physician's knife, green bone, 3-3/4", $675.**
R6185, Tested XX, long pull, candy stripe, 3-3/4" ...... **650**
P185, Tested XX, green pyremite, 3-3/4" .................... **650**
RM185, 1920-40, Tested XX, doctor's knife, Christmas tree, 3-5/8" ................................................................. **750**
3185, 1920-40, Tested XX, yellow composition, 3-5/8" ........................................................................... **400**
6185, Tested XX, red bone, Pat. No., 3-5/8" ............... **500**
6185, 1920-40, Tested XX, green bone, 3-5/8", .......... **750**
3185, 1940-64, XX, yellow composition, 3-5/8" ......... **200**
6185, 1940-64, XX, red bone, 3-5/8" .......................... **300**
3185, 1965-69, USA, flat yellow, 3-5/8" ..................... **200**
3185, 1965-69, USA, yellow composition, 3-5/8" ....... **150**
6185, 1965-69, USA, bone, 3-5/8" .............................. **150**
3185, 1970, 10 Dot, flat yellow, 3-5/8" ....................... **225**
6185, 1970, 10 Dot, bone, 3-5/8" ................................ **150**
6185, 1970, 10 Dot, delrin, rare, 3-5/8" ...................... **250**

# Case Knives Tested (1920-1971)

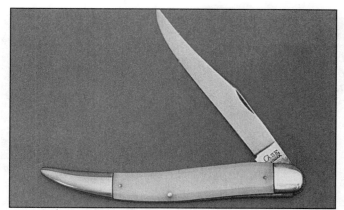

***31093, Tested XX, toothpick, yellow, hi-pull, 5", $375.***
**RM1093**, 1920-40, Tested XX, toothpick, Christmas tree, 5" ........................................................................ **650**
**GS1093**, 1920-40, Tested XX, goldstone, 5" ............... **600**
**HA1093**, 1920-40, Tested XX, high art, 5" ................. **600**
**P1093**, 1920-40, Tested XX, swirl celluloid, 5" .......... **550**
**R1093**, 1920-40, Tested XX, candy stripe, 5" ............. **600**
**RM1093**, 1920-40, Tested XX, mottled red, 5" .......... **600**
**61093**, 1920-40, Tested XX, green bone, 5" ............... **700**
**31093**, 1940-64, XX, yellow composition, 5" .............. **200**
**61093**, 1940-55, XX, toothpick, green bone, 5" ......... **500**
**61093**, 1940-64, XX, red bone, 5" .............................. **275**
**61093**, 1940-64, XX, bone, 5" .................................... **225**
**61093**, 1965-69, USA, bone, 5" .................................. **200**
**61093**, 1970, 10 Dot, bone, 5" .................................... **175**

***RM1096, Case Tested XX, Christmas yellow, 3-1/8", $600.***
**61096**, 1920-40, Tested XX, green bone, 3-1/8" .......... **650**
**R1096**, 1920-40, Tested XX, candy stripe, 3-1/8" ....... **600**
**81096**, 1920-40, Tested XX, pearl, 3-1/8" ................... **650**

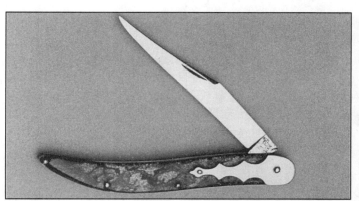

***RM193, Case Tested XX, barn door hinge, Christmas yellow handle, 5", $800.***
**91094**, 1920-40, Tested XX, onyx .............................. **450**
**R1094**, 1920-40, Tested XX, candy stripe .................. **500**
**61094**, 1920-40, Tested XX, Rogers bone ................... **650**
**RM1095**, 1920-40, Tested XX, Christmas tree, 5" ..... **700**
**B1095**, 1920-40, Tested XX, waterfall ........................ **550**
**R1095**, 1920-40, Tested XX, candy stripe, 5" ............. **550**
**31095**, 1920-40, Tested XX, yellow composition, 5"... **400**
**61095**, 1920-40, Tested XX, green bone, 5" ............... **700**
**91095**, 1945, Case's stainless imitation onyx ............. **550**
**4196X**, 1920-40, Tested XX, Case's stainless, citrus knife, white composition ........................................ **850**

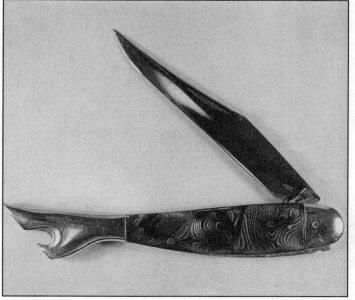

***GM1097, Tested XX, leg knife, green mottled, 5", $600.***
**GS1097**, 1920-30, Tested XX, goldstone ..................... **600**
**31097**, 1920-40, Tested XX, leg, yellow composition . **400**
**RM1097**, 1920-30, Tested XX, Christmas tree .......... **600**
**R1097**, 1920-30, Tested XX, candy stripe ................... **600**
**7197LSSP**, pakkawood .............................................. **80**
**P197LSSP**, pakkawood .............................................. **60**
**7197LSSP**, curly maple ............................................. **100**

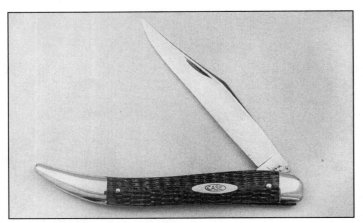

**61098**, Tested XX, green bone, 5-1/2", $550.
**RM1098**, 1920-40, Tested XX, Christmas tree, 5-1/2"
................................................................................................ 850
**R1098**, 1920-40, Tested XX, candy stripe, 5-1/2" ....... 800
**B1098**, 1920-40, Tested XX, waterfall, 5-1/2" ............ 800
**61098**, 1920-40, Tested XX, Rogers bone, 5-1/2" ........ 950
**3199EO**, 1920-40, Tested XX, yellow composition, 4-1/8"
................................................................................................ 450
**1199SHRSS**, 1940-64, XX, walnut, 4-1/8" ..................... 75
**1199SHRSS**, 1965-69, USA, walnut, 4-1/8" .................. 55
**1199SHRSS**, 1970, 10 Dot, walnut, 4-1/8" .................... 55

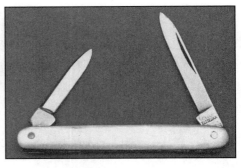

*Unknown pattern, 1920-40, Tested XX, pearl, 2-1/8", $150.*

*Unknown pattern, 1920-40, Tested XX, metal castrating knife, cord cutter, 2-5/8", $275.*

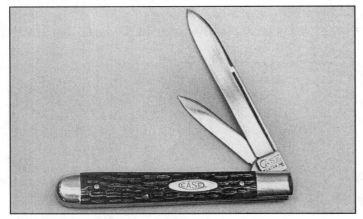

*Unknown pattern, 1920-40, Tested XX, long pull, green bone, $350.*

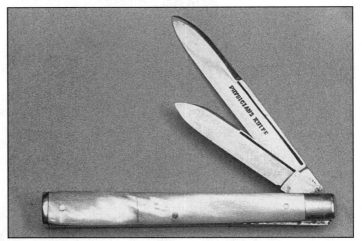

*Unknown pattern, 1920-40, Tested XX, doctor's knife, pearl, 3-3/4", $900.*

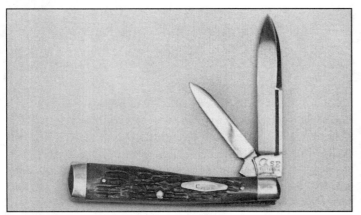

*Unknown pattern, 1920-40, Tested XX, gunstock, doctor's knife, long pull, green bone, 3", $700.*

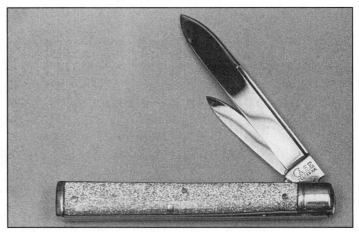

*Unknown pattern, 1920-40, Tested XX, doctor's knife, goldstone, 3-3/4", $900.*

*Unknown pattern, 1920-40, Tested XX, miniature, black & goldstone checkered handles, rare, $400.*

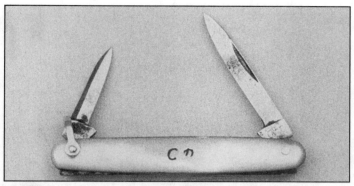

*Watch fob, Tested XX, pearl w/bail, 1-3/4", $175.*

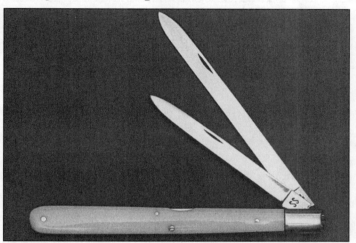

*4200SS, USA, citrus or melon tester, white composition, small & large stamp, 5-1/2", $250.*
**4200SS**, 1940-64, XX, melon tester, white composition, 5-1/2" ................................................................ 750
**4200SS**, 1965-69, USA, melon tester, serrated master blade, white composition, 5-1/2" ................. 850
**4200SS**, 1970, 10 Dot, melon tester, white composition, 5-1/2" ................................................................ 250

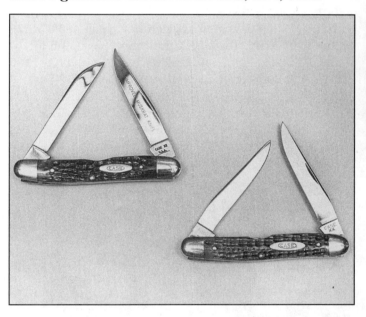

*Top: 1970, 10 Dot, muskrat, bone, Hawbaker's Special, 3-7/8", $1,500.*
*Bottom: 1940-55, XX, muskrat, green bone, 3-7/8", $1,200.*
**Muskrat**, 1920-40, Tested XX, green bone, 3-7/8" ................................................................ 2,000
**Muskrat**, 1920-40, Tested XX, yellow celluloid, rare, 3-7/8" ................................................................ 2,700
**Muskrat**, 1920-40, Tested XX, early Rogers bone, 3-7/8", ................................................................ 2,000
**Muskrat**, 1940-49, XX, rough black, 3-7/8" ............. 1,200
**Muskrat**, 1940-64, XX, red bone, 3-7/8" ..................... 600
**Muskrat**, 1940-64, XX, Rogers bone, late, 3-7/8" ....... 900
**Muskrat**, 1940-50, XX, Rogers bone, early, 3-7/8" ................................................................ 1,800
**Muskrat**, 1940-64, XX, bone, 3-7/8" ............................ 350
**Muskrat**, 1965-69, USA, bone, 3-7/8" ......................... 225
**Muskrat**, 1970, 10 Dot, bone, 3-7/8" ............................ 250

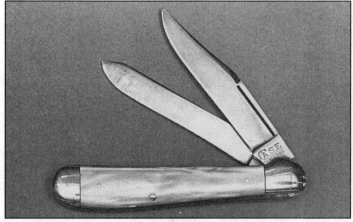

*9200LP, Tested XX, cracked ice, imitation pearl, 4", $900.*
**6200LP**, 1920-40, Tested XX, green bone, 3-15/16". 1,600
**3200LP**, 1920-40, Tested XX, yellow composition, 3-15/16" ................................................................ 900
**5200LP**, 1920-40, Tested XX, stag, 3-15/16" ........... 1,600

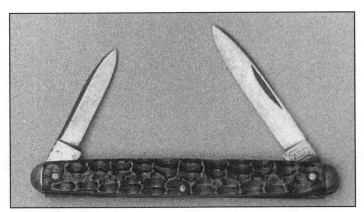

***62001**, Case Tested w/no writing below line, (Case is written in script), bone, 2-11/16", $275.*

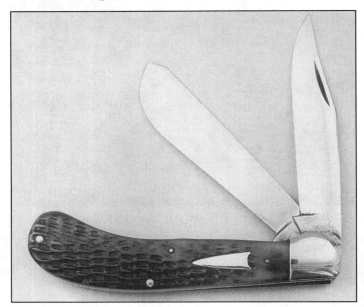

***62100**, 1920-40, Tested XX, green bone, 4-5/8", $2,000.*
**32100**, 1920-40, Tested XX, yellow composition, 4-5/8" ........................................................... **1,500**
**92100**, 1920-40, Tested XX, imitation pearl, 4-5/8" ........................................................... **1,200**

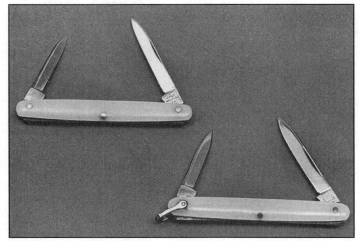

*Top: **3201**, Case Bradford, yellow, 2-5/8", $110.*
*Bottom: **3201 R**, Tested XX, yellow w/bail, 2-5/8", $100.*

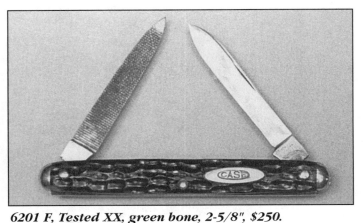

***6201 F**, Tested XX, green bone, 2-5/8", $250.*
**P2001**, 1920-40, Tested XX, blue/cream mingled, 2-5/8" ........................................................... **225**
**22001 R**, 1920-40, Tested XX, slick black, 2-5/8" ....... **150**
**62001**, 1920-40, Tested XX, green bone, 2-5/8" .......... **200**
**82001**, 1920-40, Tested XX, genuine pearl, 2-5/8" ..... **225**
**82101 R**, 1920-40, Tested XX, genuine pearl, 2-5/8".. **225**
**92101 R**, 1920-40, Tested XX, imitation pearl, 2-5/8" ........................................................... **100**
**3201**, 1920-40, Tested XX, yellow composition, 2-5/8" ........................................................... **125**
**6201**, 1920-40, Tested XX, green bone, 2-5/8" ............ **225**
**7201**, 1920-40, Tested XX, tortoise shell, 2-5/8" ........ **225**
**9201**, 1920-40, Tested XX, imitation pearl, 2-5/8"..... **100**
**9201R**, 1920-40, Tested XX, imitation pearl, 2-5/8" .. **110**

***92001T**, Tested XX, cracked ice, 2-5/8", $110.*
**3201**, 1940-64, XX, yellow composition, 2-5/8" ............ **50**
**6201**, 1940-64, XX, bone, 2-5/8" ................................. **65**
**8201**, 1940-64, XX, pearl, 2-5/8" ................................. **125**
**9201**, 1940-64, XX, imitation pearl, 2-5/8" ................... **45**
**9201**, 1940-64, XX, cracked ice, 2-5/8" ......................... **45**
**9201 R**, 1940-64, XX, imitation pearl, 2-5/8" ................ **50**
**9201 R**, 1940-64, XX, cracked ice, 2-5/8" ...................... **50**
**3201**, 1965-69, USA, yellow composition, 2-5/8" ......... **40**
**6201**, 1965-69, USA, bone, 2-5/8" ................................ **55**
**9201**, 1970, 10 Dot, imitation pearl, 2-5/8" ................... **40**
**3201**, 1970, 10 Dot, yellow composition, 2-5/8" ........... **40**
**3201**, 1970, 10 Dot, flat yellow composition, 2-5/8" ..... **55**
**6201**, 1970, 10 Dot, bone, 2-5/8" .................................. **55**

Case Knives Tested (1920-1971) 177

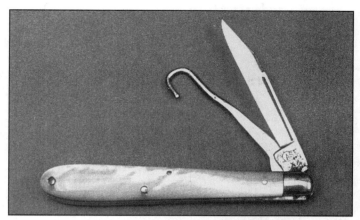

*820028, Case Tested XX, pearl w/button hook, (no lower bolsters), 2-7/8", $350.*

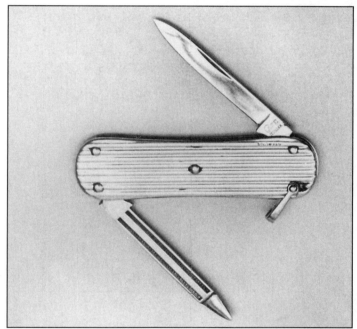

*S2, Tested XX, sterling silver, 2-1/4", $175.*

| | |
|---|---|
| **S2 LP**, XX, sterling silver, 2-1/4" | **125** |
| **S2**, XX, sterling silver, 2-1/4" | **125** |
| **S2 LP**, U.S.A, sterling silver, 2-1/4" | **150** |

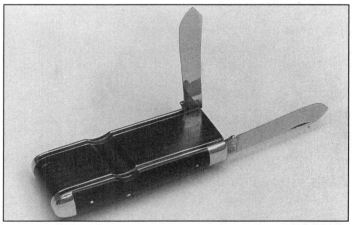

*1202, Tested XX, grafting & budding knife, G&B wood, 3-3/8", (also made in 3" long pull), $550.*

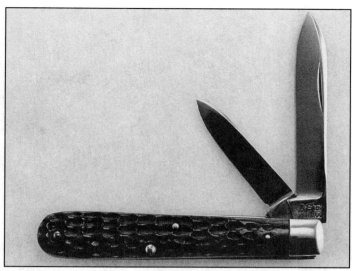

*6202, 1920-40, Tested XX, green bone, 3-3/8", $275.*

| | |
|---|---|
| **5202RAZ**, 1920-40, Tested XX, stag, 3-3/8" | **425** |
| **6202**, 1920-40, Tested XX, green bone, 3-3/8" | **275** |

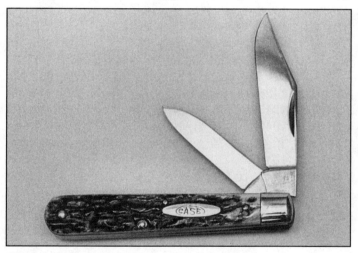

*5202-1/2, Tested XX, stag, 3-3/8", $300.*

| | |
|---|---|
| **202-1/2**, 1920-40, Tested XX, slick black, 3-3/8" | **150** |
| **6202-1/2**, 1920-40, Tested XX, green bone, 3-3/8" | **275** |
| **6202-1/2**, 1920-40, Tested XX, rough black, 3-3/8" | **175** |
| **6202-1/2EO**, 1920-40, Tested XX, green bone, 3-3/8" | **325** |
| **6202SHREO**, 1920-40, Tested XX, bone, 3-3/8" | **325** |
| **62103**, 1920-40, Tested XX, green bone, 2-7/8" | **250** |
| **62103R**, 1920-40, Tested XX, green bone, 2-7/8" | **250** |
| **82103**, 1920-40, Tested XX, genuine pearl, 2-7/8" | **275** |
| **82103R**, 1920-40, Tested XX, genuine pearl, 2-7/8" | **275** |
| **6202-1/2**, 1940-49, XX, rough black, 3-3/8" | **125** |
| **6202-1/2**, 1940-55, XX, green bone, 3-3/8" | **200** |
| **2202-1/2**, 1940-64, XX, slick black, 3-3/8" | **150** |
| **6202-1/2**, 1940-64, XX, bone, 3-3/8" | **85** |
| **6202-1/2**, 1965-69, USA, bone, 3-3/8" | **65** |
| **6202-1/2**, 1970, 10 Dot, delrin, 3-3/8" | **40** |
| **6202-1/2**, 1970, 10 Dot, bone stag, 3-3/8" | **65** |
| **62004**, 1920-40, Tested XX, Baby Barlow, green bone, 3" | **550** |

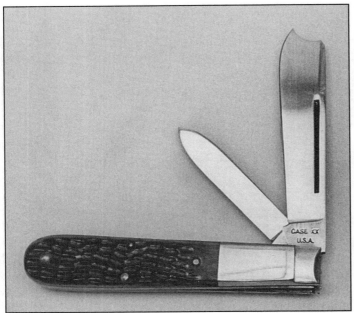

**6205RAZ, 1965-69, USA, long pull, bone, 3-3/4", $150.**
5205RAZ, 1920-40, Tested XX, stag, 3-3/4" ............... **600**
5205, 1920-40, Tested XX, stag, 3-3/4" ..................... **550**
62005, 1920-40, Tested XX, spear, green bone, 3-3/8"
................................................................................. **550**
6205RAZ, 1920-40, Tested XX, green bone, 3-3/4" ..... **600**
6205RAZ, 1940-49, XX, rough black, 3-3/4" ............... **700**
6205RAZ, 1940-55, XX, green bone, 3-3/4" ............... **550**
6205RAZ, 1940-64, XX, red bone, 3-3/4" .................... **400**
6205RAZ, 1940-64, XX, bone, 3-3/4" ......................... **275**
6205RAZ, 1970, 10 Dot, bone, 3-3/4" ........................ **150**

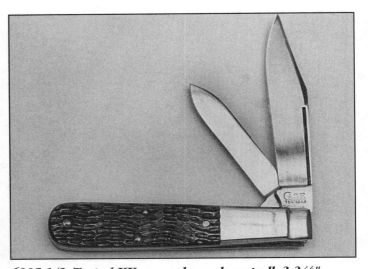

**6205-1/2, Tested XX, green bone, long pull, 3-3/4", $1,000.**
5205-1/2, 1920-40, Tested XX, stag, 3-3/4" ............. **1,200**

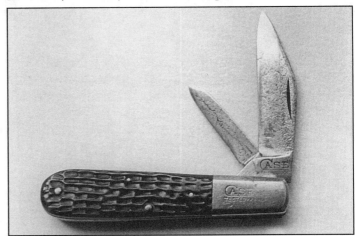

**62005-1/2, Tested XX, green bone, bolsters, stamped, 3-3/8", $700.**

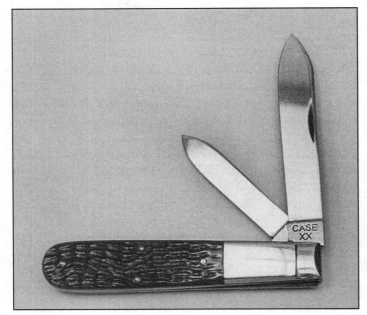

**6205, 1940-55, XX, green bone, 3-3/4", $400.**
6205, 1920-40, Tested XX, green bone, 3-3/4" ........... **650**
6205, 1940-55, XX, red bone, 3-3/4" ......................... **325**
6205, 1940-55, XX, bone, 3-3/4" ............................... **250**

**62005, 1920-40, Case Tested, green bone, 3-3/8", $700.**
5206, 1920-40, Tested XX, stag, 2-5/8" ..................... **325**
6206, 1920-40, Tested XX, green bone, 2-5/8" ........... **300**
8206, 1920-40, Tested XX, pearl, 2-5/8" .................... **300**
GS206, 1920-40, Tested XX, goldstone, 2-5/8" ........... **300**

# Case Knives Tested (1920-1971) 179

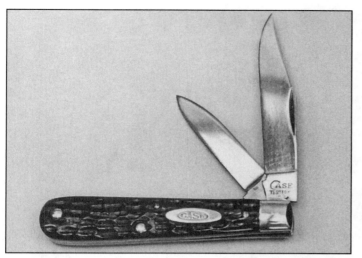

*62061/2, Tested XX, green bone, 2-5/8", $250.*

6206-1/2, 1920-40, Tested XX, rough black, 2-5/8".... **225**
5206-1/2, 1920-40, Tested XX, stag, 2-5/8" ................ **325**
8206-1/2, 1920-40, Tested XX, genuine pearl, 2-5/8"
................................................................................ **300**
6206-1/2, 1940-49, XX, rough black, 2-5/8" ............... **150**
6206-1/2, 1940-55, XX, green bone, 2-5/8" ................ **225**

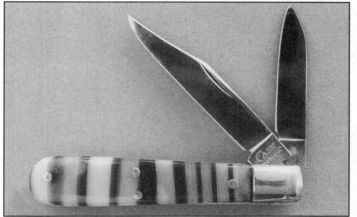

*B206-1/2, butter & molasses, waterfall handle, rare, 2-3/4", $350.*

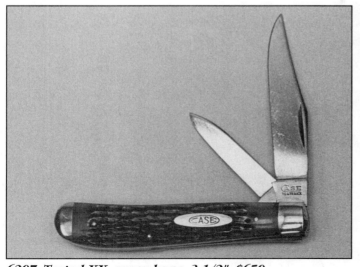

*6207, Tested XX, green bone, 3-1/2", $650.*

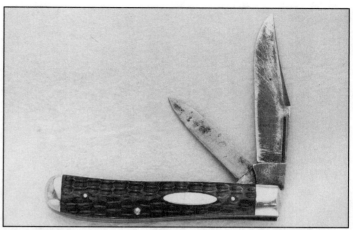

*6207LP, 1920-40, Tested XX, green bone, 3-1/2", $750.*
RM207LP, 1920-40, Tested XX, Christmas tree, 3-1/2"
................................................................................ **750**
2207, 1920-40, Tested XX, slick black, 3-1/2" ............ **500**
3207, 1920-40, Tested XX, yellow composition, 3-1/2"
................................................................................ **500**
5207, 1920-40, Tested XX, stag, rare, 3-1/2" .............. **900**
6207LP, 1920-40, Tested XX, rough black, 3-1/2" ...... **650**
6207, 1940-49, XX, rough black, 3-1/2" ..................... **450**
6207, 1940-55, XX, green bone, 3-1/2" ...................... **450**
6207, 1940-64, XX, red bone, 3-1/2" .......................... **225**
2207, 1940-64, XX, slick black, 3-1/2" ....................... **375**
6207, 1940-64, XX, bone, 3-1/2" ................................ **150**
6207, 1940-64, XX, Rogers bone early, 3-1/2" ........... **700**
6207, 1965-69, USA, bone, 3-1/2" .............................. **100**
6207, 1970, 10 Dot, bone, 3-1/2" ............................... **110**

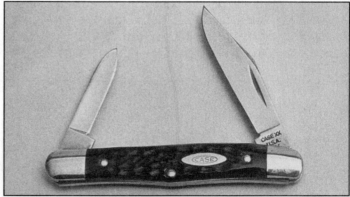

*6208, 1970, 10 Dot, bone, 3-1/4", $60.*

5208, 1920-40, Tested XX, stag, 3-1/4" ...................... **325**
6208, 1920-40, Tested XX, green bone, 3-1/4" ........... **350**
6208, Tested XX, rough black ..................................... **250**
6208, 1940-49, XX, half whittler, rough black, 3-1/4"
................................................................................ **175**
6208, 1940-49, XX, green bone, 3-1/4" ...................... **275**
6208, 1940-64, XX, red bone, 3-1/4" .......................... **150**
6208, 1940-64, XX, bone, 3-1/4" ................................ **100**
6208, 1965-69, USA, bone, 3-1/4" ................................ **75**
2209, XX, slick black, bud folding blade, rare, 3-1/4"
................................................................................ **250**

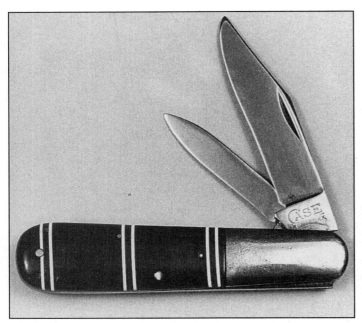

*R2009-1/2, Tested XX, candy stripe scales, 3-3/8", $650.*

**62009-1/2**, 1920-40, Tested XX, green bone, 3-5/16". **400**
**92009-1/2**, 1920-40, Tested XX, cracked ice, 3-5/16". **550**
**62009-1/2**, 1940-50, XX, saw marks, black composition 3-5/16" ................................................................. **150**
**62009-1/2**, 1940-55, XX, green bone, 3-5/16"............. **225**
**62009-1/2**, 1940-64, XX, red bone, 3-5/16"................. **125**
**62009-1/2**, 1940-64, XX, bone, 3-5/16" ....................... **110**
**62009-1/2**, 1965-69, USA, master blade in back, bone, 3-5/16" ................................................................................ **75**
**62009-1/2**, 1965-69, USA, master blade in front, bone, 3-5/16" ................................................................................ **75**
**62009-1/2**, 1970, 10 Dot, delrin, rare, 3-5/16" .......... **125**
**62009-1/2**, 1970, 10 Dot, bone stag, 3-5/16" ................ **75**

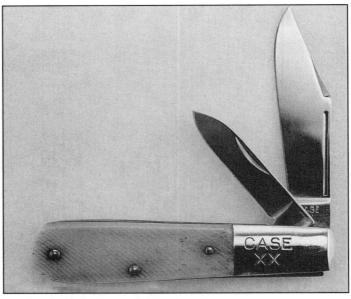

*62009-1/2, LP, 1940-55, XX, green bone, 3-5/16", $225.*

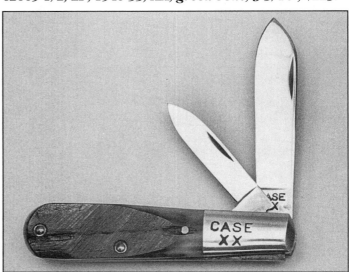

*62009, 1940-64, XX, spear blade, bone, 3-3/8", $110.*

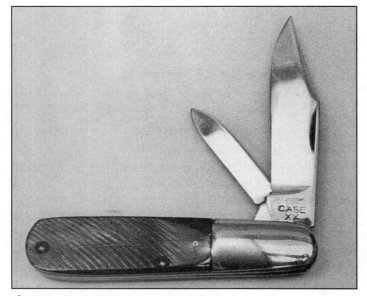

*62009-1/2, 1940-55, XX, clip blade, green bone, round bolster, 3-3/8", $200.*

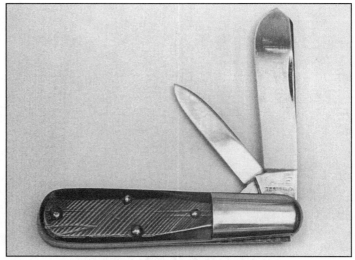

*62009, Tested XX, Barlow spey blade, green bone, 3-3/8", $500.*

## Case Knives Tested (1920-1971)

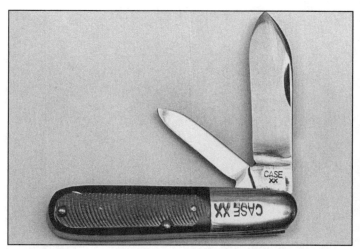

*62009, 1940-50, XX, black composition, bolster stamped upside down, 3-3/8", $125.*

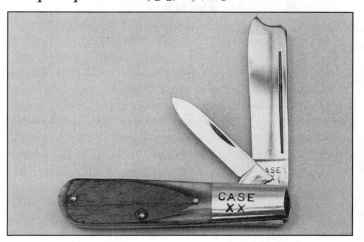

*62009RAZ, 1940-55, XX, long pull, bone, 3-3/8", $125.*
62009, 1920-40, Tested XX, green bone, 3-5/16"........ 350
62009RAZ, 1920-40, Tested XX, green bone, 3-5/16". 600
62009SH, 1920-40, Tested XX, green bone, 3-5/16"... 600
62009, 1940-64, XX, red bone, 3-5/16" ........................ 150
62009RAZ, 1940-64, XX, red bone, 3-5/16" ................ 200
62009RAZ, 1940-55, XX, green bone, 3-5/16" ............ 325
62009, 1940-55, XX, green bone, 3-5/16" ................... 225
62009, 1940-64, XX, bone, 3-5/16"............................... 100
62009RAZ, 1940-64, XX, bone, 3-5/16" ....................... 120
62009, 1940-64, XX, black composition, 3-5/16" ........ 150
62009SH, 1940-64, XX, black composition, 3-5/16" ... 160
62009, 1965-69, USA, master blade in back bone, 3-5/16" ........................................................................ 75
62009, 1965-69, USA, master blade in front bone, 3-5/16" ........................................................................ 75
62009, USA, spear, delrin,............................................... 90
62009RAZ, 1965-69, USA, master blade in front, bone, 3-5/16" ........................................................................ 90
62009, 1970, 10 Dot, delrin, 3-5/16" ............................. 50
62009, 1970, 10 Dot, bone stag, 3-5/16" ...................... 75
62009RAZ, 1970, 10 Dot, delrin, 3-5/16" ..................... 60
62009RAZ, 1970, 10 Dot, bone, 3-5/16" ....................... 90

*62109, Tested XX, spear, baby copperhead, green bone, 3-1/8", rare, $650.*
RM2109, spear blade, Christmas yellow, 3-1/8"......... 750
62109X, 1920-40, Tested XX, green bone, 3-1/8" ....... 550
62109X, 1920-40, Tested XX, rough black, 3-1/8"...... 400
62109X, 1940-49, XX, rough black, 3-1/8" .................. 250
62109X, 1940-55, XX, green bone, 3-1/8" ................... 400
62109X, 1940-64, XX, red bone, 3-1/8"........................ 200
62109X, 1940-64, XX, bone, 3-1/8" .............................. 150
62109X, 1965-69, USA, bone, 3-1/8"............................ 100
62109X, 10 Dot, (1970), bone, 3-1/8" .......................... 100

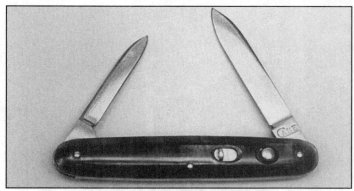

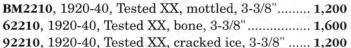

*T7210, Tested XX, double switchblade, tortoise, 3-3/8", $1,500.*
BM2210, 1920-40, Tested XX, mottled, 3-3/8".......... 1,200
62210, 1920-40, Tested XX, bone, 3-3/8" ................. 1,600
92210, 1920-40, Tested XX, cracked ice, 3-3/8" ...... 1,200

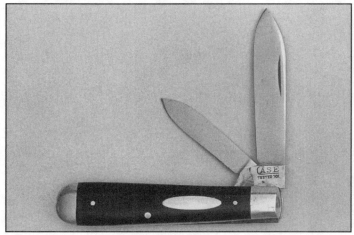

*2210, Tested XX, slick black, plain shield, 3-1/8", $150.*

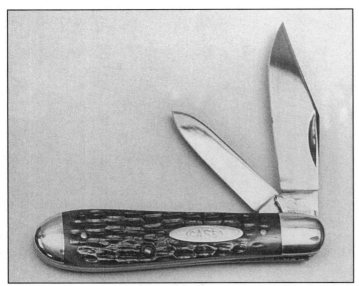

***6210-1/2, Tested XX, green bone, 3-1/8", $250.***
**3210-1/2**, 1920-40, Tested XX, yellow composition, 3-1/8" ............................................................. **400**
**5210-1/2**, 1920-40, Tested XX, stag, 3-1/8" ............... **650**

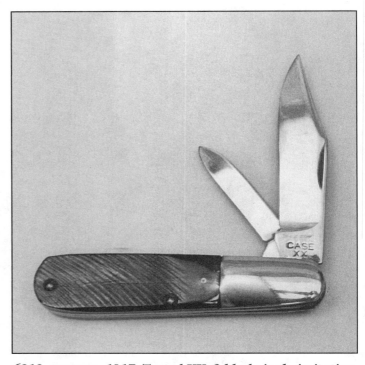

***6213, approx. 1917, Tested XX, 2-blade jack, imitation jig bone, iron bolsters, no emblem (stamp not in any previous book.). The author believes this to be a WW I military contract knife, rare, $1,000.***
**6213**, 1920-40, Tested XX, Rogers bone, 4" ............ **1,800**
**6213**, 1920-40, Tested XX, green bone, 4" .............. **1,600**

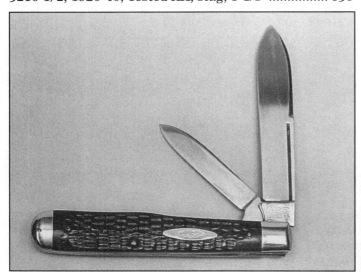

***6211 LP, Tested XX, green bone, 4-1/2", $2,000.***

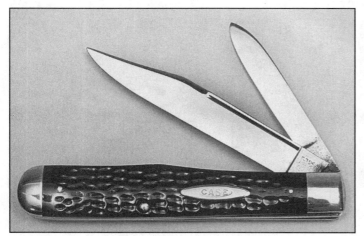

***6211-1/2, Tested XX, green bone, long pull, 4-1/2", $2,000.***

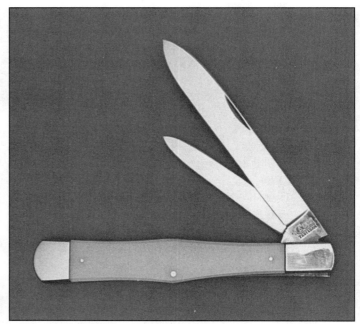

***32213, Tested XX, spear, yellow, rare, 5-1/4", $800.***
**62213**, Tested XX, spear, Rogers bone, rare, 5-3/8" **1,200**
**62213**, 1920-40, Tested XX, spear, green bone, 5-3/8"
............................................................................. **1,000**

Case Knives Tested (1920-1971) 183

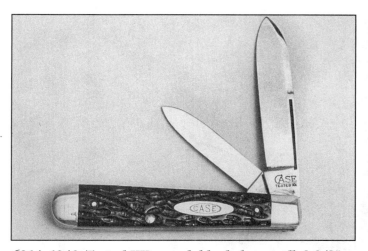

***6214, 1940, Tested XX, rough black, long pull, 3-3/8", $225.***

6214, 1920-40, Tested XX, green bone, 3-3/8" ............ 275
6214, 1940-49, XX, rough black w/shield, 3-3/8" ....... 150
6214, 1940-49, XX, rough black w/out shield, 3-3/8" ................................................................................. 135
6214, 1940-55, XX, green bone, 3-3/8" ...................... 250
6214, 1940-64, XX, red bone, 3-3/8" .......................... 150
6214, 1940-64, XX, late Rogers bone, 3-3/8" ............. 200
6214, 1940-64, XX, bone, 3-3/8" ................................. 125
6214, 1965-69, USA, bone, 3-3/8" ................................ 75
6214, 1970, 10 Dot, delrin, 3-3/8" ................................ 50
6214, 1970, 10 Dot, bone stag, 3-3/8" ......................... 75

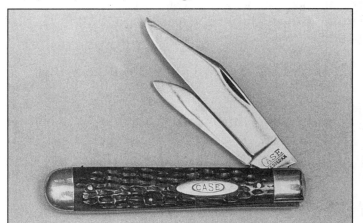

***6214-1/2, Tested XX, green bone, 3-3/8", $275.***

5214-1/2, 1920-40, Tested XX, stag, 3-3/8" ............... 325
6214-1/2, 1920-40, Tested XX, Rogers bone, 3-3/8" ... 350
6214-1/2, 1940-49, XX, rough black, 3-3/8" ............... 125
6214-1/2, 1940-55, XX, green bone, 3-3/8" ................. 225
6214-1/2, 1940-64, XX, red bone, 3-3/8" ..................... 150
6214-1/2, 1940-64, XX, bone, 3-3/8" ........................... 125
6214-1/2, 1965-69, USA, bone, 3-3/8" .......................... 75
6214-1/2, 1970, 10 Dot, delrin, 3-3/8" .......................... 50
6214-1/2, 1970, 10 Dot, bone stag, 3-3/8" ................... 75
6215, 1920-40, tested XX, small gunstock, green bone, 3" .................................................................................. 1,500
6216, 1920-40, Tested XX, green bone, 3-3/8" ........... 300

***6216EO, 1920-40, Tested XX, green bone, w/chain, 1 of 100, 3-3/8", $400.***

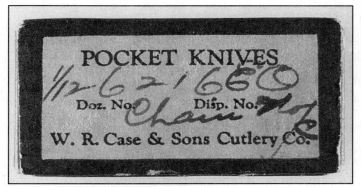

***End of box, marked 6216EO, 1/12 doz., very rare.***

6216EO, 1920-40, Tested XX, green bone, 3-3/8" ....... 350
6216, 1940-64, XX, bone, 3-3/8" ................................. 125

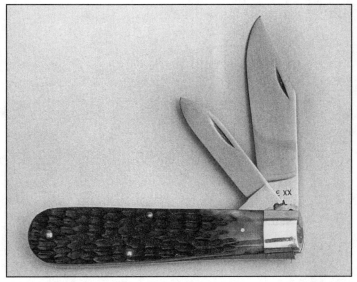

***6216-1/2, USA, bone, 3-3/8", $85.***

6216-1/2, 1920-40, Tested XX, green bone, 3-3/8" ..... 300
6216-1/2, 1940-64, XX, bone, 3-3/8" ........................... 125
7216-1/2, 1920-1940, tortoise, 3-3/8" ......................... 350

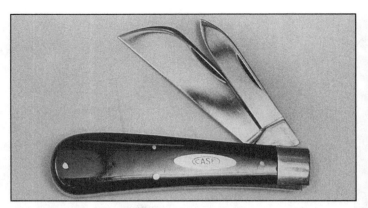

*2217, Tested XX, slick black, 3-7/8", $350.*

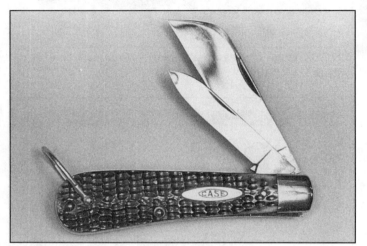

*6217R, Tested XX, green bone, 4", $550.*

6217, 1920-40, Tested XX, green bone, 4" .................. 550
6217, 1940-55, XX, green bone, 4" .............................. 450
6217, 1940-64, XX, red bone, 4" ................................. 300
2217, 1940-64, XX, slick black, 4" .............................. 250
6217, 1940-64, XX, bone, 4" ....................................... 225
6217, 1965-69, USA, wood, 4" ...................................... 75
6217, 1965-69, USA, bone stag, 4" ............................. 150
6217, 1970, 10 Dot, bone stag, 4" ............................... 175
6217, 1970, 10 Dot, laminated wood, 4" .................... 100
6219, 1920-40, Tested XX, green bone 4-1/8" ............ 650

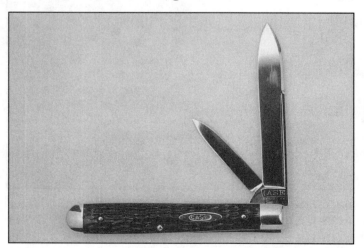

*62019LP, Tested XX, green bone, 4-1/8", $1,200.*

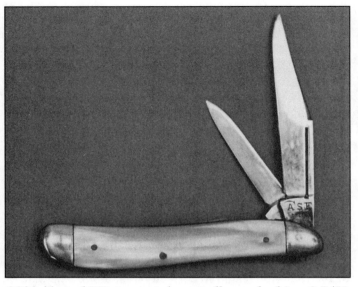

*9220, Tested XX, peanut, long pull, cracked ice, 2-7/8", $300.*

**RM220**, 1920-40, Tested XX, Christmas tree, 2-3/4"
.................................................................................... 450
**RM220SAB**, 1920-40, Tested XX, Christmas tree, 2-3/4"
.................................................................................... 550
**9220SAB** Tested XX, imitation pearl, cracked ice, ..... 400
2220, 1920-40, Tested XX, slick black, 2-3/4" ............ 250
3220, 1920-40, Tested XX, yellow composition, 2-3/4"
.................................................................................... 250
5220, 1920-40, Tested XX, stag, 2-3/4" ....................... 400
6220, 1920-40, Tested XX, rough black, 2-3/4" .......... 300
6220, Tested XX, Rogers bone, 2-7/8" ......................... 450
6220, 1920-40, Tested XX, green bone, 2-3/4" ........... 400
**6220SAB**, 1920-40, Tested XX, long pull, green bone, 2-3/4" .................................................................................... 550
8220, 1920-40, Tested XX, genuine pearl, 2-3/4" ....... 500
9220, 1920-40, Tested XX, imitation pearl, 2-3/4" ..... 300
2220, 1940-64, XX, slick black, 2-3/4" ....................... 100
3220, 1940-64, XX yellow composition, 2-3/4" ........... 100
5220, 1940-64, XX, stag, 2-3/4" .................................. 150
6220, 1940-49, XX, peanut, rough black, 2-3/4" ........ 200
6220, 1940-55, XX, green bone, 2-3/4" ....................... 350
6220, 1940-64, XX, red bone, 2-3/4" ........................... 150
6220, 1940-64, XX, Rogers bone, 2-3/4" ..................... 175
6220, 1940-64, XX, bone, 2-3/4" ................................. 100
9220, 1940-64, XX, imitation pearl, 2-3/4" ................. 150
9220, 1940-64, XX, cracked ice, 2-3/4" ...................... 150
2220, 1965-69, USA, slick black, 2-3/4" ....................... 90
3220, 1965-69, USA, yellow composition, 2-3/4" ......... 90
5220, 1965-69, USA, stag, 2-3/4" ................................ 125
6220, 1965-69, USA, bone, 2-3/4" ............................... 100
6220, 1965-69, USA, delrin, 2-3/4" ............................. 125
2220, 1970, 10 Dot, slick black, 2-3/4" ........................ 80
3220, 1970, 10 Dot, yellow composition, 2-3/4" .......... 80
3220, 1970, 10 Dot, flat yellow, 2-3/4" ....................... 100
5220, 1967, brass backsprings, 12 made .................... 350

# Case Knives Tested (1920-1971)

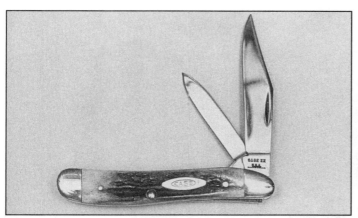

*5220, 10 Dot, stag, 2-7/8", $125.*

*Top: 6220, Tested XX, green bone, 2-3/4", $400.*
*Middle: 6220SAB LP, Tested XX, green bone, 2-3/4", $450.*
*Bottom: 6220LP, Tested XX, green bone, 2-3/4", $550.*

| | | |
|---|---|---|
| 6220, 1970, 10 Dot, bone, 2-3/4" | | 100 |
| 6220, 1970, 10 Dot, delrin, scarce, 2-3/4" | | 125 |
| 6220, 1971, 9 Dot, bone, 2-3/4" | | 100 |

*06221-1/2, Tested XX, green bone, 3-1/4", $650.*

| | | |
|---|---|---|
| 06221-1/2, Tested XX, long pull, green bone | | 700 |
| 02221-1/2, 1920-40, Tested XX, slick black, 3-1/4" | | 350 |
| 03221, 1920-1940, Tested XX, yellow, 3-1/4" | | 350 |
| 07221, 1920-40, Tested XX, spear, tortoise, 3-1/4" | | 700 |
| 06221, 1920-40, Tested XX, Wharncliffe, green bone, 3-1/4" | | 1,000 |

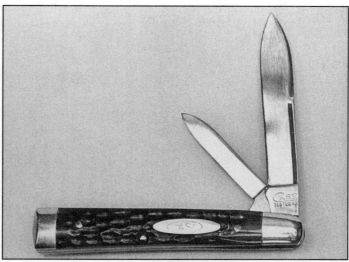

*6222, Tested, green bone, doctor's, long pull, 3-3/8", $1,200.*

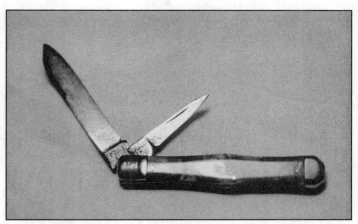

*P223, 1920-40, Tested XX, green swirl celluloid, 3-1/2", $500.*

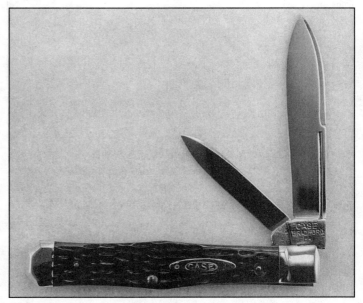

*6223, 1920-40, Tested XX, green bone, 3-1/2", $800.*

| | | |
|---|---|---|
| 6223, 1920-40, Tested XX, green bone, 3-1/2" | | 800 |
| 9223, 1920-40, Tested XX, imitation pearl, 3-1/2" | | 500 |

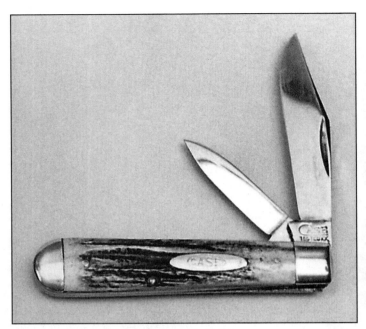

*5224-1/2, Tested XX, stag, 3", $350.*

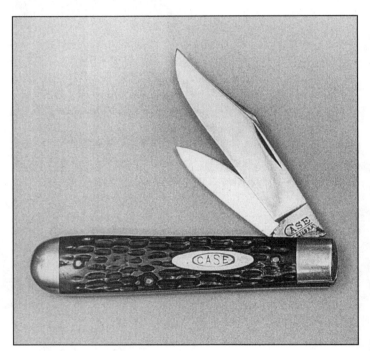

*6224-1/2, Tested XX, green bone, 3", $300.*
**RM224-1/2**, 1920-40, Tested XX, Christmas tree, 3" ............................................................................. 400
**3224-1/2**, 1920-40, Tested XX, yellow composition, 3" ............................................................................. 250
**2224SH**, 1920-40, Tested XX, slick black, 3" ............... 300
**2224RAZ**, 1920-40, Tested XX, slick black, 3" ............ 300
**3224**, 1920-40, Tested XX, yellow composition, 3" ..... 225
**6224**, 1920-40, Tested XX, green bone, 3" .................. 300
**2224SP**, 1940-64, XX, slick black, 3" ......................... 250
**2224SH**, 1940-64, XX, slick black, 3" ......................... 250
**2224RAZ**, 1940-64, XX, slick black, 3" ....................... 300

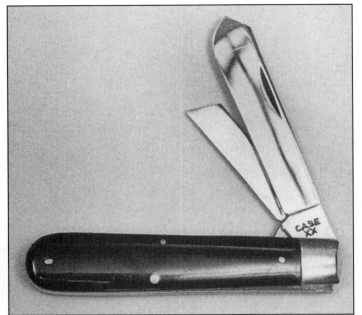

*22024SP, XX, slick black, 3", $250.*
**52024**, 1920-40, Tested XX, stag, 3" ............................ 360
**62024**, 1920-40, Tested XX, green bone, 3" ................ 300
**62024SH**, 1920-40, Tested XX, green bone, 3" ........... 350
**62024RAZ**, 1920-40, Tested XX, green bone, 3" ......... 350
**220024SP**, 1940-64, XX, slick black, "Little John Carver," (extremely rare, price quoted is for knife in the original balsa wood block & sleeve), 3" ................... 1,000
**62024**, 1940-64, XX, green bone, 3" ............................. 225

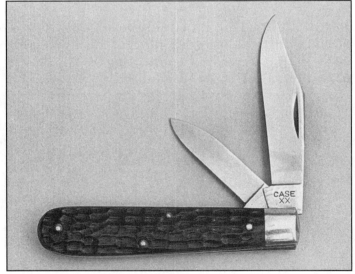

*62024-1/2, bone, 3", XX, $90.*
**52024-1/2**, 1920-40, Tested, XX, stag, 3" .................... 300
**62024-1/2**, 1920-40, Tested, XX, green bone, 3" ........ 325
**32024-1/2**, 1940-64, XX, yellow composition, 3" .......... 90
**32024-1/2**, 1965-69, USA, flat yellow, 3" ...................... 90
**62024-1/2**, 1940-55, XX, green bone, 3" ..................... 275
**32024-1/2**, 1965-69, USA, yellow composition, 3" ........ 75
**62024-1/2**, 1965-69, USA, bone, 3" ............................... 65

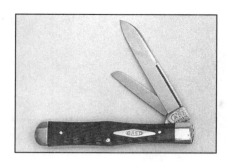

***6225LP**, Tested XX, green bone, 3", $450.*
**32025**, Tested XX, yellow spear blade, 3" ......... 350

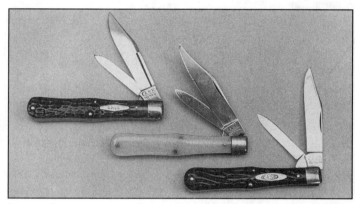

*Top: **62025-1/2**, 1920-40, Tested XX, green bone, 3", $400.*
*Middle: **32025-1/2**, 1920-40, Tested XX, yellow composition, 3", $350.*
*Bottom: **62025-1/2**, 1920-40, Tested XX, rough black, 3", $400.*
**22025-1/2**, 1920-40, Tested XX, slick black, 3" .......... 350

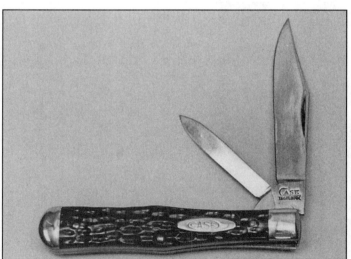

***6225-1/2**, Tested XX, Coke bottle, green bone, 3", $450.*
**5225-1/2**, 1920-40, Tested XX, stag, 3" ...................... 450
**6225-1/2**, 1920-40, Tested XX, rough black, 3" .......... 400
**6225-1/2**, 1940-49, XX, rough black, 3" ...................... 250
**6225-1/2**, 1940-55, XX, green bone, 3" ...................... 350
**6225-1/2**, 1940-64, XX, red bone, 3" .......................... 225
**6225RAZ**, 1940-64, XX, bone, 3" ................................ 300
**6225-1/2**, 1940-64, XX, bone, 3" ................................ 150
**6225-1/2**, 1965-69, USA, bone, 3" .............................. 110
**6225-1/2**, 1970, 10 Dot, bone, 3" ................................ 110

***P2026**, pyremite, 3", $600.*
**RM2026**, 1920-40, Tested XX, long pull, Christmas tree, 3" ............................................................................. 600
**82026**, 1920-40, Tested XX, long pull, genuine pearl, 3" ............................................................................. 600

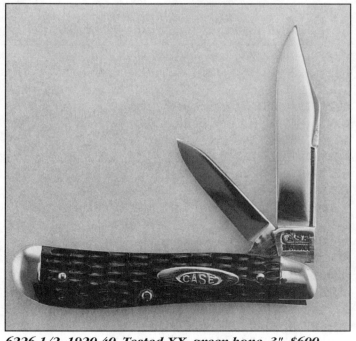

***6226-1/2**, 1920-40, Tested XX, green bone, 3", $600.*

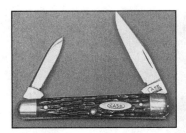 

*Left: 92027-1/2, Tested XX, long pull, imitation pearl, 2-3/4", $200.*
*Right: 62027-1/2, Tested XX, bone, 2-3/4", $200.*
**RM2027-1/2**, 1920-40, Tested XX, Christmas tree, 2-3/4" ................................................................... 300
**GS2027-1/2**, 1920-40, Tested XX, goldstone, 2-3/4" ................................................................... 250
**62027-1/2**, 1940-64, Tested XX, green bone, 2-3/4" ................................................................... 225
**82027-1/2**, Tested XX, pearl, 2-3/4" ............................ 300
**62027-1/2**, 1940-64, XX, rough black, 2-3/4" ............ 125
**62027-1/2**, 1940-64, XX, bone, 2-3/4" ......................... 90
**92027-1/2**, 1940-64, XX, cracked ice, 2-3/4" .............. 125

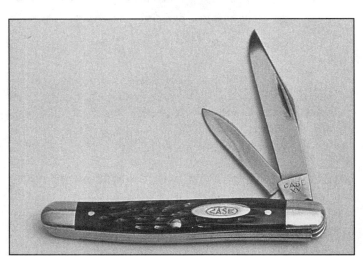

*6227, 1940-64, XX, bone, 2-3/4", $65.*
**6227**, 1920-40, Tested XX, early Rogers bone, 2-3/4" ................................................................... 230
**6227**, 1940-55, XX, green bone, 2-3/4" ....................... 200
**6227**, 1940-64, XX, red bone, 2-3/4" ........................... 125
**6227**, 1965-69, USA, bone, 2-3/4" ................................. 65
**6227**, 1970, 10 Dot, delrin, 2-3/4" ................................. 75
**6227**, 1970, 10 Dot, bone stag, 2-3/4" .......................... 65
**H2027**, 1920-40, Tested XX, mottled, 2-3/4" .............. 275
**RM2027**, 1920-40, Tested XX, spear, Christmas tree, 2-3/4" ................................................................... 325
**RM2027**, 1920-40, Tested XX, red mottled, 2-3/4" ..... 250
**62027**, 1920-40, Tested XX, green bone, 2-3/4" .......... 200
**92027**, 1920-40, Tested XX, imitation pearl, 2-3/4" ... 200
**2228**, 1920-40, Tested XX, dogleg, slick black, 3-1/2" 250
**2228EO**, 1920-40, Tested XX, slick black, 3-1/2" ....... 275
**2228PU**, 1920-40, Tested XX, slick black, 3-1/2" ....... 275
**6228**, 1920-40, Tested XX, green bone, 3-1/2" .......... 375

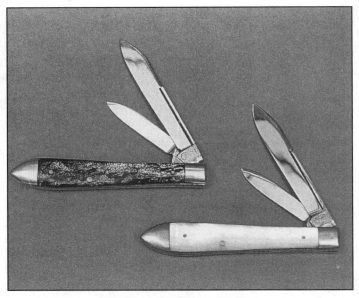

*Top: RM2028, Tested XX, long pull, Christmas yellow, 2-7/8", $550.*
*Bottom: 82028, W. R. Case & Son, Bradford, Pa., pearl, 2-7/8", LP, $550.*
**22028**, Tested XX, slick black, 3-1/2" ......................... 350
**GS2028**, Tested XX, goldstone, 3-1/2" ........................ 550
**62028**, Tested XX, rough black ................................... 350
**62028**, 1920-40, Tested XX, green bone, 3-1/2" .......... 450
**22028**. 1940-64, XX, slick black, 3-1/2" ...................... 200

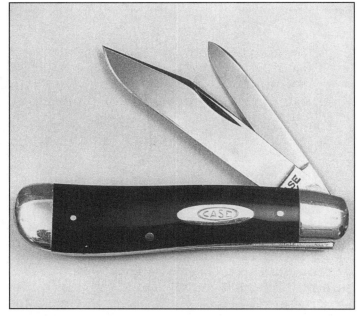

*22028-1/2, XX, slick black, 3-1/2", $110.*
**M2028-1/2**, 1920-40, Tested XX, metal, 3-1/2" .......... 200
**22028-1/2**, 1920-40, Tested XX, slick black, 3-1/2" ..... 275
**62028-1/2**, 1920-40, Tested XX, green bone, 3-1/2" ... 450
**62028-1/2**, 1940-49, XX, rough black, 3-1/2" ............. 200
**62028-1/2**, 1940-64, XX, bone, 3-1/2" ........................ 250
**62028-1/2**, 1940-50, XX, early Rogers, 3-1/2" ............. 450

# Case Knives Tested (1920-1971)

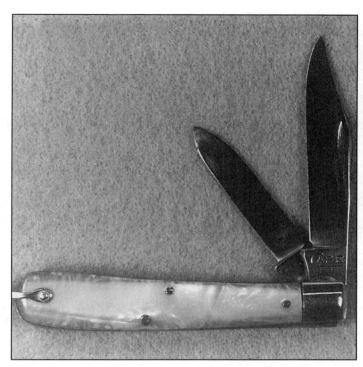

*9229-1/2R, 1920-40, Tested XX, cracked ice, 2-1/2", $250.*

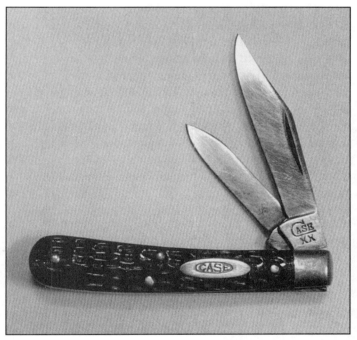

*6229-1/2, Case XX, main blade, green bone, 2-1/2", $350.*

6229-1/2, 1920-40, Tested XX, green bone, 2-1/2" ..... 300
6229-1/2, Tested XX, rough black, 2-1/2" .................. 250
7229-1/2, 1920-40, Tested XX, tortoise, 2-1/2" ........... 350
8229-1/2, 1920-1940, Tested XX, pearl, 2-1/2" ........... 300
2229-1/2, 1940-64, XX, slick black, 2-1/2" ................. 140
6229-1/2, 1940-64, XX, bone, 2-1/2" .......................... 150
2229-1/2, 1965-69, USA, slick black, rare, 2-1/2" ...... 200
6229-1/2, 1965-69, USA, bone, 2-1/2" ....................... 100

*Top: 06230LP, Tested XX, green bone, 3-1/4", $450.*
*Bottom: 06230-1/2, Tested XX, green bone, 3-1/4", $450.*

02230, 1920-40, Tested XX, black composition, 3-1/4"
................................................................................. 250
05230LP, 1920-40, Tested XX, stag, 3-1/4" ................ 450
06230, 1920-40, Tested XX, long pull, green bone, 3-1/4"
................................................................................. 450
06230SH, 1920-40, Tested XX, green bone, 3-1/4" ..... 450
06230SP, 1920-40, Tested XX, green bone, 3-1/4" ...... 450
09230, 1920-40, Tested XX, imitation pearl, 3-1/4" ... 300
02230-1/2, 1920-40, Tested XX, black composition, 3-1/4" ............................................................................. 275
05230-1/2, 1920-40, Tested XX, stag, 3-1/4" .............. 430
06230-1/2, 1920-40, Tested XX, green bone, 3-1/4" ... 450
09230-1/2, 1920-40, Tested XX, imitation pearl, 3-1/4"
................................................................................. 300

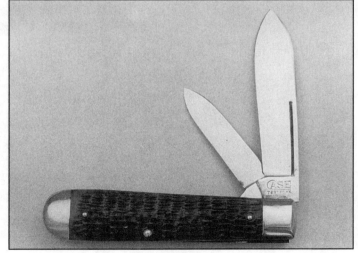

*6231, Tested XX, long pull, imitation bone, no shield, 3-3/4", $200.*

6231 LP, Tested XX, red bone, shield, 3-3/4" .............. 300
6231, 1940-64, XX, bone, 3-3/4" ................................ 200
6231, 1940-49, XX, rough black, 3-3/4" ..................... 225
6231, 1940-55, XX, green bone, 3-3/4" ...................... 350
6231, 1940-64, XX, red bone, spear, 3-3/4" ............... 250
6231, 1965-69, USA, bone, rare, 3-3/4" ...................... 450

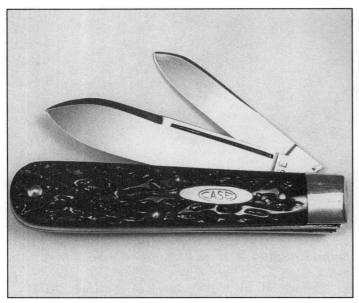

**62031, 1940-49, XX, long pull, rough black, 3-3/4", $250.**

22031, 1920-40, Tested XX, slick black, 3-3/4" .......... 250
52031, 1920-40, Tested XX, stag, 3-3/4" ..................... 450
62031, 1920-40, Tested XX, green bone, 3-3/4" .......... 450
62031, 1920-40, Tested XX, rough black, 3-3/4" ........ 300
62031, 1940-64, XX, bone, 3-3/4" ............................... 200
62031, 1940-55, XX, green bone, 3-3/4" ...................... 350
62031, 1940-55, XX, long pull, green bone, 3-3/4" ..... 400
62031, 1940-64, XX, red bone, 3-3/4" ......................... 250

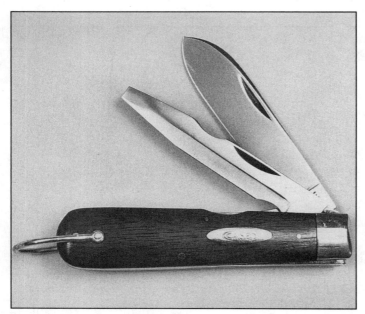

**12031 XX, electrician's knife, LR, walnut, 3-1/4", $45.**
12031 L, 1920-40, Tested XX, walnut, 3-3/4" ............. 150
12031 LR, 1965-69, USA, electrician's knife, walnut, 3-3/4" ................................................................................ 60
12031 LR, 1970, 10 Dot, electrician's knife, walnut, 3-3/4" ................................................................................ 60

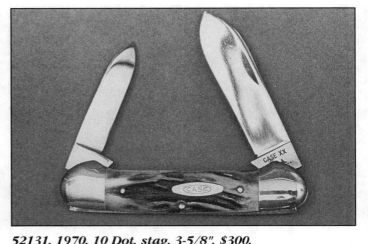

**52131, 1970, 10 Dot, stag, 3-5/8", $300.**
52131, 1920-40, Tested XX, stag, 3-5/8" .................... 800
52131, 1920-40, Tested XX, long pull, stag, 3-5/8" . 1,000
92131, 1920-40, Tested XX, cracked ice, 3-5/8" ......... 950
52131, XX, red stag ................................................... 1,000
52131 LP, XX, red stag .............................................. 1,200
52131, 1940-64, XX, stag, 3-5/8" ................................ 600
52131, 1940-55, XX, stag, long pull, 3-5/8" ................ 900
52131, 1965-69, USA, stag, 3-5/8" .............................. 300
62131, 1965-69, USA, bone, 3-5/8" ............................. 150
62131, 1970, 10 Dot, bone, 3-5/8" ............................... 150
62131, 1964, XX, bone, 3-5/8" .................................... 400

Beware: A few of these knives were made in 1964, but not sold in production; some, however, could have gotten to the collector market.

2231-1/2, 1920-40, Tested XX, flat blade, slick black, 3-3-/4" ........................................................................... 250
6231-1/2, 1920-40, Tested XX, green bone, 3-3/4" ..... 400
6231-1/2, 1920-40, Tested XX, rough black, 3-3/4" .... 250
6231-1/2, 1920-40, Tested XX, bone, 3-3/4" ............... 250
2231-1/2, 1940-64, XX, long pull is standard, slick black, 3-3/4" ....................................................................... 150
2231-1/2SAB, 1940-64, XX, long pull is standard, slick black, 3-3/4" ............................................................. 125
42311-1/2, 1940-64, XX, long pull is standard, white composition, 3-3/4" ................................................. 300
6231-1/2, 1940-64, XX, bone, long pull is standard, 3-3/4" .............................................................................. 225
6231-1/2, 1940-64, XX red bone, 3-3/4" ..................... 275
6231-1/2, 1940-55 XX, green bone, 3-3/4" ................. 330
6231-1/2, 1940-49 XX, long pull, rough black, 3-3/4" ........................................................................................ 250
2231-1/2SAB, 1965-69, USA, long pull is standard, slick black, 3-3/4" ............................................................... 60
6231-1/2, 1965-69, USA, long pull is standard, bone, 3-3/4" .............................................................................. 100
2231-1/2SAB, 1970, 10 Dot, long pull is standard, slick black, 3-3/4" ................................................................. 65
6231-1/2, 1970, 10 Dot, long pull is standard, bone, 3-3/4" .............................................................................. 100

Case Knives Tested (1920-1971) 191

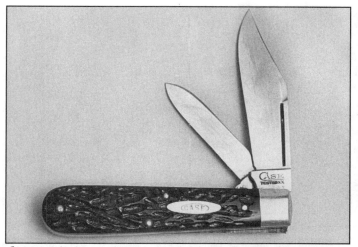

**62031-1/2, Tested XX, rough black, 3-3/4", $300.**
22031-1/2, 1920-40, Tested XX, slick black, 3-3/4".... 250
**52031-1/2**, 1920-40, Tested XX, stag, 3-3/4" ............. 400
**52031-1/2SAB**, 1920-40, Tested XX, stag, 3-3/4" ........ 450
**62031-1/2**, 1920-40, Tested XX, green bone, 3-3/4" ... 400
22031-1/2, 1940-64, XX, long pull is standard, slick black, 3-3/4" ................................................................ 225
62031-1/2, 1940-55, XX, green bone, 3-3/4" ............... 400
62031-1/2, 1940-64, XX, red bone, 3-3/4" .................... 225
62031-1/2, 1940-64, XX, long pull is standard, bone, 3-3/4" ................................................................................ 200
62031-1/2, 1940-49, XX, rough black, 3-3/4" ............. 250
62031-1/2, 1940-49, XX, long pull, rough black, 3-3/4" ................................................................................ 250

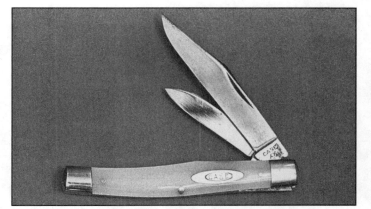

**3232, XX, yellow composition, 3-5/8", $175.**
3232, 1920-40, Tested XX, yellow composition, 3-5/8" ................................................................................ 200
**5232**, 1920-40, Tested XX, stag, 3-5/8" ...................... 300
**6232**, 1920-40, Tested XX, green bone, 3-5/8" ........... 300
6232, 1940-64, XX, late Rogers bone, 3-5/8" ............... 200
6232, 1940-50, XX, rough black, 3-5/8" ...................... 150
6232, 1940-55, XX, green bone, 3-5/8" ........................ 200
6232, 1940-64, XX, red bone, 3-5/8" ............................ 150
5232, 1940-64, XX, stag, 3-5/8" .................................... 200
6232, 1940-64, XX, bone, 3-5/8" ................................... 125
5232, 1965-69, USA, stag, 3-5/8" ................................ 125
6232, 1965-69, USA, bone, 3-5/8" ................................ 75

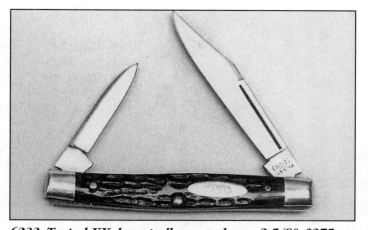

**6233, Tested XX, long pull, green bone, 2-5/8", $275.**
3233, Tested XX, long pull, yellow composition, 2-5/8" ................................................................................ 250
6233, Tested XX, long pull, rough black, 2-5/8" ......... 225
6233, Tested XX, long pull, green bone, 2-5/8" ......... 325
6233, XX, long pull, green bone, 2-5/8" ...................... 300
**RM233**, Tested XX, long pull, Christmas tree, 2-5/8" ................................................................................ 400
**GS233**, Tested Bradford, long pull, goldstone, 2-5/8" ................................................................................ 375
**8233LP**, 1920-40, Tested XX, pearl, 2-5/8" ................ 300
9233, Tested XX, long pull, cracked ice, 2-5/8" .......... 225
6233, 1940-55, XX, long pull, green bone, 2-5/8" ....... 300
3233, XX, long pull, yellow composition, 2-5/8" ........ 150
3233, XX, regular pull, yellow composition, 2-5/8" (large) ................................................................................ 75
3233, XX, regular pull, yellow composition, 2-5/8" (small) ................................................................................ 75
**5233**, (large) XX, regular pull, stag, 2-5/8" ................ 150
**6233**, (large) XX, regular pull, bone, 2-5/8" ................ 90
6233, XX, regular pull, red bone, 2-5/8" ..................... 110
6233, 1940-49, XX, long pull, rough black, 2-5/8" ..... 200
6233, 1940-49, XX, regular pull, rough black, 2-5/8" ................................................................................ 140
9233, XX, long pull, cracked ice, 2-5/8" ...................... 225
9233, (large) XX, regular pull, cracked ice, 2-5/8"...... 60
9233, (small) XX, regular pull, cracked ice, 2-5/8" ...... 60
9233, XX, cracked ice, no bolsters, rare, 2-5/8" ......... 250

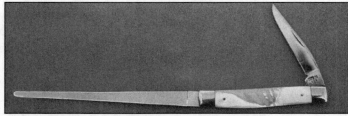

**8233, letter opener, pearl, 6-3/4", $250.**
8233, (large) XX, regular pull, pearl, 2-5/8" ............... 125
9233, XX, long pull, imitation pearl, 2-5/8" ............... 135
9233, (large) XX, regular pull, imitation pearl, 2-5/8" ................................................................................ 60

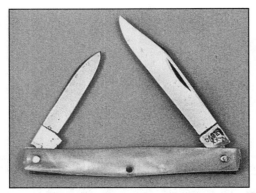

*9233, XX, cracked ice, SHAD, no bolsters, rare, 2-5/8" $250.*

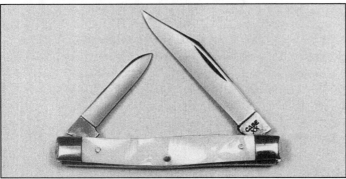

**9233, XX, cracked ice, 2-5/8", $60.**
**3233**, USA, regular pull, yellow composition, 2-5/8" ... **60**
**5233**, USA, regular pull, stag, 2-5/8" .......................... **125**
**6233**, USA, regular pull, bone, 2-5/8" .......................... **75**
**6233**, USA, regular pull, red bone, 2-5/8" .................... **75**
**9233**, USA, regular pull, cracked ice, 2-5/8" ................. **50**
**8233**, USA, regular pull, pearl, 2-5/8" ......................... **100**
**3233**, 10 Dot, regular pull, yellow composition, 2-5/8"
............................................................................................... **60**
**6233**, 10 Dot, regular pull, bone, 2-5/8" ....................... **65**
**6233**, 10 Dot, regular pull, delrin, 2-5/8" ..................... **65**
**8233**, 10 Dot, regular pull, pearl, 2-5/8" ..................... **100**
**9233**, 10 Dot, regular pull, imitation pearl, 2-5/8" ...... **50**
**5233**, 10 Dot, regular pull, stag, 2-5/8" ...................... **125**

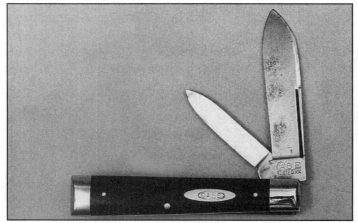

**2234, Tested XX, doctor's knife, long pull, slick black, 3-5/8", $800.**
**5234**, 1920-40, Tested XX, doctor's knife, stag, 3-5/8"
............................................................................................... **1,500**

**6234, Tested XX, green bone, 3-5/8", $1,500.**

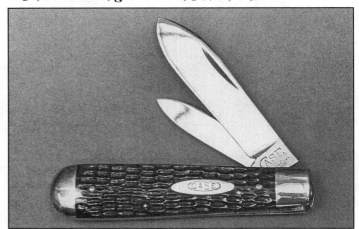

**6235, Tested XX, green bone, 3-1/4", $300.**
**6235EO**, 1920-40, Tested XX, green bone, 3-1/4" ....... **400**
**6235SH**, 1920-40, Tested XX, green bone, 3-1/4" ....... **400**
**6235**, 1940-49, XX, rough black, 3-1/4" ..................... **125**
**6235**, 1940-55, XX, green bone, 3-1/4" ...................... **250**
**6235**, 1940-64, XX, bone, 3-1/4" ................................. **125**
**6235EO**, 1940-64, XX, bone, 3-1/4" ............................ **225**
**6235**, 1940-64, XX, red bone, 3-1/4" .......................... **175**
**6235EO**, 1940-49, XX, rough black, 3-1/4" ................. **250**
**6235**, 1940-50, XX, early Rogers, 3-1/4" .................... **400**
**6235**, 1965-69, USA, bone, rare, 3-1/4" ..................... **400**

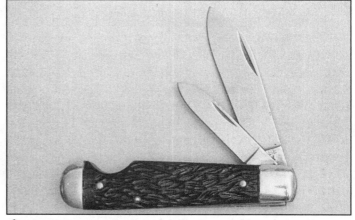

**620035EO, XX, black imitation jigged bone, 3-1/4", $90.**

**62035-1/2, Tested XX, bone, 3-1/4", $400.**

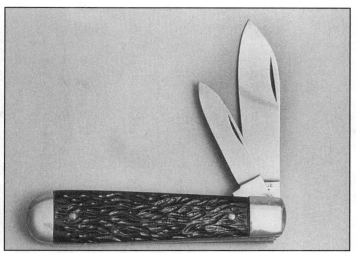

**620035, XX, imitation black bone, 3-1/4", $65.**
**620035LP**, 1940-64, XX, black plastic, 3-1/4".............. 75
**620035EO**, 1940-64, XX, black plastic, 3-1/4".............. 90

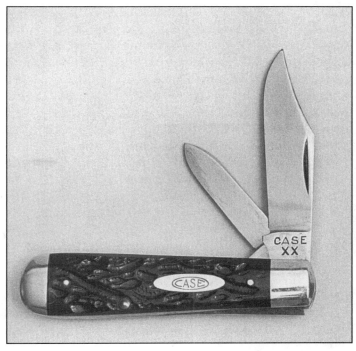

**6235-1/2, 1940-49, XX, rough black, 3-3/8", $125.**
3235-1/2, 1920-40, Tested XX, yellow composition, 3-3/8" ................................................................ 250
5235-1/2, 1920-40, Tested XX, stag, 3-3/8" ............... 350
6235-1/2, 1920-40, Tested XX, green bone, 3-3/8" ..... 300
6235-1/2PU, 1920-40, Tested XX, green bone, 3-3/8" ................................................................ 400
6235-1/2, 1940-64, XX, bone, 3-3/8" ......................... 125
6235-1/2PU, 1940-64, XX, bone, 3-3/8" ..................... 250
6235-1/2, 1940-55, XX, green bone, 3-3/8" ................ 250
6235-1/2, 1940-64, XX, red bone, 3-3/8" .................... 175
6235-1/2, 1965-69, USA, master clip blade in back, bone, 3-3/8" ............................................................. 75
6235-1/2, 1965-69, USA, master clip blade in front, bone, also w/no shield, 3-3/8" .................................. 75
6235-1/2, 1970, 10 Dot, bone, 3-1/4" ........................... 75

**620035-1/2, XX, black imitation bone, 3-1/4", $65.**

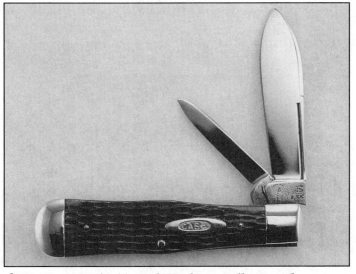

**6237 LP, 1920-40, Tested XX, long pull, green bone, 3-1/2", $1,200.**
6237-1/2, Tested XX, green bone, long pull, 3-1/2".... 650
6237-1/2, 1920-40, Tested XX, early Rogers bone .. 1,300

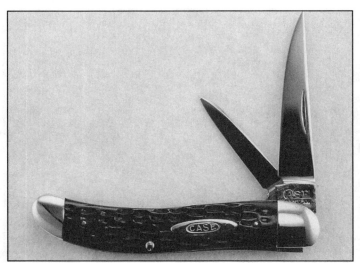

*62039, Tested XX, small sowbelly, green bone, 3-3/8", $800.*

*Top: 6240SP, Tested XX, green bone, 4-7/16", $2,000.*
*Bottom: 6240 pen, Tested XX, green bone, 4-7/16", $1,600.*

**3240SP**, 1920-40, Tested XX, yellow composition, 4-7/16" ................................................................. **1,200**
**9240SP**, 1920-40, Tested XX, imitation pearl, 4-7/16" ................................................................. **1,800**

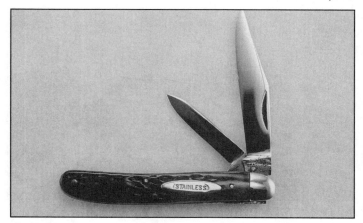

*6242, Case's stainless, Rogers bone, 2-3/4", $400.*
**6242**, 1920-40, similar to peanut, green bone, no lower bolster, 2-3/4" .............................................................. **400**

*62042, imitation black bone, 2-7/8", XX, $60.*
**52042LP**, 1920-40, Tested XX, stag, slant bolsters, 3" ................................................................. **250**
**52042**, 1920-40, Tested XX, regular pull, stag, 3" ..... **225**
**62042**, 1920-40, Tested XX, green bone, 3" ............... **200**
**82042**, 1920-40, Tested XX, genuine pearl, slant bolsters, 3" ................................................................. **325**
**92042**, 1920-40, Tested XX imitation pearl, 3" .......... **125**
**92042LP**, 1920-40, Tested XX, imitation pearl, 3" ..... **150**
**62042**, 1940-49, XX, rough black, 3" ............................ **75**
**62042**, 1940-55, XX, green bone, 3" ........................... **150**
**62042**, 1940-64, XX, red bone, 3" ............................... **110**
**62042**, 1940-64, XX, bone, 3" ....................................... **90**
**62042R**, 1940-64, XX, bone, 3" ..................................... **95**
**92042**, 1940-64, XX, imitation pearl, 3" ........................ **60**
**92042**, 1940-64, XX, cracked ice, 3" ............................. **60**
**92042R**, 1940-64, XX, imitation pearl, 3" ...................... **60**
**92042R**, 1940-64, XX, cracked ice, 3" ........................... **60**
**62042**, 1965-69, USA, bone, 3" ..................................... **55**
**62042R**, 1965-69, USA, bone, 3" ................................... **60**
**92042**, 1965-69, USA, imitation pearl, 3" ..................... **45**
**92042R**, 1965-69, USA, imitation pearl, 3" ................... **45**
**62042**, 1970, 10 Dot, bone, 3" ...................................... **50**
**62042R**, 1970, 10 Dot, bone, 3" .................................... **60**
**92042**, 1970, 10 Dot, imitation pearl, 3" ...................... **45**
**92042R**, 1970, 10 Dot, imitation pearl, 3" .................... **50**

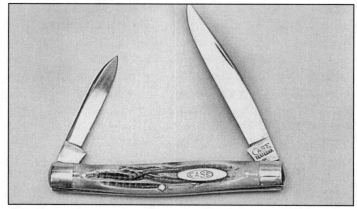

*52044, Tested XX, second-cut stag, rare, 3-1/4", $400.*
**62044F**, 1920-40, Tested XX, green bone, 3-1/4" ........ **250**
**82044**, 1920-40, Tested XX, genuine pearl, 3-1/4" ..... **250**
**82044F**, 1920-40, Tested XX, genuine pearl, 3-1/4" ... **250**

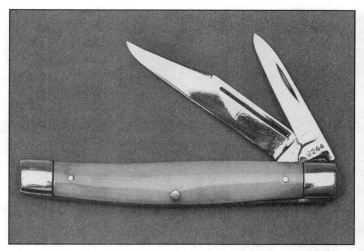

**B244, Tested XX, waterfall, long pull, 3-1/4", $250.**

| | | |
|---|---|---|
| 2244, | 1920-40, Tested XX, slick black, 3-1/4" | 150 |
| 3244, | 1920-40, Tested XX, yellow composition, 3-1/4" | 150 |
| 5244, | 1920-40, Tested XX, stag, 3-1/4" | 250 |
| 6244, | 1920-40 Tested, XX, green bone, 3-1/4 | 250 |
| 9244, | 1920-40, Tested XX, imitation pearl, 3-1/4" | 150 |
| 6244, | 1940-55, XX, green bone, 3-1/4" | 200 |
| 6244, | 1940-64, XX, red bone, 3-1/4" | 125 |
| 6244, | 1940-64, XX, bone, 3-1/4" | 90 |
| 6244, | 1965-69, USA, bone, 3-1/4" | 60 |
| 6244, | 1970, 10 Dot, bone stag, 3-1/4" | 60 |
| 6244, | 1970, 10 Dot, delrin, rare, 3-1/4" | 125 |

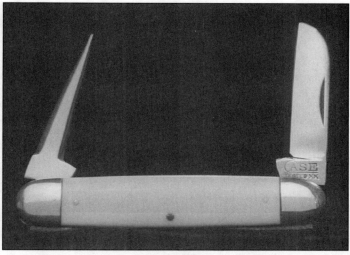

**B245PU, Tested XX, waterfall, 3-3/4", $350.**

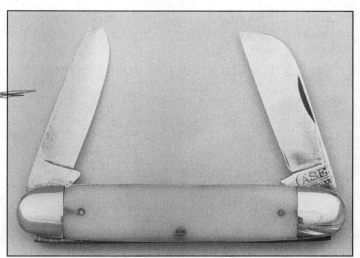

**03245, Tested XX, sheepfoot, spey blades, yellow composition, 3-3/4", $250.**

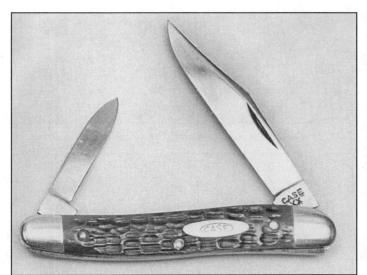

**06244, 1940-55, XX, green bone, 3-1/4", $200.**

| | | |
|---|---|---|
| 02244, | 1920-40, Tested XX, slick black, 3-1/4" | 150 |
| 05244, | 1920-40, Tested XX, stag, 3-1/4" | 250 |
| 06244, | 1920-40, Tested XX, green bone, 3-1/4" | 250 |
| 06244, | 1940-64, XX, red bone, 3-1/4" | 125 |
| 06244, | 1940-64, XX, bone, 3-1/4" | 90 |
| 06244, | 1965-69, USA, bone, 3-1/4" | 65 |
| 06244, | 1970, 10 Dot, delrin, 3-1/4" | 50 |
| 06244, | 1970, 10 Dot, bone stag, 3-1/4" | 65 |
| 08244, | 1920-40, Tested XX, genuine pearl, 3-1/4" | 300 |

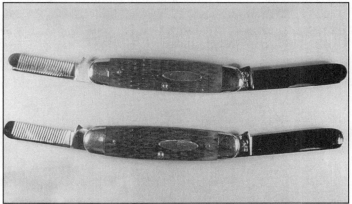

**06245, 1920-40, Tested XX, dog grooming knife, large & small stamp, green bone, 3-3/4", $650.**

| | | |
|---|---|---|
| 02245, | 1920-40, Tested XX, slick black, 3-1/4" | 200 |
| 04245B&G, | 1920-40, Tested XX, white composition, 3-3/4" | 250 |
| 04245LP, | 1920-40, Tested XX, sheepfoot, white composition, 3-3/4" | 250 |

**06245, 1920-40, Tested XX, green bone, spear (also clip), 3-3/4", $350.**
06245, 1920-40, Tested XX, dog grooming, green bone, 3-3/4" .................................................................. 650
02245-1/2, 1920-40, Tested XX, slick black, 3-3/4".... 250
05245-1/2, 1920-40, Tested XX, stag, 3-3/4" .............. 500
06245-1/2, 1920-40, Tested XX, green bone, 3-3/4" ... 400

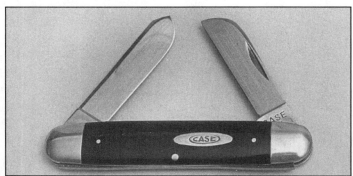

**06245, 1920-40, Tested XX, green bone, spear (also clip), 3-3/4", $350.**
06245, 1920-40, Tested XX, dog grooming, green bone, 3-3/4" .................................................................. 650
02245-1/2, 1920-40, Tested XX, slick black, 3-3/4".... 250
05245-1/2, 1920-40, Tested XX, stag, 3-3/4" .............. 500
06245-1/2, 1920-40, Tested XX, green bone, 3-3/4" ... 400

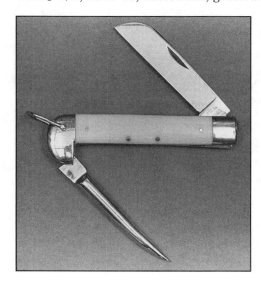

**2245SHSP, XX, slick black, 3-3/4", $200.**

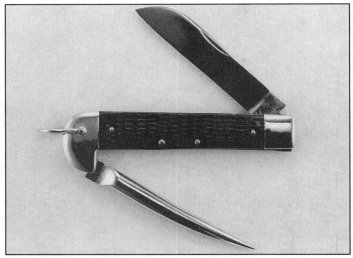

**6246R, 1920-40, Tested XX, green bone, 4-3/8", $600.**
3246R, 1940-64, XX, rigger's knife (none stainless), yellow composition, 4-3/8" ............................................ 350
6246RSS, 1940-64, XX, stainless, red bone, 4-3/8"..... 350
6246RSS, 1940-64, XX, stainless, bone, 4-3/8" .......... 250
6246RSS, 1965-69, USA, bone, stainless, 4-3/8" ........ 150
6246RSS, 1970, 10 Dot, stainless, rigger's knife bone, 4-3/8" ............................................................................. 150

**5247J LP, Tested XX, red stag, rare, 3-7/8", $1,500.**

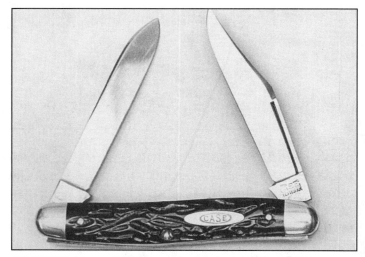

**6247J LP, Tested XX, rough black, 3-7/8", $1,200.**
5247J, 1920-40, Tested XX, stag, 3-7/8" ................. 1,500
6247J, 1920-40, Tested XX, green bone, 3-7/8" ....... 1,500

Case Knives Tested (1920-1971) 197

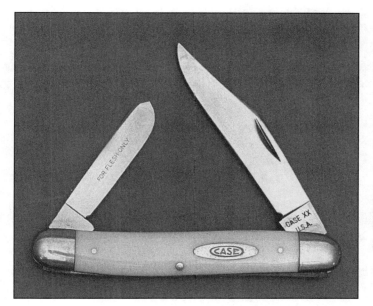

**04247SP, USA, white composition, 3-7/8", $150.**
04247SP, 1920-40, Tested XX, long pull, white composition, 3-7/8" ............................................. 400
05247SP, 1920-40, Tested XX, long pull, stag, 3-7/8" ............................................. 650
06247SP, 1920-40, Tested XX, long pull, Winterbottom bone, 3-7/8" ............................................. 1,000
06247SP, 1920-40, Tested XX, long pull, green bone, 3-7/8" ............................................. 650
06247Pen, 1920-40, Tested XX, long pull, green bone, 3-7/8" ............................................. 650
06247Pen, 1920-40, Tested XX, long pull, rough black, 3-7/8" ............................................. 500
04247SP LP, 1940-64, XX, white composition, 3-7/8" ............................................. 300
04247SP, 1940-64, XX, white composition, 3-7/8" ..... 175
05247SP, 1940-64, XX, stag, 3-7/8" ............................. 350
05247SP, 1940-64, XX, long pull, stag, 3-7/8" ............ 600
05247SP, 1940-64, XX, red stag, 3-7/8" ....................... 600
05247SP, 1940-64, long pull, red stag, 3-7/8" ............. 750
05247Pen, 1940-64, XX, stag, 3-7/8" .......................... 300
05247Pen, 1940-64, XX, long pull, stag, 3-7/8" .......... 350
05247Pen, 1940-64, XX, red stag, 3-7/8" ..................... 500
05247Pen, 1940-64, XX, long pull, red stag, 3-7/8" ... 550
06247Pen, 1940-55, XX, green bone, 3-7/8" ............... 350
06247Pen, 1940-55, XX, long pull, green bone, 3-7/8" ............................................. 450
06247Pen, 1940-49, XX, rough black, 3-7/8" ............. 300
06247Pen, 1940-49, XX, long pull, rough black, 3-7/8" ............................................. 400
06247Pen, 1940-64, XX, red bone, 3-7/8" ................... 200
06247Pen, 1940-64, XX, bone, 3-7/8" ......................... 150
06247Pen, 1940-64, XX, late red Rogers bone, 3-7/8" ............................................. 300
05247SP, 1965-69, USA, stag, 3-7/8" .......................... 300
06247Pen, 1970, 10 Dot, bone, 3-7/8" ......................... 100

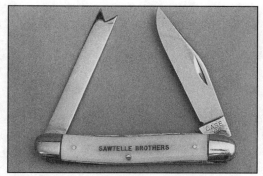

**4247FK, 1940-64, Case XX, greenskeeper, special dandelion blade, 3-7/8", $450.**
4247FK, 1965-69, USA, greenskeeper ......................... 400
4247FK, 1970, 10 Dot, greenskeeper, white composition, very scarce, 3-7/8" ............................................. 450
4247FK, 1973, 7 Dot, white composition, rare, 3-7/8" ............................................. 450

**62048SP, Tested XX, long pull, green bone, 4", $600.**
RM2048SP, 1920-40, Tested XX, Christmas tree, 4" . 700
92048, 1920-40, Tested XX, onyx, 4" ......................... 550
GS2048, 1920-40, Tested XX, goldstone, 4" .............. 550
R2048, 1920-40, Tested XX, candy stripe, 4" ............ 550
32048SP, 1940-64, XX, yellow composition, 4" ......... 125
62048SP, 1940-55, XX, green bone, 4" ....................... 350
62048SP, 1940-64, XX, red bone, 4" ........................... 150
62048SP, 1940-64, XX, Rogers bone, 4" ..................... 250
62048SP, 1940-64, XX, bone, 4" .................................. 125
32048SP, 1965-69, USA, yellow composition, 4" ......... 75
62048SP, 1965-69, USA, delrin, 4" ............................... 50
62048SP, 1965-69, USA, bone stag, 4" ...................... 100
62048SPSSP, 1965-69, USA, delrin, 4" ........................ 60
62048SPSSP, 1965-69, USA, (first model), stainless, polished, master blade etched "Tested XX Stainless", bone, 4" ............................................. 175
62048SPSSP, 1965-69, USA, stainless, polished edge, bone, 4" ............................................. 100
62048SPSSP, 1965-69, USA, stainless, polished blade, bone, 4" ............................................. 150
32048SP, 1970, 10 Dot, yellow composition, 4" ......... 100
62048SP, 1970, 10 Dot, delrin, 4" ................................ 50
62048SPSSP, 1970, 10 Dot, stainless, polished edge, delrin, 4" ............................................. 50

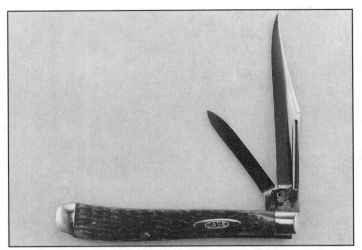

**62049LP, 1920-40, Tested XX, green bone, 4-1/8", $1,500.**
**62049PEN**, Tested XX, green bone, 4" ................... **1,500**

**6249, 1940-55, XX, copperhead, green bone, 3-15/16", $800.**
**P249**, 1920-40, Tested XX, mottled brown, 3-15/16" **1,200**
**6249**, 1920-40, Tested XX, rough black, 3-15/16" ... **1,200**
**6249**, 1920-40, Tested XX, green bone, 3-15/16"..... **1,500**
**9249**, 1920-40, Tested XX, imitation pearl, 3-15/16"
................................................................................ **1,250**
**6249**, 1940-64, XX, red bone, 3-15/16" ...................... **450**
**6249**, 1940-64, XX, early Rogers bone, 3-5/16" ....... **1,000**
**6249**, 1940-49, XX, rough black, 3-5/16" .................... **800**
**6249**, 1940-64, XX, bone, 3-15/16" ............................ **300**
**6249**, 1965-69, USA, bone, 3-15/16" .......................... **200**
**6249**, 1970, 10 Dot, bone, 3-15/16" ............................ **200**
**6250**, 1920-40, Tested XX, green bone, 4-3/8" ......... **1,800**
**6250**, 1940-55, XX, sunfish, green bone, 4-3/8" ...... **1,500**
**6250**, 1940-64, XX, red bone, 4-3/8" ......................... **650**
**6250**, 1940-64, XX, bone stag, 4-3/8" ........................ **400**
**6250**, 1940-64, XX, laminated wood, 4-3/8" ............. **200**
**6250**, 1965-69, USA, laminated wood, 4-3/8" ........... **150**
**6250**, 1965-69, USA, bone stag, 4-3/8" ..................... **500**
**6250**, 1970, 10 Dot, laminated wood, 4-3/8" ............. **150**

**6251 F, Tested XX, hobo, green bone, 5-1/4", $1,250.**
**6251**, 1920-40, Tested XX, knife-fork combination,
green bone, 5-1/4" .......................................................... **1,250**
**6251**, 1920-40, Tested XX, knife-fork combination,
Rogers bone, early, 5-1/4" ............................................. **1,400**
**9251**, 1920-40, Tested XX, knife-fork combination,
imitation onyx, 5-1/4" ..................................................... **1,000**

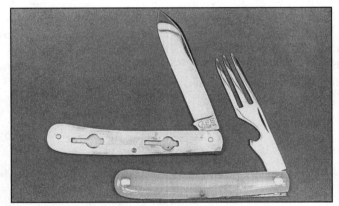

**3252, Tested XX, hobo, yellow, 3-3/4", $600.**
**6252**, 1920-40, Tested XX, hobo, knife-fork combination,
green bone, 3-3/4" .......................................................... **800**

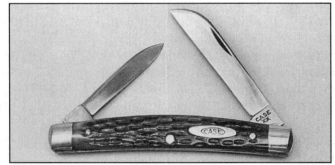

**62052, 1940-55, Tested XX, green bone, 3-1/2", $900.**
**52052**, 1920-40, Tested XX, stag, 3-1/2" ................... **900**
**62052**, 1920-40, Tested XX, early Rogers bone, 3-1/2"
............................................................................................ **1,000**
**62052**, 1940-49, XX, rough black, 3-1/2" ................... **250**
**62052**, 1940-64, XX, red bone, 3-1/2" ........................ **200**
**62052**, 1965-69, USA, bone, 3-1/2" ............................ **100**
**62052**, 1970, 10 Dot, bone, 3-1/2" .............................. **100**

Case Knives Tested (1920-1971)  199

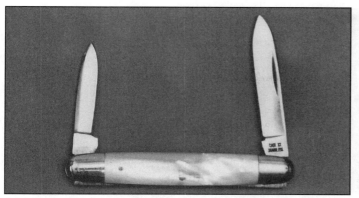

*82053SS, XX, pearl, w/bolsters, 2-3/4", $150.*

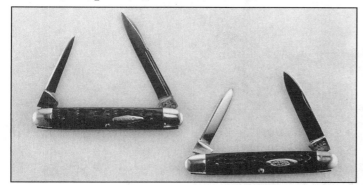

*Top: 6253LP, Tested XX, green bone, 3-1/4", $225.*
*Bottom: 6253, Tested XX, green bone, 3-1/4", $225.*

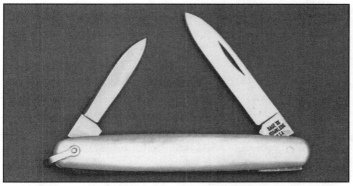

**82053SRSS, USA, pearl, 2-13/16", $90.**
**GS2053**, Tested XX, goldstone ..................................... 250
**5253**, 1920-40, Tested XX, stag, 3-1/4" ....................... 200
**5253LP**, 1920-40, Tested XX, stag, 3-1/4" ................... 250
**6253**, 1920-40, Tested XX, green bone, 3-1/4" ............ 225
**62053**, 1920-40, Tested XX, green bone, bolsters, 2-3/4"
..................................................................................... 225
**82053SR**, 1920-40, Tested XX, pearl, 2-13/16" ........... 225
**9253**, 1920-40, Tested XX, imitation pearl, 3-1/4" ..... 150
**62053SS**, 1940-64, XX, bone, bolsters, 2-3/4", ............ 175
**82053SR**, 1940-64, XX, genuine pearl, 2-13/16" ........ 100
**82053SS**, 1940-64, XX, stainless, genuine pearl, 2-13/16"
..................................................................................... 100
**62053SS**, 1965-69, USA, bone, w/bolsters, rare, 2-3/4"
..................................................................................... 225
**82053SRSS**, 1965-69, USA, stainless, genuine pearl,
2-13/16" ......................................................................... 90

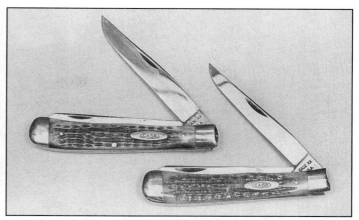

*Top: 5254, USA, reg. blade, second-cut stag, 4-1/8",*
*$800.*
*Bottom: 5254, USA, muskrat, second-cut stag, 4-1/8",*
*$1,000.*

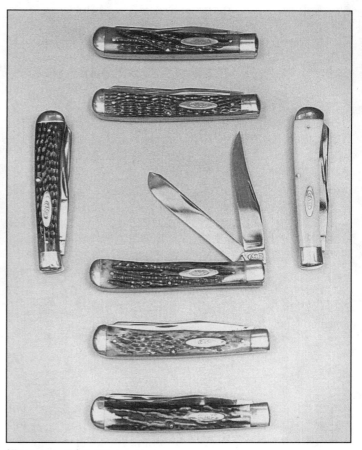

*Trapper 54 pattern*
*Top to bottom:*
*5254, Tested XX, red stag, 4-1/8", $6,000.*
*6254, Tested XX, green bone, 4-1/8", $6,000.*
*5254, (blades open), Tested XX, second-cut stag,*
*4-1/8", $6,000.*
*6254, XX w/Tested frame, Rogers bone, 4-1/8", $6,500.*
*Left: 6254, Tested XX, red bone, 4-1/8", $3,000.*
*Right: 3254, Tested XX, yellow composition, 4-1/8",*
*$3,000.*

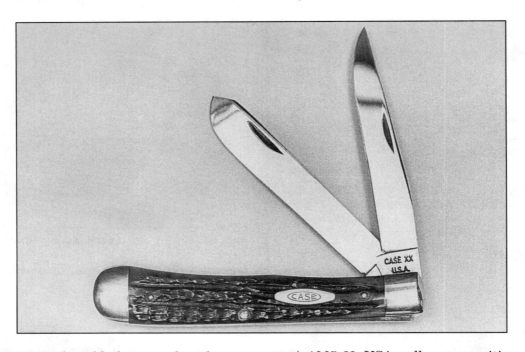

**6254, USA, trapper, muskrat blade, second-cut bone, 4-1/8", $800.**

3254, 1920-40, Tested XX, yellow composition, rare, 4-1/8" ............................................................ 3,500
5254, 1920-40, Tested XX, red stag, rare, 4-1/8" .... 6,000
5254, 1920-40, Tested XX, stag, 4-1/8" .................... 4,500
5254, 1920-40, Tested XX, second-cut stag, rare, 4-1/8" ............................................................................. 6,500
6254, 1920-40, Tested XX, green bone, 4-1/8" ......... 6,000
6254, 1920-40, Tested XX, red bone, rare, 4-1/8" .... 4,500
6254, 1920-40, Tested XX, early Rogers bone, rare, 4-1/8" ............................................................................. 6,500
9254, 1920-40, Tested XX, imitation pearl, 4-1/8" .. 4,500
6254, 1920-40, Tested XX, Winterbottom bone, 4-1/8" ............................................................................. 7,000
3254, 1940-64, XX, yellow composition, 4-1/8" .......... 300
3254, 1940-64, XX, Tested frame, first model, yellow composition, 4-1/8" ....................................................... 350
3254, 1940-64, XX, Tested frame, first model, flat yellow, 4-1/8" .................................................................. 375
5254, 1940-64, XX, stag, 4-1/8" ..................................... 650
5254, 1940-64, XX, Tested frame, first model, stag, 4-1/8" .................................................................................. 800
5254, 1940-64, XX, red stag, rare, 4-1/8" ................. 2,000
6254, 1940-55, XX, Tested frame, first model, green bone, rare, 4-1/8" ........................................................ 3,000
6254, 1940-64, XX, trapper, red bone, 4-1/8" ............. 800
6254, Tested frame, XX, first model, red bone........ 1,800
6254, 1940-64, XX, bone, 4-1/8" .................................... 700
6254, 1940-64, XX, Tested frame, first model, bone, 4-1/8" .................................................................................. 900
6254, 1940-64, XX, second-cut stag, rare, 4-1/8" .... 4,500
6254, 1940-42, XX, Tested frame, Rogers bone, rare, 4-1/8" .............................................................................. 5,500

3254, 1965-69, USA, yellow composition, 4-1/8" ....... 150
3254, 1965-69, USA, flat yellow, 4-1/8" ...................... 200
3254, 1965-69, USA, muskrat blade, flat yellow, rare, 4-1/8" .................................................................................. 600
3254, 1965-69, USA, muskrat blade, yellow composition, 4-1/8" ....................................................... 500
5254, 1965-69, USA, stag, 4-1/8" ................................... 300
5254, 1965-69, USA, muskrat blade, stag, 4-1/8" ...... 650
6254, 1965-69, USA, bone, 4-1/8" .................................. 250
6254, 1965-69, USA, muskrat blade, bone, 4-1/8" ..... 600
6254, 1965-69, USA, regular blade, second-cut, 4-1/8" .................................................................................. 800
6254SSP, 1965-69, USA, both blades stamped "Case XX, Stainless", 4-1/8" ............................................................ 750
6254SSP, 1965-69, USA, polished blades, bone, 4-1/8" .................................................................................. 350
6254SSP, 1965-69, USA, polished edge, bone, 4-1/8". 300
6254SSP, 1965-69, USA, muskrat blade, polished edge bone, 4-1/8" ...................................................................... 650
6254SSP, 1965-69, USA, muskrat blade, polished blade bone, 4-1/8" ...................................................................... 650
6254SSP, 1965-69, USA, first model, ("Tested XX Stainless" etched lengthwise on master blade) bone, 4-1/8" .................................................................................. 400
3254, 1970, 10 Dot, yellow composition, 4-1/8" ......... 150
3254, 1970, 10 Dot, flat yellow, 4-1/8" ......................... 300
5254, 1970, 10 Dot, stag, 4-1/8" .................................... 300
5254, 1970, 10 Dot, second-cut stag, very rare, 4-1/8" ............................................................................. 2,000
6254, 1970, 10 Dot, bone, 4-1/8" ................................... 250
6254SSP, 1970, 10 Dot, polished edge bone, 4-1/8".... 250
6254SSP, 1970, 10 Dot, large stamp bone, 4-1/8" ...... 450
6254SSP, 1970, 10 Dot, gut blade proto (6 made), 4-1/8" .................................................................................. 700

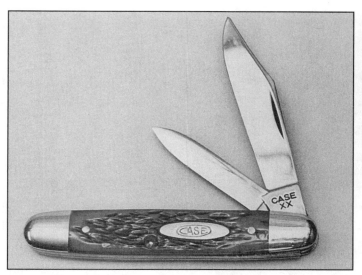

**62055, XX, Rogers bone, 3-1/2", $450.**
22055, 1920-40, Tested XX, slick black, 3-1/2" .......... 300
22055LP, 1920-40, Tested XX, slick black composition, 3-1/2" ................................................................. 350
32055, 1920-40, Tested XX, yellow composition, 3-1/2" ................................................................. 350
32055, 1920-40, Tested XX, long pull, yellow composition, 3-1/2" ....................................................... 400
62055, 1920-40, Tested XX, green bone, 3-1/2" .......... 400
62055LP, Tested XX, green bone ............................... 450
62055, 1920-40, Tested XX, long pull, rough black, 3-1/2" ................................................................. 350
92055, 1920-40, Tested XX, imitation pearl, 3-1/2"... 350
92055LP, Tested XX, imitation pearl, 3-1/2" ............... 350
62055, 1940-49, XX, rough black, 3-1/2" ..................... 250
62055, 1940-49 XX, long pull, rough black, 3-1/2" .... 350
62055, 1940-55, XX, green bone, 3-1/2" ..................... 350
62055, 1940-55, XX, long pull, green bone, 3-1/2" ..... 450
62055, 1940-64, XX, red bone, 3-1/2" ........................ 200
22055, 1940-64, XX, slick black, 3-1/2" ...................... 125
22055, 1940-64, XX, long pull, slick black, 3-1/2" ..... 200
62055, 1940-64, XX, bone, 3-1/2" ............................... 150
92055, 1940-64, XX, cracked ice, 3-1/2" ..................... 300
92055, 1940-64, XX, long pull, cracked ice, 3-1/2"..... 350
22055, 1965-69, USA, slick black, 3-1/2" .................... 185
62055, 1965-69, USA, bone, 3-1/2" ............................ 100
62055, 1970, 10 Dot, bone, 3-1/2" .............................. 100

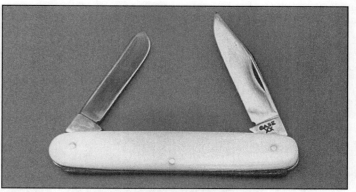

**4257, XX, white composition, 3-3/4", $75.**
4257, 1920-40, Tested XX, white composition, 3-3/4" ................................................................. 100
4257, 1940-64, XX, "Office Knife" on handle, white composition, 3-3/4" ....................................................... 125
42057, 1920-40, Tested XX, white composition, 3-5/16" ................................................................. 100
92057, 1920-40, Tested XX, imitation pearl, 3-5/16". 100
42057, 1940-64, XX, "Office Knife" on handle, white composition, 3-5/16" ....................................................... 125
42057, 1940-64, XX, office knife, plain handle, white composition, 3-5/16" ....................................................... 75

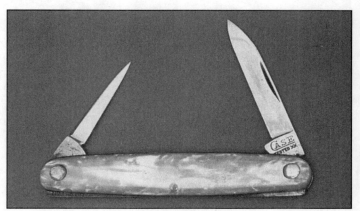

**92058, Tested XX, birdseye, French pearl, 3-1/4", $125**
32058, 1920-40, Tested XX, yellow composition, 3-1/4" ................................................................. 125
92058, 1920-40, Tested XX, imitation pearl, 3-1/4"... 125
92058, 1940-50, XX, cracked ice, 3-1/4" ..................... 125

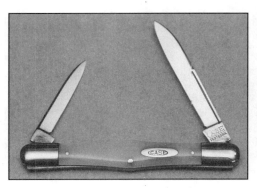

**32056, Case Tested XX, yellow/white liner, 3", $250.**

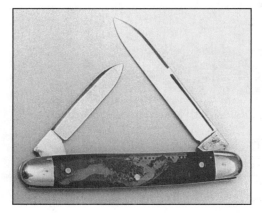

**HA2058LP, high art handles, regular bolsters, 3-1/4", $400.**

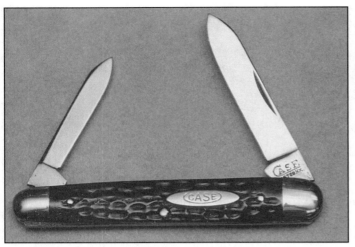

**62059, 1920-40, Tested XX, senator pen, green bone, 3-1/4", $250.**

**62059SP**, 1920-40, Tested XX, green bone, 3-1/4"...... 250
**62059**, 1920-40, citrus peeler, green bone, 3-1/4"...... 400
**62059-1/2**, 1920-40, Tested XX, green bone, 3-1/4"... 200

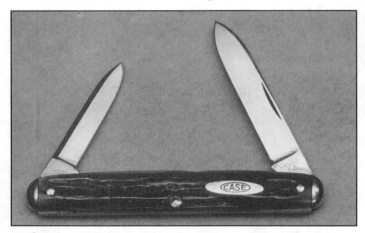

**5260, Tested XX, equal-end gentleman's knife, stag, $300.**

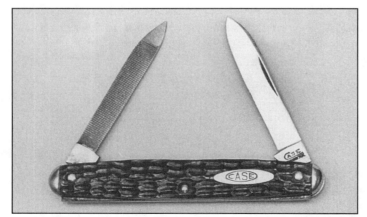

**6260F, 1920-40, Tested XX, green bone, tip bolsters, 3-7/16", $300.**

**5260**, 1920-40, Tested XX, stag, 3-7/16"...................... 300
**5260**, 1920-40, Tested XX, red stag, 3-7/16" .............. 400
**5260**, 1940-64, XX, stag, 3-7/16"................................ 300
**5260**, 1940-64, XX, red stag, 3-7/16" ......................... 400

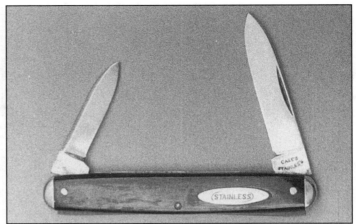

**P260T, Case's stainless (stainless shield), red plastic, 3-1/16", $300.**

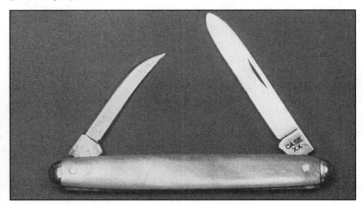

**8261, 1940-64, XX, pearl, 2-7/8", $100.**

**6261**, 1920-40, Tested XX, green bone, 2-7/8"............. 225
**6261F**, 1920-40, Tested XX, green bone, 2-7/8".......... 225
**8261**, 1920-40, Tested XX, genuine pearl, 2-7/8"....... 225
**8261F**, 1920-40, Tested XX, genuine pearl, 2-7/8"..... 250
**9261**, 1920-40, Tested XX, imitation pearl, 2-7/8"..... 125
**9261F**, 1920-40, Tested XX, imitation pearl, 2-7/8"... 125
**9261**, 1940-64, XX, imitation pearl, 2-7/8".................... 60
**9261**, 1940-64, XX, cracked ice, 2-7/8" ......................... 60
**8261**, 1965-6, USA, genuine pearl, 2-7/8" ..................... 90
**9261**, 1965-69, USA, imitation pearl, 2-7/8" ................. 60
**8261**, 1970, 10 Dot, genuine pearl, 2-7/8" .................. 100
**9261**, 1970, 10 Dot, imitation pearl, 2-7/8" .................. 60

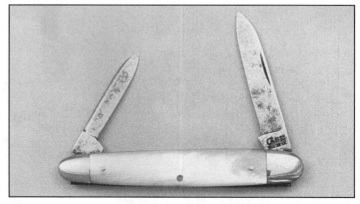

**82063, 1920-40, Tested XX, genuine pearl, 3-1/8", $225.**

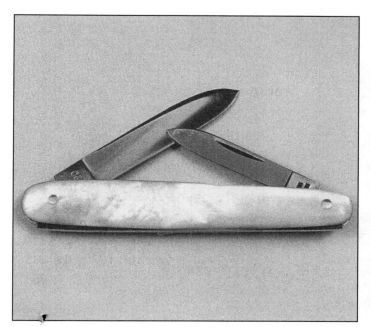

***82063, XX, pearl, SHAD, 3-1/16", $150.***
**82063**, 1920-40, Tested XX, genuine pearl, no bolster, 3-1/16" .................................................................. **200**
**82063SHADSS**, 1965-69, USA, genuine pearl, 3-1/16" ............................................................................... **300**
**62063SS**, 1940-64, XX, bone, 3-1/16" ........................... **100**
**62063**, 1940-55, XX, green bone, 3-1/16" ................... **200**

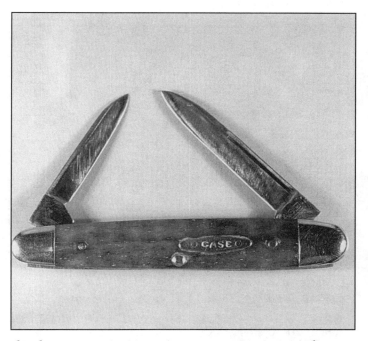

***62063LP, 1920-40, Tested XX, green bone, 3-1/16", $225.***
**62063SS**, 1940-64, XX, red bone, 3-1/16" .................... **125**

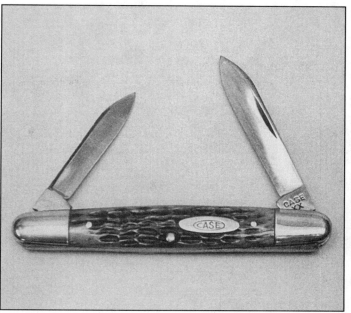

***06263, XX, nonstainless, green bone, 3-1/8", $225.***
**05263**, 1920-40, Tested XX, nonstainless, stag, 3-1/8" ............................................................................. **250**
**06263**, 1920-40, Tested XX, green bone, 3-1/8" .......... **225**
**08263**, 1920-40, Tested XX, genuine pearl, 3-1/8" ..... **250**
**06263SS**, 1940-55, XX, stainless, green bone, 3-1/8" ............................................................................. **200**
**06263SS**, 1940-64, XX, red bone, 3-1/8" ..................... **125**
**05263**, 1940-64, XX, nonstainless, stag, 3-1/8" .......... **300**
**05263SS**, 1940-64, XX, stag, 3-1/8" ............................ **150**
**06263**, 1940-64, XX, bone, 3-1/8" ............................... **125**
**06263SS**, 1940-64, XX, bone, 3-1/8" ........................... **100**
**05263SS**, 1965-69, USA, stag, 3-1/8" .......................... **100**
**06263FSS**, 1965-69, USA, bone, 3-1/8" ........................ **65**
**06263SSP**, 1965-69, USA, polished blade, bone, 3-1/8" ............................................................................... **65**
**06263SSP**, 1965-69, USA, polished edge, bone, 3-1/8" ............................................................................... **65**
**06263SSP**, 1965-69, USA, master blade etched "Tested XX Stainless," first model, brushed finish bone, 3-1/8" ............................................................................. **100**
Also polished finish.
**05263SS**, 1970, 10 Dot, stag, 3-1/8" ............................ **125**
**06263SS**, 1970, 10 Dot, bone, 3-1/8" ............................ **65**
**06263SSP**, 1970, 10 Dot, polished blade, bone, 3-1/8" ............................................................................... **65**
**06263FSSP**, 1970, 10 Dot, polished blade, bone, 3-1/8" ............................................................................... **65**
**06263FS**, 1970, 10 Dot, bone, 3-1/8" ............................ **65**

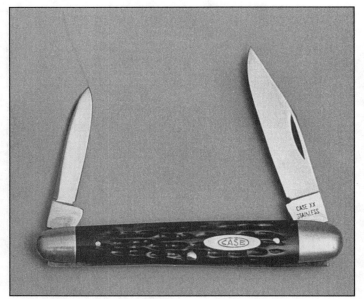

***62063-1/2, XX, stainless, bone, 3-1/16", $200.***
62063-1/2, 1920-40, Tested XX, green bone, 3-1/16". **250**
**82063-1/2**, 1920-40, Tested XX, genuine pearl, 3-1/16" ............................................................................ **250**
**92063-1/2**, 1920-40, Tested XX, imitation pearl, 3-1/16" ............................................................................ **175**
62063-1/2, 1940-55, XX, green bone, 3-1/16" ............ **225**
62063-1/2SS, 1940-64, XX, red bone, 3-1/16" ............ **125**
92063-1/2, 1940-64, XX, imitation pearl, 3-1/16" ...... **100**

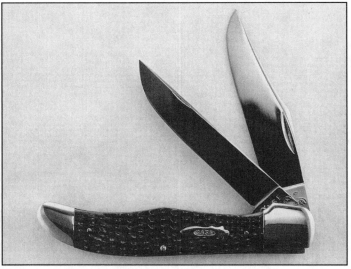

***6265, Tested XX, flat, thin frame, green bone, rare, 5-1/4", $1,500.***

***6265, Top thin frame; bottom regular frame. There really is a difference.***

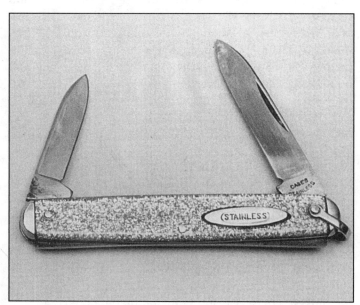

***GS264R, Case's stainless, goldstone, 3-1/8", $250.***
**6264T**, 1920-40, Tested XX, green bone, tip bolster, 3-1/8" ............................................................................ **250**
**6264TF**, 1920-40, Tested XX, green bone, 3-1/8" ....... **250**
**8264T**, 1920-40, Tested XX, genuine pearl, 3-1/8" ..... **275**
**8264TF**, 1920-40, Tested XX, genuine pearl, 3-1/8" ... **275**
**9264TF**, 1920-40, Tested XX, imitation pearl, 3-1/8" ............................................................................ **150**

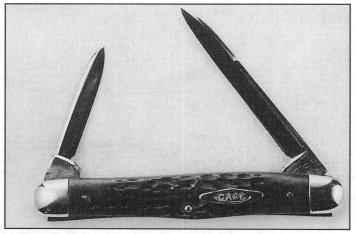

***6265LP, Tested XX, pattern number stamped on back of master blade, green bone, rare, 3-1/4", $400.***
**3265SAB**, 1920-40, Tested XX, yellow composition, 5-1/4" ............................................................................ **700**
**3265**, 1920-40, Tested XX, flat blade, yellow composition, 5-1/4" ............................................................................ **700**
**5265SAB**, 1920-40, Tested XX, stag, 5-1/4" ............... **800**
**5265**, 1920-40, Tested XX, flat blade stag, 5-1/4" ...... **850**
**5265**, 1920-40, Tested XX, flat blade, second-cut stag, 5-1/4" ............................................................................ **1,200**
**6265**, 1920-40, Tested XX, second-cut stag, 5-1/4" . **1,200**
**6265SAB**, 1920-40, Tested XX, green bone, 5-1/4" ..... **800**

# Case Knives Tested (1920-1971)

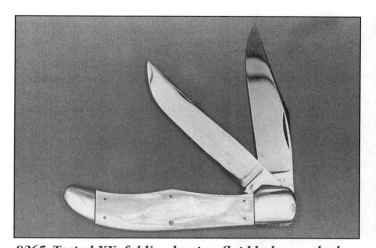

*9265, Tested XX, folding hunter, flat blade, cracked ice, 5-1/4", $800.*

**6265SAB**, 1940, Tested XX, rough black, 5-1/4" ......... **700**
**6265**, 1920-40, Tested XX, flat blade, green bone, 5-1/4" ................................................................ **1,000**
**9265SAB**, 1920-40, Tested XX, imitation pearl, 5-1/4" ................................................................ **900**
**9265**, 1920-40, Tested XX, flat blade, imitation pearl, 5-1/4" ................................................................ **900**
**5265**, 1940-64 XX, flat master blade, stag, 5-1/4" .. **1,000**
**5265SAB**, 1940-64, XX, stag, 5-1/4" ............................ **450**
**5265SABDR**, 1964, XX, stag, 5-1/4" ............................ **500**
**5265SAB**, 1940-64, XX, second-cut stag, 5-1/4" ....... **1,000**
**5265SAB**, 1940-64, XX, red stag, 5-1/4" ...................... **600**

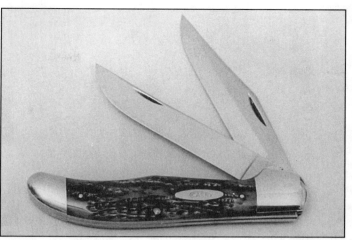

*6265Sab, XX, green bone, second-cut, grooved, $1,200 mint.*

**5265SABDR**, 1965-69, USA, stag, 5-1/4" ................... **250**
**5265SAB**, XX frame, USA, stag, bolsters not drilled ................................................................ **350**
**5265SABDR**, 1965-69, USA, XX frame, stag, 5-1/4" .. **300**
**6265SAB**, 1965-69, USA, XX frame, bone, 5-1/4" ....... **400**
**6265SABDR**, 1965-69, USA, skinning blade serrated, bone, 5-1/4" ................................................................ **450**
**6265SABDR**, 1965-69, USA, XX frame, wood, 5-1/4". **125**

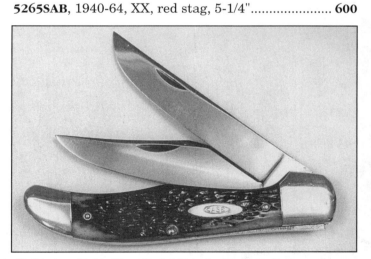

*6265SAB, 1940-64, XX, folding knife, late Rogers bone, 5-1/4", $750.*

**6265**, 1940-49, XX, flat blade, green bone, 5-1/4" ...... **850**
**6265SAB**, 1940-64, XX, red bone, 5-1/4" ...................... **450**
**6265**, 1940-64, XX, flat blade, red bone, 5-1/4" .......... **700**
**6265**, 1940-64, XX, flat ground master, bone, 5-1/4". **500**
**6265SAB**, 1940-64, XX, laminated wood, 5-1/4" ......... **175**
**6265SAB**, 1940-64, XX, bone, 5-1/4" ............................ **300**
**6265SAB**, 1940-50, XX, folding hunter, rough black, 5-1/4" ................................................................ **450**
**6265**, 1940-49, XX, flat blade, rough black, 5-1/4" .... **550**
**6265SAB**, 1940-55, XX, green bone, 5-1/4" ................. **700**

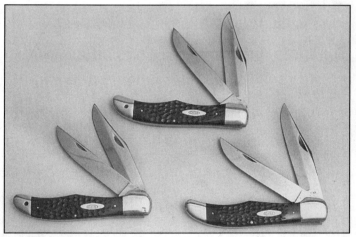

*Folding hunters*
*Top: 6265SAB, USA frame, pakkawood, drilled bolsters, 5-1/4", $100.*
*Left: 6265SAB, USA on XX frame, pakkawood, drilled bolster, 5-1/4", $125.*
*Right: 6265SAB, USA on XX frame, pakkawood, bolster not drilled, 5-1/4", $125. Pig's eye bolsters-pin made for Florida State Conservation Dept.*
*6265 for skinning alligators. Nickel pins broke easily, so they were changed to steel pins. Not in production, $150.*

**6265SAB-DR**, 1965-69, USA, wood, 5-1/4" .................... **80**
**6265SAB-DR**, 1965-69, USA, XX frame, bone, 5-1/4" ................................................................ **450**
**5265SAB-DR**, 1970, 10 Dot stag, 5-1/4" ...................... **300**
**6265SAB-DR**, 1970, 10 Dot wood, 5-1/4" .................... **100**

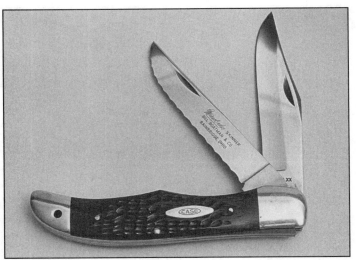

***6265SAB/DR, USA, Bill Boatman, folding hunter, serrated edge, pakkawood, 5-1/4", $225.***
**6265SAB**, 1940-64, XX, Bill Boatman, serrated, red bone, 5-1/4" .................................................................. 550
**6265SAB**, 1940-64, XX, Bill Boatman Special, small blade, serrated, laminated wood, 5-1/4", ..................... 300
**6265SAB**, 1940-64, XX, Bill Boatman Special, small blade, serrated, bone, 5-1/4" ..................................... 500
**6265SAB DR**, 1940-64, XX, Bill Boatman Special, small blade, serrated, bone, 5-1/4" ............................... 500
**6265SAB DR**, 1940-64, XX, Bill Boatman, serrated, small blade, laminated wood, 5-1/4" ........................... 250
**6265SAB DR**, 1965-69, USA, Bill Boatman, serrated, small blade, wood, 5-1/4" .......................................... 250
**6265SAB DR**, 1970, 10 Dot, Bill Boatman, wood, 5-1/4" ......................................................................... 250

Note: All Boatman serrated-blade folding hunters are quite scarce.

***06267, USA, bone, 3-1/4", $175.***
06267, 1940, Tested XX, rough black, 3-1/4" .............. 250
06267, 1920-40, Tested XX, cracked ice, 3-1/4" ......... 250
06267, 1920-40, Tested XX, early Rogers bone, 3-1/4" ................................................................................. 350
06267, 1920-40, Tested XX, green bone, 3-1/4" ......... 325
06267, 1940-64, XX, long pull, bone, 3-1/4" ............... 200

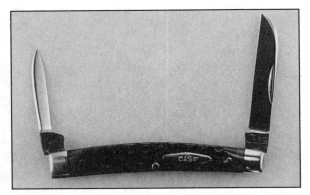

*Top: 6269, 1920-40, Tested XX, green bone, 3", $350*
*Bottom: 6268, 1920-40, Tested XX, green bone, 3-1/4", $350.*

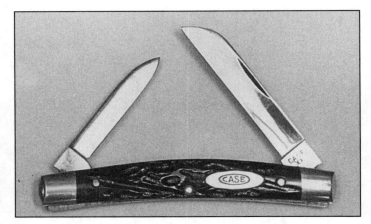

***6269, 1940-49, XX, rough black, 3", $150.***
6269, 1920-40, Tested XX, rough black, 3" ............... 300
6269, 1920-40, Tested XX, green bone, 3" ................. 350
8269, 1920-40, Tested XX, genuine pearl, 3" ............. 400
9269, 1920-40, Tested XX, imitation pearl, 3" ........... 300
6269LP, 1940-49, XX, rough black, 3" ....................... 200
6269, 1940-55, XX, green bone, 3" ............................. 250
6269LP, 1940-55, XX, green bone, 3" ......................... 350
6269, 1940-64 XX, red bone, 3" .................................. 150
6269, 1940-64, XX, bone, 3" ....................................... 110
6269, 1965-69, USA, bone, 3" ....................................... 85
6269, 1970, 10 Dot, bone ............................................... 85
6270F, 1920-40, Tested XX, bone, 3" .......................... 500

Case Knives Tested (1920)

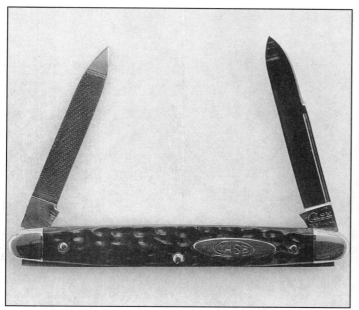

**6271 Tested XX, FLP, green bone, 3-1/4", $400.**

**8271**, 1940-64, XX, regular pull, pearl, 3-1/4" ........... **250**
**8271**, XX, pearl, straight bolsters & pins, 3-1/4" ....... **250**
**RM271**, Case's stainless, red-black Christmas tree, also goldstone, 3-1/4" .................................................. **300**
**6271F**, 1920-40, Tested XX, bone, flat bolsters, 3-1/4" ................................................................................ **250**
**8271**, 1920-40, Tested XX, genuine pearl, 3-1/4" ....... **250**
**8271F**, 1920-40, Tested XX, genuine pearl, 3-1/4" ..... **250**
**9271**, XX, cracked ice ................................................. **200**
**6271**, 1940-64, XX, red bone, 3-1/4" ........................... **200**
**6271 SS**, 1940-64, XX, bone, 3-1/4" ............................ **200**
**8271**, 1940-64, XX, long pull, genuine pearl, 3-1/4" .. **300**
**8271SS**, 1940-64, XX, genuine pearl, 3-1/4" ............... **250**
**8271SS**, 1940-64, XX, long pull, genuine pearl, 3-1/4" ................................................................................ **300**
**8271SSFLP**, 1940-64, XX, genuine pearl, 3-1/4" ......... **300**
**8271F**, 1940-64, XX, genuine pearl, 3-1/4" .................. **300**
**8271F**, 1940-64, XX, long pull, genuine pearl, 3-1/4" ................................................................................ **300**
**22074-1/2PU**, 1920-40, Tested XX, slick black, 3-1/4" ................................................................................ **250**
**62074-1/2**, 1920-40, Tested XX, green bone ............... **350**

*[handwritten: 62074½ LONG PULL CROWN BLADE]*

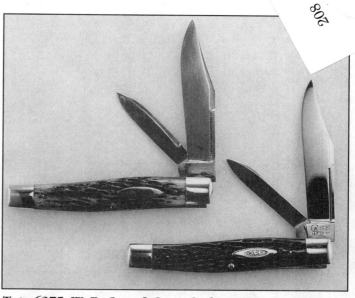

*Top: 6275, W. R. Case & Sons Cutlery Co., pen, early Rogers bone, 4-1/4", $1,500.*
*Bottom: 6275, Tested XX, pen, green bone, 4-1/4", $1,200.*

**5275SP**, 1920-40, Tested XX, long pull, stag, 4-1/4" ................................................................................ **1,200**
**6275SP LP**, 1920-40, Tested XX, green bone, 4-1/4" ................................................................................ **1,200**
**6275SP**, 1920-40, Tested XX, rough black, 4-1/4" ...... **800**
**6275SP**, 1940-50, XX, long pull, rough black, 4-1/4" ................................................................................ **800**
**6275SP**, 1940-64, XX red bone, 4-1/4" ....................... **450**
**6275SP**, 1940-64, XX, long pull, red bone, 4-1/4" ....... **500**
**6275SP**, 1940-64, XX, bone, 4-1/4" .............................. **200**
**6275SP**, 1940-55, XX, regular pull, green bone, 4-1/4" ................................................................................ **550**
**6275SP**, 1965-69, USA, bone, 4-1/4" ............................ **150**
**6275SP**, 1970, 10 Dot, bone, 4-1/4" .............................. **150**
**6276**, 1920-40, Tested XX, green bone, 3-5/8" ............ **550**

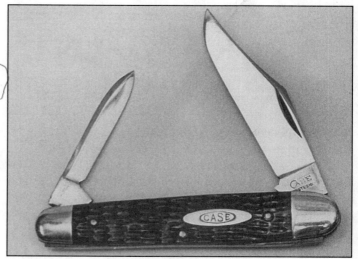

*6276-1/2, Tested XX, sleeveboard, green bone, 3-5/8", $450.*

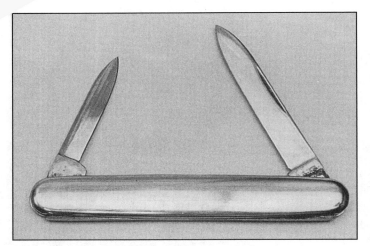

*M279, Tested XX, all metal, 3-1/8", $95.*

*M279, Case's stainless, sterling, 3-1/8", $250*

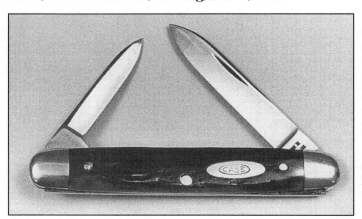

*5279SS, XX, red stag, 3-1/8", $225.*
RM279, 1920-40, Tested XX, Christmas tree, 3-1/8"
................................................................................. 300
GM279, 1920-40, Tested XX, green mottled, 3-1/8" ... 200
M279R, 1920-40, Tested XX, metal, 3-1/8" ................. 90
2279, 1920-40, Tested XX, slick black, 3-1/8" ............ 100
3279, 1920-40, Tested XX, yellow composition, 3-1/8"
................................................................................. 125
3279R, 1920-40, Tested XX, yellow composition, 3-1/8"
................................................................................. 125

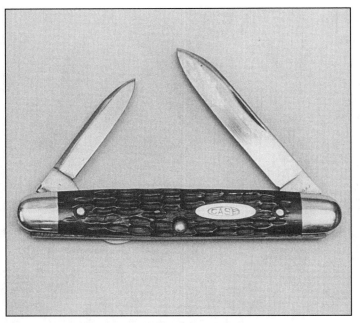

*6279, Tested XX, green bone, 3-1/8", $250.*
*8279SHAD, 1920-40, Tested XX, genuine pearl, 3-1/8", $225.*
82079, 1920-40, Tested XX, genuine pearl, 3-1/4" ..... 250
M279SS, 1940-64, XX, metal, 3-1/8" ............................ 40
6279SS, 1940-64, XX, red bone, 3-1/8" ...................... 125
6279, 1940-64, XX, bone, 3-1/8" ................................. 125
6279SSF, 1940-64, XX, bone, 3-1/8" ........................... 125
6279SS, 1940-64, XX, bone, 3-1/8" ............................. 100

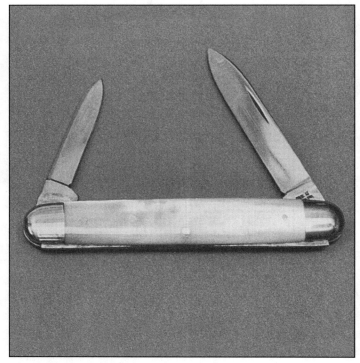

*8279, Tested XX, pearl, 3-1/8", $150.*

*8279F, Tested XX, pearl, 3-1/8", $200.*

| | |
|---|---|
| 8279, 1940-64, XX, genuine pearl, 3-1/8" | 150 |
| 8279SS, 1940-64, XX, genuine pearl, 3-1/8" | 125 |
| 9279, 1940-64, XX, imitation pearl, 3-1/8" | 100 |
| 9279SSHAD, 1940-64, XX, cracked ice, 3-1/8" | 45 |
| 9279SS, 1940-64, XX, cracked ice, bolsters, 3-1/8" | 100 |
| M279SC, 1965-69, USA, stainless, 3-1/8" | 45 |
| 2279SSHAD, 1940-64, XX, slick black, 3-1/8" | 100 |
| M279SS, 1965-69, USA, polished stainless, 3-1/8" | 40 |
| M279SS, 1965-69, USA, stainless, 3-1/8" | 40 |
| M279SSF, 1965-69, USA, stainless, 3-1/8" | 40 |
| 5279SS, 1965-69, USA, stag, 3-1/8" | 300 |
| 6279SS, 1965-69, USA, bone, 3-1/8" | 75 |
| 6279SS, 1965-69, USA, transition (XX to USA) bone, 3-1/8" | 135 |
| M279SCSS, 1970, 10 Dot, stainless, 3-1/8" | 40 |
| M279SSF, 1970, 10 Dot, stainless, 3-1/8" | 30 |
| 6279SS, 1970, 10 Dot, bone, 3-1/8" | 45 |
| M279SS, 1970, 10 Dot, metal, 3-1/8" | 45 |
| M279SSF, 1940-64, XX, metal, 3-1/8" | 35 |
| 5279, 1940-64, XX, stag, 3-1/8" | 300 |
| 5279SS, 1940-64, XX, stag, 3-1/8" | 150 |
| 6279, 1940-49, XX, rough black, 3-1/8" | 150 |
| 6279SS, 1940-49, XX, rough black, 3-1/8" | 125 |
| 6279SSF, 1940-49, XX, rough black, 3-1/8" | 125 |
| 6279, 1940-55, XX, green bone, 3-1/8" | 225 |
| 6279SS, 1940-55, XX, green bone, 3-1/8" | 200 |
| 6279SSF, 1940-55, XX, green bone, 3-1/8" | 200 |

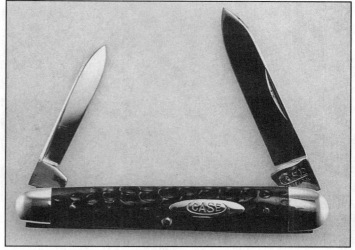

*62079, Tested XX, green bone, 3-1/4", $300.*

| | |
|---|---|
| 62079, Tested XX, spear blade, green bone, 3-1/4" | 300 |
| 92079, Tested XX, imitation pearl, 3-1/4" | 200 |
| 62079-1/2, 1920-40, Tested XX, green bone, 3-1/4" | 250 |
| 82079-1/2, 1920-40, Tested XX, genuine pearl, 3-1/4" | 275 |
| 92079-1/2, 1920-40, Tested XX, cracked ice, 3-1/4" | 200 |
| 62079-1/2, 1940-64, XX, bone, 3-1/4" | 150 |
| 62079-1/2SS, 1940-55, XX, green bone, 3-1/4" | 200 |
| 62079-1/2, 1940-49, XX, rough black, 3-1/4" | 150 |

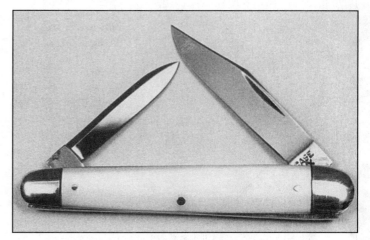

*82079-1/2, 1940-64, XX, pearl, 3-1/4", $150.*

| | |
|---|---|
| 82079-1/2SS, 1940-64, XX, genuine pearl, 3-1/4" | 100 |
| 92079-1/2, 1940-64, XX, imitation pearl, 3-1/4" | 100 |
| 92079-1/2, 1940-64, XX, cracked ice, 3-1/4" | 100 |
| 82079-1/2SS, 1965-69, USA, genuine pearl, 3-1/4" | 90 |
| 82079-1/2SS, 1970, 10 Dot, genuine pearl, 3-1/4" | 90 |
| 6281, 1920-40, Tested XX, doctor's knife, green bone, 3-1/8" | 1,200 |
| 8281, 1920-40, Tested XX, doctor's knife, pearl, 3-1/8" | 1,200 |
| 9281, 1920-40, Tested XX, doctor's knife, imitation pearl, 3-1/8" | 900 |
| GS281, 1920-40, Tested XX, doctor's knife, goldstone, 4" | 1,000 |

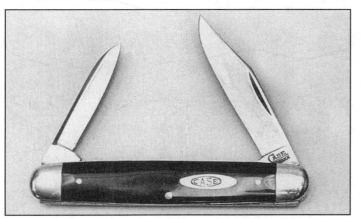

*2279-1/2, Tested XX, slick black, 3-1/4", $150.*

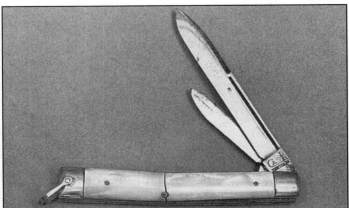

*9282R, Tested XX, doctor's knife, long pull, imitation cracked ice, handle cracked, 2-3/4", $600.*
**B282**, 1920-40, Tested XX, doctor's knife, waterfall, 2-3/4" ................................................................. 700
**B282**, 1920-40, Tested XX, imitation onyx, 2-3/4" ..... 600
**5282**, 1920-40, Tested XX, stag, 2-3/4" ...................... 800
**6282**, 1920-40, Tested XX, green bone, 2-3/4" ........... 700
**6282**, 1920-40, Tested XX, early Rogers bone, 2-3/4" 800
**8282**, 1920-40, Tested XX, genuine pearl, 2-3/4" ....... 800

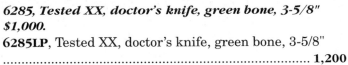

*6285, Tested XX, doctor's knife, green bone, 3-5/8" $1,000.*
**6285LP**, Tested XX, doctor's knife, green bone, 3-5/8" ................................................................................ 1,200

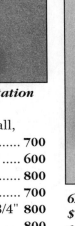

*62082, 1920-40, Tested XX, doctor's knife, long pull, green bone, 2-7/8", $850.*

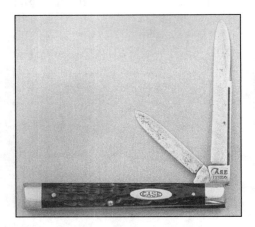

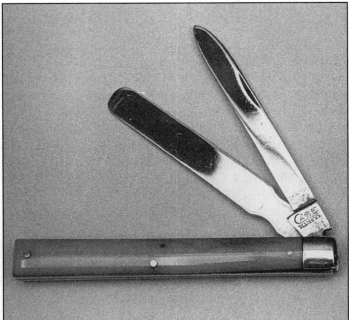

*B285, Tested XX, doctor's knife, waterfall, 3-5/8", $1,000.*
**RM285**, 1920-40, Tested XX, Christmas tree, 3-5/8" ................................................................................ 1,200
**3285**, 1920-40, Tested XX, yellow composition, 3-5/8" .................................................................................. 750
**7285**, 1920-40, Tested XX, tortoise, 3-5/8" ............. 1,000

*6285 doctor's knife w/bolsters, green bone, 3-5/8", Tested XX, $1,500.*

Case Knives Tested (1920-1971) 211

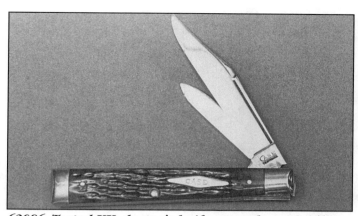

*62086, Tested XX, doctor's knife, green bone, 3-1/4", $900.*
**52086**, 1920-40, Tested XX, stag, 3-1/4"................. **1,000**
**62086**, 1920-40, Tested XX, early Rogers bone, 3-1/4"
......................................................................... **1,000**
**82086**, 1920-40, Tested XX, genuine pearl, 3-1/4".. **1,000**
**92086R**, 1920-40, Tested XX, imitation pearl, 3-1/4"
......................................................................... **750**

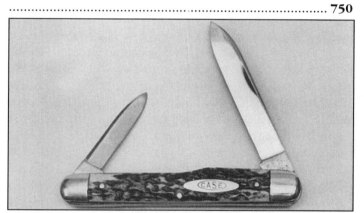

*5287, Tested XX, gunstock, stag, 3-1/2", $900.*
**8287**, 1920-40, Tested XX, pearl, 3-1/2" ................. **1,000**

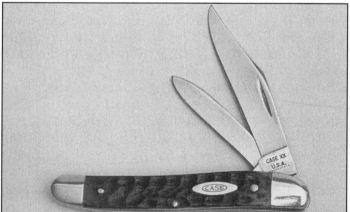

*62087, 10 Dot, bone, odd shield, 3-1/4", $65.*
**22087**, 1920-40, Tested XX, slick black, 3-1/4" ......... **135**
**42087**, 1920-40, Tested XX, white composition, 3-1/4"
......................................................................... **150**
**62087**, 1920-40, Tested XX, green bone, 3-1/4" ......... **175**
**22087**, 1940-64, XX, slick black, 3-1/4" ........................ **65**
**52087**, 1940-64, XX, stag, 3-1/4" ................................. **125**

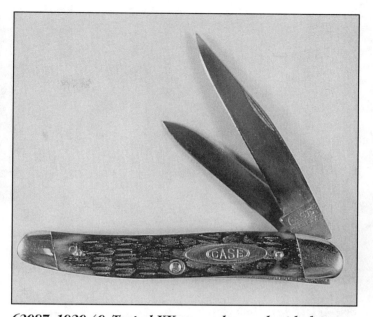

*62087, 1920-40, Tested XX, green bone, slant bolsters, rare, 3-1/4", $250.*
**62087**, 1940-64, XX, bone, 3-1/4" ................................. **75**
**62087**, 1940-49, XX, rough black, 3-1/4" .................... **125**
**62087**, 1940-55, XX, green bone, 3-1/4" ..................... **150**
**62087**, 1940-64, XX, red bone, 3-1/4" ......................... **100**
**22087**, 1965-69, USA, slick black, 3-1/4" ..................... **65**
**52087**, 1965-69, USA, stag, 3-1/4" ............................... **125**
**62087**, 1965-69, USA, bone, 3-1/4" ............................... **65**
**22087**, 1970, 10 Dot, slick black, 3-1/4" ....................... **65**
**52087**, 1970, 10 Dot, stag, 3-1/4" ................................. **125**
**62087**, 1970, 10 Dot, delrin, 3-1/4" ............................... **45**

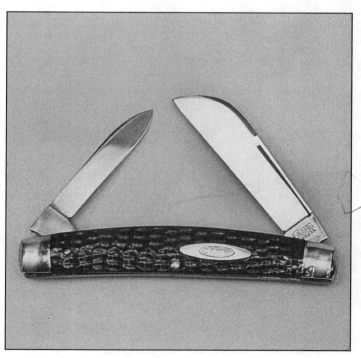

*6288, 1920-40, Tested XX, long pull, green bone, 4-1/8", $2,700.*

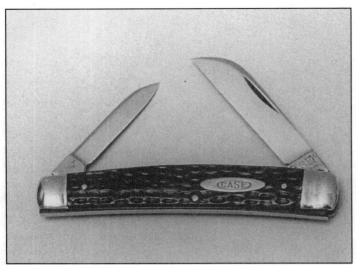

*62089, Tested XX, congress, green bone, 3-3/4", $2,800.*

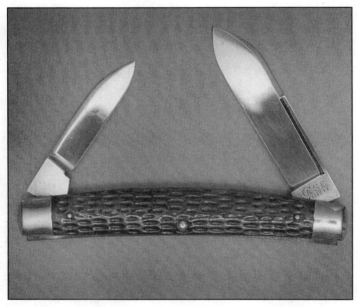

*6288LP, Case Tested XX, spear master blade, both blades stamped, green bone, no shield, 4-1/8", $2,500.*

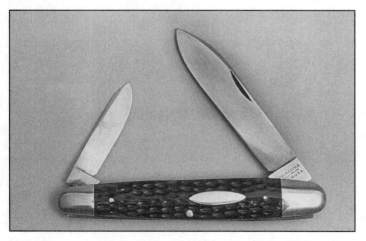

*6291, contract knife made by Case for Winchester, green bone, 4-1/2", $2,700.*

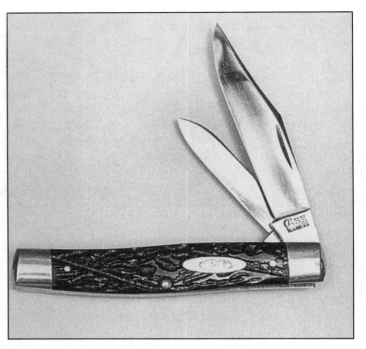

**6292, 1920-40, Tested XX, rough black, 4" $350.**
3292, 1920-40, Tested XX, yellow composition, 4"..... **300**
6292, 1920-40, Tested XX, green bone, 4"................. **350**
6292, 1940-49, XX, rough black, 4" ........................... **225**
6292, 1940-55, XX, green bone, 4"............................. **300**
6292, 1940-64, XX, red bone, 4"................................. **200**
6292, 1940-64, XX, bone, 4" ...................................... **150**
6292, 1965-69, USA, bone, 4" .................................... **100**
6292, 1970, 10 Dot, bone, 4" ..................................... **100**
32093F, 1920-40, Tested XX, yellow composition, 5"
............................................................................... **300**
62093F, 1920-40, Tested XX, green bone, 5" ............. **400**
32093F, 1945, Case's stainless, yellow celluloid, 5"
............................................................................... **300**
62093F, 1945, Case's stainless, green bone, 5" .......... **400**
6294, 1920-40, Tested XX, green bone, 4-1/4"......... **1,200**
6294LP, 1920-40, Tested XX, green bone, 4-1/4"..... **1,500**
6294LP, 1920-40, Tested XX, red bone, 4-1/4" ........ **1,200**
6294JL.P, 1920-40, Tested XX, green bone, 4-1/4"
............................................................................... **2,700**
6294LP, 1920-40, Tested XX, 2-blade gunboat, early Rogers bone, 4-1/4".................................................. **3,500**
6294, 1940-55, XX, green bone, 4-1/4" ..................... **800**
6294, 1940-64, XX, red bone, 4-1/4" ......................... **600**
6294LP, 1940-64, XX, red bone, 4-1/4" ..................... **900**
6294, 1940-64, XX, bone, 4-1/4"................................ **400**
6294LP, 1940-64, XX, bone, rare, 4-1/4".................... **700**

Case Knives Tested (1920-1971)   213

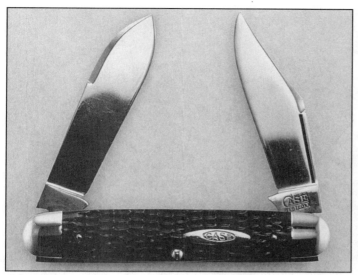

*6294J, Tested XX, green bone, 4-1/4", $2,700.*

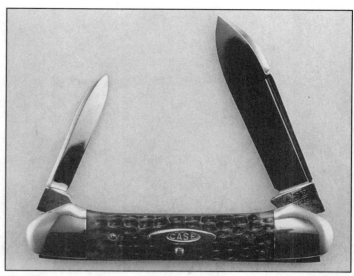

*6294X, Tested XX, gunboat, green bone, 4-1/4", $4,000.*

*6294J, Tested XX, green bone, flat grooved bolsters, 4-1/4", $3,000.*

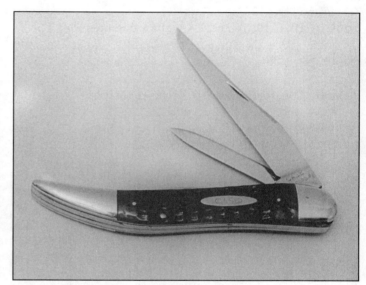

*62094, green bone, 4-1/4", $550.*

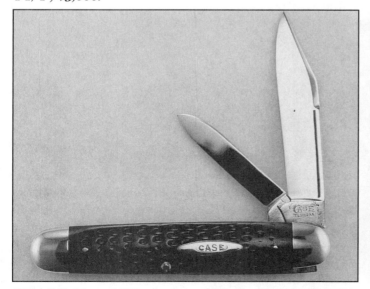

*6294-1/2, Tested XX, cigar, green bone, 4-1/4", $1,250.*

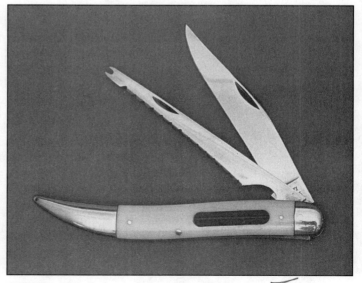

*32095F, XX, fish scaler, yellow, 5", $125.*

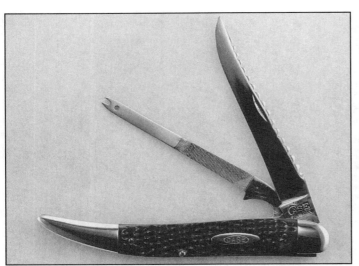

**62095F, 1920-40, Tested XX, green bone, 5", $450.**
RM2095F, 1920-40, Tested XX, fisherman's knife, Christmas tree, 5" ............................................. 450
32095F, 1920-40, Tested XX, yellow composition, 5" ............................................................................ 300
32095FSS, 1920-40, Tested XX, yellow composition, 5" ............................................................................ 300
32095F, Case's stainless, yellow composition ............ 300
32095F, 1940-41, XX, flat yellow, 5" ......................... 150
32095FSS, 1965-69, USA, yellow composition, 5" ...... 100
32095FSS, 1970, 10 Dot, yellow composition, 5" ........ 100

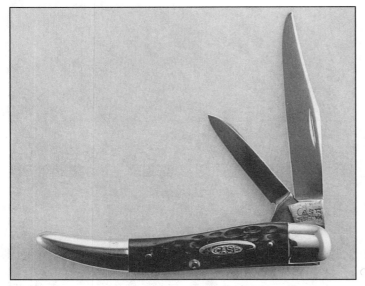

**62096, Tested XX, toothpick, green bone, 3-1/8", $450.**
RM2096, 1920-40, Tested XX, Christmas yellow, 3-1/8" ................................................................ 450
R2096, 1920-40, Tested XX, candy stripe, 3-1/8" ....... 450
62096, 1920-40, Tested XX, Rogers bone, 3-1/8" ........ 450
62096, 1920-40, Tested XX, Rogers bone, early, 3-1/8" ................................................................ 450
62096, 1920-40, Tested XX, green bone, 3-1/8" .......... 450
Note: RM2096, R2096 & the three 62096s are toothpick patterns.

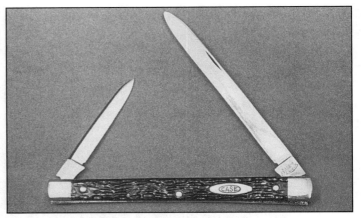

**6296X, Case's stainless, green bone, 4-1/4" $1,500.**
9296X, Case's stainless, cracked ice, 4-1/4" **1,250**

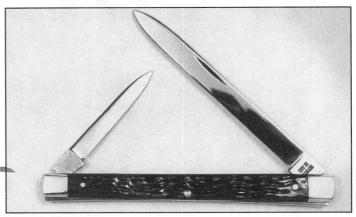

**6296XSS, XX, bone, 4-1/4", $450.**
6296X, 1920-40, Tested XX, stainless, green bone, half-oval, 4 -1/4" ............................................................ 1,500
6296X, XX, clip point, rare ........................................... 600
6296XSS, XX, red bone, 4-1/4" ..................................... 600
6296XSS, 1940-55, XX, green bone, 4-1/4" .............. 1,200
6296XSS, 1965-69, USA, bone, 4-1/4" ......................... 800

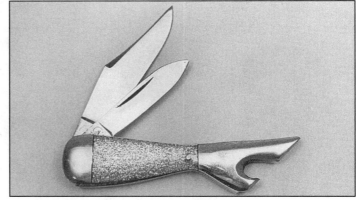

**GS297, Case Tested XX, leg, goldstone, 3-1/4", $400.**
R297, 1920-40, Tested XX, small leg, candy stripe.... 400
RM297, 1920-40, Tested XX, small leg, Christmas tree ................................................................ 450
3297, 1920-40, Tested XX, small leg, yellow composition ................................................................ 350
8297, 1920-40, Tested XX, small leg, genuine pearl.. 500

## Case Knives Tested (1920-1971)

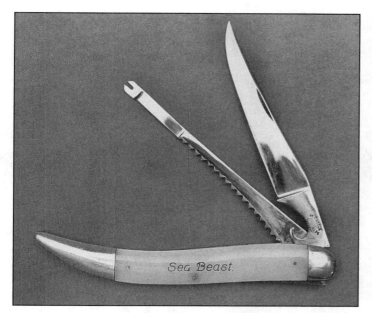

**92098F, Case's stainless, sea beast, imitation onyx, 5-1/2", $400.**
**RM2098F**, 1920-40, Tested XX, Christmas tree, 5-1/2" ................................................................ **600**
**92098F**, 1920-40, Tested XX, imitation onyx, 5-1/2" ................................................................ **400**
**32098F**, 1920-40, Tested XX, yellow composition, 5-1/2" ................................................................ **350**
**62098F**, 1920-40, Tested XX, green bone, 5-1/2"........ **650**
**62098F**, Case's stainless, green bone, 5-1/2".............. **600**

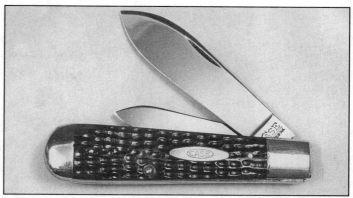

**6299, 1920-1940, Tested XX, green bone, 4-1/8", $500.**
**6299**, Tested XX, rough black ..................... **350**
**5299**, 1920-40, Tested XX, stag, 4-1/8" ....................... **700**
**6299**, 1940-64, XX, bone, 4-1/8" ................................. **450**
**6299**, 1940-49, XX, rough black, 4-1/8" ...................... **300**
**6299**, 1940-55, XX, green bone, 4-1/8" ...................... **500**
**GM2099R**, 1920-40, Tested XX, green mottled, 2-7/8" ................................................................ **150**
**82099R**, 1920-40, Tested XX, genuine pearl, 2-7/8"... **200**
Note: GM2099R & 82099R are senator/lobster.

**5299-1/2, 1965-69, USA, stag, 4-1/8", $225.**
**3299-1/2**, 1920-40, Tested XX, yellow composition, 4-1/8" ....................................................................... **300**
**5299-1/2**, 1920-40, Tested XX, stag, 4-1/8" ................ **700**
**6299-1/2**, 1920-40, Tested XX, green bone, 4-1/8" .. **1,000**
**6299-1/2**, 1940-55, XX, green bone, 4-1/8" ................ **600**
**3299-1/2**, 1940-64, XX, yellow composition, 4-1/8".... **150**
**3299-1/2**, 1940-64, XX, "A" blade, yellow composition, 4-1/8" ....................................................................... **175**
**3299-1/2**, 1940-64, XX, "A" blade, flat yellow, 4-1/8". **200**
**5299-1/2**, 1940-64, XX, stag, 4-7/8" .......................... **250**
**5299-1/2**, 1940-64, XX, "A" blade, stag, 4-1/8"........... **350**
**3299-1/2**, 1965-69, USA, yellow composition, 4-1/8". **100**
**3299-1/2**, 1970, 10 Dot, yellow composition, 4-1/8"... **100**
**3299-1/2**, 1970, 10 Dot, flat yellow, 4-1/8" ................ **125**
**5299-1/2**, 1970, 10 Dot, stag, 4-1/8" ......................... **225**

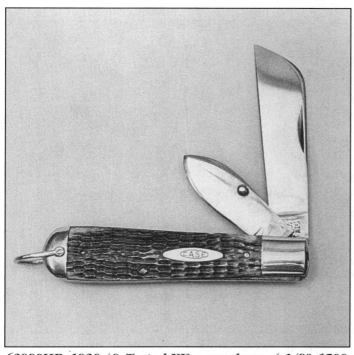

**6299SHR, 1920-40, Tested XX, green bone, 4-1/8", $500.**

*Unknown pattern, 1920-40, Tested XX, 2- blade, Case (in script) w/no Tested XX, Christmas handles, 3-1/16", $400.*

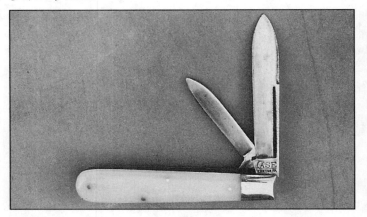
*Unknown pattern, 1920-40, Tested XX, 2-blade jack, yellow celluloid, 3-3/4", $450.*

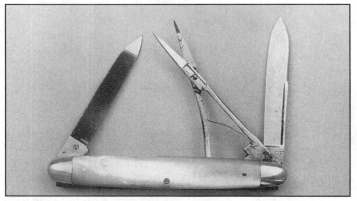
*Unknown pattern, 1920-40, Tested XX, equal end, blade, scissors, file, pearl, 3-1/4", $400.*

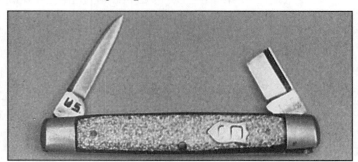
*Unknown pattern, Case Tested XX, US stamp, goldstone, broken spear master, rare stamp, $200.*

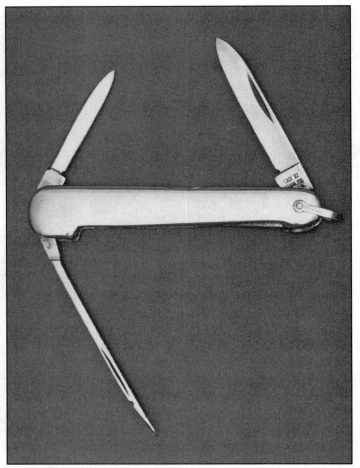

*M3102R, XX, all metal, 2-3/4", $50.*

| | | |
|---|---|---|
| **M3102R**, 1920-40, Tested XX, metal | | 110 |
| **M3102RSS**, 1965-69, USA, metal | | 50 |
| **M3102RSS**, 1970, 10 Dot, metal | | 50 |

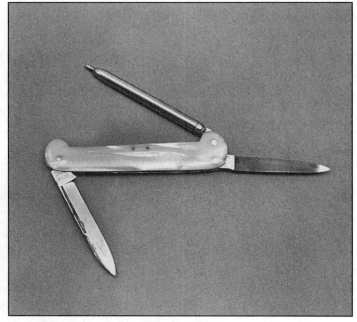
*83102F LP, Tested XX, ball point pen, cracked ice, $225.*

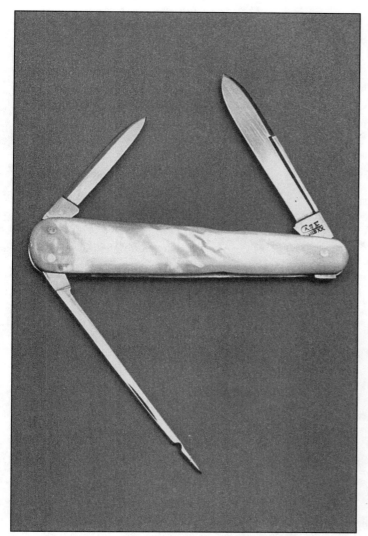

**83102, 1920-40, Tested XX, pearl, 2-3/4", $225.**
63102, 1920-40, Tested XX, green bone, flat bolsters
........................................................................................ 250
83102SS, 1940-64, XX, genuine pearl........................ 200

**T3105SS file, Toledo scale, dots on handles, 3-1/8", $100.**
T3105SS, 1940-64, XX, metal, older knife has no dots on handle .................................................................. 250

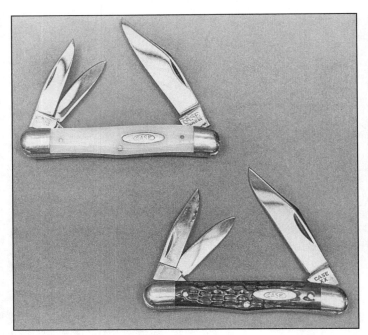

**Top: 3308, 1920-40, Tested XX, yellow composition, 3-1/4", $500.**
**Bottom: 6308, 1940-55, XX, green bone, 3-1/4", $500.**

| | |
|---|---|
| 6308, Tested XX, rough black | 500 |
| 2308, 1920-40, Tested XX, slick black, 3-1/4" | 500 |
| 5308, 1920-40, Tested XX, stag, 3-1/4" | 850 |
| 6308, 1920-40, Tested XX, green bone, 3-1/4" | 800 |
| 8308, 1920-40, Tested XX, genuine pearl, 3-1/4" | 800 |
| 6308, 1940-49, XX, rough black, 3-1/4" | 350 |
| 6308, 1940-64, XX, red bone, 3-1/4" | 300 |
| 6308, 1940-64, XX, bone, 3-1/4" | 250 |
| 6308, 1965-69, USA, bone, 3-1/4" | 150 |
| 6308, 1970, 10 Dot, bone, 3-1/4" | 150 |

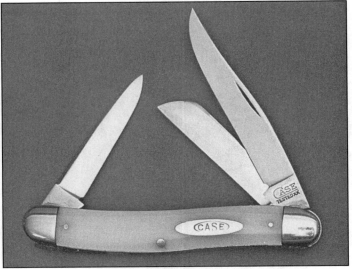

*3318HE, Tested XX, yellow celluloid, 3-1/2", $300.*

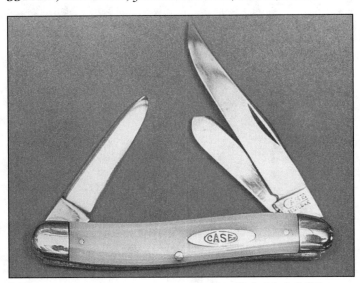

*3318 HP, Tested XX, spey, yellow celluloid, 3-1/2", $300.*

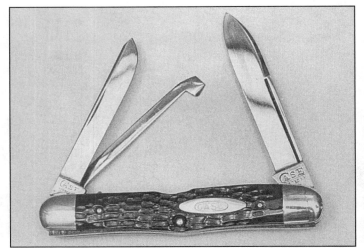

**63109, Tested XX, 3-backspring whittler, citrus peeler & cap lifter, long pull, green bone, 3-5/8", $1,250.**

| | |
|---|---|
| 63109, 1920-40, Tested XX, green bone | 1,200 |
| 93109, 1920-40, Tested XX, cracked ice | 1,000 |
| RM3109, 1920-40, Tested XX, Christmas tree | 1,250 |
| 83109X, 1920-40, Tested XX, pearl | 1,250 |

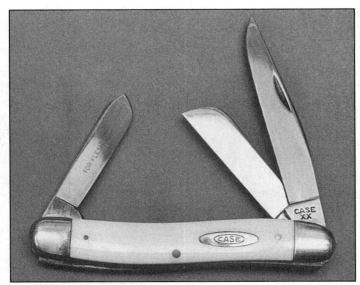

*4318HP, XX, white composition, 3-1/2", $125.*

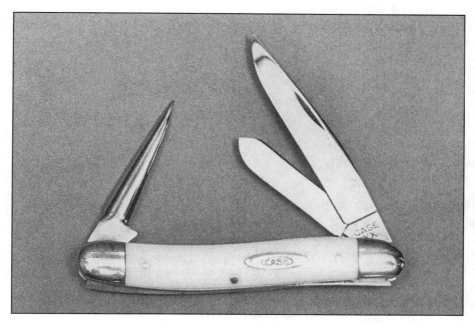

**4318PU, XX, white composition, 3-1/2", $225.**
RM318HE, Tested XX, Christmas tree ...................... 700
RM318SHPEN, 1920-40, Tested XX, Christmas tree, 3-1/2" ................................................................. 700
3318SHPEN, 1920-40, Tested XX, yellow composition, 3-1/2" ................................................................. 300
3318SHSP, 1920-40, Tested XX, yellow composition, 3-1/2" ................................................................. 300
3318SPPEN, 1920-40, Tested XX, yellow composition, 3-1/2" ................................................................. 300
5318SHSP, 1920-40, Tested XX, stag, 3-1/2" .............. 600
6318SHPU, 1920-40, Tested XX, green bone, 3-1/2" .. 600
6318SPPU, 1920-40, Tested XX, green bone, 3-1/2" ... 600
6318SPPen, 1920-40, Tested XX, green bone, 3-1/2" ................................................................. 600
6318SHPEN, 1920-40, Tested XX, green bone, 3-1/2" ................................................................. 600
6318SHPEN, 1920-40, Tested XX, green bone, 3-1/2" ................................................................. 600
6318SHpen, 1940-64, XX, red Rogers bone ............... 450
8318SHSP, 1920-40, Tested XX, genuine pearl, 3-1/2" ................................................................. 750
9318SHPEN, 1920-40, Tested XX, cracked ice, 3-1/2" ................................................................. 400
9318SHPU, 1920-40, Tested XX, cracked ice, 3-1/2" .. 450
3318SHPEN, 1940-64, XX, yellow composition, 3-1/2" ................................................................. 100
4318SHSP, 1940-64, XX, white composition, 3-1/2"... 100
4318SH, 1940-64, XX, master blade, California clip, white composition, 3-1/2" ...................................... 25
6318SPPU, 1940-49, XX, rough black, 3-1/2" ............ 300
6318SHSP, 1940-49, XX, rough black, 3-1/2" ............ 250
6318SHPEN, 1940-49, XX, rough black, 3-1/2" ......... 250
6318SPPU, 1940-55, XX, green bone, 3-1/2" ............. 400

6318SHSP, 1940-55, XX, green bone, 3-1/2" .............. 350
6318SHSP, 1940-55, XX long pull, green bone, 3-1/2" ................................................................. 425
6318SHPEN, 1940-55, XX, green bone, 3-1/2" ............ 350
6318SPPU, 1940-64, XX, red bone, 3-1/2" .................. 300
6318SHSP, 1940-64, XX, red bone, 3-1/2" .................. 200
6318SHPEN, 1940-64, XX, red bone, 3-1/2" ............... 200
6318SPPU, 1940-64, XX, bone, 3-1/2" ....................... 200
6318SHSP, 1940-64, XX, bone, 3-1/2" ....................... 150
6318SHSPSSP, 1964, XX to USA transition, bone, 3-1/2" ................................................................. 300
6318SHPEN, 1940-64, XX, bone, 3-1/2" ..................... 150
9318HP, 1940-64, XX, cracked ice, 3-1/2" ................. 300
3318SHPEN, 1965-69, USA, yellow composition, 3-1/2" ................................................................. 100
4318SHSP, 1965-69, USA, white composition, 3-1/2" ................................................................. 100
6318SPPU, 1965-69, USA, bone, 3-1/2" ..................... 100
6318SHSP, 1965-69, USA, bone, 3-1/2" ..................... 100
6318SHPEN, 1965-69, USA, bone, 3-1/2" ................... 100
6318HPSS, 1965-69, USA, polished blades, 3-1/2" ..... 125
6318HSSPSSP, 1965-69, USA, polished, bone, 3-1/2" ................................................................. 100
6318HP, 1965-66, USA, polished, stainless, 3-1/2" ................................................................. 125
6318SHSPSSP, 1965-69, USA, first model, bone, etched "Tested XX Stainless", 3-1/2" ..................... 150
3318SHPEN, 1970, 10 Dot, yellow composition, 3-1/2" ................................................................. 100
4318SHSP, 1970, 10 Dot, white composition, 3-1/2" .. 110
6318SPPU, 1970, 10 Dot, bone, 3-1/2" ....................... 125
6318SHPEN, 1970, 10 Dot, bone, 3-1/2" ..................... 100
6318SHSP, 1970, 10 Dot, bone, 3-1/2" ....................... 100
6318HPSSP, 1970, 10 Dot, polished, bone, 3-1/2" ...... 100

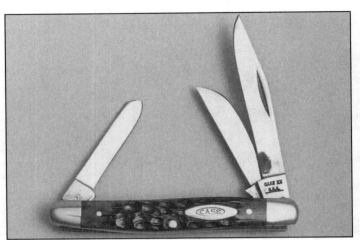

**6327SHSP, 1970, 10 Dot, bone, 2-3/4", $100.**
6327SHSP, 1940-64, XX, bone, 2-3/4" .......................... **110**
9327SHSP, 1940-64, XX, imitation pearl, 2-3/4" .......... **65**
9327SHSP, 1940-64, XX, cracked ice, 2-3/4" ................ **65**
6327SHSP, 1965-69, USA, bone, 2-3/4" ....................... **90**
9327SHSP, 1965-69, USA, 2-3/4" ................................ **60**
6327SHSP, 1970, 10 Dot, delrin, scarce, 2-3/4" .......... **100**
9327SHSP, 1970, 10 Dot, 2-3/4" ................................. **60**

**13031 LR, XX, electrician's knife, walnut, 3-3/4", $75.**
13031LR, 1965-69, USA, electrician's knife, walnut, 3-3/4" ........................................................................... **60**
13031LR, 1970, 10 Dot, electrician's knife, walnut, 3-3/4" ........................................................................... **60**

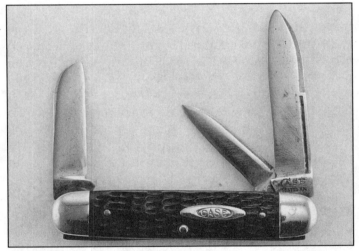

**6330, 1920-40, Tested XX, green bone, 3-1/4", $750.**

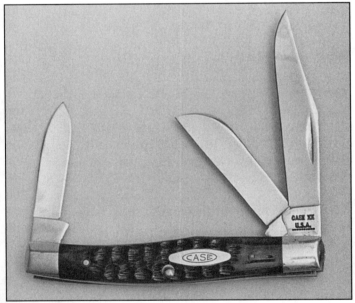

**6332, 1970 10 Dot, bone, 3-5/8", $100.**
5332, 1920-40, Tested XX, stag, 3-5/8" ..................... **500**
6332, 1920-40, Tested XX, green bone, 3-5/8" .......... **500**
5332, 1940-64, XX, stag, 3-5/8" ................................ **200**
5332LP, 1940-64, XX, stag, 3-5/8" ............................ **350**
6332, 1940-49, XX, rough black, 3-5/8" ................... **250**
6332, 1940-55, XX, green bone, 3-5/8" .................... **350**
6332, 1940-64, XX, red bone, 3-5/8" ........................ **225**
6332, 1940-64, XX, late Rogers bone, 3-5/8" ........... **250**
6332, 1940-64, XX, bone, 3-5/8" ............................... **150**
6332, 1965-69, USA, bone, 3-5/8" ............................ **100**
5332, 1965-69, USA, stag, 3-5/8" .............................. **150**
5332, 1970, 10 Dot, stag, 3-5/8" ................................ **150**

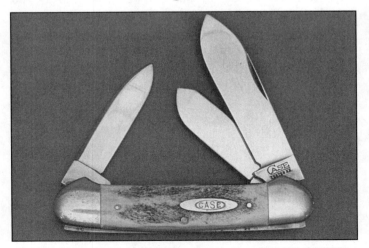

**53131, 1920-40 Tested XX, canoe, stag, 3-5/8", $2,500.**

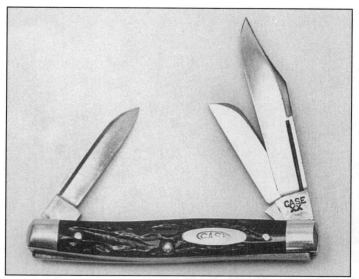

**6333, 1940-49, XX, long pull, rough black, 2-5/8", $150.**

| | |
|---|---|
| 6333, 1940, Tested XX, long pull, rough black, 2-5/8" | **200** |
| 6333, 1920-40, Tested XX, green bone, 2-5/8" | **225** |
| 9333, 1920-40, Tested XX, cracked ice, 2-5/8" | **140** |
| 6333, 1940-49, XX, rough black, 2-5/8" | **90** |
| 6333, 1940-55, XX, green bone, 2-5/8" | **225** |
| 6333LP, 1940-55, XX, green bone, 2-5/8" | **250** |
| 6333, 1940-64, XX, bone, 2-5/8" | **100** |
| 6333, 1940-64, XX, early Rogers bone, 2-5/8" | **175** |
| 9333, 1940-64, XX, imitation pearl, 2-5/8" | **60** |
| 9333, 1940-64, XX, long pull, imitation pearl, 2-5/8" | **125** |
| 9333, 1940-64, XX, long pull, cracked ice, 2-5/8" | **125** |
| 9333, 1940-64, XX, cracked ice, 2-5/8" | **60** |
| 6333, 1965-69, USA, bone, 2-5/8" | **90** |
| 9333, 1965-69, USA, imitation pearl, 2-5/8" | **50** |
| 6333, 1970, 10 Dot, delrin, 2-5/8" | **50** |
| 6333, 1970, 10 Dot, bone stag, 2-5/8" | **90** |
| 9333, 1970, 10 Dot, imitation pearl, 2-5/8" | **60** |
| 83042, 1920-40, Tested XX, whittler, pearl | **550** |

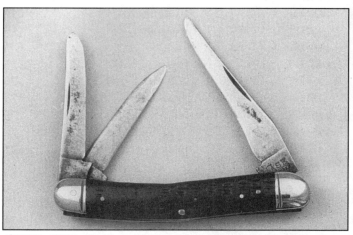

**63038, 1920-40, Tested XX, 3-backspring whittler, 3 blade, green bone, 3-3/8", $1,200.**

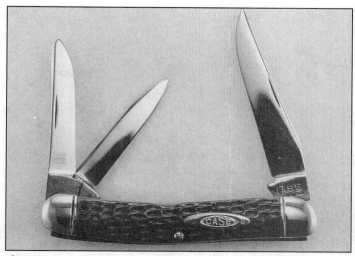

**63038, Tested XX, green bone, 3-3/8", $1,500.**

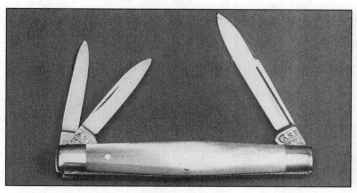

**83042, 1920-40, Tested XX, whittler, pearl, $700.**

| | |
|---|---|
| 93042, 1920-40, Tested XX, imitation pearl | **550** |
| 63042, 1920-40, Tested XX, early Rogers bone | **700** |

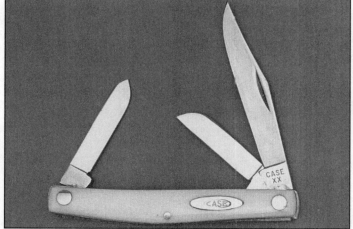

**33044HP, 1964, XX, birdseye, yellow composition, 3-1/4", $150.**

| | |
|---|---|
| 33044HP, 1964, XX, made only in 1964, flat yellow, 3-1/4" | **150** |
| 33044SHSP, 1965-69, USA, birdseye, yellow composition, 3-1/4" | **100** |
| 33044SHSP, 1970, 10 Dot, birdseye, yellow composition, 3-1/4" | **100** |
| 33044SHSP, 1970, 10 Dot, flat yellow, 3-1/4" | **125** |

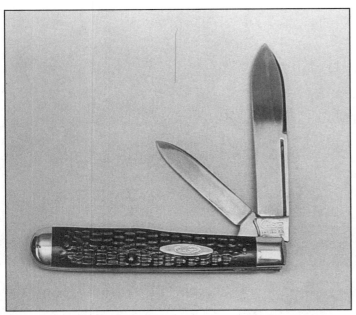

*GS344, small blades have Case Tested XX, goldstone, $350.*

**GS344**, 1920-40, Tested XX, goldstone, 3-1/4"............ **350**
**RM344SHSP**, 1920-40, Tested XX, Christmas tree, 3-1/4"
.................................................................................. **400**
**RM3044F**, 1920-40, Tested XX, Christmas tree, 3-1/4"
.................................................................................. **425**
**B344PU**, 1920-30, Tested XX, imitation onyx, 3-1/4"
.................................................................................. **400**

*6344, 1920-40, Tested XX, green bone, 3-1/4", $350.*
**6344SHSP**, 1920-40, Tested XX, green bone, 3-1/4"
.................................................................................. **350**
**6344SHPEN**, 1920-40, Tested XX, green bone, 3-1/4"
.................................................................................. **350**
**6344SHPU**, 1920-40, Tested XX, green bone, 3-1/4"
.................................................................................. **400**
**6344SPPU**, 1920-40, Tested XX, green bone, 3-1/4"
.................................................................................. **400**
**6344SPPEN**, 1920-40, Tested XX, green bone, 3-1/4"
.................................................................................. **350**
**8344SHSP**, 1920-40, Tested XX, genuine pearl, 3-1/4"
.................................................................................. **450**
**9344SHPEN**, 1920-40, Tested XX, imitation pearl, 3-1/4"
.................................................................................. **250**
**6344SHSP**, 1940-55, XX, green bone, 3-1/4"............... **300**
**6344SHPEN**, 1940-55, XX, green bone, 3-1/4"............ **300**
**6344SHSP**, 1940-64, XX, red bone, 3-1/4".................. **150**
**6344SHPEN**, 1940-64, XX, red bone, 3-1/4"................ **150**
**6344SHSP**, 1940-64, XX, bone, 3-1/4" ........................ **125**
**6344SHPEN**, 1940-64, XX, bone, 3-1/4" ..................... **125**
**6344SHPEN**, 1965-69, USA, bone, 3-1/4" .................... **75**
**6344SHSP**, 1965-69, USA, bone, 3-1/4" ....................... **75**
**6344SHPEN**, 1970, 10 Dot, bone, 3-1/4" ...................... **75**
**6344SHSP**, 1970, 10 Dot, bone, 3-1/4" ......................... **75**
**6344SHSP**, 1970, 10 Dot, delrin, rare, 3-1/4" ............. **125**

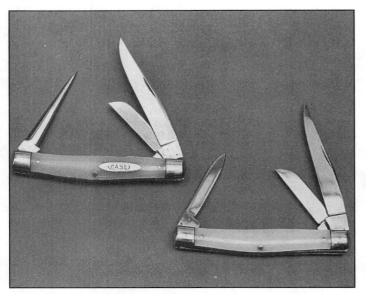

*Top: 3344PU, 1920-40, Tested XX, yellow celluloid w/ shield, 3-1/4", $250.*
*Bottom: 3344, 1920-40, Tested XX, yellow celluloid no shield, 3-1/4", $200.*
**3344SPPU**, 1920-40, Tested XX, yellow composition, 3-1/4" ........................................................................ **250**
**5344SHSP**, 1920-40, Tested XX, stag, 3-1/4" ............. **400**
**5344SHPEN**, 1920-40, Tested XX, stag, 3-1/4" .......... **400**

Case Knives Tested (1920-1971) 223

**63045, 1920-40, Tested XX, green bone, 3-5/8", $300.**
6345, 1920-40, Tested XX, green bone, 3-5/8"............ **400**
6345PU, 1920-40, Tested XX, green bone, 3-5/8"....... **450**

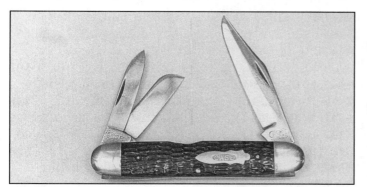

**6345-1/2SAB, 1920-40, Tested XX, whittler, green bone, 3-5/8", $1,800.**

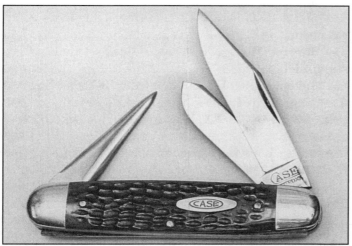

**6345-1/2 PU, 1920-1940, Tested XX, green bone, 3-3/4", $650.**
2345-1/2PU, 1920-40, Tested XX, slick black, 3-5/8". **325**
6345-1/2, 1920-40, Tested XX, imitation bone, 3-5/8"
.................................................................................... **225**
6345-1/2, 1920-40, Tested XX, green bone, 3-5/8"..... **500**
6345-1/2SH, 1920-40, Tested XX, green bone, 3-5/8"
.................................................................................... **500**
6345-1/2, 1920-40, Tested XX, rough black, 3-5/8".... **350**

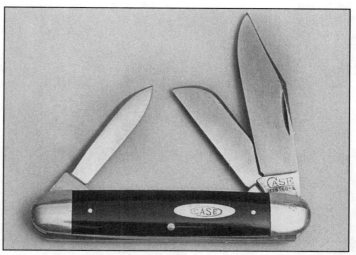

**2345-1/2, 1920-40, Tested XX, slick black, 3-5/8", $300.**
2345-1/2SH, 1940-64, XX, slick black, 3-5/8"............. **175**
2345-1/2P, 1940-64, XX, long pull, slick black, 3-5/8"
.................................................................................... **250**
6345-1/2SH, 1940-49, XX, rough black, 3-5/8".......... **275**
6345-1/2SH, 1940-55, XX, green bone, 3-5/8"............ **450**
6345-1/2SH, 1940-64, XX, red bone, 3-5/8"................ **550**
6345-1/2SH, 1940-64, XX, bone, 3-5/8"...................... **250**
2345-1/2SH, 1965-69, USA, slick black, 3-5/8".......... **200**
6345-1/2SH, 1965-69, USA, bone, rare, 3-5/8"............ **500**

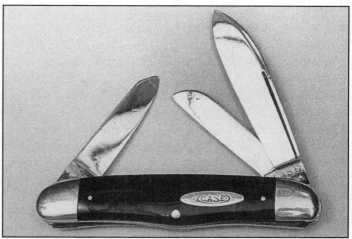

**23046, Tested XX, humpback, long pull, slick black, 3-3/8", $550.**
33046, 1920-40, Tested XX, yellow composition, 3-5/8"
.................................................................................... **600**
43046, 1920-40, Tested XX, white composition, 3-5/8"
.................................................................................... **600**
63046, 1920-40, Tested XX, green bone, 3-5/8"....... **1,000**
6345-1/2PU, XX, red bone............................................ **450**
M346, 1940-50, XX, English Navy contract, metal, "Metal stampings Ltd.", 3-5/8" ................................. **135**
M346, 1940-64, XX, metal, "Case XX Made For USA Navy", 3-5/8"............................................................. **150**
M346, 1940-50, XX, Canadian Navy contract, aluminum, 3-5/8"....................................................... **150**

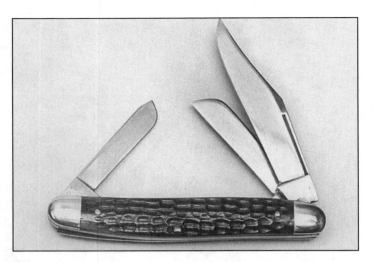

**6347HP**, 1920-40, Tested XX, long pull, green bone 3-7/8", $650.

**RM347SPPU**, 1920-40, Tested XX, long pull, Christmas tree, 3-7/8" ............................................................. 800
**RM347SPPen**, 1920-40, Tested XX, long pull, Christmas tree, 3-7/8" ............................................................. 800
**RM347SHPU**, 1920-40, Tested XX, long pull, Christmas tree, 3-7/8" ............................................................. 850
**M347SPPen**, 1920-40, Tested XX, long pull, metal, 3-7/8" ........................................................................... 350
**M347SPPU**, 1920-40, Tested XX, long pull, metal, 3-7/8" ........................................................................... 400
**3347SHSP**, 1920-40, Tested XX, long pull, yellow composition, 3-7/8" ..................................................... 500
**3347SPPen**, 1920-40, Tested XX, long pull, yellow composition, 3-7/8" ..................................................... 500
**3347SPPU**, 1920-40, Tested XX, long pull, yellow composition, 3-7/8" ..................................................... 550
**3347SHPU**, 1920-40, Tested XX, long pull, yellow composition, 3-7/8" ..................................................... 550
**5347SHSP**, 1920-40, Tested XX, long pull, stag, 3-7/8" ............................................................................ 900
**5347SHPen**, 1920-40, Tested XX, long pull, stag, 3-7/8" ............................................................................ 900
**6347SHSP**, 1920-40, Tested XX, green bone, 3-7/8" ... 700
**6347SHSP**, 1920-40, Tested XX, long pull, green bone, 3-7/8" ...................................................................... 800
**6347SHPen**, 1920-40, Tested XX, green bone, 3-7/8". 700
**6347SHPen**, 1920-40, Tested XX, long pull, green bone, 3-7/8" ...................................................................... 800
**6347SHPU**, 1920-40, Tested XX, green bone, 3-7/8" .. 800
**6347SHPU**, 1920-40, Tested XX, long pull, green bone, 3-7/8" ...................................................................... 850
**6347SPPen**, 1920-40, Tested XX, green bone, 3-7/8" . 700
**6347SPPen**, 1920-40, Tested XX, long pull, green bone, 3-7/8" ...................................................................... 800
**6347SPPU**, 1920-40, Tested XX, green bone, 3-7/8" ... 750
**6347SPPU**, 1920-40, Tested XX, long pull, green bone, 3-7/8" ...................................................................... 850

**6347PUPen**, 1920-40, Tested XX, green bone, 3-7/8". **750**
**6347PUPen**, 1920-40, Tested XX, long pull, green bone, 3-7/8" ...................................................................... 850
**6347JSH**, 1920-40, Tested XX, long pull, green bone, 3-7/8" .................................................................... 1,800
**6347JSPU**, 1920-40, Tested XX, long pull, green bone, 3-7/8" .................................................................... 1,800
**6347SHSP**, 1920-40, Tested XX, long pull, rough black, 3-7/8" ...................................................................... 650
**6347SPPU**, 1920-40, Tested XX, long pull, rough black, 3-7/8" ...................................................................... 700
**6347SHPU**, 1920-40, Tested XX, long pull, rough black, 3-7/8" ...................................................................... 700
**6347SHSP**, 1920-40, Tested XX, long pull, early Rogers bone, 3-7/8" .................................................................. 1,200
**9347SHSP**, 1920-40, Tested XX, cracked ice, 3-7/8" ... 600
**9347SPPen**, 1920-40, Tested XX, cracked ice, 3-7/8". 600
**9347SPPU**, 1920-40, Tested XX, long pull, cracked ice, 3-7/8" ...................................................................... 650
**9347JPU**, 1920-40, Tested XX, long pull, cracked ice, 3-7/8" .................................................................... 1,500
**3347SPPU**, 1920-40, Tested XX, yellow composition, 3-7/8" ...................................................................... 450
**5347SHSP**, 1920-40, Tested XX, stag, 3-7/8" ............. 700
**5347SHSP**, 1920-40, Tested XX, red stag, 3-7/8"..... 1,200
**5347HP**, Tested XX, second-cut stag, rare .............. 1,500
**5347SHSP**, 1920-40, Tested XX, long pull, red stag, 3-7/8" .................................................................... 1,500
**5347SHSP**, 1940-64, Tested XX, long pull, stag, 3-7/8" ...................................................................................... 750
**5347SHSP**, 1940-64, XX, stainless steel, all blades stamped, stag, 3-7/8" ...................................................... 450
**5347SHSP**, 1940-64, XX, stainless steel, all blades stamped, red stag, 3-7/8" ............................................. 700
**6347SPPen**, 1940-49, XX, rough black, 3-7/8"............ 350
**6347SHSP**, 1940-49, XX, rough black, 3-7/8" ............ 350
**6347SHSP**, 1940-49, XX, long pull, rough black, 3-7/8" ...................................................................................... 550
**6347SHPU**, 1940-49, XX, rough black, 3-7/8"............. 400
**6347SHPU**, 1940-49, XX, long pull, rough black, 3-7/8" ...................................................................................... 650
**6347SPPU**, 1940-49, XX, long pull, rough black, 3-7/8" ...................................................................................... 650
**6347SHSP**, 1940-55, XX, green bone, 3-7/8" ............. 500
**6347SHSP**, 1940-55, XX, long pull, green bone, 3-7/8" ...................................................................................... 650
**6347SHPU**, 1940-55, XX, green bone, 3-7/8" ............. 550
**6347SHPU**, 1940-55, XX, long pull, green bone, 3-7/8" ...................................................................................... 650
**6347SPPU**, 1940-55, XX, green bone, 3-7/8" ............. 550
**6347SPPU**, 1940-55, XX, long pull, green bone, 3-7/8" ...................................................................................... 650
**6347SPPen**, 1940-55, XX, green bone, 3-7/8" ............ 550

**6347SPPen**, 1940-55, XX, long pull, green bone, 3-7/8"
............................................................................ 650
**6347SHSP**, 1940-55, XX, stainless steel, all blades stamped, green bone, 3-7/8"............................. 750
**6347SHSP**, 1940-64, XX, late Rogers bone, 3-7/8" ..... 400
**6347SHPU**, 1940-64, XX, late Rogers bone, 3-7/8" ..... 450
**6347SPPU**, 1940-64, XX, late Rogers bone, 3-7/8" ..... 450
**6347SHSP**, 1940-64, XX, stainless steel, all blades stamped, late Rogers bone, 3-7/8" ............................... 550
**6347SHSP**, 1940-64, XX, late red Rogers bone, 3-7/8"
............................................................................ 500
**6347SHSP**, 1940-64, XX, late red Rogers bone, stainless steel, all blades stamped, 3-7/8" ........................ 650
**6347SHSP**, 1940-64, XX, red bone, 3-7/8"................... 400
**6347SPPU**, 1940-64, XX, red bone, 3-7/8"................... 450
**6347SPPen**, 1940-64, XX, red bone, 3-7/8".................. 400
**6347SHSPSSP**, 1940-64, XX, stainless steel, all blades stamped, red bone, 3-7/8" .................................. 550
**6347SPPU**, 1940-64, XX, long pull, second-cut bone, 3-7/8" ................................................................. 1,250
**6347SHSP**, 1940-64, XX, bone, 3-7/8" ......................... 225
**6347SPPen**, 1940-64, XX, bone, 3-7/8" ....................... 225
**6347SPPU**, 1940-64, XX, bone, 3-7/8" ........................ 250
**6347SHPen**, 1940-64, XX, bone, 3-7/8" ....................... 225
**6347SHPU**, 1940-64, XX, bone, 3-7/8" ........................ 250
**6347SHSP**, 1940-64, XX, stainless steel, all blades stamped, bone, 3-7/8" ............................................ 400
**3347SHSP**, 1965-69, USA, yellow composition, 3-7/8"
............................................................................ 100
**3347SHSP**, 1965-69, USA, flat, yellow composition, 3-7/8" ..................................................................... 125
**5347SHSP**, 1965-69, USA, stag, 3-7/8" ....................... 225
**5347SHSPS**, 1965-69, USA, stainless steel, all blades stamped, stag, 3-7/8" .............................................. 450
**5347SHSPS**, 1965-69, USA, stainless steel, polished blades, large stamp, stag, 3-7/8" ................................ 450
**5347SHSPS**, 1965-69, USA, transition USA-XX, stag, 3-7/8" ..................................................................... 550
**6347SHSP**, 1965-69, USA, bone, 3-7/8" ...................... 125
**6347SPPen**, 1965-69, USA, bone, 3-7/8" ..................... 125
**6347SPPU**, 1965-69, USA, bone, 3-7/8" ...................... 150
**6347SHSPSSP**, 1965-69, USA, first model, all blades stamped "Case XX Stainless USA", bone, 3-7/8" ....... 400
**6347SHSPSSP**, 1965-69, USA, first model, brushed finish, bone, 3-7/8" ....................................................... 225
**6347SHSPSSP**, 1965-69, USA, bone, 3-7/8" ............... 150
**6347SHSPS**, 1965-69, USA, polished, all blades small stamped, bone, 3-7/8" ............................................ 400
**6347SHSPS**, 1965-69, USA, polished blades, small stamp, bone, 3-7/8" ........................................................ 200
**6347SHSPS**, 1965-69, USA, polished blades, large stamp, bone, 3-7/8" ........................................................ 200
**3347SHSP**, 1970, 10 Dot, yellow composition, 3-7/8". 100

**3347SHSP**, 1970, 10 Dot, flat, yellow composition, 3-7/8" ..................................................................... 125
**5347SHSP**, 1970, 10 Dot, stag, 3-7/8" ......................... 225
**5347SHSPS**, 1970, 10 Dot, stainless, stag, 3-7/8" ....... 400
**5347SHSP**, 1970, 10 Dot, transition 10 Dot-USA, stag, 3-7/8" ..................................................................... 500
**6347SHSP**, 1970, 10 Dot, bone, 3-7/8" ........................ 125
**6347SPPen**, 1970, 10 Dot, bone, 3-7/8"....................... 125
**6347SPPU**, 1970, 10 Dot, bone, 3-7/8" ....................... 150
**6347SHSPSSP**, 1970, 10 Dot, bone, 3-7/8" ................. 150
**630047SPPen**, 1920-40, Tested XX, iron bolsters, iron liners, no shield, wide backsprings, green bone, 3-7/8"
............................................................................ 600
**630047SHSP**, 1920-40, Tested XX, iron bolsters, iron liners, no shield, wide backsprings, green bone, 3-7/8"
............................................................................ 600

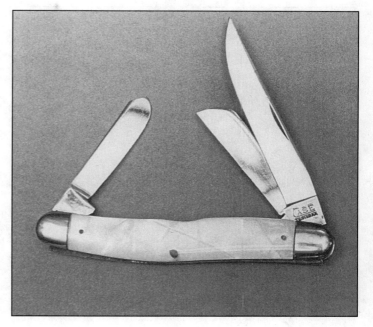

***93047, 1920-40, Tested XX, cracked ice, 3-7/8", $700.***
**B3047**, 1920-40, Tested XX, waterfall, 3-7/8" ......... 1,000
**43047**, 1920-40, Tested XX, white composition, 3-7/8"
............................................................................ 600
**63047**, 1920-40, Tested XX, rough black, 3-7/8" ........ 600
**53047**, 1940-64, XX, stag, 3-7/8" ................................ 400
**53047**, 1940-64, XX, red stag, 3-7/8" ......................... 550
**63047**, 1940-64, XX, bone, 3-7/8".............................. 250
**63047**, 1940-64, XX, red bone, 3-7/8"........................ 350
**63047**, 1940-55, XX, green bone, 3-7/8" .................... 700
**63047**, 1940-49, XX, rough black, 3-7/8" ................... 450
**93047**, 1940-64, XX, cracked ice, 3-7/8" .................... 350
**53047**, 1965-69, USA, stag, 3-7/8" ............................. 250
**63047**, 1965-69, USA, bone, 3-7/8" ........................... 200
**53047**, 1970, 10 Dot, stag, 3-7/8" .............................. 250
**63047**, 1970, 10 Dot, bone, 3-7/8" ............................ 150

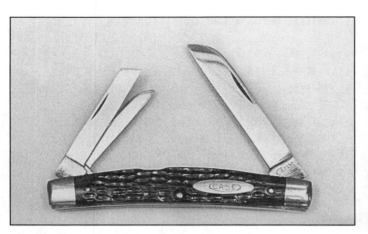

***63052**, 1920-40, Tested XX, congress whittler, green bone, 3-1/2", $3,500.*
***3352**, 1920-40, Tested XX, hobo, 3-piece (knife, fork & spoon), yellow, 3-3/4", 700*

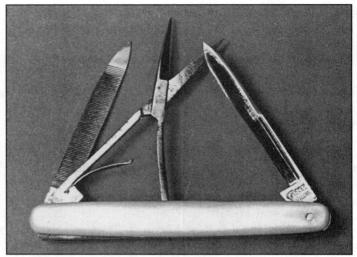

***8361FSC**, 1920-40, Tested XX, pearl, 2-7/8", $350.*
**2361F**, 1920-40, Tested XX, whittler, slick black, 2-7/8" ................................................................. **350**
**8361**, 1920-40, Tested XX, whittler, pearl, 2-7/8" ...... **400**

***23055PU**, 1940-60, XX, slick black, 3-1/2", $400.*
**23055**, 1920-40, Tested XX, slick black, 3-1/2" .......... **400**
**23055PU**, 1920-40, Tested XX, slick black, 3-1/2" ...... **450**
**33055**, 1920-40, Tested XX, yellow composition, 3-1/2" ................................................................. **450**
**63055**, 1920-40, Tested XX, green bone, 3-1/2" .......... **650**
**63055PU**, 1920-40, Tested XX, green bone, 3-1/2" ..... **700**
**63055**, 1920-40, Tested XX, rough black, 3-1/2" ........ **500**
**63055PU**, 1920-40, Tested XX, rough black, 3-1/2" .... **500**
**63056**, 1920-40, Tested XX, green bone, 3" ................ **650**
**83056**, 1920-40, Tested XX, pearl, 3" ........................ **700**
**6358**, 1920-40, Tested XX, whittler, green bone, 2-7/8" ................................................................. **700**
**8358**, 1920-40, Tested XX, whittler, pearl, 2-7/8" ...... **800**
**8360**, 1920-40, Tested XX, whittler, pearl, 3-7/16" .... **800**

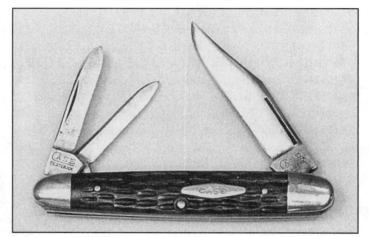

***63063-1/2**. Tested XX, long pull, green bone, 3-1/16", $650.*
**93063-1/2**, 1920-40, Tested XX, long pull, cracked ice, 3-1/16" ................................................................. **600**

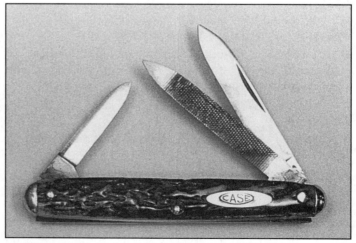

***5364TF**, 1920-40, Tested XX, stag, 3-1/8", $300.*

Case Knives Tested (1920-1971) 227

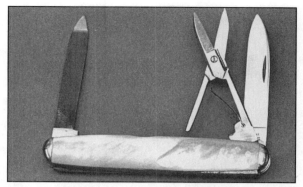

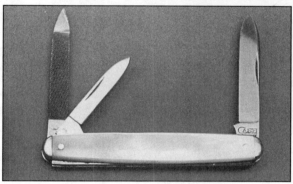

*Top: 8364, TSCI SS, 1940-64 XX, not a whittler, pearl, 3-1/8", $150.*
*Bottom: 8364TF, 1920-40, Tested XX, whittler, pearl, rare, 3-1/8", $550.*

**8364T** 1920-40, Tested XX, genuine pearl, 3-1/8" ...... **300**
**8364SC**, 1920-40, Tested XX, genuine pearl, 3-1/8".. **300**
**8364SSSC**, 1965-64, USA, stainless, genuine pearl, 3-1/8" ................................................................ **150**
**8364SSSC**, 1970, 10 Dot, stainless, genuine pearl, 3-1/8" ................................................................ **150**

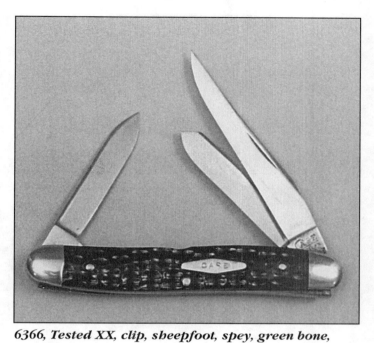

*6366, Tested XX, clip, sheepfoot, spey, green bone, 3-3/16", $550.*
**6366PEN**, 1920-40, Tested XX, green bone, 3-1/8" ..... **550**
**8366HE**, 1920-40, Tested XX, pearl, 3-1/8" ............... **550**

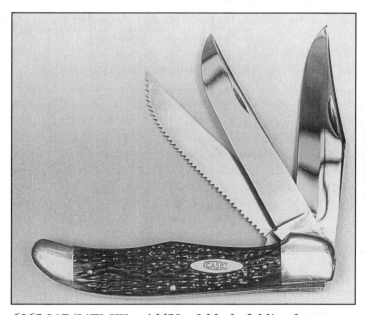

*6365 SAB/SAW, XX, mid-'50s, 3-blade folding-hunter prototype, 3 backsprings, bone, very rare, 5-1/4", $5,000.*

*9367, Case Tested XX, imitation onyx, 3-1/4", $400.*
**6367**, 1920-40, Tested XX, green bone, 3-1/4" ............ **450**
**8367**, 1920-40, Tested XX, genuine pearl .................. **500**
**63067**, 1920-40, Tested XX, whittler, green bone ...... **800**
**B3067**, 1920-40, Tested XX, whittler, waterfall, 3-1/4" ................................................................ **800**
**6368**, 1920-40, Tested XX, congress, green bone, 3-1/4" ................................................................ **3,500**

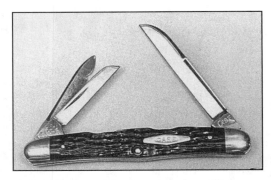

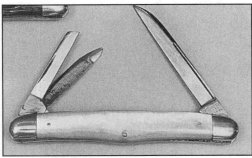

***Top: 6370FLP, 1920-40, Tested XX, green bone, 3-1/8", $900.***
***Bottom: 8370FLP, 1920-40, Tested XX, pearl, 3-1/8", $900.***

**6370LP**, 1920-40, Tested XX, green bone ................... **900**
**8370LP**, 1920-40, Tested XX, genuine pearl .............. **750**
**8371**, 1920-40, Tested XX, genuine pearl, 3-1/4" .... **1,200**
**6373**, 1920-40, Tested XX, Wharncliffe whittler, green bone, 3-1/2" ............................................................. **2,000**
**63074**, 1920-40, Tested XX, Rogers bone, 3-1/2" ........ **800**

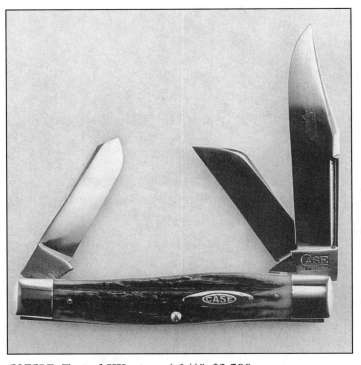

***5375LP, Tested XX, stag, 4-1/4", $2,500.***
**5375**, 1920-40, Tested XX, long pull, second-cut stag, 4-1/4" ............................................................... **3,000**
**5375**, 1920-40, Tested XX, long pull, stag, 4-1/4" ............................................................... **2,500**
**6375**, 1920-40, Tested XX, long pull, green bone, 4-1/4" ............................................................... **2,800**
**6375LP**, 1920-40, Tested XX, Winterbottom bone, 4-1/4" ............................................................... **4,000**
**5375**, 1940-64, XX, stag, 4-1/4" ..................... **450**
**5375**, 1940-64, XX, long pull, stag, 4-1/4" ................. **800**
**6375**, 1940-49, XX, rough black, 4-1/4" ..................... **500**
**6375**, 1940-49, XX, long pull, rough black, 4-1/4" ............................................................... **700**
**6375**, 1940-55, XX, green bone, 4-1/4" ..................... **800**
**6375**, 1940-55, XX, long pull, green bone, 4-1/4" ............................................................... **1,500**
**6375**, 1940-64, XX, red bone, 4-1/4" ......................... **500**
**6375**, 1940-64, XX, long pull, red bone, 4-1/4" ........... **800**
**5375**, 1965-69, USA, stag, 4-1/4" ................................ **350**
**5375**, 1965-69, USA, second-cut stag, 4-1/4" .......... **1,500**
**6375**, 1965-69, USA, bone, 4-1/4" .............................. **250**
**5375**, 1970, 10 Dot, stag, 4-1/4" ................................. **350**
**6375**, 1970, 10 Dot, bone, 4-1/4" ................................ **250**

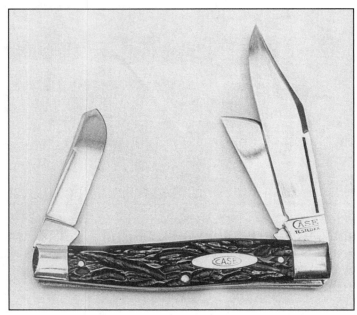

***6375LP, 1920-40, Tested XX, rough black, 4-1/4", $1,250.***

Case Knives Tested (1920-1971) 229

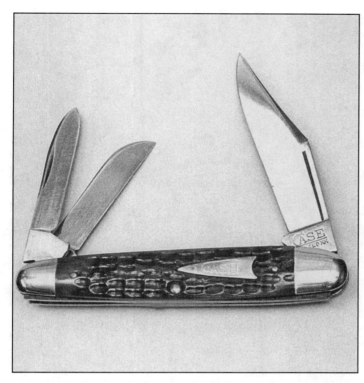

**6376-1/2LP, Tested XX, whittler, green bone, 3-5/8", $1,250.**
2376-1/2, 1920-40, Tested XX, slick black, 3-5/8" ...... **700**
5376-1/2, 1920-40, Tested XX, stag, 3-5/8" ................ **900**
6376-1/2, 1920-40, Tested XX, green bone, 3-5/8" ..... **900**

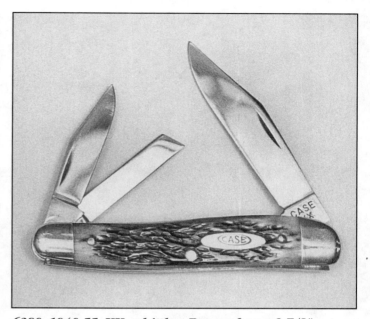

**6380, 1940-55, XX, whittler, Rogers bone, 3-7/8", $2,000.**
6380, 1920-40, Tested XX, flat blade, early Rogers bone, 3-7/8" ............................................................................ **3,000**
6380, 1920-40, Tested XX, whittler, flat blade, green bone, 3-7/8" ............................................................... **3,000**
6380, 1940-55, XX, whittler, green bone, 3-7/8" ..... **1,500**
6380, 1940-64, XX, red bone, 3-7/8" .......................... **600**
6380, 1940-64, XX, bone, 3-7/8" .................................. **400**
6380, 1965-69, USA, bone, 3-7/8" ............................... **300**
6380, 1970, 10 Dot, bone, 3-7/8" ................................ **300**
83081, 1920-40, Tested XX, lobster, genuine pearl, 3" ..................................................................................... **250**

**6379-1/2F, 1920-40, Tested XX, green bone, 3-1/4", $700.**
6379-1/2, 1920-40, Tested XX, green bone, 3-1/4" ..... **700**

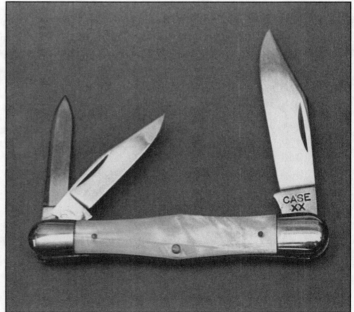

**9383, 1940-55, XX, cracked ice, 3-1/2", $500.**
9383SAB, 1940-55, XX, cracked ice, 3-1/2" ................ **750**

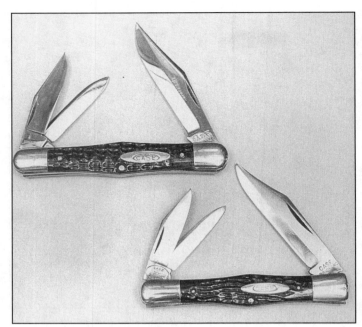

*Top: 6383SAB, 1920-40, Tested XX, green bone, 3-1/2", $1,000.*
*Bottom: 6383SAB, Case Bradford, green bone, square bolsters, 3-1/2", 1,500.*

**B383**, 1920-40, Tested XX, imitation onyx, 3-1/2" ..... **600**
**2383**, 1920-40, Tested XX, slick black, 3-1/2" ............ **500**
**GS383**, 1920-40, Tested XX, goldstone, 3-1/2" ........... **900**
**5383**, 1920-40, Tested XX, stag, 3-1/2" .................... **1,200**
**5383SAB**, 1920-40, Tested XX, stag, 3-1/2" ............ **1,500**
**6383**, 1920-40, Tested XX, green bone, 3-1/2" ........... **900**
**6383LP**, 1920-40, Tested XX, green bone, rare, 3-1/2"
........................................................................... **1,500**
**8383**, 1920-40, Tested XX, genuine pearl, 3-1/2" .... **1,500**
**9383**, 1920-40, Tested XX, imitation pearl, 3-1/2" ..... **750**
**2383**, 1940-64, XX, slick black, 3-1/2" ....................... **250**
**2383SAB**, 1940-64, XX, slick black, 3-1/2" ................. **450**
**5383**, 1940-64, XX, stag, 3-1/2" ................................. **500**
**5383SAB**, XX, stag, 3-1/2" ......................................... **700**
**5383**, 1940-50, XX, red stag, 3-1/2" ............................ **700**
**6383**, 1940-49, XX, rough black, 3-1/2" ..................... **400**
**6383**, 1940-55, XX, green bone, 3-1/2" .................... **1,250**
**6383**, 1940-64, XX, red bone, 3-1/2" .......................... **450**
**6383**, 1940-64, XX, bone, 3-1/2" ................................ **350**
**9383**, 1940-64, XX, imitation pearl, 3-1/2" ................ **400**
**9383SAB**, 1940-64, XX, imitation pearl, 3-1/2" ......... **700**
**2383**, 1965-69, USA, slick black, 3-1/2" ..................... **200**
**5383**, 1965-69, USA, stag, 3-1/2" ............................... **350**
**6383**, 1965-69, USA, bone, 3-1/2" .............................. **200**
**5383**, 1970, 10 Dot, stag, 3-1/2" ................................. **350**
**6383**, 1970, 10 Dot, bone, 3-1/2" ................................ **200**
**63083**, 1920-40, Tested XX, green bone, 3-3/16"........ **400**
**83083**, 1920-40, Tested XX, genuine pearl, 3-3/16" .... **350**
Note: 63083 & 83083 are both lobsters.

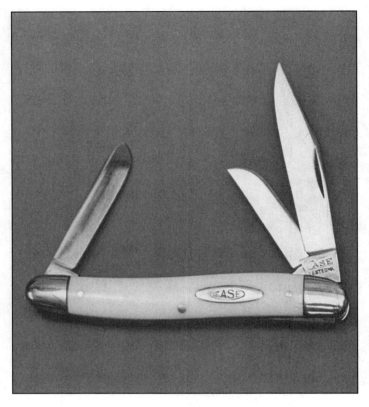

*43087, 1920-40, Tested XX, white composition, 3-1/4", $250.*

**23087SHPEN**, 1920-40, Tested XX, slick black, 3-1/4"
........................................................................... **200**
**63087SPPEN**, 1920-40, Tested XX, green bone, 3-1/4"
........................................................................... **350**
**63087SPPEN**, 1940-49, XX, rough black, 3-1/4" ......... **250**
**63087SPPEN**, 1940-55, XX, green bone, 3-1/4"........... **300**
**63087PEN**, 1940-55, XX, red Rogers bone, 3-1/4" ...... **175**
**63087SPPEN**, 1940-64, XX, red bone, 3-1/4" .............. **150**
**23087SHPEN**, 1940-64, XX, slick black, 3-1/4" ........... **100**
**53087SHPEN**, 1940-64, XX, stag, 3-1/4" ..................... **150**
**63087SPPEN**, 1940-64, XX, bone, 3-1/4" ..................... **125**
**23087SHPEN**, 1965-69, USA, slick black, 3-1/4".......... **65**
**53087SHPEN**, 1965-69, USA, stag, 3-1/4" .................. **125**
**23087SHPEN**, 1965-69, USA, bone, 3-1/4" ................... **75**
**23087SHPEN**, 1970, 10 Dot, slick black, 3-1/4"............ **65**
**53087SHPEN**, 1970, 10 Dot, stag, 3-1/4" .................... **125**
**63087SHPEN**, 1970, 10 Dot, delrin, 3-1/4" ................... **60**
**63087SHPEN**, 1970, 10 Dot, bone, 3-1/4" ..................... **75**
**5387**, 1920-40, Tested XX, gunstock whittler, stag,
3-1/2" .................................................................... **2,000**
**8387**, 1920-40, Tested XX, gunstock whittler, pearl,
3-1/2" .................................................................... **2,000**

# Case Knives Tested (1920-1971)   231

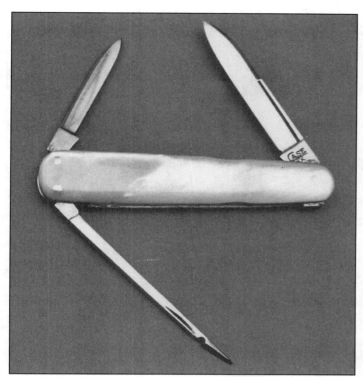

*83088, Tested XX, lobster, pearl, 3-1/8", $300.*
**83088SS**, 1940-64, XX, genuine pearl, 3-1/8" ............ **300**
**83089SCI**, 1920-40, Tested XX, genuine pearl, 3-1/16"
...................................................................................... **300**
**83089SCISSF**, 1940-64, XX, genuine pearl, 3-1/16" ... **200**
**83089SCSSF**, 1965-69, USA, genuine pearl, 3-1/16"
...................................................................................... **325**

*5391, 1940-42, XX, stag, 4-1/2", $2,500.*

*6391, Tested XX, green bone, 4-1/2", $6,500.*
**3391**, 1920-40, Tested XX, yellow composition, rare,
4-1/2" ............................................................................ **2,500**
**5391**, 1920-40, Tested XX, red stag, 4-1/2" ............ **3,500**
**5391**, 1920-40, Tested XX, stag, 4-1/2" ................... **3,000**
**5391LP**, 1920-40, Tested XX, red stag, rare, 4-1/2"
...................................................................................... **8,000**
**6391**, 1920-40, Tested XX, Winterbottom, rare, 4-1/2"
...................................................................................... **8,000**
**5391**, 1940-42, XX, red stag, 4-1/2" ........................ **3,000**

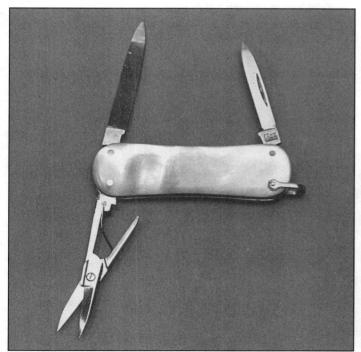

*83090SCI, 1920-40, Tested XX, pearl lobster, 2-1/4", $275.*
**83090SCRSS**, 1940-64, XX, genuine pearl, 2-1/4" ...... **200**

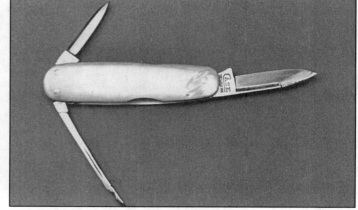

*83091, 1920-40, Tested XX, genuine pearl, 2-1/4", $250.*
**GM3091**, 1920-40, Tested XX, gold plate, 2-1/4" ........ **250**

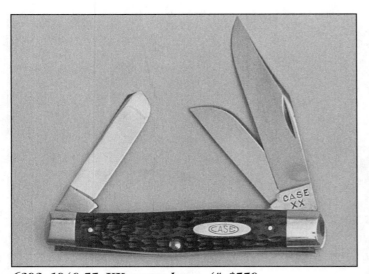

**6392, 1940-55, XX, green bone, 4", $550.**
9392PU, 1920-40, Tested XX, onyx, 4" ....................... 600
5392, 1920-40, Tested XX, stag, 4" ............................ 750
6392, 1920-40, Tested XX, green bone, 4" .................. 750
**6392PU**, 1920-40, Tested XX, green bone, 4" ............. 800
**6392HP**, 1920-40, Tested XX, rough black, 4" ........... 500
5392, 1940-64, XX, stag, 4" ........................................ 400
6392, 1940-49, XX, rough black, 4" ............................ 350
6392, 1940-49, XX, long pull, rough black, 4" ............ 450
6392, 1940-55, XX, green bone, 4" ............................. 450
6392, 1940-64, XX, red bone, 4" ................................. 325
6392, 1940-64, XX, bone, 4" ....................................... 150
5392, 1965-69, USA, stag, 4" ...................................... 275
6392, 1965-69, USA, bone, 4" ..................................... 150
6392, USA, transition (master blade USA/spey blade 10 Dots), bone, 4" ............................................................. 300
5392, 1970, 10 Dot, stag, 4" ........................................ 300
6392, 1970, 10 Dot, bone, 4" ....................................... 150
6392, 1970, 10 Dot to USA, bone, 4" .......................... 300

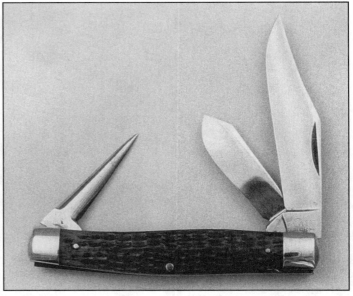

**63092, 1920-40, Tested XX, punch, green bone, 4", $600.**
33092, 1920-40, Tested XX, birdseye, yellow composition, 4" ............................................................. 300
33092, 1965-69, USA, birdseye, yellow composition, 4" ................................................................................. **125**
33092, USA, birdseye, 2 blades stamped USA, yellow composition, rare ........................................................ 300
33092, 1970, 10 Dot, birdseye, yellow composition, 4" ................................................................................. **125**
33092, 1970, 10 Dot, flat, yellow, 4" .......................... 140
5393, 1920-40, Tested XX, stag, 3-15/16" ................... 850
6393, 1920-40, Tested XX, green bone, 3-15/16" ........ 800
**6393R**, 1920-40, Tested XX, green bone, 3-15/16" ..... 850
9393, 1920-40, Tested XX, imitation pearl, 3-15/16" ................................................................................. 600
93093, 1920-40, Tested XX, imitation pearl, 3-15/16" ................................................................................. 500

Note: 5393 through 93093 are stockman/transition.

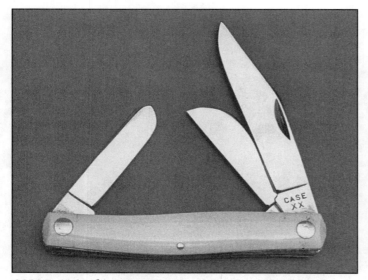

**33092, 1940-64, XX, yellow, w/out shield, 4", $100; w/ shield, $150.**
33092, 1940-64, XX, flat, yellow, 4" ........................... 125

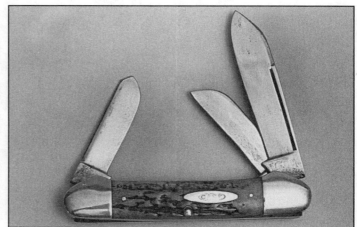

**5394LP, 1920-40, Tested XX, gunboat, stag, 4-1/4", $4,500.**
6394, 1920-40, Tested XX, green bone, 4-1/4" ......... 4,000

## Case Knives Tested (1920-1971)   233

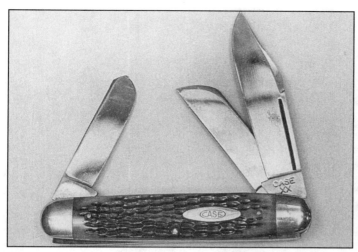

**6394-1/2, 1940-55, XX, long pull, green bone, 4-1/4", $3,000.**
**5394-1/2**, 1920-40, Tested XX, stag, 4-1/4" ............. **5,000**
**6394-1/2**, 1920-40, Tested XX, green bone, 4-1/4" .. **4,000**
**6394-1/2**, 1940-64, XX, red bone, 4-1/4" .................. **4,000**
**6394-1/2LP**, 1940-64, XX, red bone, 4-1/4" .............. **3,200**

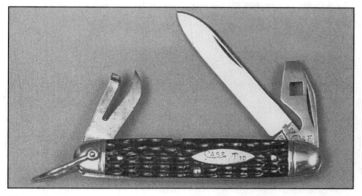

*Tested XX, Scout Jr. w/skate wrench, or could be Ford Model-T coil adjustment wrench or gaslight wrench, green bone, Scout shield, rare, 3-3/8", $1,000.*

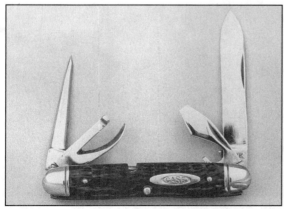

*Shown: 64090, 1920-40, Tested XX, Scout Jr., 4 blade, green bone, 3-3/8", $600.*
*Not shown: 64090, 1920-40, Tested XX, Scout Jr., genuine pearl, 3-3/8", $900;*
*Also not shown: 64090, 1920-40, Tested XX, Scout Jr., slick black, 3-3/8", $550.*

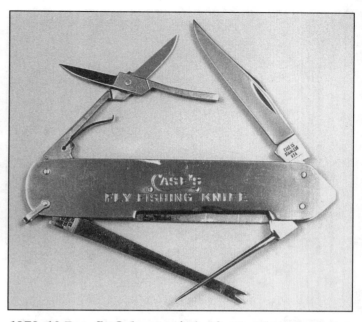

*1970, 10 Dot, fly fisherman's knife, stainless steel, 3-7/8", $350.*
**Fly fisherman**, 1920-40, Tested XX, nonstainless steel, 3-7/8" ................................................................ **800**
**Fly fisherman**, 1920-40, Tested XX, stainless, 3-7/8" ................................................................................ **750**
**Fly fisherman**, 1940-64, XX, stainless, 3-7/8" ......... **400**
**Fly fisherman**, 1940-64, XX (XX to USA), stainless, 3-7/8" ................................................................ **400**
**Fly fisherman**, 1965-69, USA (USA to 10 Dot), stainless, 3-7/8" ................................................... **350**
**Fly fisherman**, 1965-69, USA, stainless, 3-7/8" ...... **350**
**Fly fisherman**, 1970, 10 Dot, Transition (10 Dot to 9 Dot), stainless, 3-7/8" ................................................. **350**
**Fly fisherman**, 1970, 10 Dot, Transition (10 Dot to USA), stainless, 3-7/8" ............................................... **350**

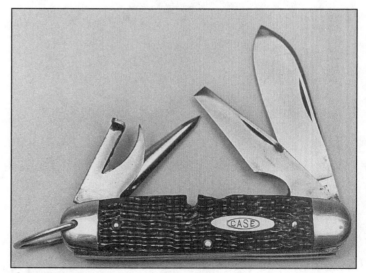

*6445R, 1920-40, Tested XX, Camp Scout or utility, green bone, 3-3/4", $450.*

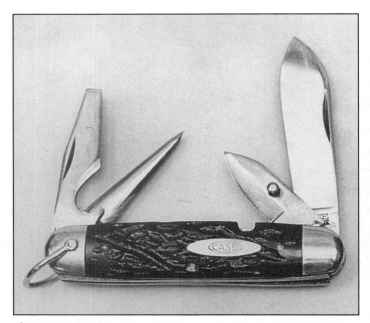

**6445R, 1920-40, Tested XX, rough black, 3-3/4", $325.**
B445R, 1920-40, Tested XX, imitation onyx, 3-3/4" .................................................................. 450
6445R, 1920-40, Tested XX, Navy knife, red fiberloid, 3-3/4" .......................................................... 350
9445R, 1920-40, Tested XX, imitation pearl, 3-3/4" .. 450

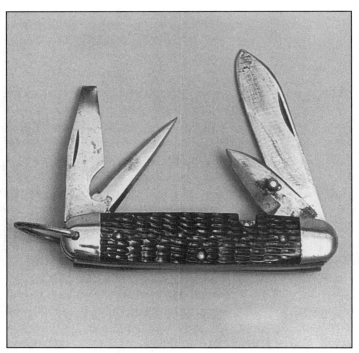

*64045R, Tested XX, Scout, green bone, no shield, 3-5/8", $350.*

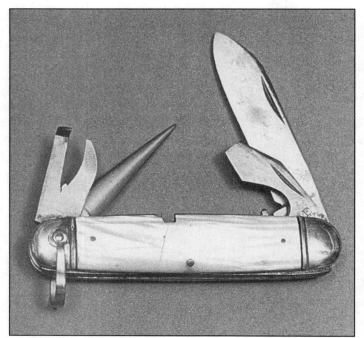

*9445R, 1920-40, Tested XX, cracked ice, 3-3/4", $450.*
6445R, 1940-49, XX, rough black, 3-3/4" ..................... 250
6445R, 1940-50, XX, imitation jig bone, 3-3/4" ............ 90
6445R, 1940-64, XX, red bone, 3-3/4" ......................... 250
6445R, 1940-64, XX, bone, 3-3/4" ............................... 200
6445R, 1965-69, USA, bone, 3-3/4" ............................. 125
6445R, 1970, 10 Dot, bone, 3-3/4" ............................... 150
64045, 1940-49, XX, rough black, 3-3/4" .................... 100

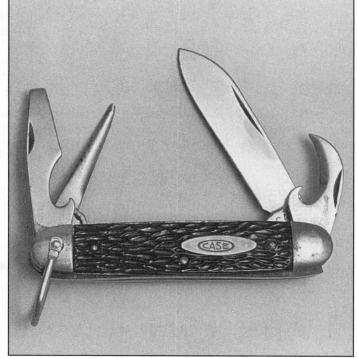

*640045R. 1940-50, XX, Scout, black plastic, 3-5/8", $75.*
640045R, 1920-40, Tested XX, green bone, 3-3/4" .................................................................. 350
640045R, 1940-64, XX, brown plastic, 3-3/4" ............... 65
640045R, 1965-69, USA, black plastic, 3-3/4" ............... 50
640045R, 1970, 10 Dot, brown plastic, 3-3/4" .............. 60

# Case Knives Tested (1920-1971) 235

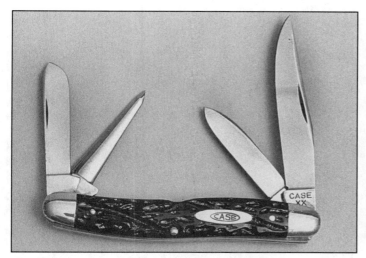

***64047PU, 1940-49, XX, rough black, 4", $600.***
**64047PU**, 1920-40, Tested XX, rough black, 4" .......... 800
**64047PU**, 1920-40, Tested XX, green bone, 4" ........ **1,250**
**94047PU**, 1920-40, Tested XX, imitation pearl, 4" .... 800
**64047PU**, 1940-55, XX, green bone, 4" ...................... 900
**64047PU**, 1940-64, XX, red bone, 4" .......................... 500
**64047PU**, 1940-64, XX, bone, 4" ................................ 350
**64047PU**, 1965-69, USA, bone, 4" .............................. 250
**64047PU**, 1970, 10 Dot, bone, 4" ................................ 250

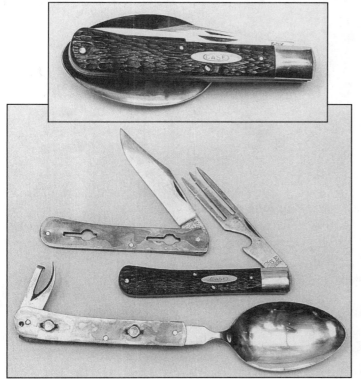

***A & C-352B 1920-40, Tested XX, hobo 6452, green bone, 3-3/4", clip blade, $1,000.***
**3452**, 1920-40, Tested XX, yellow celluloid, 3-3/4" .... 600
**M452**, 1920-40, Tested XX, metal, 4" ........................ 550
**GS452**, 1920-40, Tested XX, goldstone, rare, 4" ...... **1,200**
**6452**, 1920-40, Tested XX, spear blade, green bone, 4"
............................................................................................ 800

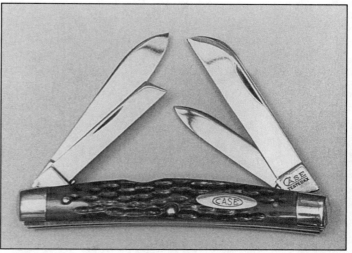

***64052, XX to Tested XX, congress transition, red bone, rare, 3-1/2", $3,000.***

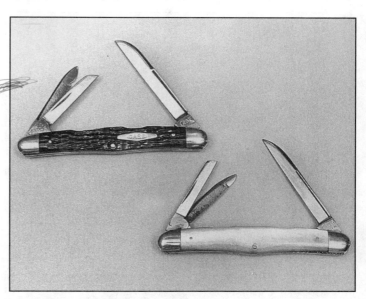

***64052, Case Tested XX, green bone, rare, 3-1/2", $3,000.***
**54052**, 1920-40, Tested XX, stag, 3-1/2" .................. **3,500**
**64052**, 1920-40, Tested XX, green bone, 3-1/2" ........ **3,500**
**64052**, Tested XX, Rogers bone .............................. **3,800**
**54052**, 1940-64, XX, stag, 3-1/2" ................................ 700
**54052**, 1940-64, XX (XX to USA), stag, 3-1/2" ........... 800
**64052**, 1940-55, XX, green bone, 3-1/2" .................... 900
**64052**, 1940-64, XX, red bone, 3-1/2" ........................ 500
**64052**, 1940-64, XX, bone, 3-1/2" ................................ 400
**64052**, 1940-64, XX (XX to USA), bone, 3-1/2" .......... 500
**54052**, 1965-69, USA, stag, 3-1/2" .............................. 350
**54052**, 1965-69, USA (USA to 10 Dot), stag, 3-1/2" ... 500
**64052**, 1965-69, USA, bone, 3-1/2" ............................ 250
**64052**, 1965-69, USA (USA to 10 Dot), bone, 3-1/2" .. 350
**54052**, 1970, 10 Dot stag, 3-1/2" ................................ 350
**54052**, 1970, 10 Dot (10 Dot to USA), stag, 3-1/2" .... 500
**64052**, 1970, 10 Dot, bone, 3-1/2" .............................. 300
**64052**, 1970, 10 Dot (10 Dot to USA), bone, 3-1/2" .... 350

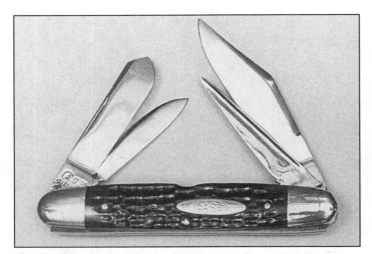

**64055PU, 1920-40, Tested XX, green bone, 3-1/2", $1,600.**
64055PU, 1940-55, XX, green bone, 3-1/2" ............. **1,500**

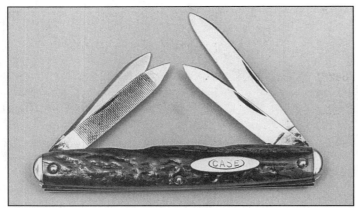

**5460T, 1920-40, Tested XX, stag, 3-3/8", $550.**
5460T 1920-40, Tested XX, red stag, 3-3/8" ............... **600**
8460 1920-40, Tested XX, genuine pearl, 3-3/8" ........ **650**

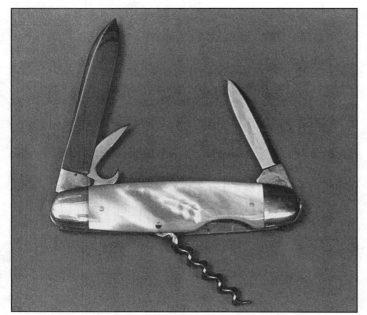

**84062K, 1920-40, Tested XX, pearl, 3-1/4", $800.**
94062K, 1920-40, Tested XX, imitation onyx, 3-1/4". **700**

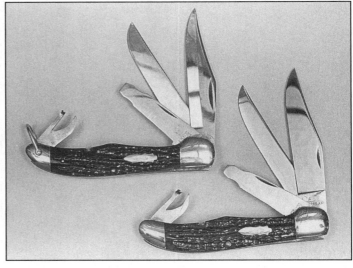

**6465SAB-R, Tested XX, folding hunter, saber blade, green bone, 5-1/4", $3,000.**
6465 green bone, flat blade...................................... **3,000**

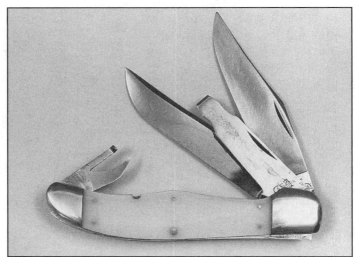

**3465, 1920-1940, Tested XX, folding hunter, flat blade, yellow celluloid, rare, 5-1/4", $3,000**
9465CI, 1920-40, Tested XX, French pearl handle. **3,000**

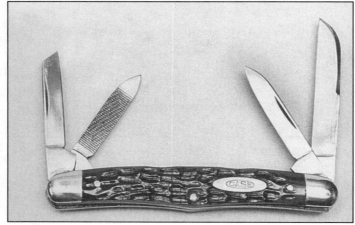

**6470F, 1920-40, Tested XX, green bone, 3-1/8", $900.**
6470, 1920-40, Tested XX, green bone, 3-1/8"........... **900**

Case Knives Tested (1920-1971) 237

**64081, Tested XX, gunstock whittler, lobster claw file, green bone, 3", $1,500.**
**64081**, Tested XX, gunstock whittler, lobster claw file, Rogers bone, 3" .......................................... **1,600**
**84081**, Tested XX, gunstock whittler, lobster claw file, genuine pearl, 3" ...................................... **1,600**

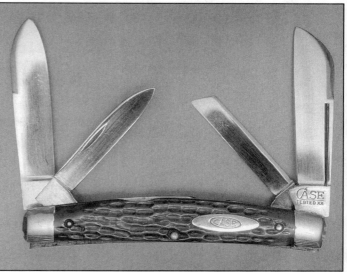

**6488LP, Case Tested XX, red bone, XX shield, 4-1/8", $5,000.**
**5488LP**, 1920-40, Tested XX, stag, 4-1/8" ................ **8,000**
**6488LP**, 1920-40, Tested XX, Winterbottom bone, 4-1/8" ................................................................ **12,000**
**6488LP**, 1920-40, Tested XX, green bone, 4-1/8" ..... **8,000**
**6488LP**, 1920-40, Tested XX, Rogers bone, 4-1/8" ................................................................ **10,000**
**6488LP**, 1920-40, Tested XX, rough black, 4-1/8" .. **6,000**
**6488**, 1940-49, XX, rough black, regular pull, rare, 4-1/8" ................................................................. **1,200**
**6488LP**, 1940-49, XX, rough black, 4-1/8" ............... **1,800**

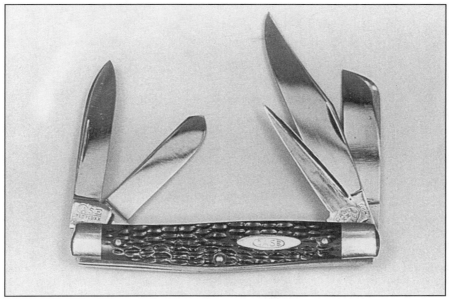

**6592, Tested XX, transitional, green bone, 3-7/8", $4,000.**
**9592**, Tested XX, cracked ice, 3-7/8" ....................... **3,500**

# Price Guide for Case Plain Stag Sets, Engraved and Serial Numbered Sets, and Individual Stag Knives (1976-1984)

| Pattern | Value Plain | Value Engraved | Remarks |
|---|---|---|---|
| **1976 4 Dot Razor Edge (Grey Etch)** | | | |
| 5111-1/2 L | $175 | none made | 15,000 made |
| 5172 | $175 | none made | of each knife. |
| 5233 | $85 | none made | No engraved bolster |
| 5254 | $125 | none made | knives made in 1976. |
| 5265 SAB | $150 | none made | |
| 52087 | $85 | none made | |
| 5347 | $125 | none made (7) | |
| Set of all 7 | $850 | none made | |
| 4 sheath knives for above set - - - - $500 - - - - - - 5,000 sets made. | | | |
| **1977 3 Dot Blue Scroll (Blue Etch)** | | | |
| 5111-1/2 L | $175 | $350 | 19,000 made of each |
| 5172 | 175 | $225 | plain bolster knife. |
| 52131 | 100 | $175 | 1,000 made of each |
| 5233 | 85 | $125 | engraved bolster knife. |
| 52033 | 100 | none made | No engraved knife made. |
| 5254 | 125 | $200 | Also made in 2 Dot (rare). |
| 5265 SAB | 150 | $200 | |
| 52087 | 85 | $100 | Also made in 2 Dot (rare). |
| 5347 | 125 | $175 | |
| Set of all 8 | $950 | $1250 | Not including 52033. |
| 4 sheath knives for above set - - - - $500 - - - - - 5,000 sets made. | | | |
| **1978 2 Dot Red Case (Red Etch)** | | | |
| Muskrat | $150 | $200 | 14,000 made of each |
| 5220 | $85 | $125 | plain bolster knife. |
| 52032 | $85 | $100 | 1,000 made of each |
| 5279 | $85 | $150 | engraved bolster knife. |
| 5254 | $125 | $200 | Also made in 1 Dot (rare). |
| 52087 | $85 | $100 | |
| 5347 | $125 | $175 | |
| Set of all 7 | $600 | $825 | |
| 4 sheath knives for above set - - - - $500 - - - - - 5,000 sets made. | | | |
| **1979 1 Dot Bradford Centennial (Brown Etch)** | | | |
| 5207 SP | $85 | $150 | 7,500 made of each |
| 52027 | $65 | $85 | plain bolster knife. |
| 5249 | $100 | $150 | 1,000 made of each |
| 5275 | $100 | $125 | engraved bolster knife. |
| 5292 | $85 | $100 | |
| 5318 | $85 | $100 | |
| Set of all 6 | $475 | $650 | |
| 4 sheath knives for above set - - - - $600 - - - - - 5,000?? sets made. | | | |
| **1980 10 Dot 75th Anniversary (Green Etch)** | | | |
| 5207 SP | $85 | $150 | 7,500 made of each |
| 5208 | $85 | $125 | plain bolster knife. |
| 52109 X | $85 | $125 | 1,000 made of each |
| 5235-1/2 | $65 | $85 | engraved bolster knife. |
| 5244 | $65 | $85 | |
| 5275 | $85 | $100 | |
| 5318 | $85 | $100 | |
| Set of all 7 | $500 | $700 | |
| Note: no sheath knives made for this set. | | | |
| **1981 9 Dot Plain Set (No Etch)** | | | |
| 5149 | $95 | $135 | 5,000 made of each |
| Muskrat | $150 | $200 | plain bolster knife. |
| 52027 | $65 | $85 | 1,000 made of each |
| 5235-1/2 | $65 | $85 | engraved bolster knife. |
| 5254 | $100 | $150 | |
| 53131 | $125 | $175 | |
| Set of all 6 | $500 | $700 | |
| Note: no sheath knives made for this set. | | | |
| **1983 Second-Cut Stag Set** | | | |
| Muskrat | $100 | $175 | 700 made of each |
| 5220 | $85 | $125 | plain bolster knife. |
| 52131 | $100 | $175 | 300 made of each |
| 5254 | 125 | $175 | engraved bolster knife. |
| 5383 | 125 | $175 | |
| Set of all 5 | $550 | $800 | |
| Note: all blades are new grind, except master blade of 5383. | | | |
| **1984 Second-Cut Stag Set** | | | |
| 5205 R | $85 | $100 | 600 made of each |
| 5207 SP | $85 | $150 | plain bolster knife. |
| 52033 | $85 | $100 | 400 made of each |
| 5318 | $85 | $100 | engraved bolster knife. |
| 5380 | $175 | $275 | |
| Set of all 5 | $500 | $750 | |

# Price Guide for Case Stag Sets, Truck, Miscellaneous Sets, and Single Knives

| DESCRIPTION | Year Made | #Ks | #Made | Price | Notes |
|---|---|---|---|---|---|
| #1 Stag Collector Set | USA-10 Dot | 23 | 2,000 | | |
| #2 Stag Collector Set | USA-10 Dot | 12 | 700 | $2,500 | w/5 sheath kn.&7 folders |
| Congress Set—all have serial numbers | 1984 | 3 | 2,000 | $350 | w/wood&glass displ. box |
| Mint congress Set w/engraved bolsters | 1984 | 3 | 500 | $450 | w/wood&glass displ. box |
| Whittler Set w/engraved bolsters | 1983 | 3 | 2,500 | $400 | w/wood&glass displ. box |
| 75th Anniversary Canoe Set | 1980 | 3 | 5,000 | $500 | w/wood&glass displ. box |
| Gunboat Set | 1985 | 3 | 2,500 | $400 | w/wood&glass displ. box |
| Barlow Set | 1982 | 3 | 5,000 | $300 | w/wood&glass displ. box |
| Pearl Set | 1982 | 3 | 1,000 | $750 | w/wood&glass displ. box |
| Texas Toothpick Set | 1984 | 3 | 2,500 | $350 | w/wood&glass displ. box |
| Rainbow Trapper Set (stainless) | 1988 | 5 | 500 | $850 | w/wood box |
| Rainbow Trapper Set (Damascus) | 1989 | 5 | 500 | $1,100 | w/wood box |
| Double Eagle Bicen. (523-7) | 1976 | 1 | 2,500 | $300 | w/wood chest |
| American Spirit Bicen. (5165) | 1976 | 1 | 10,000 | $150 | w/glass-top display |
| Chief Crazy Horse Kodiak | 1982 | 1 | 5,000 | $450 | w/box & leather sheath |
| #1 NASA Original Astronaut Knife, M-1 | 1970, '71 | 1 | 2,495 | $350 | w/wood&glass displ. box |
| #2 Astronaut Knife-M-1, 25th Anniv. NASA Commem. | 1983 | 1 | 1,000 | $250 | w/wood display plaque |
| #3 Astronaut Knife-First Steps on the Moon-7/20/69 | 1989 | 1 | 1,000 | $200 | w/display plaque |
| Sidewinder | 1980-1982 | 1 | ? | $300 | w/leather pouch & box |
| Texas Lockhorn | 1980 &'81 | 1 | ? | $175 | w/leather pouch & box |
| Bulldog (5172)—"X-X" | 1940-1964 | 1 | ? | $500 | w/wood box |
| Bulldog (5172)—"Transition" | 1965-1966 | 1 | ? | $450 | w/wood box |
| Bulldog (5172)—"USA" | 1966-1969 | 1 | ? | $300 | w/wood box |
| Buffalo (P172)—USA | 1965-1969 | 1 | ? | $135 | w/wood box |
| Buffalo (P172)—Dots | 1971-1980 | 1 | ? | $100 | w/wood box |
| #1 Case/Ertl Truck—1932 Ford panel | 1995 | 1 | 2,500 | $500 | This is bank/ no knife |
| #2 Case/Ertl Truck—1957 Chevy stake body | 1996 | 1 | 2,500 | $600 | w/6227PW red bone |
| #3 Case/Ertl Truck—1950 Chevy pickup | 1997 | 1 | 2,500 | $350 | w/6220 brown bone |
| #4 Case/Ertl Truck—1940 Ford pickup | 1998 | 1 | 2,500 | $250 | w/610096 black bone |
| #5 Case/Ertl Truck—1947 Studebaker pickup | 1999 | 1 | 2,500 | $225 | w/6201 blue bone |
| #6 Case/Ertl Truck—1947 Dodge canopy delivery | 2000 | 1 | 2,500 | $200 | w/TH 61165 white bone |
| #7 Case/Ertl Truck—1951 Ford pickup | 2001 | 1 | 2,500 | $175 | w/6225-1/2 cran. bone |
| #8 Case/Ertl Truck—1946 Dodge power wagon | 2002 | 1 | 2,500 | $150 | w/61749 L red bone |
| #8-A Case/Ertl Truck—1946 Dodge power wagon | 2002 | 1 | 250 | $350 | w/81749 L abalone |
| #8-B Case-Coke/Ertl Truck—1925 Kenworth | 2002 | 1 | 2,500 | $125 | w/610096 dark red bone |
| #9 Case/Ertl Truck—1918 Mack flatbed | 2003 | 1 | 2,500 | $135 | w/6215 green bone |
| #9-A Case/Ertl Truck—1918 Mack flatbed | 2003 | 1 | 250 | $350 | w/6215 abalone |
| #9-B Case/Ertl Truck-Bank—1912 Ford Model "T" | 2003 | 1 | 2,500 | $100 | w/610096 red bone |
| #9-C Case/Ertl Truck-Bank—1936 Ford panel | 2003 | 1 | 2,500 | $50 | This is bank/ no knife |

Premium Guide To Knives & Razors, 6th Edition

# Case Fixed Blade Hunting Knives

By Bradley Wood

Over the years, W. R. Case & Sons has produced a vast assortment of fixed blade hunting knives[1] with many varied and beautiful handle materials. I have attempted to outline the predominant stag handled[2] variations that exist while also providing as much production data as possible on other handle materials. I compiled the information using the 1934 and 1941 price lists, as well as price lists from 1950 to 2003, except for the years 1951, 1953, 1954, 1960, 1973, and 1988. I also reviewed the 1938 Case catalog[3] as well as Case catalog numbers 60, 61, 66, 67, 68, 69, 70, 71, 77, 81, the two white binder Case catalogs from the early 1980s, the maroon covered 1986/87 catalog, and the Case catalog for each year from 1988 to 2003.

*Bradley Wood*

## General Information

**Chrome plating**: Due to information contained in the foreword of the January 1, 1934 price list, a reliable date for when Case first began to chrome plate hunting knife blades has been located. The 1934 price list described the attributes of chrome plating and stated that hunting knives with a "chrome finish" were part of a "new line" and that Case recommended this "new process" very highly. As such, this provides the collector with a way of determining whether a given hunting knife was made prior to 1934 or after 1934 (at least approximately so) by determining whether the blade is chrome plated or not.

In addition, the October 15, 1982 price list was the last list to contain any hunting knife patterns with chrome-plated blades[4]. After this list, all regular production hunting knives were listed in stainless steel. Therefore, it appears that Case chrome plated its hunting knife blades from about 1934 to about 1983.

**Carson, Cody and others**: In Case's earlier years, some hunting knives were stamped on the back tang with different names. The names I have seen are: BOONE, CARSON, CENTO, CODY, EXPERT, HOBO[5], SCOUT, and X-PERT. In my experience, all these knives, except for the HOBO marked pattern, were stamped on the front tang with the "Curved Tail C" Tested stamping and had non-chrome plated blades. Since the blades weren't chromed, they were all probably produced prior to 1934.

**Tang stamps in the USA era**[6]: Unlike Case pocketknives[7], the Case XX USA tang stamp was used from 1965 to 1979 on Case hunting knives. It is very important to realize that in the 1970s Case did not use the pocketknife dotting system on its hunting knives. For example, a Case hunting knife produced in 1975 has only the Case XX USA tang stamp with no dots underneath, whereas a Case pocketknife from the same year had five dots underneath the stamp. Also, it's interesting to note that on hunting knives the "USA" in the Case XX USA stamp does not have periods after the letters, but on pocketknives the "USA" has a period after each letter[8].

**USA leather sheaths**: An interesting change occurred in leather sheaths during the USA era. The interior of the belt loop on the USA sheaths were initially finished with smooth leather (as were sheaths produced during the XX era) and then transitioned into sheaths in which the interior of the belt loop was left unfinished[9]. The sheaths appear to have transitioned to the unfinished variety sometime around the time the Razor Edge stag set was introduced[10].

## Stag Handles[11]

Case has produced many variations within its stag handled hunting knife line. I have detailed some of these variations below as well as some patterns first introduced in the 1980s or thereafter. In addition, the stag tables present information as to the stag patterns listed in price lists over the years.

**Split stags**: Case produced at least 13 patterns of hunting knives with "split stag" handles. Split stags are characterized by a handle with the front and back stag slabs resting against one another instead of being separated by the blade. The split stag patterns I have encountered are as follows: 515, 523-5, 5024*, 5025-5,

557, 557SAB, 578, 5324, 5325-5, 5325-6, 5326*, 5361, and 5362. I also believe a split stag 523-6 exists.

**Pigstickers**: Case produced both a 563-5* and 563-6* "pigsticker" pattern in stag. These patterns exhibit either a five- or six-inch saber ground blade, respectively, with nickel silver bolsters on both ends of the handle and with the Case stamp on the top or bottom bolster[12]. Case also produced a 562-5* stag pigsticker that had a saber-ground five-inch blade fashioned with no top bolster and with an integral guard[13] instead of a bottom bolster. I also believe a 562-6* exists (a six-inch version of the 562-5*).

**Slab sides**: Case produced at least six patterns with "slab side" stag handles. Slab sides are characterized by having have either an integral front guard or a nickel silver front guard but no pommel. The stag slab side patterns produced were as follows: 552-5*, 564*, 564SAB*, 567*, 5161* and an unknown pattern with a Bowie knife style blade[14]. Except for the Bowie pattern, all the slab sides were marked with the CASE stamp (all capital letters with serifs)[15].

**Finn variations**: Several interesting variations exist within the "Finn" family (M5Finn, 5Finn, and 516-5) of stag patterns. For example, all three patterns were produced with both non-concave and concave ground blades. In addition, all three were produced with and without black bands beneath their pommels in the XX era[16]. I believe knives without the black bands were produced before knives with the black band. During the XX era, both the M5Finn and 5Finn were produced with brightly polished stainless steel blades in addition to chrome plated blades. Lastly, the 5Finn and 516-5 were produced in the early USA era with second-cut stag handles.

**Etched tang stamps**: I have seen three Case stag hunting knives with tang stamps that were acid etched "case" instead of the mark being stamped into the metal. The patterns were a 523-5, 5025-5, and a 557. I am not sure why an etching would have been used in place of a tang stamp. One could speculate, however, that it was used when the regular tang stamp had broken.

**Pommel transition**: In the XX era, pommels were changed from a round or square style (depending on the pattern) to the "knight's head" style pommel[17]. The knight's head style carried on into the USA era with all USA hunting knives having the knight's head pommel. With the exception of the 557 SAB pattern[18], I believe the change from round or square pommels to the knight's head style occurred somewhat close to the end of the XX era.

The round pommel stag patterns that were also made with knight's head pommels in the XX era were as follows: 523-6, 5025-6, 557, 557SAB, 5325-6, and 5361. The square pommel patterns that were later made with knights head pommels in the XX era were as follows: 5Finn, 516-5, and 523-5[19].

**XX to USA transitions**: Just as with Case pocketknives, Case stag hunting knives also exhibit a XX to USA transition period. In my experience, pattern numbers were not stamped on the back tangs of Case hunting knives manufactured prior to the use of the Case XX USA tang stamp[20]. However, at some point in the USA era, Case began to stamp pattern numbers on the back tangs of its hunting knives[21]. I believe the pattern number stamping began early on in the USA era because both the 557 and 5325-6 patterns can be found in the USA era with and without pattern numbers on the back tang, and both patterns were discontinued sometime between January 2, 1967 and March 1, 1968.

I believe that Case USA hunting knives without pattern numbers on their back tangs are XX to USA transitions. The stag patterns produced both with and without pattern numbers in the USA era were as follows: M5Finn, 5Finn, 516-5, TwinFinn, 523-3 1/4, 523-5, 523-6, 557, 5325-6 and 5361.

In addition, two other XX to USA transitions exist. The XX to USA transition 561 Deluxe Knif-ax[22] exhibited a knife blade with a Case (sans serif) stamp, whereas the ax featured the Case XX USA stamp. The Kodiak also underwent a XX to USA transition in which "Handmade in U.S.A." on the transition Kodiak was etched and filled in with black paint on the back of the blade[23] instead of being stamped on the back tang as were later USA Kodiaks. This knife was also furnished with the same alligator-hide-pattern stamped-leather sheath as was the XX Kodiak.

**USA tang stamp variations**: As is encountered with certain Case USA pocketknives, the Kodiak Hunter, 516-5, 523-5, 523-6, and 5361 were all produced in the USA era with both a small Case XX USA tang stamp, as well as one that was noticeably larger. On the 516-5 and 5361, the small USA stamp appears on knives without pattern numbers, whereas the large stamp appears on knives with pattern numbers. However, on the 523-5, the small USA stamp appears on knives both with and without pattern numbers, but I have only seen the large stamp version on 523-5s without pattern numbers. As to the 523-6, I have seen both the large and small USA stamp appear on knives with pattern numbers as well as without pattern numbers. With the Kodiak, both the large and small stamp appear to have been used interchangeably through the USA era. Lastly, an "extra small" version of the USA stamp exists on the post-transition Kodiak.

In addition, two other USA Kodiak tang stamp variations exist, which I believe are from 1978 and 1979[24]. The Kodiak tang stamping for 1978 had a dot both before the "XX" and after the "XX" in the "Case XX USA" stamping[25]. Similarly, in 1979 the Kodiak stamping had one dot before the "XX," but the dot after the "XX" was deleted[26]. As with the regular "Case XX USA" stamp on the Kodiak, both a small and large variation of the 1979 stamp exist.

**Long handled 5Finns and 516-5s**: In addition to the regular length handle, the 5Finn and 516-5 were both produced in the USA era with a stag handle that was approximately 3/4-inch longer (5Finn) and 1/2-inch longer (516-5) than the regular production handle. These longer-handled variations had chrome-plated blades and had handles of the same length and contour as the stainless-steel bladed 5Finn SSP and 516-5 SSP in the stag sets produced in the late 1970s[27]. The stag TwinFinn set was also produced with the longer handle 516-5 and with a longer sheath than the regular TwinFinn sheath to accommodate the longer-handled 516-5.

**Patterns introduced in the 1980s or thereafter**: Numerous stag handled hunting knife patterns were first introduced during the 1980s or thereafter. The following are twelve such patterns of which I am aware: Bowie, Camp Knife, Custom Hunter, DE15505 (Case Germany hunting knife produced in 2001), 5300 (Apache), 5400 (Cheyenne), 547-5 SS, 562-4 1/2 SS (Double-edged "Boot Hunter" style hunting knife), 578-3 1/2 SS, 581-6SS, 592-4D (Damascus blade) and 596-2 3/4D (Damascus blade).

## Stag Tables

I listed in the tables below only pattern numbers that were listed in Case price lists, and I have listed the pattern numbers exactly as they appeared in those lists. The columns in the tables list the years of price lists reviewed and the rows list the pattern numbers. An "x" appears in a column whenever a particular pattern

| Stag | 1-1-34 | 1938 | 1-1-41 | 1-1-50 | 1-1-52 | 6-1-55 | 8-1-56 | 4-1-57 | 9-1-58 | 12-1-59 | 9-15-61 |
|---|---|---|---|---|---|---|---|---|---|---|---|
| Kodiak | | | | | | | | | | | |
| M5Finn | | x | x | x | x | x | x | x | x | x | x |
| M5Finn ss | | | | x | x | | | | | | |
| 5Finn | | x | x | x | x | x | x | x | x | x | x |
| 5Finn ss | | | | x | x | | | | | | |
| 5Finn cc ss** | | | | x | x | | | | | | |
| 516-5 | | x | x | x | x | x | x | x | x | x | x |
| TwinFinn | | x | x | x | x | x | x | x | x | x | x |
| 501 | | x | | | | | | | | | |
| 515 | x | x | x | x | x | | | | | | |
| 523-3¼ | | | | | | | | | | x | x |
| 523-5 | x | x | x | x | x | x | x | x | x | x | x |
| 523-6 | x | x | x | x | x | x | x | x | x | x | x |
| 5025-5 | x | x | x | x | x | x | x | x | | | |
| 5025-6 | | | | | | | | | | | |
| 557 | x | x | x | x | x | x | x | x | x | x | x |
| 557SAB | x | x | x | | | | | | | | |
| 561Deluxe | | x | x | x | x | x | x | x | x | x | x |
| 578 | x | x | x | x | x | x | x | x | x | | |
| 5324 | x | | | | | | | | | | |
| 5325-5 | x | x | x | x | x | x | x | x | x | x | x |
| 5325-6 | x | x | x | x | x | x | x | x | x | x | x |
| 5361 | x | x | x | | | | | x | x | x | |
| 5362 | x | | x | | | | | | | | |

** The "cc" designation denotes a concave ground blade.

was listed in the corresponding price list[28]. I only labeled a pattern as "disct'd" (discontinued) if the noted price list stated the pattern was discontinued. However, by studying the tables, one can be fairly certain when particular stag patterns were discontinued due to their disappearance from subsequent price lists.

| Stag, Con't | 3-1-62 | 7-1-63 | 2-1-64 | 2-1-65 | 1-1-66 | 1-1-67 | 3-1-68 | 4-1-69 | 1-1-70 | 1-1-71 |
|---|---|---|---|---|---|---|---|---|---|---|
| Kodiak** | | x | x | x | x | x | x | x | x | x |
| M5Finn | x | x | x | x | x | x | x | x | x | disct'd |
| M5Finn ss | | | | | | | | | | |
| 5Finn | x | x | x | x | x | x | x | x | x | disct'd |
| 5Finn ss | | | | | | | | | | |
| 5Finn cc ss | | | | | | | | | | |
| 516-5 | x | x | x | x | x | x | x | x | x | disct'd |
| TwinFinn | x | x | x | x | x | x | x | x | x | disct'd |
| 501 | | | | | | | | | | |
| 515 | | | | | | | | | | |
| 523-3¼ | x | x | x | x | x | x | x | x | x | disct'd |
| 523-5 | x | x | x | x | x | x | x | x | x | disct'd |
| 523-6 | x | x | x | x | x | x | x | x | x | disct'd |
| 5025-5 | | | | | | | | | | |
| 5025-6 | | x | x | disct'd | | | | | | |
| 557 | x | x | x | x | x | x | | | | |
| 557SAB | | | | | | | | | | |
| 561Deluxe | x | x | x | x | x | x | x | x | x | disct'd |
| 578 | | | | | | | | | | |
| 5324 | | | | | | | | | | |
| 5325-5 | x | disct'd | | | | | | | | |
| 5325-6 | x | x | x | x | x | x | | | | |
| 5361 | x | x | x | x | x | x | x | x | x | disct'd |
| 5362 | | | | | | | | | | |

**The Kodiak was the only hunting knife that survived the discontinuance of stag in 1970. It remained in Case's line until stag was again discontinued in 2000 (an April 14, 2000, fax from the Case National Sales Office announced the "stag interruption").

Although the chrome-plated M5Finn, 5Finn, 516-5, and 523-5 patterns listed above were discontinued as of January 1, 1971, they were all produced in later years with stainless steel blades. For example, the M5Finn SSP, 5Finn SSP, 516-5 SSP and 523-5 SSP were all part of the stag sets of the late 1970s such as the Razor Edge Set. In addition, for periods in the 1980s and 90s, these patterns were made with round one-piece stag handles with a brass guard and butt cap and brightly polished stainless steel blades (and "SS" was used in the pattern numbers instead of "SSP").

In addition, the stag TwinFinn was put back into production for a short period in the 1990s, but with the 516-5 SS and M5Finn SS having round stag handles with a brass guard and butt cap, brightly polished stainless blades, and a redesigned sheath. The stag TwinFinn SS was first listed in a 1990 Case products flyer of "new fixed blades" and was no longer listed as of the March 1, 1995 price list.

Lastly, the 523-3 1/4 was redesigned as the "523-3 1/4SSP" and was produced with a flat-ground stainless blade (instead of a chrome-plated saber ground blade) and etched with a colorful pheasant etching. The earlier versions of the knife were shipped in a multi-color box with a hunting scene on the lid and text stating it was a "Small Game Knife." The Small Game Knife was first listed in the November 1, 1978, price list and remained in Case's hunting-knife line until stag was discontinued in 2000.

## Bone Handles

Case produced a great variety of bone-handled hunting knives. Some of the bone-handled patterns seen today on the collector's market were not listed in Case price lists. Examples of such patterns are the "small," "medium," and "large" Bowie patterns (actual pattern numbers unknown). However, the bone-handled patterns listed in the Case price lists I reviewed are as follows:

The following patterns were listed[29] in the January 1, 1934 price list and discontinued[30] between January 2, 1941 and January 1, 1950: 161, 62-5, 63-5, 64, 652[31] and 67. In addition, the 0600 Fish SS[32] and the 62-6 were listed in the January 1, 1934 price list and noted in the January 1, 1941 list as being discontinued once stock was depleted. Furthermore, the following patterns were listed in the January 1, 1934 price list and discontinued prior to the date the 1938 catalog was printed[33]: 0606 Fish SS[34], 066 Fish SS, 600 Fish, and 63-6. Finally, the 6700 F and the 661 Knif-ax were first listed in the 1938 catalog and were discontinued between January 2, 1941 and January 1, 1950.

## Leather Handles

From the beginning, leather handles were a staple of Case's hunting-knife line. Production data on the patterns that were included in Case price lists is as follows:

(i) **M3Finn**[35] - Listed in the January 1, 1950 price list and discontinued between January 2, 1978 and November 1, 1978; (ii) **3Finn**[36] - Listed in the 1938 Case catalog and discontinued between October 16, 1982 and September 1, 1983; (iii) **3TwinFinn** - Listed in the January 1, 1950 price list and discontinued between January 2, 1978 and November 1, 1978; (iv) **309** - Listed in the 1938 Case catalog and discontinued between January 2, 1941 and January 1, 1950; (v) **315** - Listed in the January 1, 1934 price list and discontinued between January 2, 1971 and January 1, 1972; (vi) **315-4 1/4** - Listed in the January 1, 1950 price list and discontinued between January 2, 1952 and June 1, 1955; (vii) **315-4 3/4** - Listed in the June 1, 1955 price list and discontinued between January 2, 1976 and January 1, 1977; (viii) **316-5** - Listed in the January 1, 1950 price list and discontinued between January 2, 1978 and November 1, 1978; (ix) **322-5** - Listed in the 1938 Case catalog and discontinued between January 2, 1941 and January 1, 1950; (x) **322 1/2-5** - Listed in the January 1, 1950 price list and discontinued between February 2, 1965 and January 1, 1966; (xi) **323-3 1/4** - Listed in the December 1, 1959 price list and discontinued between January 2, 1978 and November 1, 1978; (xii) **323-5**[37] - Listed in the January 1, 1934 price list and discontinued between October 16, 1982 and September 1, 1983; (xiii) **323-6**[38] - Listed in the January 1, 1934 price list and discontinued between October 16, 1982 and September 1, 1983; (xiv) **324** - Listed in the January 1, 1934 price list and discontinued between January 2, 1934 and the date the 1938 Case catalog was printed; (xv) **3025-5** - Listed in the January 1, 1934 price list and discontinued between April 2, 1957 and September 1, 1958; (xvi) **3025-6** - Listed in the 1938 Case catalog and discontinued between February 2, 1964 and February 1, 1965; (xvii) **325-5** - Listed in the January 1, 1934 price list and discontinued between January 2, 1972 and September 1, 1974; (xviii) **325-6** - Listed in the January 1, 1934 price list and discontinued between January 2, 1972 and September 1, 1974; (xix) **326** - Listed in the 1938 Case catalog and discontinued between January 2, 1941 and January 1, 1950; (xx) **0361SS** - Listed in the January 1, 1934 price list and discontinued between January 2, 1934 and the date the 1938 Case catalog was printed; (xxi) **361** - Listed in the January 1, 1934 price list and discontinued between January 2, 1934 and the date the 1938 Case catalog was printed; (xxii) **362** - Listed in the January 1, 1934 price list and discontinued between January 2, 1972 and September 1, 1974; (xxiii) **364SAB** - Listed in the 1938 Case catalog and discontinued between January 2, 1978 and November 1, 1978; (xxiv) **365** - Listed in the January 1, 1934 price list and discontinued between January 2, 1972 and September 1, 1974; (xxv) **365SAB** - Listed in the 1938 Case catalog and discontinued between October 16, 1982 and September 1, 1983; (xxvi) **366** - Listed in the 1938 Case catalog and discontinued between October 16, 1982 and September 1, 1983; (xxvii) **378** - Listed in the January 1, 1934 price list and discontinued between September 2, 1958 and December 1, 1959; (xxviii) **92** - Listed in the January 1, 1934 price list and discontinued between January 2, 1941 and January 1, 1950; and (xxix) **380 Combo and 580 Combo** (a leather-handled and wood-handled ax, respectively, combined with a 316-5) - Both listed in the December 1, 1959 price list and discontinued between January 2, 1972 and September 1, 1974.

**The leather "Finn" series in stainless:** The M3Finn SSP, 3Finn SSP, and 316-5 SSP were listed in the February 1, 1965 price list and discontinued between March 2, 1989 and March 1, 1990. In addition, the 3TwinFinn SSP is listed in the January 1, 1978 price list and discontinued between March 2, 1989 and March 1, 1990. However, in the April 1, 1991 price list, all of these patterns except for the 3Finn SSP[39] were again listed but with just an "SS" in their pattern numbers. All four were in current production as of February 1, 2003 price list.

## Celluloid Handles[40]

Case produced many celluloid handled patterns. The celluloid patterns listed in the Case price lists I reviewed were as follows:

The following celluloid[41] handled hunting knives were listed in the January 1, 1934 price list and discontinued between January 2, 1941 and January 1, 1950: Midget*, Asst. Cataline (a dagger), 352, 923-5*, 923-6*, 952, 957, 957SAB, 9362*, 964 and 97*. In addition, the following patterns were listed in the January 1, 1934 price list and discontinued between January 2, 1934 and the date the 1938 catalog was printed: M15, F52, 3361, 392, R92, 457, 457SAB, Finn, 9325-5, F78, PS78, 978, and PS97. Furthermore, the following patterns were listed in the 1938 catalog and discontinued once stock was depleted, as noted in the January 1, 1941 price list: E23-5* and M9Finn*.

The following patterns were only listed in the January 1, 1941 price list: E22-5* and C23-5*. In addition, the E66 was only listed in the 1938 catalog. Furthermore, the 9Finn was listed in the 1938 catalog and discontinued between January 2, 1952 and June 1, 1955. Lastly, the 961 Knif-ax was listed in the January 1, 1934 price list and the 961 Deluxe Knif-ax[42] was listed in the 1938 catalog, with both being discontinued between December 2, 1959 and September 15, 1961.

Some information can be gleaned from the 1938 Case catalog as to the type of celluloid handle denoted by the letter designations. For example, the E23-5 was listed with having a "mottled pearl, black and red composition handle," whereas the RE66 was listed as having a "mottled pearl and brown composition handle." The 352 was listed as having a "cream color composition" handle, whereas the 957 was listed with an "imitation composition pearl" handle. In addition, on page 343 of the 1942 Stoeger Arms Catalog ("The Shooter's Bible"), the R92 was listed as having a "mottled black agate composition handle."

## Plastic Handles[43]

The following is a listing of the most commonly encountered plastic-handled hunting knives produced by Case:

(i) **BOWIE** - This pattern was based on the V44 fighting knife manufactured during WWII. This knife featured a detailed etching of a frontiersman with a coonskin cap (Davy Crockett) towards the end of the blade. This version of the Bowie knife was listed in the February 1, 1965 price list and was discontinued between March 2, 1990 and April 1, 1991[44]. White and black plastic-handled versions of this knife are still produced today; (ii) **2Finn** - Listed in the March 1, 1968 price list and discontinued between June 2, 1987 and March 1, 1989 (not shown in the 1988 catalog). Beginning with the September 1, 1983 price list, it was listed as a 2Finn SS with a stainless steel blade instead of a chrome-plated blade; (iii) **200 (Cherokee)** - Listed in the January 1, 1967 price list and discontinued between October 2, 1980 and October 1, 1981; (iv) **216-5** - Listed in the January 1, 1971 price list and discontinued between June 2, 1987 and March 1, 1989 (not shown in the 1988 catalog). Beginning with the September 1, 1983 price list, it was listed as a 216-5SS with a stainless-steel blade instead of a chrome-plated blade; (v) **223-5** - Listed in the March 1, 1968 price list and discontinued between June 2, 1987 and March 1, 1989 (not shown in the 1988 catalog). Beginning with the September 1, 1983 price list, it was listed as a 223-5SS with a stainless-steel blade instead of a chrome-plated blade; (vi) **223-6** - Listed in the March 1, 1968 price list and discontinued between October 16, 1982 and September 1, 1983; (vii) **300 (Apache)** - Listed in the February 1, 1965 price list and discontinued between October 2, 1980 and October 1, 1981; (viii) **303 (throwing knife)** - Listed in the January 1, 1934 price list and discontinued between January 16, 1985 and March 1, 1986; (ix) **304 (double throwing knife set)** - Listed in the October 1, 1981 price list and discontinued between October 16, 1982 and September 1, 1983; (x) **305 (double throwing knife set)** - Listed in the October 1, 1981 price list and discontinued between October 16, 1982 and September 1, 1983; and (xi) **400 (Cheyenne)** - Listed in the January 1, 1967 price list and discontinued between October 2, 1980 and October 1, 1981.

## Wood Handles

**Fish knives:** Case produced several fish knives over the years with wood handles. Some of the more notable wood-handled fish knives were as follows:

(i) **500 Fish**[45] - Listed in January 1, 1934 price list and discontinued between January 2, 1941 and January 1, 1950. This is the same pattern as the 5700 CHR, except the 500 Fish has an integral guard; (ii) **5700 CHR**[46] - Listed in the 1938 catalog and discontinued between January 2, 1972 and September 1, 1974; and (iii) **7 Fish** - Listed in the January 1, 1934 price list and discontinued between January 2, 1941 and January 1, 1950.

**Named models:** Beginning in the late 1970s, Case developed many wood-handled hunting knives with particular names as listed below:

(i) **R503SSP (Arapaho)** - Listed in the November 1, 1978 price list and discontinued between June 2, 1987 and March 1, 1989 (not shown in the 1988 catalog); (ii) **P62-4 1/2 SS (Boot Hunter)** - Listed in the November 1, 1978 price list and discontinued between April 2, 1992 and April 1, 1993; (iii) **Caribou Skinner** - Listed in the October 1, 1981 price list and discontinued between January 16, 1985 and March 1, 1986; (iv) **R803 SSP (Choctaw)** - Listed in the October 1, 1981 price list and discontinued between January 16, 1985 and March 1, 1986; (v) **Desert Prince** - Listed in the October 1, 1981 price list and discontinued between January 16, 1985 and

March 1, 1986; (vi) **R703 SSP (Kiowa)** - Listed in the November 1, 1978 price list and discontinued between June 2, 1987 and March 1, 1989 (not shown in the 1988 catalog); (vii) **Kodiak** - Listed in the January 1, 2001 price list and discontinued between January 2, 2002 and February 1, 2003; (viii) **P51 SSP (Lil' Devil)** - Listed in the November 1, 1978 price list and discontinued between October 16, 1982 and September 1, 1983; and (ix) **R603 SSP (Pawnee)** - Listed in the November 1, 1978 price list and discontinued between January 16, 1985 and March 1, 1986.

**Pigsticker:** The wood-handled "pigsticker" exhibited a double-edged dagger-style six-inch blade and was listed as a 162-6 in the January 1, 1934 price list and as a 562 in the 1938 catalog. Later, it was designated as a 562-6 in the 1955 price list, with the 562-6 pattern number remaining until it was last listed in the December 1, 1959 price list. This knife was also produced with a single edge, but the pattern number of this variation is not known.

**Marlin spike:** Case produced a walnut-handled hunting knife with a marlin spike contained in its sheath, which was designated as a 147 pattern. The 147 was listed in the January 1, 1941 price list and was discontinued between September 2, 1974 and June 1, 1975.

**261 and 261 Deluxe:** The 261 Knif-ax was listed in the January 1, 1934 price list and was discontinued between January 2, 1967 and March 1, 1968. The 261 Deluxe Knif-ax was listed in the 1938 catalog and was discontinued between December 2, 1959 and September 15, 1961.

## Hard Rubber Handles

Case produced several hard rubber handled hunting knives over the years. Some of the hard rubber handled patterns were as follows:

(i) **206** - Listed in the January 1, 1941 price list and discontinued between January 2, 1941 and January 1, 1950; (ii) **208-5** - Listed in the January 1, 1934 price list and discontinued between January 2, 1941 and January 1, 1950; (iii) **209-5** - Listed in the January 1, 1934 price list and discontinued between January 2, 1950 and July 1, 1952; (iv) **262** - Listed in the January 1, 1934 price list and discontinued between January 2, 1934 and the date the 1938 catalog was printed; and (v) **27F** - Listed in the January 1, 1941 price list and discontinued between January 2, 1941 and January 1, 1950.

## Pearl Handles and Metal Handles

To my knowledge, Case only produced one genuine pearl-handled and one metal-handled hunting knife in regular production, each of which is listed below, respectively:

(i) **M8Finn** - Listed in the January 1, 1941 price list, with this price list also noting the M8Finn was discontinued once stock was depleted; and (ii) **709** - Listed in the January 1, 1934 price list and discontinued between January 2, 1941 and January 1, 1950.

## Endnotes

1. Note that the term "fixed blade hunting knife" is used instead of merely "hunting knife" or "sheath knife" so as to exclude any folding knives furnished with sheaths. As such, any references in this article to "hunting knife" refers only to Case fixed-blade hunting knives. I did not include information on commemoratives or military patterns, nor did I attempt to cover in any comprehensive way the patterns introduced during the 1980s or thereafter.

2. References to "stag" in this article refers to genuine stag and not bone stag.

3. I have stated this catalog is from 1938, as that is the approximate date of publication attributed to it by James S. Giles. *The First 100 Years: A Pictorial and Historical Review of W. R. Case & Sons Cutlery,* (Tennessee: Smoky Mountain Knife Works, 1989) 50.

4. That is, all hunting knife patterns listed in the September 1, 1983 and later price lists as well as Case catalogs included an "SS" or "SSP" designation.

5. The Hobo marked pattern featured a handle that accepted three interchangeable hunting knife blades just like the Sportsman Set. The difference between the Hobo and Sportsman handles was that the Hobo handle featured a short throw blade latch identical to the earliest design locking mechanism on Knif-ax sets, whereas the Sportsman handle had a blade-locking latch similar to the spring release on the Case 5161L or 5171L switchblade pocketknives. The front tangs of the blades in both sets were marked with the "W. R. Case & Sons Bradford, PA." stamp.

6. References to the "USA era" in this article refer to the 1965 to 1979 period. Please note that I have no Case production information that verifies that Case switched in 1965 to the "Case XX USA" stamping on hunting knives, nor do I have any information which indicates the contrary. As such, I have kept with accepted practice and listed 1965 as the date the USA stamp was first used on Case hunting knives.

7. On Case pocketknives, the Case XX USA stamp was only used from 1965 to 1969.

8. However, with the Case XX Stainless USA stamping, neither the hunting-knife stamp nor the pocketknife stamp have periods in the "USA".

9. That is, the interior of the belt loop exhibits a split leather appearance.

10. The only exception to this appears to have been the small sheath supplied with hunting knives such as the M5Finn SSP and M3Finn SSP, which continued to be

produced with a smooth finish to the interior of the belt loop until sometime in the late 1970s or early 1980s.

11. Note that any patterns marked in this section with an asterisk (*) indicate an educated guess as to the pattern number, as these patterns were not listed in any Case price lists or catalogs I reviewed. It is also important to understand that, except for the tables, the information presented in this section is based primarily on my personal observations and opinions rather than Case literature.

12. On the Bradford version of a 563-5* I have seen, the top bolster was marked Case Bradford, Pa. on one side and Case's Tested XX on the other. It stands to reason that Bradford-stamped hunting knives marked "Case's Tested XX" on the back tang or bolster were not manufactured until late 1914 at the earliest, as the Tested XX trademark was not transferred from Case Brothers to W. R. Case & Sons until October 21, 1914. That is the date indicated on the trademark transfer in the United States Patent Office. For a copy of this trademark transfer, see pgs. 64 and 65 of Jim Sargent and Jim Schleyer's book, *Case Factory Endorsed Pocket Price Guide: W. R. Case & Sons Knives, 3rd Ed.*, Virginia: Knife Nook, 1985.

13. An integral guard is formed as part of the blade itself rather than being made from a separate piece of metal.

14. This knife was designed just like the 1991 NKCA Bowie and, in fact, the 1991 NKCA Bowie was patterned on this knife.

15. I believe the CASE stamp (all capital letters with serifs) was used not only in the XX era, but also in earlier years. For example, I have seen this stamp on two different Case hunting knives (a 6025-5 and a 5362) for which the blades were not chrome plated. As discussed above, this would strongly suggest the knives were manufactured prior to 1934. The 1938 Case catalog also shows several hunting knife patterns with this stamp.

16. References to the "XX era" refer to the 1940 to 1964 period.

17. The knight's head style of pommel somewhat resembles the profile of an armored knight's headpiece.

18. The 557SAB pattern last appeared in the January 1, 1941 price list, but yet was made with both round and knight's head pommels.

19. The 523-5 was also produced with a round pommel, but this pommel is much more scarce than the square pommel.

20. The only exception to this rule of which I am aware was the 337-6"Q WWII military leather-handled pattern, in which the pattern number was stamped on the back tang. Other than this, I know of no other pre-USA hunting knife in which the pattern number was stamped on the back tang.

21. Note that I have also seen leather-handled USA patterns both with and without pattern numbers on their back tangs. However, unlike the USA stag patterns, I cannot state with certainty that all the USA leather patterns were produced both with and without pattern numbers, as I have not personally observed the no-pattern number variation on all USA leather-handled hunting knives.

22. I have used the spelling "Knif-ax" throughout this article, since that is the spelling most often encountered in Case catalogs. However, spellings of "Knife-ax", "Knifax" and "Knife Axe" are also encountered in Case literature.

23. This is the same manner that the "Handmade in U.S.A." marking was applied to the XX Kodiak.

24. I believe these stampings are from 1978 and 1979, respectively, because the "red etch" series of Case hunting knives from 1978 exhibit the "two dot" USA stamp and the 1979 "Bradford Centennial" series exhibit the "one dot" USA stamp.

25. Note the dots are not underneath the stamp, as would be seen on a 1978 Case pocketknife.

26. Note the dot is not underneath the stamp as would be seen on a 1979 Case pocketknife. This type of stamp is also seen on the earliest version of the Small Game Knife (523-3 1/4 SSP).

27. The late 1970s sets were the Razor Edge Set, the Blue Scroll Set, the Red Etch Set, and the Bradford Centennial Set.

28. The only exception to this is that the "1938" column refers to the 1938 Case catalog and not a price list.

29. Anytime in this article a pattern is noted as "listed" in a given year's price list or catalog, it means that is the earliest price list or catalog to which I had access that first listed the pattern.

30. When listing the date of discontinuance of patterns in this article, I stated a range of years, with the beginning of the range referring to the day after the date of the last price list that listed the pattern and the end of the range being the next most recent price list to which I had access that no longer listed the pattern. As such, dates of discontinuance could have varied from the dates listed in this article. However, I believe relying on Case price lists in this manner should provide reliable information on dates of discontinuance of patterns.

31. The 652 pattern again appears in the September 1, 1961 price list but is then designated as a 652-5. The 652-5 was then listed as discontinued in the January 1, 1967 price list. No bone-handled hunting knives appear in price lists from January 1, 1967 until the March 1, 1998 price list, which then contains the 647-5 SS and 678-3 1/2 SS bone-handled patterns.

32. The "0" at the beginning of this pattern number (as well as the other pattern numbers which begin with "0" in this section and the 0361SS in the leather-handled section below) indicates a stainless steel blade.

33. Anywhere in this article a particular pattern is stated as discontinued between January 2, 1934 and the date the 1938 catalog was printed, it means that the pattern was listed in the January 1, 1934 price list but

was not in the 1938 catalog (nor the 1941 price list or other subsequent lists to which I had access).

34. I am uncertain of the blade design for the 0606Fish SS and the 066 Fish SS patterns, as they were not pictured in any Case catalogs to which I had access.

35. Case manufactured a brightly polished stainless-steel version of the M3Finn ("M3Finn ss"), which was listed in the January 1, 1950 price list and discontinued between January 2, 1952 and June 1, 1955.

36. Case manufactured two brightly polished stainless-steel versions of the 3Finn ("3Finn ss" and "3Finn cc ss," with the "cc" denoting a concave ground blade). The knives were listed in the January 1, 1950 price list and discontinued between January 2, 1952 and June 1, 1955.

37. The chrome-plated 323-5 and 365SAB patterns were also made with stainless-steel blades. The first listing of the 323-5SS and 365SABSS patterns was in the September 1, 1983 price list. The 323-5SS and 365SABSS were not listed in the March 1, 1990 list through the January 1, 2002 list. However, they then appeared again in the February 1, 2003 list and corresponding catalog, but the 365SAB SS pattern was then designated as a "365-5 SS" pattern.

38. In the January 1, 1941 price list, the 323-6 was listed as being discontinued once stock was depleted and did not show up again in price lists until the February 1, 1965 price list.

39. The 3Finn SSP was not listed again after the March 1, 1989 list until the February 1, 2003 list and was then designated as a 3Finn SS.

40. Patterns marked with an asterisk (*) in this section mean the January 1, 1941 price list stated that the pattern was discontinued once stock was depleted.

41. Celluloid is also sometimes referred to as "composition" in Case literature.

42. The difference between the "Deluxe" and regular 961 (as is true with all other Case Knif-ax combinations with the "Deluxe" designation) was that the ax of the 961 Deluxe had a flared forged head, whereas the ax that came with the 961 had a standard flat head.

43. Case used different wording over the years to describe plastic-handled hunting knives. For example, in earlier catalogs, Case stated that the handle on the 303 throwing knife was fiber but later described it as plastic. Also, early in production, the 200, 300, 400, 2Finn, 216-5, 223-5 and 223-6 were described as having a "Hy-car" handle, but later the handles were described as plastic and then synthetic. Lastly, the Bowie Knife was originally described as having a hard rubber handle, but later the handle was described as plastic and then synthetic.

44. As seen in the picture in the 1991 catalog, the etch on the Bowie had changed from a coonskin-capped frontiersman to a picture of Jim Bowie on the blade with "Jim Bowie 200th Anniversary 1790-1990."

45. Note that the 500 Fish pattern and the 7 Fish pattern noted below were labeled "Fish" in the January 1, 1934 price list but were designated merely with an "F" in the 1938 catalog and later price lists.

46. In the 1938 catalog, the 5700CHR was listed as having a walnut handle but the 700CHR was listed as having a beech handle. Also, the 5700CHR was designated in the January 1, 1950 and later lists as a 5700F.

Copyright ©2004 by Bradley Wood. All rights reserved.

**Tony Clemmons**

## Stag Handles

*Unknown pattern, stag, Case Bradford PA, Case's Tested XX on back tang, rare, 8", $400.*

*Unknown pattern, stag, W. R. Case & Sons Cutlery Co., Case's Tested XX on back tang, rare, 8-3/8", $400.*

# Case Fixed Blade Hunting Knives 249

*Unknown pattern, stag slabs, W. R. Case & Sons, Bowie, rare, 9-7/8", $325.*

*Unknown pattern, stag, curved tail C stamp on front guard, blade ground very thin, rare, 7-1/4", $200.*

**Unknown pattern**, stag, KA-BAR style blade, blood groove, butt cap, very scarce, 9-1/4" .......................... **275**

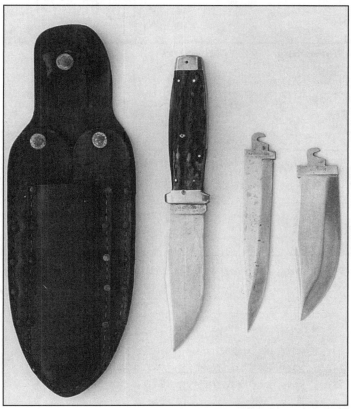

*Hobo Set, stag, W. R. Case & Sons, HOBO on back tang, 3 blades, rare, $2,500.*

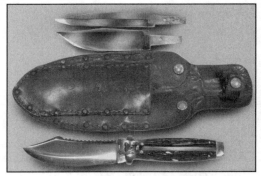

*Sportsmen Set, stag, W. R. Case & Sons, Case's Tested XX on back tang, 3 blades, rare, $2,500.*

**M5Finn**, stag, Case Tested XX (straight line), very scarce, 6" .................................................................. **220**

**M5Finn**, stag, long tail C, 6" ........................................ **200**

**M5Finn**, stag, short tail C, scarce, 6" .......................... **175**

*M5Finn, red stag, **CASE** (sans serif), no black band below pommel, non-concave blade, 6", $150.*

*M5Finn, stag, **CASE** (sans serif), no black band below pommel, concave ground blade, 6", $125.*

*M5Finn, stag, Case XX Stainless, scarce, 6", $175.*

*M5Finn, stag, **CASE** (sans serif), black band below pommel, 6-1/8", $110.*

*M5Finn, stag, **CASE** (sans serif), black band below pommel, tall pommel, 6-1/4", $110.*

**M5Finn**, stag, USA, no pattern number on back tang (XX to USA transition), 6-1/4" ...................... **120**

**M5Finn**, stag, USA, 6-1/4" ........................................... **100**

*5Finn, stag, long tail C, backward slanting square pommel, 7-3/4", $200.*

*5Finn, stag, short tail C, 7-3/4", $175.*

**5Finn**, stag, short tail C, small stamp, 7-3/4" ........... **175**

5Finn, stag, big C, scarce, 7-3/4", $175.

5Finn, second-cut stag, USA, very scarce, 7-7/8", $250.

5Finn, stag, short tail C, "stainless" in a half moon on back of tang, non-concave ground blade, rare, 7-3/4", $300.

5Finn, stag, USA, no pattern number on back tang (XX to USA transition), 7-7/8", $135.

5Finn, stag, Case's stainless, scarce, 7-7/8", $225.

5Finn, stag, USA, 7-7/8", $100.

5Finn, stag, Case XX Stainless, scarce, 7-7/8", $200.

5Finn, stag, USA, long handle, 8-5/8", $140.

5Finn, stag, **CASE** (sans serif), square pommel, no black band below pommel, 7-7/8", $125.

516-5, stag, long tail C, 9", $200.

5Finn, stag, **CASE** (sans serif), short square pommel, black band below pommel, 7-7/8", $125.

516-5, stag, short tail C, 9", $150.

5Finn, stag, **CASE**(sans serif), knight's head pommel, 7-7/8", $125.

516-5, stag, big C, 9", $175.

5Finn, second-cut stag, **CASE** (sans serif), very scarce, 7-7/8", $275.

516-5, stag, **CASE** (sans serif), no black band below pommel, non-concave ground blade, 9", $140.

Case Fixed Blade Hunting Knives 251

*516-5, stag, **CASE** (sans serif), no black band below pommel, concave ground blade, 9", $125.*

*516-5, stag, **CASE** (sans serif), short square pommel, black band below pommel, 9", $125.*

*516-5, stag, **CASE** (sans serif), knight's head pommel, 9", $125.*

*516-5, second-cut stag, USA, very scarce, 9", $225.*

516-5, stag, USA, small stamp, no pattern number on back tang (XX to USA transition), 9" .......................... 125

*516-5, stag, USA, large stamp, 9", $100.*

516-5, stag, USA, long handle, 9" ................................ 110

516-5, red stag, USA, long handle, 9" ......................... 120

TwinFinn, stag, long tail C stamp on both knives, basketweave sheath, very scarce .............................. 475

TwinFinn, stag, big C 516-5 & CASE (sans serif) M5Finn, both knives w/flat ground blades (Tested to XX transition) ................................................................. 350

TwinFinn, stag, CASE (sans serif) stamp on both knives, concave ground blade on 516-5 & flat ground blade on M5Finn (flat-ground to concave-ground transition) ..................................................................... 300

TwinFinn, stag, CASE (sans serif) stamp on 516-5, Case XX Stainless stamp on M5Finn ........................ 325

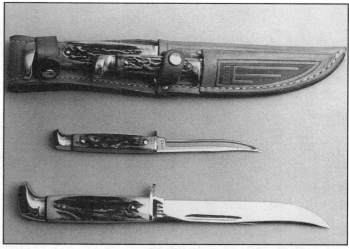

*516-5, TwinFinn, stag, **CASE** (sans serif), knight's head pommel, $275.*

TwinFinn, stag, USA, no pattern number on back tang of either knife (XX to USA transition) ....................... 300

TwinFinn, stag, USA ...................................................... 250

TwinFinn, stag, USA, long handle 516-5 .................... 275

501, stag, W. R. Case & Sons (three lines), double-edge garter knife, 8" ............................................................ 350

*515, split stag, Case Tested XX (straight line), 7-3/4", $250.*

*515, split stag, Case Tested XX in oval, 7-3/4", $250.*

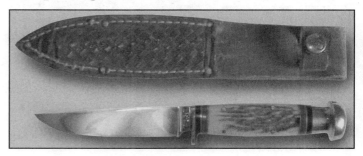

*515, split stag, long tail C, 7-3/4", $250.*

*515, stag, **CASE** (sans serif), split stag, nickel spacers, 7-3/4", $225.*

*523-3-1/4, stag,* **CASE** *(sans serif), 6-1/4", $135.*

*523 3 1/4, stag,* **CASE** *(sans serif), tall pommel, 6-1/4", $135.*

523 3 1/4, stag, USA, no pattern number on back tang (XX to USA transition), 6-1/4" ...................... 135

523 3 1/4, stag, USA, 6-1/4" ...................... 125

523 3 1/4, stag, USA (1979 stamp), pheasant etched blade, colorful box, 7" ...................... 90

*523-5, stag, CASE (serifs), split stag, hunting dog scene etch, very rare, 9", $300.*

523-5, stag, CASE (serifs), backward slanting square pommel, 9" ...................... 175

*523-5, stag, CASE (serifs), round pommel, very scarce, 9", $225.*

*523-5, stag,* **CASE** *(sans serif), small square pommel, 9", $140.*

*523-5, stag,* **CASE** *(sans serif), knight's head pommel, 9", $140.*

*523-5, stag, case (etched stamp), rare, 9", $250.*

*523-5, stag, USA, large stamp, no pattern number on back tang (XX to USA transition), 9", $175.*

*523-5, stag, USA, small stamp, no pattern number on back tang (XX to USA transition), 9", $175.*

*523-5, stag, USA, small stamp, 9", $130.*

523-6, stag, CASE (serifs), round pommel, 10-1/4", $175

523-6, stag, CASE (serifs), knight's head pommel, 10-1/4" ...................... 175

523-6, stag, USA, large stamp, no pattern number on back tang (XX to USA transition), 10-1/4" ................. 195

*523-6, stag, USA, large stamp, 10-1/4", $150.*

*523-6, stag, USA, small stamp, 10-1/4", $150.*

*5024, split stag, CASE (serifs), small blood groove, rare, 8-3/4", $325.*

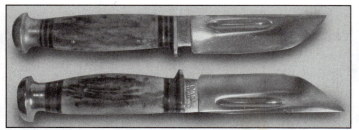

*5324, split stag, curved tail C, CODY on back tang, 9-1/4", $275.*

Case Fixed Blade Hunting Knives 253

*5025-5, split stag, curved tail C, 9-1/2", $300.*

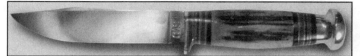

*5025-5, split stag, CASE (serifs), 9-1/4", $250.*

*5025-5, stag, CASE (serifs), 9-1/8", $200.*

*5025-5, stag, **CASE** (sans serif), 9-1/8", $200.*

*5025-6, stag, CASE (serifs), flat blade, round pommel, very scarce, 10-3/8", $235.*

*5025-6, stag, CASE (serifs), flat blade, knight's head pommel, very scarce, 10-3/8", $235.*

*5325-5, split stag, Case Bradford PA, Case's Tested XX on back tang, saber ground blade, 9-5/8", $350.*

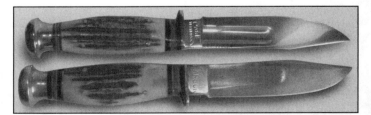

*5325-5, split stag, curved tail C, CARSON on back tang, 9-1/2", $300.*

*5325-5, stag, CASE (serifs), small blood groove, 9-1/4", $225.*

*5325-5, red stag, CASE (serifs), 9-1/8", $200.*

*5325-5, stag, CASE (serifs), 9-1/8", $200.*

*5325-5, stag, **CASE** (sans serif), 9-1/8", $200.*

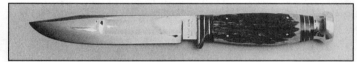

*5325-6, split stag, W. R. Case & Sons, Case's Tested XX on back tang, saber ground blade, 10-1/2", $450.*

5325-6, split stag, Case Bradford PA, Case's Tested XX on back tang, saber ground blade, 10-1/2" ................. **450**

5235-6, split stag, curved tail C, CARSON on back tang, 10-5/8" ........................................................................... **375**

5325-6, split stag (thin slabs), CASE (serifs), 10-1/2" ........................................................................................... **275**

5325-6, stag, CASE (sans serif), round pommel, 10-3/8" ........................................................................................... **225**

5325-6, stag, CASE (sans serif), knight's head pommel, 10-3/8" ................................................................................ **225**

*5325-6, stag, USA, no pattern number on back tang (XX to USA transition), 10-3/8", $250.*

*5325-6, stag, USA, 10-3/8", $200.*

**5326**, split stag, CASE (serifs), Woodcraft shaped blade, 8-3/8" .................................................................. **250**

**551**, CASE (serifs), basketweave sheath, 5-3/4" blade, 10-5/8" ................................................................ **1,400**

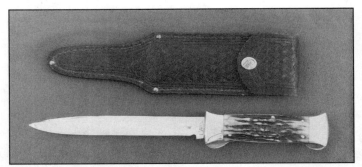

*551, long tail C, basketweave sheath, 5-3/4" blade, 10-5/8", $1,400.*

*552-5, stag slabs, CASE (serifs), very scarce, 8-7/8", $225.*

*557, split stag, Case's Tested XX on front guard, 7-1/2", $225.*

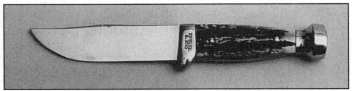

*557, stag, Case's Tested XX on front guard, round nickel silver split pommel, 7", $200.*

*557, second-cut stag, long tail C on front guard, round nickel silver split pommel, 6-3/4", $200.*

*557, stag, long tail C, 7", $185.*

*557, stag, CASE (serifs), 6-7/8", $175.*

*557, stag, **CASE** (sans serif), 6-7/8", $150.*

*557, red stag, case (etched stamp), rare, 6-7/8", $250.*

*557, stag, **CASE** (sans serif), knight's head pommel, 6-7/8", $160.*

**557**, stag, USA, no pattern number on back tang (XX to USA transition), very scarce, 6-7/8" ........................... **250**

*557, stag, USA, very scarce, 6-7/8", $220.*

*557SAB, split stag, Case's Tested XX on front guard, 7-5/8", $225.*

**557SAB**, stag, big C, round pommel, 6-7/8" ................ **185**

**557SAB**, stag, CASE (serifs), 6-7/8" ........................... **185**

*557SAB, stag, CASE (serifs), 6-7/8", $185.*

**561 Deluxe**, stag, Case's Tested XX ........................ **1,000**
Add $150 for original box.

**561 Deluxe**, stag, Case Tested XX on axe, CASE (sans serif) on blade (Tested XX to XX transition).............. **900**

**561 Deluxe**, stag, CASE (sans serif) on knife blade & CASE XX USA on axe (XX to USA transition) .......... **750**
Add $100 for original box.

Case Fixed Blade Hunting Knives 255

**561 deluxe**, stag, USA ... **700** Add $100 for original box.

*5161, stag, CASE (serifs), Outers pattern, very scarce, 7-1/2", $225.*

**5361**, split stag, W. R. Case & Sons Cutlery Co. Bradford PA, Case's Tested XX on back tang, saber ground blade, 8-1/8" ........................................................ **300**

*5361, split stag, Case Bradford PA, Case's Tested XX on back tang, 8-3/8", $275.*

*5361, split stag, Case stainless (curved tail C), rare, 8-1/2", $350.*

**5361**, split stag, curved tail C, SCOUT on back tang, 8-1/2" ........................................................................... **250**

**5361**, stag, CASE (serifs), scarce, 8-1/2" ..................... **200**

**5361**, stag, USA, small stamp, no pattern number on back tang (XX to USA transition), scarce, 8-1/2" ....... **210**

**5361**, stag, USA, large stamp, 8-1/2" .......................... **180**

**562-5**, stag, Case Bradford PA, Case's Tested XX in oval on back tang, very scarce, 9-3/8" ................................ **225**

**5362**, split stag, CASE (serifs), 8-5/8" ........................ **250**

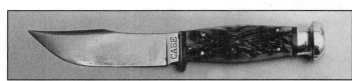

*5362, second-cut split stag, CASE (serifs), rare, 8-5/8", $300.*

**563-5**, stag, Case's Tested XX on front top bolster, Case Bradford PA on back top bolster, very scarce, 9-1/4" ................................................................................... **275**

**563-6**, stag, Case's Tested XX on front top bolster, very scarce, 10-1/8" ................................................................ **300**

**564**, stag slabs, CASE (serifs), very scarce, 7-7/8" .... **225**

*564SAB, stag slabs, CASE (serifs), very scarce, 7-7/8", $225.*

**567**, stag slabs, CASE (serifs), very scarce, 8-3/4" .... **225**

**578**, stag, CASE (serifs), 8-1/8" .................................. **200**

*5300, stag, Apache, 2,000 made in 1981 only, 9-5/8", $130.*

*5400, stag, Cheyenne, 2,000 made in 1981 only, 9-3/8", $130.*

*Razor edge set, stag, USA (1976), M5Finn, 5Finn, 516-5, 523-5, $550. Same set w/blue scroll etch, 1977 only, $550. Same set w/red etch, 1978 only, $550. Same set w/Bradford Centennial etch, 1979 only, $550.*

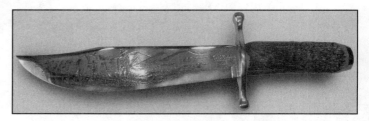

*Bowie, stag, 1980 stamp, Wild West (cowboy), plaque, 14-3/8", $265.*

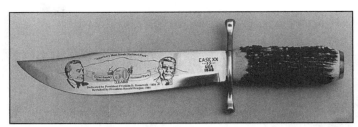

*Bowie, stag, 1984 stamp, Great Smoky Mountains 50th Anniversary, presentation box w/medallion, 14-3/8", $250.*

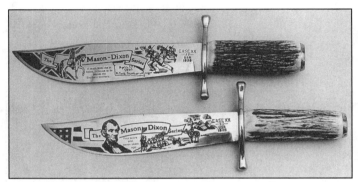

*Bowie, stag, 1984 stamp, Mason-Dixon Series, presentation box, 14-3/8", $225 each.*

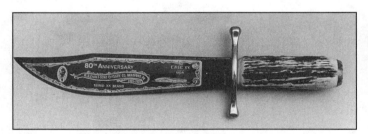

*Bowie, stag, 80th anniversary, 3,000 made in 1985, plaque, 14-3/8", $250.*

*Kodiak hunter, stag, CASE (serifs), thumb grooves on top of blade, "Handmade in U.S.A." etched on back of blade (no black), alligator-hide stamped leather sheath, 10-3/4", $350.*

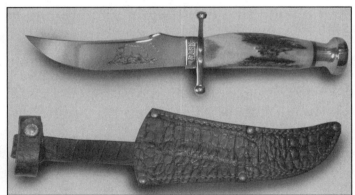

*Kodiak hunter, stag, CASE (serifs), "Handmade in U.S.A." in black on back of blade, alligator-hide stamped leather sheath, 10-3/4", $300.*

**Kodiak hunter**, stag, XX to USA transition, large USA front tang stamp, "Handmade in U.S.A." in black on back of blade, alligator-hide stamped leather sheath, scarce, 10-3/4" ............................................................ **325**

**Kodiak hunter**, stag, USA, small stamp, 10-3/4" ...... **150**

**Kodiak hunter**, stag, USA (1978 stamp), 10-3/4" ...... **150**

**Kodiak hunter**, stag, USA ( small 1979 stamp), 10-3/4" ............................................................................................ **150**

**Kodiak hunter**, stag, USA (large 1979 stamp), 10-3/4" ............................................................................................ **150**

# Case Fixed Blade Hunting Knives

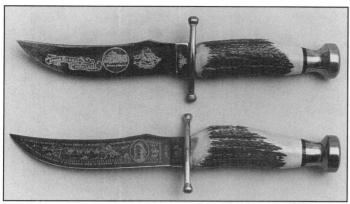

*Kodiak hunter, stag, experimental handle.*

*Top: Kodiak hunter, stag, Texas Sesquicentennial, 10-3/4", $300. Bottom: Kodiak hunter, stag, Chief Crazy Horse, blue & gold etched blade, 10-3/4", $400.*

## Bone Handles

**Unknown pattern**, Bowie style blade, Rogers bone, W. R. Case & Son, very rare ................................. 450

*Unknown pattern (6361-5?), Rogers bone, Case (script), round nickel silver split pommel, rare, $400.*

*Unknown pattern, Rogers bone, fish knife, sheath marked Kingfisher, $150.*

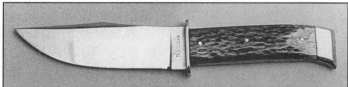

*Unknown pattern, Rogers bone, Case's Tested XX, rare, 8", $350.*

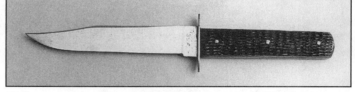

*Unknown pattern, green bone, Case Bradford PA, Case's Tested XX on back tang, similar to a 652 except flat blade & full guard, $200.*

*Unknown pattern, Rogers bone, Case Bradford PA, Case's Tested XX on back tang, rare, 8-1/4", $400.*

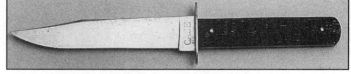

*Unknown pattern, green bone, CASE (serifs), similar to a 652 except flat blade & full guard, $150.*

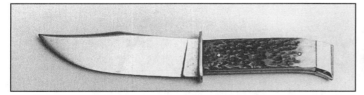

*Unknown pattern, Rogers bone, W. R. Case & Sons, Case's Tested XX on back tang, rare, 8-1/4", $400.*

*Unknown pattern, green bone, CASE (serifs), double edge sticker, 10-1/2", $400.*

Unknown pattern, early brown Rogers bone, Case Tested XX (straight line), similar to a 657 pattern except no pommel, 7-1/2", $150.

Unknown pattern, green bone, Case Tested XX (arch), pistol grip shaped handle, flat blade, guard, rare, 8-1/4", $225.

Small Bowie, Rogers bone, Case Bradford PA, Case's Tested XX on back tang, 8-3/4", $250.

Small Bowie, green bone, curved tail C, BOONE on back tang, 8-3/4", $250.

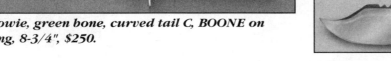

Small Bowie, green bone, Case Tested XX (straight line), $250.

Medium Bowie, Rogers bone, W. R. Case & Sons, Case's Tested XX on back tang, 10", $325.

Medium Bowie, green bone, Case Bradford PA, Case's Tested XX on back tang, 10", $325.

Large Bowie, Rogers bone, W. R. Case & Sons, Case's Tested XX on back tang, very rare, $500.

0600F, brown bone, Case Bradford PA, STAINLESS on back tang, $225.

0600F, Rogers bone, Case Stainless (etched script), rare, $225.

0600F, green bone, Case Stainless (script), 8-3/8", $200.

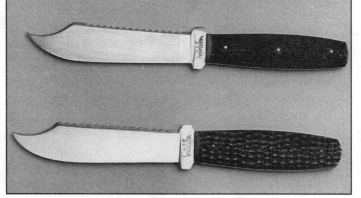

Top: 0600F, green bone, curved tail C, STAINLESS on back tang, 8-7/8", $175.
Bottom: 0600F, green bone, Case Stainless, 8-7/8", $185.

Case Fixed Blade Hunting Knives

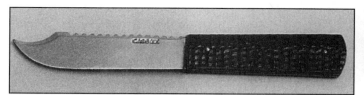

6700F, green bone, CASE XX (curly XXs), scarce, 8-3/8", $200.

161, green bone, curved tail C, 7-1/2", $125.

6025-5, second-cut green bone, CASE (serifs), nonchromed blade, very scarce, $250.

161 Rogers bone, curved tail C, 7-1/2", $125.

Top: 651, second-cut green bone, long tail C, basketweave sheath, rare, 5-3/4" blade, 10-5/8" overall, $1,500.
Bottom: 551, stag, $1,400.

161, green bone, Case stainless (script), scarce, 7-1/4", $225.

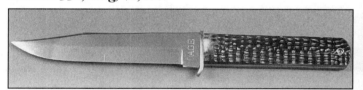

652, green bone, CASE (serifs), 8-3/4", $200.

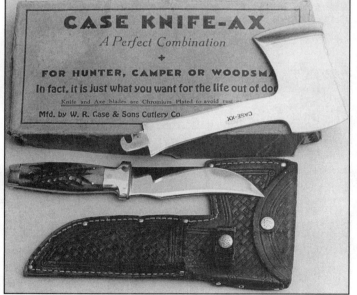

661, second-cut green bone, Case-XX, basketweave sheath, $1100 (w/box). Subtract $150 w/out original box.

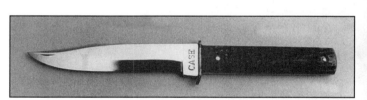

652-5, red bone, CASE (serifs), 8-3/4", $175.

657, green bone, tapered butt, Case Tested XX (straight line), rare, 6-3/4", $225.

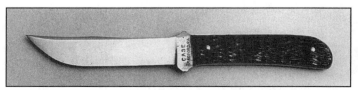

161, green bone, Case Bradford PA, Case's Tested XX on back tang, 7-1/2", $150.

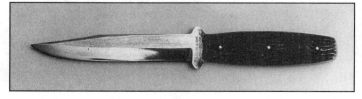

62-5, green bone, W. R. Case & Sons, Case's Tested XX on back tang, 9-1/4", $200.

*62-5, Rogers bone, Case Bradford PA, Case's Tested XX on back tang, 9-1/4", $200.*

*62-5, green bone & Rogers bone, curved tail C, CENTO on back tang of both, $200 each.*

*63-5, Rogers bone, Case Bradford PA on lower bolster, $225.*

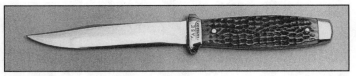

*63-5, green bone, curved tail C on lower bolster, $225.*

*63-5, green bone, long tail C, fighter-style front guard, $250.*

*63-6, green bone, Case Bradford PA on top bolster, $300.*

*64, green bone, long tail C, 8", $175.*

*64, green bone, CASE (serifs), 8", $140.*

*67, green bone, CASE (serifs), 7-3/4", $160.*

## Leather Handles

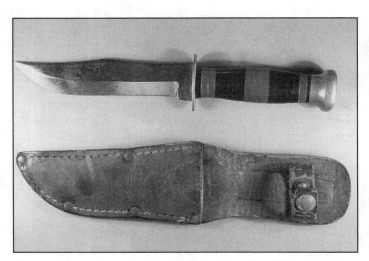

*Unknown pattern, leather, Case Bradford PA, 9-7/8", $100.*

*Unknown pattern (3024?), leather w/black, red & brass spacers, Case Bradford PA, similar to a 324 but w/a flat blade, $150.*

*Unknown pattern (361-5?). leather, **CASE** (stamped on aluminum guard), 8-3/4", $150.*

# Case Fixed Blade Hunting Knives

*Unknown pattern (361-5?), leather, case (script), 8-3/4", $150.*

*3Finn SS, leather, Case XX Stainless, polished stainless blade, scarce, 8", $75.*

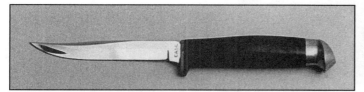

*M3Finn, leather, **CASE** (sans serif), 6-1/4", $35.*

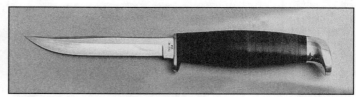

*3Finn, leather, USA, 8-3/4", $30.*

*M3Finn SS, leather, Case XX stainless, polished stainless blade, scarce, 6-1/4", $75.*

*3TwinFinn, leather, USA, $90.*

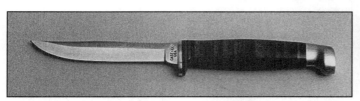

*M3FinnSSP, leather, USA (1978 stamp), 6-1/4", $30.*

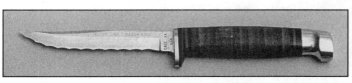

*M3FinnSSP, leather, 1982 stamp, miracle edge, $90.*

*Top: 709, hollow aluminum match container handle, CASE (serifs), compass in cap, survival knife, 9", $200. Bottom: 309, leather, CASE (serifs), hollow leather match container handle, compass in cap, survival knife, 9-1/2", $225.*

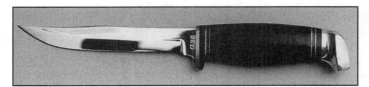

*3Finn, leather, short tail C, 7-3/4", $60.*

*3Finn, leather, **CASE** (sans serif), 8", $30.*

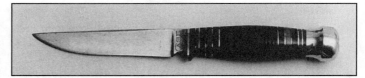

*315, leather w/colored spacers, Case Tested XX, 7-3/4", $75.*

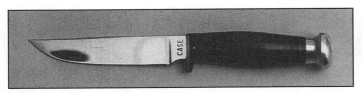

*315, leather, CASE (sans serif), 7-3/4", $35.*

*315-4-3/4, leather, CASE (sans serif), 8-7/8", $40.*

*315-4-3/4, leather, USA, 8-7/8", $40.*

*316-5, leather, CASE (sans serif), 9", $40.*

*316-5, leather, USA, 9-3/8", $40.*

*322-5, leather w/black, red & brass spacers, big C, $75.*

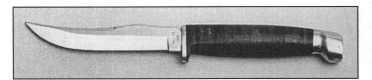

*323-3-1/4, leather, USA, 6-1/2", $40.*

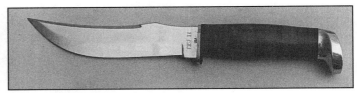

*323-5, leather, USA, 9", $45.*

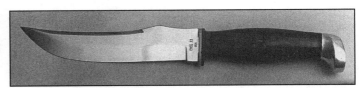

*323-6, leather, USA, 10-1/2", $50.*

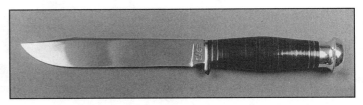

*3025-6, leather w/black, red & brass spacers, CASE (serifs), 10-1/2", $100.*

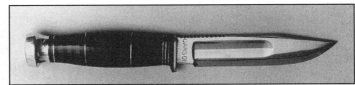

*325-5, leather w/black, red & brass spacers, curved tail C, CARSON on back tang, $150.*

*325-5, leather, CASE (serifs), 9", $75.*

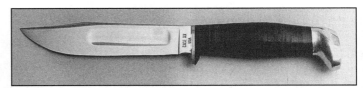

*325-5, leather, USA, 9", $75.*

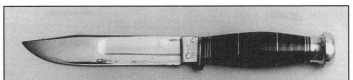

*325-6, leather w/black, red & brass spacers, curved tail C, CARSON on back tang, $150.*

Case Fixed Blade Hunting Knives 263

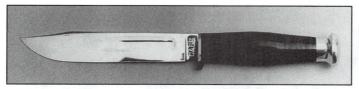

*325-6, leather, CASE (serifs), 10-1/2", $90.*

*362, leather w/black, red & brass spacers, curved tail C, 9-1/4", $100.*

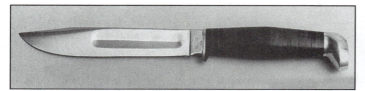

*325-6, leather, USA, 10-1/2", $90.*

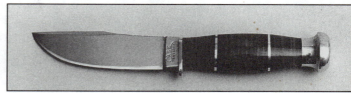

*362, leather w/aluminum spacers, curved tail C, $125.*

*357, leather, CASE (sans serif), scarce, $80.*

*362, leather, CASE (serifs), 8-3/4", $75.*

*0361SS, leather w/black, red, bone & brass spacers, Case Stainless (script), 8-1/2", $200.*

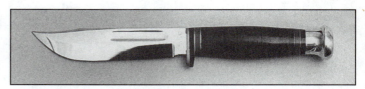

*364SAB, leather w/black, red & brass spacers, big C, 8-3/4", $75.*

*361, leather w/black, red, bone & brass spacers, curved tail C, SCOUT on back tang, 8-1/2", $150.*

*364SAB, leather, CASE (sans serif), 8-1/4", $45.*

*361, leather, CASE (serifs), scarce, 8", $150.*

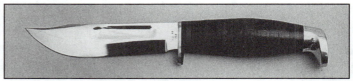

*364SAB, leather, USA, 8", $40.*

*362, leather w/black, red & brass spacers, Case Bradford PA, Case's Tested XX on back tang, $150.*

*365, leather w/bone & brass spacers, CASE (serifs), 9", $75.*

*365, leather w/black, red & brass spacers, CASE (serifs), 9-1/4", $55.*

*366, leather, USA, 8-1/4", $30.*

*365, leather, CASE (serifs), knight's head pommel, 9-1/4", $50.*

*365SAB, leather, CASE (serifs), 9", $55.*

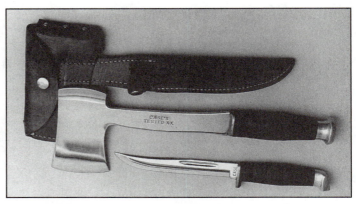

*380 combination, leather-handled axe & 316-5, Axe-Case's Tested XX, 316-5-CASE (sans serif), Tested to XX transition, deluxe head axe, $150.*

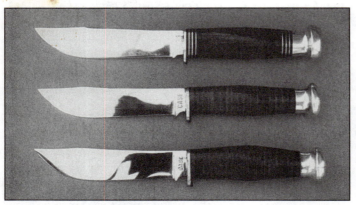

*Three Case 366 pattern hunters: Top: Tested, leather w/black, red & brass spacers, $75. Middle: CASE (sans serif-large stamp), leather, $45. Bottom: CASE (sans serif-small stamp), leather, $45.*

*380 combination, leather-handled axe & 316-5, Axe-Case XX USA, 316-5 CASE (sans serif), XX to USA transition, $150.*

## Celluloid Handles

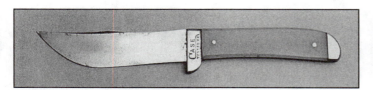

*Unknown pattern, yellow celluloid, curved tail C stamp on front guard, 7-1/2", $125.*

*Unknown pattern (RM52? or maybe F52?), blue mottled pearl celluloid, CASE (serifs), very scarce, 9", $235.*

*Unknown pattern, mingled celluloid, black, green & pink, CASE, 5-3/8", $100.*

*Small Bowie, mottled green w/brown celluloid, Case Tested XX (straight line), $250.*

Case Fixed Blade Hunting Knives 265

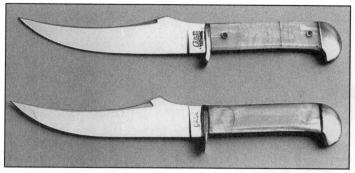

*Top: Midget, cracked ice handle, Case Tested XX (straight line), rare, 5-1/4", $175.*
*Bottom: Midget, imitation pearl celluloid, **CASE** (sans serif), rare, 5", $175.*

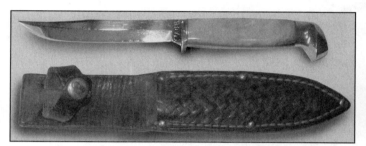

*9Finn, long tail C, greenish swirl celluloid, 7-3/4", $120.*

*M15, cracked ice, Case Tested XX (straight line), $150.*

*E23-5, mottled pearl & greenish-gray handle, CASE (serifs), 9-1/4", $225.*

*B325-5, waterfall handles, CASE (serifs), 9-1/2", $300.*

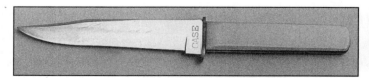

*352, yellow celluloid, CASE (serifs), 9", $125.*

*952, cracked ice, CASE (serifs), 9", $150.*

*957, cracked ice, Case's Tested XX on front guard, 7-1/2", $150.*

*957, green pearl celluloid, CASE (serifs), 6-7/8", $125.*

*957SAB, cracked ice, Case's Tested XX on front guard, 7", $150.*

*957SAB, mottled brown & white celluloid, CASE (serifs), $150.*

*957SAB, mottled celluloid, CASE (serifs), rare, 7", $150.*

*RM61, mottled pearl & brown celluloid, CASE (serifs), $225.*

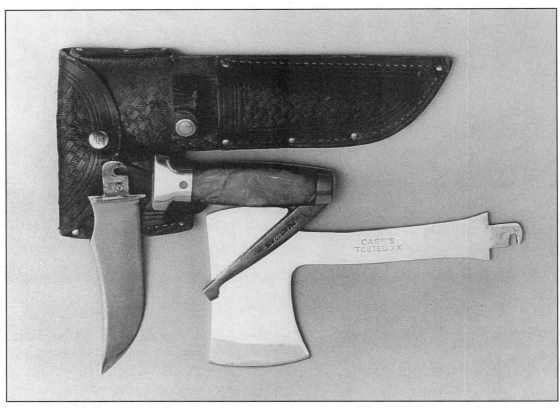

*961, "indestructible" pearl celluloid, Case's Tested XX, basketweave sheath, $700. Add $150 for original box.*

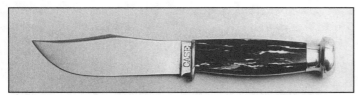

*M61, mottled celluloid, CASE (serifs), 8-1/2", $225.*

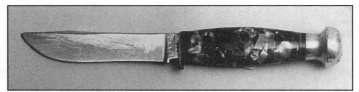

*RE66, mottled pearl, grey & black celluloid, long tail C, 8", $125.*

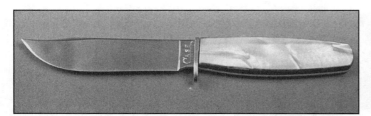

*964, greenish pearl pyremite, curved tail C, 8", $150.*

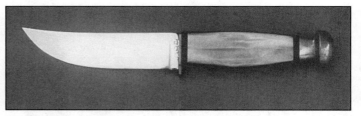

*978, imitation pearl celluloid, CASE (serifs), 8-1/8", $125.*

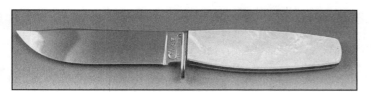

*964, cracked ice, curved tail C, 8", $150.*

# Plastic Handles

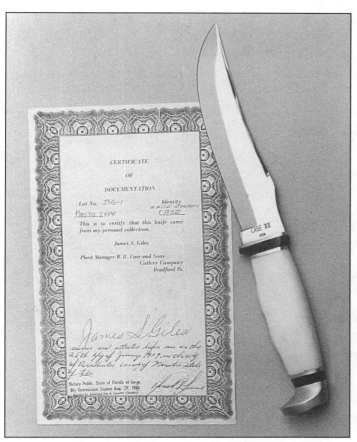

*JSG-1, white delrin, USA, one-of-a-kind prototype, 10-1/4", $150.*

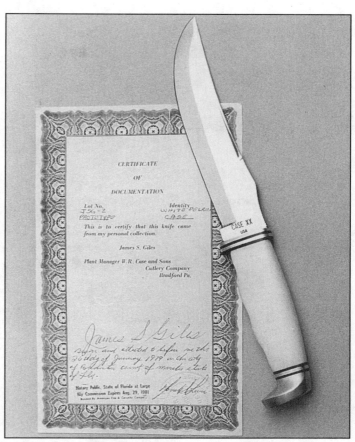

*JSG-2, white delrin, USA, one-of-a-kind prototype, 10-1/4", $150.*

*Top: Cheyenne (400), black composition, Case XX Stainless USA, 9-3/4", $50.*
*Middle: Cherokee (200), black composition, Case XX Stainless USA, 8-3/8", $50.*
*Bottom: Apache (300), black composition, Case XX Stainless USA, 10", $50.*

*2Finn, black composition, USA, 8-1/2", $40.*

*223-6, black composition, USA (1979 stamp), 10-1/4", $40.*

*223-5, black composition, USA (1979 stamp), 9-1/2", $40.*

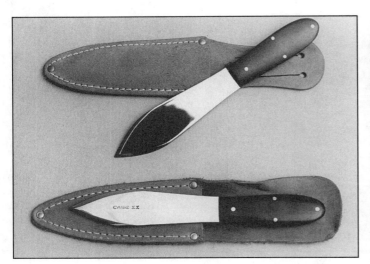

*Top: 303, red plastic, throwing knife 7-7/8", $30. Bottom: 303, red plastic, CASE XX (curly XXs), throwing knife, $45.*

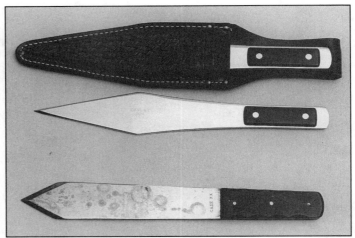

*Top: 304, set of two red plastic handled throwing knives w/double sheath, 12", $150. Bottom: Barnum & Bailey Circus throwing knife, CASE XX, heavy professional type, very scarce, 12", $150.*

## Wood Handles

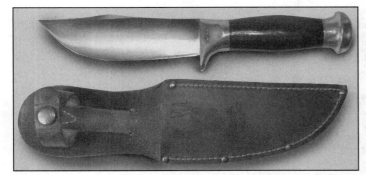

*Unknown pattern (1361-5?), walnut, **CASE** (stamped on aluminum guard), 8-1/4", $125.*

*Top: Desert Prince, pakkawood, 10-1/2", $80. Bottom: Caribou Skinner, pakkawood, 1981 stamp, $150.*

Case Fixed Blade Hunting Knives 269

*Unknown pattern (1361?), walnut w/black, red & brass spacers, W. R. Case & Sons, Case Tested XX in oval on back tang, 8-1/2", $200.*

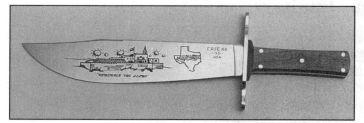

*Alamo Bowie, 1986 stamp, walnut presentation case, 13-7/8", $150.*

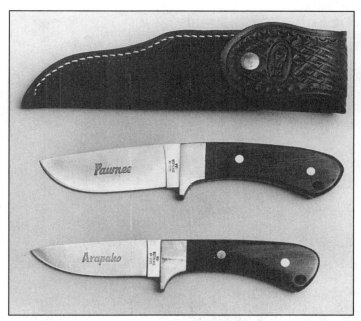

Top: *R603SSP (Pawnee), pakkawood, Case XX Stainless USA (1979 stamp), 9", $50.* Bottom: *R503SSP (Arapaho), pakkawood, Case XX Stainless USA (1979 stamp), 8-1/2", $50.*

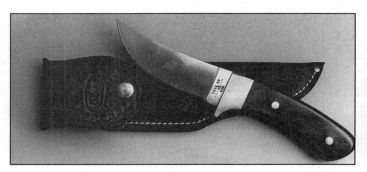

*R703SSP (Kiowa), pakkawood, 1980 stamp, 9-1/4", $50.*

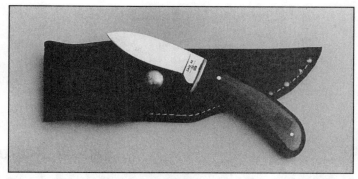

*P51SSP (Lil' Devil), pakkawood, 1980 stamp, 6-1/4", $50.*

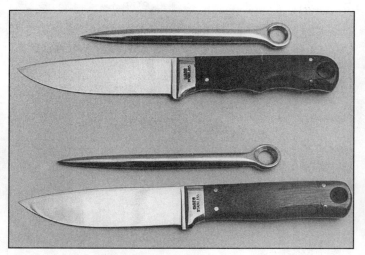

Top: *147 (Marlin Spike), ebony handle, Case's stainless, 8", 75.*
Bottom: *147 (Marlin Spike), walnut handle, Case's stainless, 8", 75.*

*5700CHR, walnut, fish knife, $45.*

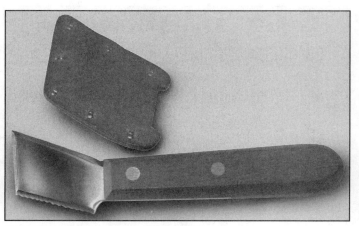

*77F SS, walnut, fish scaler, $40.*

*162 or 562, walnut, CASE XX, double-edge blade, 10-1/2", $225.*

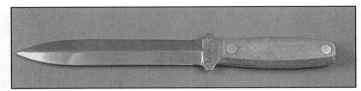

*162 or 562, beech, CASE XX, double-edge blade, 10-1/2", $225.*

## Hard Rubber Handles

*208-5, checkered hard rubber, CASE (serifs), flat blade, 9-1/2", $60.*

*262, checkered hard rubber w/red & brass spacers, curved tail C, Tested logo on handle, 9-1/4", $200.*

*208-5, checkered hard rubber, CASE (serifs), flat blade, 9-1/2", Tested logo on handle, $60.*

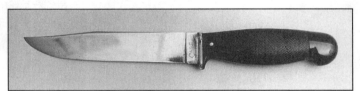

*208-6, checkered hard rubber, curved tail C, EXPERT on back tang, flat blade, $75.*

*209-5, checkered hard rubber, CASE (serifs), Tested logo on handle, saber ground blade, $75.*

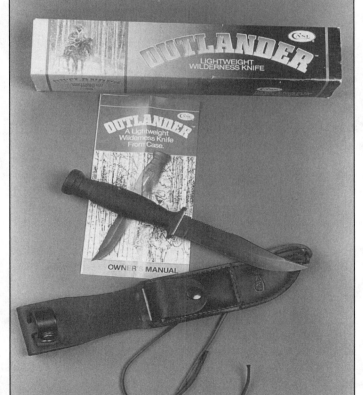

*209-5, checkered mottled brown hard rubber, CASE (serifs), Tested logo on handle, saber ground blade, $95.*

*Outlander wilderness knife, black rubber handle w/ thermometer, 10-1/2", 1986, sheath contains a honing stone, whistle, match, $65.*

## Garter Knives

**Mingled celluloid handle**, rare, Case Bradford PA... 400
**Genuine pearl handle**, W. R. Case & Sons ................ 400
**Stag handle**, silver ferrel, rare, W. R. Case & Sons... 350

**Ivory handle**, Case Bradford PA, rare, 7-1/2" ........... 350
**Goldstone handle**, Case Bradford PA, rare, 7-3/8" ... 400
**Yellow celluloid handle**, Case's Bradford PA, rare .. 400

# Little Valley Knife Association, Little Valley, New York (1898–1905) and Crandall Cutlery Co., Bradford, Pennsylvania (1904–1912)

Bob Crandall of Rochester, New York, has been collecting pocketknives since 1977. He is a member of the NKCA and NCCA. His interest focused on Crandall and Little Valley Knife Association brands when he learned he was a distant relative of Herbert E. Crandall, the founder of these companies. He obtained his first Crandall and LVKA pocketknives in 1978. These knives are numbers 74 and 86 in his overall collection, which now includes nearly 2,000 knives and razors, about 160 of which are Crandall related. His other cutlery interests include old pearl handled American pocketknives and English silver-bladed fruit knives with pearl handles from the nineteenth century.

*Bob Crandall*

## HISTORY OF LVKA/CRANDALL CUTLERY COMPANY

By Bob Crandall

Herbert E. Crandall (1876-1922) operated two cutlery firms. The first was Little Valley Knife Association in Little Valley, New York, from about 1898 until about 1905. The second was Crandall Cutlery Company in Bradford, Pennsylvania, from about 1904 until about 1912. Herbert's main connection to the cutlery business was through marriage in 1897. His wife, Theresa Case, was W. R. Case's daughter. Thus, he became brother-in-law to J. Russell Case and Harvey N. Platts, and was related to so many pioneers of American cutlery it's possible to mention only a few: Jean, John D., and Andrew Case of Case Brothers; J. B. F. Champlin of Cattaraugus and Kinfolks; Browns of Union Razor, Union Cutlery, and Kabar).

Herbert's first firm, LVKA., was a marketing effort with the products manufactured by Platts and Napanoch. His second company, Crandall Cut. Co., also encompassed design and manufacturing. That business introduced several novel ideas. One I like was the patented automatic opening knife called "The Crandall." Another was the sunken joints later promoted by his cousin Emerson Case at Robeson as "Pocketeze." Some Crandall knives used blade plating to resist rust before stainless steel was invented in 1911. The long tailed C mark was first used by Crandall and later used by W. R. Case & Sons during Case Tested years after Herbert sold his business to J. Russell Case. The razor side of the business had several patented and novel ideas also. One was a stropping device called "Sure Edge." I think cousin Emerson took that idea to Robeson also and changed it to ShurEdge!

Although I am distantly related to Herbert Crandall, I don't know how he obtained his skills in the cutlery business before he opened LVKA in his 20s. Neither do I know much about his short life after he sold Crandall Cutlery Company to his brother-in-

*Herbert Crandall*

law. He spent a few years associated with W. R. Case, but quickly disappeared from the cutlery business, and at age 46 disappeared from this world. His daughter Rhea, however, stayed involved a bit longer. Her second husband John O'Kain became president of W. R. Case, as did her son J. Russell Osborne (a son by her first husband). Her grandson John R. Osborne Jr., became vice president of manufacturing and was very close to his great-uncle J. Russell Case. And then in 1953, at the death of her uncle J. Russell Case, Rhea Crandall Osborne O'Kain inherited the W. R. Case & Sons Cutlery Company. It remained family owned until 1972. Perhaps we should pay more attention to the importance of women in our cutlery collecting and businesses!

## Little Valley Knife Association Pocketknife Marks

In the mark descriptions below, a semicolon (;) indicates separate lines on the knife tangs. The numbers under "Master Blades" and "Total Blades" refers to the number of knife blades in my collection of 15 knives that have those marks either on the master blade or in total. So far, all blades in a given knife have the same mark, other than the reproduction, which is the only knife with unmarked blades.

|  | Master Blades | Total Blades |
|---|---|---|
| **Mark #1** L. V. KNIFE ASS'N (curved); LITTLE VALLEY; N.Y. | 3 | 5 |
| **Mark #2** LITTLE VALLEY (curved); KNIFE ASSN.; LITTLE VALLEY, N.Y. | 2 | 4 |
| **Mark #3** LITTLE VALLEY KNIFE (arc); ASS'N; LITTLE VALLEY, N.Y. | 7 | 15 |
| **Mark #4** L. V. K. ASS'N; LITTLE VALLEY, N.Y. | 2 | 4 |

## Explanation of Text Under LVKA Pocketknife Photos

1 First is the handle material. Wood was the most common, with jigged bone next. Pearl, celluloid, and stag are rare. I believe most of the LVKA knives were made by Platts at the Eldred plant.
2. Next is the length of the closed knife to the nearest sixteenth of an inch.
3. The mark number refers to the list of LVKA marks described above. It is the mark on the master blade; however, the marks on the other blades are generally the same.
4. The condition is the standard NKCA grading for the knife pictured as judged by me.
5. The price is my estimate for the dollar value of the knife shown given its condition.

*Ebony, mark #1, very good, 3-5/8", $125.*

*Ebony, mark #4, near mint, 3-3/8", $350.*

## Little Valley Knife Association/Crandall Cutlery Company

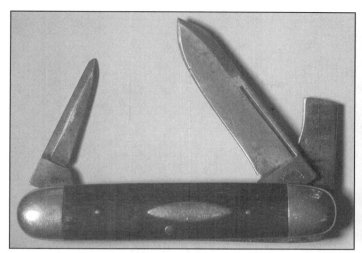

*Ebony, mark #3, poor, 3-5/8", $25.*

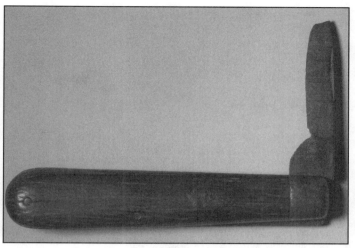

*Walnut, mark #1 (on small blade), poor, 3-1/4", $20.*

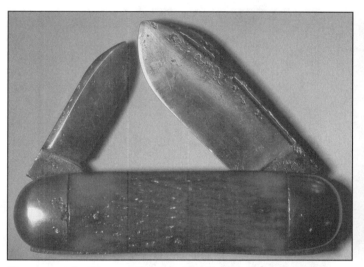

*Bone, mark #3, excellent (pitted), 4-3/16", $1,000.*

*Cocobolo, mark #3, excellent, 4", $300.*

*Bone, mark #4, excellent, 3-3/8", $250.*

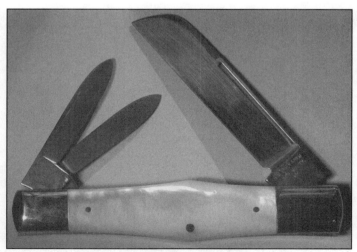

*Pearl, mark #1, reproduction, mint, 3-3/4", $65.*

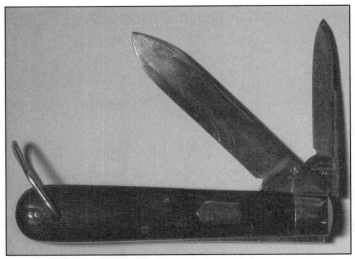

*Ebony, mark #1, excellent, 3-1/4", $200.*

*Ebony, mark #3, very good, 3-3/8", $140.*

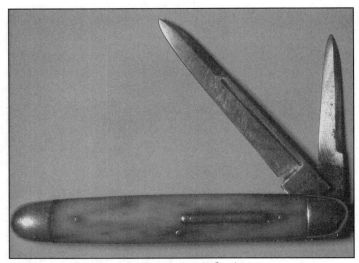

*Bone, mark #2, very good, 3-3/16", $100.*

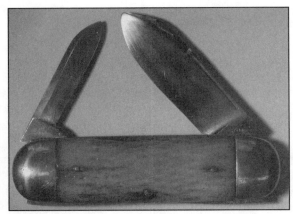

*Bone, mark #3, very good, 3-5/8", $400.*

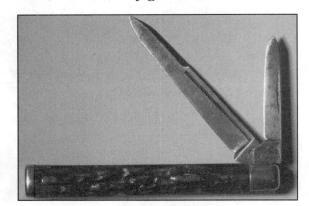

*Stag, mark #3, very good, 3", $500.*

*Ebony, mark #3, very good, 3-7/8", $150.*

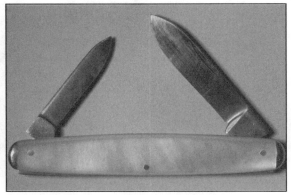

*Pearl, mark #2, excellent, 3", $150.*

# Little Valley Knife Association Razors

(All marks stamped and all blades etched "I Must Kut" unless otherwise noted.)

In the mark descriptions below, a semicolon (;) indicates separate lines on the actual marks as seen on the razor tang.

**Mark #1**
LITTLE VALLEY (curved downward); KNIFE ASS'N; LITTLE VALLEY N.Y. (curved upward)

**Mark #2**
LITTLE VALLEY KNIFE (curved downward); ASSOCIATION; LITTLE VALLEY N.Y. (curved upward)

**Mark #3**
L. V. KNIFE ASS'N; LITTLE VALLEY; N.Y.

**Mark #4**
LITTLE VALLEY KNIFE (curved downward); ---- ASS'N ----; LITTLE VALLEY, N.Y.

**Mark #5**
LITTLE VALLEY; KNIFE ASS'N

It's been said that LVKA razors were made by Napanoch. That may well have been true in the later years of LVKA; however, Napanoch did not begin business until 1900, and LVKA was definitely selling product by 1898. I would guess that perhaps Herbert was buying product from one of his new in-laws (Platts, Champlin at Cattaraugus, or Brown, but probably not Case, since they were jobbers also until about 1900).

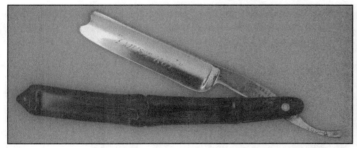

*Tortoiseshell celluloid, travel razor, mark #1, excellent, $150.*

*Slick black celluloid, mark #1, near mint, $100.*

*Black Gutta Percha, mark #2, near mint, $80.*

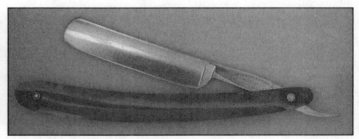

*Orange candy stripe celluloid, mark #2, excellent, $150.*

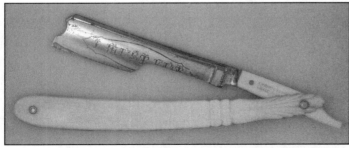

*"Classic," smooth bone, covered tang, mark #3, poor, $20.*

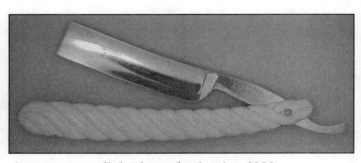

*Cream rope celluloid, mark #1, mint, $200.*

*Cream & rust rope celluloid, mark #1, excellent, $100.*

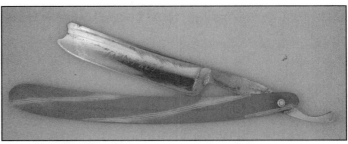

*Orange & yellow striped celluloid, mark #1, excellent, $150.*

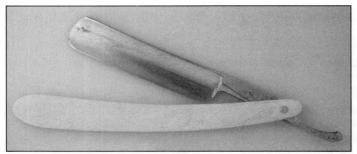

*Cream celluloid w/flowing hair, mark #4 (etched, not stamped), near mint, no "I Must Kut" etch, $200.*

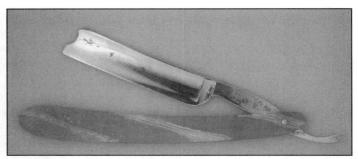

*Orange & cream striped celluloid w/wreaths, mark #1, excellent, $200.*

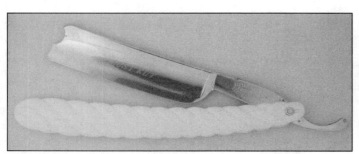

*Cream rope celluloid, mark #1, near mint, $175.*

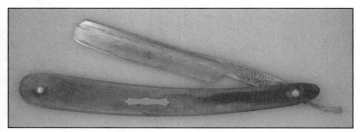

*Horn w/NS shield, mark #5, excellent, etched "I Must Cut" (Cut spelled w/"C" rather than "K"), $100.*

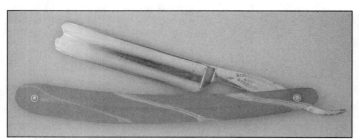

*Orange candy stripe celluloid, mark #2, near mint, $150.*

*"Classic" brown marbled celluloid, mark #1, excellent, no "I Must Kut" etch, $175.*

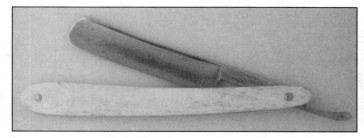

*Smooth bone, no "I Must Kut" etch, mark #4, excellent, $125.*

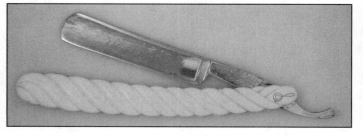

*Cream rope celluloid, mark #1, very good, $100.*

# Crandall Pocketknife Marks

In the mark descriptions below, a semicolon (;) indicates separate lines on the knife tangs. The numbers under "Master Blades" and "Total Blades" refers to the number of knife blades in my collection of 90 knives that have those marks either on the master blade or in total.

| | Master Blades | Total Blades |
|---|---|---|
| **Mark #1**<br>Crandall (long tail C) ; BRADFORD, PA.<br>This original Crandall mark was a forerunner of the long tail Case Tested mark. It was also used starting in the 1990s on Crandall reproductions made in Germany (Germany was stamped in ink on the back of some master blades) for the "Case Family Classics" series. The reproduction mark can be distinguished from the original in that, on the reproduction, Bradford, Pa. is shorter than Crandall. | 14 | 26 |
| **Mark #2**<br>CRANDALL; CUT. CO.; BRADFORD; PA.<br>The most common mark used on original Crandall knives. | 21 | 52 |
| **Mark #3**<br>CRANDALL; CUTLERY CO.; BRADFORD; PA. | 6 | 10 |
| **Mark #4**<br>CRANDALL CUTLERY CO.<br>I have seen this mark on a Crandall sunfish, but my sunfish has mark #7. | 0 | 0 |
| **Mark #5**<br>CRANDALL (curved); CUT. CO.; BRADFORD<br>I have not verified this mark. If there is a PA. under the BRADFORD (under the bolster?) it becomes mark #10. | 0 | 0 |
| **Mark #6**<br>CRANDALL; CUTLERY CO.; BRADFORD, PA. | 4 | 5 |
| **Mark #7**<br>CRANDALL; CUTLERY CO.; BRADFORD<br>The only original Crandall mark I have seen with BRADFORD but without PA. | 12 | 19 |
| **Mark #8**<br>CRANDALL; CUTLERY CO.; BRADFORD<br>All knives in my collection and all I have seen with this mark have been counterfeit. Some original knives with mark #3 have the PA. under the bolster, and it looks like this mark. It may have been one of those that the counterfeiter copied. | 3 | 6 |
| **Mark #9**<br>CRANDALL CUTLERY CO (curved); BRADFORD PA. | 2 | 2 |
| **Mark #10**<br>CRANDALL (curved); CUT. CO.; BRADFORD; PA.<br>The second most common original mark. | 20 | 55 |
| **Mark #11**<br>CRANDALL; BRADFORD; PA.<br>Both knives I have with this mark have small pen blades that would not hold a more complex mark. | 2 | 4 |
| **Mark #12**<br>THE; CRANDALL (curved); - -; PATENTED<br>The one knife in my collection with this mark is a unique automatic opening pattern. I have searched in vain for the patent to which this applies. | 1 | 1 |
| **Mark #13**<br>Crandall (long tail C); BRADFORD, PA.; U.S.A.<br>Used starting in the 1990s on all blades of certain Crandall reproductions in the "Case Family Classics" made in the U.S.A. | 2 | 6 |
| **Mark #14**<br>CRANDALL CUT. CO. (curved) ; BRADFORD, PA.<br>The one knife I have with this mark on the master blade has an unmarked small blade. | 1 | 1 |
| **Mark #15**<br>CRANDALL CUT. CO.; BRADFORD PA.<br>The one knife I have with this mark is a very unusual pattern and may be counterfeit. | 1 | 1 |
| **Unmarked**<br>Only two original Crandall knives in my collection have unmarked blades. The one unmarked master blade is a saw. The other may have been replaced. The Crandall reproductions of the 1990s made in Germany had all blades except the master unmarked. But later in the 2000s, these reproductions had all blades marked! | 1 (saw) | 8 |

## Explanation of Listings Under Crandall Pocketknife Photos

1. First is the handle material. Bone stag was a common material, also called wormgroove bone. It was bone that was jigged to look like stag and varied in color from tan to dark brown. Other types of bone jigging may indicate knives made for Crandall by other manufacturers. Pearl, wood and celluloid were also common.
2. Next is the length of the closed knife to the nearest sixteenth of an inch.
3. The mark number refers to the list of Crandall marks shown and described. It is the mark on the master blade. The marks on the other blades are often different, but are always one of the marks described.
4. The condition is the standard NKCA grading for the knife pictured as judged by me.
5. The price is my estimate for the dollar value of the knife shown given its condition. Be aware that, over time, values change. All blades are open in the pictures; therefore, the pattern can be determined. If the condition seems incorrect from the picture, it may be that the side not showing affects it.

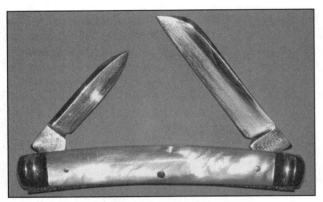

*Pearl, mark #2, near mint, 3-5/8", $450.*

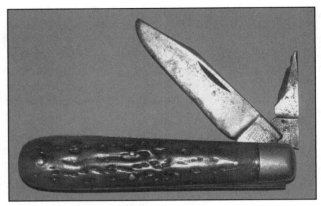

*Bone, mark #2, fair, 3-1/2", $25.*

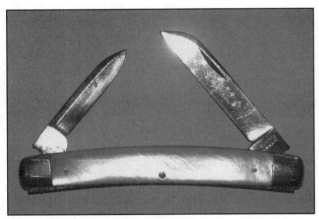

*Pearl, mark #1, excellent, 3-11/16", $250.*

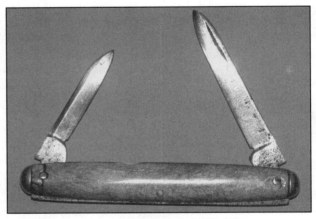

*Celluloid, mark #10, good, 3-1/4", $50.*

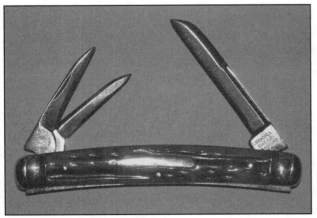

*Bone, mark #2, good, 3-11/16", $100.*

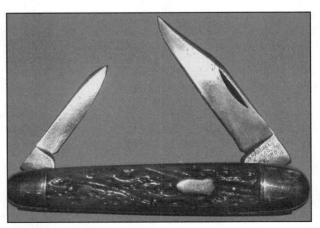

*Bone, mark #2, very good, 3-9/16", $150.*

Little Valley Knife Association/Crandall Cutlery Company 279

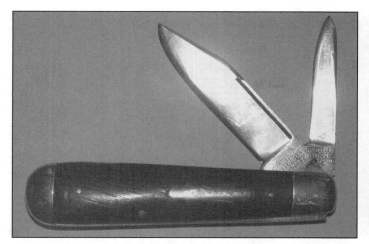

*Ebony, mark #6, very good, 3-9/16", $150.*

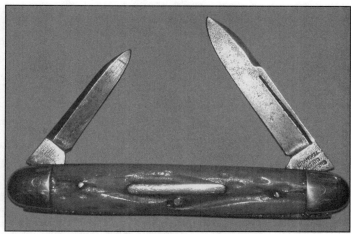

*Bone, mark #2, very good, 3-1/4", $100.*

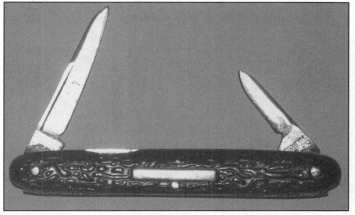

*Composition, mark #11, good, 2-3/4", $20.*

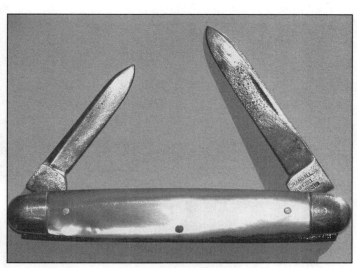

*Pearl, mark #2, very good, 3-1/16", $75.*

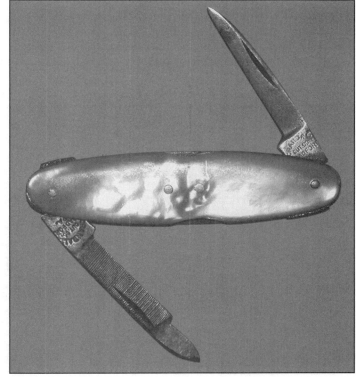

*Pearl, mark #10, very good, 2-1/4", $50.*

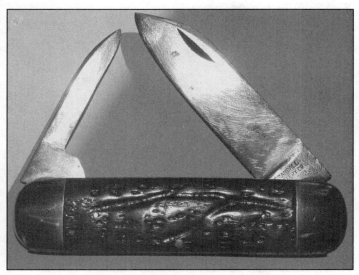

*Bone stag, mark #7, very good, 4-7/16", $300.*

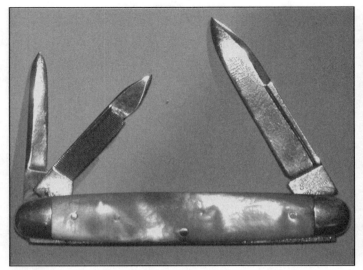

*Pearl, mark #10, excellent, 3", $110.*

*Pearl, mark #1, reproduction, mint, 3", $42.*

*Walnut, mark #10, near mint, 2-5/8", $150.*

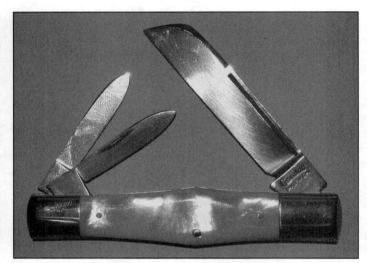

*Pearl, mark #1, reproduction, mint, 3-3/4", $64.*

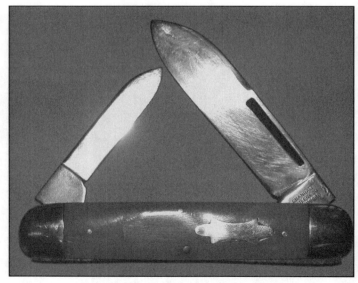

*Celluloid, mark #8, near mint, 4-1/4", counterfeit.*

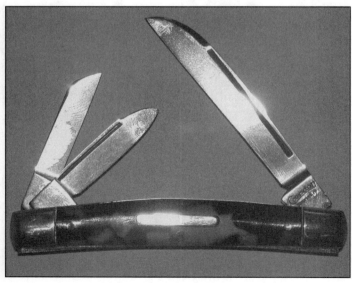

*Celluloid, mark #1, reproduction, mint, 3", $23.*

# Little Valley Knife Association/Crandall Cutlery Company

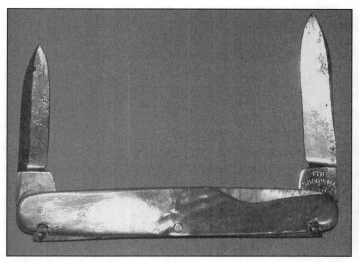

*Pearl, auto opening, mark #12, excellent (crack), 3-1/16", $500.*

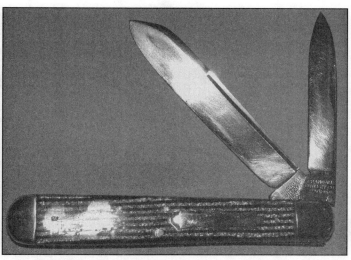

*Celluloid, mark #8, near mint, 4-1/4", counterfeit.*

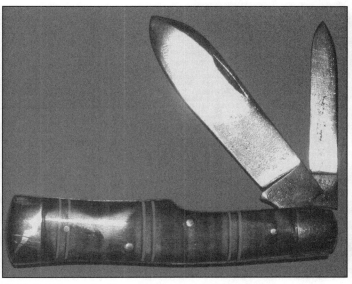

*Celluloid, mark #1, excellent, 3-5/8", $600.*

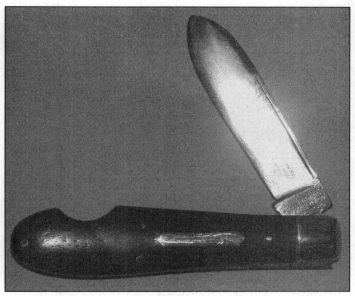

*Cocobolo, mark #3, excellent, 3-5/8", $100.*

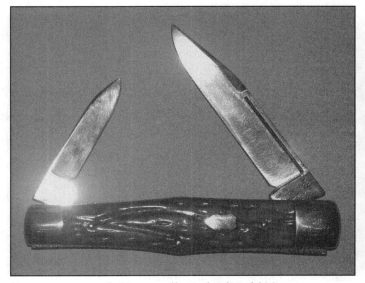

*Bone stag, mark #3, excellent, 4-1/8", $400.*

*Stag, mark #13, reproduction, mint, 4-1/2", $50.*

*Bone stag, mark #14, excellent, 3-3/8", $300.*

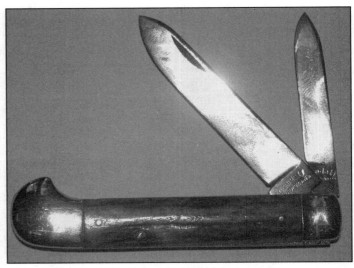

*Stag, mark #1, excellent, 3-5/8", $600.*

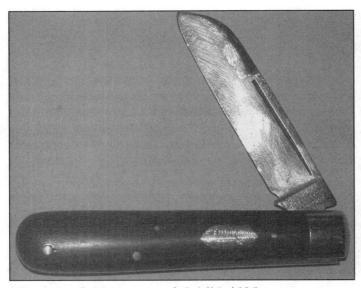

*Wood, mark #3, very good, 3-1/2", $125.*

*Bone stag, mark #1, very good, 3-1/2", #250.*

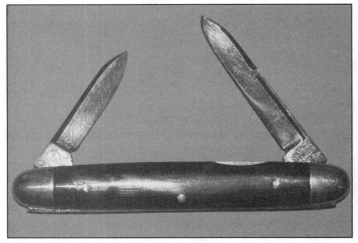

*Celluloid, mark #10, near mint, 2-5/8", $75.*

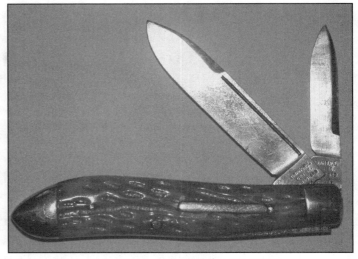

*Bone stag, mark #2, near mint, 3-1/2", $500.*

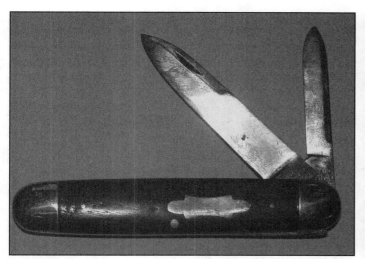

*Cocobolo, mark #7, very good, 4-3/16", $150.*

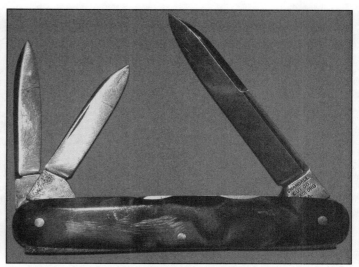

*Celluloid, mark #2, excellent, 3-3/4", $400.*

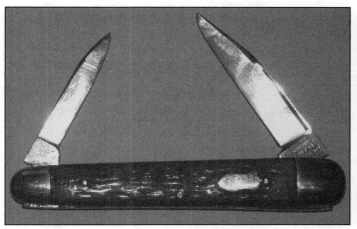

*Bone, mark #2, very good, 3-9/16", $100.*

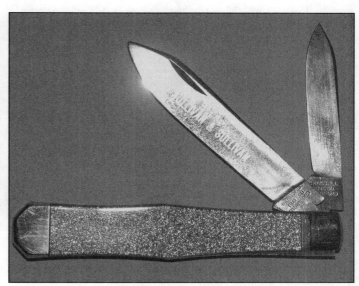

*Celluloid, mark #2, near mint, 3-9/16", $500.*

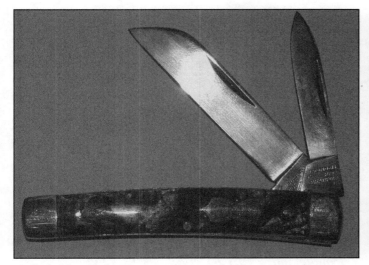

*Celluloid, mark #8, near mint, 3-3/4", counterfeit.*

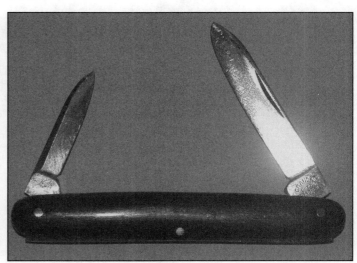

*Horn, mark #2, excellent, 3", $100.*

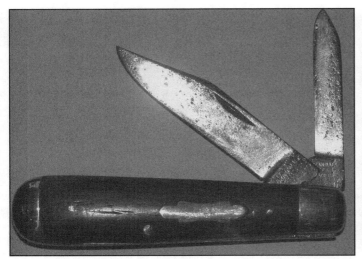

*Cocobolo, mark #2, very good, 3-9/16", $125.*

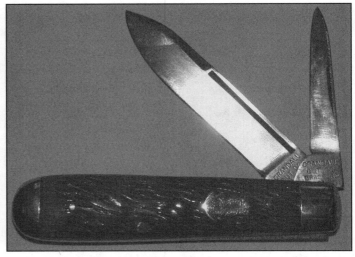

*Peachseed bone, mark #2, very good, 3-1/2", $200.*

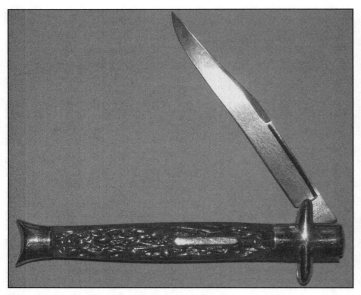

*Bone, mark #2, excellent, 3-7/8", $300.*

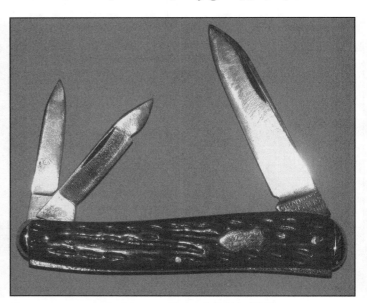

*Bone stag, mark #7, excellent, 3-1/4", $350.*

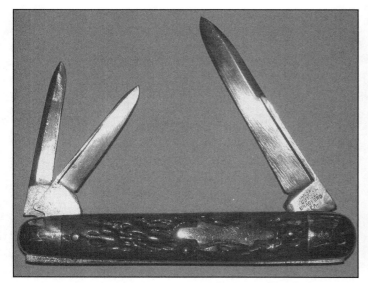

*Bone, mark #2, very good, 3-5/8", $300.*

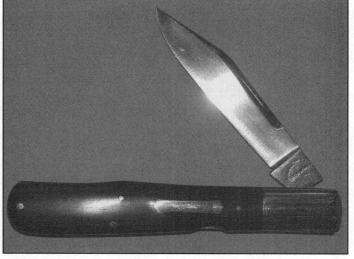

*Cocobolo, mark #9, very good, 4-3/8", $200.*

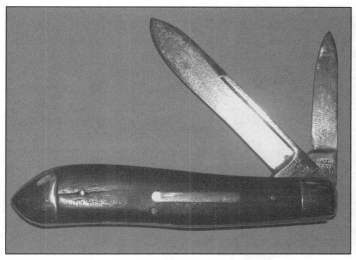

*Cocobolo, mark #2, very good, 3-1/2", $150.*

*Aluminum, mark #1, near mint, 2-7/8", $40.*

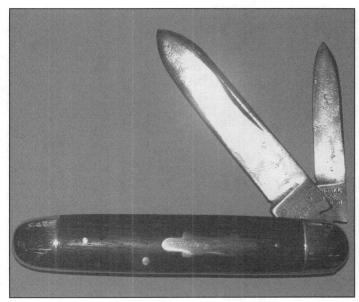

*Cocobolo, mark #7, very good, 3-1/4", $100.*

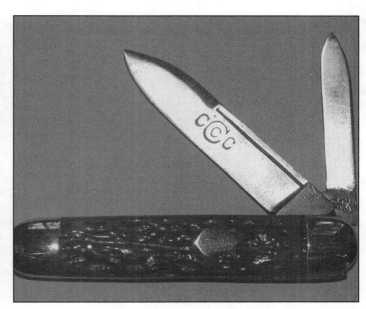

*Bone stag, mark #1, near mint, 3-5/8", $500.*

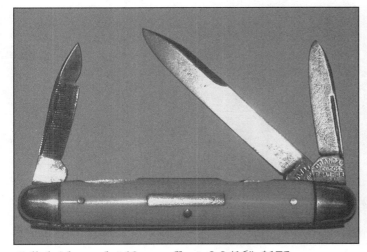

*Celluloid, mark #10, excellent, 2-9/16", $175.*

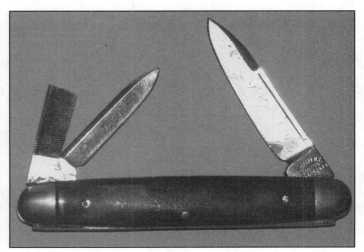

*Celluloid, mark #10, good, 3-1/16", $75.*

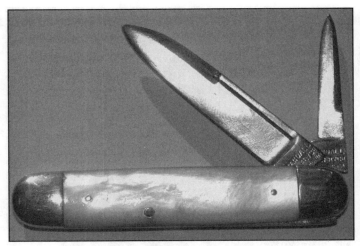

*Pearl, mark #6, very good, 3-5/8", $250.*

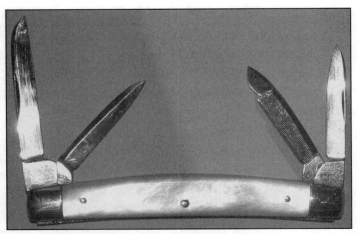

*Pearl, mark #10, excellent, 3-5/16", $350.*

*Pearl, mark #2, near mint, 3-3/4", $500.*

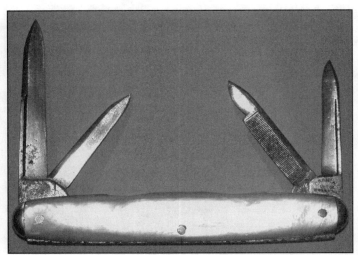

*Pearl, mark #2, very good, 3-1/4", $250.*

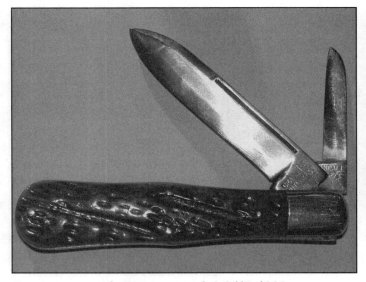

*Bone stag, mark #7, very good, 3-3/4", $300.*

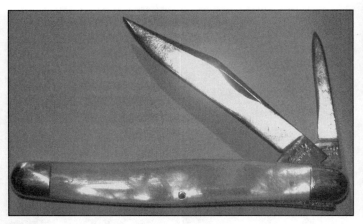

*Pearl, mark #1, very good, 3-3/4", $125.*

## Little Valley Knife Association/Crandall Cutlery Company

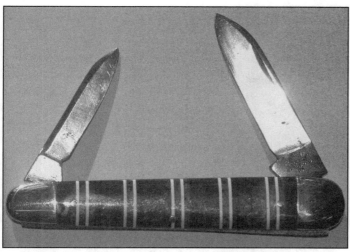

*Celluloid, mark #10, excellent, 3-5/8", $200.*

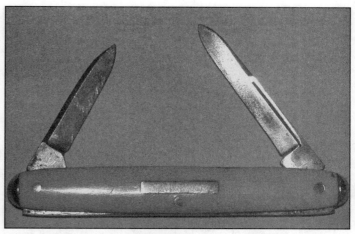

*Celluloid, mark #10, very good, 2-9/16", $40.*

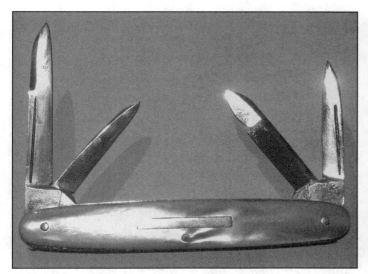

*Pearl, mark #10, very good, 3-1/4", $150.*

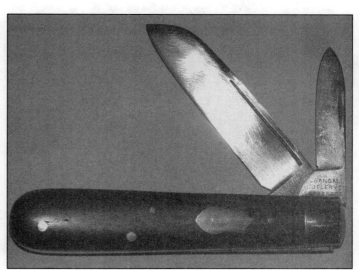

*Cocobolo, mark #3, excellent, 3-1/2", $150.*

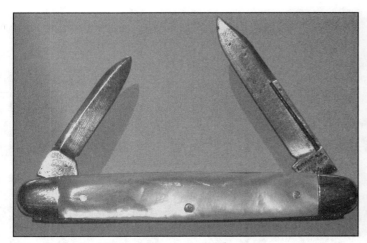

*Pearl, mark #11, excellent, 2-9/16", $75.*

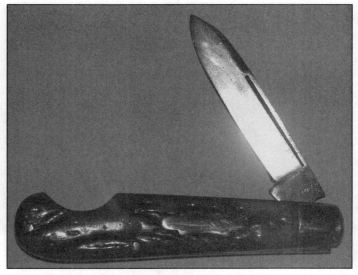

*Bone stag, very good, 3-1/2", $75.*

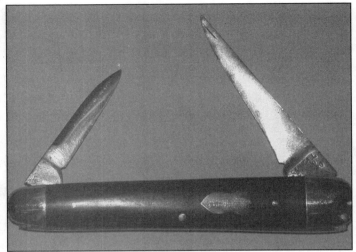
*Cocobolo, mark #10, good, 3-1/2", $25.*

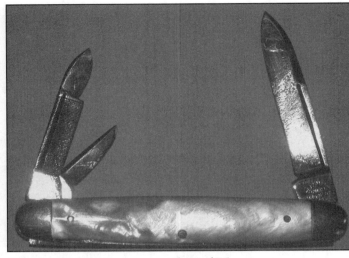
*Pearl, mark #10, very good, 3", $75.*

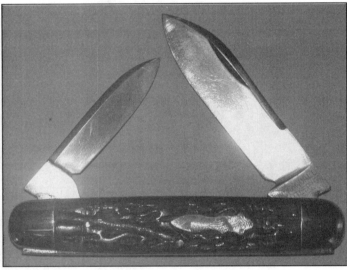
*Bone stag, mark #7, near mint, 3-7/16", $400.*

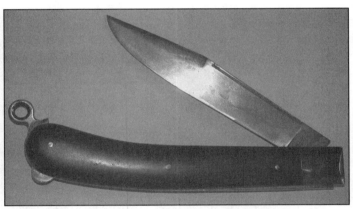
*Composition, mark #15, excellent, 7-1/4", value is a mystery!*
*This knife is a mystery. Is it real or counterfeit? It has a unique Crandall mark #15. Why would someone counterfeit such an odd knife? It's so odd, it may be real. Why not counterfeit an original pattern?*

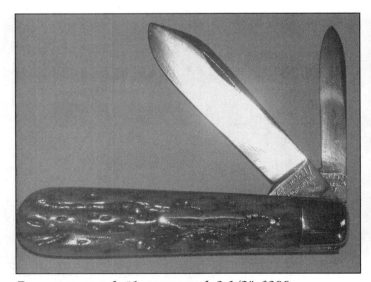
*Bone stag, mark #1, very good, 3-1/2", $200.*

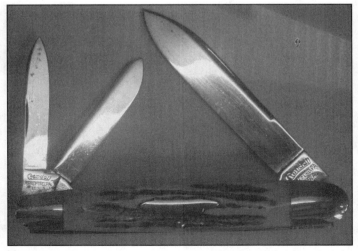
*Stag, mark #13, reproduction, near mint, 4-1/2", $50.*

### Case
(left, top to bottom)
Case 5254, XX, USA, trapper, muskrat blade, stag, 4-1/8", $650.
Case 5254, 10 Dot, XX, USA, trapper, stag, 4-1/8", $300.
Case 3254, XX, USA, trapper, flat yellow, 4-1/8", $300.
(right, top to bottom)
Case 6254SSP, XX, USA, trapper, 2nd model, bone, 4-1/8", $300.
Case 6254, Tested XX, trapper, Rogers bone, 4-1/8", $6,500.
Case 6254, XX, trapper, bone, 4-1/8", $700.

### Case
Case W165SAB SSP, Moby Dick with genuine natural bone scrimshawed with whaling scene, brass liners, and engraved nickel silver bolsters, $150.

### Case 1976 Bicentennial Set
(top) Case 523-7SS, Double Eagle hunting knife with genuine stag handle, 2,500 made, $300.
(bottom) Case 516SSP, pocketknife with genuine stag handle, $175.

### Case
R. Case, Bradford, Germany, abalone, early 1900s, 1-7/8", $250.

### Case 75th Anniversary of Case Cutlery Co. Canoe Set
Case 5394SSP.
Case 53131SSP.
Case 52131SSP.
The blade on each knife is etched with one of Case's 3 factories and the factory date, engraved brass bolsters, genuine stag handles, $400.

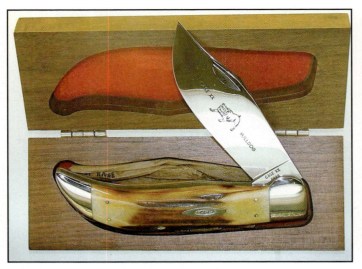

**Case**
Case, 5172, XX USA, bulldog with box, stag handles, 5-1/2", $350.

**Case**
Eight Case knives, showing colorful handle materials used from early 1900 to around 1940, $250 to $1,000.

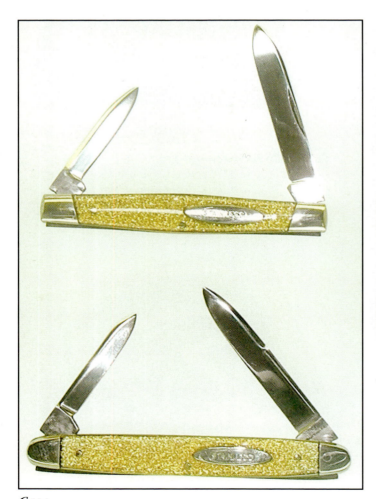

**Case**
(top) Case GS2042, Bradford PA, goldstone handles, 2-7/8", $250.
(bottom) Case GS271LP, Bradford PA, goldstone handles, 3-1/4", $350.

**Case**
(top) Case 3465, Tested XX, folding hunter, 4 blade, flat blade, 5-1/4", $3,000.
(top left) Case 6265, XX, folding hunter, flat, green bone, $850.
(top right) Case RM172, Tested XX, clasp knife, Christmas-tree handle, $2,500.
(center) Case 5172L, Bradford, Pa., zipper (switchblade), stag, 5-1/2", $9,000.
(bottom left) Case 6365SAB, XX proto, 3-backspring folding hunter, 3 blade, (saw blade), $5,000.
(bottom right) Case 6465, Tested XX, folding hunter, 4 blade, flat blade, 5-1/4", $3,000.

**Case**
Vintage Case knife patterns from 1915-1965, showing various color handle materials used: green bone, red bone, rough black, imitation pearl, Winterbottom bone, second-cut stag, pearl, stag, goldstone, yellow celluloid, French pearl, wormgroove bone, and imitation onyx. $250 to $1,500.

**Case**
Vintage Case 65 folding hunters, $250-$1,500.

**Case**

(top to bottom)

Case 3465, Tested XX, folding hunter, 4-blade, flat blade, yellow composition, $3,000.
Case 5111-1/2 L, 9 Dot, cheetah, genuine stag, $500.
Case 22028, Tested XX, dogleg jack, black composition, $350.
Case 4100SS, USA, citrus knife, white composition, $150.
Case 1203LR, XX, electrician's knife, walnut, $450.

**Case**

(top to bottom)

Case 6100, Tested XX, honeycomb green bone, $1,100.
Case 6394-1/2, XX, cigar, red bone, $4,000.
Case RM2020, peanut, Christmas tree, $450.
Case B239-1/2, Case Bros., sowbelly, waterfall, $650.
Case 5375, XX, L.P., stockman, red stag, $800.
Case 6488, Tested XX, L.P., congress, Winterbottom bone, $12,000.
Case 9265, Tested XX, folding hunter, cracked ice, $800.

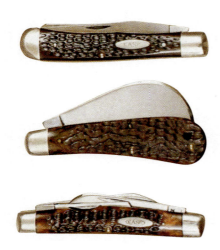

**Case**

(top to bottom)

Case 6254SSP, 1970s, trapper, delrin, $65.
Case 61011, 1970s, hawkbill, pakkawood, $40.
Case 6488, 1970s, congress, bone, $450.

**Case**

(left to right)

Case 6254, USA, trapper, second-cut bone, $800.
Case 6143, prototype Daddy Barlow, jigged bone, $300.
Case 62031LP, XX, jack, rough black, $250.
Case 6299, Tested XX, teardrop jack, green bone, $500.
Case 6265SAB, XX, folding hunter, Rogers bone, $750.
Case 6296X, XX, citrus knife, red bone, $600.

***Case***
*Case Kodiak hunter, Chief Crazy Horse commemorative box and plaque $400.*

***Case***
*Case 5257, 2 blades, genuine stag, 3", $450. This extremely old knife from Case Brothers Cutlery Company, Little Valley, New York, dates from as early as 1912.*

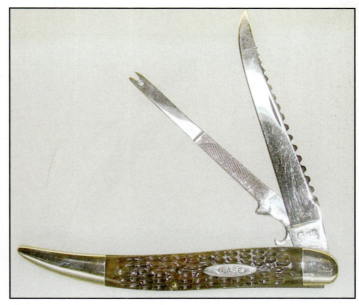

***Case***
*Case 62095F, Tested XX, fish knife, green bone handles, 5", $450.*

***Case***
*Case C91050, Tested XX, flat blade, cracked ice handles, 5-3/8", $850.*

**Case**
Case 6235 1/2, Tested XX, rough black, 3-3/8", $200.

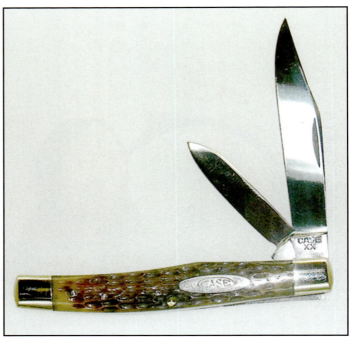

**Case**
Case 6232, XX, green bone handles, 3-5/8", $200.

**Case**
Case 5265 SAB, Dr., XX, folding hunter, stag, 5-1/4", $500.

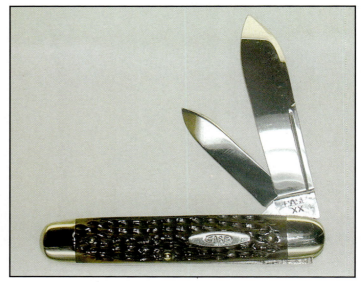

**Case**
Case 6294 LP, XX, green bone handles, 4-1/4", $1,500.

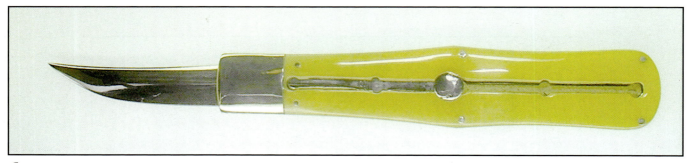

**Case**
Case PB 31050 SAB, Tested XX, blade graduated in increments of about 1", $700.

**Case**
Case 62131, canoe, 2 blades, jigged bone, distinctive canoe shape, with etching of an Indian and canoe on the master blade, 3-5/8", $40.

**Case**
Case 2138SS, sodbuster single-blade utility knife, 4-1/2", $30. Using black composition handle material, these knives are built for heavy duty use around ranch or farm.

**Case**
Case 62009 1/2, Barlow, 2 blades, appaloosa bone, 3-5/16", $50. Barlows are very old but still popular.

**Case**
Case 61011, XX, hawkbill, Rogers bone, 4", $300.

**Case**
(top) Case 62024 1/2, USA, barehead jack, genuine jigged red bone, 3", $65.
(bottom) Case 6216 1/2, CASE XX, barehead jack, genuine jigged red bone, 3-3/8", $125.

**Case**
Case 61024 1/2, XX, barehead jackknives, genuine jigged bone, 3", $55 each. These knives, stamped CASE XX, date to 1940-1964.

**Case**
(top) Case 62032, serpentine jack, 2 blade, jigged bone, square bolsters, 3-5/8", $40.
(bottom) Case 62087, serpentine jack, 2 blade, jigged bone, 3-1/4", $40.

**Case**
(top to bottom)
Case 6308, whittler, 3 blade, delrin, $35.
Case 6383, whittler, 3 blade, 3-1/2", $35.
Case 6308, whittler, 3 blade, jigged-bone, 3-1/4", $40.

**Case**
Case SR6244, smooth red-bone serpentine jackknives, 3-1/4", $45. Smooth red bone was one of Case's innovations.

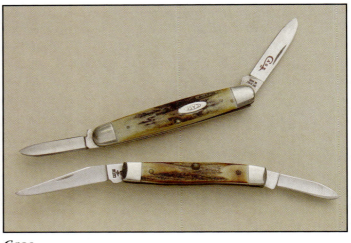

**Case**
(top) Case 5279 SSP, 2-blade senator, genuine stag, $65.
(bottom) Case 52033, small serpentine pen, genuine stag, $85.

**Case**
Case 6308, jigged red-bone whittler, 3-1/4", $50. Made in the mid-1970s.

**Case**
Case 6208, red bone 1/2 whittler knives, 3-1/4", $40. A whittler has 3 blades, with a double thick main blade opposite two smaller blades. This prevents the main blade from folding up on the hands of the whittler.

**Case**
*(top to bottom)*
Case GS172, Tested XX, clasp, 5-1/2", $2,500.
Case RM172, Tested XX, clasp, $2,500.
Case 3172, Tested XX, clasp, $1,500.

**Case**
*(top to bottom)*
Case 6265SAB, XX, rough black, 5-1/4", $450.
Case 9265, Tested XX, flat blade, French-pearl cracked-ice, 5-1/4", $800.
Case GYP172 Tested XX, clasp, celluloid, 5-1/2", $2000.
Case, 5172L, Bradford, Pa., zipper switchblade, genuine stag, 5-1/2", $8,000.

**Case**
W. R. Case & Sons, 1905-1914, GS3109, 3-backspring whittler, goldstone, 3-5/8", $1,200.

**Case**
*(left)* Case XX, folding hunter, red wormgroove handles, 5-1/4", $450.
*(right)* Case 64052, 10 Dot 1970, XX USA, congress, bone handles, 3-1/2", $300.

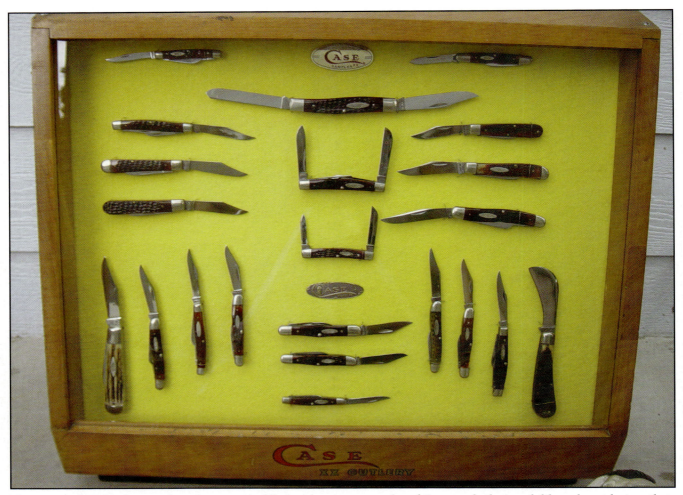

*This original W. R. Case cutlery showcase is filled with mint examples of Case pocketknives (although not knives that originally came with the showcase). The showcase was found in an old hardware store and dates to the early 1970s. What a great way to display Case knives! The knives range from $35 to $200 each.*

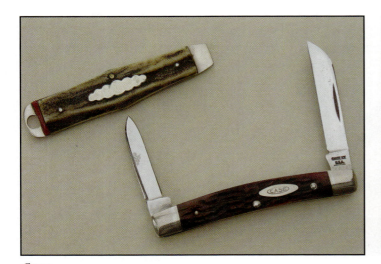

**Case**
*Case 6269, congress, 2 blade, jigged red bone, 3", $65. Made in the early 1970s. This knife is pictured next to a custom-made blade opener.*

**Case**
*Case 06263 SSP, senator pen, jigged red bone, $40. Etched "Tested XX razor edge" on the master blade, it's shown with an original W. R. Case & Sons bamboo celluloid razor, $125.*

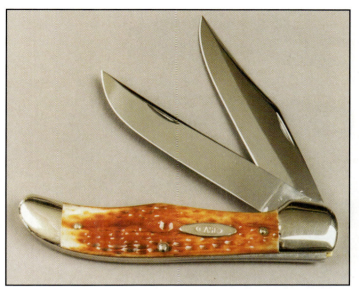

**Case**
*Case 6265SAB, XX, red bone, 5-1/4", $450.*

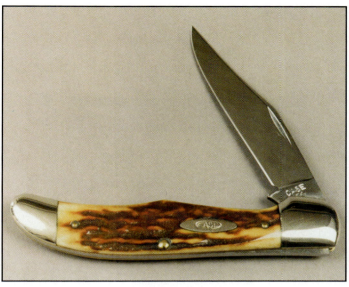

**Case**
*Case 5165, XX, flat, red stag, 5-1/4", $700.*

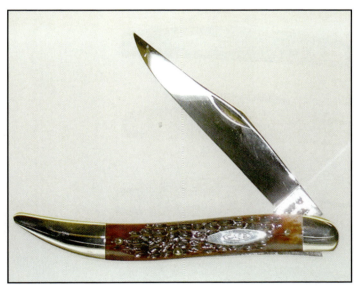

**Case**
*Case 61093, 8 Dot 1972, XX USA, toothpick, red bone handles, 5", $125.*

**Case**
*(top) Case 6205 RAZ, XX, rough black, 3-3/4", $700.*
*(middle) Case 6249, XX, "Copper Head," rough black, 4", $800.*
*(bottom) Case Tested XX, muskrat, rough black, 4", $1,200.*

**Case**
*(left to right)*
*Case 9383 SAB, XX, whittler, imitation onyx, 3-1/2", $700.*
*Case 6383, 7 Dot 1973, XX USA, whittler, bone, 3-1/2", $100.*
*Case 2383, XX, whittler, smooth black, 3-1/2", $250.*
*Case 6383 SAB, XX, whittler, green bone, 3-1/2", $1,250.*
*Clauss, Fremont, Ohio, USA, whittler, made by Case on contract, Winterbottom bone, 3-1/2", $1,000.*

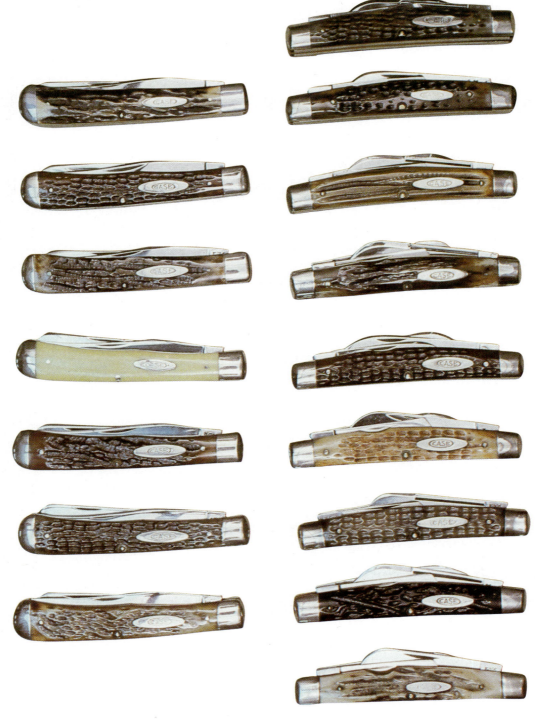

**Case #54 Trappers**
(left, top to bottom)
5254, Tested XX, genuine stag, $4,500.
6254, Tested XX, red bone, $4,500.
6254, Tested XX, second-cut stag, $6,000.
Yellow composition, $4,000.
5254, Tested XX, red stag, $6,000.
6254, Tested XX, green bone, $6,000.
6254, XX Tested frame, Rogers bone, $6,500.

**Case #88 Congresses**
(right, top to bottom)
6488, L.P., Tested XX, green bone, $8,000.
6488, XX, reg. pull, bone, $1,000.
6488, L.P., Tested XX, Winterbottom bone, $12,000.
5488, L.P., Tested XX, genuine stag, $8,000.
6488, XX, reg. pull, red bone, $1,200.
5488, XX, reg. pull, second-cut stag, $1,500.
6488, Tested XX, L.P., green bone, $8,000.
6488, Tested XX, L.P., rough black, $6,000.
5488, XX, reg. pull, genuine white stag, $1,200.

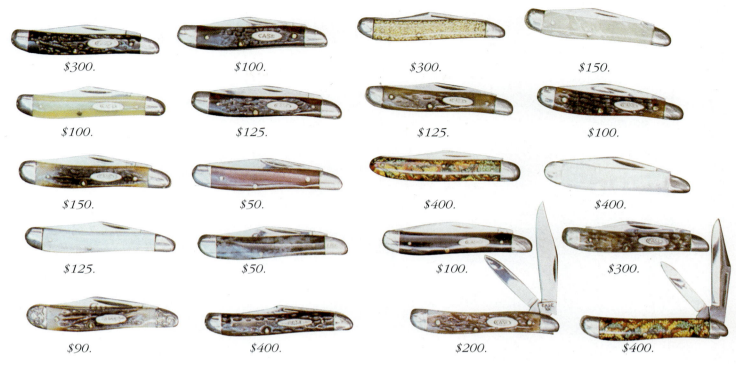

**Case**
*This display of Case peanuts shows 20 variations of handle materials, stampings, and pulls.*

**Case**
An extremely rare original Case Bros. Tested XX Cutlery advertisement. With the designation of Little Valley (New York) and Kane (Pennsylvania), this sign can be dated between 1907 and 1909. Made of bright pink celluloid, it shows some signs of being slightly burned but still retains its complete logo. The sign itself (excluding the wood framing) measures 8-1/2" x 10-1/2", $300 to $500.

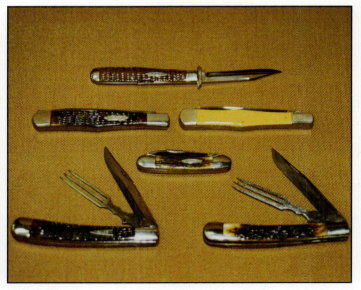

**Case**
(top) Case 6111-1/2L, Tested XX, green bone, $1,800.
(top left) Case 62213, Tested XX, swell center, green bone, $1,000.
(top right) Case 32213, Tested XX, yellow celluloid, $800.
(center) Case 53131, Tested XX, canoe, 3 blade, stag, $2,500.
(bottom left) Case 6251F, Bradford, Pa., hobo, knife and fork, green bone, arrow shield, $1,250.
(bottom right) W. R. Case & Sons, 6251F, Bradford, Pa., hobo, old Rogers bone, $1,400.

**Case**
Case 6375, moose, jigged amber bone, 4-1/4", $100. This special knife was the Rocky Mountain Blade Collector's Club knife for 1994, as the RMBC logo on the spey blade indicates.

**Case**
(top) Case 64052, 1974, 6 Dot, 4-blade congress, genuine, jigged red bone, 3-1/2", $85.
(bottom) Case 64052, 1979, 1 Dot, 4-blade congress, genuine, jigged red bone, 3-1/2", $65.

**Case**
(top to bottom)
Case 9333, XX, penknife, 3 blades, imitation pearl, $50.
Case 9333, 1970, XX, penknife, 3 blades, imitation pearl, $50.
Case 8233, XX, penknife, genuine pearl, $90.
Case 9233, penknife, pearl composition, $50.
The second number indicates the number of blades in the knife.

**Case Peanuts**
(left to right)
3220, yellow delrin, 3220, 2-7/8", $30.
RM220, Christmas tree celluloid, 2-7/8", $45.
GS220, goldstone celluloid, 2-7/8", $45.
6220 SP, jigged red bone, with a special long spey blade not usually found on peanut-style jackknives, $45.

**Case**
Case 6292, XX, Texas jack, late Rogers bone, 4", $350.

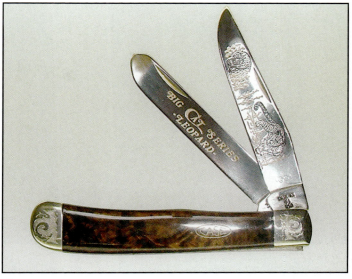

**Case**
Case trapper, etched blade, engraved bolsters, imitation tortoise handles, 4-1/8", $150.

**Case**
Case 6275SP, 2 blades, jigged bone, 4-3/8", $65. The "SP" designation is for a spey blade, the second blade on this pocketknife. This knife, made in the mid-1970s, was designed for the serious hunter/trapper.

**Case**
Case 6254, 1970s, trapper, 2 blade, jigged red-bone, 4-1/8", $50. Trapper patterns are perhaps the most desirable Case knife pattern.

**Case**
Case A6250, Museum Founders Knife, elephant toenail with appaloosa handle, $175. Shown is 1 of set of 4.

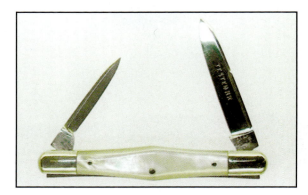

**Case**
Case Bros. Cut. Co., 8258, equal end, swell center, pearl handles, 3", $400.

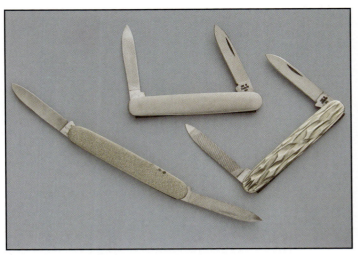

**Case**
Case M279, metal gentleman's penknives, 3-1/8", $40 each. Made in the late 1970s, these knives have a file blade as the second blade.

**Case**
(top and bottom) Case 6220 peanuts, smooth red bone, 2-7/8", $40 each.
(center) Case 6220 peanut, brown and white appaloosa bone, 2-7/8", $40.

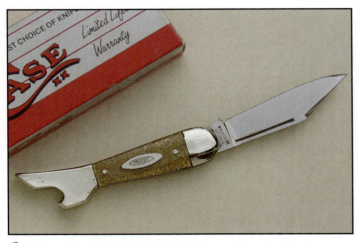

**Case**
Case GS197, lady's leg knife, goldstone celluloid, 3-1/4", $65.

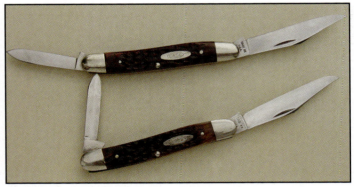

**Case**
Case 06247 PEN, 1970s, jigged red bone, 3-7/8", $60 each.

**Case**
Case 61050, Tested XX, zipper release switchblade, green bone handles, 5-3/8", $7,500.

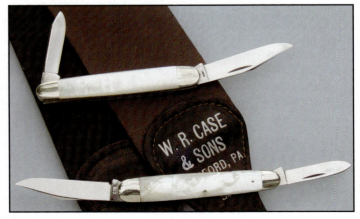

**Case**
Case pearl penknives photographed on an original Case razor strop. Both knives bear pattern number 82079 (the first number designating genuine pearl handle material). Notice that the top Case knife has no pins showing, while the bottom knife has the more traditional center pin and pins holding the pearl sides to the knife. Top knife, $75; bottom knife, $85.

**Case**
Case 61215 1/2, Tested, switchblade, brown jigged bone handles, 5", $2,500.

**Case**
Case 61214 1/2, Tested, switchblade, brown jigged bone handles, 4-1/8", $2,500.

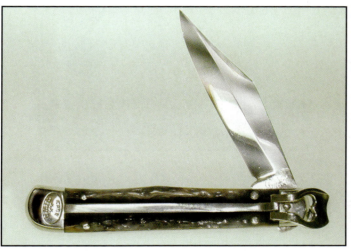

**Case**
Case 5171 L, Tested XX, switchblade, hinge and strap, stag handles, 5-1/4", $3,500.

**Case**
31212-1/2, Case Tested, switchblade, yellow celluloid handles, 4", $1,500.

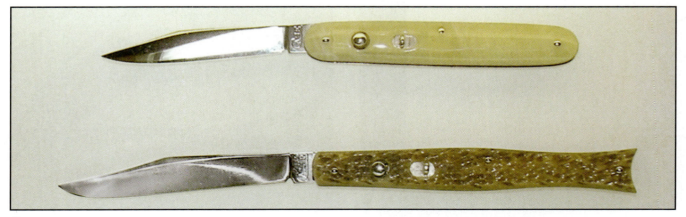

**Case**
(top) Case Tested, 91210 1/2, switchblade, imitation onyx, 3-1/2", $800.
(bottom) Case Tested, 61213 1/2, switchblade, early Rogers bone, 4", 1,800.

**Case**
Case SR6347 1/2, 1980, premium stockman, 3-blade, smooth red bone, 3-7/8", $60 each.

**Case**
Case 63047, 1970s, premium stockman, 3 blade, jigged bone, 3-7/8". The spey blade is clearly etched "for flesh only," a designation for blades designed for castrating livestock, $75.

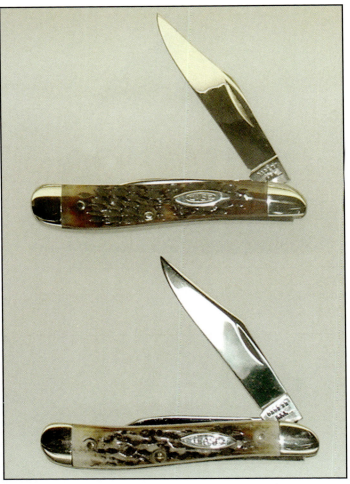

**Case**
(top) Case 6220, 10 Dot 1970, XX USA, peanut, bone, 2-7/8", $100.
(bottom) Case 5220, 10 Dot 1970, XX USA, peanut, stag, 2-7/8", $125.

**Case**
W. R. Case & Sons, Bradford, Pa., 52131 LP, genuine stag handles, $1,500.

**Case**
Case 6172, Bradford, Pa., zipper release switchblade, stag handles, 5-1/2", $9,000.

307

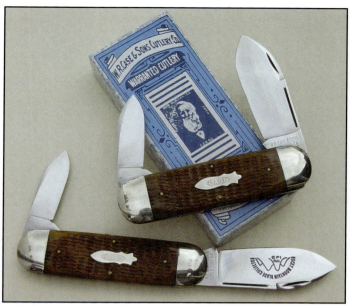

**Case**
Case 6250, elephant toenails, with genuine jigged honey bone handles. The bottom knife is the Rocky Mountain Blade Collectors club knife for 1996, 4-1/2", $150.

**Case**
Case 6220 peanuts, 2-bladed serpentine jacks.
(top) Maple handle, 2-7/8", $50.
(bottom two) 1970, 10 Dot, jigged red bone, $100 each.

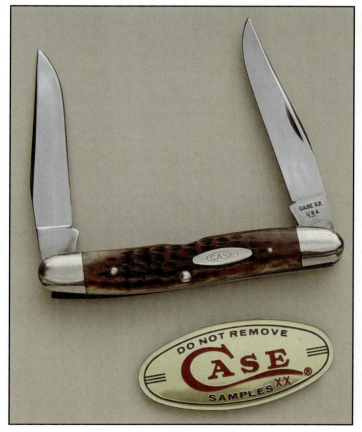

**Case**
Case muskrat knife, jigged bone, 3-7/8". This knife was made in 1977, $75.

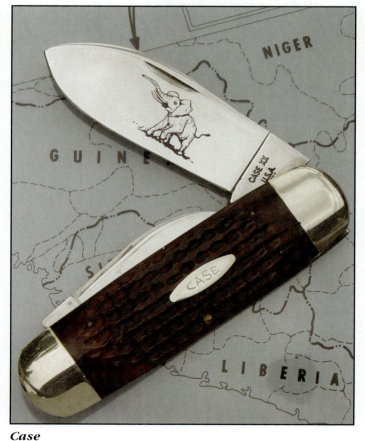

**Case**
Case 6250 elephant toenail (so named because of its massive size and unique shape), mid-1970s. This example has an elephant etched on the blade, pakkawood handles, and is 4-1/2", $100.

**Case**
Case 6375, premium stockman, genuine jigged bone, 4-1/4", $75. This knife was made in 1977 and is Case's largest stockman.

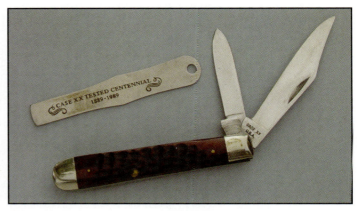

**Case**
Case 6214 1/2, USA, swell-end jack, 2 blade, red bone, 3-3/8", $65. A Case Centennial (1889-1989) knife opener has been photographed with this knife.

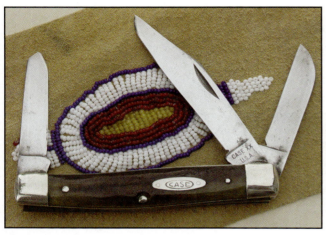

**Case**
Case 5392, premium stockman, genuine stag, 4". This knife dates to 1965-69, $275.

**Case**
Kentucky 1976 Bicentennial, set of three knives, handles made of green delrin, wood, and stag, with plaque, $125.

**Case**
(top) Case 5220, genuine stag (the "5" designating stag handles), $125.
(bottom) Case 8220, 1980s, genuine pearl (the "8" designating genuine pearl handles), $85.

**Case**
Case 5299 1/2, swell-end jack, 2 blade, genuine stag, 4". Slabs of genuine stag handle material, ready to be installed, surround the knife. $200.

**This colorful assortment of sheath knives includes Case, Case Tested, W. R. Case, and Jean Case.**
(top to bottom)
361-4 1/2, Tested XX, leather and brass spacer, $250.
M361-4 1/2, XX, brown marbled pyremite, $250.
RM52-5, XX, blue agate pyremite, $225.
Jean Case Cutlery Co., amber celluloid, $225.
RM361, XX, cream and black pyremite, $250.
B325-5, XX, waterfall (rare), $300.

**Case**
(top) Case 957, XX, brown and white celluloid handle, saber blade, 3-3/4", $150.
(middle) Case GS 57 SAB, goldstone celluloid handle, split bolster with round pommel, 3-1/2" blade, $200.
(bottom) Case, 366-4, Tested XX, early celluloid, 3-1/2" blade, $150.

(top to bottom)
Jean Case, L.V.N.Y., stag handle and pommel, 5" blade, $250.
Unknown pattern, Case XX, stag handle, flat pommel, saber blade, 9-1/4", $350.
Case 661-4-1/2, Tested XX, W. R. Case & Sons, Brad., Pa., Rogers bone, flat nickel silver bolster, rare, $400.
Case 6361-5, Rogers bone, round nickel silver split bolster, Case script on blade, rare, $400.

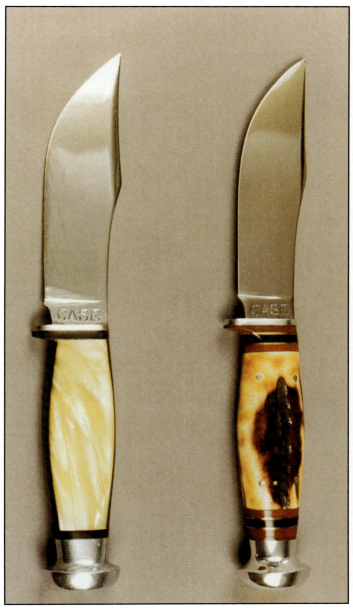

**Case**
(left) Case 9362, XX, cracked ice with black spacers, 8-3/4", $300.
(right) Case 5362, XX, split stag, 8-3/4", $300.

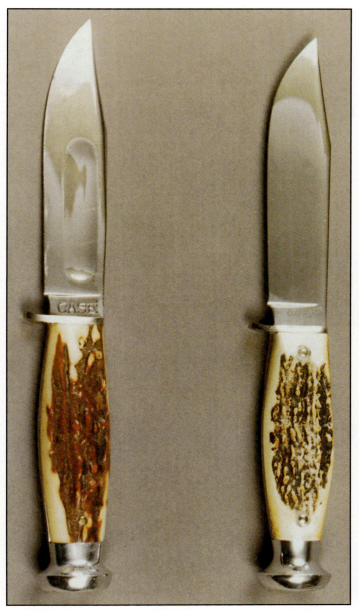

**Case**
(left) Case 5325-5, XX, red stag, 9-1/8", $200.
(right) Case 5325-5, XX, stag, 9-1/8", $200.

**Case**
*Jean Case sheath knife, amber handle with red, black, and brass spacers, brass butt and guard, $225.*

**Case**

Case 561, Tested XX, leather sheath, deluxe knife/axe combination, genuine stag, $600.

**Case**

Case 961, Tested XX, imitation pearl celluloid with black liners, short hinge release lock, knife/axe combination, rare, $750.

**Case**

Case 561, XX U.S.A, leather sheath, deluxe knife/axe combination, genuine stag, $600.

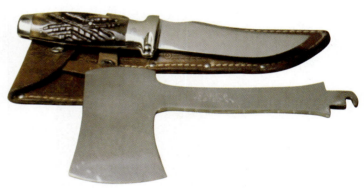

**Case**

Case 661, Tested XX, leather sheath, knife/axe combination, second-cut green bone, $650.

**Case**

Case 961, Tested XX, imitation onyx celluloid knife/axe combination, basketweave sheath, $600.

**Case**

Case 261, Tested XX, leather sheath, walnut handle, knife/axe combination, $500.

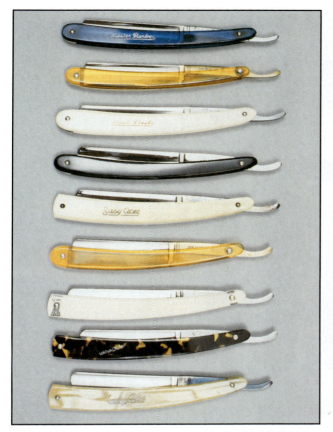
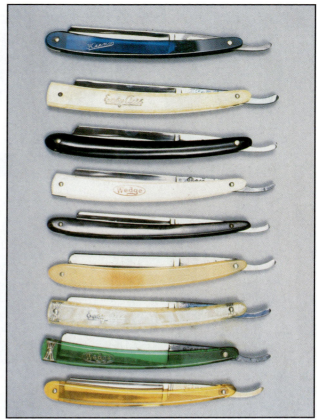
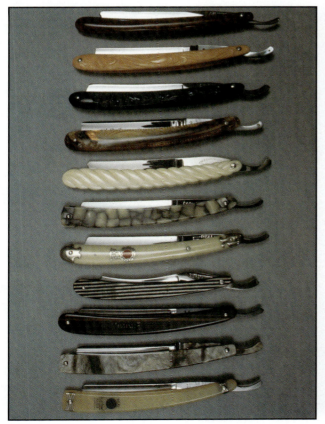

**Case**
*These Case razors exhibit a wide range of exotic and fanciful handle materials and designs that have made collecting so popular throughout the years. Prices range from $50 each to $400 each.*

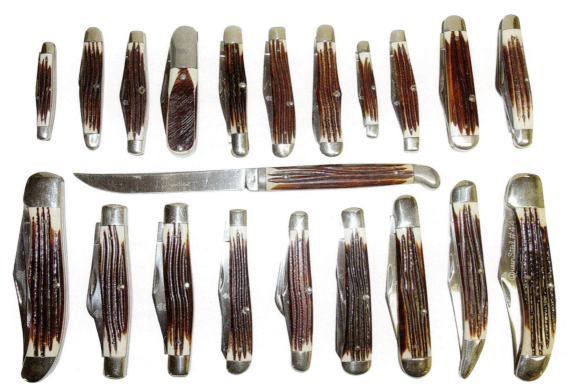

### Queen
*Twenty-one Queen cutlery patterns with the scarce burnt orange composition handle material, late '60s era. Prices range from $35 each to $150 each.*

### Schatt & Morgan
*These colorful knives were produced by Schatt & Morgan Cutlery Co., the forerunner of the Queen City Cutlery Co. and the Queen Cutlery Co. Prices range from $150 each to $750 each.*

### Queen
*(top to bottom)*
Queen NKCA 10th Anniversary (1972-1982) with emblem, genuine stag handle, 1,200 made, $80-$100.
Queen 58, Coke bottle with red imitation Winterbottom bone handle, $80-$100.
Queen 11, Winterbottom bone handle, $70-$90.
Queen serpentine jack with imitation red Winterbottom bone handle, $60-$80.

**Queen**
Queens with older handle materials.
(top to bottom)
Queen 35, small serpentine, with rough black handle, rare Q Stainless stamp, $40.
Queen 15, congress with brown Rogers bone, rare Q Stainless stamp, $85.
Queen 20, folding outdoors knife with green Rogers bone, rare Q Stainless stamp, $125.

**Queen**
These Queens also exhibit older handle materials.
(top to bottom)
Queen 9, stockman with green Winterbottom bone, rare Q Stainless stamp, $135-$150.
Queen 19, heavy duty trapper with white and brown Winterbottom bone, rare satin finished blades, Q Steel stamp, $200-$225.
Queen 46, folding fishing knife with rare light brown Winterbottom bone, blade etched (no tang stamp), $100-$125.

**Queen**
This display of eleven Queen stag handle knives and six Queen smoke pearl handle knives represent all recent Queen patterns that were made with these natural materials. Stag handled knives, $60 to $150 each. Average price of smoke pearl handle knives is $200 each.

**Queen**
Queen rare stockman, 3 blade, red Winterbottom stag, $55. The stamping on the master blade indicates this knife was made after 1984.

**Queen**
Queen single-bladed trapper, genuine Winterbottom bone, 4-1/8", $40. Queen was one of a very few companies to use this unique handle material. The thin blade proved very useful in skinning all sorts of animals.

**Queen**
Queen unusual 2-blade penknife, genuine Rogers jigged bone, "big Q" stamping, dates from 1932-1945, 2-1/2", $50.

**Queen**
Queen small stockman, Winterbottom bone (a material favored by Queen Cutlery Company). This stockman contains the typical 3 blades: a pen blade, a sheepfoot blade, and a master blade, $50.

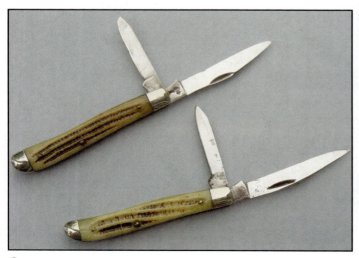

**Queen**
Queen serpentine peanuts, 2 blades, Winterbottom bone, $40 each.

**Queen**
Queen serpentine jackknife, 2 blade, Winterbottom bone, 3-1/2", $40. Winterbottom is characterized by a long, deep, row-like jigging pattern, usually darkened, and lighter, almost translucent bone material.

**Remington**
(top to bottom)
Remington R1253L, brown bone, 5-3/8", $3,000.
Remington R1273, brown bone, 5-3/8", $4,500.
Remington R293, H.T.T, brown bone, 5-3/8", $3,500.
Remington R1263, brown bone, 5-3/8", $4,000.

**Remington**
(left, top to bottom)
Remington 1253L, bone, 5-3/8", $3,000.
Remington 1273, bone, 5-3/8", $4,500.
Remington R293 HTT, bone, 5-3/8", $3,500.
Remington R1263, bone, 5-3/8", $4,000.
Remington R1613, bone, 5", $6,000.
Remington R953, cartridge, bone, 5", $700.
Remington R953, toothpick, bone, 5", $300.
Remington R3843, utility, bone, 3-5/8", $600.

(right, top to bottom)
Remington R1128, cocobolo, 4-1/2", $4,000.
Remington R1123, bone, 4-1/2", $3,000.
Remington R1303, bone, 4-5/8", $3,500.
Remington R1306, stag, 4-5/8", $2,500.
Remington R4243, bone, 4-3/4", $3,500.
Remington R4353, bone, 4-1/4", $3,500.
Remington R4466, stag, 3-3/4", $8,500.
Remington R1173, bone, 3-1/2", $7,000.

**Remington**
Remington R2403, switchblade, brown jigged bone, 5", $2,200.

**Remington**
Remington R6836, humpback whittler, genuine stag, $1,200.

**Remington**
Remington R4283, 5-blade sowbelly, bone, $8,000.

**Remington**
(top to bottom)
Remington R1128, cocobolo, 4-1/2", $4,000.
Remington R1303, brown bone, 4-5/8", $3,500.
Remington R1306, genuine stag, 4-5/8", $2,500.
Remington R1123, brown bone, 4-1/2", $3,000.

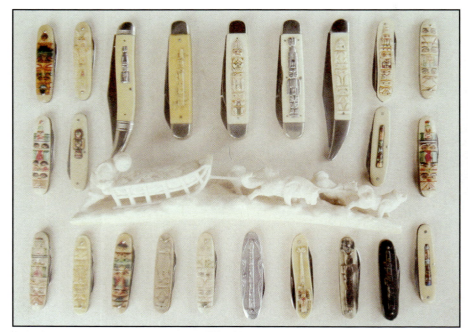
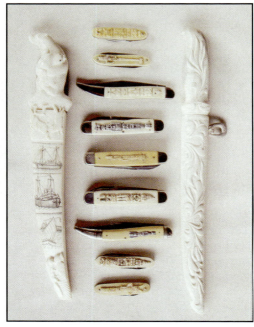

**Remington Totem Pole Knives (1917-1940)**
*Most have ivory handles that are hand carved by native Alaskans. Some have ivory handles with sterling totem pole inlays. All totem pole knives are quite rare. Prices range from $350 to $4,000 each.*

**Remington**
*Remington knives, showing eight different colorful handles. Prices range from $100 to $300 each. Remington used the term "pyremite" for this handle material.*

***Remington***
*1920s Remington display for official Boy Scout knives, $200+.*

**Remington**
*Boxed assortment of Scout knives, which were introduced in the late 1920s to early 1930s, $8,000.*

***Remington***
*Remington R3475, 3-bladed whittler, 3-1/4", $300. The acorn shield on the yellow celluloid (pyremite) handle sides indicates that this Remington has a punch blade included. At top is an original Remington blade opener, $25.*

**Remington**
Remington, stockman, brown jigged bone, 3-7/8", $400.

**Remington**
(left to right)
R219, teardrop easy opener jack with brass handle, $225.
R555, equal end jack with candy stripe handle, $225.
R3855, pruner with imitation ivory handle, $350.
R4405, serpentine with Christmas tree handle, $300.
R4679, serpentine with nickel silver handle, $150.
R2215, jack with multicolor handle, $125.
R1915, serpentine jack with candy stripe handle, $150.

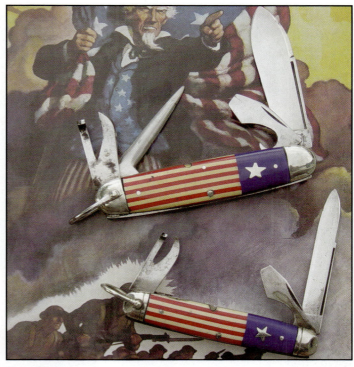

**Remington**
Remington red, white, and blue, 4-blade "flag" scout utility knives.
(left) R3335, 3-3/4", $450.
(right) R4235, 3-3/8", $450.

**Remington**
Remington fancy celluloid-handled pocketknives, each with 3 blades. Although they look like duplicates, other than the handle material, they are different patterns. The top, handled in yellow celluloid, has a pattern number of R4825, while the bottom knife, handled in red celluloid has a pattern number of R4845. If you look carefully, you will see that the yellow knife has straight sides, while the red knife has a slight serpentine shape to it, thus the different pattern numbers. These knives are known as Remington "straight lines" because "Remington" is stamped in a straight line on the tang. Both measure 3-1/4" and are valued at $125.

**Remington**
Remington showroom countertop advertising board, 1930s, $200+.

**Remington Serpentine Jack Two-Blade Knives**
R1825 may be Remington's most common pattern.
(top to bottom)
*Grey cracked ice celluloid, $150.
Camouflage-type celluloid, $150.
French ivory celluloid, $150.*

**Remington**
*Remington 2-bladed serpentine-style jacks, 3-5/8", $125 each. These two knives have the same style but slightly different bone coloration. Both have long pulls on the master blade. Although this was perhaps Remington's best-known pattern, it has no pattern number stamped on the back of the blades.*

**Remington**
*Remington 8243 Easy (EZ) Opener, 2 blades, jigged bone, stamped, 3-5/8", $250. At top, original blade opener, $25.*

**Remington**
*Remington R3133, 4", $900. This knife is unusual because it contains three backsprings, not the normal two. With its acorn shield, it contains a punch blade.*

**Remington**
*"Curtis Baby Ruth Candy and Gum" serpentine jackknife, $150. This jigged black-handled jackknife was made specifically by Remington for the Curtis Candy Company in the 1930s and has no pattern number because it's an advertising knife. If a store ordered a certain number of cases of candy and gum from the Curtis company, it received one of these knives with the unique Curtis logo.*

**Remington**
*(top) Remington R2105, swell-end penknife, 2 blade, onyx celluloid, 3", $110.
(bottom) Remington R7945 "watch fob" knife with bail, green cracked-ice celluloid, $75.*

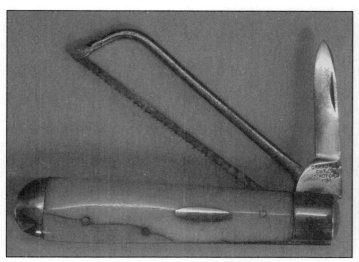

*Smooth bone, mark #2, (on small blade), very good, 3-7/16", $300.*

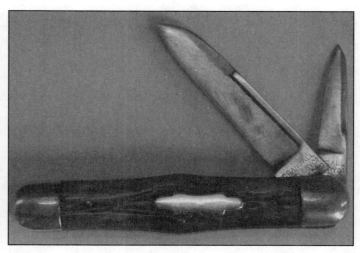

*Bone stag, mark #7, very good, 3-5/8", $125.*

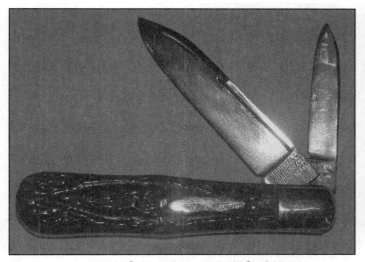

*Bone stag, mark #6, excellent, 3-13/16", $450.*

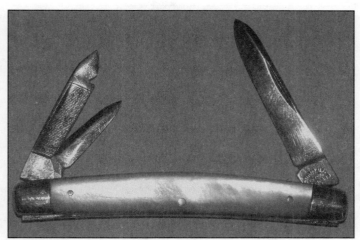

*Pearl, mark #10, very good, 3-5/16", $150.*

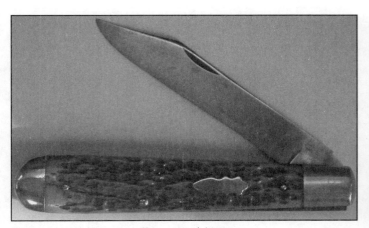

*Bone, mark #7, excellent, 5", $400.*

*Bone stag, mark #10, excellent, 3-3/4", $300.*

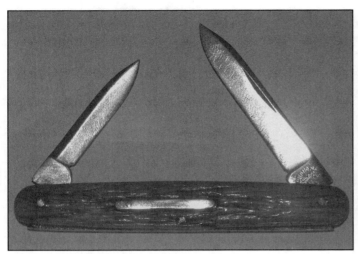

*Tan bone, mark #10, very good, 3", $75.*

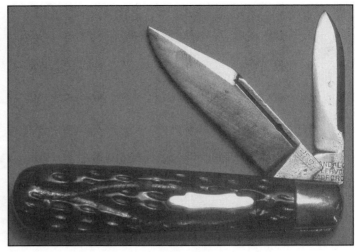

*Bone stag, mark #7, very good, 3-1/2", $200.*

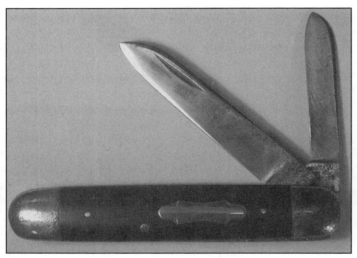

*Ebony, mark #7, very good, 3-5/8", $150.*

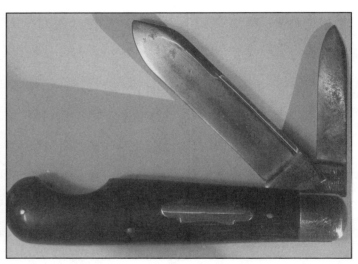

*Ebony, mark #7, very good, 3-9/16", $125.*

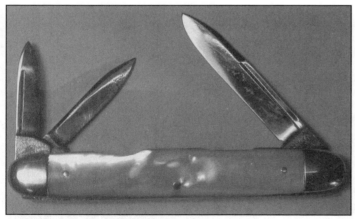

*Pearl, mark #10, very good, 3-1/4", $175.*

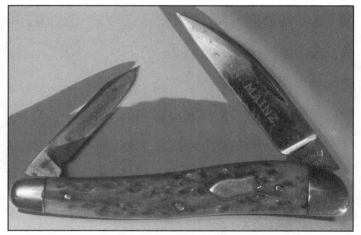

*Bone stag, mark #1, near mint, 3-1/4", $325.*

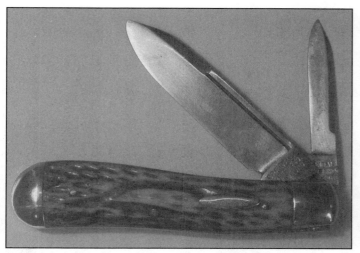
*Bone stag, mark #3, excellent, 3-1/2", $450.*

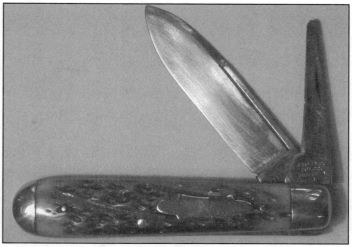
*Bone stag, mark #7, excellent, 3-1/2", $400.*

*Peachseed bone, mark #7, near mint, 4", $1,200.*

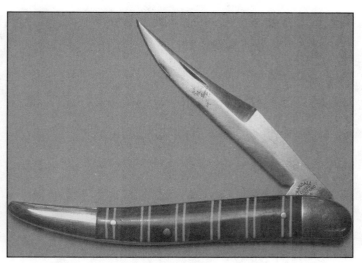
*Celluloid, mark #10, excellent, 4-1/4", $275.*

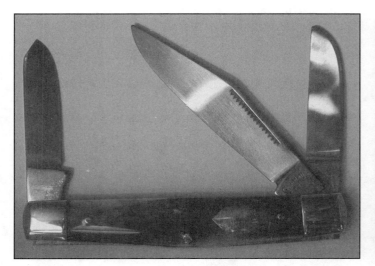
*Celluloid, mark #1, reproduction, mint, 3-9/16", $30.*

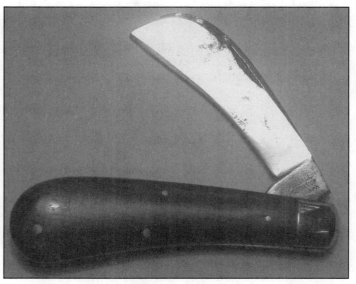
*Wood, mark #6, very good, 4", $75.*

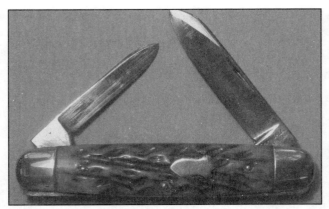

*Bone stag, mark #2, excellent, 3-1/4", $200.*

*Dark bone stag, mark #10, near mint, 3-1/4", $200.*

*Celluloid, mark #10, very good, 3-1/16", $75.*

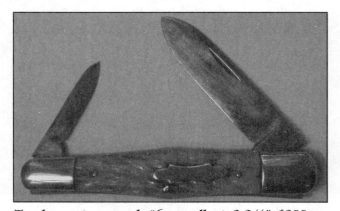

*Tan bone stag, mark #6, excellent, 3-3/4", $300.*

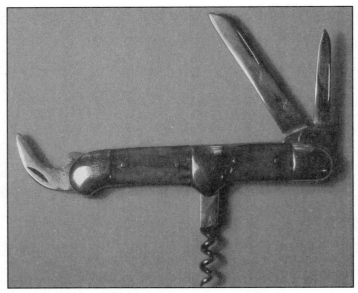

*Bone stag, mark #1, very good, 3", $250.*

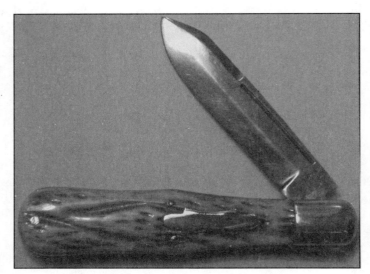

*Bone stag, mark #3, very good, 3-3/4", $150.*

*Bone stag, mark #7, very good, 4-7/16", $300.*

# Crandall Razors

(All marks stamped and all blades etched "I Must Kut," unless otherwise noted.)
In the mark descriptions below, a semicolon (;) indicates separate lines on the actual marks as seen on the razor tang.

**Mark #1**
CRANDALL CUT. CO.; BRADFORD, PA.

**Mark #2**
CRANDALL CUT. Co.; BRADFORD, PA.
(Only minor difference from mark #1 involving the o in Co.)

**Mark #3**
CRANDALL CUT. Co.; BRADFORD, PA.

**Mark #4**
CRANDALL CUTLERY Co (curved); BRADFORD, PA.

**Mark #5**
CRANDALL CUTLERY Co; BRADFORD, PA.

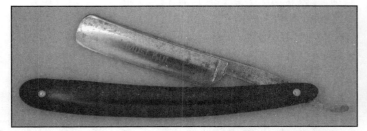

*Slick black celluloid, mark #1, blade excellent, handle fair, $45.*

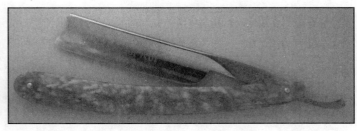

*Tan marbled celluloid, mark #3, near mint, $150.*

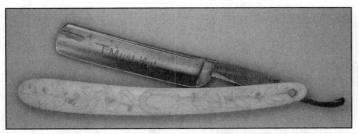

*Ivory celluloid w/vine & wreath, mark #1, excellent, $100.*

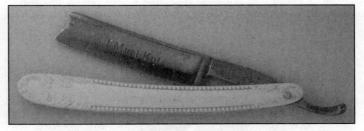

*Ivory celluloid w/beaded border, mark #3, excellent, $100.*

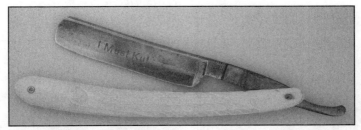

*Ivory celluloid w/feathers & covered tang, mark #2, excellent, $125.*

*Ivory celluloid w/vine & flowing hair, mark #1, excellent, $125.*

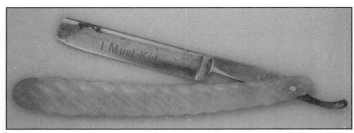

*Translucent cream rope celluloid, mark #3, very good, $75.*

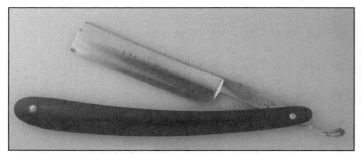

*Slick back celluloid, mark #3, near mint, $100.*

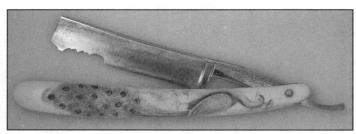

*Ivory celluloid w/green peacock, mark #1, excellent (w/deep nicks), $50.*

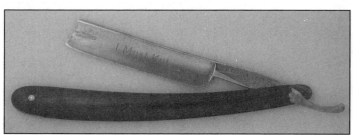

*Slick black celluloid, blade mark #3, excellent, handle fair, $35.*

*Brown & ivory mottled celluloid, mark #1, excellent, $125.*

*Slick black celluloid, mark #1, mint (w/nicks in blade), $25.*

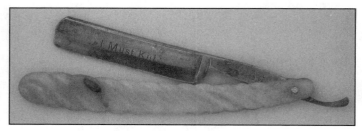

*Translucent cream rope celluloid, mark #3, excellent, $75.*

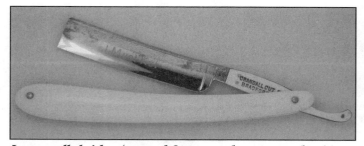

*Ivory celluloid w/carved & covered tang, mark #1, excellent, $150.*

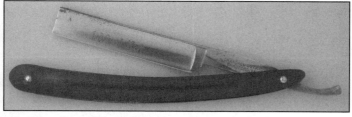

*Slick back celluloid, mark #1, near mint, $75.*

Little Valley Knife Association/Crandall Cutlery Company 327

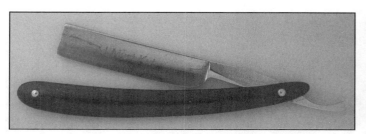

*Slick black celluloid, mark #1, near mint, $75.*

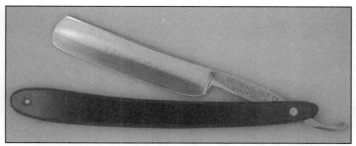

*Black Plastic w/beveled edges, mark #1, near mint, $75.*

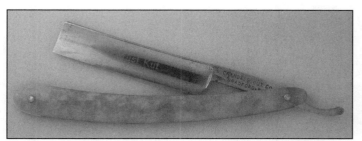

*Orange mottled celluloid, mark #3, near mint, $125.*

*Slick black celluloid, mark #1, excellent, (w/broken tang), $20.*

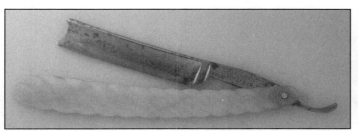

*Translucent cream rope celluloid, mark #1, excellent, $100.*

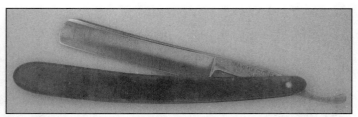

*Tortoiseshell celluloid, no "I Must Kut" etch, mark #1, excellent, $125.*

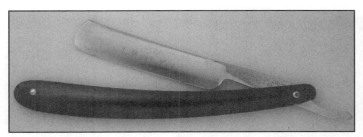

*Slick black celluloid, mark #2 (etched, not stamped), near mint, $100.*

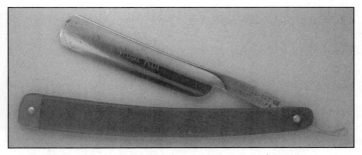

*Clear red celluloid, mark #1, near mint, $100.*

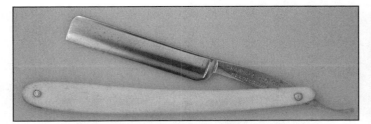

*Smooth white bone, mark #1, excellent, $100.*

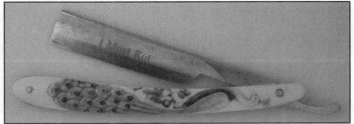

*Ivory celluloid, w/green & brown peacocks, mark #1, near mint, $300.*

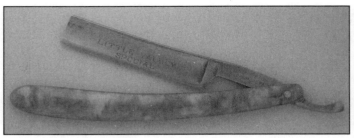

*Yellow w/green marbled celluloid, mark #4, excellent, stamped "LITTLE VALLEY SPECIAL," $250.*

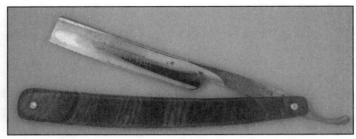

*Green striated celluloid, mark #1, excellent, $200.*

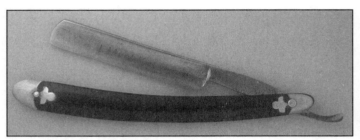

*Slick black celluloid, fancy NS end caps, mark #1, excellent, $125.*

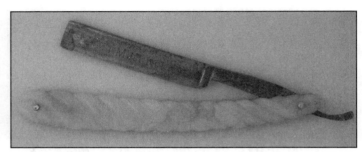

*Cream rope, celluloid, mark #1, very good, $75.*

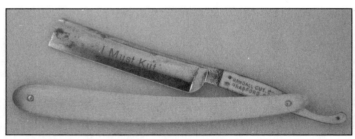

*Ivory celluloid w/carved & covered tang, mark #1, excellent, $125.*

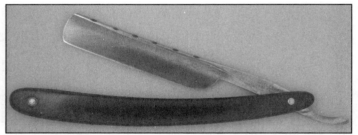

*Black plastic w/beveled edges, worked back, mark #5, excellent, etched "I Must Cut" (Cut spelled w/"C" rather than "K"), $100.*

*Cream celluloid, w/red vines, mark #1, excellent, $125.*

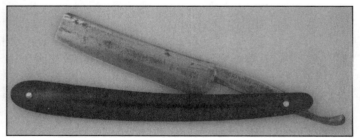

*Slick black celluloid, mark #1, very good, no "I Must Kut" etch, $75.*

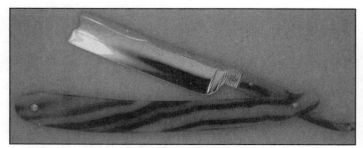

*Butter & molasses celluloid, worked back, mark #1, near mint, covered/engraved tang, no "I Must Kut" etch, $400.*

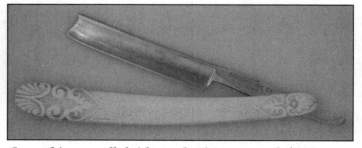

*Carved ivory celluloid, mark #1, very good, $100.*

# The Continuing Hawbaker Saga

By Ralph H. Scruton

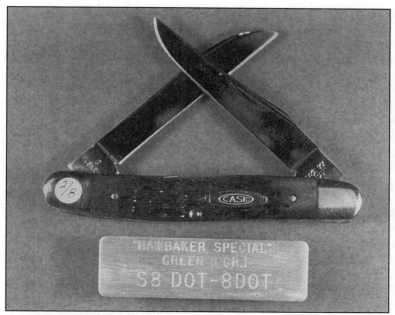

*Hawbaker Special*

Sometime back while browsing the Web, I noticed an unusual Hawbaker Special knife for sale. Of course, that perked my interest. The first thing I did was contact the seller about the markings, and he verified them right away. After bidding and winning, I received the knife and discovered it was stamped correctly, but the seller had mistakenly misidentified it. While we all make mistakes, we usually can correct them. In writing *Facts on the Hawbaker Knife*, an article that appeared in *Knife World* in May 1987, I find that I made some mistakes and that there are a lot more interesting facts that I think Hawbaker collectors should be aware of.

## Hawbaker's Writings

Mr. S. Stanley Hawbaker started in the mail-order business in 1934 in Greencastle, Pennsylvania. It wasn't until 1945 that he moved into the old mill in Fort Loudon, Pennsylvania, that is the home for the business today. He was an avid storyteller, and he became a prolific writer. His first attempt, a book titled *Trapping and Trailing*, was quite a success. In this publication, he wrote about his 20 years experience on the trapline and the 60 years

*S. Stanley Hawbaker*

of trapping secrets his grandfather had shared with him. A copy of this book in any condition is very desirable for a Hawbaker collector, and today, a copy in excellent condition would bring $200 to $250, maybe more.

In 1940, for the 1940-41 trapping season, he published his first issue of *Hawbaker's Catalog*, a mail-order catalog for the trapper. The catalogs have been published yearly to date, even after his demise in 1983, as they have been continued, along with the business, by his very capable son, Edwin M. Hawbaker. These catalogs are also collectible, with some of the very early ones bringing as much as several hundred dollars. In fact, I have offered up to $250 for a 1940-41 issue in mint condition and have had no takers. In 1941, Hawbaker wrote *Trapping North America Furbearers*. This book has flourished and is now in its eighteenth edition, which is still available, of course.

Along came 1951, and S. Stanley Hawbaker, with his foresight for the future, saw that the sportsmen of America needed a superb hunting, fishing, and trapping magazine. Thus, he launched *The American Woodsman*, with his brother Lyman as the editor and himself as the publisher. This magazine was far ahead of its time, as it provided first-class stories and tips rather than pulp fiction. In addition, its covers were exquisite works of art. Many of the covers were done by wildlife artists who are now nationally recognized: Sawyer, Lee, Gemmil, Pray, Sherwan, Morrow, Klingbail, Oughton, Hill, Staffan, Hexom, Peacock, Stevenson, and McCallister. From the first issue of July 1951 through the November-December 1955 issue, each copy of *The American Woodsman* sold for 25 cents. These colorful magazines make excellent reading on cold winter nights, plus they're attractive additions to any Hawbaker collection.

Then came *The Trapper Magazine,* published from January 1954 through December 1958. It was printed mostly in Hawbaker's own print shop and was a little crude or "rough around the edges," as one might say, especially compared to *The American Woodsman*. In fact, a few issues were a combination of magazine and catalog. S. Stanley, as he was often called, wrote many books about trapping and hunting various species of furbearing animals. Following are a few of his works: *Mink*; *Mink & Muskrat*; *Fox & Coyote*; *Raccoon*; *Beaver & Otter*; *Red & Gray Fox*; *How to Use Lure & Bait;* and *The Art of Hunting Deer & Bear*.

## Hawbaker's First Knives

The first knives made for Hawbaker's Trading Post were custom sheath knives. It's been claimed that they were made by a prisoner. Not true. They were made by D. M. Hutchinson, a guard at "The Rock," a federal prison in central Pennsylvania. My source tells me he lived in State College, Pennsylvania. It is reported that during World War II, Mr. Hutchinson furnished all inductees that he heard of with one of his hand-made knives. The knives are advertised in Hawbaker's 1947 catalog as three models made exclusively for S. Stanley Hawbaker and Sons. The models were the General Eisenhower, General McArthur, and General Patton. Also, he reportedly sent one of these to each of these men.

## Hawbaker Miniature Knives

Also at the forefront of Hawbaker collectibles are his miniature traps, which were produced as tie bars and key chains. The traps were handmade by Melvin B. Koch of Lititz, Pennsylvania. From 1925 to 1975, Koch worked as a tool and die maker at Woodstream Corp., which manufactured animal traps. Koch made the stamping and forming dies for the miniature traps. Then he assembled them by hand, each one having nine hand-riveted points of assembly.

This reminds me of a humorous incident that happened at a *Blade* show in Knoxville, Tennessee. A friend and I had our knives in display cases. Along came a "one-in-every-show" guy. (He's the one who picks up every knife and opens and closes it.) Well, we had some of these miniature traps in our display. Lo and behold, he tripped one of these beauties with the back of his middle finger, and it snapped on loose skin. Of course it didn't hurt him, but he did a no-no by pulling on it. Being a double-spring miniature Oneida Newhouse bear trap, the harder he pulled on it, the tighter it gripped. You have to compress both springs to release it. We laughed at him for awhile, then turned him loose.

## The Hawbaker Special

Let's get to the Hawbaker Special as we know it today. First, no knife belongs in a Hawbaker collection that has not been commissioned or sold by S. Stanley Hawbaker & Sons. It's very gratifying to the Hawbakers to know that all knives made with this blade configuration are recognized as "Hawbaker Specials," but this doesn't mean that they are part of a Hawbaker collection.

The first knife made in this blade configuration was a muskrat made by Schrade Cutlery Co., of Walden, New York, sometime between 1904 and 1938. I have an example of this in my collection; therefore, I am pretty positive these were in existence before the Hawbaker business was. So why don't we just call these other knives what they are, just muskrat knives, not "so and so" Hawbaker muskrats. I believe that to use another man's name to sell something is called infringement.

We now know that S. Stanley Hawbaker & Sons sold unmarked peachseed bone Schrade Cutlery and Schrade Walden knives. Also there was a rough black in Schrade Cutlery sold in his business along with first- and second-generation York Cutlery knives. Moving to the W. R. Case generation, we find that two models of the XXs were made—one with the early type rough jigging, and the second with the more easily recognized finer jigging. According to the "Hawbaker Update" article with the letter from Edwin M. Hawbaker that appeared in *Knife World*, January 1992, the flow of counterfeit Hawbaker Specials seems to have slowed. Still, beware of the 7 dot-7 dot bone handle knives, as a few of them seem to surface now and then.

Other knives that we overlooked in this collection were the 1982 red and greens that were returned to the factory because of the quality of the color in the scales. These will be the same as the regular knives with the omission of the blade etching. It was deemed that these returned knives could not be sold with the original blade etchings, but they fit right into your collection. That adds up to 37 knives in my collection of Hawbaker Specials, plus the Queen Pearl, "Changing of the Guard—Into the Millennium" that also is "Honoring Changing of the Guard, From Father: S. Stanley Hawbaker, To Son: Edwin M. Hawbaker—The Tradition Goes On," for a grand total of 38 knives. Five hundred of these knives were produced and some are still available. For more information, contact one of the following:

1. NKCA, P.O. Box 21070, Chattanooga, TN 37424. Phone 423-892-5007.
2. S. Stanley Hawbaker & Sons, 258 Hawbaker Drive South, Fort Loudon, PA 17224. Phone: 717-369-3615.
3. Ralph H. Scruton (contact information below).

When I began collecting Hawbaker Specials, I thought a collector could only go so far. But the more you're out and about, the more you become aware of how diversified and intriguing S. Stanley Hawbaker collectibles are. Not only are there knives and publications, but the memorabilia is almost endless. We have found matchbooks, pens, lead and mechanical pencils, swim-through-handle fish bowls, shipping containers, large and small calendars, plates, and miniature traps, to name a few things.

I am always interested in hearing from any and all Hawbaker collectors. You may reach me by writing to Ralph H. Scruton, 914 Hykes Rd., Greencastle, PA 17225; by calling (717) 597-8511; by faxing (717) 598-8289; or by e-mailing rhsjr@innernet.net.

| Date | Maker | Handle | # Ordered | # Shipped | Date Shipped | Blade Variations | Hawbaker Variations | Value |
|---|---|---|---|---|---|---|---|---|
| 1904-38 | Schrade Cut. | peach-seed bone | unknown | unknown | unknown | improved muskrat | not etched | $750 |
| 1938-73 | Schrade Walden | peach-seed bone | unknown | unknown | unknown | improved muskrat | not etched | $875 |
| 1955 | York Deep-Etch | jigged bone | 600 | 600 | Dec. '55 | improved muskrat | Hawbaker Special | $900 |
| Oct. '56 | York #1 & #2 | jigged bone | 600 | 600 | March '57 | improved muskrat | Hawbaker Special | $900 |
| 1958 | York #2 | jigged bone | 600 | 538 | Aug. '58 | improved muskrat | Hawbaker Special | $900 |
| Sept. '61 | Case*(note 1) | jigged bone | 600 | 180 | Nov. '61 | Case XX | Case XX | $1,200 |
| | | | | 180 | Dec. '61 | Case XX | Case XX | $1,200 |
| | | | | 235 | Feb. '62 | Case XX | Case XX | $1,200 |
| Sept. '63 | Case | jigged bone | 600 | 180 | Oct. '63 | Case XX | Case XX | $1,200 |
| | | | | 411 | Oct. '64 | Case XX | Case XX | $1,200 |
| Sept. '66 | Case | jigged bone | 600 | 180 | Oct. '66 | Case XX, USA | Case XX, USA | $1,100 |
| | | | | 420 | Oct. '67 | Case XX, USA | Case XX, USA | $1,100 |
| July '69 | Case | jigged bone | 600 | 180 | Aug. '69 | Case XX, USA | Case XX, USA | $1,100 |
| | | | | 144 | Oct. '69 | Case XX, USA | Case XX, USA | $1,100 |
| | | | | 282 | July '70 | Case XX, USA | 10 Dots | $950 |
| | | | | | | 10 Dots | 10 Dots | $1,000 |
| May '71 | Case | jigged bone | 180 | 182 | May '71 | 10 Dots | Case XX, USA | $1,200 |
| | | | | | | 10 Dots | 9 Dots | $1,150 |
| | | | | | | 9 Dots | Case XX, USA | $1,500 (rare) |
| | | | | | | 9 Dots | 10 Dots | $1,150 |
| Nov. '71 | Case | jigged bone | 600 | 300 | Jan. '72 | 9 Dots | 9 Dots | $275 |
| | | | | 311 | Oct. '72 | 8 Dots | 7 Dots | $175 |
| Apr. '73 | Case | delrin | 600 | 180 | June '73 | 7 Dots | 7 Dots | $225 |
| | | | | 462 | Sept. '73 | 7 Dots | 7 Dots | $225 |
| Nov. '73 | Case*(note 2) | delrin | 600 | 600 | March '74 | 7 Dots | 7 Dots | $225 |
| | | jigged bone | Approx. 4% | | | 7 Dots | 7 Dots 1 nail gr. | $600 |
| | | jigged bone | Approx. 4% | | | 7 Dots | 7 Dots 2 nail gr. | $600 |
| Sept. '74 | Queen | imitation Winterbottom | | | Oct. '74 | improved muskrat | Hawbaker Special | $350 |
| Mar. '78 | Case | jigged bone | 1,000 | 1,000 | Apr. '78 | 3 Dots | 9 Dots | $175 |
| | | | | | | 3 Dots | 7 Dots | $200 |
| | | | | | | 3 Dots | 2 Dots | $200 |
| | | | | | | 2 Dots | 9 Dots | $200 |
| | | | | | | 2 Dots | 7 Dots | $185 |
| | | | | | | 2 Dots | 2 Dots | $200 |
| Oct. '81 | Case | jigged green bone | 1,000 | 1,000 | 1982 | S 9 Dots | 8 Dots 1 nail gr. | $250 |
| | | | | | | S 9 Dots | 8 Dots 2 nail gr. | $135 |
| Nov. '81 | Case | jigged red bone | 1,000 | 1,000 | 1982 | S 9 Dots | 8 Dots 1 nail gr. | $250 |
| | | | | | | S 9 Dots | 8 Dots 2 nail gr. | $135 |
| June '82 | Case | jigged green bone | 1,000 | 1,114 | 1982 | S 8 Dots | 8 Dots 1 nail gr. | $135 |
| | | | | | | S 8 Dots | 8 Dots 2 nail gr. | $135 |
| June '82 | Case | jigged red bone | 1,000 | 681 | 1982 | S 8 Dots | 8 Dots 1 nail gr. | $135 |
| | | | | | | S 8 Dots | 8 Dots 2 nail gr. | $135 |
| Apr. '87 | Case | stag 50th Anniv. | 1,000 | 1,000 | June '87 | SS 3 Dots | Stag Hawbaker Spl | $325 |
| Apr. '87 | Case | stag 50th Anniv. | 3 | 3 | May 1987 | SS 3 Dot | serial #000 | $750 |
| Mar.' 99 | Queen | Pearl Millennium | 500 | 500 | Jul. 1999 | improved muskrat | Hawbaker Special | $225 |
| Nov.' 99 | Queen | Pearl | 500 | 500 | Nov. 1,000 | Going into Millennium | Hawbaker Special | $250 |

Note 1: Some first model XX-XX Hawbaker Specials were shipped in the first order. (These had the early Case XX jigging—very coarse jigging compared to later jigging.) $1,500

Note 2: Case jigged bone approximately 4 percent of the 1,200 ordered in delrin, both one and two nail grooves. $1,200

# A Short History Of Queen Cutlery

By David A. Krauss, Ph.D.

One of the last manufacturers of traditional bench-made American cutlery resides in Titusville, Pennsylvania. Remarkably, its factory continues to produce knives in much the same way as they were produced there over 100 years ago. Queen City Cutlery Company incorporated in 1922 and shortened its name to "Queen Cutlery Company" in January of 1946. Queen may very well be the oldest, as well as the last, American cutlery factory that truly makes knives "the old fashioned way." Queen was founded by five supervisors who had been fired from the Schatt & Morgan Cutlery Company. The two companies competed in Titusville for about 11 years, until Queen City Cutlery was able to purchase Schatt & Morgan. The story of Queen City Cutlery is so woven from the threads of Schatt & Morgan Cutlery that one needs to know a little of that history also.

But first, a brief overview is in order. Students of American cutlery history know that until the end of the Civil War, most of the higher-grade cutlery used by Americans was both produced and imported from Sheffield, England. Solingen, Germany, supplied a majority of the remainder of common goods during that time. This situation changed abruptly beginning with the McKinley Act of 1890, and continuing with other tariffs introduced in 1894 and 1897. The tariffs placed high duties on all imported cutlery. Suddenly, American cutlery importers had to start becoming manufacturers or change their line of work. Fueled by the protectionist economic policy of the time, and aided by immigrating cutlers, abundant natural resources, and American mechanical ingenuity, U.S. manufacturers were free to create their own type of cutlery making, unburdened by guilds or European traditions. Thus, the so-called "Golden Age" of American cutlery began. By 1918 and the end of the First World War, America was using its cutlery expertise to become the preeminent supplier of quality cutlery until the Great Depression of 1929, but we are getting ahead of ourselves. Let's go back to Schatt & Morgan, and the origins of Queen Cutlery.

John W. Schatt and Charles B. Morgan established the Schatt & Morgan Cutlery Company in 1895. Initially founded as the "New York Cutlery Company" (not to be confused with the well-known New York Knife Company), the pair opened an office in New York City sometime in 1896. Although they started out importing, they quickly realized that to remain in business they would have to become manufacturers. So sometime in 1896 or early in 1897 they moved to Schatt's hometown of Gowanda, New York, and in July of 1897 they purchased the Platts' cutlery plant there. The Platts then moved to Eldred, Pennsylvania, (The former Gowanda factory site now has a plaque noting the Platts' tenure there.)

Schatt and Morgan hired Arthur Orchird to run the Gowanda facility. Their cutlery manufactured in Gowanda was marked with a two-line S&M tang stamp with either "GOWANDA NY" or "NEW YORK" on the second line. The company was housed in Gowanda from 1897 until 1902, at which time they moved to the Titusville, Pennsylvania, factory and incorporated there that same year. Schatt & Morgan went bankrupt in the late 1920s, and was sold to Queen City Cutlery in August of 1933 at a sheriff's auction. The five supervisors who had been fired from Schatt & Morgan back in 1922 were able to return to the place where they had started. At that time C. B. Morgan, former president of Schatt & Morgan, ended up working for the very men he had previously dismissed. Queen resides in that same Titusville factory to this day, so the story of the modern day Queen Cutlery Company really begins with its predecessor, Schatt & Morgan.

Titusville, Pennsylvania, became famous in 1859 as the birthplace of the petroleum industry when Edwin Drake drilled the first successful oil well there. Because of this association with oil, Titusville became known as the Queen City (hence Queen City Cutlery Company). In 1860, the population was 243. When the city incorporated six years later, the population was 8,000. Such was and is the power of petroleum. However, by the mid-1870s other towns in the area were producing more oil. Standard Oil was beginning to create an essential monopoly, and Titusville was being passed by because it would not become a one-industry town. An industrial association was formed to attract new industries to Titusville. Schatt & Morgan was invited to town and was offered both financial incentives and larger facilities. In Gowanda, they were employing 125 men and were making a profit. Optimism and expansion were the words of the day. Schatt, Morgan, and their new plant manager and treasurer, Jessie Crouch, signed papers in October of that year, and as noted above, moved the business to Titusville. (Morgan would buy Schatt out in 1911 and Schatt would remain in Gowanda, becoming the manager of an opera house there.)

In 1903, Schatt & Morgan was manufacturing 40,000 dozen knives per year in Titusville and had 12 salesmen on the road with sales all around the country according to newspaper reports of the day. Several building expansions were undertaken to keep up with production, beginning as early as 1907. In less than five years, the company had doubled the size of its facility to keep up with an ever-increasing demand for its cutlery. The Schatt & Morgan catalog #2 published in 1911 noted, "Although comparatively young as knife manufacturers, we have already grown to be one of the largest and best known houses of the United States." These facilities would end up being owned and operated by Queen Cutlery.

The First World War altered the growth of Schatt & Morgan, due to the rationing of materials needed for the war effort, but primarily due to the short supply of skilled workers. The great influenza epidemic of 1918 also took its toll in Titusville and elsewhere. In addition, Morgan was active in local politics and had served as mayor from 1916 to 1919. In 1919, Schatt & Morgan Cutlery expanded again and built a one-story building across the street from the factory to house the boiler, electric generator, and air compressor for the factory. However, by then the heyday for Schatt & Morgan was beginning to fade, and the story gets a little complicated in the ten years between 1919 and 1929. (Morgan served as mayor again between 1924 and 1927.) It's about at this point where the five men who would start Queen City Cutlery Company first enter the story.

As if the effect of the First World War was not bad enough for Schatt & Morgan, its longtime plant superintendent, Jessie Crouch, died in 1921, only two years after the company built the new power plant building. The company was further crippled by the 1922 firing of five of their most skilled workers, all supervising department heads. These were the men who in that same year would incorporate their own business: Queen City Cutlery Company. These department heads apparently had been making skeleton knives (knives without handle scales) on the sly since around 1918 and then wholesaling them out on their own, but were discovered in 1922 and promptly let go. The Schatt & Morgan workforce subsequently dropped about 30 percent, or from about 90 to 60 workers that year, probably as a result of firing those supervisors.

By 1923. C. B. Morgan was quoted in the daily newspaper, the *Titusville Herald,* as stating "I think that we as well as most manufacturers made a mistake during the rush of war times that more apprentices were not kept at work…now we find ourselves short of skilled workers." (Some of those skilled workers in Titusville were working for Queen). That same year, Morgan accepted the Republican nomination for mayor again, and was also quoted denying rumors that the company had been sold to Remington. (It had been offered to "a syndicate" but was not purchased). Schatt & Morgan had extreme difficulty in purchasing new materials and making money by the later 1920s, but their terminal problems really began when they fired those five men in 1922. Those men incorporated Queen City Cutlery, moved about a mile away, and began manufacturing cutlery themselves. Ironically, 11 years later they returned to the factory, and on August 21, 1933, they were able to purchase the business and all its contents at a sheriff's auction.

The five men who founded Queen City Cutlery were Frank Foresther (1883-1939), Geza Revitzky (1880-1979), E. Clarence Erickson (1897-1961), Jesse F. Barker (1895-1970), and Harry L Matthews (1897-1967). Harry Matthews married Geza Revitzky's daughter, and their two sons were active in the business until 1975. Frank Foresther's son, Louis, was also active in the company from 1939 until his death in 1956. Clarence Erickson's daughter Eleanor married Walter Bell, who became president in 1961 when his father-in-law died. Bell was president of the company in 1969 when it passed out of family hands and was purchased by Servotronics Corporation. Bell retired in 1972. As of the beginning of 2004, the president of Queen Cutlery Company is Bob Breton. Retired master cutler and cutlery designer Fred Sampson still lives in Titusville and remains helpful in resolving some of the questions collectors have regarding Queen's products over the years.

Now let's go back to 1922 and the beginnings of Queen City Cutlery. At that time, the fledgling company was working out of a garage, but six months later it had moved into a building on Spring Street that had formerly been used as a mill. Queen City was never located more than a mile or so away from the Schatt & Morgan factory. Queen City would stay at the Spring Street location for the next ten years, purchasing new equipment and enlarging the facility in 1927. By that time they were employing twenty-five men and five women and had four salesmen on the road.

It is important to note that Queen City Cutlery was an innovator and a pioneer in using functional stainless steel in American pocket cutlery. (Stainless is defined as having at least 11 percent chromium in the alloy.) As early as 1926, Queen City Cutlery was listed in the regional trade publications as manufacturers of "high grade stainless steel cutlery." Stainless steel had been introduced in England in 1914 and first patented in America in 1915, but the change in blade material was initially opposed by many cutlers, as often happens when new technologies are introduced in an existing field. The new steel could not be forged by hand, and cutlers of the day simply did not understand how to properly temper and harden the new material, as it did not follow the rules of carbon steel that generations of cutlers had been used to. This led to poor products and a poor reputation for the new material.

By February of 1927, the *Titusville Herald* noted, however, that "the company [Queen City] has for some time been using what is known as stainless steel in the manufacturing of pocket knives and its output is eagerly sought in all parts of the country." Queen was the primary innovator of this change from carbon steel to a stainless steel formulation that was well suited for blades and backsprings. Queen was the first American cutlery company to successfully introduce a large variety of stainless steel cutlery to the market. Even though almost 90 percent of cutlery had carbon steel blades until the late 1940s, Queen had been successfully producing a line of stainless steel knives since the mid 1920s. Queen used "stainless" on its tang stamps from about the mid-1940s to the mid-1950s. Around 1955 or 1956, Queen decided to change the markings on its knives from "stainless" to "Queen Steel" because cutlery retailers and the public generally did not know that Queen had perfected the new material.

"Queen Steel" was a type of 440 stainless steel developed by the Cyclops Steel Company. Originally called Eames Petroleum Ironworks, Cyclops was a specialty steel plant in Titusville. The first nickel-chromium steel produced in America was made there under the leadership of Cyclops' chief metallurgist Charles Evans in 1917. Queen worked closely with Cyclops to develop its 400 series stainless steel products. Queen's willingness to experiment and push the limits of cutlery steel was also evident in 1999 when it began using ATS-34 steel on master blades, and again in 2002 when it started using both D-2 and 420HC steels for blades.

As noted above, Queen City Cutlery Company shortened its name to Queen Cutlery Company in January of 1946. This simple act led to some legal difficulties with the Henry Sears & Son Cutlery Company in Minnesota, who saw the change as an infringement on its name. Henry Sears was already using the word "Queen" on some of their straight razors and knife blades. They were also using the name on some of their knife handle shields. Henry Sears & Son threatened Queen Cutlery with legal action in 1948. This prompted numerous "cease and desist" letters between companies and a trip in the middle of winter to Minnesota, where Queen president, E. Clarence Erickson, and the company lawyer, Roland Mahaney met with the Henry Sears people. In 1956, Queen hired a trademark registration company to file "Certificates of Registration" in all contiguous 48 states to protect their claim, and over time Queen prevailed. Henry Sears & Son went out of business in 1958 due to other economic reasons and the case never went to court. On another legal front, the reader may wish to know that in 1950 Queen was granted a patent for an Erickson designed automatic (switchblade) knife, which was manufactured for a few years until the 1958 Switchblade Act made those items illegal. Queen then disposed of the unused parts by mixing them with concrete that was being used to make a driveway in Titusville.

Queen used a wide variety of handle materials over the years; some of the most expensive and rare being "smoked pearl." In addition to mother-of-pearl, the company also has used various horn, bone, stag, and woods, as well as numerous synthetic materials to haft their knives. Although Rogers jigged bone was used on many of its early knives, by the mid to late 1940s, Queen began producing most of its knives in Winterbottom bone. Winterbottom bone was originally produced in the Winterbottom factory in Egg Harbor, New Jersey, and from about 1950 to 1959, Queen used that style of jigged bone almost exclusively. Today, Queen is well known for its use of Winterbottom bone and it continues to produce some knives with both bone and synthetic handles in that distinctive jigging style. Synthetic handles of plastic and nylon materials were used more and more beginning in the 1950s, and Queen began hafting most of its knives in synthetic Winterbottom style by 1959.

Overall the 1950s and 1960s were not good decades for traditional American cutlery, as inexpensive Asian and European cutlery flooded the market, while at the same time the U.S. became less rural and more industrialized, creating less need for pocketknives for day-to-day cutting chores. Not only did Queen begin using Delrin Winterbottom and other less expensive synthetic handle materials, it also stopped tang stamping their knives around 1960 to further reduce production costs in an effort to remain competitive. Queen resumed tang stamping in 1972. From 1922 to 1955, Queen used approximately 20 different tang stamps; see "The History of Queen Tang Stamps" and the variety of tang stamps on the Queen knives that follow.

Queen Cutlery was family owned and operated until 1969, when it was sold to Servotronics Corporation of Buffalo, New York. Second generation family members stayed on for a few more years, but by the mid-1970s all had retired and the company leadership was entirely taken over by Servotronics. (Servotronics had also purchased Ontario Cutlery in 1967 and owns both companies to this day.)

Knife collecting began to gain popularity just about the time the company was sold to Servotronics. As noted above, Queen returned to tang stamps in 1972 as a way to benefit from the renewed interest in quality traditional pocket cutlery. Around that time, the company also began to issue limited edition knives, commemoratives, and other different "series" and styles of knives, which they continue to do to the present. For example it began the Master Cutler series in the 1970s, the Stag series of the 1980s, and reintroduced Schatt & Morgan series in 1991, a Robeson series in 1995, and a "File & Wire" series in 1998 respectively. Current Queen Cutlery knives are made with both users and collectors in mind, and of course it continues its extensive contract work. (Ironically, even today the Queen mark is not as popular as some of the cutlery marks that Queen produces under contract, as those knives are really "Queen"-made products, regardless of what their various tang stamps purport).

Collectors and users of cutlery, as well as anyone with an interest in American manufacturing history, can be grateful that Queen continues to manufacture all its pocketknives in the original Schatt & Morgan factory in Titusville. Quality cutlery is produced there today in essentially the same way as it was produced there over 100 years ago—real bench-made cutlery with a human touch. The company remains a remarkable constant in small-scale American manufacturing and is the third oldest industry in Titusville. Readers may wish to know that Queen opened a factory store there in 1998, where one can purchase cutlery. And tours of the facility are given when factory-planned events occur. All collectors should be pleased that quality continues at the Queen Cutlery Company.

© copyright 2004. Used by permission.

David Krauss is the author of *American Pocketknives: The History of Schatt & Morgan and Queen Cutlery*. His book is available at americanpocketknives.com.

**Queen Cutlery Inc. Collectors**

P.O. Box 109, Titusville, Pennsylvania 16354
e-mail: queen1922@aol.com · website: queencutlerycollectors.com

© Queen Cutlery Company, All Rights Reserved, Used Herein With Permission

# History of Queen Cutlery Tang Stamps

## 1890 To 1930

**S⊠M Titusville PA**

**Schatt-Morgan Cutlery Co. Titusville Pa**

**SCHATT &MORGAN CUTLERY CO. TITUSVILLE PA**

**QUEEN CITY TITUSVILLE PA.**
About 1925 - 1932

**QUEEN CITY**
About 1922 - 1932

**Q C C C**
About 1930 - 1932

## 1930 To 1950

**Queen City**
About 1925 - 1945

**QUEEN CUT. CO.**
About 1932 - 1949

About 1932 - 1955

UEEN
About 1958 - 1960

**QUEENCUTLERYCO TITUSVILLE, PA.**
About 1932 - 1950

About 1935 - 1955

About 1946 - 1948

## 1950 To 1960

 STAINLESS
About 1946 - 1948

 STAINLESS
About 1946 - 1950

 STAINLESS
About 1946 - 1948

 STAINLESS
About 1946 - 1948

 STAINLESS
About 1946 - 1949

 STEEL
About 1949 - 1958

## 1960 To Present Day

 STEEL
About 1958 - 1960

1972 Only

About 1973 - 1975

 76
1976 Only

1976 Only

**QUEEN CUTLERY Titusville Pa**
1991-1996

Starting in 1984
Dated after 1990

**MADE IN USA 2000**
1997 - 2000

# Queen / Schatt & Morgan Cutlery

*Pictured left to right, back row: Jim Sargent, David Clark, Howard Drake, and Fred Fisher.*
*Pictured left to right, front row: David Krauss, Mike Sullivan, and Linda Fisher.*

#7, Queen City, senator pen, 2 blade, imitation onyx handles, brass liners, NS bolsters, bail, no etch, block Queen City tang stamp, 2-1/2", $40-$50.

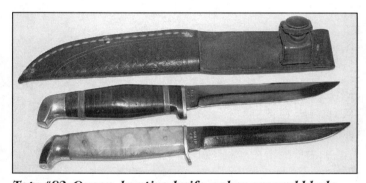

Top: #82, Queen, hunting knife, saber ground blade, stacked leather handles, no etch, block Queen City tang stamp, 4" blade, $65-$75.
Bottom: #82, Queen, hunting knife, saber ground blade, cracked ice handles, no etch, block Queen City tang stamp, 4" blade, $65-$75.

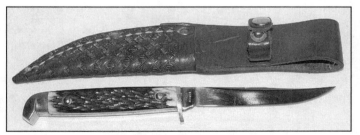

#85, Queen, hunting knife, Rogers bone handles, no etch, block Queen City tang stamp, 3" blade, $45-$60.

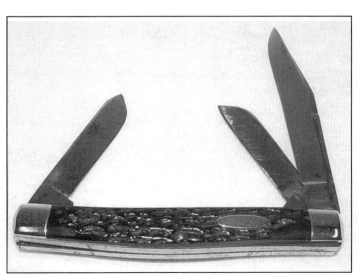

#26, Queen, stockman, 3 blade, Rogers bone handles w/shield, brass liners, NS bolsters, no etch, block Queen City tang stamp, 3-1/4", $80-$90.

#85, Queen, hunting knife, saber ground blade, cracked ice handles, no etch, block Queen City tang stamp, 3" blade, $45-$60.

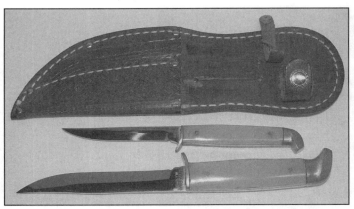

*Queen City, twin set hunting knives, amber handles, no etch, block Queen City tang stamp, 4" & 3" blades, $130-$150.*

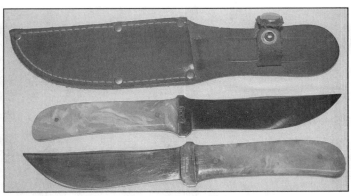

*Top: Queen City, outers, waterfall handles, no etch QCCC tang stamp, 4" blade, $145-$160.*
*Bottom: Queen City, outers, waterfall handles, no etch, block Queen City tang stamp, 4" blade, $125-$145.*

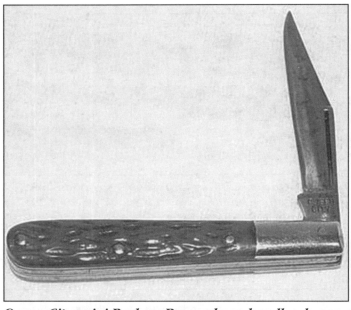

*Queen City, mini Barlow, Rogers bone handles, brass liners, bare head NS bolster, no etch, block Queen City tang stamp, 2-1/4" blade, $80-$90.*

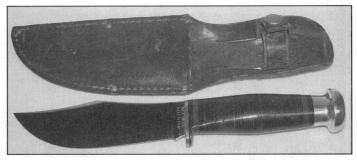

*Queen City, hunting knife, stacked leather handles, no etch, block Queen City Titusville, Pa tang stamp, 4-3/4" blade, $65-$85.*

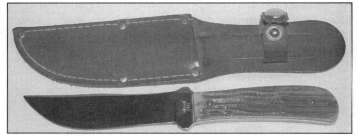

*Queen City, outers, peachseed bone handles, no etch, block Queen City tang stamp, 4" blade, $110-$135.*

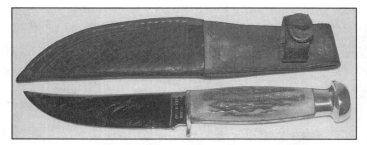

*Queen City, hunting knife, stag handles, no etch, block Queen City Titusville, Pa tang stamp, 4-1/4" blade, $75-$90.*

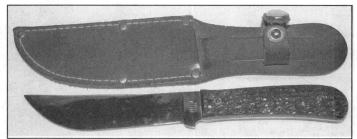

*Queen City, outers, jigged bone handles, no etch, block Queen City tang stamp, 4" blade, $150-$160.*

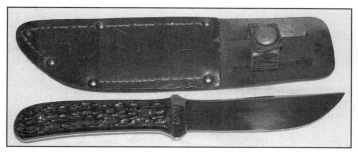

*Queen City, outers, jigged bone handles, no etch, QCCC tang stamp, 4" blade, $100-$125.*

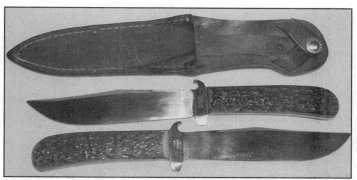

*Queen City, camp knife, jigged bone handles, no etch, block Queen City tang stamp, 5" blade, $125-$150.*

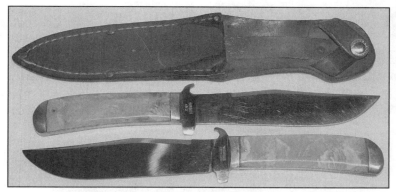

*Queen City, camp knife, waterfall handles, no etch, block Queen City tang stamp, 5" blade, $150-$175.*

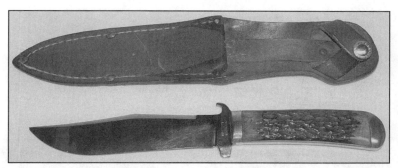

*Queen City, camp knife, jigged bone handles, no etch, block Queen City Titusville tang stamp, 5" blade, $125-$150.*

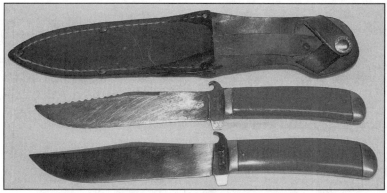

*Queen City, camp knife, red celluloid handles, no etch, block Queen City tang stamp, 5" blade, $125-$135.*

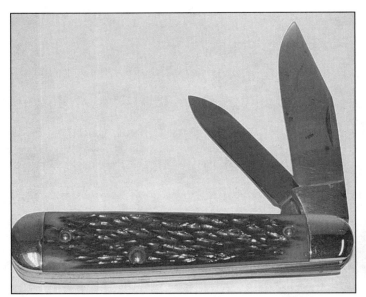

#10, Queen, heavy duty jack, 2 carbon steel blades, Rogers bone handles, brass liners, NS bolsters, Queen Cutlery script etch, no tang stamp, 4-1/8", $140-$150.

#19, Queen, trapper, 2 blade, burnt stag handles, brass liners, NS bolsters, no etch, script Queen City tang stamp, 4-1/8", $70-$80.

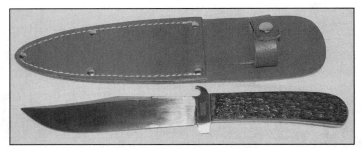

Queen City, camp knife, jigged bone handles, no etch, block Queen City tang stamp, 5" blade, $125-$150.

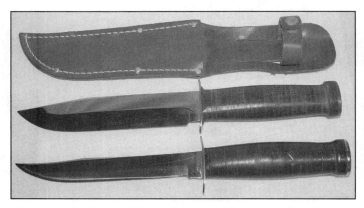

Top: Queen City, military knife, wide blade, stacked leather handles, no etch, script Queen City tang stamp, 6" blade, $75-$100.
Bottom: Queen City, military knife, narrow blade, stacked leather handles, no etch, script Queen City tang stamp, 6" blade, $75-$100.

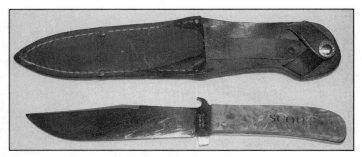

Queen City, camp knife, red & white handles w/Scout on handle, no etch, block Queen City tang stamp, 5" blade, $125-$135.

#36, Queen, lockback, 1 blade, Rogers bone handles, brass liners, NS bolster, Queen Q Cutlery script etch, no tang stamp, 4-1/2", $250-$300.

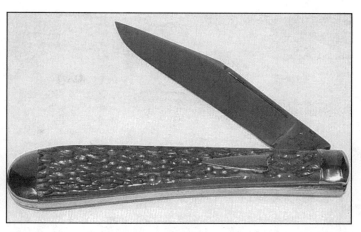

Queen City, reverse dogleg trapper, 1 blade, brown pick bone handles, 4-3/8", $195-$220.

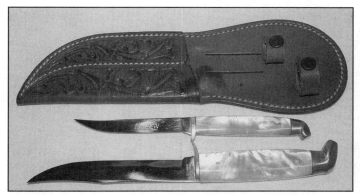

#81, Queen, twin set hunting knives, simulated mother-of-pearl handles, no etch, Queen City tang stamp, 4" & 3" blades, $115-$125.

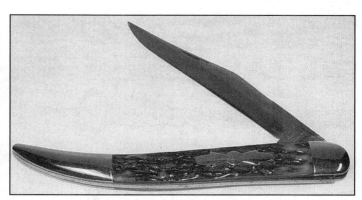

Queen City, toothpick, 1 blade, brown jigged bone handles, hammered pins, propeller shield, 5", $175-$250.

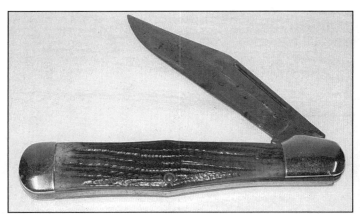

Queen City, folding hunter, Coke bottle, 1 blade, early Winterbottom bone handles, NS bolsters, no etch, Queen City tang stamp, 5-1/4", $250-$300.

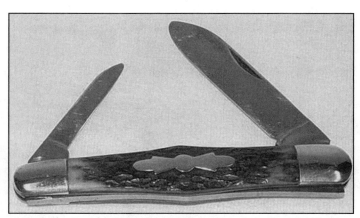

Queen City, swell-center opposite-end jack, 2 blade, Rogers bone handles, NS bolsters, propeller shield, 3-3/4", $130-$150.

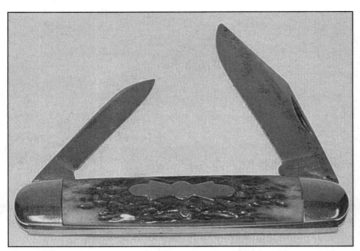

*Queen City, equal-end jack, 2 blade, unsharpened, perfect jigged bone handles, NS bolsters, hammered pins, propeller shield, 3-5/8", $150-$200.*

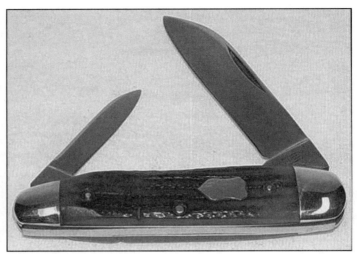

*Queen City, sleeveboard, 2 blade, early Winterbottom bone handles, NS bolsters, brass liners, 3-1/2", $300-$350.*

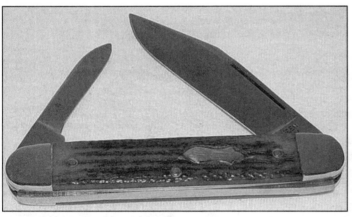

*Queen City, cigar, 2 blade, NS bolsters & shield, brass liners, 4-1/4", $175-$225.*

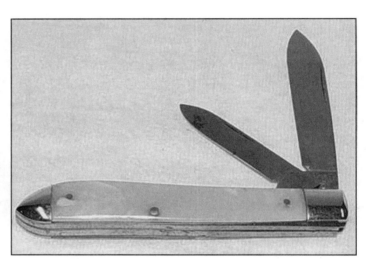

*Queen City, jack, 2 blade, imitation onyx handles, 3", $145-$175.*

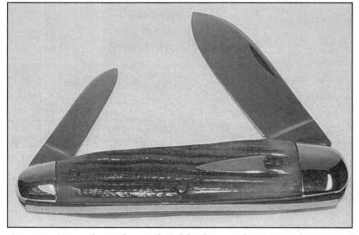

*Queen City, sleeveboard, 2 blade, early Winterbottom bone handles, NS bolsters & shield, 4", $300-$400.*

*Queen City, farmer's jack, 2 blade, candy stripe handles, NS bolsters, pins & liners, 4-1/2", $200-$250.*

*Queen City, farmer's jack, 2 blade, Rogers bone handles, steel bolsters, 4-5/8", $200-$250.*

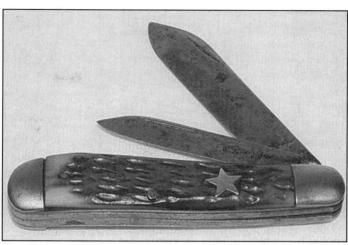

*Queen City, dogleg jack, 2 blade, jigged bone handles w/star shield, hammered pins, brass liners, iron bolsters, 3-1/2", $200-$250.*

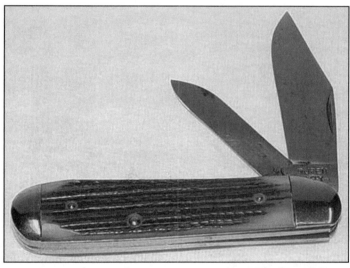

*Queen City, heavy jack, 2 blade, early Winterbottom bone handles, steel bolsters, $150-$200.*

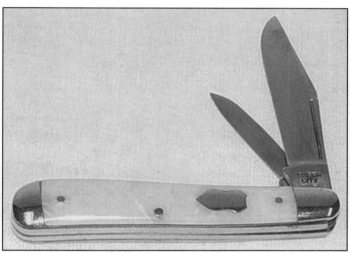

*Queen City, dogleg jack, 2 blade, imitation onyx handles, NS shields, 2-7/8", $165-$180.*

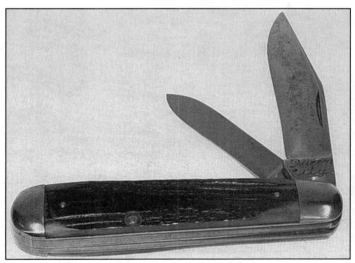

*Queen City, heavy jack, 2 blade, early Winterbottom bone handles, steel bolsters, 3-3/4", $150-$200.*

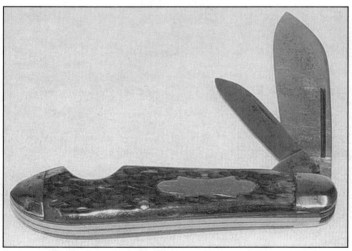

*Queen City, easy opener jack, 2 blade, Rogers bone handles, NS shield, iron bolsters, 3-3/4", $180-$250.*

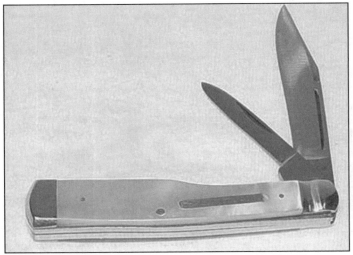

*Queen City, gunstock, pearl handles, NS bolsters & bar shield, brass liners, 3", $300-$350.*

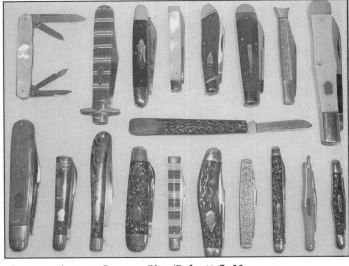

*Group picture Queen City/Schatt & Morgan.*

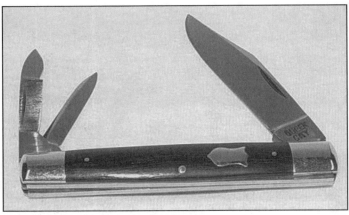

*Queen City, split backspring whittler, 3 blade w/one small file blade, ebony handles, NS federal shield, brass liners, 3-1/2", $200-$250.*

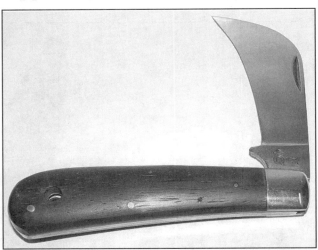

*#1, Queen, pruning or hawkbill, one 3" blade, rosewood handles, brass liners, NS bolsters, no etch, QUEEN STEEL tang stamp, 4-1/8", $25-$35.*

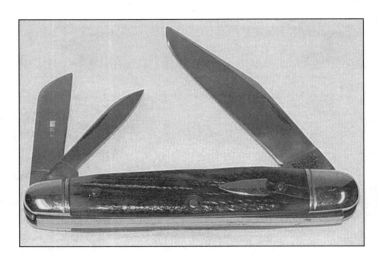

*Queen City, split backspring whittler, 3 blade, early Winterbottom bone handles, grooved bolsters, NS arrow shield, 3-3/4", $300-$350.*

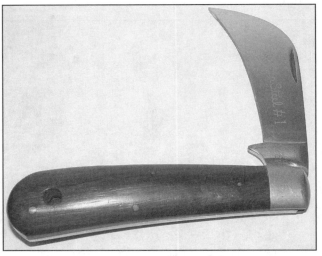

*#1, Queen, pruning or hawkbill, one 3" blade, rosewood handles, brass liners, NS bolsters, Queen Steel #1 etch, Q STEEL tang stamp, 4-1/8", $25-$35.*

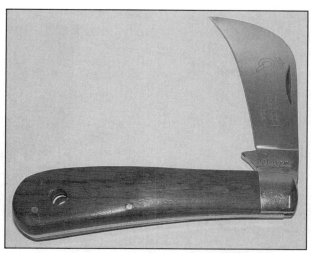

*#1, Queen, pruning or hawkbill, one 3" blade, rosewood handles, brass liners, NS bolsters, 4-1/8", Queen Steel #1 Made in U.S.A. etch, QUEEN tang stamp, $25-$35.*

*#2, Queen, serpentine jack, 2 blade, Winterbottom bone handles, brass liners, NS bolsters, no etch, big Q tang stamp, 3-1/4", $45-$60.*

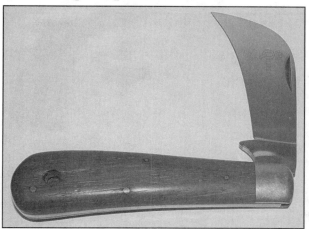

*#1, Queen, pruning or hawkbill, one 3" blade, rosewood handles, brass liners, NS bolsters, Queen Steel #1 etch, no tang stamp, 4-1/8", $25-$35.*

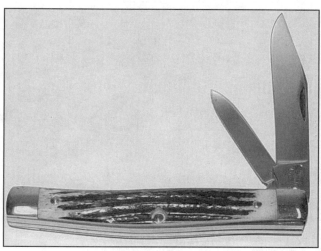

*#2, Queen, serpentine jack, 2 blade, Winterbottom bone handles, brass liners, NS bolsters, no etch, QUEEN STEEL tang stamp, 3-1/4", $45-$60.*

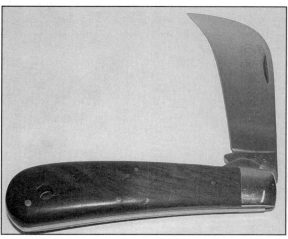

*#1, Queen, pruning or hawkbill, one 3" blade, rosewood handles, brass liners, NS bolsters, Queen Steel #1L etch, Q 22-72 tang stamp, 4-1/8", $25-$35.*

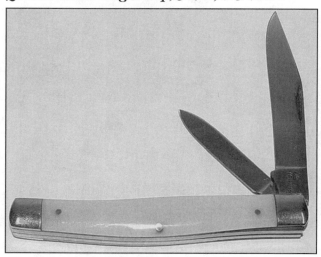

*#2, Queen, serpentine jack, 2 blade, amber handles, brass liners, NS bolsters, no etch, QUEEN STEEL tang stamp, 3-1/4", $30-$45.*

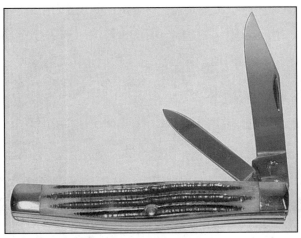

*#2, Queen, serpentine jack, 2 blade, Winterbottom bone handles, brass liners, NS bolsters, no etch, Q STEEL tang stamp, 3-1/4", $45-$60.*

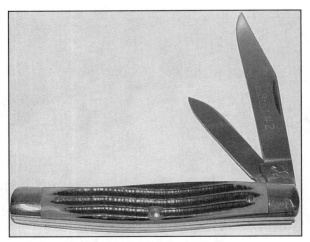

*#2, Queen, serpentine jack, 2 blade, Winterbottom bone handles, brass liners, NS bolsters, Queen Steel #2 etch, Q STEEL tang stamp, 3-1/4", $45-$60.*

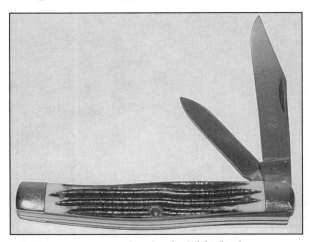

*#2, Queen, serpentine jack, 2 blade, burnt orange imitation Winterbottom bone handles, brass liners, NS bolsters, Queen Steel #2 etch, Q STEEL tang stamp, 3-1/4", $50-$65.*

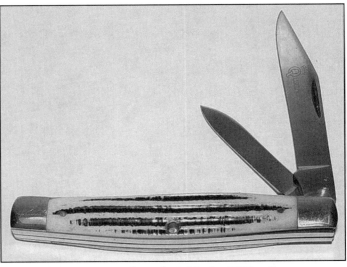

*#2, Queen, serpentine jack, 2 blade, Winterbottom bone handles, brass liners, NS bolsters, Queen Steel #2 etch, no tang stamp, 3-1/4", $45-$60.*

*#2, Queen, serpentine jack, 2 blade, black Micarta handles, brass liners, NS bolsters, Gamekeeper 302 U.S.A. etch, Q76 tang stamp, 3-1/4", $35-$40.*

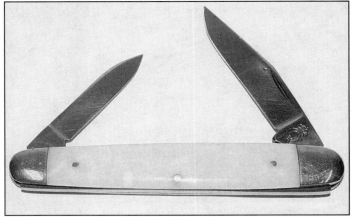

*#3, Queen, sleeveboard pen, 2 blade, imitation pearl handles, brass liners, NS bolsters, no etch, big Q tang stamp, 3-5/16", $40-$60.*

Queen / Schatt & Morgan Cutlery   347

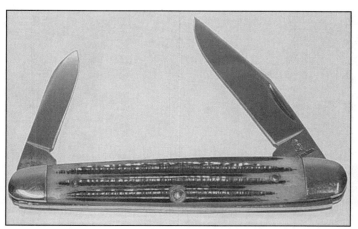

#3, Queen, sleeveboard pen 2 blade, Winterbottom bone handles, brass liners, NS bolsters, no etch, Q STAINLESS tang stamp, 3-5/16", $70-$80.

#3, Queen, sleeveboard pen, 2 blade, Rogers bone handles, brass liners, NS bolsters, Queen etch, no tang stamp, 3-5/16", $60-$80.

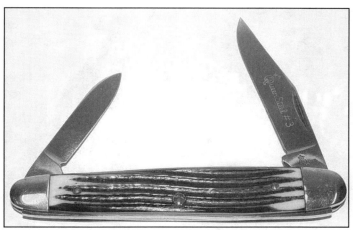

#3, Queen, sleeveboard pen, 2 blade, burnt orange imitation Winterbottom bone handles, brass liners, NS bolsters, Queen Steel #3 etch, Q STEEL tang stamp, 3-5/16", $70-$80.

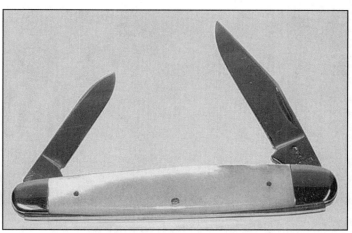

#4, Queen, sleeveboard pen, 2 blade, pearl handles, brass liners, NS bolsters, no etch, Q STAINLESS tang stamp, 3-5/16", $100-$125.

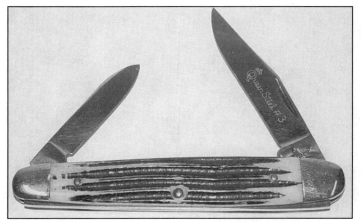

#3, Queen, sleeveboard pen, 2 blade, Winterbottom bone handles, brass liners, NS bolsters, Queen Steel #3 etch, Q STEEL tang stamp, 3-5/16", $40-$60.

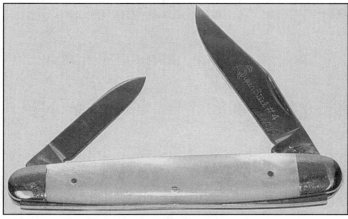

#4, Queen, sleeveboard pen, 2 blade, pearl handles, brass liners, NS bolsters, Queen Steel #4 etch, Q STEEL tang stamp, 3-5/16", $50-$60.

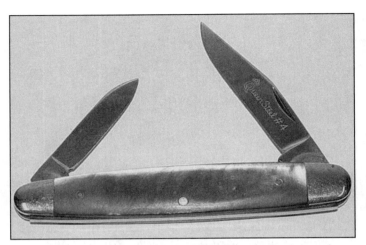

#4, Queen, sleeveboard pen, 2 blade, smoked pearl handles, brass liners, NS bolsters, 3-5/16", Queen Steel #4 etch, no tang stamp, $200-$225.

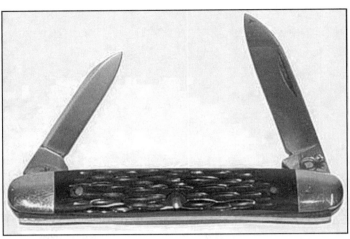

#5, Queen, senator pen, 2 blade, rough black imitation bone handles, brass liners, NS bolsters, no etch, big Q tang stamp, 2-1/2", $30-$40.

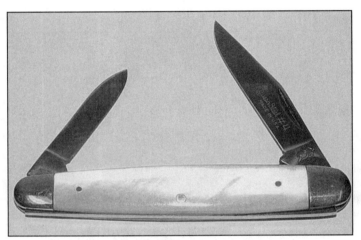

#4, Queen, sleeveboard pen, 2 blade, pearl handles, brass liners, NS bolsters, Queen Steel #4 Made in the U.S.A. etch, Q 22-72 tang stamp, 3-5/16", $40-$50.

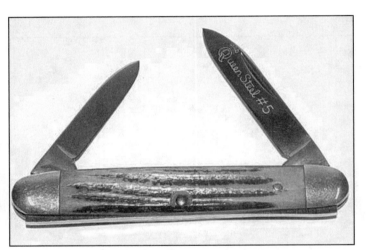

#5, Queen, senator pen, 2 blade, Winterbottom bone handles, brass liners, NS bolsters, Queen Steel #5 etch, no tang stamp, 2-1/2", $30-$40.

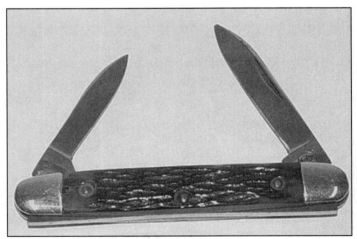

#5, Queen, senator pen, 2 blade, Rogers bone handles, brass liners, NS bolsters, 2-1/2", no etch, big Q tang stamp, $30-$40.

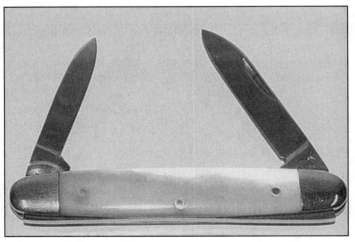

#6, Queen, senator pen, 2 blade, pearl handles, brass liners, NS bolsters, no etch, big Q tang stamp, 2-1/2", $40-$50.

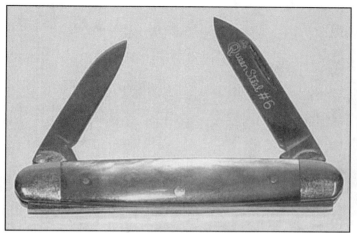

#6P, Queen, senator pen, 2 blade, smoked pearl handles, brass liners, NS bolsters, Queen Steel #6 etch, no tang stamp, 2-1/2", $150-$175.

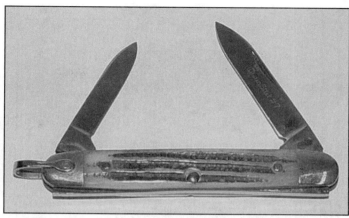

#7, Queen, senator pen, 2 blade, Winterbottom bone handles, brass liners, NS bolsters, bail, Queen Steel #7 etch, big Q tang stamp, 2-1/2", $40-$50.

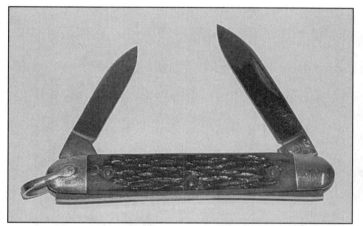

#7, Queen, senator pen, 2 carbon steel blades, Rogers bone handles, brass liners, NS bolsters, bail, no etch, big Q tang stamp, 2-1/2", $40-$50.

#8, Queen, senator pen, 2 blade, pearl handles, brass liners, NS bolsters, bail, no etch, big Q tang stamp, 2-1/2", $40-$50.

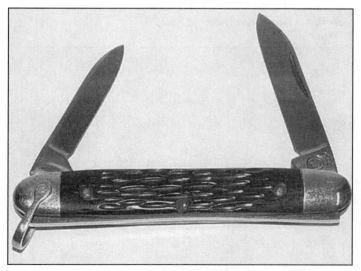

#7, Queen, senator pen, 2 blade, rough black imitation bone handles, brass liners, NS bolsters, bail, no etch, big Q tang stamp, 2-1/2", $40-$50.

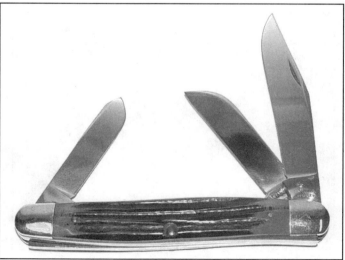

#9, Queen, stockman, 3 blade, Winterbottom bone handles, brass liners, NS bolsters, no etch, QUEEN STAINLESS tang stamp, all tangs stamped STAINLESS, 4", $135-$150.

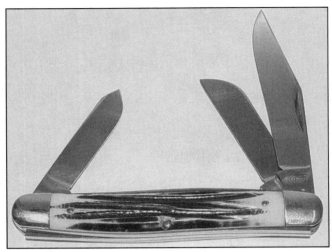

#9, Queen, stockman, 3 blade, Winterbottom bone handles, brass liners, NS bolsters, no etch, QUEEN STEEL tang stamp, 4", $100-$120.

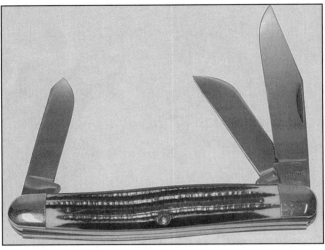

#9, Queen, stockman, 3 blade, burnt orange imitation Winterbottom bone handles, brass liners, NS bolsters, Queen Steel #9 etch, Q STEEL tang stamp, 4", $100-$120.

#9, Queen, stockman, 3 blade, Winterbottom bone handles, brass liners, NS bolsters, no etch, Q STEEL tang stamp, 4", $85-$100.

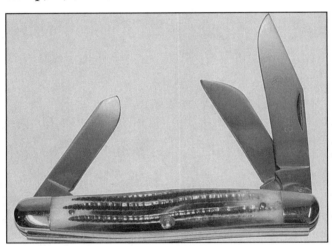

#9, Queen, stockman, 3 blade, Winterbottom bone handles, brass liners, NS bolsters, Queen Steel #9 etch, no tang stamp, 4", $75-$90.

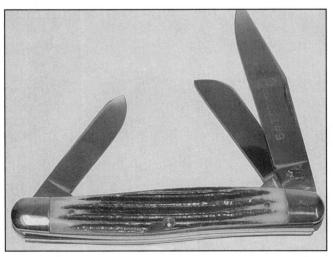

#9, Queen, stockman, 3 blade, Winterbottom bone handles, brass liners, NS bolsters, Queen Steel #9 etch, Q STEEL tang stamp, 4", $85-$100.

#9A, Queen, stockman, 3 blade, amber handles, brass liners, NS bolsters, no etch, QUEEN STEEL tang stamp, 4", $70-$80.

Queen / Schatt & Morgan Cutlery 351

#9A, Queen, stockman, 3 blade, amber handles, brass liners, NS bolsters, Queen Steel #9A etch, Q STEEL tang stamp, 4", $70-$80.

#10, Queen, heavy duty jack, 2 blade, stag handles, brass liners, NS bolsters, Stag Series 6110 Made in U.S.A. etch, big Q tang stamp, 4-1/8", $100-$120.

#309, Queen, stockman, 3 blade, black Micarta handles, brass liners, NS bolsters, Queen Steel #309 etch, Q 22-72 tang stamp, 4", $35-$50.

#10, Queen, heavy duty jack, 2 carbon steel blades, Rogers bone handles, brass liners, NS bolsters, no etch, crown over Queen tang stamp, 4-1/8", $110-$130.

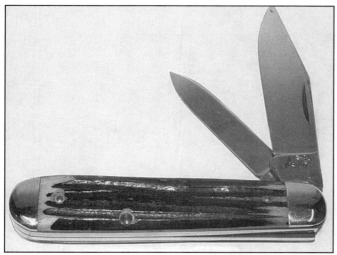

#10, Queen, heavy duty jack, 2 blade, Winterbottom bone handles, brass liners, NS bolsters, no etch, big Q tang stamp, 3-11/16", $100-$120.

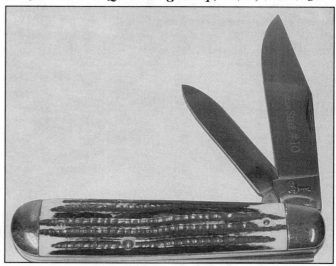

#10, Queen, heavy duty jack, 2 blade, Winterbottom bone handles, brass liners, NS bolsters, Queen Steel #10 etch, Q STEEL tang stamp, 3-11/16", $80-$95.

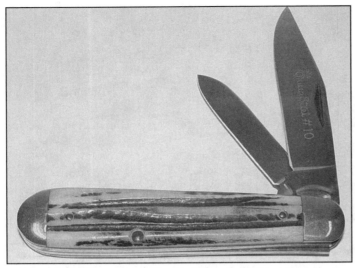

#10, Queen, heavy duty jack, 2 blade, Winterbottom bone handles, brass liners, NS bolsters, Queen Steel #10 etch, no tang stamp, 3-11/16", $80-$95.

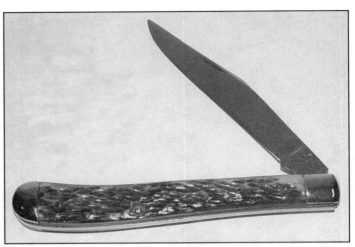

#11, Queen, utility, 1 carbon steel blade, Rogers bone handles, brass liners, NS bolsters, no etch, crown over Queen tang stamp, 4-1/8", $110-$125.

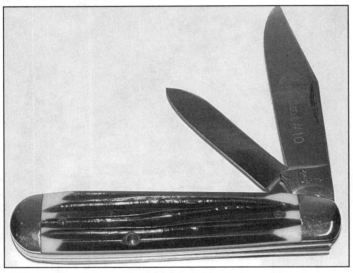

#10, Queen, heavy duty jack, 2 blade, burnt orange imitation Winterbottom bone handles, brass liners, NS bolsters, Q Steel #10 etch, no tang stamp, 3-11/16", $90-$110.

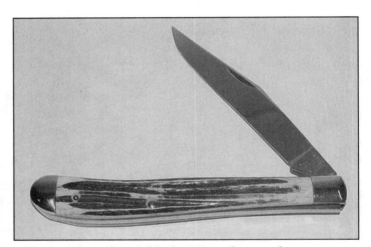

#11, Queen, utility, 1 blade, Winterbottom bone handles, brass liners, NS bolsters, no etch, QUEEN CUT. CO. STAINLESS tang stamp, 4-1/8", $125-$150.

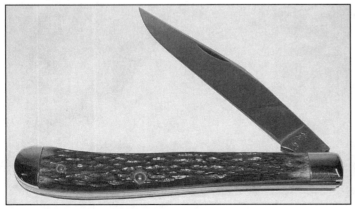

#11, Queen, utility, 1 blade, Rogers bone handles, brass liners, NS bolsters, no etch, big Q tang stamp, 4-1/8", $110-$125.

#11, Queen, utility, 1 blade, Winterbottom bone handles, brass liners, NS bolsters, no etch, Q on side over STAINLESS tang stamp, 4-1/8", $120-$135.

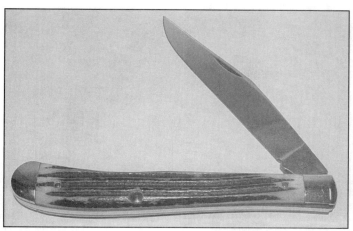

*#11, Queen, utility, 1 blade, Winterbottom bone handles, brass liners, NS bolsters, no etch, QUEEN STAINLESS tang stamp, 4-1/8", $120-$135.*

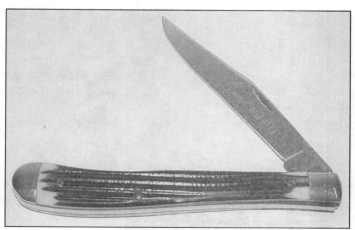

*#11, Queen, utility, 1 blade, burnt orange imitation Winterbottom bone handles, brass liners, NS bolsters, Queen Steel #11 etch, Q STEEL tang stamp, 4-1/8", $80-$100.*

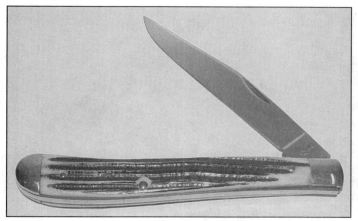

*#11, Queen, utility, 1 blade, Winterbottom bone handles, brass liners, NS bolsters, no etch, QUEEN STEEL tang stamp, 4-1/8", $80-$100.*

*#11, Queen, utility, 1 blade, imitation Winterbottom bone handles, brass liners, NS bolsters, Irish Spring etch, Queen tang stamp, 4-1/8", $50-$60 w/box.*

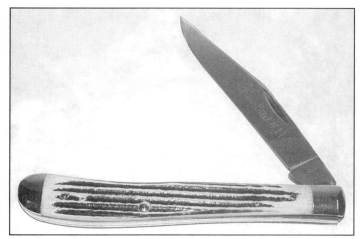

*#11, Queen, utility, 1 blade, Winterbottom bone handles, brass liners, NS bolsters, Queen Steel #11 etch, Q STEEL tang stamp, 4-1/8", $70-$90.*

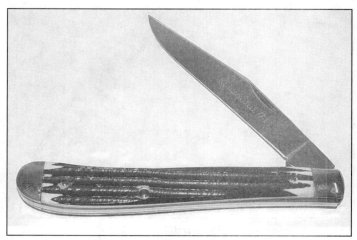

*#11, Queen, utility, 1 blade, Winterbottom bone handles, brass liners, NS bolsters, Queen Steel #11 etch, no tang stamp, 4-1/8", $70-$90.*

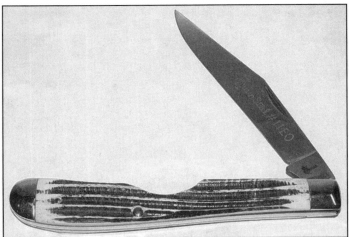

*#11EO, Queen, easy open utility, 1 blade, Winterbottom bone handles, brass liners, NS bolsters, Queen Steel #11EO etch, Q STEEL tang stamp, 4-1/8", $50-$60.*

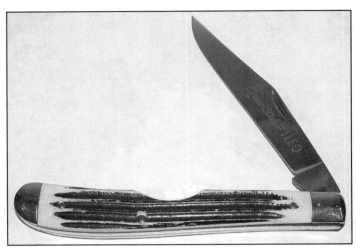

*#11EO, Queen, easy open utility, 1 blade, Winterbottom bone handles, brass liners, NS bolsters, Queen Steel #11EO etch, no tang stamp, 4-1/8", $50-$60.*

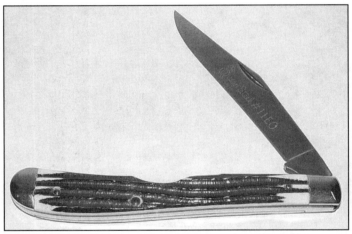

*#11EO, Queen, easy open utility, 1 blade w/glazed finish, Winterbottom bone handles, brass liners, NS bolsters, Queen Steel #11EO etch, Q STEEL tang stamp, 4-1/8", $130-$150.*

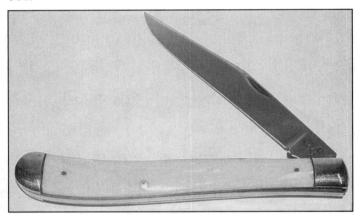

*#12, Queen, utility, 1 blade, simulated pearl handles, brass liners, NS bolsters, no etch, Q STAINLESS tang stamp, 4-1/8", $80-$100.*

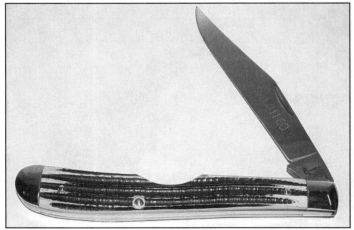

*#11EO, Queen, easy open utility, 1 blade, Winterbottom bone handles, brass liners, NS bolsters, Queen Steel #11EO etch, QUEEN tang stamp, rare, 4-1/8", $70-$90.*

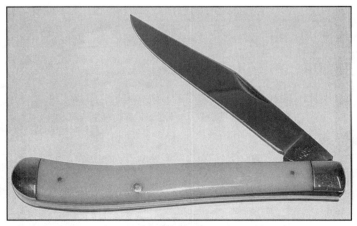

*#13, Queen, utility, 1 blade, amber handles, brass liners, NS bolsters, no etch, QUEEN STEEL tang stamp, 4-1/8", $40-$60.*

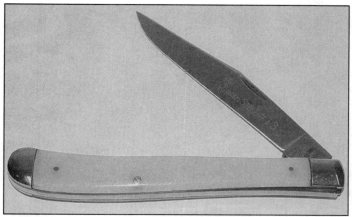

*#13, Queen, utility, 1 blade, amber handles, brass liners, NS bolsters, Queen Steel #13 etch, Q STEEL tang stamp, 4-1/8", $35-$50.*

*#14, Queen, peanut, 2 blade, Rogers bone handles, brass liners, NS bolsters, no etch, Q STAINLESS tang stamp, rare, 2-3/4", $90-$110.*

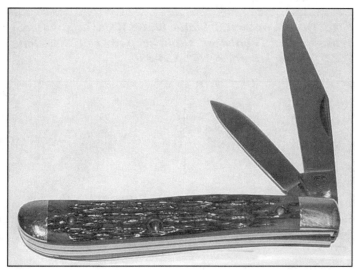

*#14, Queen, peanut, 2 blade, Rogers bone handles, brass liners, NS bolsters, no etch, QUEEN STEEL tang stamp, rare, 2-3/4", $90-$110.*

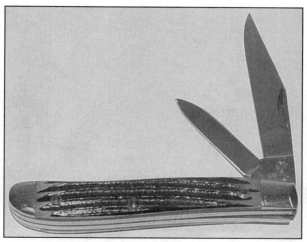

*#14, Queen, peanut, 2 blade, Winterbottom bone handles, brass liners, NS bolsters, no etch, QUEEN STEEL tang stamp, 2-3/4", $70-$85.*

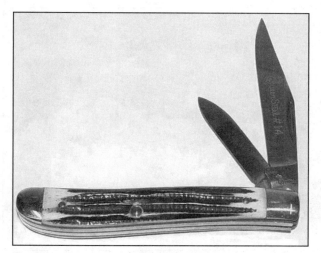

*Peanut, Queen #14, 2 blade, Winterbottom bone handles, brass liners, NS bolsters, Queen Steel #14 etch, Q STEEL tang stamp, 2-3/4", $40-$60.*

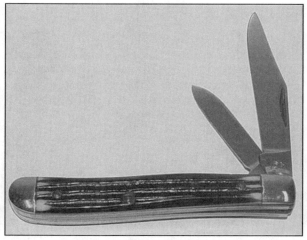

*#14, Queen, peanut, 2 blade, burnt orange imitation Winterbottom bone handles, brass liners, NS bolsters, Queen Steel #14 etch, Q STEEL tang stamp, 2-3/4", $50-$75.*

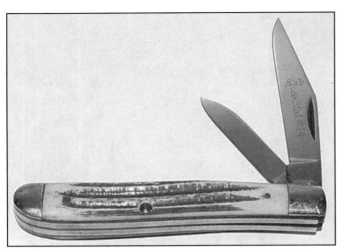

#14, Queen, peanut, 2 blade, Winterbottom bone handles, brass liners, NS bolsters, Queen Steel #14 etch, no tang stamp, 2-3/4", $40-$60.

#14P, Queen, peanut, 2 blade, pearl handles, brass liners, NS bolsters, Queen Steel #14P etch, intermediate Q tang stamp, 2-3/4", $80-$100.

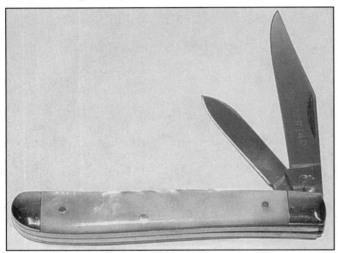

#14P, Queen, peanut, 2 blade, pearl handles, brass liners, NS bolsters, Queen Steel #14P etch, Q STEEL tang stamp, 2-3/4", $80-$100.

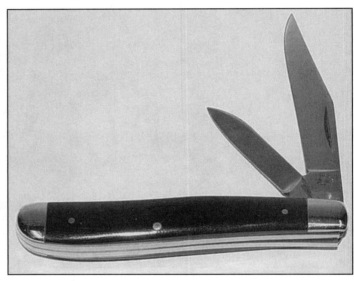

#314, Queen, peanut, 2 blade, black Micarta handles, brass liners, NS bolsters, Gamekeeper 314 U.S.A. etch, Q 22-72 tang stamp, 2-3/4", $35-$40.

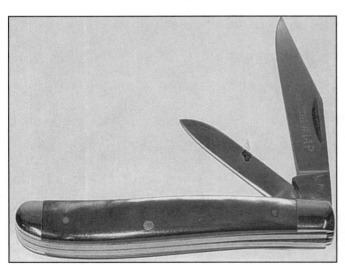

#14P, Queen, peanut, 2 blade, smoked pearl handles, brass liners, NS bolsters, Queen Steel #14P etch, no tang stamp, 2-3/4", $275-$300.

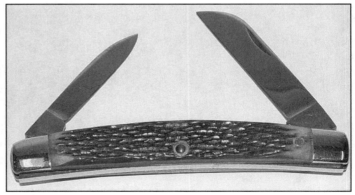

#15, Queen, half congress, 2 carbon steel blades, Rogers bone handles, brass liners, NS bolsters, no etch, big Q tang stamp, 3-1/2", $80-$100.

#15, Queen, half congress, 2 blade, Rogers bone handles, brass liners, NS bolsters, no etch, Q STAINLESS tang stamp, 3-1/2", $90-$100.

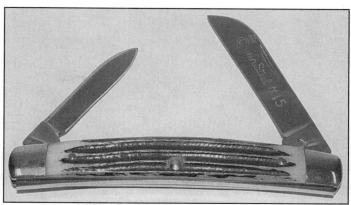

#15, Queen, half congress, 2 blade, Winterbottom bone handles, brass liners, NS bolsters, Queen Steel #15 etch, Q STEEL tang stamp, 3-1/2", $70-$90.

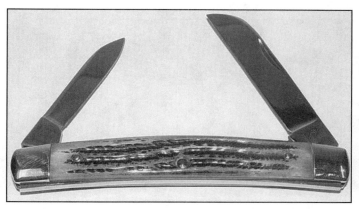

#15, Queen, half congress, 2 blade, Winterbottom bone handles, brass liners, NS bolsters, no etch, Q STAINLESS tang stamp, 3-1/2", $90-$100.

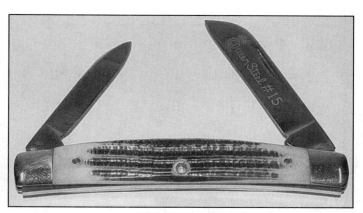

#15, Queen, half congress, 2 blade, Winterbottom bone handles, brass liners, NS bolsters, Queen Steel #15 etch, no tang stamp, 3-1/2", $70-$90.

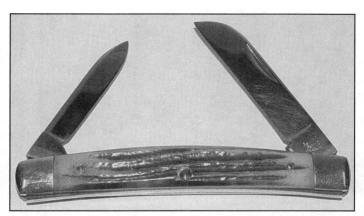

#15, Queen, half congress, 2 blade, Winterbottom bone handles, brass liners, NS bolsters, no etch, QUEEN STEEL tang stamp, 3-1/2", $90-$100.

#16, Queen, stockman, 3 blade, Rogers bone handles, brass liners, NS bolsters, no etch, big Q tang stamp, 3-1/4", $50-$70.

*#16, Queen, stockman, 3 blade, Winterbottom bone handles, brass liners, NS bolsters, no etch, Q STAINLESS tang stamp, 3-1/4", $50-$70.*

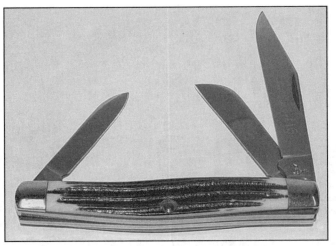

*#16, Queen, stockman, 3 blade, burnt orange imitation Winterbottom bone handles, brass liners, NS bolsters, Queen Steel #16 etch, Q STEEL tang stamp, 3-1/4", $50-$70.*

*#16, Queen, stockman, 3 blade, Winterbottom bone handles, brass liners, NS bolsters, 3-1/4", no etch, QUEEN STEEL tang stamp, $50-$70.*

*#16A, Queen, stockman, 3 blades, amber handles, brass liners, NS bolsters, no etch, QUEEN STEEL tang stamp, 3-1/4", $40-$50.*

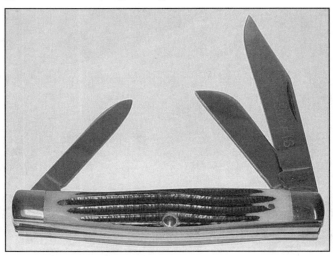

*#16, Queen, stockman, 3 blade, Winterbottom bone handles, brass liners, NS bolsters, Queen Steel #16 etch, Q STEEL tang stamp, 3-1/4", $50-$60.*

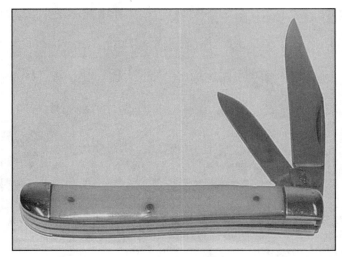

*#17, Queen, peanut, 2 blade, amber handles, brass liners, NS bolsters, no etch, Q STAINLESS tang stamp, 2-3/4", $60-$75.*

#18, Queen, heavy duty jack, 2 carbon steel blades, Rogers bone handles, brass liners, NS bolsters, no etch, big Q tang stamp, 3-11/16", $100-$120.

#18, Queen, heavy duty jack, 2 blade, Winterbottom bone handles, brass liners, NS bolsters, no etch, big Q tang stamp, 3-11/16", $80-$100.

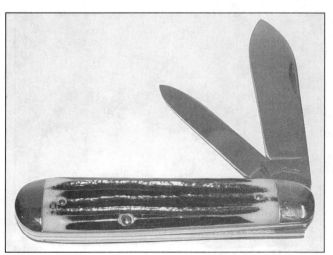

#18, Queen, heavy duty jack, 2 blade, Winterbottom bone handles, brass liners, NS bolsters, Queen Steel #18 etch, Q STEEL tang stamp, 3-11/16", $80-$95.

#18, Queen, heavy duty jack, 2 blade, Winterbottom bone handles, brass liners, NS bolsters, Queen Steel #18 etch, no tang stamp, 3-11/16", $80-$95.

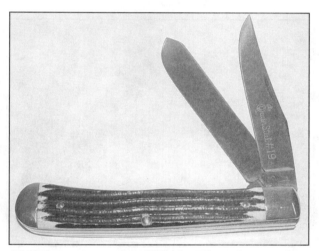

#19, Queen, trapper, 2 blade, Winterbottom bone handles, brass liners, NS bolsters, Queen Steel #19 etch, Q STEEL tang stamp, 4-1/8", $150-$170.

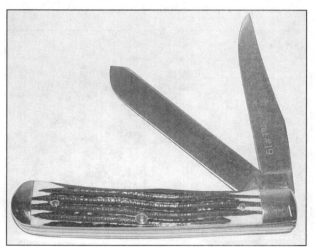

#19, Queen, trapper, 2 blade, Winterbottom bone handles, glazed finish, brass liners, NS bolsters, Queen Steel #19 etch, Q STEEL tang stamp, 4-1/8", $200-$225.

*#19, Queen, trapper, 2 blade, burnt orange imitation Winterbottom bone handles, NS bolsters, brass liners, Queen Steel #19 etch, Q STEEL tang stamp, 4-1/8", $100-$125.*

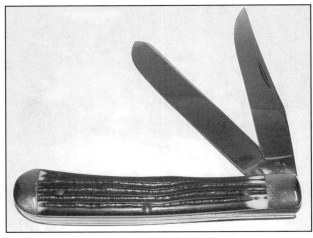

*#19, Queen, trapper, 2 blade, imitation Winterbottom bone handles, brass liners, NS bolsters, Queen Steel #19 etch, Q 22-72 tang stamp, 4-1/8", $50-$75.*

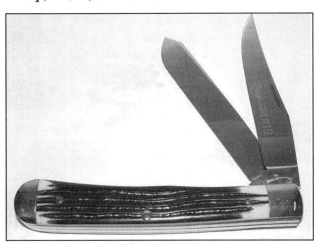

*#19, Queen, trapper, 2 blade, burnt orange imitation Winterbottom bone handles, brass liners, NS bolsters, Queen Steel #19 etch, QUEEN tang stamp, 4-1/8", $100-$125.*

*#19, Queen, trapper, 2 blade, stag handles, brass liners, NS bolsters, Stag Series Stag Trapper 8160 1 of 800 etch, Q81 USA tang stamp, 4-1/8", $80-$100.*

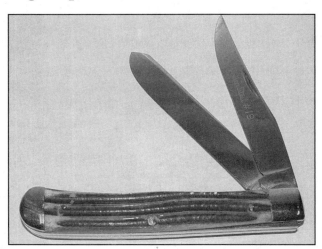

*#19, Queen, trapper, 2 blade, Winterbottom bone handles, brass liners, NS bolsters, Queen Steel #19 etch, no tang stamp, 4-1/8", $140-$150.*

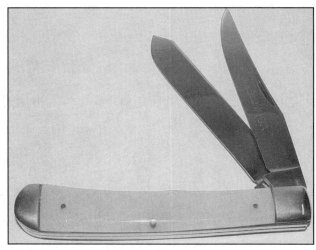

*#19A, Queen, trapper, 2 blade, amber handles, brass liners, NS bolsters, Queen Steel #19A etch, no tang stamp, 4-1/8", $50-$75.*

Queen / Schatt & Morgan Cutlery  361

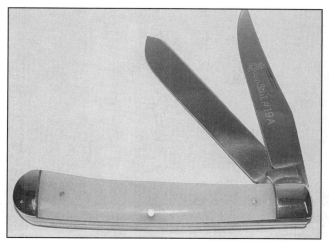

*#19A, Queen, trapper, 2 blade, amber handles, brass liners, NS bolsters, Queen Steel #19A etch, Q STEEL tang stamp, 4-1/8", $50-$75.*

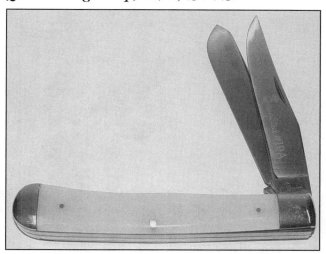

*#19A, Queen, trapper, 2 blade, amber handles, glazed finish, brass liners, NS bolsters, Queen Steel #19A etch, Q STEEL tang stamp, 4-1/8", $100-$125.*

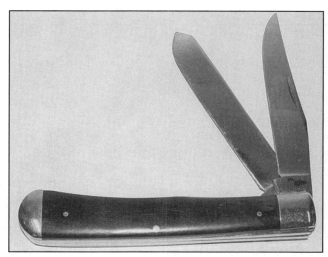

*#19B, Queen, trapper, 2 blade, slick black handles, brass liners, NS bolsters, 4-1/8", Queen Steel #19B Made in U.S.A. etch, Queen w/Dot tang stamp, $80-$90.*

*#19B, Queen, trapper, 2 blade, slick black handles, brass liners, NS bolsters, Queen Steel #19B Made in U.S.A. etch, Q76 tang stamp, 4-1/8", $50-$75.*

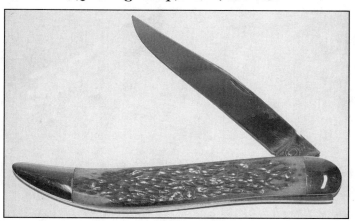

*#20, Queen, Texas toothpick, 1 blade, Rogers bone handles, brass liners, NS bolsters, no etch, big Q tang stamp, 5", $150-$170.*

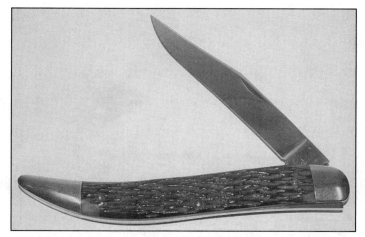

*#20, Queen, Texas toothpick, 1 blade, Rogers bone handles, brass liners, NS bolsters, no etch, big Q tang stamp on front, STAINLESS tang stamp on back, 5", $160-$180.*

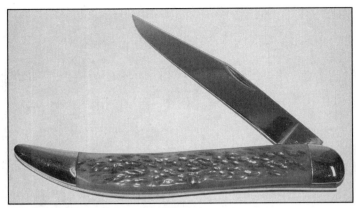

*#20, Queen, Texas toothpick, 1 blade, Rogers bone handles, brass liners, NS bolsters, no etch, Q STAINLESS tang stamp, 5", $160-$180.*

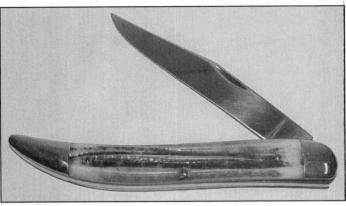

*#20, Queen, Texas toothpick, 1 blade, Winterbottom bone handles, brass liners, NS bolsters, no etch, QUEEN STEEL tang stamp, 5", $120-$150.*

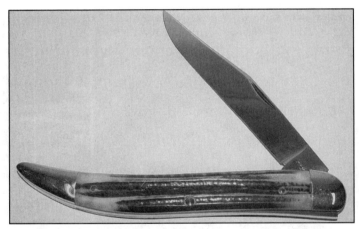

*#20, Queen, Texas toothpick, 1 blade, Winterbottom bone handles, brass liners, NS bolsters, no etch, Q STAINLESS tang stamp, 5", $120-$150.*

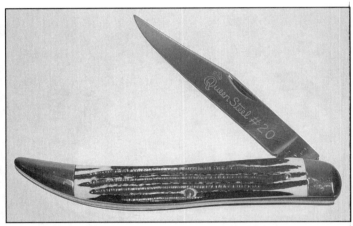

*#20, Queen, Texas toothpick, 1 blade, Winterbottom bone handles, brass liners, NS bolsters, Queen Steel #20 etch, Q STEEL tang stamp, 5", $120-$150.*

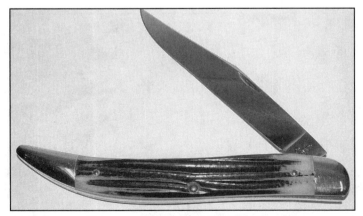

*#20, Queen, Texas toothpick, 1 blade, Winterbottom bone handles, brass liners, NS bolsters, no etch, Q STEEL tang stamp, 5", $120-$150.*

*#20, Queen, Texas toothpick, 1 blade, burnt orange imitation Winterbottom handles, brass liners, NS bolsters, Queen Steel #20 etch, Q STEEL tang stamp, 5", $140-$170.*

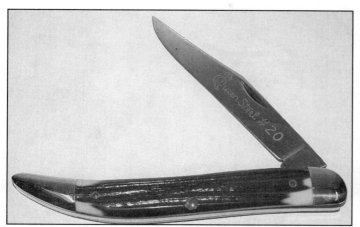

#20, Queen, Texas toothpick, 1 blade, imitation Winterbottom bone handles, brass liners, NS bolsters, Queen Steel #20 etch, no tang stamp, 5", $40-$60.

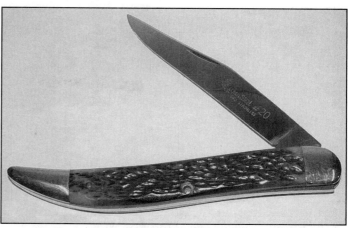

#20, Queen, Texas toothpick, 1 blade, Rogers bone handles, brass liners, NS bolsters, Queen Steel #20 440 Stainless etch, Q78 tang stamp, 5", $80-$100.

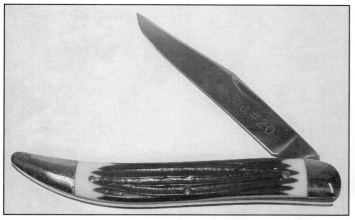

#20, Queen, Texas toothpick, imitation Winterbottom bone handles, brass liners, NS bolsters, 1 blade, Queen Steel #20 etch, Q 22-72 tang stamp, 5", $40-$60.

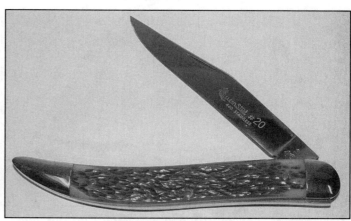

#20, Queen, Texas toothpick, 1 blade, Rogers bone handles, brass liners, NS bolsters, Queen Steel #20 440 Stainless etch, Q79 tang stamp, 5", $90-$110.

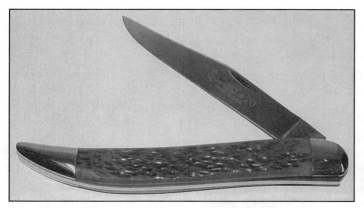

#20, Queen, Texas toothpick, 1 blade, Rogers bone handles, brass liners, NS bolsters, Queen Steel #20 MADE IN U.S.A. etch, Q76 tang stamp, 5", $70-$90.

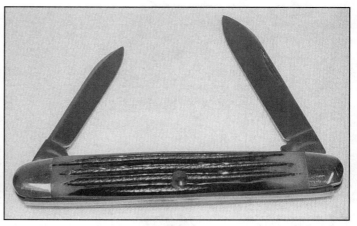

#21, Queen, sleeveboard, 2 blade, Winterbottom bone handles, brass liners, NS bolsters, no etch, QUEEN STEEL tang stamp, 3-5/16", $40-$60.

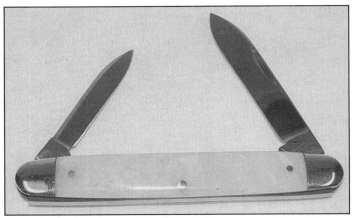

*#21, Queen, sleeveboard, 2 blade, imitation pearl handles, brass liners, NS bolsters, no etch, QUEEN STEEL tang stamp, 3-5/16", $40-$60.*

*#22, Queen, Barlow, 2 blade, sawn bone handles, brass liners, no etch, QUEEN STEEL tang stamp, 3-1/2", $80-$100.*

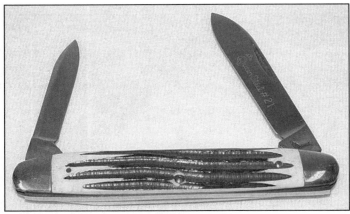

*#21, Queen, sleeveboard, 2 blade, Winterbottom bone handles, brass liners, NS bolsters, Queen Steel #21 etch, Q STEEL tang stamp, 3-5/16", $40-$60.*

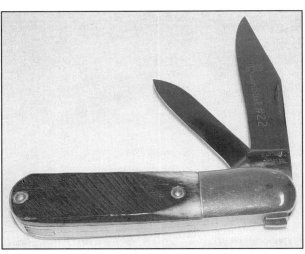

*#22, Queen, Barlow, 2 blade, sawn bone handles, aluminum frame, Queen Steel #22 etch, PAT. NO. 2728139 tang stamp, 3-1/2", $60-$80.*

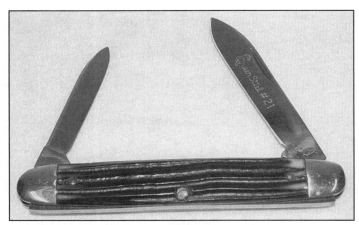

*#21, Queen, sleeveboard, 2 blade, burnt orange imitation Winterbottom bone handles, brass liners, NS bolsters, Queen Steel #21 etch, Q STEEL tang stamp, 3-5/16", $60-$75.*

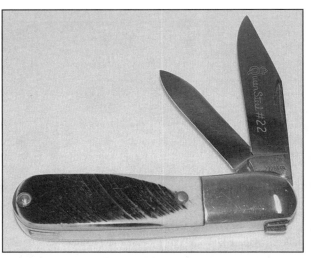

*#22, Queen, Barlow, 2 blade, burnt orange imitation Winterbottom bone handles, aluminum frame, Queen Steel #22 etch, PAT. NO. 2728139 tang stamp, 3-1/2", $60-$80.*

#22, Queen, Barlow, 2 blade, sawn bone handles, brass liners, Drake Well w/picture etch, Q 22-72 tang stamp, 3-1/2", $60-$80.

#23, Queen, Barlow, 2 blade, sawn bone handles, aluminum frame, Queen Steel #23 etch, PAT. NO. 2728139 tang stamp, 3-1/2", $60–$80.

#22, Queen, Barlow, 2 blade, wooden handles, brass liners, Rawhide Series 8075 440 stainless etch, Q80 USA tang stamp, 3-1/2", $60-$80.

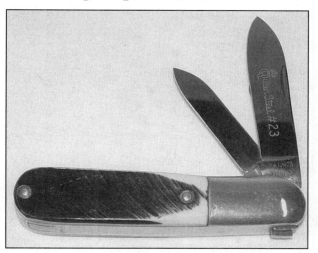

#23, Queen, Barlow, 2 blade, burnt orange imitation Winterbottom bone handles, aluminum frame, Queen Steel #23 etch, PAT. NO 2728139 tang stamp, 3-1/2", $60-$80.

#23, Queen, Barlow, 2 blade, sawn bone handles, steel liners, no etch, big Q tang stamp, 3-1/2", $60-$80.

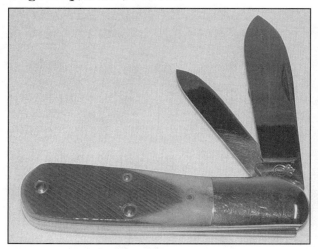

#23, Queen, Barlow, 2 blade, sawn bone handles, no etch, intermediate Q tang stamp, 3-1/2", $60-$80.

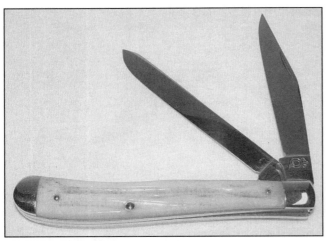

#24, Queen, slim trapper, 2 blade, Winterbottom bone handles, brass liners, NS bolsters, no etch, big Q tang stamp, 4", $100-$120.

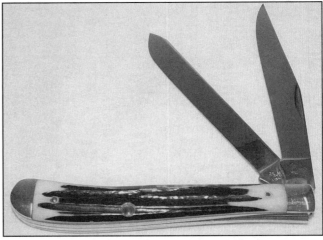

#24, Queen, slim trapper, 2 blade, Winterbottom bone handles, brass liners, NS bolsters, no etch, QUEEN STEEL tang stamp, 4", $100-$130.

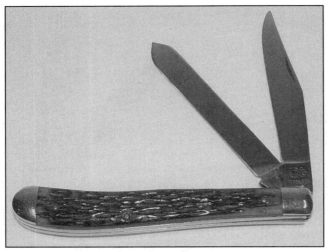

#24, Queen, slim trapper, 2 blade, Rogers bone handles, brass liners, NS bolsters, no etch, Q on side over STAINLESS tang stamp, 4", $120-$150.

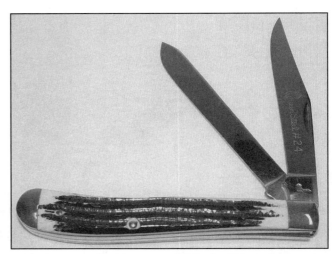

#24, Queen, slim trapper, 2 blade, Winterbottom bone handles, brass liners, NS bolsters, Queen Steel #24 etch, Q STEEL tang stamp, 4", $90-$110.

#24, Queen, slim trapper, 2 blade, Winterbottom bone handles, brass liners, NS bolsters, no etch, Q on side over STAINLESS tang stamp, 4", $120-$150.

#24, Queen, slim trapper, 2 blade, burnt orange imitation Winterbottom handles, brass liners, NS bolsters, Queen Steel #24 etch, Q STEEL tang stamp, 4", $100-$125.

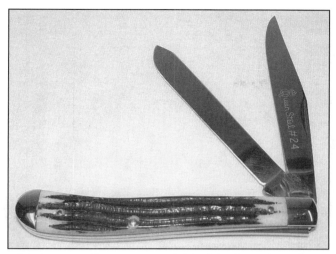

*#24, Queen, slim trapper, 2 blade, Winterbottom bone handles, brass liners, NS bolsters, Queen Steel #24 etch, no tang stamp, 4", $70-$90.*

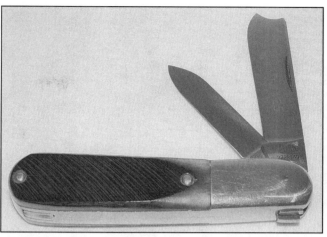

*#25, Queen, Barlow, 2 blade, sawn bone handles, aluminum frame, Queen Steel #25 etch, PAT. NO. 2728139 tang stamp, 3-1/2", $60-$80.*

*#24B, Queen, slim trapper, 2 blade, imitation slick black handles, brass liners, NS bolsters, Queen Steel #24B Made in USA etch, Q76 tang stamp, 4", $60-$80.*

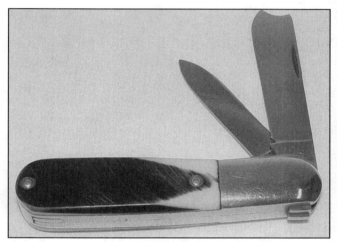

*#25, Queen, Barlow, 2 blade, burnt orange imitation sawn bone handles, aluminum frame, Queen Steel #25 etch, PAT. NO. 2728139 tang stamp, 3-1/2", $60-$80.*

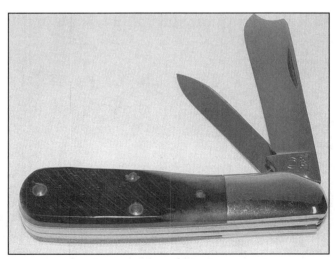

*#25, Queen, slim trapper, 2 blade, sawn bone handles, brass liners, no etch, big Q tang stamp, 3-1/2", $100-$120.*

*#25, Queen, Barlow, 2 blade, sawn bone handles, aluminum frame, Queen Steel #25 etch, Q STEEL tang stamp, 3-1/2", $60-$80.*

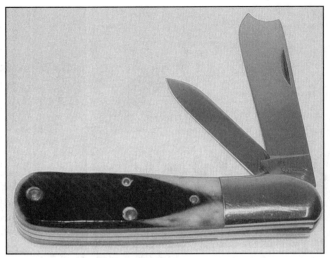

#25, Queen, Barlow, 2 blade, sawn bone handles, brass liners, no etch, Q STEEL tang stamp, 3-1/2", $60-$80.

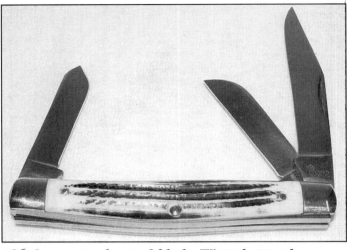

#26, Queen, stockman, 3 blade, Winterbottom bone handles, brass liners, NS bolsters, no etch, QUEEN STEEL tang stamp, 3-1/4", $90-$110.

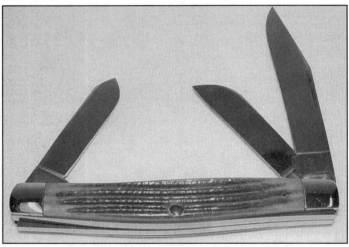

#26, Queen, stockman, 3 blade, Winterbottom bone handles, brass liners, NS bolsters, no etch, Q STAINLESS tang stamp, 3-1/4", $90-$110.

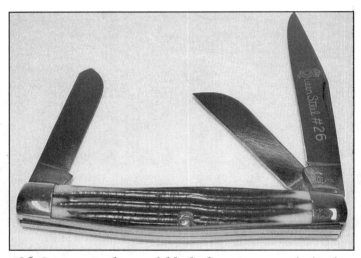

#26, Queen, stockman, 3 blade, burnt orange imitation Winterbottom bone handles, brass liners, NS bolsters, Queen Steel #26 etch, Q STEEL tang stamp, 3-1/4", $50-$75.

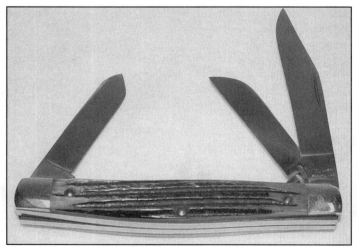

#26, Queen, stockman, 3 blade, Winterbottom bone handles, brass liners, NS bolsters, no etch, QUEEN STAINLESS tang stamp, 3-1/4", $90-$110.

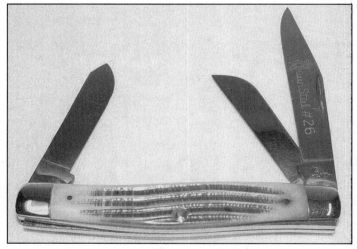

#26, Queen, stockman, 3 blade, Winterbottom bone handles, brass liners, NS bolsters, Queen Steel #26 etch, Q STEEL tang stamp, 3-1/4", $40-$60.

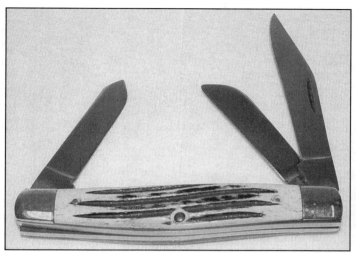

#26, Queen, stockman, 3 blade, Winterbottom bone handles, brass liners, NS bolsters, Queen Steel #26 Made in U.S.A. etch, no tang stamp, 3-1/4", $40-$60.

#27, Queen, Barlow, 2 blade, sawn bone handles, aluminum frame, Queen Steel #27 etch, Q STEEL tang stamp, 3-1/2", $60-$80.

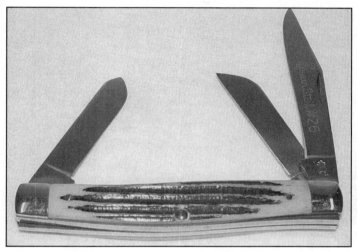

#26, Queen, Stockman, 3 blade, Winterbottom bone handles, brass liners, NS bolsters, Queen Steel #26 etch, intermediate Q tang stamp, 3-1/4", $40-$60.

#28, Queen, large jack, 2 carbon steel blades, Winterbottom bone handles, brass liners, NS bolsters, no etch, big Q tang stamp, 4-1/2", $140-$160.

#26A, Queen, Stockman, 3 blade, amber handles, brass liners, NS bolsters, no etch, QUEEN STEEL tang stamp, 3-1/4", $40-$50.

#28, Queen, large jack, 2 blade, Winterbottom bone handles, brass liners, NS bolsters, no etch, Q STAINLESS tang stamp, 4-1/2", $150-$175.

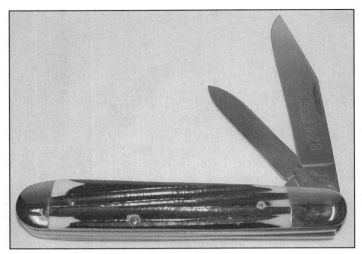

*#28, Queen, large jack, 2 blade, Winterbottom bone handles, brass liners, NS bolsters, Queen Steel #28 etch, Q STEEL tang stamp, 4-1/2", $100-$130.*

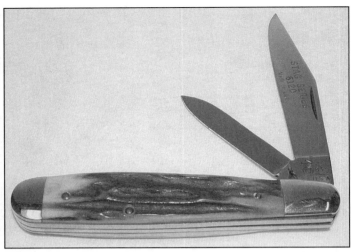

*#28, Queen, large jack, 2 blade, stag handles, brass liners, NS bolsters, Stag Series 6120 Made in USA etch, Q83 USA tang stamp, 4-1/2", $80-$100.*

*#28, Queen, large jack, 2 blade, burnt orange imitation Winterbottom bone handles, brass liners, NS bolsters, Queen Steel #28 etch, Q STEEL tang stamp, 4-1/2", $120-$150.*

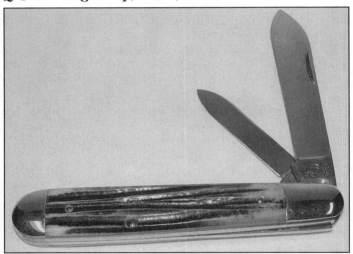

*#29, Queen, large jack, 2 carbon steel blades, Winterbottom bone handles, brass liners, NS bolsters, no etch, big Q tang stamp, 4-1/2", $140-$160.*

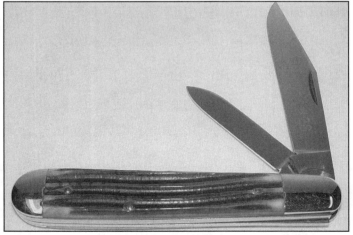

*#28, Queen, large jack, 2 blade, brown Winterbottom bone handles w/deep grooves, brass liners, NS bolsters, Queen Steel #28 etch, no tang stamp, 4-1/2", $90-$110.*

*#29, Queen, large jack, 2 blade, Winterbottom bone handles, brass liners, NS bolsters, no etch, Q STAINLESS tang stamp, 4-1/2", $150-$175.*

#29, Queen, large jack, 2 blade, Winterbottom bone handles, brass liners, NS bolsters, Queen Steel #29 etch, Q STEEL tang stamp, 4-1/2", $100-$130.

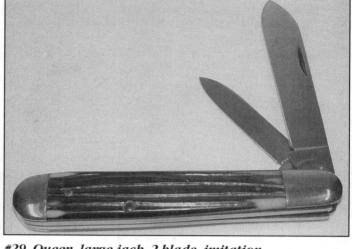

#29, Queen, large jack, 2 blade, imitation Winterbottom bone handles, brass liners, NS bolsters, 4-1/2", Queen Steel #29 etch, no tang stamp, $50-$70.

#29, Queen, large jack, 2 blade, burnt orange imitation Winterbottom bone handles, brass liners, NS bolsters, Queen Steel #29 etch, Q STEEL tang stamp, 4-1/2", $120-$150.

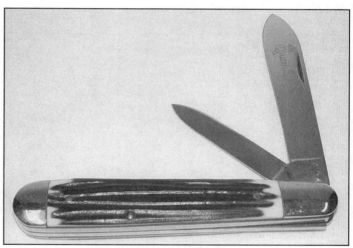

#29, Queen, large jack, 2 blade, imitation Winterbottom bone handles, brass liners, NS bolsters, Queen Steel #29 etch, Q 22-72 tang stamp, 4-1/2", $50-$70.

#29, Queen, large jack, 2 blade, Winterbottom bone handles, brass liners, NS bolsters, Queen Steel #29 etch, no tang stamp, 4-1/2", $90-$110.

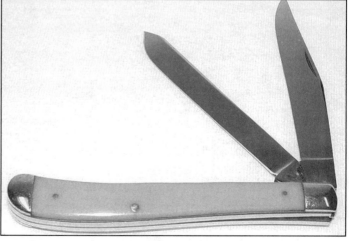

#30, Queen, slim trapper, 2 blade, amber handles, brass liners, NS bolsters, no etch, QUEEN STEEL tang stamp, 4", $50-$70.

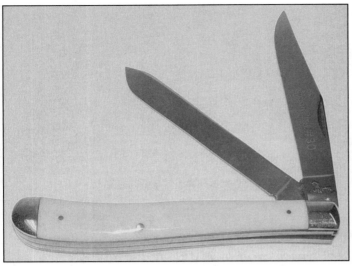

#30, Queen, slim trapper, 2 blade, amber handles, brass liners, NS bolsters, Queen Steel #30 etch, Q STEEL tang stamp, 4", $40-$55.

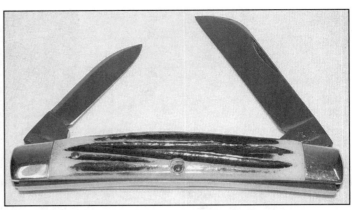

#31, Queen, large congress, 2 blade, Winterbottom bone handles, brass liners, NS bolsters, no etch, QUEEN STEEL tang stamp, 4", $100-$125.

#31, Queen, large congress, 2 carbon steel blades, Winterbottom bone handles, brass liners, NS bolsters, no etch, big Q tang stamp, 4", $70-$90.

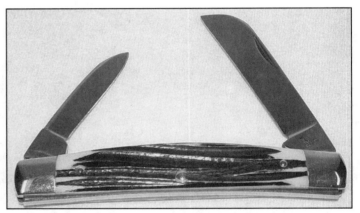

#31, Queen, large congress, 2 blade, Winterbottom bone handles, brass liners, NS bolsters, no etch, Q STEEL tang stamp, 4", $70-$90.

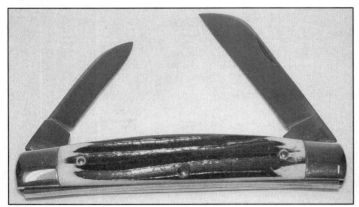

#31, Queen, large congress, 2 blade, Winterbottom bone handles, brass liners, NS bolsters, no etch, QUEEN STAINLESS tang stamp, 4", $100-$125.

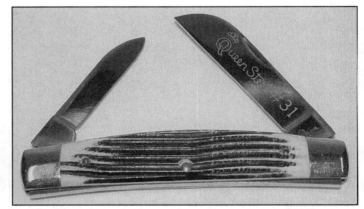

#31, Queen, large congress, 2 blade, Winterbottom bone handles, fine jigged bone, six grooves, brass liners, NS bolsters, Queen Steel #31 etch, Q STEEL tang stamp, 4", $70-$90.

# Queen / Schatt & Morgan Cutlery 373

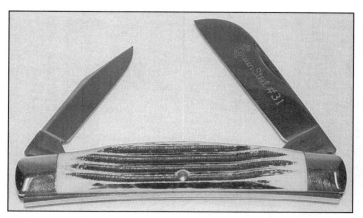

#3 brownish orange color, brass liners, NS bolsters, Queen Steel #31 etch, no tang stamp, 4", $70-$90.

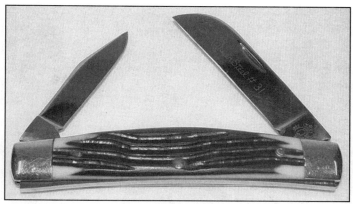

#31, Queen, large congress, 2 blade, imitation Winterbottom bone handles, brass liners, NS bolsters, Queen Steel #31 etch, Q 22-72 tang stamp, 4", $40-$60.

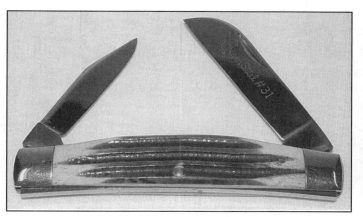

#31, Queen, large congress, 2 blade, Winterbottom bone handles, coarse jigged bone, 3 grooves, brownish orange color, brass liners, NS bolsters, Queen Steel #31 etch, no tang stamp, 4", $70-$90.

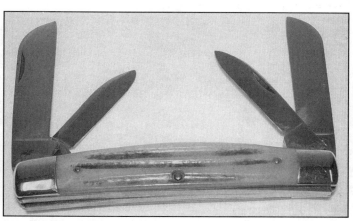

#32, Queen, large congress, 4 carbon steel blades, Winterbottom bone handles, brass liners, NS bolsters, no etch, big Q tang stamp, 4", $125-$150.

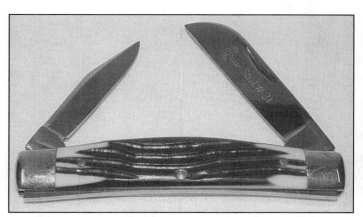

#31, Queen, large congress, 2 blade, imitation Winterbottom bone handles, brass liners, NS bolsters, Queen Steel #31 etch, no tang stamp, 4", $40-$60.

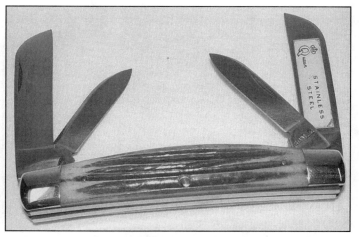

#32, Queen, large congress, 4 blade, Winterbottom bone handles, brass liners, NS bolsters, paper sticker on blade, Queen stainless steel, QUEEN STAINLESS tang stamp on sheepfoot blade, STAINLESS tang stamp on pen blade, 4", $180-$200.

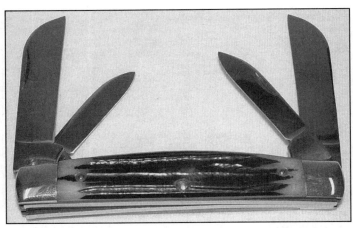

*#32, Queen, large congress, 4 blade, Winterbottom bone handles, brass liners, NS bolsters, no etch, QUEEN STEEL tang stamp, 4", $150-$170.*

*#32, Queen, large congress, 4 blade, Winterbottom bone handles, brass liners, NS bolsters, Queen Steel #32 etch, Q STEEL tang stamp, 4", $125-$150.*

*#32, Queen, large congress, 4 blade, Winterbottom bone handles, brass liners, NS bolsters, no etch, Q STEEL tang stamp, 4", $125-$150.*

*#33, Queen, congress, 4 carbon steel blades, Rogers bone handles, brass liners, NS bolsters, no etch, big Q tang stamp, 3-1/2", $160-$175.*

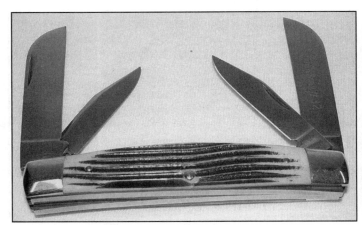

*#32, Queen, large congress, Winterbottom bone handles, fine jigged bone, brass liners, NS bolsters, 4 blade, Queen Steel #32 etch, Q STEEL tang stamp, 4", $125-$150.*

*#33, Queen, congress, 4 blade, Rogers bone handles, brass liners, NS bolsters, no etch, Q STAINLESS tang stamp, 3-1/2", $180-$200.*

Queen / Schatt & Morgan Cutlery 375

#33, Queen, congress, 4 blade, Rogers bone handles, brass liners, NS bolsters, paper sticker "Queen Steel" on sticker, no etch, Q STAINLESS tang stamp, 3-1/2", $180-$200.

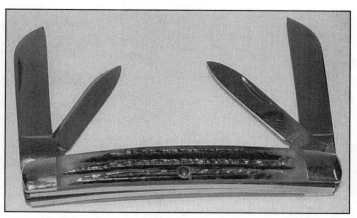

#33, Queen, congress, 4 blade, Winterbottom bone handles, brass liners, NS bolsters, no etch, QUEEN STEEL tang stamp, 3-1/2", $120-$150.

Congress, Queen #33, 4 blade, Rogers bone handles, brass liners, NS bolsters, Queen Steel etch (unusual), QUEEN STEEL tang stamp, 3-1/2", $150-$175.

#33, Queen, congress, 4 blade, Winterbottom bone handles, brass liners, NS bolsters, no etch, Q STEEL tang stamp, 3-1/2", $100-$130.

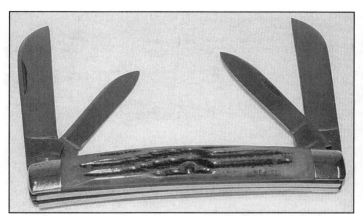

#33, Queen, congress, 4 blade, Winterbottom bone handles, brass liners, NS bolsters, no etch, Q STAINLESS tang stamp, 3-1/2", $180-$200.

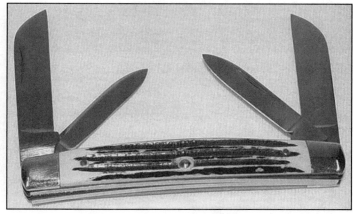

#33, Queen, congress, 4 blade, Winterbottom bone handles, brass liners, NS bolsters, Queen Steel #33 etch, Q STEEL tang stamp, 3-1/2", $100-$130.

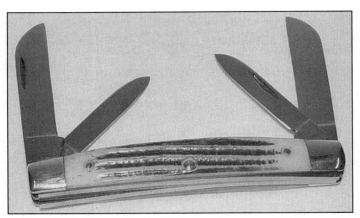

#33, Queen, congress, 4 blade, Winterbottom bone handles, brass liners, NS bolsters, Queen Steel #33 etch, no tang stamp, 3-1/2", $100-$130.

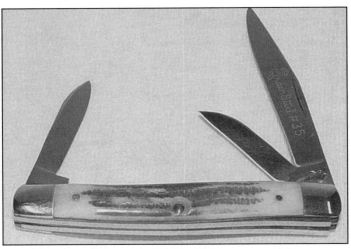

#35, Queen, small serpentine, 3 blade, Winterbottom bone handles, brass liners, NS bolsters, Queen Steel #35 etch, Q STEEL tang stamp, 2-5/8", $40-$50.

#33, Queen, congress, 4 blade, Rogers bone handles, brass liners, NS bolsters, Queen Steel #33 etch, no tang stamp, 3-1/2", $100-$130.

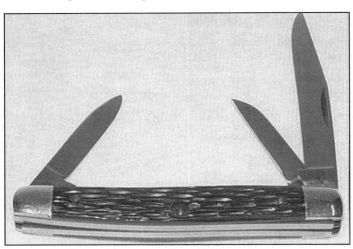

#35, Queen, small serpentine, 3 blade, rough black imitation bone handles, brass liners, NS bolsters, no etch, Q STAINLESS tang stamp, 2-5/8", $40-$60.

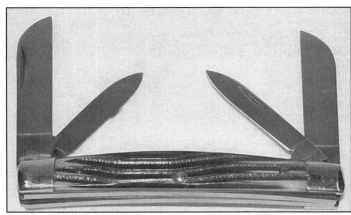

#33, Queen, congress, 4 blade, imitation Winterbottom bone handles, brass liners, NS bolsters, Queen Steel #33 etch, no tang stamp, 3-1/2", $60-$80.

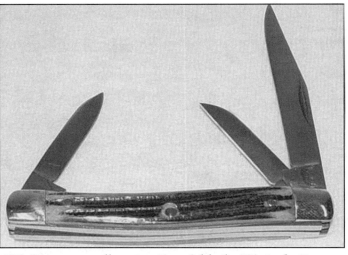

#35, Queen, small serpentine, 3 blade, Winterbottom bone handles, brass liners, NS bolsters, 2-5/8", Queen Steel #35 etch, Q STEEL tang stamp, $40-$50.

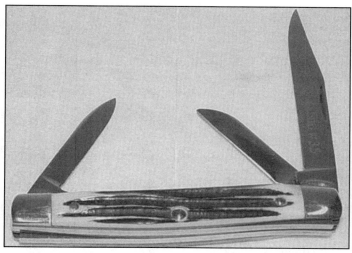

#35, Queen, small serpentine, 3 blade, Winterbottom bone handles, brass liners, NS bolsters, Queen Steel #35 etch, intermediate Q tang stamp, 2-5/8", $40-$50.

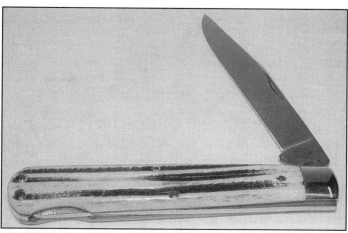

#36, Queen, lockback, 1 blade, brown Winterbottom bone handles, brass liners, NS bolster, no etch, Q STEEL tang stamp, 4-1/2", $150-$160.

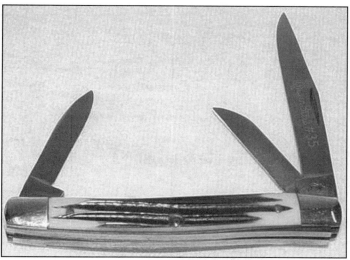

#35, Queen, small serpentine, 3 blade, burnt orange imitation Winterbottom bone handles, brass liners, NS bolsters, Queen Steel #35 etch, intermediate Q tang stamp, 2-5/8", $40-$50.

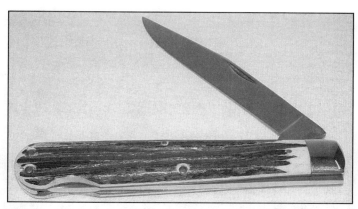

#36, Queen, lockback, 1 blade, Winterbottom bone handles, brass liners, NS bolster, Queen Cutlery TITUSVILLE, PA. etch, no tang stamp, 4-1/2", $75-$100.

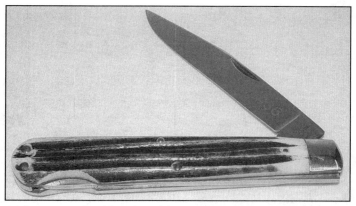

#36, Queen, lockback, 1 blade, Winterbottom bone handles, brass liners, NS bolster, Queen Steel #36 etch, Q STEEL tang stamp, 4-1/2", $160-$175.

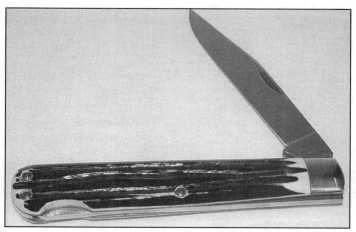

#36, Queen, lockback, 1 blade, Winterbottom bone handles, brass liners, NS bolster, Queen Steel #36 etch, no tang stamp, 4-1/2", $80-$100.

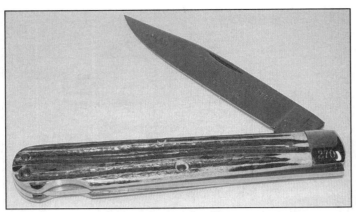

#36, Queen, lockback, 1 blade, Winterbottom bone handles, brass liners, NS bolster, old pattern lockback 6155, Made in USA 1 of 700 engraved, Q83 tang stamp, 4-1/2", $100-$125.

#37, Queen, stockman, 3 blade (one is punch blade), imitation Winterbottom bone handles, brass liners, NS bolster, Queen Steel #37 etch, no tang stamp, 4-1/2", $60-$75.

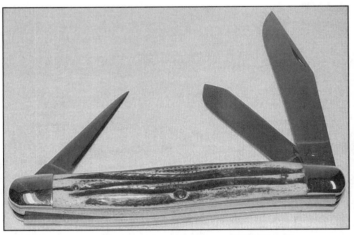

#37, Queen, stockman, 3 carbon steel blades (one is punch blade), Winterbottom bone handles, brass liners, NS bolster, no etch, big Q tang stamp, 4-1/2", $170-$185.

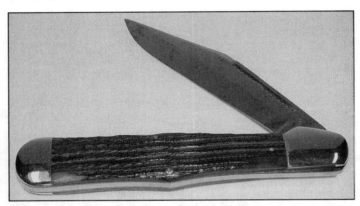

#38, Queen, swell center, 1 jumbo carbon steel blade, early brown Winterbottom bone handles, brass liners, NS bolster, NS hammered pins, no etch, big Q tang stamp, 5-1/4", $275-$325.

#37, Queen, stockman, 3 blade (one is punch blade), Winterbottom bone handles, brass liners, NS bolster, paper sticker Queen Steel on blade, QUEEN STEEL tang stamp, 4-1/2", $170-$185.

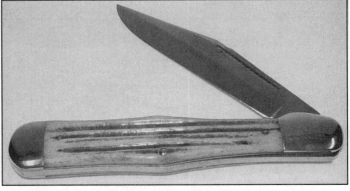

#38, Queen, swell center, 1 jumbo blade, Winterbottom bone handles, brass liners, NS bolster, no etch, big Q tang stamp, 5-1/4", $250-$300.

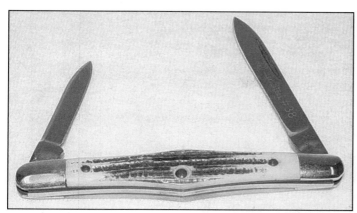

#38, Queen, swell-center pen, 2 blade, Winterbottom bone handles, brass liners, NS bolster, Queen Steel #38 etch, Q STEEL tang stamp, 3", $130-$150.

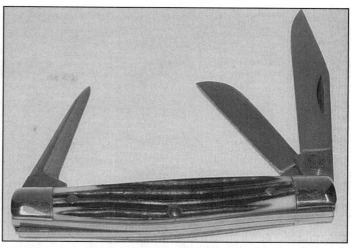

#38, Queen, stockman, 3 blade w/punch, imitation Winterbottom bone handles, brass liners, NS bolster, Queen Steel #38 etch, Q 22-72 tang stamp, 3-1/4", $35-$50.

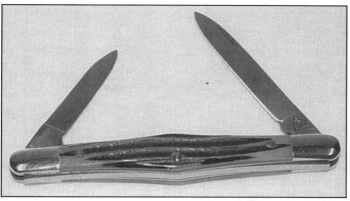

#38, Queen, swell-center pen, 2 blade, Winterbottom bone handles, brass liners, NS bolster, no etch, Q USA tang stamp, 3", $40-$60.

#38, Queen, stockman, 3 blade w/punch, amber handles, brass liners, NS bolster, Queen Steel #38 etch, no tang stamp, 3-1/4", $35-$50.

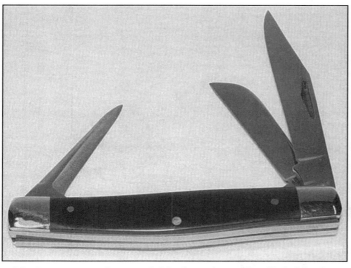

#38, Queen, stockman, 3 blade w/punch, slick black handles, brass liners, NS bolster, Queen Steel #38B Made in USA etch, Q 22-72 tang stamp, 3-1/4", $35-$50.

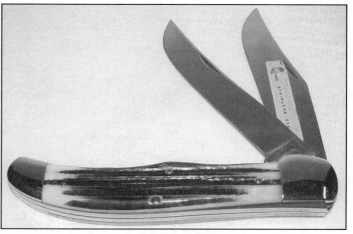

#39, Queen, folding hunter, 2 blade, Winterbottom bone handles, brass liners, NS bolster, FINEST Q STAINLESS etch w/paper sticker, big Q tang stamp w/ second blade stamped STAINLESS, 5-1/4", $250-$270.

#39, Queen, folding hunter, 2 blade, Winterbottom bone handles, brass liners, NS bolster, FINEST Q STAINLESS etch, big Q w/STAINLESS stamped through Q tang stamp w/second blade stamped STAINLESS, 5-1/4", $200-$250.

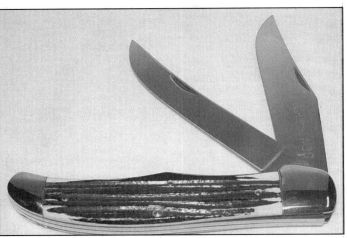

#39, Queen, folding hunter, 2 blade, Winterbottom bone handles, brass liners, NS bolster, Queen Steel #39 etch, Q STEEL tang stamp, 5-1/4", $150-$175.

#39, Queen, folding hunter, 2 blade, Winterbottom bone handles, brass liners, NS bolster, Queen Steel etch, Q STAINLESS tang stamp w/second blade stamped Q STAINLESS, 5-1/4", $200-$250.

#39, Queen, folding hunter, 2 blade, burnt orange imitation Winterbottom bone handles, brass liners, NS bolster, Queen Steel #39 etch, Q STEEL tang stamp, 5-1/4", $160-$180.

#39, Queen, folding hunter, 2 blade, Winterbottom bone handles, brass liners, NS bolster, no etch, Q STEEL tang stamp, 5-1/4", $150-$175.

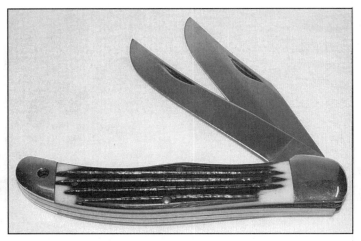

#39, Queen, folding hunter, 2 blade, imitation Winterbottom bone handles, brass liners, NS bolster, Queen Steel #39 etch, Q STEEL tang stamp, 5-1/4", $75-$100.

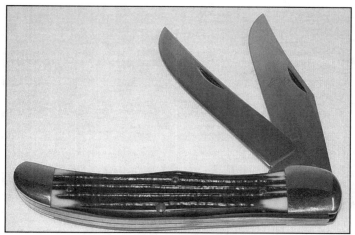

#39, Queen, folding hunter, 2 blade, imitation Winterbottom bone handles, brass liners, NS bolster, Queen Steel #39 etch, no tang stamp, 5-1/4", $75-$100.

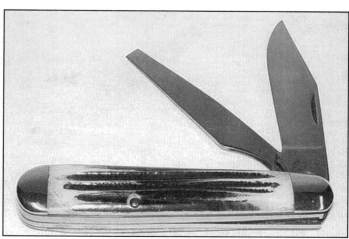

#40, Queen, heavy duty screwdriver, 2 blade, Winterbottom bone handles, brass liners, NS bolster, no etch, big Q tang stamp, 3-11/16", $150-$170.

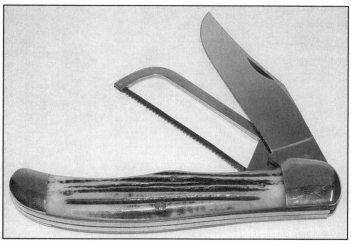

#39, Queen, folding hunter, 2 blade, secondary blade is saw blade, Winterbottom bone handles, brass liners, NS bolster, no etch, no tang stamp, 5-1/4", $125-$150.

#40, Queen, electrician, 2 blade, Winterbottom bone handles, brass liners, NS bolster, no etch, big Q tang stamp, 3-11/16", $150-$170.

#39, Queen, folding hunter, 2 blade, stag handles, brass liners, NS bolster, NSGA Show 1 of 150 etch, Q80 tang stamp, 5-1/4", $125-$150.

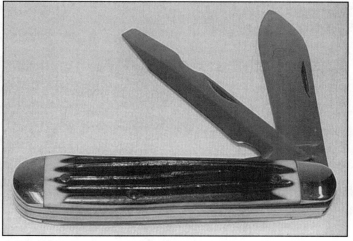

#40, Queen, electrician, 2 blade, imitation Winterbottom bone handles, brass liners, NS bolster, Queen Steel #40 etch, no tang stamp, 3-11/16", $35-$50.

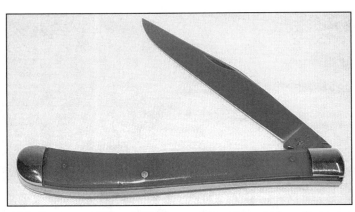

*#41, Queen, utility, 1 blade, red handles, brass liners, NS bolsters, no etch, Q STAINLESS tang stamp, 4-1/8", $60-$80.*

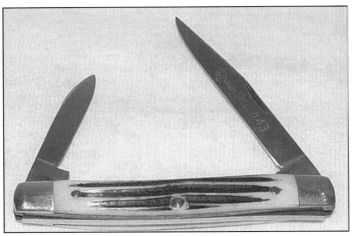

*#43, Queen, small serpentine, 2 blade, Winterbottom bone handles, brass liners, NS bolsters, Queen Steel #43 etch, big Q tang stamp, 2-5/8", $35-$45.*

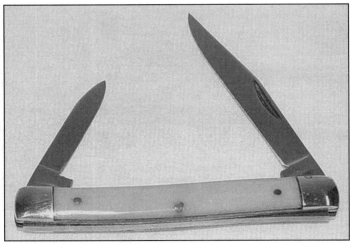

*#42, Queen, small serpentine, 2 blade, amber handles, brass liners, NS bolsters, no etch, QUEEN STEEL tang stamp, 2-5/8", $25-$35.*

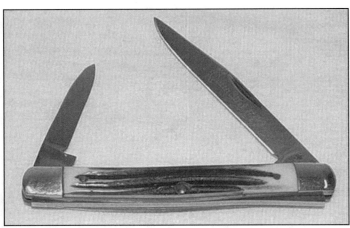

*#43, Queen, small serpentine, 2 blade, burnt orange imitation Winterbottom bone handles, brass liners, NS bolsters, Queen Steel #43 etch, big Q tang stamp, 2-5/8", $35-$45.*

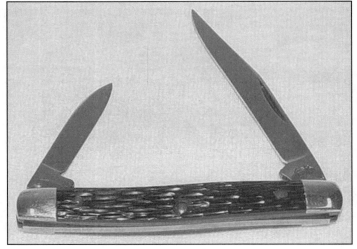

*#43, Queen, small serpentine, 2 blade, rough black imitation bone handles, brass liners, NS bolsters, no etch, big Q tang stamp, 2-5/8", $35-$45.*

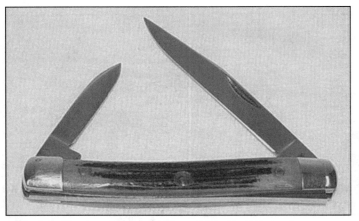

*#43, Queen, small serpentine, 2 blade, Winterbottom bone handles, brass liners, NS bolsters, no etch, QUEEN STEEL tang stamp, 2-5/8", $35-$45.*

Queen / Schatt & Morgan Cutlery 383

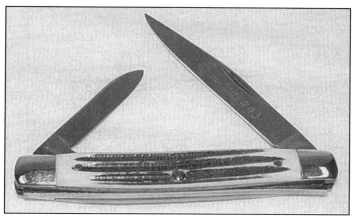

#43, Queen, small serpentine, 2 blade, Winterbottom bone handles, brass liners, NS bolsters, Queen Steel #43 etch, Q STEEL tang stamp, 2-5/8", $35-$45.

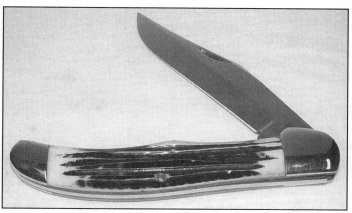

#44, Queen, folding hunter, 1 blade, Winterbottom bone handles, brass liners, NS bolster, no etch, QUEEN STEEL tang stamp, 5-1/4", $160-$175.

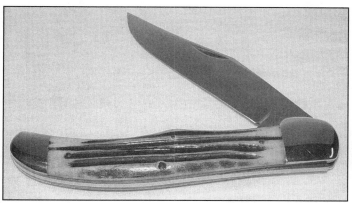

#44, Queen, folding hunter, 1 blade, Winterbottom bone handles, brass liners, NS bolster, FINEST Q STAINLESS etch, Q STAINLESS tang stamp, 5-1/4", $170-$190.

#44, Queen, folding hunter, 1 blade, Winterbottom bone handles, brass liners, NS bolster, Queen Steel #44 etch, Q STEEL tang stamp, 5-1/4", $125-$150.

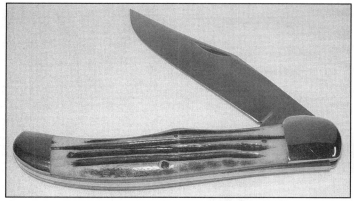

#44, Queen, folding hunter, 1 blade, Winterbottom bone handles, brass liners, NS bolster, Queen Steel etch, Q STAINLESS tang stamp, 5-1/4", $170-$190.

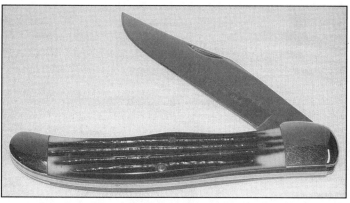

#44, Queen, folding hunter, 1 blade, burnt orange imitation Winterbottom bone handles, brass liners, NS bolster, Queen Steel #44 etch, Q STEEL tang stamp, 5-1/4", $140-$160.

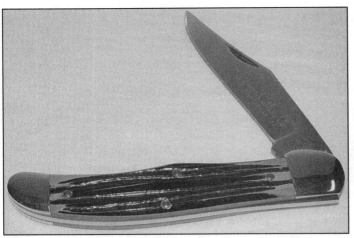

#44, Queen, folding hunter, short frame, 1 blade, Winterbottom bone handles, brass liners, NS bolster, Queen Cutlery Co Titusville, PA etch, Q USA tang stamp, 5-1/4", $80-$100.

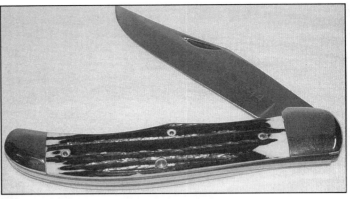

#44, Queen, folding hunter, 1 blade, Winterbottom bone handles, brass liners, NS bolster, Queen Steel #44 etch, no tang stamp, 5-1/4", $125-$150.

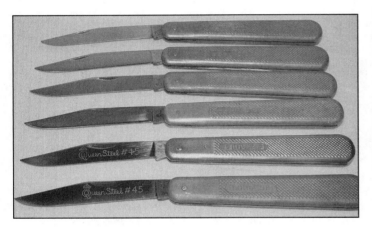

(top to bottom)
#45, Queen, Big Chief, 1 blade, aluminum handles, enclosed spring, no etch, Q STAINLESS tang stamp w/ Pat Pending stamped on backside of blade, 5", $15-$25.
#45, Queen, Big Chief, 1 blade, aluminum handles, enclosed spring, no etch, QUEEN STAINLESS tang stamp w/Pat Pending stamped on backside of blade, 5", $15-$25.
#45, Queen, Big Chief, 1 blade, aluminum handles, enclosed spring, no etch, QUEEN STEEL tang stamp w/ Pat Pending stamped on backside of blade, 5", $15-$25.
#45, Queen, Big Chief, 1 blade, aluminum handles, enclosed spring, no etch, Q STEEL tang stamp w/Pat Pending stamped on backside of blade, 5", $15-$25.
#45, Queen, Big Chief, 1 blade, aluminum handles, enclosed spring, Queen Steel #45 etch, Patent no 2728139 tang stamp, 5", $15-$25.
#45, Queen, Big Chief, 1 blade w/satin finish, aluminum handles, enclosed spring, Queen Steel #45 etch, Patent no 2728139 tang stamp, 5", $15-$25.

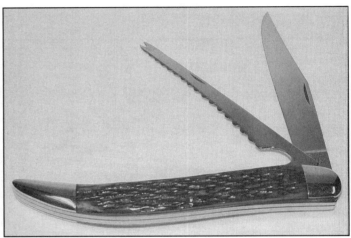

#46, Queen (previously #19), fish knife, 2 blade w/ secondary blade hook disgorger & scaler, Rogers bone handles w/out sharpening stone, brass liners, NS bolster, no etch, big Q tang stamp, 5", $150-$175.

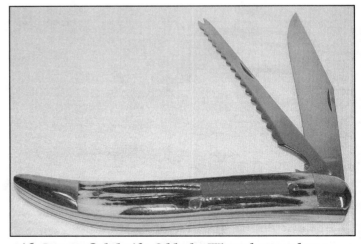

#46, Queen, fish knife, 2 blade, Winterbottom bone handles w/rectangular sharpening stone, brass liners, NS bolster, no etch, Q STAINLESS tang stamp, secondary blade magnetic hook disgorger & scaler w/"STAINLESS" tang stamp, 5", $175-$200.

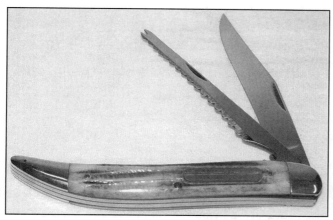

#46, Queen, fish knife, 2 blade, Winterbottom bone handles w/flat oval sharpening stone, brass liners, NS bolster, no etch, QUEEN STEEL tang stamp, secondary blade magnetic hook disgorger & scaler w/"STAINLESS" tang stamp, 5", $175-$200.

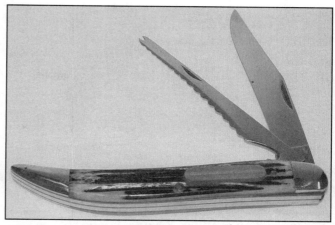

#46, Queen, fish knife, 2 blade w/secondary blade hook disgorger & scaler, Winterbottom bone handles w/flat oval sharpening stone, brass liners, NS bolster, no etch, Q STEEL tang stamp, 5", $100-$125.

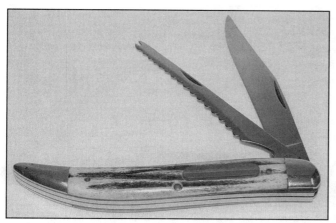

#46, Queen, fish knife, Winterbottom bone handles w/flat oval sharpening stone, brass liners, NS bolster, 2 blade, no etch, QUEEN STEEL tang stamp, w/secondary blade hook disgorger & scaler, 5", $175-$200.

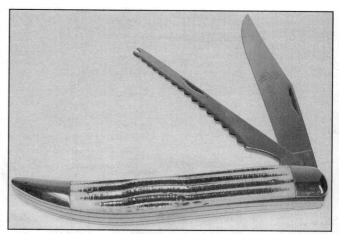

#46, Queen, fish knife, 2 blade w/secondary blade hook disgorger & scaler, Winterbottom bone handles w/out flat oval sharpening stone, brass liners, NS bolster, Queen Steel #46 etch, Q STEEL tang stamp 5", $125-$150.

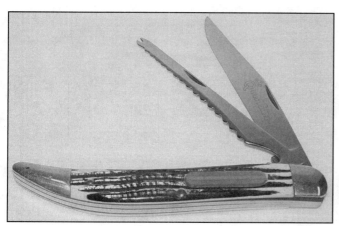

#46, Queen, fish knife, 2 blade w/secondary blade hook disgorger & scaler, Winterbottom bone handles w/flat oval sharpening stone, brass liners, NS bolster, Queen Steel #46 etch, Q STEEL tang stamp, 5", $100-$125.

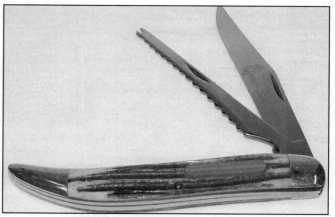

#46, Queen, fish knife, 2 blade w/secondary blade hook disgorger & scaler, Winterbottom bone handles w/flat oval sharpening stone, brass liners, NS bolster, Queen Steel #46 etch, no tang stamp, 5", $100-$125.

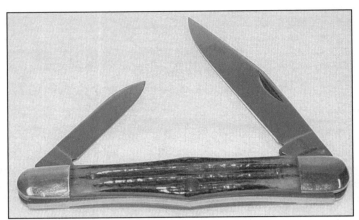

*#47, Queen, half whittler, 2 blade, Winterbottom bone handles, brass liners, NS bolsters, no etch, Q STAINLESS tang stamp, 3-1/2", $80-$100.*

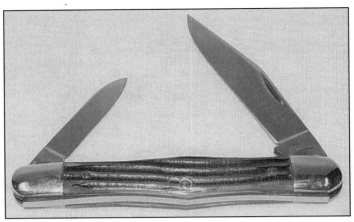

*#47, Queen, half whittler, 2 blade, Winterbottom bone handles, brass liners, NS bolsters, Queen Steel #47 etch, Q STEEL tang stamp, 3-1/2", $60-$75.*

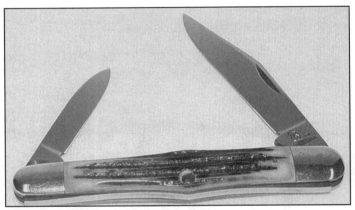

*#47, Queen, half whittler, 2 blade, Winterbottom bone handles, brass liners, NS bolsters, no etch, QUEEN STAINLESS tang stamp, 3-1/2", $80-$100.*

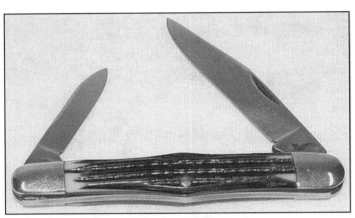

*#47, Queen, half whittler, 2 blade, burnt orange imitation Winterbottom bone handles, brass liners, NS bolsters, Queen Steel #47 etch, Q STEEL tang stamp, 3-1/2", $60-$80.*

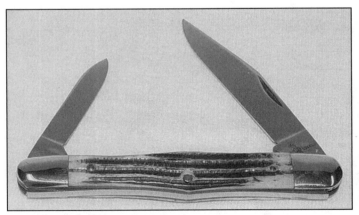

*#47, Queen, half whittler, 2 blade, Winterbottom bone handles, brass liners, NS bolsters, no etch, QUEEN STEEL tang stamp, 3-1/2", $80-$100.*

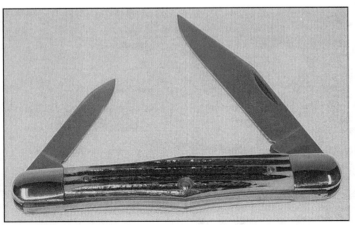

*#47, Queen, half whittler, 2 blade, Winterbottom bone handles, brass liners, NS bolsters, Queen Steel #47 etch, no tang stamp, 3-1/2", $60-$75.*

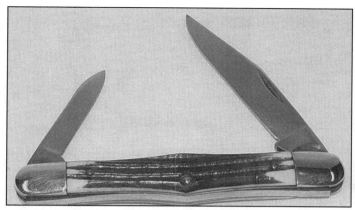

#47, Queen, half whittler, 2 blade, burnt orange imitation Winterbottom bone handles, brass liners, NS bolsters, Queen Steel #47 etch, no tang stamp, 3-1/2", $60-$80.

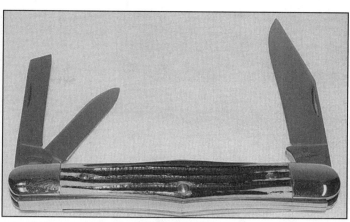

#48, Queen, whittler, 3 blade, Winterbottom bone handles, brass liners, NS bolsters, Queen Steel #48 etch, Q STEEL tang stamp, 3-1/2", $100-$125.

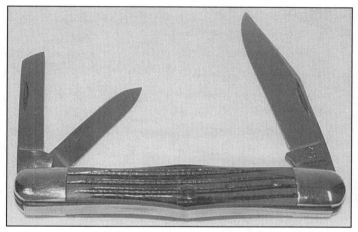

#48, Queen, whittler, 3 blade, Winterbottom bone handles, brass liners, NS bolsters, no etch, Q STAINLESS tang stamp, 3-1/2", $160-$180.

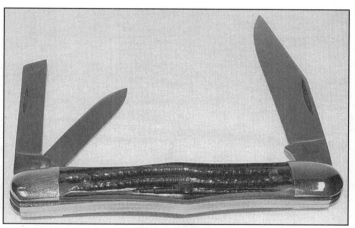

#48, Queen, whittler, 3 blade, Winterbottom bone handles, brass liners, NS bolsters, no etch, Q STEEL tang stamp, 3-1/2", $100-$125.

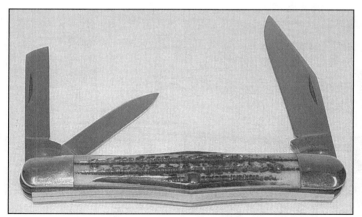

#48, Queen, whittler, 3 blade, Winterbottom bone handles, brass liners, NS bolsters, no etch, QUEEN STAINLESS tang stamp, 3-1/2", $160-$180.

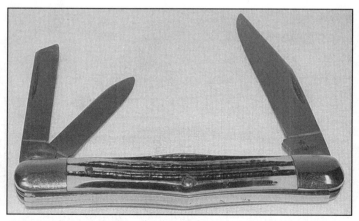

#48, Queen, whittler, 3 blade, burnt orange imitation Winterbottom bone handles, brass liners, NS bolsters, Queen Steel #48 etch, Q STEEL tang stamp, 3-1/2", $100-$125.

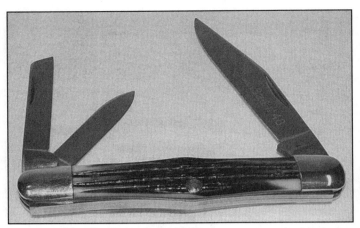

#48, Queen, whittler, 3 blade, burnt orange imitation Winterbottom bone handles, brass liners, NS bolsters, Queen Steel #48 etch, QUEEN tang stamp, 3-1/2", $100-$125.

#49, Queen, large stockman, 3 blade, Winterbottom bone handles, brass liners, NS bolsters, no etch, QUEEN STAINLESS tang stamp, 4-1/4", $175-$200.

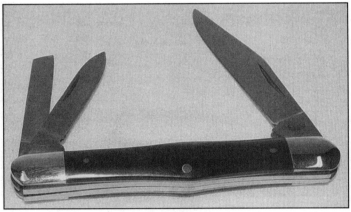

#48, Queen, whittler, 3 blade, slick black handles, brass liners, NS bolsters, Queen Steel #48B etch, QUEEN tang stamp, 3-1/2", $30-$50.

#49, Queen, large stockman, 3 blade, Winterbottom bone handles, brass liners, NS bolsters, no etch, Q STEEL tang stamp, 4-1/4", $100-$130.

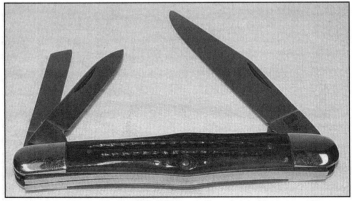

#48, Queen, whittler, 3 blade, Winterbottom bone handles, brass liners, NS bolsters, Queen Steel #48 Made in USA etch, Q76 tang stamp, 3-1/2", $30-$50.

#49, Queen, large stockman, 3 blade, Winterbottom bone handles, brass liners, NS bolsters, Queen Steel #49 etch, Q STEEL tang stamp, 4-1/4", $100-$130.

#49, Queen, large stockman, 3 blade, Winterbottom bone handles, brass liners, NS bolsters, glazed finish, Queen Steel #49 etch, no tang stamp, 4-1/4", $150-$175.

#49, Queen, large stockman, 3 blade, Winterbottom bone handles, brass liners, NS bolsters, Queen Steel #49 Made in USA etch, Queen 22-72 tang stamp, 4-1/4", $100-$130.

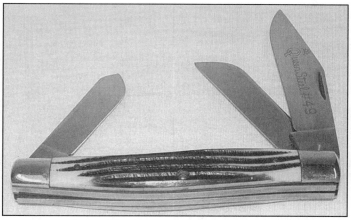

#49, Queen, large stockman, 3 blade, burnt orange imitation Winterbottom bone handles, brass liners, NS bolsters, Queen Steel #49 etch, Q STEEL tang stamp, 4-1/4", $100-$130.

#50, Queen, salesman sample, 2 blade, celluloid handles, brass liners, NS bolsters, no etch, no tang stamp, 3-1/2", $70-$90.

#49, Queen, large stockman, 3 blade, Winterbottom bone handles, brass liners, NS bolsters, Queen Steel #49 Made in USA etch, no tang stamp, 4-1/4", $100-$130.

#51, Queen, dogleg, 2 blade, Winterbottom bone handles, brass liners, NS bolsters, no etch, Q STAINLESS tang stamp, 3-1/2", $100-$125.

#51, Queen, dogleg, 2 blade, Winterbottom bone handles, brass liners, NS bolsters, no etch, QUEEN STEEL tang stamp, 3-1/2", $70-$90.

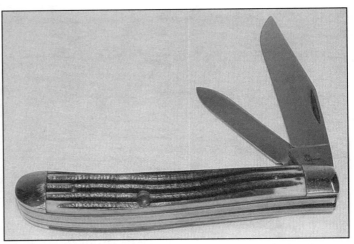

#51, Queen, dogleg, 2 blade, burnt orange imitation Winterbottom bone handles, brass liners, NS bolsters, Queen Steel #51 etch, Q STEEL tang stamp, 3-1/2", $60-$80.

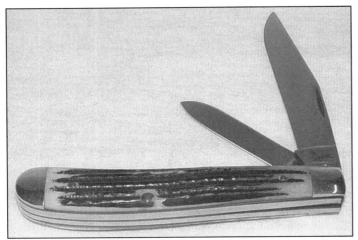

#51, Queen, dogleg, 2 blade, Winterbottom bone handles, brass liners, NS bolsters, no etch, Q STEEL tang stamp, 3-1/2", $60-$80.

#51, Queen, dogleg, 2 blade, Winterbottom bone handles, brass liners, NS bolsters, Queen Steel #51 etch, no tang stamp, 3-1/2", $60-$80.

#51, Queen, dogleg, 2 blade, Winterbottom bone handles, brass liners, NS bolsters, Queen Steel #51 etch, Q STEEL tang stamp, 3-1/2", $60-$80.

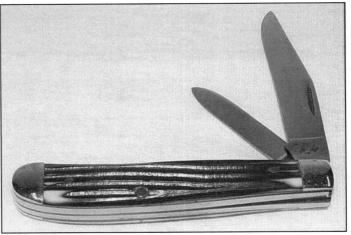

#51, Queen, dogleg, 2 blade, imitation Winterbottom bone handles, brass liners, NS bolsters, Queen Steel #51 Made in USA etch, Q 22-72 tang stamp, 3-1/2", $40-$60.

*#52, Queen, moose, 2 blade, Winterbottom bone handles, brass liners, NS bolsters, no etch, Q STAINLESS tang stamp, 4-1/4", $135-$150.*

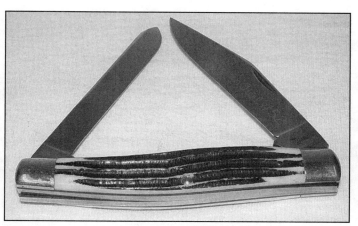

*#52, Queen, moose, 2 blade, Winterbottom bone handles, brass liners, NS bolsters, Queen Steel #52 etch, Q STEEL tang stamp, 4-1/4", $100-$125.*

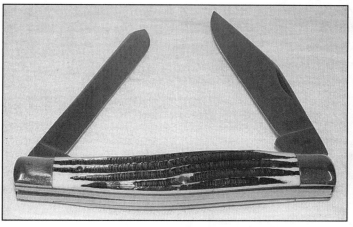

*#52, Queen, moose, 2 blade, Winterbottom bone handles, brass liners, NS bolsters, glazed finish, Queen Steel #52 etch, Q STEEL tang stamp, 4-1/4", $135-$150.*

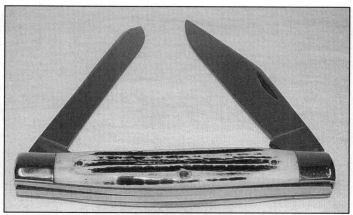

*#52, Queen, moose, 2 blade, Winterbottom bone handles, brass liners, NS bolsters, Queen Steel #52 etch, no tang stamp, 4-1/4", $100-$125.*

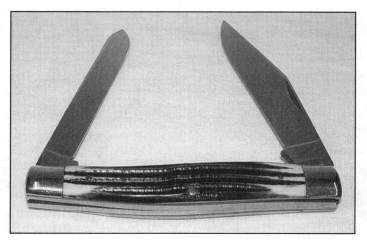

*#52, Queen, moose, 2 blade, burnt orange imitation Winterbottom bone handles, brass liners, NS bolsters, Queen Steel #52 etch, Q STEEL tang stamp, 4-1/4", $100- $125.*

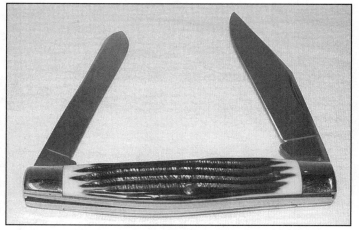

*#52, Queen, moose, 2 blade, imitation Winterbottom bone handles, brass liners, NS bolsters, Queen Steel #52 etch, Q 22-72 tang stamp, 4-1/4", $50-$70.*

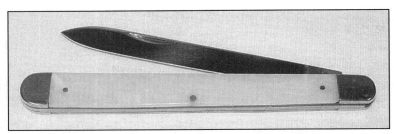

*#53, Queen, citrus fruit, 1 blade, simulated pearl handles, brass liners, NS bolsters, no etch, QUEEN STEEL tang stamp, 4-5/8", $70-$100.*

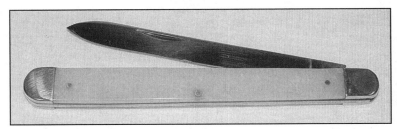

*#53, Queen, citrus fruit, 1 blade, simulated pearl handles, brass liners, NS bolsters, no etch, Q STEEL tang stamp, 4-5/8", $75-$100.*

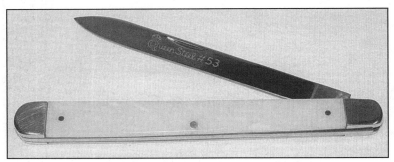

*#53, Queen, citrus fruit, 1 blade, simulated pearl handles, brass liners, NS bolsters, Queen Steel #53 etch, no tang stamp, 4-5/8", $75-$100.*

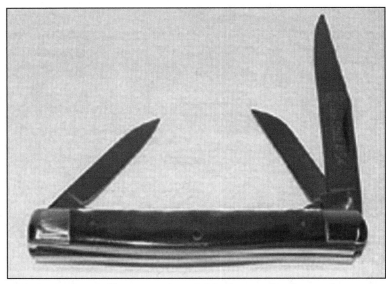

*#54, Queen, small serpentine, 3 blade, smoked pearl handles, brass liners, NS bolsters, Queen Steel #54 etch, no tang stamp, 2-5/8", $350-$375.*

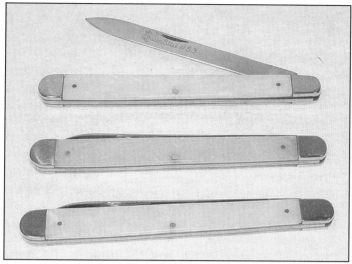

#53, Queen, three citrus fruit knives, 1 blade, simulated pearl handles, brass liners, NS bolsters, 4-5/8", $75-$100.

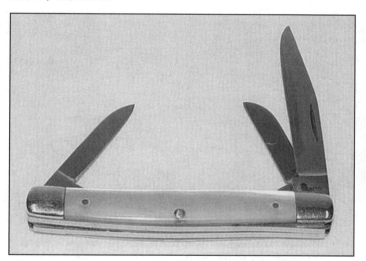

#54, Queen, small serpentine, 3 blade, pearl handles, brass liners, NS bolsters, no etch, QUEEN tang stamp, 2-5/8", $40-$60.

#55, Queen, sleeveboard pen, 2 blade, cracked ice handles, w/Queen Cutlery Co on handle, brass liners, NS bolsters, Queen Steel #55 MADE IN U.S.A. etch, QUEEN tang stamp, 3-5/16", $45-$60.

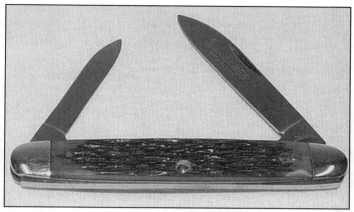

#55, Queen, sleeveboard pen, 2 blade, Rogers bone handles, brass liners, NS bolsters, Queen Steel #55 MADE IN U.S.A. etch, Q76 tang stamp, 200 made, 3-5/16", $45-$60.

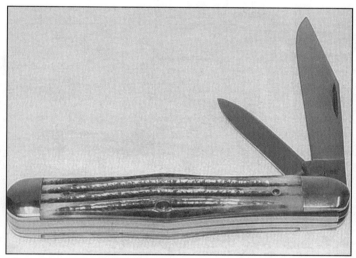

#56, Queen, swell center, 2 blade, Winterbottom bone handles, brass liners, NS bolsters, no etch, QUEEN STEEL tang stamp, 3-1/2", $80-$100.

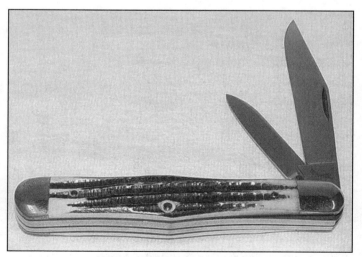

#56, Queen, swell center, 2 blade, Winterbottom bone handles, brass liners, NS bolsters, Queen Steel #56 etch, QUEEN STEEL tang stamp, 3-1/2", $80-$100.

*#56, Queen, swell center, 2 blade, Winterbottom bone handles, brass liners, NS bolsters, Queen Steel #56 etch, Q STEEL tang stamp, 3-1/2", $80-$100.*

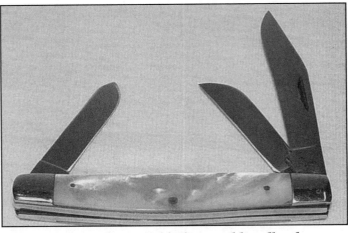

*#57, Queen, stockman, 3 blade, pearl handles, brass liners, NS bolsters, Queen Steel #57 Made in USA etch, QUEEN tang stamp, 3-1/4", $60-$80.*

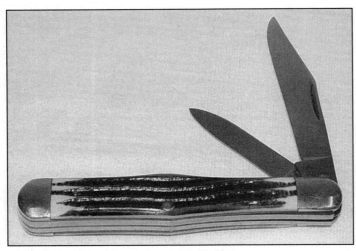

*#56, Queen, swell center, 2 blade, burnt orange imitation Winterbottom bone handles, brass liners, NS bolsters, Queen Steel #56 etch, Q STEEL tang stamp, 3-1/2", $80-$100.*

*#57, Queen, stockman, 3 blade, smoked pearl handles, brass liners, NS bolsters, Queen Steel #57 etch, no tang stamp, 3-1/4", $300-$325.*

*#56, Queen, swell center, 2 blade, imitation Winterbottom bone handles, brass liners, NS bolsters, Queen Steel #56 etch, no tang stamp, 3-1/2", $80-$100.*

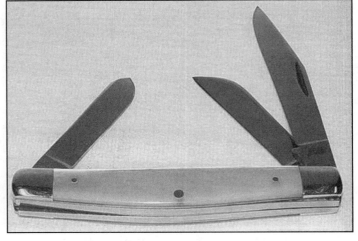

*#57, Queen, stockman, 3 blade, pearl handles, brass liners, NS bolsters, Queen Steel #57 etch, intermediate Q tang stamp, 3-1/4", $60-$80.*

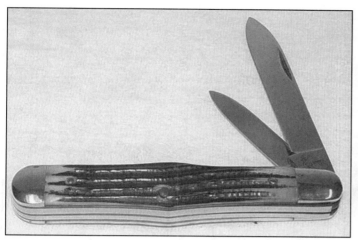

#58, Queen, swell center, 2 blade, Winterbottom bone handles, brass liners, NS bolsters, no etch, QUEEN STEEL tang stamp, 3-1/2", $80-$100.

#58, Queen, swell center, 2 blade, imitation Winterbottom bone handles, brass liners, NS bolsters, Queen Steel #58 etch, Q STEEL tang stamp, 3-1/2", $80-$100.

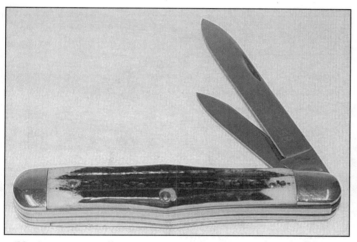

#58, Queen, swell center, 2 blade, Winterbottom bone handles, brass liners, NS bolsters, Queen Steel #58 etch, Q STEEL tang stamp, 3-1/2", $80-$100.

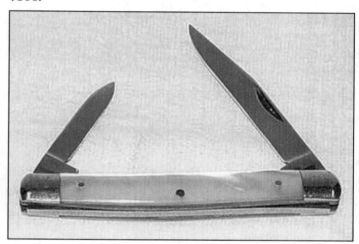

#59, Queen, small serpentine, 2 blade, pearl handles, brass liners, NS bolsters, no etch, QUEEN STEEL tang stamp, 2-5/8", $40-$60.

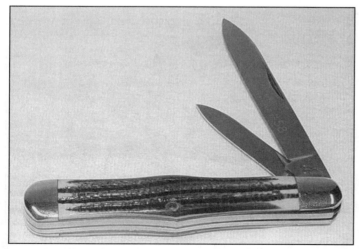

#58, Queen, swell center, 2 blade, burnt orange imitation Winterbottom bone handles, brass liners, NS bolsters, Queen Steel #58 etch, Q STEEL tang stamp, 3-1/2", $80-$100.

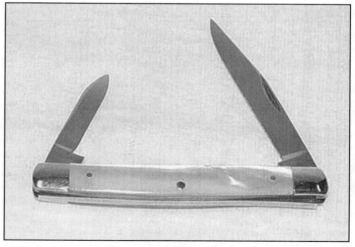

#59, Queen, small serpentine, 2 blade, pearl handles, brass liners, NS bolsters, Queen Steel #59 etch, Q STEEL tang stamp, 2-5/8", $40-$60.

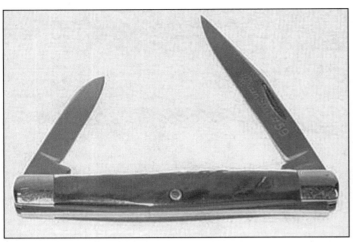

#59, Queen, small serpentine, 2 blade, smoked pearl handles, brass liners, NS bolsters, Queen Steel #59 etch, no tang stamp, 2-5/8", $175-$200.

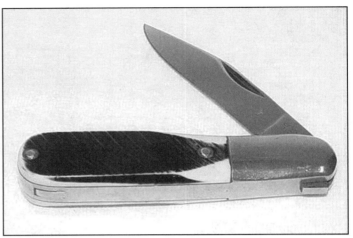

#60, Queen, Barlow, 1 blade, burnt orange imitation sawn bone handles, aluminum frame, no etch, PAT. NO. 2728139 tang stamp, 3-1/2", $60-$80.

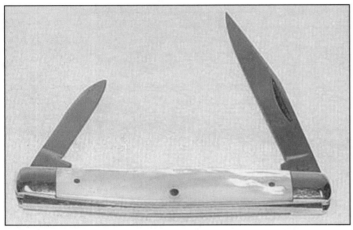

#59, Queen, small serpentine, 2 blades, pearl handles, brass liners, NS bolsters, Queen Steel #59 etch, intermediate Q tang stamp, 2-5/8", $40-$60.

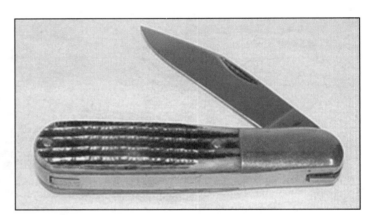

#60, Queen, Barlow, 1 blade, Winterbottom bone handles, aluminum frame, no etch, Q STEEL tang stamp, 3-1/2", $60-$80.

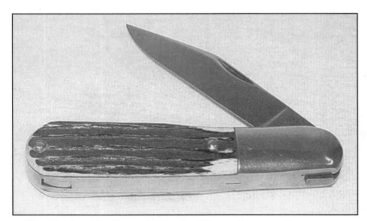

#60, Queen, Barlow, 1 blade, Winterbottom bone handles, aluminum frame, no etch, QUEEN STEEL tang stamp w/PAT. PENDING stamped on rear tang, 3-1/2", $60-$80.

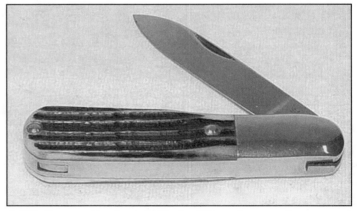

#60S, Queen, Barlow, 1 blade, Winterbottom bone handles, aluminum frame, no etch, QUEEN STEEL tang stamp, 3-1/2", $60-$80.

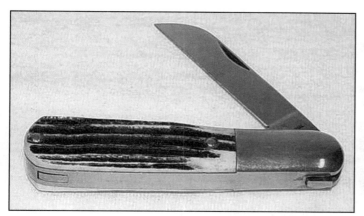

#60SH, Queen, Barlow, 1 blade, Winterbottom bone handles, aluminum frame, no etch, Q STEEL tang stamp, 3-1/2", $60-$80.

#61, Queen, stockman, 3 blade, burnt orange imitation Winterbottom bone handles, brass liners, NS bolsters, Queen Steel #61 etch, Q STEEL tang stamp, 3-5/8", $80-$100.

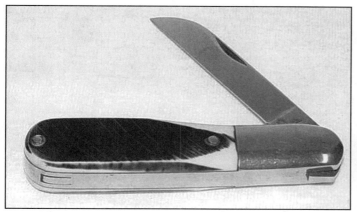

#60SH, Queen, Barlow, 1 blade, burnt orange imitation sawn bone handles, aluminum frame, no etch, Q STEEL tang stamp, 3-1/2", $60-$80.

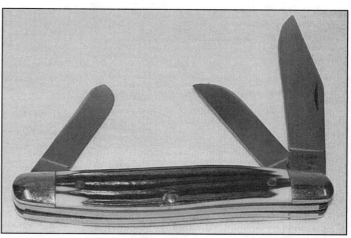

#61, Queen, stockman, 3 blade, imitation Winterbottom bone handles, brass liners, NS bolsters, Queen Steel #61 Made in USA etch, Q 22-72 tang stamp, 3-5/8", $50-$70.

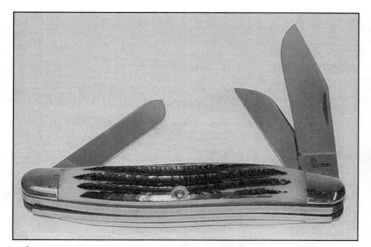

#61, Queen, stockman, 3 blade, Winterbottom bone handles, brass liners, NS bolsters, Queen Steel #61 etch, Q STEEL tang stamp, 3-5/8", $80-$100.

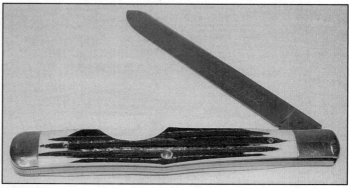

#62, Queen, large lasy open, 1 blade, no nail nick, Winterbottom bone handles, brass liners, NS bolsters, glazed finish, Queen Steel #62 etch, Q STEEL tang stamp, 5-1/4", $180-$200.

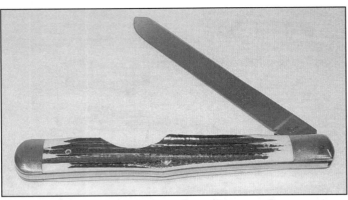

#62, Queen, large lasy open, 1 blade, no nail nick, Winterbottom bone handles, brass liners, NS bolsters, Queen Steel #62 etch, Q STEEL tang stamp, 5-1/4", $150-$175.

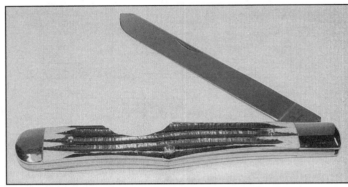

#62, Queen, large lasy open, 1 blade, Winterbottom bone handles, brass liners, NS bolsters, Queen Steel #62 etch, Q STEEL tang stamp, 5-1/4", $100-$120.

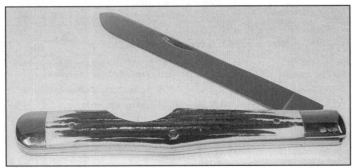

#62, Queen, large lasy open, 1 blade, Winterbottom bone handles, brass liners, NS bolsters, Queen Steel #62 etch, no tang stamp, 5-1/4", $100-$120.

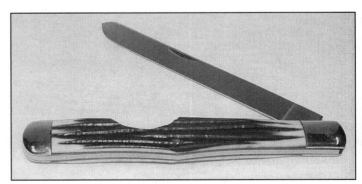

#62, Queen, large lasy open, 1 blade, imitation Winterbottom bone handles, brass liners, NS bolsters, Queen Steel #62 etch, no tang stamp, 5-1/4", $60-$75.

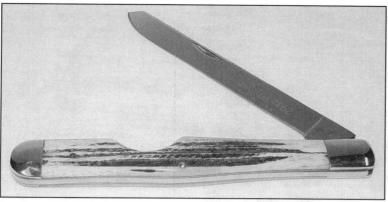

#62, Queen, large lasy open, 1 blade, Winterbottom bone handles, brass liners, NS bolsters, Queen Steel #62 MADE IN U.S.A. etch, long tail Queen tang stamp, 5-1/4", $70-$85.

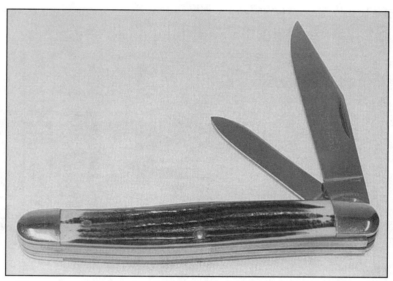

#63, Queen, stockman, 2 blade, burnt orange imitation Winterbottom bone handles, brass liners, NS bolsters, Queen Steel #63 etch, Q STEEL tang stamp, 4", $90-$100.

#63, Queen, stockman, 2 blade, Winterbottom bone handles, brass liners, NS bolsters, Queen Steel #63 etch, no tang stamp, 4", $90-$100.

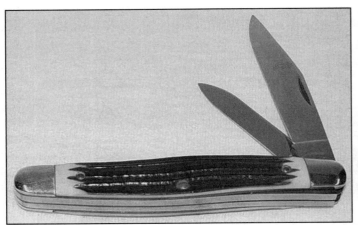

#63, Queen, stockman, 2 blade, imitation Winterbottom bone handles, brass liners, NS bolsters, Queen Steel #63 etch, no tang stamp, 4", $40-$60.

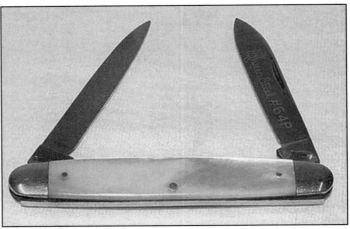

#64P, Queen, sleeveboard pen, 1 blade, one nail file, pearl handles, brass liners, NS bolsters, Queen Steel #64 etch, Q STEEL tang stamp, 3-5/16", $125-$150.

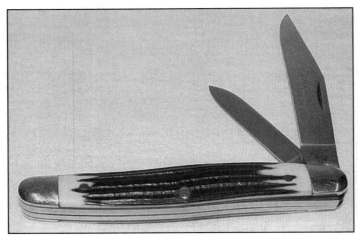

#63, Queen, stockman, 2 blade, imitation Winterbottom bone handles, brass liners, NS bolsters, Queen Steel #63 Made in USA etch, Q 22-72 tang stamp, 4", $40-$60.

#65, Queen, jack, 2 blade, burnt orange imitation Winterbottom bone handles, aluminum frame, no etch, PAT. NO. 2728139 tang stamp, 3-3/4", $60-$80.

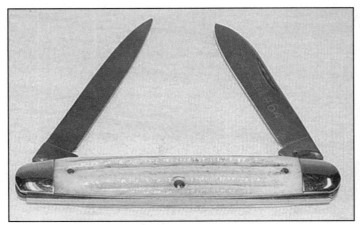

#64, Queen, sleeveboard pen, 1 blade, one nail file, Winterbottom bone handles, brass liners, NS bolsters, Queen Steel #64 etch, Q STEEL tang stamp, 3-5/16", $125-$150.

#66, Queen, muskrat, 2 blade, Winterbottom bone handles, brass liners, NS bolsters, Queen Steel #66 etch, Q STEEL tang stamp, 4", $175-$200.

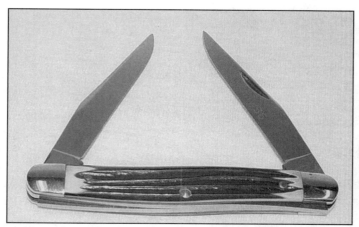

#66, Queen, muskrat, 2 blade, imitation Winterbottom bone handles, brass liners, NS bolsters, Queen Steel #66 etch, no tang stamp, 4", $40-$60.

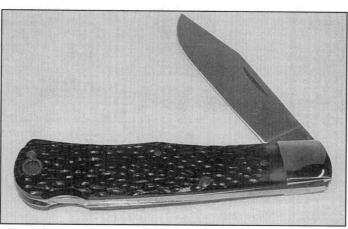

#1440, Queen, mountain man, 1 blade, imitation bone handles, stainless liners, NS bolsters, The Mountain Man Queen Steel #1440 Made in USA etch, no tang stamp, 4-1/2", $70-$90.

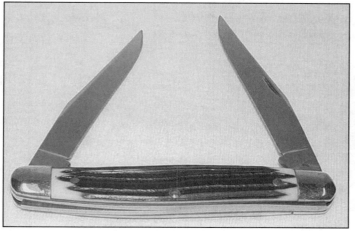

#66, Queen, muskrat, 2 blade, imitation Winterbottom bone handles, brass liners, NS bolsters, Queen Steel #66 Made in USA etch, Q 22-72 tang stamp, 4", $40-$60.

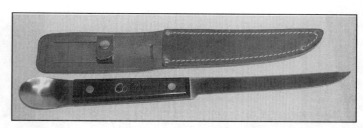

#71, Queen, Coho knife, rosewood handles, no etch, no tang stamp, 6-1/4" blade, $35-$45.

#66, Queen, muskrat, 2 blades, smooth burnt bone handles, brass liners, NS bolsters, Queen Steel BB3 Made in USA etch, Q92 tang stamp, 4", $50-$70.

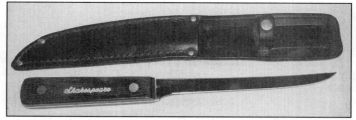

#72 (prototype), Queen, hunting knife, laminated wood handles w/Shakespeare inscription, no etch, no tang stamp, 6-1/4" blade, $45-$65.

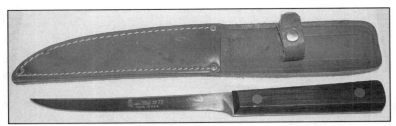

#72, Queen, hunting knife, rosewood handles, Queen Steel
#72 Made in USA etch, no tang stamp, 6-1/4" blade, $40-$55.

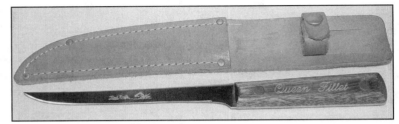

#72, Queen, fillet, oak handles, Queen Fillet Trout Knife etch, no tang stamp, 6-1/4" blade, $40-$50.

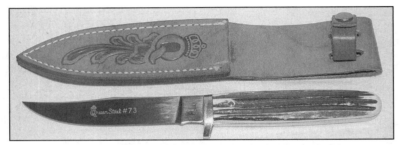

#73, Queen, hunting knife, Winterbottom bone handles, Queen Steel #73 etch, QUEEN tang stamp, 4" blade, $55-$65.

#73, Queen, hunting knife, Winterbottom bone handles, Queen Steel #73 etch, no tang stamp, 4" blade, $55-$65.

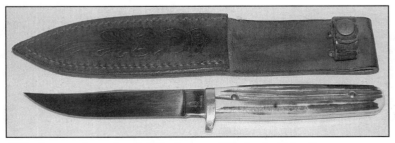

#73, Queen, hunting knife, brown Winterbottom bone handles, no etch, Q STAINLESS tang stamp, 4" blade, $50-$75.

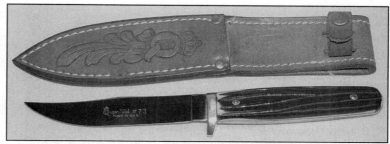

*#73, Queen, hunting knife, imitation Winterbottom bone handles, Queen Steel #73 Made in USA etch, no tang stamp, 4" blade, $45-$55.*

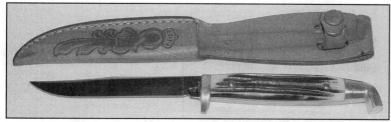

*Hunting knife, Queen #74, brown Winterbottom bone handles, no etch, Q STAINLESS tang stamp, 3-3/4" blade, $55-$75.*

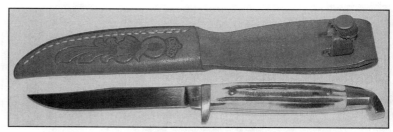

*#74, Queen, hunting knife, brown Winterbottom bone handles, no etch, Q STEEL tang stamp, 3-3/4" blade, $50-$70.*

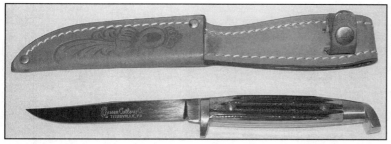

*#74, Queen, hunting knife, brown Winterbottom bone handles, Queen Cutlery Co. Titusville PA etch, no tang stamp, 3-3/4" blade, $50-$70.*

*#74, Queen, hunting knife, burnt orange imitation Winterbottom bone handles, Queen Steel #74 etch, no tang stamp, 3-3/4" blade, $55-$65.*

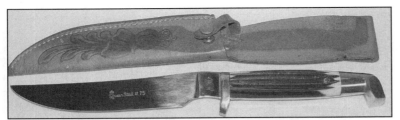

#75, Queen, hunting knife, imitation Winterbottom bone handles, Queen Steel #75 etch, big Q tang stamp, 6" blade, $75-$85.

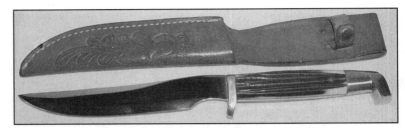

#75, Queen, hunting knife, imitation Winterbottom bone handles, Queen Steel #75 etch, no tang stamp, 6" blade, $50-$75.

#75, Queen, hunting knife, Winterbottom bone handles, Queen Steel #75 etch, Q STEEL tang stamp, 6" blade, $75-$100.

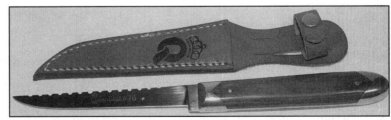

#76, Queen, hunting knife, rosewood handles, Queen Steel #76 etch, no tang stamp, 4-1/4" blade, $35-$45.

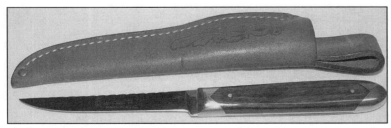

#76, Queen, hunting knife, rosewood handles, Queen Steel #76 Made in USA etch, no tang stamp, 4-1/4" blade, $35-$45.

Queen / Schatt & Morgan Cutlery 405

#77, Queen, hunting knife, Winterbottom bone handles, no etch, sideways Q STAINLESS tang stamp, 5" blade, $75-$85.

#77, Queen, hunting knife, Winterbottom bone handles, no etch, Q STEEL tang stamp, 5" blade, $50-$75.

#77, Queen, hunting knife, imitation Winterbottom bone handles, Queen Steel #77 etch, no tang stamp, 5" blade, $45-$55.

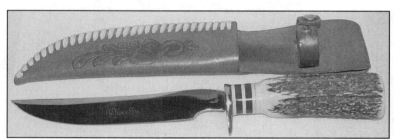

#78, Queen, hunting knife, stag handles, Queen Steel etch, small Q tang stamp, 7" blade, $150-$175.

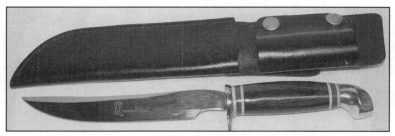

#78, Queen, hunting knife, rosewood handles, Queen Steel etch, no tang stamp, 7" blade, $175-$190.

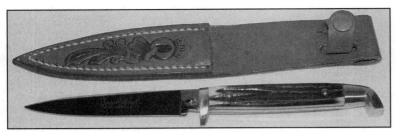

*#79, Queen, hunting knife, burnt orange imitation Winterbottom bone handles, Queen Cutlery Co. Titusville, Pa etch, QUEEN STEEL tang stamp, 3-3/4" blade, $100-$140.*

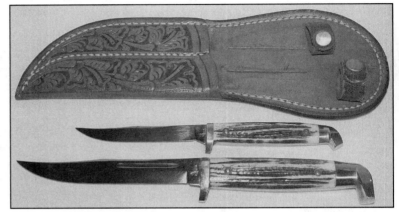

*#80, Queen, twin set hunting knives, brown Winterbottom bone handles, no etch, Q STEEL tang stamp, 4" & 3" blades, $100-$125.*

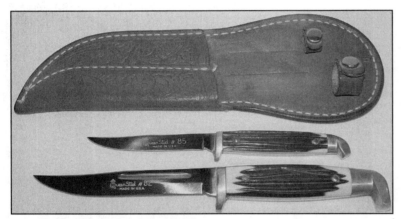

*#80, Queen, twin set hunting knives, imitation Winterbottom bone handles, Queen Steel #80 Made in USA etch, no tang stamp, 4" & 3" blades, $70-$90.*

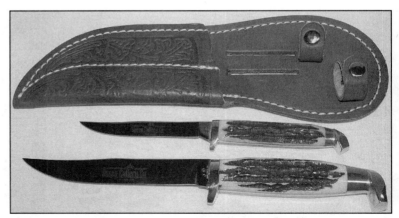

*#81, Queen, twin set hunting knives, carved stag handles, Queen Cutlery Co. Tool Steel etch, Q Titusville, Pa tang stamp, 4" & 3" blades, $50-$70.*

*#82, Queen, hunting knife, Winterbottom bone handles, Finest Stainless etch, big Q tang stamp, 4-1/4" blade, $50-$75.*

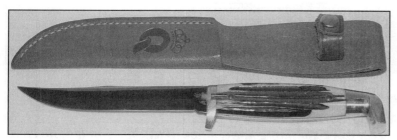

*#82, Queen, hunting knife, Winterbottom bone handles, no etch, big Q tang stamp w/STAINLESS on back, 4-1/4" blade, $50-$75.*

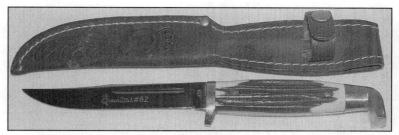

*#82, Queen, hunting knife, imitation Winterbottom bone handles, Queen Steel #82 etch, intermediate Q tang stamp, 4-1/4" blade, $35-$45.*

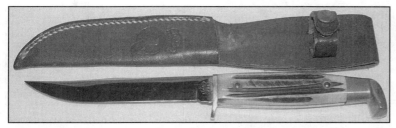

*#82, Queen, hunting knife, Winterbottom bone handles, no etch, crown over QUEEN tang stamp, 4-1/4" blade, $50-$65.*

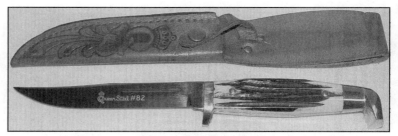

*#82, Queen, hunting knife, Winterbottom bone handles, Queen Steel #82 etch, no tang stamp, 4-1/4" blade, $45-$55.*

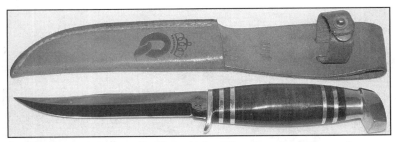

*#82, Queen, hunting knife, stacked leather handles w/ aluminum spacers, no etch, Q tang stamp w/STAINLESS on back, 4-1/4" blade, $50-$65.*

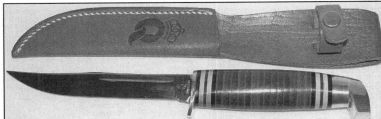

*#84, Queen, hunting knife, stacked leather handles, no etch, Q STAINLESS tang stamp, 4-1/4" blade, $50-$70.*

*#82, Queen, hunting knife, stacked leather handles, Queen Steel #84 Made in USA etch, no tang stamp, 4-1/4" blade, $45-$55.*

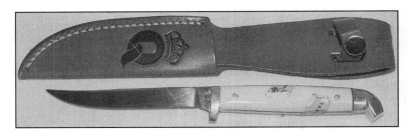

*#85, Queen, hunting knife, imitation ilvory handles w/paper sticker, no etch, Q tang stamp w/STAINLESS on back, 3" blade, $50-$65.*

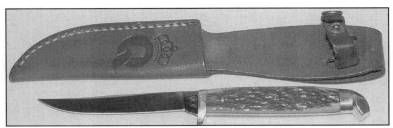

*#85, Queen, hunting knife, Rogers bone handles, no etch, Q tang stamp w/STAINLESS on back, 3" blade, $50-$60.*

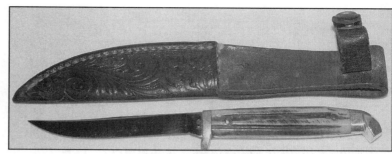

*#85, Queen, hunting knife, Winterbottom bone handles, no etch, Q tang stamp w/ STAINLESS on back, 3" blade, $50-$60.*

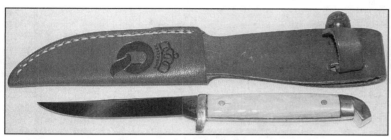

*#85, Queen, hunting knife, imitation ivory handles, no etch, Q tang stamp, 3" blade, $50-$60.*

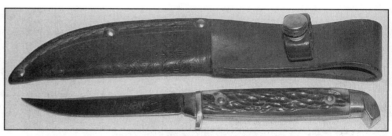

*#85, Queen, hunting knife, Rogers bone handles, Queen etch, no tang stamp, 3" blade, $45-$55.*

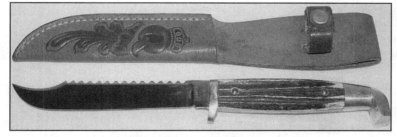

*#87, Queen, fish knife, Winterbottom bone handles, no etch, Q STAINLESS tang stamp, 4-1/2" blade, $60-$80.*

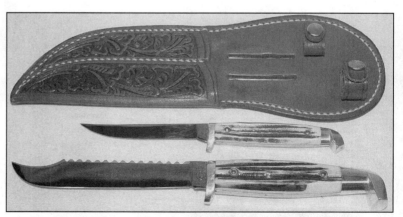

*#88, Queen, twin set, brown Winterbottom bone handles, 4-1/2" & 3" blades, Finest Stainless etch, big Q tang stamp on 4-1/2" blade, Finest Stainless etch, big Q tang stamp w/ STAINLESS on back of 3" blade, $100-$125.*

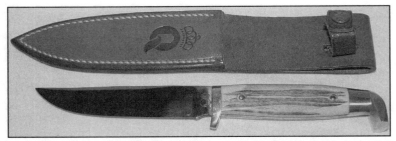

#89, Queen, hunting knife, brown Winterbottom bone handles, no etch, sideways big Q tang stamp, 4" blade, $50-$65.

#89, Queen, hunting knife, brown Winterbottom bone handles, no etch, sideways big Q tang stamp w/STAINLESS on back, 4" blade, $50-$75.

#89, Queen, hunting knife, Winterbottom bone handles, no etch, Q STEEL tang stamp, 4" blade, $50-$60.

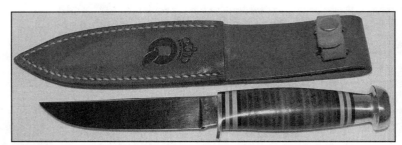

#90, Queen, hunting knife, stacked leather handles, no etch, Q tang stamp w/STAINLESS on back, 4" blade, $45-$65.

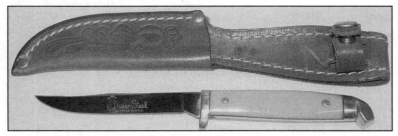

#91, Queen, hunting knife, amber handles, Queen Steel Made in USA etch, no tang stamp, 3" blade, $40-$50.

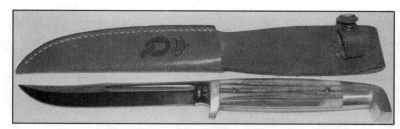

#95, Queen, hunting knife, brown Winterbottom bone handles, no etch, sideways Q STAINLESS tang stamp, 5" blade, $50-$65.

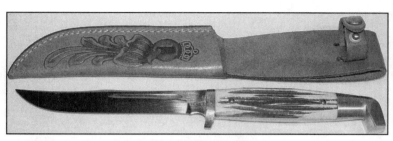

#95, Queen, hunting knife, Winterbottom bone handles, no etch, Q STEEL tang stamp, 5" blade, $45-$55.

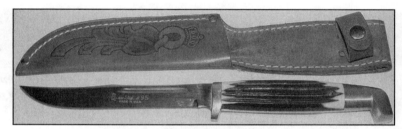

#95, Queen, hunting knife, imitation Winterbottom bone handles, Queen Steel #95 Made in USA etch, no tang stamp, 5" blade, $35-$45.

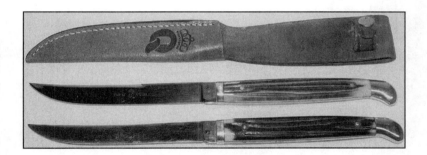

Top: #96, Queen, fillet knife, Winterbottom bone handles, Finest Stainless etch, Q tang stamp, 4-1/2" blade, $50-$75.
Bottom: #96, Queen, fillet knife, burnt orange imitation Winterbottom bone handles, Queen Steel etch, Q STEEL tang stamp, 4-1/2" blade, $55-$65.

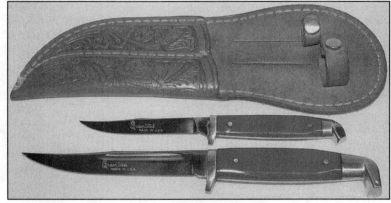

#97, Queen, twin set hunting knives, red handles, Queen Steel Made in USA etch, no tang stamp, 4" & 3" blades, $100-$125.

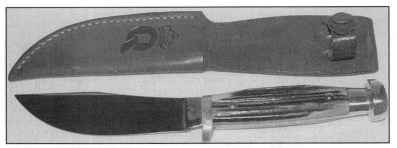

*#98, Queen, hunting knife, brown Winterbottom bone handles, no etch, Q tang stamp w/STAINLESS on back, 4" blade, $60-$80.*

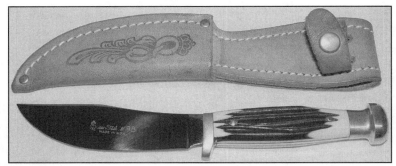

*#98, Queen, hunting knife, imitation Winterbottom bone handles, Queen Steel #98 Made in USA etch, no tang stamp, 4" blade, $40-$50.*

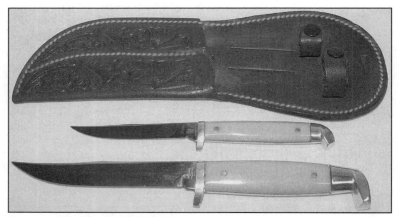

*#99, Queen, twin set hunting knives, amber handles, no etch, Queen over STAINLESS tang stamp, 4" & 3" blades, $110-$135.*

*#99, Queen, hunting knife, red handles, no etch, Q STAINLESS tang stamp, 3" blade, $55-$65.*

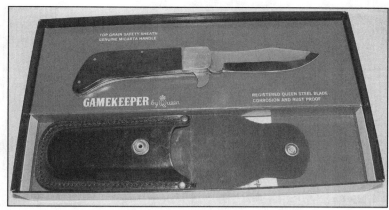

#390, Queen, gamekeeper knife, Micarta handles, no etch, Q STEEL USA tang stamp, 4-1/4" blade, $75-$90. More than one version.

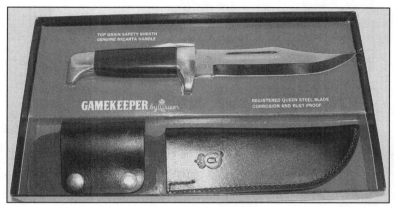

#394, Queen, gamekeeper knife, Micarta handles, no etch, Q STEEL USA tang stamp, 6" blade, $125-$150.

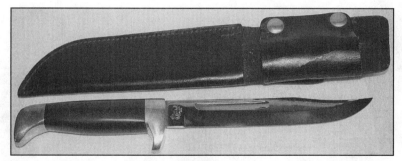

#395, Queen, gamekeeper knife, Micarta handles, no etch, Q STEEL USA tang stamp, 7" blade, $130-$160.

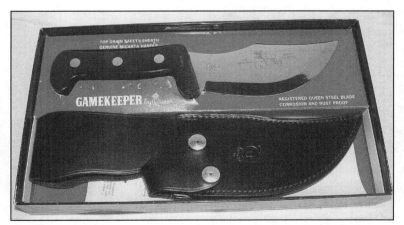

#399, Queen, gamekeeper knife, Micarta handles, moose skinner, The Original Moose Skinner w/moose image etch, Q STEEL USA tang stamp, 5-1/2" blade, $80-$100.

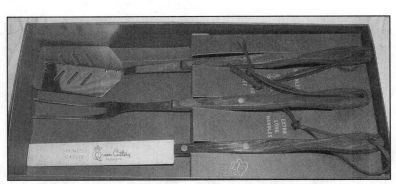

*BBQ set, rosewood handles, no etch, Queen STAINLESS tang stamp.*

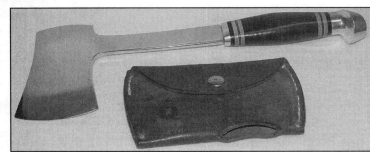

*#SBA80, Queen, archer's axe, stacked leather handle, no etch, Q tang stamp, $35-$45.*

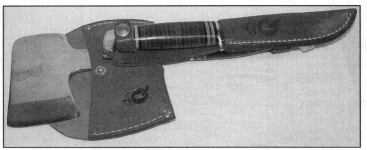

*#KA80, Queen, knife-axe combination, stacked leather handle, no etch, Q tang stamp, $160-$180 w/knife, $130-$150 w/out knife.*

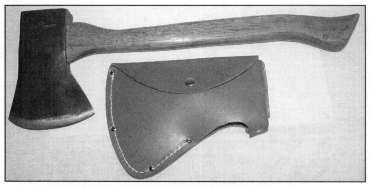

*#SBA78, Queen, single bit camp axe, 16" hickory handle, $225-$250.*

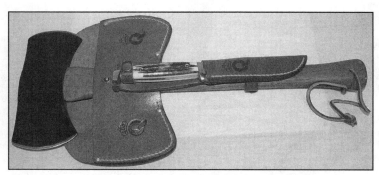

*#DBA79, Queen, double bit one-pound utility axe, 15" hickory handle, $325-$350 w/knife, $275-$300 w/out knife.*

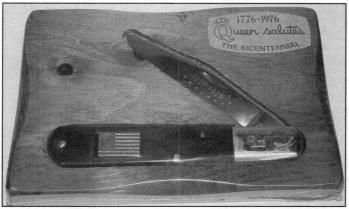

*Bicentennial commemorative granddaddy Barlow, 1776-1976 etch w/stars around date, Q76 tang stamp, 5", $35-$45 in display block.*

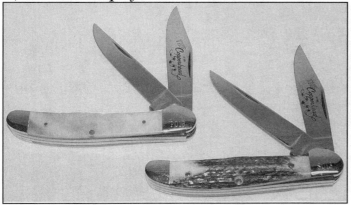

*The Copperhead Set*
*Top: Two blade, pearl handles, brass liners, NS bolsters, The Copperhead 1 of 500 etch, Q81 tang stamp, 6-3/8".*
*Bottom: Two blade, stag handles, brass liners, NS bolsters, The Copperhead 1 of 500 etch, Q81 tang stamp, 6-3/8".*
*Could be bought individually or as a set w/matching serial numbers. All knives are numbered, $75-$85 each, $150-$160 pair.*

*Limited Edition, 2 blade, stag handles, brass liners, NS bolsters, Limited Edition 1980 etch, Q80 tang stamp, 6". One canoe & mini trapper. Knives are serial numbered. $75-$85 each, $150-$160 pair.*

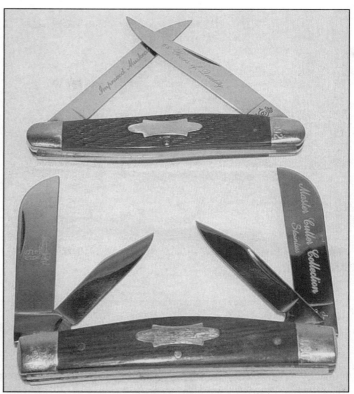

*Top: #32, Queen, large congress, 4 blade, wood handles, brass liners, NS bolsters, Master Cutler Collection etch, big Q tang stamp, 4", $70-85.*
*#66, Queen, muskrat, 2 blade, jigged bone handles,*
*Bottom: brass liners, NS bolsters, 66 Years of Quality on primary blade etch, Improved Muskrat on secondary blade etch, big Q tang stamp, 4", $70-$85. Both knives made in 1988 for 66th anniversary.*

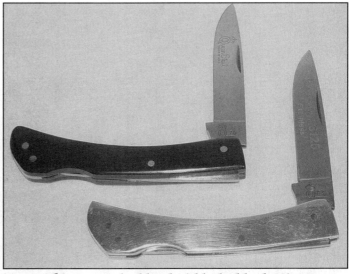

*Top: #365, Queen, lockback, 1 blade, black Micarta handles, brass liners, NS bolsters, Queen Steel Made in U.S.A. etch, Q76 tang stamp, 7", $30-40.*
*Bottom: #6125, Queen, lockback, 1 blade, aluminum handles, brass liners, NS bolsters, Queen 6125 Stainless etch, Q83 tang stamp, 7", $30-$40.*

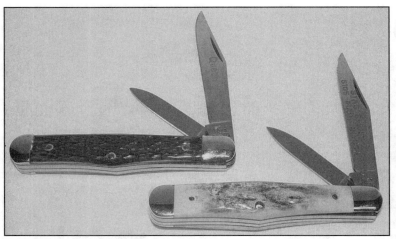
*Whittlers, Rogers bone whittler & stag whittler, $60 to $70 each.*

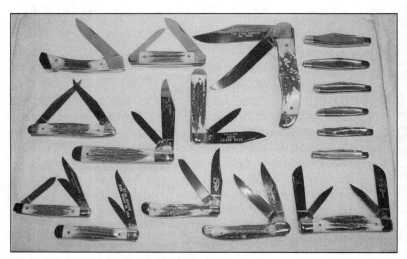
*Group stag & smoked pearl knives.*

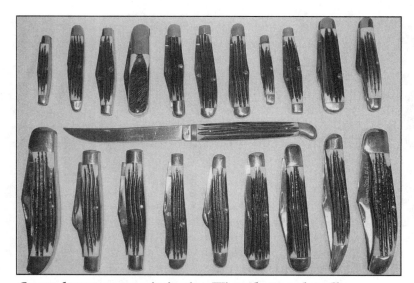
*Group burnt orange imitation Winterbottom handles.*

Kitchen cutlery, nine pieces, Winterbottom bone handles:
(left to right)
S300 slicer, 10" blade.
SS300 sharpening steel, 12-1/2".
CF300 carving fork, 10-1/2".
SF101 steak fork, 9".
H300 steak carver, 6-3/4" blade.
U101 steak knife, 4-11/16" blade.
P300SH sheepfoot paring knife, 2-1/4" blade.
C300 carver, 9" blade.
P300 paring knife, 3" blade.
$20 to $30 each.

# Remington

When Eliphalet Remington started his arms manufacturing plant in 1816, he had no idea this new venture would lead to the eventual production of some of the most highly prized and sought after knives in the world.

Upon his death, the arms company passed to his sons, who soon sold to Marcellus Hartley of Union Metallic Cartridge Company. When Hartley died, his grandson Marcellus Dodge took over both Remington and the Union Metallic Cartridge Company. Since the Remington name was better known, the Union Metallic Cartridge name was dropped; however, most of the knives have UMC stamped within the Remington circle on the tang.

It took more than a century and World War I to spur the company into manufacturing these highly prized knives.

Remington was a major manufacturer of bayonets for WW I and upon the war's end, the company found itself with a tremendous production capability but no contracts; hence, the decision to enter the pocketknife market, which it did in February 1920.

From this beginning, things progressed well within an ever-increasing number of patterns. In 1929, Remington felt the crunch of the Depression and sold controlling interest to the DuPont Company in 1933.

With the war looming ever closer in Europe, the U.S. government began gearing up, and increasing arms contracts pushed pocketknives aside.

Pal Cutlery Company bought the cutlery equipment in approximately 1940.

## Remington Pattern Numbers

The Remington pattern number was stamped on the reverse side of the tang, with either the circle stamp or the straight line. The "circle" was reserved for the higher-quality knives. Some stamps were inked on.

The "R" preceding a number denotes that it is a pocketknife and the last digit reveals the handle material.

## Handle Materials

1. Redwood
2. Black composition
3. Bone
4. Pearl
5. Pyremite
6. Genuine stag
7. Ivory or white bone
8. Cocobolo wood
9. Metal-stainless, nickel, brass, etc.
0. Horn-buffalo, cow
CH. Designates knife with chain.

Author's note: Remington manufactured advertising knives for many companies, but the author has seen very few Remington advertising knives with a pattern number.

## Tips for Remington Collectors

Since Remington only made pocketknives for about 20 years (1920-1940), and Pal Cutlery Company purchased them in approximately 1940 and continued to use parts in inventory to make transition knives after the purchase, very few authentic Remington parts are available to use in counterfeit knives. As a result, you will generally find very poor quality imported copies of Remington patterns and junk knives made from worn authentic parts.

Generally speaking, most counterfeiting of Remington knives occurs with the smaller, less-common patterns, rather than the famous bullet patterns. However, I have seen some counterfeited bullets as well.

As with all knife manufacturers, Remington had a few inconsistencies in various patterns, which causes

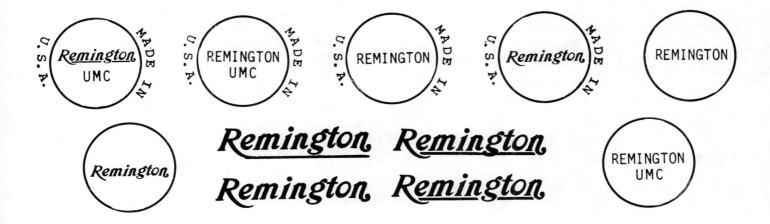

confusion. The following are tips all serious Remington collectors and dealers should know:

## Bullet Patterns
Remington produced 13 bullet patterns:

R293    This is a H.T.T. (Hunter, Trader, Trapper) pattern with two long blades—clip and spey—both with long pulls. The length is 5-1/4". It should have a bullet shield and brown bone handles.

R1123    This is a thick trapper pattern with two long blades with regular pulls. The length is 4-1/2". It has a bullet shield, brown bone handles, and a lanyard hole. It also has grooved bolsters.

R1128    This pattern is identical to the R1123, except it has cocobolo handle material instead of brown bone.

R1173    This pattern is referred to as the baby bullet. It looks like the R1123, except its length is 3-1/2" (1" shorter). It also has bone handles.

R1253L    This is a long hobo pattern, which is a lockback. The length is 5-1/4". It has a bullet shield and brown bone handles. This pattern has one clip blade with a long pull. It sometimes can be found with a bail.

R1263    This pattern has a hobo frame. The length is 5-3/8". It has two blades. The front one is a short pen blade with a regular pull. The back one is a long clip blade with a long pull. It has brown bone handles, a bullet shield, and grooved bolsters.

R1273    This pattern is identical to the R1263, except the long blade in the back is a spear blade instead of a clip blade. This long slender blade also has a long pull.

R1303    The frame of this pattern is the same size and shape as the R1123 (4-1/2"). However, this is a single blade lockback knife. The blade has a regular pull. It also has a bullet shield, brown bone handles, and a lanyard hole.

R1306    This pattern is the same as the R1303, except it has stag handles instead of bone. Some R1306s have a thumb groove on the top of the blade. If the knife has two handle rivets near the bolster, it will have the groove on top of the blade. If there is only one rivet, it will not have the thumb groove.

R1613BL    This is a toothpick pattern. The length is 5". It has a bullet shield, brown bone handles, and grooved bolsters. Remington also made this knife with a cartridge shield instead of a bullet shield. The pattern number is the same, except it does not have "BL" at the end of the number.

R4243    This is a big camp knife pattern. The length is 4-3/4". It has flat grooved bolsters, a bullet shield, brown bone handles, and a bail. This pattern has four blades. A can opener and a punch blade are on one end. The other end has a short sheepfoot blade with a long pull in the front and a long clip blade with a long pull in the back.

R4353    This pattern is referred to as the big muskrat. The length is 4-1/2". It has a blade at each end with regular pulls. The handles are brown bone, and it has a bullet shield.

R4466    This pattern is referred to as the baby muskrat. The length is 3-3/4". It has stag handles, a bullet shield, and grooved bolsters. It has one blade at each end and each blade has a regular pull. Blades are clip and spey.

If you count the stamp variations on the 13 patterns and pin placements on the R1306, probably 25 to 30 different bullet combinations exist; however, the above 13 patterns constitute a complete set. In the past couple of years, a complete set of near-mint bullets sold for approximately $40,000. You can see why these knives are attractive to counterfeiters.

**Additional Information about Bullet Patterns:**
On almost all of the R1128 cocobolo-handled bullets, the "8" in the pattern number looks like it has been stamped over a "3." This is not unusual and should not cause you to be alarmed. Apparently, the factory must have restamped existing R1123 blades for this knife.

A few authentic Pal bullets were made. The master blade was made by Pal and stamped Pal Blade Co. Because the examples found were used, it is uncertain whether there was an original blade etch.

On the R4353 big muskrat, the master blade is supposed to be a plain unmarked blade. However, a few did have a Remington blade etching. Normally, two-bladed bullets had a Remington etch on the big spey blade.

## Tips on Remington Patterns That Are Not Bullets

The R3943 sleeveboard pattern normally only has a blade etch and no tang stamp. However, a few were made with both a tang stamp and blade etch.

Remington also made another advertising knife with a special stamp on the front tang. It was made for Quickpoint in St. Louis, Missouri.

Most Remington patterns with a punch blade have an acorn shield. Some exceptions are the R4283 five-blade sowbelly, the R3843 six-blade utility knife, some R100 patterns, the 4243 camp bullet, and some official Scout knives. There may be others as well.

Remington made three patterns with five blades. They are the R3143 stockman, R4283 sowbelly, and R3843 Scout. Remington did not make a knife with more than five blades.

Remington actually made a knife with smoked pearl handles about 1920, before Queen Cutlery, which is often credited with first using smoked pearl handle material.

Remington produced three types of dog-groomer knives. The R4733 was made with and without an Airedale dog-head shield. There was also a thinner version made, which had no pattern number or shield. All three knives had two dog-groomer blades, one at each end.

Other than the bullet patterns, Remington made very few folding knives with stag handles. They are all considered to be rare and very collectible.

For about four years, Remington inked on pattern numbers and blade markings. This was not just on cheaper patterns. This process was used from about 1936 to 1940 (Remington was bought by Pal Cutlery Co. in 1940).

Remington produced many various advertising knives. Most of these did not have pattern numbers on them. Roughly five percent of these knives did have a number on the blade. This probably occurred because some blades in inventory already had numbers on them and they were pulled out of inventory to complete an order or finish a production run of a certain advertising knife.

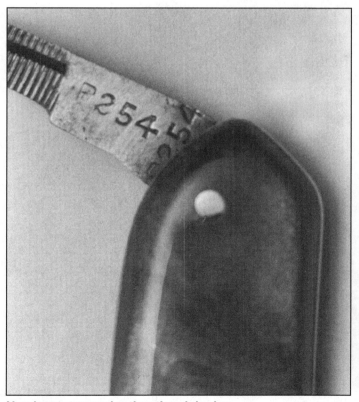

**Numbers stamped rather than inked on.**

## Examples of Remington Tang Stamps

Remington used about a dozen different tang stamps in its 20 years of pocketknife production. These were all variations of either the circle stamp or the straight-line stamp. For example, these are the more frequently used stamps, and the years used.

## Other Facts about Remington Knives

- Knives w/REMINGTON UMC within a circle were made from 1921 to 1924.
- Knives w/MADE IN USA outside of the circle were made from 1924 to 1933.
- Knives w/REMINGTON in the circle and MADE IN USA outside the circle were made from 1933 to 1935.
- Same as above, but w/REMINGTON in script instead of block were made from 1935 to 1940.

Note: All prices given are mint value.

| Description | Price |
| --- | --- |
| RA1, redwood, 3-3/8" | 125 |
| R015, pyremite | 100 |
| R15, 2 blade, small leg, grey swirl pyremite, Remington Circle UMC, 3-1/4" | 300 |
| R17, switchblade/pull ball, white composition, 2-3/4" | 250 |
| R21CH, jack, redwood bl., chain, 3-3/8" | 150 |
| R23CH, 2-blade jack, bone, 3-3/8" | 150 |
| R23CH, 2 blade w/chain, imitation black bone, Remington UMC, 3-3/8" | 150 |
| RLO24, letter opener | 150 |
| R25, 2-blade jack, white pyremite, 3-3/8" | 125 |
| R31, redwood, 3-3/8" | 125 |
| R32, 2-blade jack, black, 3-3/8" | 125 |
| R35, pyremite, 3-3/8" | 125 |

*RA1, redwood, 3-3/8", $125.*

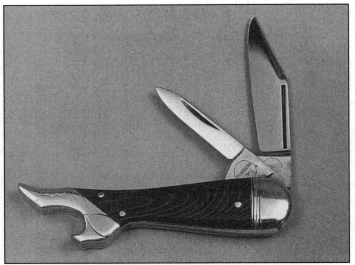

R15, 2 blade, small leg, grey swirl pyremite, Remington Circle UMC, 3-1/4", $300.

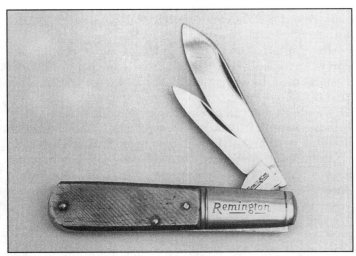

RB040, Barlow spear, regular pull, brown bone, 3-3/8", $150.

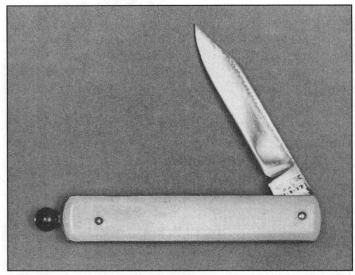

R17, switchblade/pull ball, white composition, 2-3/4", $250.

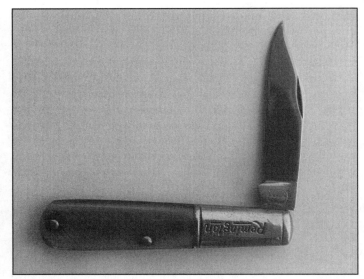

RB041, Barlow, bone, 3-3/8", $150.

R23CH, 2-blade w/chain, imitation black bone, Remington UMC, 3-3/8", $150.

RB43, Barlow, 2-blade, long pull, Remington Circle UMC, 3-3/8", $175.

Remington 421

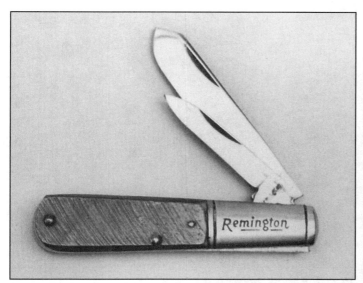

*RB44, Barlow (clip), brown bone, 3-3/8", $150.*

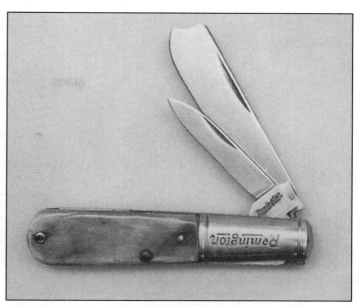

*RB47, Barlow, brown bone, 3-3/8", $200.*

*RB45, Barlow (spey), brown bone, 3-3/8", $175.*

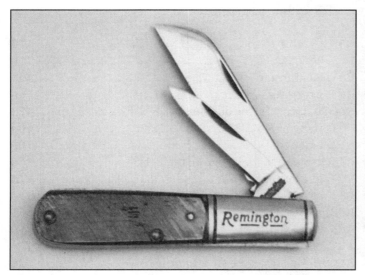

*RB46, Barlow (sheepfoot), brown bone, 3-3/8", $200.*

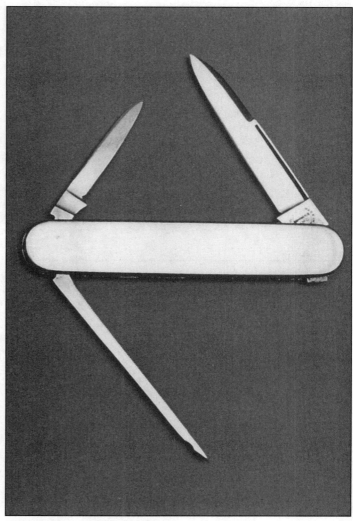

*R64, lobster, metal, $100.*

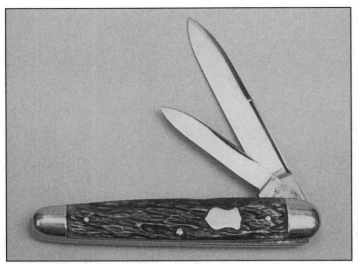

*R73, 2-blade jack, brown bone, 3-1/8", $140.*

*RC090, Barlow, pyremite handle, 3-3/8", $125.*

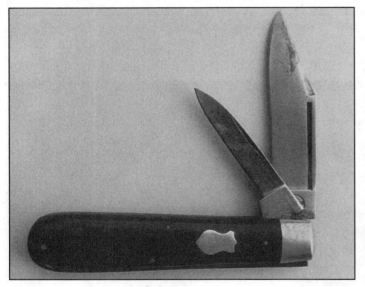

*R81, redwood, 3-1/2", $110.*

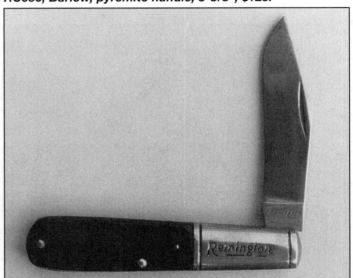

*RC091, Barlow, horn, 3-3/8", $125.*

| Description | Price |
|---|---|
| **RLO35**, letter opener | 125 |
| **RB040**, Barlow, spear blade, brown bone, 3-3/8" | 150 |
| **RB040**, Barlow spear, regular pull, brown bone, 3-3/8" | 150 |
| **RB041**, Barlow, bone, 3-3/8" | 150 |
| **RB43**, Barlow, 2-blade, LP, Remington Circle UMC, 3-3/8" | 175 |
| **RB44**, Barlow (clip), brown bone, 3-3/8" | 150 |
| **RB44W**, white, 3-3/8" | 150 |
| **R473**, bone, slant bolster, 3-1/4" | 250 |
| **RB45**, Barlow (spey), brown bone, 3-3/8" | 175 |
| **RB46**, Barlow (sheepfoot), brown bone, 3-3/8" | 200 |
| **RB47**, Barlow, brown bone, 3-3/8" | 200 |
| **R51**, redwood | 90 |
| **R52**, black | 160 |
| **R53**, bone | 180 |

| Description | Price |
|---|---|
| **R55**, pyremite | 170 |
| **R63**, bone | 170 |
| **R64**, lobster, metal | 100 |
| **R65**, pyremite | 100 |
| **RLO70**, fancy letter opener | 175 |
| **R71**, redwood, 3-1/8" | 100 |
| **R72**, black, 3-1/8" | 100 |
| **R73**, 2-blade jack, brown bone, 3-1/8" | 140 |
| **R75**, pyremite, 3-1/8" | 125 |
| **R81**, redwood, 3-1/2" | 110 |
| **R82**, black, 3-1/2" | 115 |
| **R83**, bone, 3-1/2" | 150 |
| **R85**, pyremite, 3-1/2" | 125 |
| **RC090**, Barlow, pyremite handle, 3-3/8" | 125 |
| **R91**, redwood | 130 |
| **RC091**, Barlow, horn, 3-3/8" | 125 |

# Remington 423

*R100A, bone, Hildelgo steel etch, 3-3/8", $300.*

*R100B, etched Remington standard dollar knife, bone. Note: punch blade but no acorn shield, $400.*

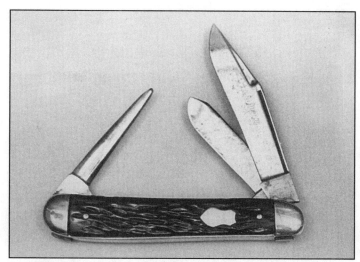

*R100R, punch blade, long pull, brown bone, enclosed backspring, 3-3/8", $300.*

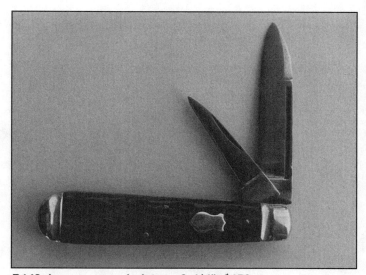

*R143, bone, recess bolsters, 3-1/4", $150.*

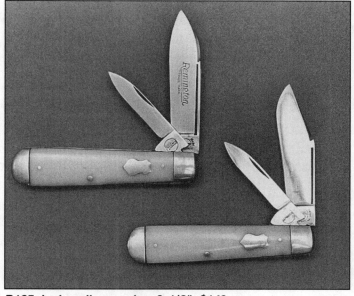

*R165, jack, yellow scales, 3-1/2", $140.*

| Description | Price |
|---|---|
| **R92**, black | 140 |
| **R93**, bone | 165 |
| **R95**, pyremite | 130 |
| **R100**, bone backsprings not covered, 3-1/4" | 160 |
| **R100A**, bone, Hildelgo steel etch, 3-3/8" | 300 |
| **R100B**, bone, etched Remington standard dollar knife, Note: punch blade but no acorn shield | 400 |
| **R100R**, punch blade, long pull, brown bone, enclosed backspring, 3-3/8" | 300 |
| **R102A**, black composition, 3-1/8" | 200 |
| **R102CH**, black, 3-1/2" | 140 |
| **R103CH**, bone, 3-1/2" | 150 |
| **R105B**, punch blade, pyremite, 3-3/8" | 150 |
| **R108CH**, cocobolo | 100 |
| **R111**, redwood | 100 |
| **R112**, black | 100 |

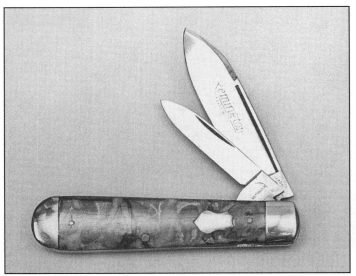

*R165, jack, pyremite, 3-1/2", $165.*

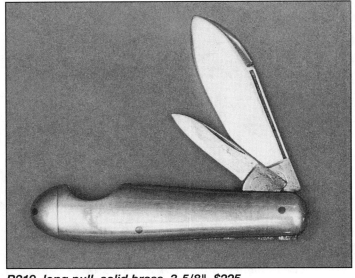

*R219, long pull, solid brass, 3-5/8", $225.*

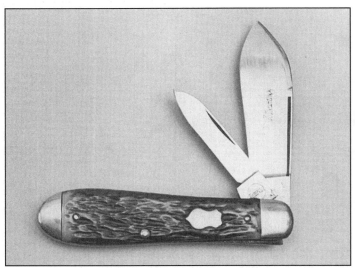

*R173, jack, teardrop, brown bone, 3-3/4", $250.*

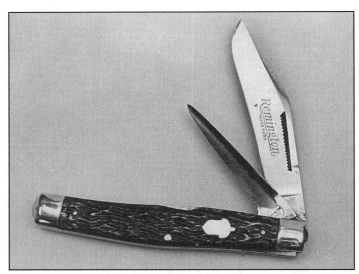

*R273, Texas jack, brown bone, acorn shield, 4", $300.*

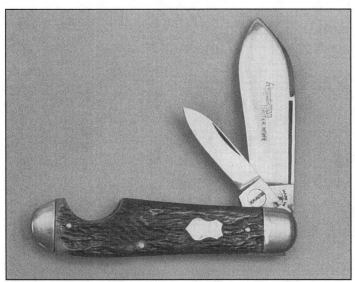

*R203, jack/easy opener, brown bone, 3-5/8", $275.*

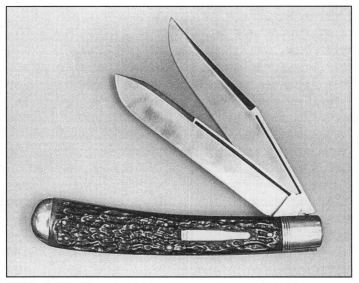

*R293, H.T.T. (Hunter, Trader, Trapper), long pull, brown bone, bullet shield, 5-1/4", $3,500.*

| Description | Price |
|---|---|
| R113, bone | 145 |
| R115, pyremite | 115 |
| R122, black, 3-1/2" | 135 |
| R123, bone, 3-1/2" | 150 |
| R125, pyremite, 3-1/2" | 135 |
| R131, redwood | 135 |
| R132, black | 135 |
| R133, bone | 160 |
| R135, pyremite | 150 |
| R141, redwood, 3-1/4" | 125 |
| R142, black, 3-1/4" | 125 |
| R143, bone, recess bolsters, 3-1/4" | 150 |
| R145, pyremite, 3-1/4" | 150 |
| R151, redwood, 3-1/2" | 140 |
| R152, black, 3-1/2" | 140 |
| R153, bone, 3-1/2" | 160 |
| R155, pyremite, 3-1/2" | 140 |
| R161, 2-blade jack, redwood, 3-1/2" | 140 |
| R162, 2-blade jack, black, 3-1/2" | 140 |
| R163, 2-blade jack, bone, 3-1/2" | 160 |
| R165, jack, yellow scale, 3-1/2" | 140 |
| R165, jack, pyremite, 3-1/2" | 165 |
| R171, redwood, 3-3/4" | 150 |
| R172, black, 3-3/4" | 150 |
| R173, jack, teardrop, brown bone, 3-3/4" | 250 |
| R175, pyremite, 3-3/4" | 175 |
| R181, redwood, 3-5/8" | 150 |
| R183, bone, 3-5/8" | 180 |
| R185, pyremite, 3-5/8" | 155 |
| R191, redwood | 140 |
| R192, black | 140 |
| R193, bone | 180 |
| R195, pyremite | 160 |
| R201, easy opener jack, redwood, 3-5/8" | 150 |
| R202, easy opener jack, black, 3-5/8" | 150 |
| R203, jack/easy opener, brown bone, 3-5/8" | 275 |
| R205, easy opener jack, pyremite, 3-5/8" | 200 |
| R211, redwood | 150 |
| R212, easy opener jack, black, 3-5/8" | 150 |
| R213, easy opener jack, bone, 3-5/8" | 180 |
| R219, long pull, solid brass, 3-5/8" | 225 |
| R222, black | 130 |
| R223, bone | 180 |
| R225, pyremite | 150 |
| R228, cocobolo | 140 |
| R232, black | 140 |
| R233, bone | 180 |
| R235, pyremite | 160 |
| R238, cocobolo | 130 |
| R242, black | 180 |
| R243, bone | 200 |

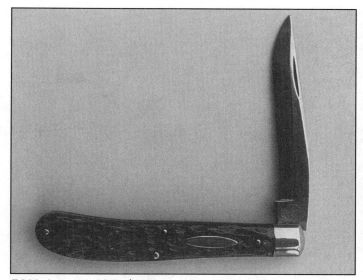

*R303, bone, 3-3/4", $250.*

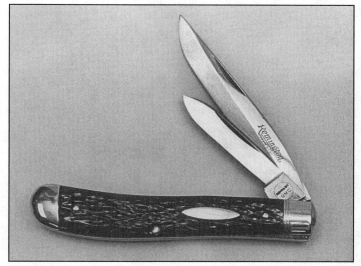

*R313, trapper w/pen, saber, brown bone, 3-7/8", $600.*

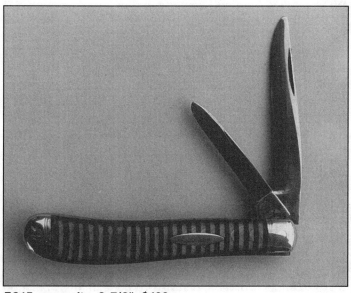

*R315, pyremite, 3-7/8", $400.*

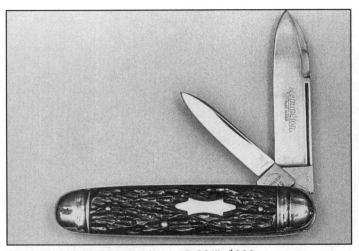
*R333, equal end, brown bone, 3-3/4", $200.*

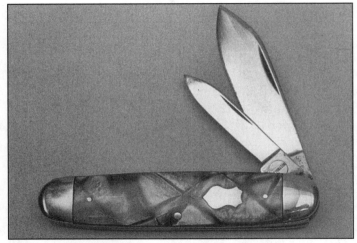
*R365, jack, gold swirl pyremite, 3-3/4", $225.*

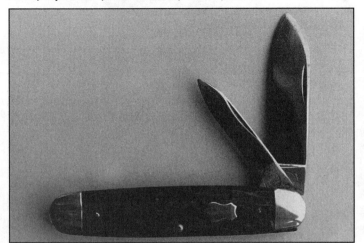
*R363, bone, 3-3/4", $200.*

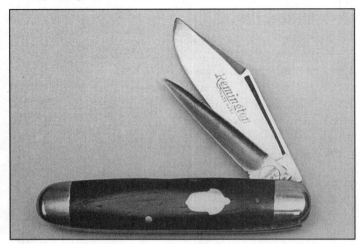
*R378, equal end jack, cocobolo, acorn shield, 3-3/4", $250.*

| Description | Price |
|---|---|
| R245, pyremite | 180 |
| R248, cocobolo | 160 |
| R252, black | 150 |
| R253, bone | 180 |
| R255, pyremite | 170 |
| R258, cocobolo | 150 |
| R262, black, 4" | 140 |
| R263, 2-blade jack, bone, 4" | 225 |
| R272, black | 225 |
| R273, Texas jack, brown bone, acorn shield, 4" | 300 |
| R275, jack, pyremite, candy stripe, 4" | 300 |
| R275, pyremite, 4" | 300 |
| R282, black | 170 |
| R283, bone | 200 |
| R293, H.T.T. (Hunter, Trader, Trapper), long pull, brown bone, bullet shield, 5-1/4" | 3,500 |
| R303, bone, 3-3/4" | 250 |
| R305, pyremite, 3-3/4" | 250 |
| R313, trapper w/pen, saber, brown bone, 3-7/8" | 600 |
| R315, pyremite, 3-7/8" | 400 |

| Description | Price |
|---|---|
| R322, black | 160 |
| R323, bone | 180 |
| R325, pyremite | 170 |
| R328, cocobolo | 160 |
| R333, equal end, brown bone, 3-3/4" | 200 |
| R341, redwood | 170 |
| R342, black | 170 |
| R343, bone | 200 |
| R352, 2 blade equal-end jack, black, 3-3/4" | 200 |
| R353, 2 blade equal end jack, bone, 3-3/4" | 225 |
| R355, 2 blade equal jack, pyremite, 3-3/4" | 200 |
| R358, cocobolo, 3-3/4" | 175 |
| R363, bone, 3-3/4" | 200 |
| R365, jack, gold swirl pyremite, 3-3/4" | 225 |
| R372, equal-end jack, black, 3-3/4" | 175 |
| R373, equal-end jack, bone, 3-3/4" | 200 |
| R375, equal-end jack, pyremite, 3-3/4 | 200 |
| R378, equal end jack, cocobolo, acorn shield, 3-3/4" | 250 |
| R391, teardrop jack, redwood, 3-3/8" | 160 |
| R392, teardrop jack, black, 3-3/8" | 160 |

Remington 427

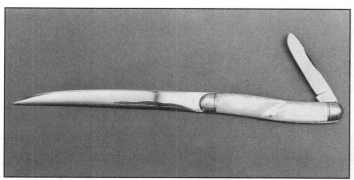

*R393, teardrop jack, bone, 3-3/8", $225*

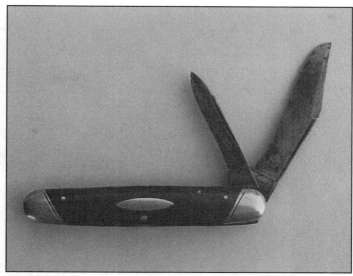

*R475, pyremite, slant bolsters, 3-1/4", $250.*

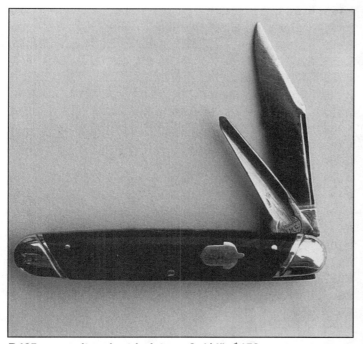

*R465, pyremite, slant bolsters, 3-1/4", $150.*

*R485, pyremite, 3-1/2", $175.*

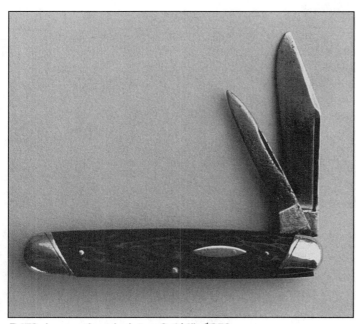

*R473, bone, slant bolster, 3-1/4", $250.*

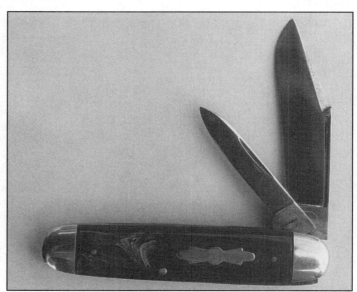

*R515, pyremite, 3-1/2", $225.*

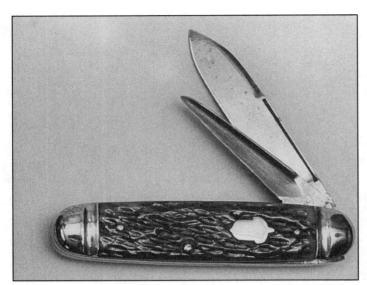

*R553, brown bone, acorn shield, 3-1/4", $200.*

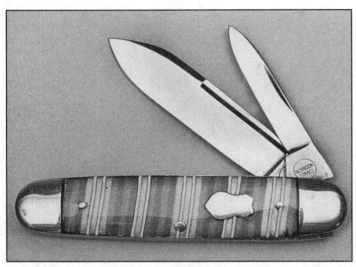

*R555, jack, candy-stripe scales, Remington Circle UMC, 3-1/4", $225.*

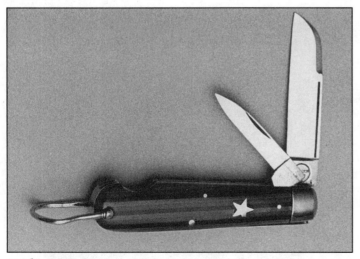

*R565, 2 blade, red, white & blue w/star, Remington Circle, 3-1/2", $350.*

| Description | Price |
|---|---|
| **R393**, teardrop jack, bone, 3-3/8" | 225 |
| **R402**, black | 150 |
| **R403**, bone | 185 |
| **R405**, pyremite | 170 |
| **R410**, buffalo horn | 150 |
| **R412**, black | 150 |
| **R415**, pyremite | 170 |
| **R423**, bone | 170 |
| **R432**, black, 3-1/2" | 250 |
| **R435**, pyremite, 3-1/2" | 250 |
| **R443**, bond | 450 |
| **R444**, doctor's knife, spatula blade, pearl | 500 |
| **R453**, bone | 360 |
| **R455**, pyremite | 300 |
| **R463**, equal-end jack, bone, 3-1/4" | 170 |
| **R465**, pyremite, slant bolsters, 3-1/4" | 150 |
| **R475**, pyremite, slant bolsters, 3-1/4" | 250 |
| **R482**, black, 3-1/2" | 150 |
| **R483**, bone, 3-1/2" | 180 |
| **R485**, pyremite, 3-1/2" | 175 |
| **R488**, equal end, 2 blade spear, cocobolo, 3-1/2" | 150 |
| **R493**, bone | 180 |
| **R495**, pyremite | 180 |
| **R503**, bone | 180 |
| **R505**, pyremite | 180 |
| **R512**, equal-end jack, black, 3-1/2" | 200 |
| **R513**, equal-end jack, bone, 3-1/2" | 225 |
| **R515**, pyremite, 3-1/2" | 225 |
| **R523**, bone | 200 |
| **R525**, pyremite | 200 |
| **R551**, redwood, 3-1/4" | 150 |
| **R552**, black, 3-1/4" | 150 |
| **R553**, brown bone, acorn shield, 3-1/4" | 200 |
| **R555**, jack, candy-stripe scales, Remington Circle UMC, 3-1/4" | 225 |
| **R565**, 2 blade, red, white & blue w/star, Remington Circle, 3-1/2" | 350 |
| **R572**, black | 150 |
| **R575**, pyremite, 3-1/4" | 225 |
| **R583**, bone | 200 |
| **R585**, pyremite | 200 |
| **R590**, 2 blades, buffalo horn, slant bolsters, 3-1/4" | 250 |
| **R593**, jack, 2 blades, bone, slant bolsters, 3-1/4" | 250 |
| **R595**, jack, 2 blades, pyremite, slant bolsters, 3-1/4" | 250 |
| **R603**, small serpentine jack, bone, 3-3/8" | 125 |
| **R605**, jack, gold swirl pyremite, 3-3/8" | 150 |
| **R609**, metal, 3-3/8" | 140 |
| **R613**, bone | 200 |
| **R615**, pyremite | 200 |
| **R622**, black, 4" | 200 |
| **R623**, bone, 4" | 275 |

*R575, pyremite, 3-1/4", $225*

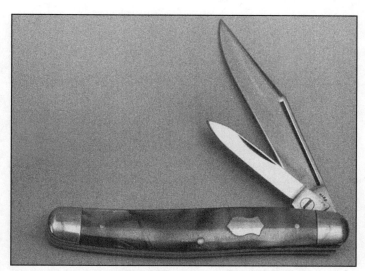

*R605, jack, gold swirl pyremite, 3-3/8", $150.*

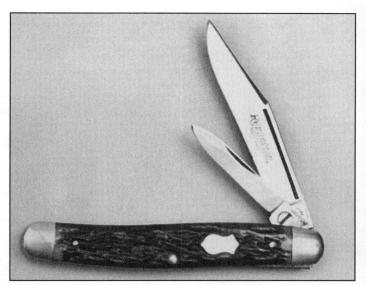

*R603, small serpentine jack, bone, 3-3/8", $125.*

| Description | Price |
|---|---|
| **R625**, pyremite, 4" | 275 |
| **R629**, lobster, metal, w/bail, 2-3/4" | 90 |
| **R633**, bone | 200 |
| **R635**, pyremite | 200 |
| **R643**, bone | 250 |
| **R645**, switchblade, candy stripe, 4" | 1,000 |
| **R645**, pyremite | 250 |
| **R653**, bow tie, bone, 3-7/8" | 400 |
| **R655**, pyremite, bow tie, 3-7/8" | 450 |
| **R663**, bone | 300 |
| **R668**, cocobolo | 275 |
| **R672**, 2 blade dogleg jack, black, 3" | 175 |
| **R673**, bone, 3" | 200 |
| **R674**, 2 blade dogleg jack, pearl, 3" | 225 |
| **R675**, 2 blade, dogleg jack, pyremite, 3" | 200 |

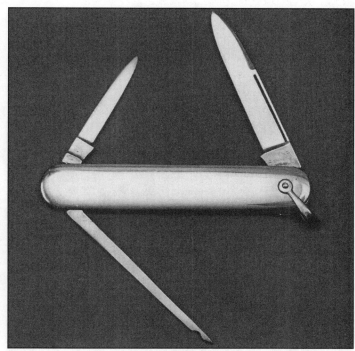

*R629, lobster, metal, w/bail, 2-3/4", $90.*

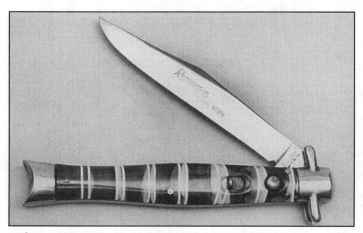

*R645, switchblade, candy stripe, 4", $1,000.*

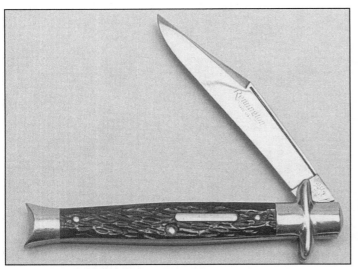

*R653, bow tie, bone, 3-7/8", $400.*

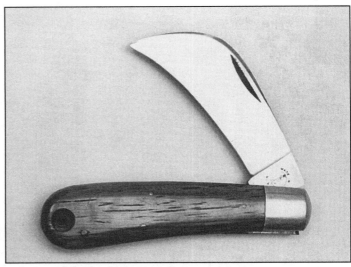

*R698, hawkbill, cocobolo, 4", $125.*

*R673, bone, 3", $200.*

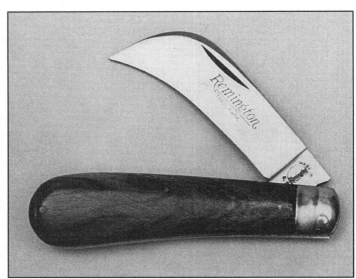

*R708, hawkbill, cocobolo, 3-5/8", $125.*

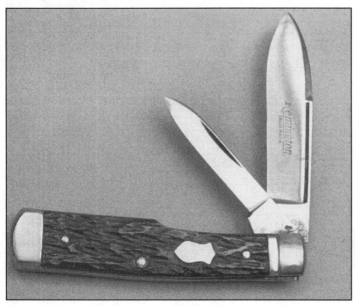

*R683, gunstock, long pull, brown bone, 3", $550.*

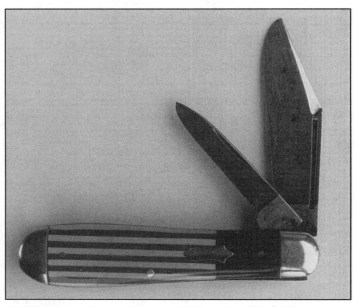

*R775, pyremite, red, white & blue, 3-1/2", $400.*

| Description | Price |
|---|---|
| **R677**, 2 blade dogleg jack, ivory, 3" | 200 |
| **R682**, gunstock, black, 3" | 450 |
| **R683**, gunstock, long pull, brown bone, 3" | 550 |
| **R684**, gunstock, pearl, 3" | 650 |
| **R685**, gunstock, pyremite, 3" | 500 |
| **R693**, hawkbill, bone, 4" | 175 |
| **R698**, hawkbill, cocobolo, 4" | 125 |
| **R703**, small hawkbill, bone, 3-5/8" | 200 |
| **R706**, small hawkbill, genuine stag, 3-5/8" | 250 |
| **R708**, hawkbill, cocobolo, 3-5/8" | 125 |
| **R713**, bone, 3-3/4" | 225 |
| **R718**, 2 blade hawkbill, cocobolo, 3-3/4" | 200 |
| **R723**, large 1 blade hawkbill, bone, 4-1/2" | 250 |
| **R728**, large 1 blade hawkbill, cocobolo, 4-1/2" | 225 |
| **R732**, black | 120 |
| **R733**, bone | 160 |
| **R735**, pyremite | 140 |
| **R738**, cocobolo | 120 |
| **R743**, bone | 160 |
| **R745**, pyremite | 135 |
| **R753**, bone, 3-1/2" | 275 |
| **R755**, pyremite, red, white & blue, 3-1/2" | 350 |
| **R756**, genuine stag, 3-1/2" | 400 |
| **R763**, bone | 200 |
| **R772**, black | 150 |
| **R773**, bone | 175 |
| **R775**, pyremite, red, white & blue, 3-1/2" | 400 |
| **R783**, bone | 190 |
| **R793**, bone | 230 |
| **R803**, bone, 3" | 100 |
| **RC803**, bone, 3" | 50 |
| **R805**, pyremite | 100 |
| **R813**, bone | 220 |
| **R823**, bone | 170 |
| **R825**, pyremite | 135 |
| **R833**, 2 blade serpentine, long spey, bone, 3-5/8" | 275 |
| **R835**, 2 blade serpentine, long spey, pyremite, 3-5/8" | 275 |
| **R843**, bone | 170 |
| **R845**, pyremite | 140 |
| **R853**, bone | 175 |
| **R855**, pyremite | 150 |

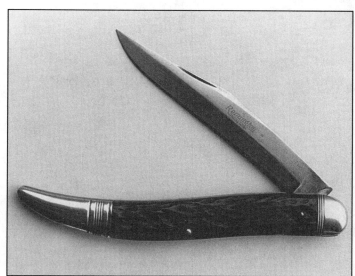

*R933, saber blade, bone, 5", $450.*

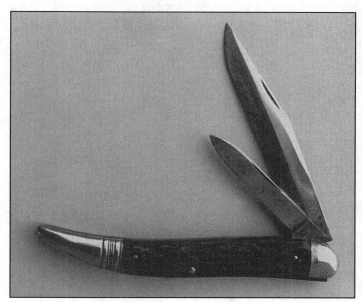

*R943, bone, 5", $500.*

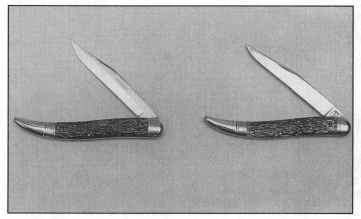

**Toothpicks**
Left: *R953, saber blade, brown bone, grooved bolster, 5", $500.*
Right: *R953, flat blade, brown bone, grooved bolster, no shield, 5", $300.*

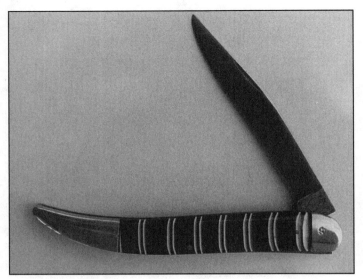

*R955, pyremite candy stripe, 5", $350.*

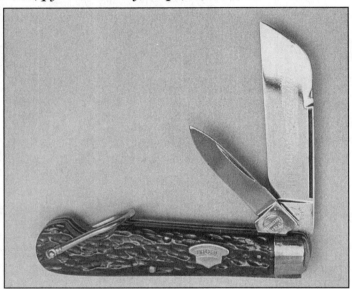

*R963, Scout/easy opener, sheepfoot blade, bone, Scout hat shield, bail, $800.*

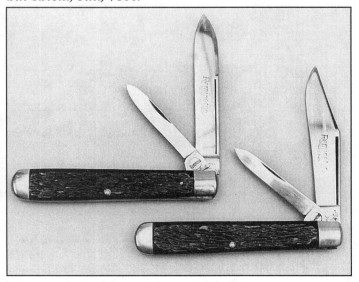

*R973, jack, imitation bone, 4-1/4", $450.*

| Description | Price |
|---|---|
| **R863**, bone | 210 |
| **R865**, pyremite | 150 |
| **R873**, 2 blade sleeve board jack, bone, 3-1/8" | 110 |
| **R874**, 2 blade sleeve board jack, pearl, 3-1/8" | 125 |
| **R875**, 2 blade sleeve board jack, pyremite, 3-1/8" | 110 |
| **R881**, redwood | 120 |
| **R882**, black | 125 |
| **R883**, bone | 160 |
| **R892**, black | 140 |
| **R893**, bone | 200 |
| **R895**, pyremite | 170 |
| **R901**, redwood | 140 |
| **R913**, bone, # front tang | 200 |
| **R921**, 1 blade maize, redwood, 4-1/8" | 200 |
| **R932**, black | 250 |
| **R933**, saber blade, bone, 5" | 450 |
| **R935**, 2 blade toothpick, pyremite, 5" | 350 |
| **R942**, 2 blade toothpick, black, 5" | 450 |
| **R943**, bone, 5" | 500 |
| **R945**, pyremite, 5" | 500 |
| **R953**, saber blade, brown bone, grooved bolster, 5" | 500 |
| **R953**, flat blade, brown bone, grooved bolster, no shield, 5" | 300 |
| **R953**, brown bone, 5" | 300 |
| **R953**, brown bone, Remington UMC, round bullet shield, 5" | 700 |
| **R955**, pyremite candy stripe, 5" | 350 |
| **R962**, black, 4-1/4" | 225 |
| **R963**, Scout/easy opener, sheepfoot blade, bone, Scout hat shield, ball | 800 |
| **R965**, pyremite, 4-1/4" | 225 |
| **R973**, jack, imitation bone, 4-1/4" | 450 |
| **R982SAB**, 2 dogleg jack, black, 2-7/8" | 150 |
| **R983**, 2 blade dogleg jack, SAB, bone, 2-7/8" | 300 |
| **R985**, 2 blade dogleg jack, SAB, pyremite, 2-7/8" | 300 |
| **R992**, black, 3-1/4" | 115 |
| **R993**, bone, 3-1/4" | 130 |
| **R995**, jack, blue & white composition, 3-1/4" | 125 |
| **R1002**, 2 blade jack, black, grooved, front bolsters, 3-5/8" | 200 |
| **R1003**, 2 blade jack, bone, grooved, front bolsters, 3-3/8" | 225 |
| **R1005**, 2 blade jack, pyremite, grooved, front bolsters, 3-5/8" | 225 |
| **R1012**, 2 blade jack, black, 3-5/8" | 150 |
| **R1013**, 2 blade jack, bone, 3-5/8" | 200 |
| **R1022**, large English-style jack, black, 4-1/4" | 500 |
| **R1023**, large English-style jack, bone, 4-1/4" | 500 |
| **R1032**, 2 blade teardrop jack, black, 3-3/8" | 100 |
| **R1033**, 2 blade teardrop jack, bone, 3-3/8" | 115 |

Remington 433

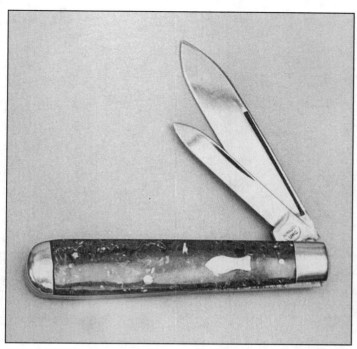

*R995, jack, blue & white composition, 3-1/4", $125.*

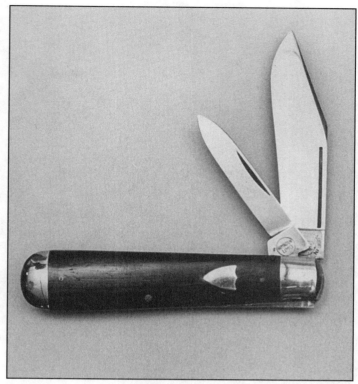

*R1071, cocobolo (shows 2 blade styles), 3-3/8", $150.*

*R1063, pyremite, 3-3/8", $200.*

| Description | Price |
| --- | --- |
| **R1035**, 2 blade teardrop jack, pyremite, 3-3/8" | 100 |
| **R1042**, 2 blade jack, black, 3-3/8" | 150 |
| **R1043**, 2 blade jack, bone, 3-3/8" | 200 |
| **R1045**, 2 blade jack, pyremite, 3-3/8" | 175 |
| **R1051**, 1 blade budding knife, redwood, 3-1/2" | 125 |
| **R1053**, 2 blade jack, bone, 3-1/2" | 125 |
| **R1055**, 2 blade jack, punch, pyremite, 3-3/8" | 150 |
| **R1061**, 2 blade jack, redwood, 3-3/8" | 90 |
| **R1063**, 2 blade jack, bone, 3-3/8" | 130 |

*R1073, bone, 3-3/8", $200.*

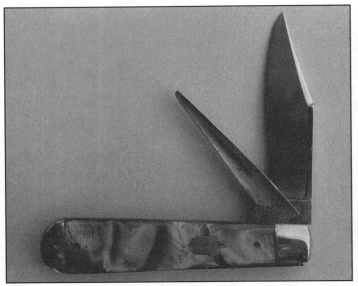

**R1075, punch, pyremite, 3-3/8", $200.**

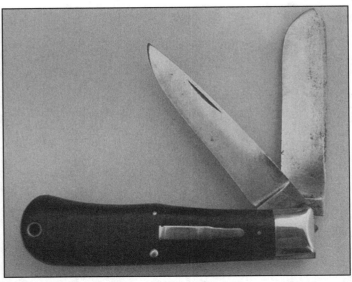

**R1128, bullet, cocobolo, 4-1/2", $4,000.**

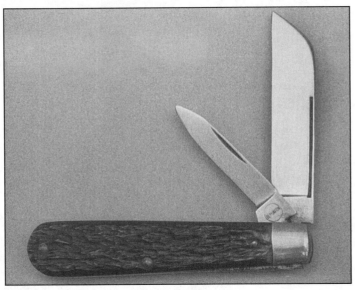

**R1103, brown bone, 3-3/8", $135.**

**R1143, barehead English jack, bone, 4-3/8", $500**

**Top: R1123, brown bone, bullet shield, 4-1/2", $3,000.**
**Bottom: R1173, brown bone, baby bullet, 3-1/2", $7,000.**

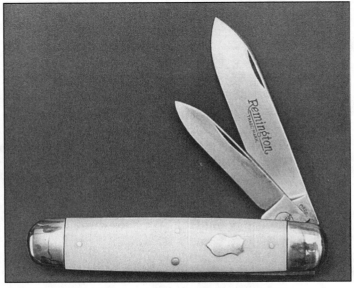

**R1225, jack, white composition, 4-1/4", $275.**

| Description | Price |
|---|---|
| **R1063**, barehead jack, bone, 3-3/8" | 200 |
| **R1063**, pyremite, 3-3/8" | 200 |
| **R1071**, cocobolo (shows 2 blade styles), 3-3/8" | 150 |
| **R1072**, 2 blade jack, black, 3-3/8" | 125 |
| **R1073**, bone, 3-3/8" | 200 |
| **R1075**, punch, pyremite, 3-3/8" | 200 |
| **R1082**, 1 blade sheepfoot, LP, black, 3-3/8" | 80 |
| **R1083**, 1 blade sheepfoot, LP, bone, 3-3/8" | 100 |
| **R1085**, 1 blade sheepfoot, LP, pyremite, 3-3/8" | 100 |
| **R1092**, black | 75 |
| **R1093**, bone | 90 |
| **R1102**, 2 blade barehead jack, black, 3-3/8" | 95 |
| **R1103**, brown bone, 3-3/8" | 135 |
| **R1112**, black | 95 |
| **R1113**, bone, 3-3/8" | 125 |
| **R1123**, bullet shield, brown bone, 4-1/2" | 3,000 |
| **R1128**, bullet, cocobolo, 4-1/2" | 4,000 |
| **R1133**, bone | 160 |
| **R1143**, barehead English jack, bone, 4-3/8" | 500 |
| **R1173**, baby bullet, brown bone, 3-1/2" | 7,000 |
| **R1182**, black | 125 |
| **R1192**, black | 100 |
| **R1193**, bone | 125 |
| **R1202**, black | 140 |
| **R1203**, bone | 150 |
| **R1212**, black | 235 |
| **R1213**, bone | 300 |
| **R1222**, black, 4-1/4" | 250 |
| **R1223**, bone, 4-1/4" | 300 |
| **R1225**, jack, white composition, 4-1/4" | 275 |
| **R1232**, black, 3-5/8" | 150 |
| **R1233**, swell center, Coke, saber spear, LP spear, bone | 300 |
| **R1240**, Daddy Barlow, long pull, bone, 5" | 300 |
| **R1240**, Daddy Barlow, long pull, bone, 5" | 300 |
| **R1240**, Barlow, brown bone, 5" | 300 |
| **R1241**, Daddy Barlow, redwood, 5" | 285 |
| **R1242**, Daddy Barlow, black, 5" | 300 |
| **R1243**, Daddy Barlow, bone, 5" | 300 |
| **R1245C**, Barlow, cracked ice, 5" | 400 |
| **R1253L**, long pull, lockback, brown bone, bullet shield, 5-1/4" | 3,000 |
| **R1255**, pyremite, candy stripe, 4-1/4" | 400 |

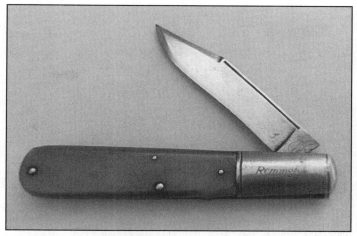

*R1240, Remington Daddy Barlow, long pull, bone, 5", $300.*

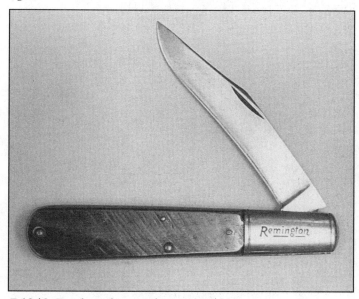

*R1240, Barlow, brown bone, 5", $300*

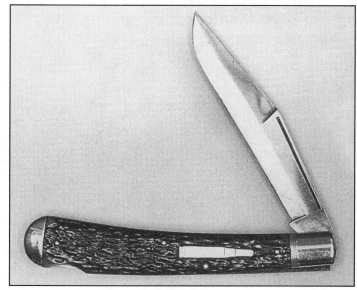

*R1253L, long pull, lockback, brown bone, bullet shield, 5-1/4", $3,000.*

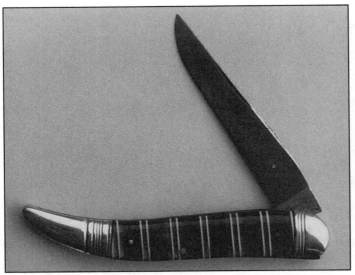

***R1255**, pyremite, candy stripe, 4-1/4", $400.*

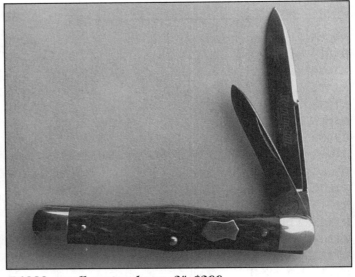

***R1283**, swell center, bone, 3", $200.*

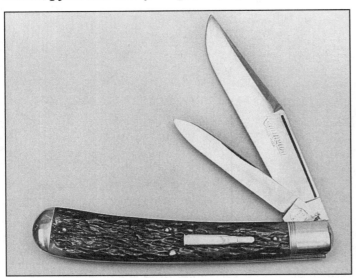

***R1263**, Remington bullet, brown bone, 5-3/8", $4,000.*

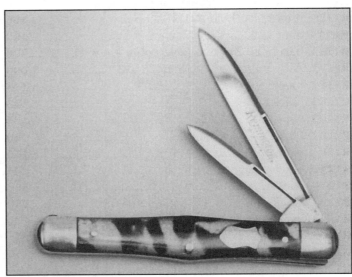

***R1285**, swell center, tortoise shell, 3", $200.*

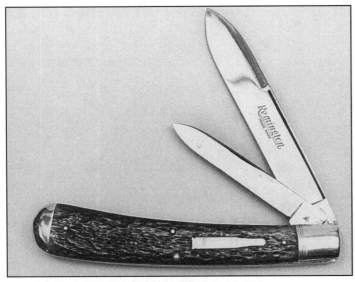

***R1273**, bullet, brown bone, 5-3/8", $4,500.*

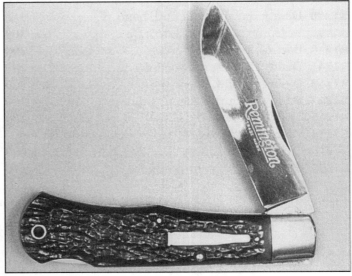

***R1303**, bullet, lockback, brown bone, bullet shield, 4-1/2", $3,500.*

| Description | Price |
|---|---|
| **R1263**, bullet, brown bone, 5-3/8" | 4,000 |
| **R1273**, bullet, brown bone, 5-3/8" | 4,500 |
| **R1283**, swell center, bone, 3" | 200 |
| **R1284**, pearl, 3" | 250 |
| **R1285**, swell center, tortoise shell, 3" | 200 |
| **R1295**, pyremite | 225 |
| **R1303**, bullet, lockback, brown bone, bullet shield, 4-1/2" | 3,500 |
| **R1306**, bullet, stag, thumb groove on top of blade, 4-5/8" | 2,500 |
| **R1315**, 2 blade, dogleg jack, bone, 3" | 160 |
| **R1323**, 2 blade dogleg, bone, | 200 |
| **R1324**, 2 blade dogleg jack, pearl, 3" | 225 |
| **R1325**, pyremite, 3" | 200 |
| **R1333**, bone | 90 |
| **R1339**, all metal, 3" | 80 |
| **R1343**, bone, 4-1/4" | 300 |
| **R1353**, bone | 215 |
| **R1363**, bone | 215 |
| **R1373**, bone, lockback, 4-1/4" | 300 |
| **R1379**, metal, 4-1/4" | 250 |
| **R1383**, fish scaler, lockback, brown bone, 4-1/4" | 500 |
| **R1389**, metal | 200 |
| **R1399**, metal, 3-1/2" | 100 |
| **R1409**, metal | 100 |
| **R1413**, bone | 115 |
| **R1423**, bone | 115 |
| **R1437**, ivory | 200 |
| **R1447**, ivory | 200 |
| **R1457**, ivory | 200 |
| **R1465**, budding knife, pyremite, 3-5/8" | 225 |
| **R1477**, florist knife, ivory, 4" | 225 |
| **R1483**, bone | 175 |
| **R1485**, pyremite | 175 |
| **R1493**, bone | 160 |
| **R1495**, pyremite | 160 |
| **R1535**, florist knife, imitation ivory, 3-3/4" | 100 |
| **R1545**, florist knife, imitation ivory, w/bail, 3-3/4" | 100 |
| **R1555**, budding knife, imitation ivory, 3-1/2" | 200 |
| **R1568**, cocobolo | 120 |
| **R1572**, black, 3" | 100 |
| **R1573**, bone, 3" | 100 |
| **R1573CH**, imitation bone, regular pull, w/chain, 3" | 150 |
| **R1593**, bone, 3-1/8" | 150 |
| **R1595**, pyremite, 3-1/8" | 150 |
| **R1608**, cocobolo | 75 |
| **R1613**, round cartridge shield, 5" | 1,200 |
| **R1613BL**, toothpick bullet, brown bone, bullet shield, grooved bolsters | 6,000 |
| **R1615**, pyremite, 5" | 500 |

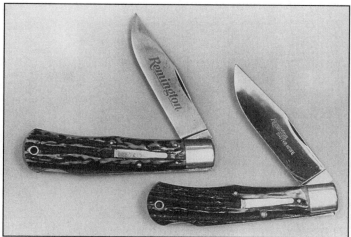

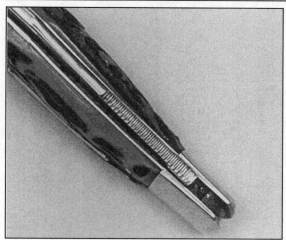

*Top photo: The author has observed many R1303 and R1306 bullets and has found that the knives w/two handle rivets at the front bolster have the thumb groove on the blade. The knives w/one rivet do not have the thumb groove.*
*Bottom photo: R1306, bullet, stag, thumb groove on top of blade, 4-5/8", $2,500.*

*R1383, fish scaler, lockback, brown bone, 4-1/4", $500.*

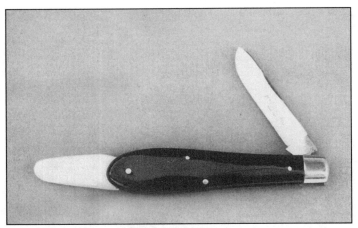

*R1465, budding knife, pyremite, 3-5/8", $225.*

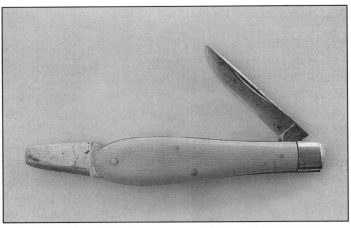

*R1555, budding knife, imitation ivory, 3-1/2", $200.*

*R1477, florist knife, ivory, 4", $225.*

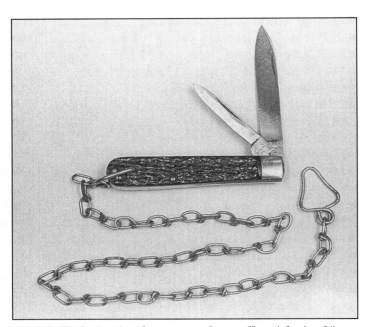

*R1573CH, imitation bone, regular pull, w/chain, 3", $150.*

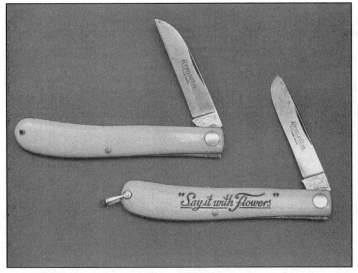

*Top: R1535, florist knife, imitation ivory, 3-3/4", $100.*
*Bottom: R1545, florist knife, imitation ivory, w/bail, 3-3/4", $100.*

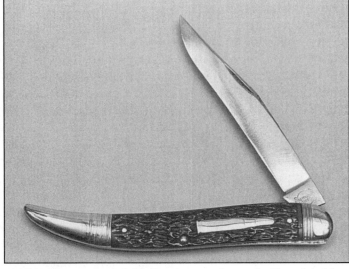

*R1613BL, toothpick bullet, brown bone, bullet shield, grooved bolsters, $6,000.*

| Description | Price |
|---|---|
| **R1622**, 2 blade jack, black, 3" | 100 |
| **R1623**, 2 blade jack, bone, 3" | 115 |
| **R1623CH**, imitation bone | 125 |
| **R1630**, buffalo horn | 400 |
| **R1630**, fish scaler, Daddy Barlow, brown bone, lockback, Remington Circle, UMC, rare, 5" | 600 |
| **R1644**, pearl, 2-7/8" | 200 |
| **R1645**, pyremite, 2-7/8" | 175 |
| **R1653**, peanut, brown bone, 2-7/8" | 200 |
| **R1655**, pyremite, candy stripe, 2-7/8" | 200 |
| **R1668**, cocobolo | 160 |
| **R1671**, redwood, 3-3/8" | 100 |
| **R1685**, feathered budding knife, pyremite, 3-3/4" | 150 |
| **R1687**, feathered budding knife, ivory | 150 |
| **R1688**, feathered budding knife, cocobolo | 150 |
| **R1707**, ivory | 125 |
| **R1715**, feathered budding knife, pyremite, 4-1/4" | 150 |
| **R1717**, feathered budding knife, ivory, 4-1/4" | 150 |
| **R1723**, 2 blade jack sheepfoot, bone, 3-1/2" | 150 |
| **R1751**, redwood, 3-1/2" | 80 |
| **R1752**, black, 3-1/2" | 80 |
| **R1753**, bone, 3-1/2" | 100 |
| **R1755**, pyremite, 3-1/2" | 80 |
| **R1763**, bone | 115 |
| **R1772**, black | 150 |
| **SR1773**, easy opener, bone | 200 |
| **R1782**, black, 3-1/2" | 150 |
| **R1783**, jack, teardrop, brown bone, 3-1/2" | 200 |
| **R1785**, pyremite, 3-1/2" | 150 |
| **R1803**, bone | 100 |
| **R1823**, bone, wild duck shield, 3-5/8" | 225 |
| **R1823**, long pull, brown bone, 3-5/8" | 125 |
| **R1823**, bone, Babe Ruth shield, 3-5/8" | 225 |
| **R1823**, bone, wild duck shield, 3-5/8" | 225 |
| **R1825**, long pull, imitation tortoise, 3-5/8" | 150 |
| **R1833**, bone | 150 |
| **R1853**, 2 blade equal-end jack, bone, 3-3/8" | 150 |
| **R1855**, 2 blade equal-end jack, pyremite, 3-3/8" | 150 |
| **R1863**, bone, 3-3/8" | 150 |
| **R1873**, bone, 3-5/8" | 150 |
| **R1882**, 2 blade jack, razor blade, black, 3" | 200 |
| **R1903**, bone | 100 |
| **R1905**, pyremite | 100 |
| **R1913**, bone, 3-3/8" | 140 |

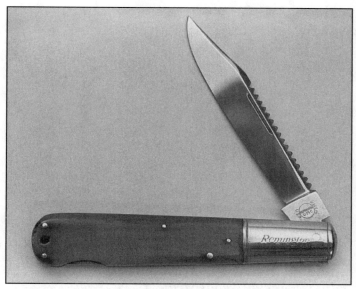

*R1630, fish scaler, Daddy Barlow, brown bone, lockback, Remington Circle, UMC, rare, 5", $600.*

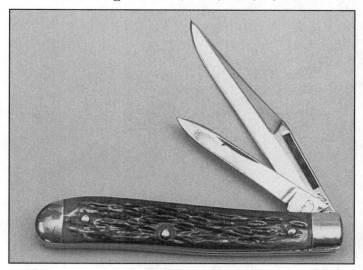

*R1653, peanut, brown bone, 2-7/8", $200.*

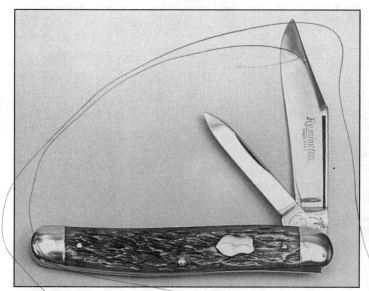

*R1823, bone, wild duck shield, 3-5/8", $225.*

*R1655, pyremite, candy stripe, 2-7/8", $200.*

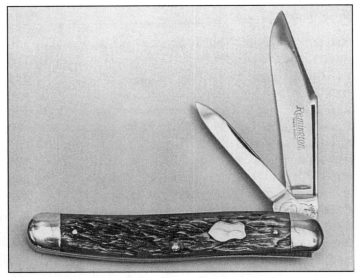

*R1823, long pull, brown bone, 3-5/8", $125.*

*SR1773, easy opener, bone, $200.*

*R1823, bone, Babe Ruth shield, 3-5/8", $225*

*R1823, bone, wild duck shield, 3-5/8", $225*

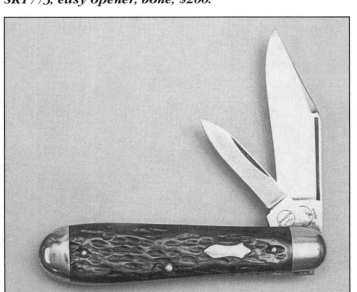

*R1783, jack, teardrop, brown bone, 3-1/2", $200.*

| Description | Price |
| --- | --- |
| **R1915**, long pull, candy stripe, 3-3/8" | **150** |
| **R1962**, black | **100** |
| **R1973**, bone | **185** |
| **R1995**, feathered budding knife, pyremite, 4-1/4" | **150** |
| **R2013**, smoker's knife, brown bone, slant bolsters | **300** |
| **R2043**, bone, 3-1/4" | **100** |
| **R2045**, pyremite, 3-1/4" | **100** |
| **R2053**, bone, 3-1/4" | **125** |
| **R2055**, waterfall pyremite, 3-1/4" | **150** |

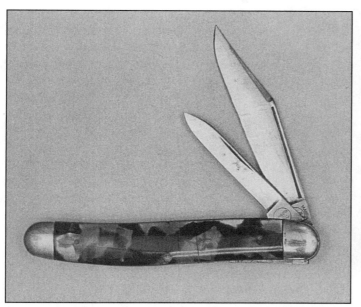

*R1825, imitation tortoise, long pull, 3-5/8", $150.*

*R1873, bone, 3-5/8", $150.*

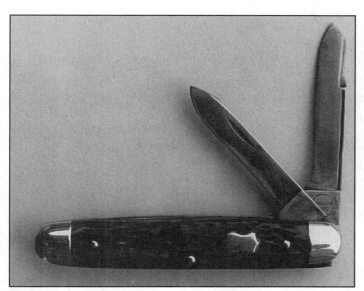

*R1863, bone, 3-3/8", $150.*

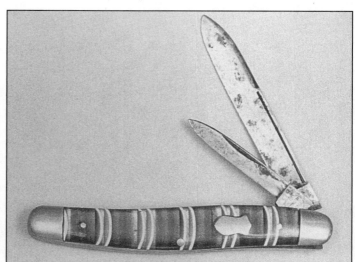

*R1915, long pull, candy stripe, 3-3/8", $150.*

| Description | Price |
|---|---|
| **R2065**, 2 blade teardrop jack, pyremite, 3-1/8" | **125** |
| **R2075**, 2 blade teardrop jack, pyremite, 3-1/8" | **125** |
| **R2083**, bone, 3-1/4" | **100** |
| **R2085**, pyremite | **100** |
| **R2093**, bone, 3-1/8" | **100** |
| **R2095**, black & white composition, 3-1/8" | **100** |
| **R2103**, 2 blade jack, bone, 3-1/8" | **110** |
| **R2105**, pyremite 3-1/8" | **110** |
| **R2111**, redwood | **120** |
| **R2203**, bone, 3-3/8" | **125** |

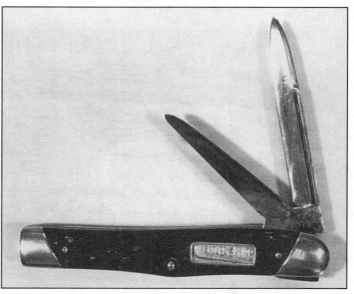

*R2013, smoker's knife, brown bone, slant bolsters, $300.*

*R2055, waterfall pyremite, 3-1/4", $150.*

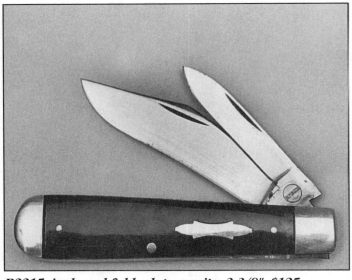

*R2215, jack, red & black pyremite, 3-3/8", $125.*

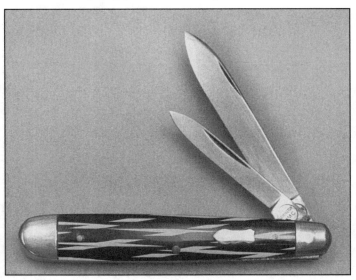

*R2095, black & white composition, 3-1/8", $100.*

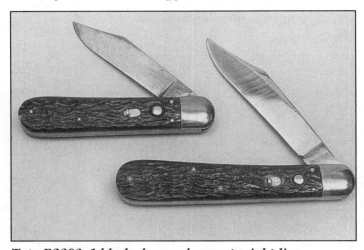

*Top: R2303, 1 blade, brown bone, straight-line (stamp), 4-1/8", $2,200.*
*Bottom: R2403, 1 blade, brown bone, straight-line (stamp), 5", $2,200.*

*R2105, pyremite, 3-1/8", $110.*

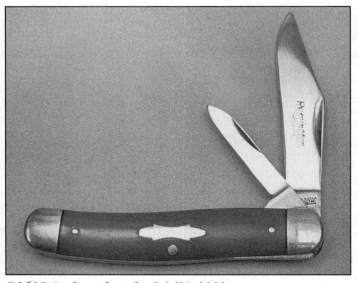

*R2605, jack, red scale, 3-3/8", $110.*

*R3033, rail splitter, bone, rare, 3-7/8", $900.*

*R-?, unknown, cocobolo, slant bolsters, rare, 3-3/4", $900.*

| Description | Price |
|---|---|
| **R2215**, jack, red & black pyremite, 3-3/8" | 125 |
| **R2223**, bone, 3-3/8" | 75 |
| **R2303**, switchblade, brown bone, straight-line (stamp), 4-1/8" | 2,200 |
| **R2403**, switchblade, brown bone, straight-line (stamp), 5" | 2,200 |
| **R2503**, bone | 75 |
| **R2505B**, pyremite | 75 |
| **R2505M**, pyremite | 75 |
| **R2505R**, pyremite | 75 |
| **R2603**, serpentine jack, bone, 3-3/8" | 125 |
| **R2605**, jack, red scale, 3-3/8" | 110 |
| **R3003**, bone | 285 |
| **R3005**, pyremite | 250 |
| **R3013**, bone | 285 |
| **R3015**, pyremite | 250 |
| **R3033**, bone | 330 |
| **R3033**, rail splitter, bone, rare, 3-7/8" | 900 |
| **R-?**, unknown, cocobolo, slant bolsters, rare, 3-3/4" | 900 |
| **R3035**, pyremite | 300 |
| **R3050**, buffalo horn, 4" | 450 |
| **R3054**, stockman, genuine pearl, 4" | 800 |
| **R3055**, pyremite, 4" | 400 |
| **R3056**, genuine stag, 4" | 500 |

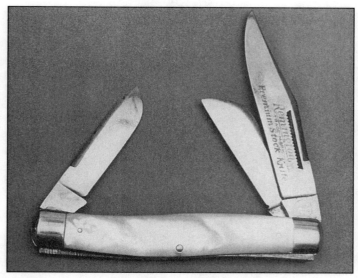

*R3054, stockman, genuine pearl, 4", $800.*

*R3055, pyremite, 4", $400.*

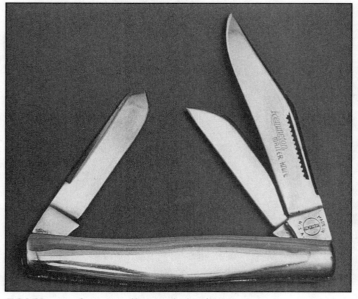

*R3059, stockman, all metal, 4", $350.*

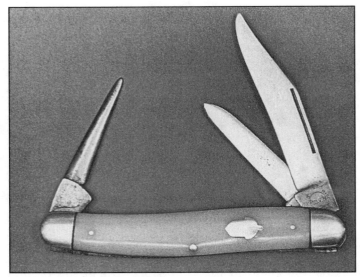

R3065, stockman, punch blade, long pull, yellow, 4", $300.

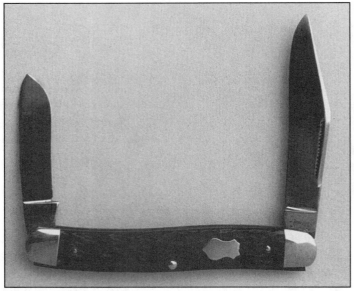

R3113, bone, round bolsters, 4", $300.

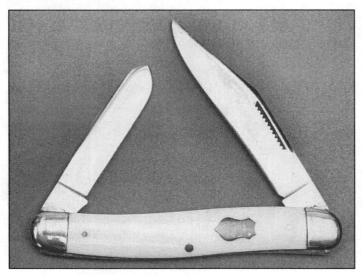

R3115, serpentine, imitation ivory, 4", $250.

R3133, 4 blade stockman, bone, rare, 4", $900.

R3143, 5 blade, bone, rare, 4", $6,500.

R3153, equal end, brown bone, acorn shield, 3-1/2", $300.

*R3163, 3 blade cattle, bone, 3-1/2", $500.*

*R3183, cattle, bone, 3-1/2", $700.*

| Description | Price |
|---|---|
| **R3062**, black, 4" | 400 |
| **R3063**, stockman, punch blade, long pull, bone, 4" | 350 |
| **R3064**, pearl, 4" | 800 |
| **R3065**, stockman, punch blade, long pull, yellow, 4" | 300 |
| **R3070**, buffalo horn | 600 |
| **R3073**, stockman whittler, bone, 4" | 800 |
| **R3075**, pyremite | 700 |
| **R3083LP**, bone | 400 |
| **R3085**, pyremite | 400 |
| **R3093**, bone | 250 |
| **R3095**, pyremite | 250 |
| **R3103**, bone | 300 |
| **R3105**, pyremite | 235 |
| **R3113**, bone, round bolsters, 4" | 300 |
| **R3115**, serpentine, imitation ivory, 4" | 250 |
| **R3115G**, pyremite, 4" | 350 |
| **R3115W**, pyremite, 4" | 350 |
| **R3123**, 2 blade moose, bone, 3-7/8" | 350 |
| **R3133**, bone, 4" | 300 |
| **R3133**, 4 blade stockman, bone, rare, 4" | 900 |
| **R3143**, 5 blade, bone, rare, 4" | 6,500 |
| **R3153**, equal end, brown bone, acorn shield, 3-1/2" | 300 |
| **R3155**, pyremite | 250 |
| **R3155B**, pyremite | 250 |
| **R3163**, 3 blade cattle, bone, 3-1/2" | 500 |
| **R3165**, 3 blade cattle, pyremite, 3-1/2" | 500 |
| **R3183**, cattle, bone, 3-1/2" | 700 |
| **R3185**, cattle, pyremite, acorn-punch, 3-1/2" | 400 |
| **R3193**, bone | 265 |
| **R3202**, black | 260 |
| **R3203**, bone, 3-1/2" | 265 |
| **R3212**, black | 300 |
| **R3213**, bone | 300 |
| **R3215**, pyremite | 260 |
| **R3222**, black | 225 |

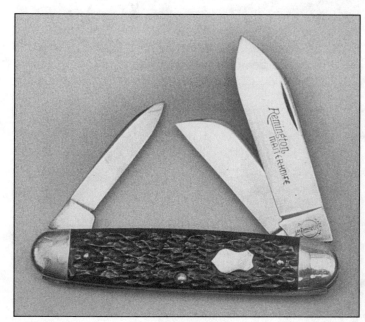

*R3273, cattle, equal end, brown bone, 3-3/4", $450.*

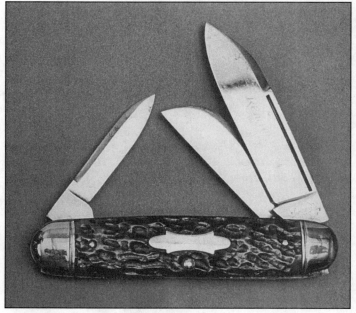

*R3273, cattle, equal end, long pull, brown bone, grooved bolster, 3-3/4", $500.*

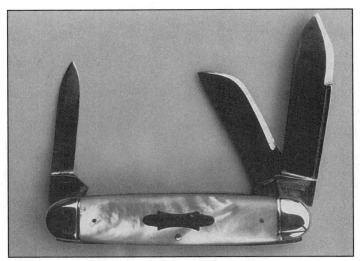

*R3274, cattle, genuine pearl, 3-3/4", $800.*

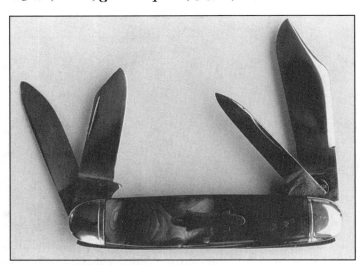

*R3305, pyremite, 3-3/4", $700.*

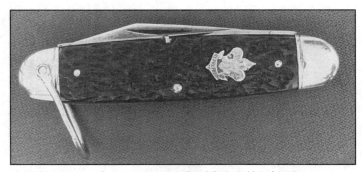

*R3333, Scout, bone, trans. shield, 3-3/4", $350.*

*R3333, utility, bone, plain shield, 3-3/4", 325.*

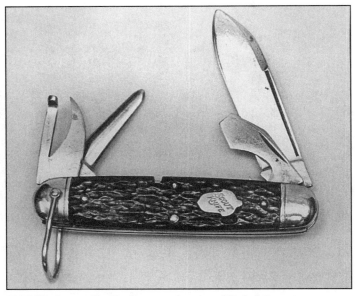

*R3333, Scout knife, brown bone, official Scout, acorn shield, bail, 3-3/4", $450.*

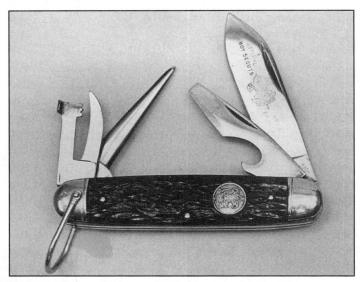

*RS3333, brown bone, official Scout shield, "Be Prepared," bail, 3-3/4", $350.*

*RS3333, Scout knife, brown bone, Scout shield, acorn shape, 3-3/4", $375*

Remington 447

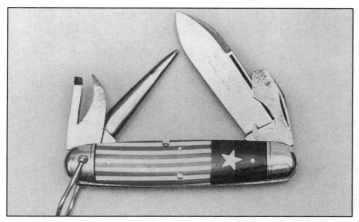

*R3335, Scout knife, red, white & blue, 3-3/4", $450.*

| Description | Price |
|---|---|
| **R3223**, bone | 250 |
| **R3225**, pyremite | 225 |
| **R3232**, black | 200 |
| **R3233**, bone | 260 |
| **R3235**, pyremite | 260 |
| **R3242**, black, 3-3/4" | 260 |
| **R3243W**, pyremite, 3-3/4" | 300 |
| **R3253**, bone | 300 |
| **R3255**, pyremite | 300 |
| **R3263**, bone | 300 |
| **R3265**, pyremite | 300 |
| **R3273**, cattle, equal end, brown bone, 3-3/4" | 450 |
| **R3273**, cattle, equal end, long pull, brown bone, grooved bolster, 3-3/4" | 500 |
| **R3274**, cattle, genuine pearl, 3-3/4" | 800 |
| **R3275**, pyremite, 3-3/4" | 500 |
| **R3283**, bone | 275 |
| **R3285**, pyremite | 250 |
| **R3293**, bone | 275 |
| **R3295**, pyremite | 250 |
| **R3302**, 4 blade equal end, black, 3-3/4" | 500 |
| **R3303**, 4 blade equal end, bone, 3-3/4" | 600 |
| **R3305**, pyremite, 3-3/4" | 700 |
| **R3312**, black, 3-3/4" | 300 |
| **R3313**, bone, 3-3/4" | 400 |
| **R3315B**, pyremite | 400 |
| **R3322**, black | 200 |
| **R3333**, Scout, trans. shield, bone, 3-3/4" | 350 |
| **R3333**, utility, bone, plain shield, 3-3/4" | 325 |
| **R3333**, Scout knife, brown bone, official Scout, acorn shield, bail, 3-3/4" | 450 |
| **RS3333**, brown bone, official Scout shield, "Be Prepared," bail, 3-3/4" | 350 |
| **RS3333**, Scout knife, brown bone, Scout shield, acorn shape, 3-3/4" | 375 |
| **R3334**, Scout knife, (utility), genuine pearl, bail, 3-3/4" | 650 |
| **RS3334**, Scout knife, pearl | 650 |

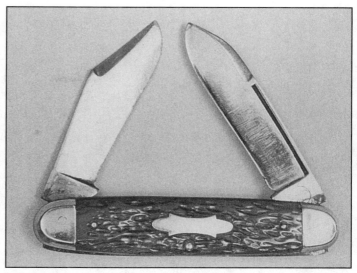

*R3363, J pattern, long pull, brown bone, 3-3/4", $400.*

*Unknown, $1,500.*

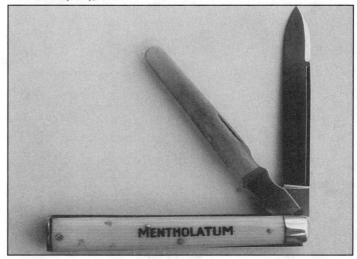

*Unknown, physician's knife, spatula blade, imitation ivory, $800.*

*Unknown, pyremite, $750.*

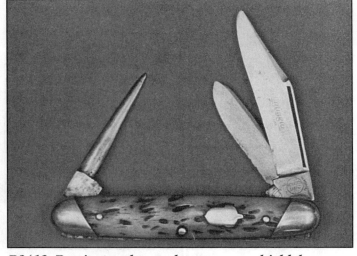

*R3413, Remington, brown bone, acorn shield, long pull, slant bolsters, 3-3/8", $250*

*R3373, bone, 3-3/4", $175.*

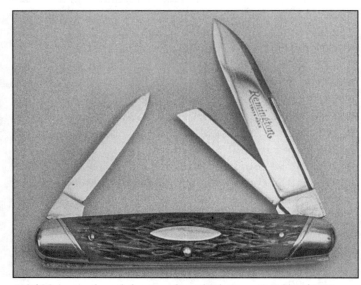

*R3423, equal end, bone, slant bolsters, 3-1/4", $350.*

*R3395, pyremite, 3-3/4", $200.*

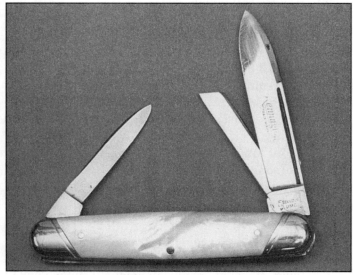

*R3424, equal end, pearl, slant bolsters, 3-3/8", $450.*

| Description | Price |
|---|---|
| **R3335**, Scout knife, red, white & blue, 3-3/4" | 450 |
| **Unknown**, physician's knife, spatula blade, imitation ivory, | 800 |
| **Unknown**, pyremite, | 75 |
| **R3352**, black, 3-3/4" | 300 |
| **R3353**, 2 blade equal-end J pattern, bone, 3-3/4" | 400 |
| **R3363**, J pattern, long pull, brown bone, 3-3/4" | 400 |
| **R3372**, 2 blade equal end, black, 3-3/4" | 200 |
| **R3373**, bone, 3-3/4", | 175 |
| **R3375**, 2 blade equal end, pyremite, 3-3/4" | 200 |
| **R3382**, black | 200 |
| **R3383**, bone | 215 |
| **R3385S**, pyremite | 200 |
| **R3393**, 2 blade equal end, bone, 3-3/4" | 200 |
| **R3395**, pyremite, 3-3/4" | 200 |
| **R3395T**, 2 blade, birdseye rivet, 3-3/4" | 200 |
| **R3403**, bone | 250 |
| **R3405J**, pyremite | 225 |
| **R3413**, brown bone, long pull, acorn shield, slant bolsters, 3-3/8" | 250 |
| **R3414**, pearl | 300 |
| **R3415H**, pyremite, 3-3/8" | 225 |
| **R3423**, equal end, bone, slant bolsters, 3-1/4" | 350 |
| **R3424**, equal end, pearl, slant bolsters, 3-3/8" | 450 |
| **R3424**, whittler, equal end, pearl, slant bolsters, 3-3/8" | 500 |
| **R3425P**, pyremite, 3-3/8" | 400 |
| **R3432**, black | 200 |
| **R3433**, bone | 200 |
| **R3435**, pyremite | 200 |
| **R3442**, black, 3-1/4" | 170 |
| **R3443**, 2 blades, brown bone, 3-1/4" | 225 |
| **R3453**, whittler, bone, 3-1/4" | 500 |
| **R3455**, saber blade, pyremite, slant bolsters, 3-1/4", | 500 |
| **R3463**, whittler, bone | 350 |
| **R3475J**, pyremite, 3-1/4" | 300 |
| **R3475K**, pyremite, 3-1/4" | 300 |
| **R3480**, small stockman, buffalo horn, 3-3/8" | 200 |
| **R3483**, small stockman, bone, 3-3/8" | 225 |
| **R3484**, small stockman, pearl, 3-3/8" | 300 |
| **R3485**, equal end, gold-swirl pyremite, 3-3/8" | 200 |
| **R3489**, metal | 175 |
| **R3494**, pearl, 3-3/8" | 300 |
| **R3495M**, pyremite, 3-3/8" | 250 |
| **R3499**, NS, 3-3/8" | 200 |
| **R3500BU**, buffalo horn | 200 |
| **R3503**, bone | 215 |
| **R3504**, pearl | 300 |
| **Unknown**, pyremite, 5", | 300 |

*Unknown*

*Unknown, pyremite, 5", $300.*

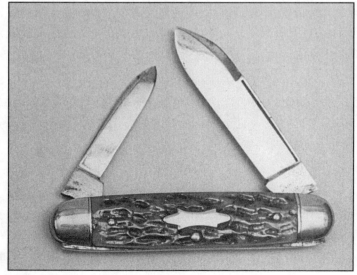

*R3443, 2 blades, brown bone, 3-1/4", $225.*

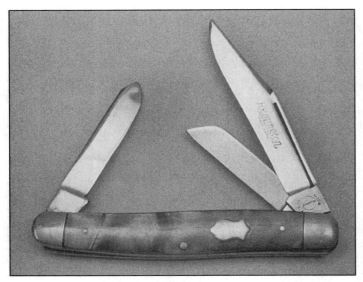

**R3485, equal end, gold-swirl pyremite, 3-3/8", $200.**

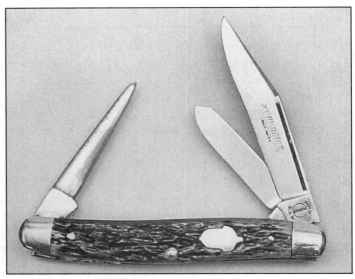

**R3513, serpentine, brown bone, acorn shield, 3-3/8", $200.**

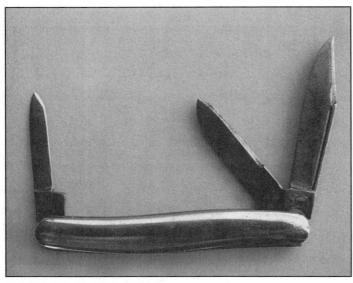

**R3499, NS, 3-3/8", $200.**

**R3553, brown bone, square bolsters, 4", $550.**

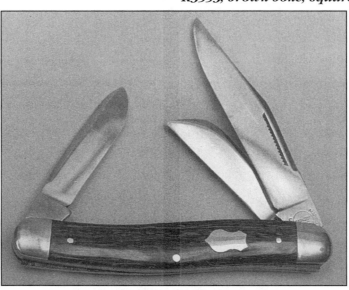

**R3555, stockman, mingled red scale, 4", $400.**

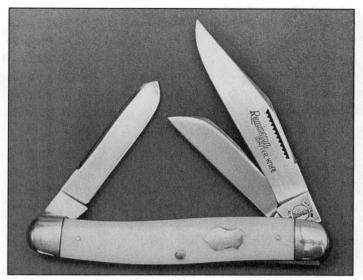

*R3557, stockman, imitation ivory, 4", $350.*

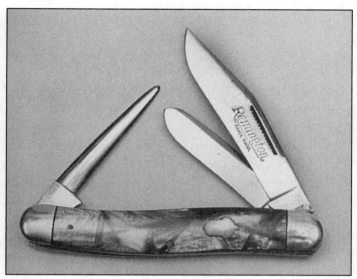

*R3565, stockman, brown swirl pyremite, acorn shield, 4", $400.*

*R3563, bone, acorn shield, 4", $500.*

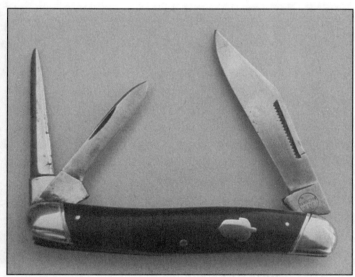

*R3580, whittler, punch, buffalo horn, 4", $400.*

| Description | Price |
|---|---|
| **R3513**, serpentine, brown bone, acorn shield, 3-3/8" | 200 |
| **R3514**, pearl, 3-3/8" | 225 |
| **R3515**, pyremite, 3-3/8" | 200 |
| **R3520BU**, buffalo horn, 3 blade whittler, 3-3/8" | 400 |
| **R3523**, bone, 3 blade whittler, 3-3/8" | 300 |
| **R3524**, pearl, 3 blade whittler, 3-3/8" | 400 |
| **R3525**, pyremite, 3 blade whittler, 3-3/8" | 300 |
| **R3533**, brown bone, 2 blade stockman, 3-5/8" | 225 |
| **R3545**, pyremite | 150 |
| **R3553**, brown bone, square bolsters, 4" | 550 |
| **R3554**, pearl, square bolsters, stockman, 4" | 600 |

| Description | Price |
|---|---|
| **R3555**, stockman, mingled red scale, 4" | 400 |
| **R3555G**, pyremite, 3-7/8" | 500 |
| **R3557**, stockman, imitation ivory, 4" | 350 |
| **R3563**, bone, acorn shield, 4" | 500 |
| **R3565**, stockman, brown swirl pyremite, acorn shield, 4" | 400 |
| **R3565D**, pyremite, 3-7/8" | 350 |
| **R3573**, bone | 240 |
| **R3575**, pyremite | 200 |
| **R3580**, whittler, punch, buffalo horn, 4" | 400 |
| **R3583**, bone, whittler, 4" | 500 |
| **R3585**, pyremite, 4" | 450 |

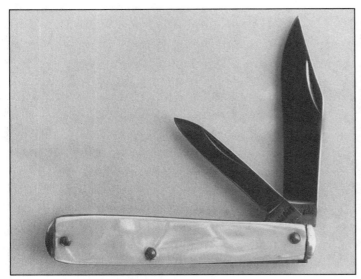
*Unknown, cracked ice.*

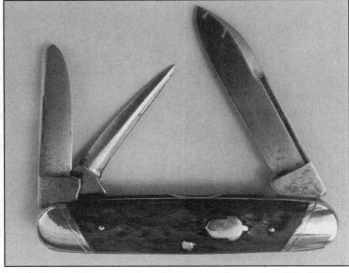
*R3683, Remington, 3 backsprings, bone, 3-1/2", $500.*

*Budweiser advertisement*

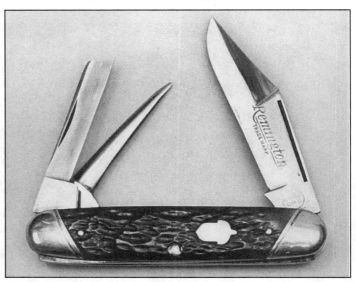
*R3693, whittler, saber blade, brown bone, acorn shield, slant bolsters, 3-1/2", $500.*

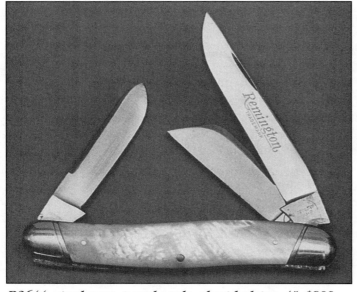
*R3644, stockman, pearl scale, slant bolster, 4", $800.*

| Description | Price |
|---|---|
| **Budweiser advertisement** ................................................. | |
| **R3593**, bone ................................................................ | 300 |
| **R3595**, pyremite ........................................................... | 300 |
| **R3596**, genuine stag.................................................... | 350 |
| **R3600**, buffalo horn..................................................... | 200 |
| **R3603**, bone ................................................................ | 215 |
| **R3604**, pearl ................................................................ | 300 |
| **R3605**, pyremite ........................................................... | 215 |
| **R3613**, bone ................................................................ | 200 |
| **R3615**, pyremite ........................................................... | 200 |
| **R3620BU**, buffalo horn................................................. | 175 |
| **R3623**, bone ................................................................ | 200 |
| **R3625**, pyremite ........................................................... | 175 |
| **R3633**, bone ................................................................ | 150 |
| **R3635**, pyremite ........................................................... | 140 |
| **R3643**, stockman, bone, slant bolsters, 4" ................. | 500 |

| Description | Price |
|---|---|
| R3644, stockman, pearl scale, slant bolster, 4" | 800 |
| R3645, pyremite, 4" | 500 |
| R3653, punch, long spar, bone, 3-7/8" | 400 |
| R3655, pyremite, long spey | 400 |
| R3665, pyremite | 300 |
| R3675, pyremite | 300 |
| R3683, 3 backsprings, bone, 3-1/2" | 500 |
| R3685C, whittler, pyremite, 3-1/2" | 500 |
| R3693, whittler, saber blade, brown bone, acorn shield, slant bolsters, 3-1/2" | 500 |
| R3700BU, buffalo horn, 4" | 300 |
| R3703, bone, 4" | 400 |
| R3704, pearl, 4" | 500 |
| R3705, pyremite, 4" | 400 |
| R3710BU, buffalo horn | 225 |
| R3713, bone, 3-7/8" | 300 |
| R3714, pearl, 3-7/8" | 400 |
| R3715, pyremite, 3-7/8" | 300 |
| R3722, black composition | 850 |
| R3723, whittler, big sleeveboard, bone | 1,000 |
| R3725, pyremite | 850 |
| R3732, black | 330 |
| R3733, bone | 385 |
| R3735, pyremite | 330 |
| R3843, utility, brown bone, 3-5/8" | 600 |
| R3853, bone, 4" | 450 |
| R3855, pruner, imitation ivory, 4" | 350 |
| R3858, cocobolo, 4" | 400 |
| R3863, Scout knife, brown bone, acorn shield, 3-3/4" | 300 |
| R3870BU, 3 blade stockman, buffalo horn, 4" | 400 |
| R3873, 3 blade stockman, bone, 4" | 500 |
| R3874, 3 blade stockman, pearl, 4" | 700 |
| R3875A, 3 blade stockman, pyremite, 4" | 500 |
| R3883, 4 blade stockman, bone, 4" | 1,500 |
| R3885, 4 blade stockman, pyremite, 4" | 1,500 |
| R3893, bone, 3-7/8" | 150 |
| R3895, pyremite | 150 |
| R3903, 2 blade J pattern, bone, 3-7/8" | 300 |
| R3923, 3 blade stockman, bone | 400 |
| R3926, genuine stag | 500 |
| R3932, black | 350 |
| R3933, bone | 400 |
| R3935, pyremite | 350 |
| R3942, large sleeveboard, ebony, 3-5/8" | 500 |
| R3943, sleeveboard, Rogers bone, 3-5/8" | 600 |
| R3943, sleeveboard, brown bone, 3-5/8" | 600 |
| R3953, bone, 3-3/4" | 200 |
| R3955, pyremite, 3-3/4" | 190 |
| R3962, black, 3-3/4" | 190 |
| R3963, bone | 215 |
| R3965, pyremite | 190 |

*R3843, utility, brown bone, 3-5/8", $600.*

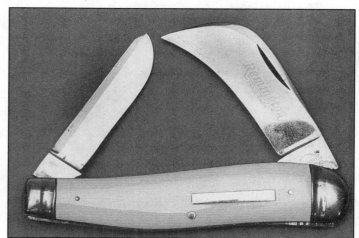

*R3855, pruner, imitation ivory, 4", $350.*

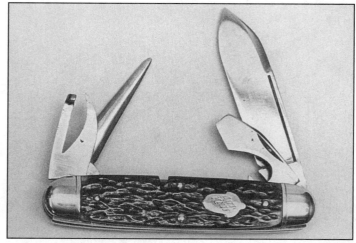

*R3863, Scout knife, brown bone, acorn shield, 3-3/4", $300.*

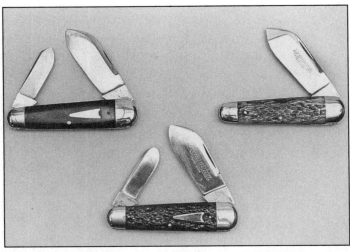

*Top left: R3942, large sleeveboard, ebony, 3-5/8", $500.*
*Top right: R3943, sleeveboard, Rogers bone, 3-5/8", $600.*
*Bottom: R3943, sleeveboard, brown bone, 3-5/8", $600.*

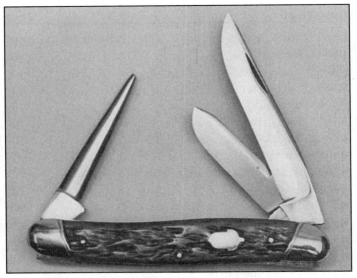

*R4073, serpentine, saber blade, brown bone, acorn shield, slant bolsters, 4", $450.*

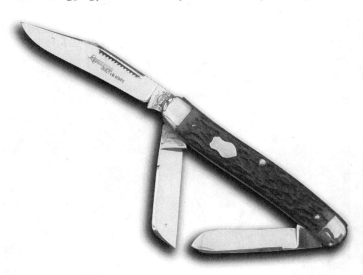

*R3993, stockman, bone, 3-5/8", $300.*

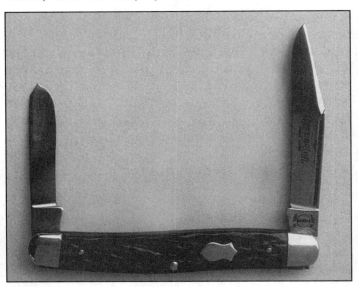

*R4103, bone, 3-3/8", $225.*

*R3993, bone, stockman, 3-5/8", 300.*

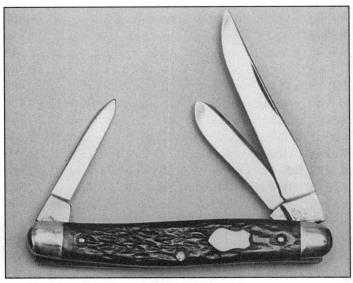

*R4133, stockman, bone, 3-3/8", $225.*

| Description | Price |
|---|---|
| R3973, 3 blade stockman, bone, 3-3/4" | 300 |
| R3983, bone | 200 |
| R3985, pyremite | 200 |
| R3993, stockman, bone, 3-5/8" | 300 |
| R3995, 3 blade stockman, pyremite | 300 |
| R4003, 2 blade serpentine, bone | 150 |
| R4005, 2 blade serpentine, pyremite, 3-3/8" | 125 |
| R4013, bone | 150 |
| R4015, pyremite | 150 |
| R4023, bone | 240 |
| R4025, pyremite | 200 |
| R4033, 3 blade serpentine, bone, 3-5/8" | 350 |
| R4035, 3 blade serpentine, pyremite, 3-5/8" | 225 |
| R4045, stockman, pyremite, 3-5/8" | 300 |
| R4053, bone | 215 |
| R4055, pyremite | 200 |
| R4063, bone | 200 |
| R4065, pyremite | 200 |
| R4073, serpentine, saber blade, brown bone, acorn shield, slant bolsters, 4" | 450 |
| R4075, pyremite, 4" | 300 |
| R4083, bone, 3-7/8" | 240 |
| R4085, pyremite, 3-7/8" | 240 |
| R4093, bone | 225 |
| R4095, pyremite | 225 |
| R4103, bone, 3-3/8" | 225 |
| R4105, pyremite, 3-3/8" | 225 |
| R4113, bone, 3-7/8" | 225 |
| R4113, bone | 240 |
| R4114, pearl, 3-7/8" | 325 |
| R4123, bone | 300 |
| R4124, pearl | 325 |
| R4133, stockman, bone, 3-3/8" | 225 |
| R4134, stockman, pearl, 3-3/8" | 400 |
| R4135, pyremite, 3-3/8" | 200 |
| R4143, 2 blade, bone, tip bolsters, 3-3/8" | 175 |
| R4144, 2 blade, pearl, tip bolsters, 3-3/8" | 250 |
| R4145, 2 blade, pyremite, tip bolsters, 3-3/8" | 200 |
| R4163, bone | 215 |
| R4173, bone | 200 |
| R4175, pyremite | 200 |
| R4200, buffalo horn | 215 |
| R4203, bone | 240 |
| R4223, 3 blade cattle, equal-end, bone, 3-1/4" | 300 |
| R4225, 3 blade cattle, equal-end, pyremite | 300 |
| R4233, bone | 350 |
| RS4233, bone, note different acorn shield, 3-3/8" | 300 |
| RS4233, bone, note different long screwdriver blade & smooth bolsters, 3-3/8" | 350 |
| RS4233, little Scout knife, brown bone, Scout shield, pinched bolsters, 3-3/8" | 400 |

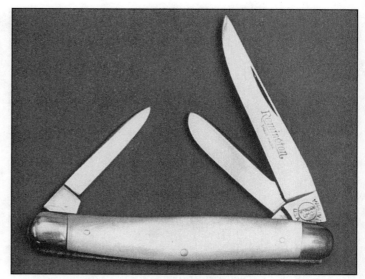

*R4134, stockman, pearl, 3-3/8", $400.*

*RS4233, bone, note different acorn shield, 3-3/8", $300.*

*RS4233, bone, note different long screwdriver blade & smooth bolsters, 3-3/8", $350.*

**RS4233, little Scout knife, brown bone, Scout shield, pinched bolsters, 3-3/8", $400.**

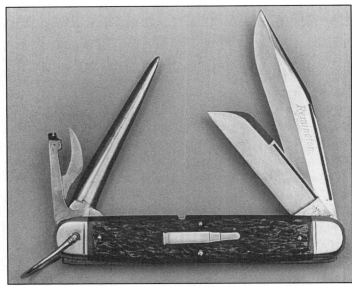

**R4243, camp bullet, long pull, brown bone, bullet shield, 4-3/4", $3,500.**

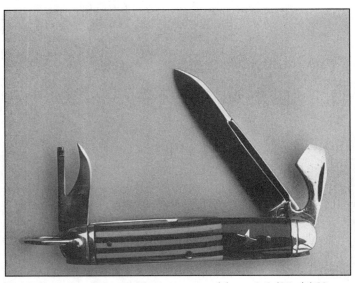

**R4235, red, white & blue, star emblem, 3-3/8", $450.**

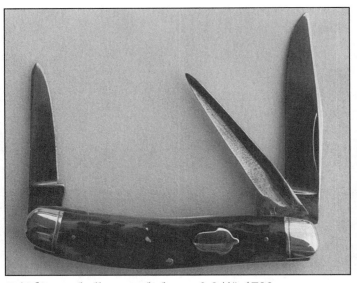

**R4263, sowbelly, punch, bone, 3-3/4", $700.**

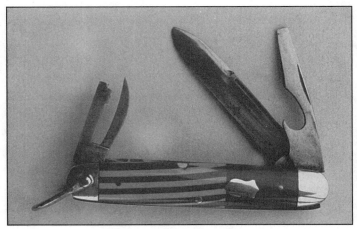

**R4235, red, white &blue handle, plain shield, 3-3/8", $450.**

**R4273, sowbelly, 3 blades, brown bone, 3-3/4", $1,200.**

Remington 457

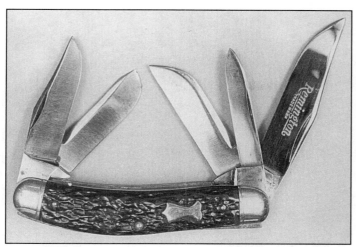

*R4283, sowbelly, brown bone, 3-3/4", $8,000.*

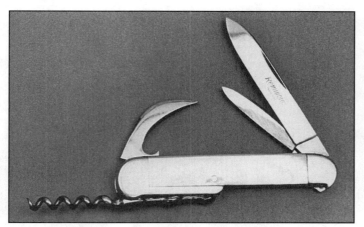

*R4334, bartender's knife, pearl, 3-1/2", $400.*

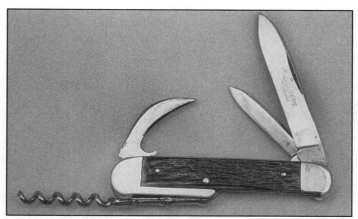

*R4336, bartender's knife, stag, 3-1/2", $400.*

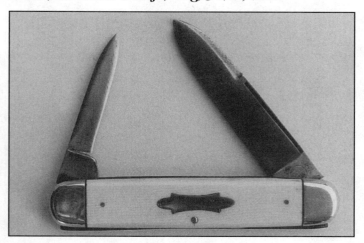

*R4345, imitation ivory, 4-1/4", $300.*

| Description | Price |
|---|---|
| **R4234**, pearl, 3-3/8" | 500 |
| **R4235**, red, white & blue, star emblem, 3-3/8" | 450 |
| **R4235**, red, white & blue, plain shield, 3-3/8" | 450 |
| **R4243**, camp bullet, brown bone, long pull, bullet shield, 4-3/4" | 3,500 |
| **R4253**, bone | 235 |
| **R4263**, sowbelly, punch, bone, 3-3/4" | 700 |
| **R4273**, sowbelly, 3 blades, brown bone, 3-3/4" | 1,200 |
| **R4274**, sowbelly, 3 blade, genuine pearl, 3-3/4" | 1,200 |
| **R4283**, sowbelly, brown bone, 3-3/4" | 8,000 |
| **R4293**, bone | 250 |
| **R4303**, bone | 250 |
| **R4313**, bone, 3-7/8" | 250 |
| **R4334**, bartender's knife, pearl, 3-1/2" | 400 |
| **R4336**, bartender's knife, stag, 3-1/2" | 400 |
| **R4343**, bone, 4-1/4" | 450 |
| **R4345**, imitation ivory, 4-1/4" | 300 |
| **R4353**, bullet/big muskrat, brown bone, bullet shield, 4-1/4" | 3,500 |
| **R4363**, bone | 300 |
| **R4365**, pyremite | 300 |

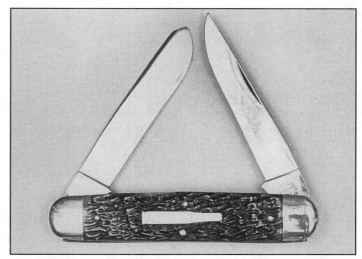

*R4353, bullet/big muskrat, brown bone, bullet shield, 4-1/4", $3,500.*

| Description | Price |
|---|---|
| **R4373**, Girl Scout knife, bone, 3-3/8" | 400 |
| **R4375**, pyremite, 3-3/8" | 275 |
| **R4383**, bone, 3-3/8" | 225 |
| **R4384**, pearl, 3-3/8" | 300 |

*R4373, Girl Scout knife, bone, 3-3/8", $400.*

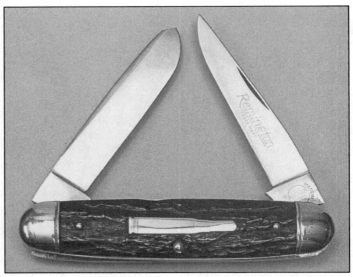

*R4466, baby muskrat, stag, shield, 3-3/4", $8,500.*

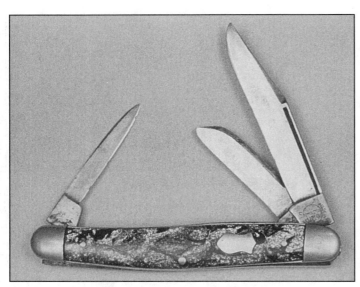

*R4405, Christmas tree, long pull, 3-3/8", $250.*

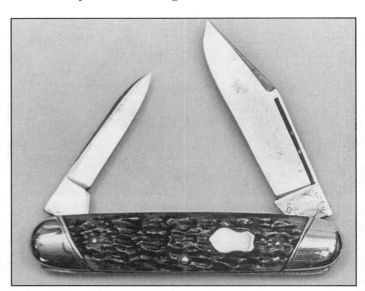

*R4473, slant bolsters, 3-1/4", $250.*

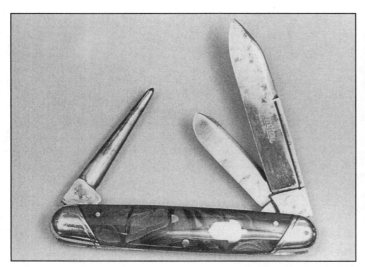

*R4425, pyremite, long pull, acorn shield, slant bolsters, 3-3/8", $300.*

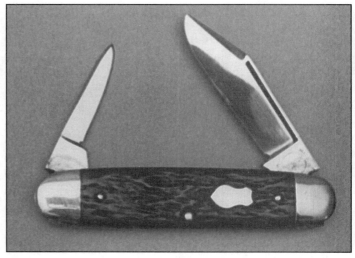

*R4473, 2 blades, LP, brown bone, straight bolsters, 3-1/4", $225.*

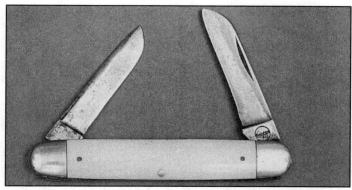

*R4497, florist's knife, imitation ivory, 3-3/4", $200.*

| Description | Price |
|---|---|
| R4394, pearl | 400 |
| R4403, bone, 3-3/8" | 225 |
| R4405, Christmas tree, long pull, 3-3/8" | 250 |
| R4413, bone | 200 |
| R4425, pyremite, long pull, acorn shield, slant bolsters, 3-3/8" | 300 |
| R4433, bone, 3-1/4" | 285 |
| R4443, bone | 200 |
| R4466, baby muskrat, stag, shield, 3-3/4" | 8,500 |
| R4473, slant bolsters, 3-1/4" | 250 |
| R4473, 2 blades, LP, brown bone, straight bolsters, 3-1/4" | 225 |
| R4483, 3 blade cattle, equal-end, bone, 3-1/2" | 285 |
| R4493, bone | 200 |
| R4497, florist's knife, imitation ivory, 3-3/4" | 200 |
| R4505, 3 blade serpentine, pyremite, 3-7/8" | 350 |
| R4506, 3 blade serpentine, genuine stag, 3-7/8" | 450 |
| R4513, brown bone, acorn shield, etched "Great Western," 4" | 700 |
| R4523, Spanish Boy Scout shield, bone, 3-3/4" | 300 |
| R4533, bone | 200 |
| R4548, electrician's knife w/lockblade, release in handle, 2 blades, cocobolo wood, Remington Circle UMC, rare, 3-3/4" | 450 |
| R4555, pyremite | 215 |
| R4563, 3 blade stockman, bone, 4-1/4" | 600 |
| R4573, bone | 250 |
| R4583, bone | 200 |
| R4593, muskrat, bone, etch blade, rare, 4" | 400 |
| R4593, muskrat, brown bone, square bolsters, 4" | 300 |
| R4593, muskrat, brown bone, round bolsters, 4" | 300 |
| R4593, muskrat, saber blade, brown bone, square bolster, 4" | 400 |
| R4603, equal end, brown bone, acorn shield, 3-1/4" | 300 |
| R4605, pyremite, 3-1/4" | 225 |
| R4613, bone, 3" | 175 |
| R4615, gold swirl, 3" | 200 |
| R4615, dogleg jack, pyremite, 3" | 200 |
| R4623, equal end, brown bone, 3-3/8" | 200 |

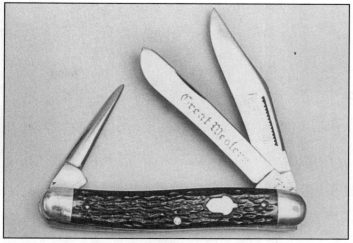

*R4513, brown bone, acorn shield, etched "Great Western," 4", $700.*

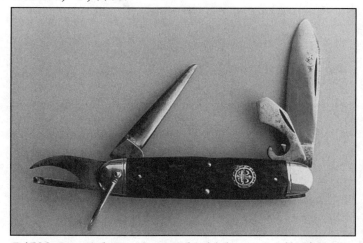

*R4523, Spanish Boy Scout shield, bone, 3-3/4", $300.*

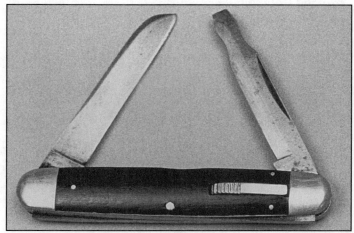
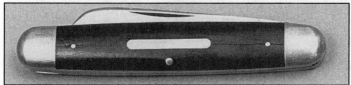

*R4548, electrician knife w/lockblade, release in handle, 2 blades, cocobolo wood, Remington Circle UMC, rare, 3-3/4", $450.*

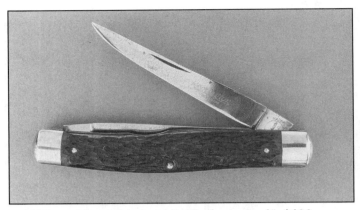

*R4593, muskrat, bone, etch blade, rare, 4", $400.*

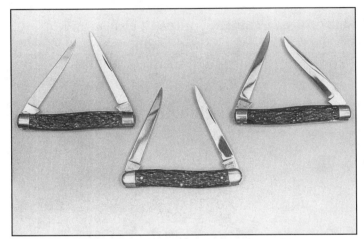

Top left: *R4593, muskrat, brown bone, square bolsters, 4", $300.*
Middle: *R4593, muskrat, brown bone, round bolsters, 4", $300.*
Top right: *R4593, muskrat, saber blade, brown bone, square bolster, 4", $400.*

*R4603, equal end, brown bone, acorn shield, 3-1/4", $300.*

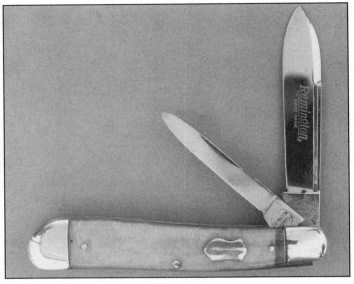

*R4615, gold swirl, 3", $200.*

*R4623, equal end, brown bone, 3-3/8", $200.*

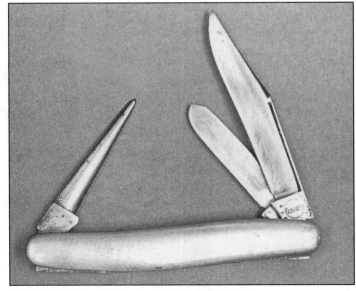

*R4679, all metal, long pull, 3-3/8", $150.*

Remington 461

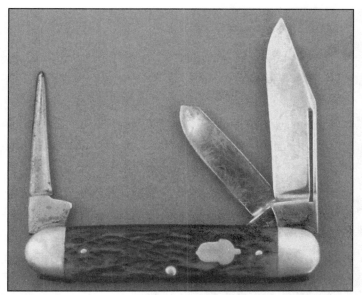
*R4683PU, brown bone, acorn shield, 3-1/4", $275.*

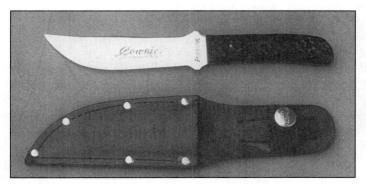
*RH4, blade 4-1/2", overall 7-1/2", $125.*

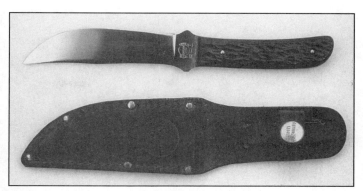
*RH4, blade 4-1/2", overall 7-1/2", $125.*

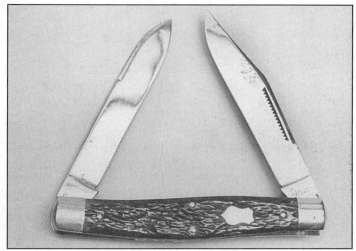
*R4703PU, brown bone, moose, 4-1/4", $500.*

| Description | Price |
|---|---|
| **R4625**, pyremite, 3-3/8" | 200 |
| **R4633**, 3 blade equal end, bone, 3-3/8" | 200 |
| **R4635**, 3 blade equal end, pyremite, 3-3/8" | 200 |
| **R4643**, 3 blade serpentine, bone, 3-3/8" | 175 |
| **R4679**, all metal, long pull, 3-3/8" | 150 |
| **R4683PU**, brown bone, acorn shield, 3-1/4" | 275 |
| **R4685**, 3 blade equal end, punch, pyremite, 3-1/4" | 250 |
| **RH4**, blade 4-1/2", overall 7-1/2" | 125 |
| **RH4**, blade 4-1/2", overall 7-1/2" | 125 |
| **R4695**, pyremite | 200 |
| **R4703**, moose, brown bone, 4-1/4" | 500 |
| **R4713**, bone | 400 |
| **R4723**, Girl Scout, brown bone, bail, 3-3/4" | 400 |
| **R4733**, dog grooming knife, bone, regular shield, etched, 3-3/4" | 350 |
| **R4733**, dog grooming knife, brown bone, no shield, 3-3/4" | 300 |
| **R4733**, dog grooming knife, brown bone, Airdale doghead shield, 3-3/4" | 350 |

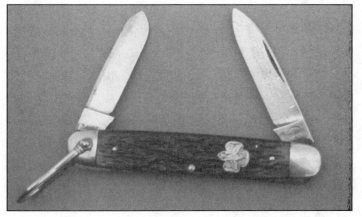
*R4723, Girl Scout, brown bone, bail, 3-3/4", $400.*

| Description | Price |
|---|---|
| **no number**, dog grooming knife, brown bone, no shield, 3-3/8" | 300 |
| **R4733**, dog grooming knife, bone, plain round emblem, 3-3/4" | 350 |
| **RS4773**, Scout knife, brown bone, 3-3/8" | 300 |
| **RS4783**, Scout knife, brown bone, w/emblem, 3-1/2" | 300 |
| **R4813**, bone | 125 |
| **R4815**, pyremite | 125 |

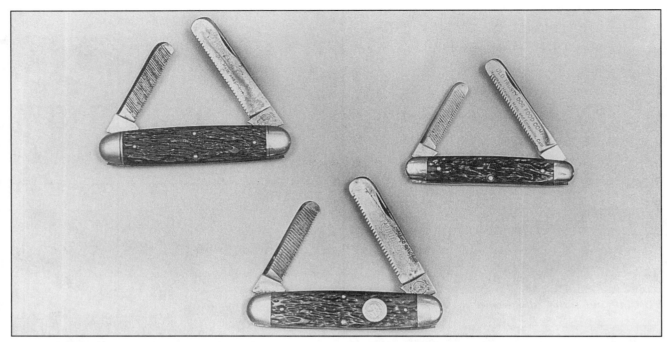

*Top left: R4733, dog grooming knife, brown bone, no shield, 3-3/4", $300.*
*Bottom: R4733, dog grooming knife, brown bone, Airdale doghead shield, 3-3/4", $350.*
*Top right: no number, dog grooming knife, brown bone, no shield, 3-3/8", $300.*

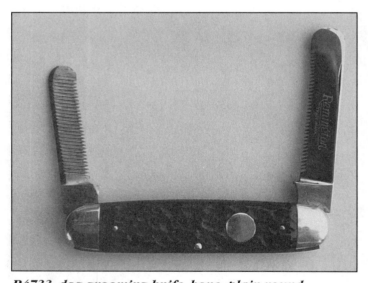

*R4733, dog grooming knife, bone, plain round emblem, 3-3/4", $350.*

*RS4773, Scout knife, brown bone, 3-3/8", $300.*

| Description | Price |
|---|---|
| **R4823**, bone | 100 |
| **R4825**, pyremite | 100 |
| **R4832**, black composition, 3-3/8" | 150 |
| **R4833**, bone | 150 |
| **R4835**, pyremite | 150 |
| **R4843**, imitation bone, 3-3/8" | 110 |
| **R4845**, straight line, slick black, 3-3/8" | 125 |
| **R4853**, bone | 125 |
| **R4855**, pyremite | 125 |

| Description | Price |
|---|---|
| **R4565**, pyremite | 125 |
| **R4863**, bone | 125 |
| **R6013**, brown bone, fluted bolsters, 3-1/4" | 450 |
| **R6014**, congress, pearl, 3" | 250 |
| **R6014**, genuine pearl, slant fluted bolsters, rare, 3-1/4" | 500 |
| **R6015**, pyremite, fluted bolsters, 3-1/4" | 400 |
| **R6023**, bone | 235 |
| **R6024**, pearl | 300 |

*RS4783, Scout knife, brown bone, w/emblem, 3-1/2", $300.*

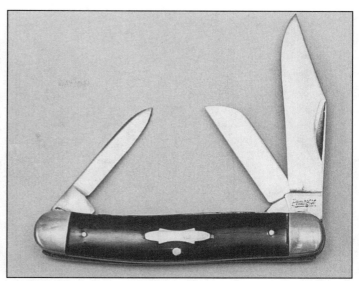

*R4845, straight line, slick black, 3-3/8", $125.*

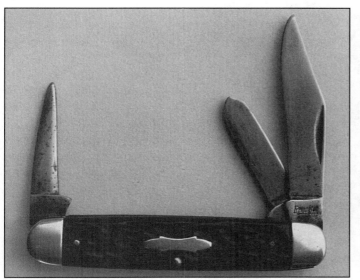

*R4832, black composition, 3-3/8", $150.*

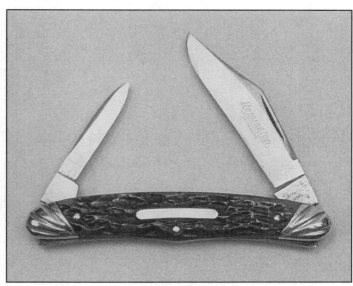

*R6013, brown bone, fluted bolsters, 3-1/4", $450.*

*R4843, imitation bone, 3-3/8", $110.*

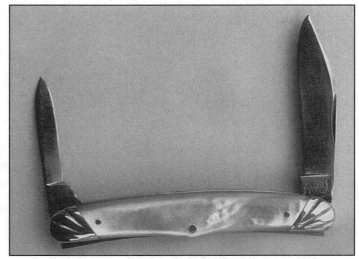

*R6014, genuine pearl, slant fluted bolsters, rare, 3-1/4", $500.*

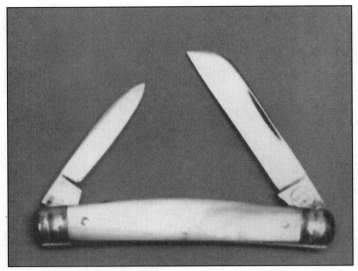

**R6014, congress, pearl, 3", $250.**

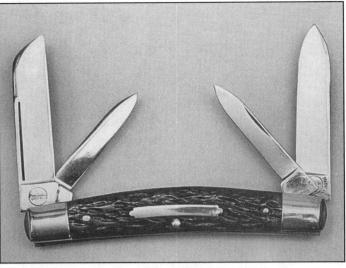

**R6043, congress, brown bone, 4-1/8", $800.**

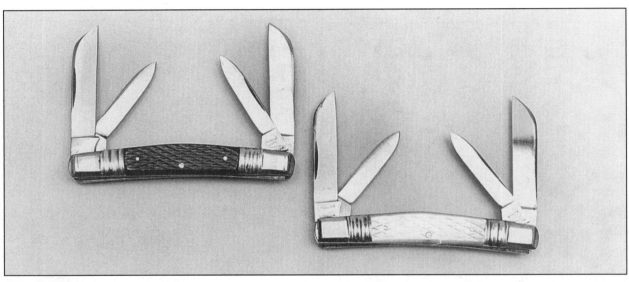

**Congresses**
**Left: R6032, black composition, scale, extended grooved bolsters, 3-1/2", $600.**
**Right: R6034, pearl, extended grooved bolsters, 3-1/2", $700.**

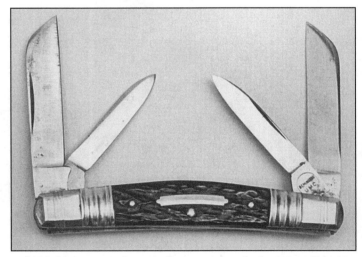

**R6033, congress, brown bone, extended grooved bolsters, 3-1/2", $400.**

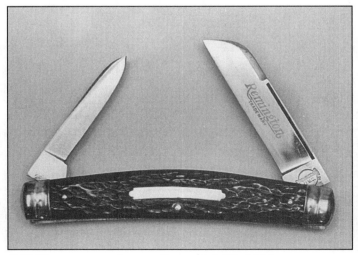

**R6063, congress, brown bone, 4-1/4", $300.**

Remington 465

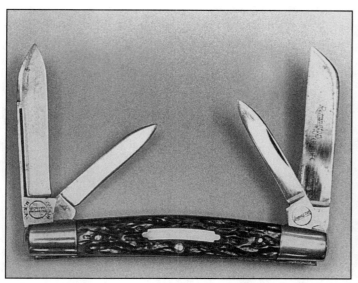
*R6073, long pull, brown bone, 3-3/4", $450.*

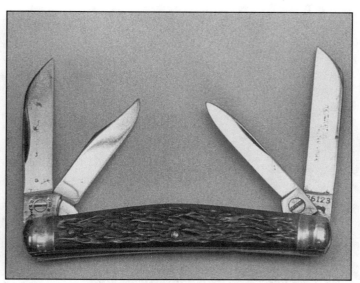
*R6123, congress, brown bone, grooved bolsters, 3-1/2", $350.*

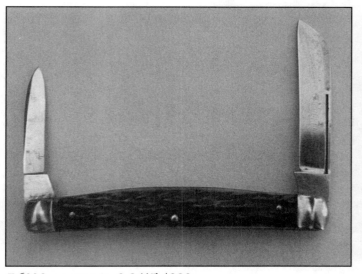
*R6093, congress, 3-3/4'" $200.*

*R6133, whittler, brown bone, threaded bolsters, 3-1/2", $650.*

| Description | Price |
|---|---|
| **R6025**, pyremite | 200 |
| **R6032**, congress, black composition, extended grooved bolsters, 3-1/2" | 600 |
| **R6033**, congress, brown bone, extended grooved bolsters, 3-1/2" | 400 |
| **R6034**, congress, pearl, extended grooved bolsters, 3-1/2" | 700 |
| **R6043**, congress, brown bone, 4-1/8" | 800 |
| **R6053**, bone, 4-1/8" | 550 |
| **R6063**, congress, brown bone, 4-1/4" | 300 |

| Description | Price |
|---|---|
| **R6073**, long pull, brown bone, 3-3/4" | 450 |
| **R6093**, congress, 3-3/4'" | 200 |
| **R6103**, bone, 3" | 175 |
| **R6105**, pyremite, 3" | 150 |
| **R6113**, bone | 275 |
| **R6123**, congress, brown bone, grooved bolsters, 3-1/2" | 350 |
| **R6133**, whittler, brown bone, threaded bolsters, 3-1/2" | 650 |

*R6143, 2 blades, brown bone, Remington Circle congress, UMC, 3-1/2", $200.*

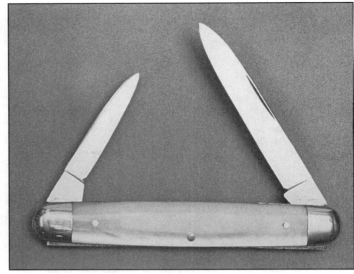

*R6194, equal end, pearl, 3-3/8", $175.*

*R6163, congress, bone, 4", $500.*

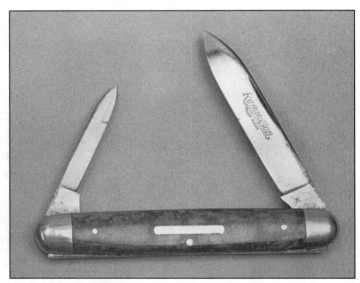

*R6195, equal end, brown mottled, 3-1/4", $140.*

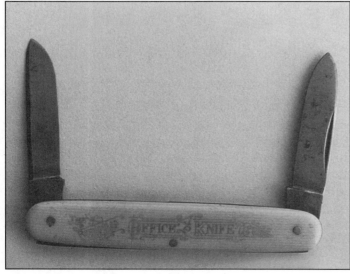

*R6175, office knife, pyremite, 3-3/4", $150.*

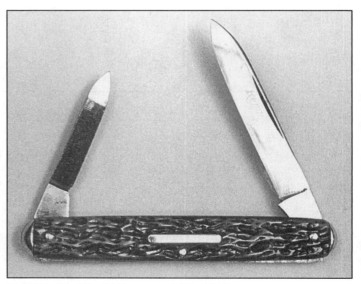

*R6203, file blade, bone, 3-1/4", $150.*

Remington 467

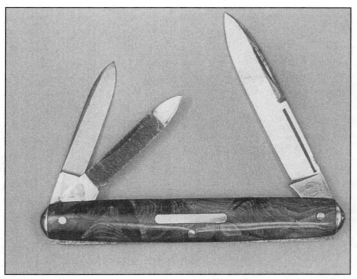

*R6225, whittler, long pull & regular pull, green-swirl pyremite, 3-1/4", $300.*

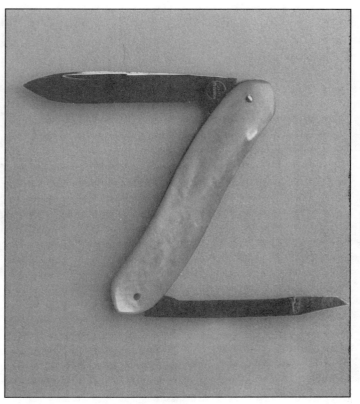

*R6244, lobster, pearl, 3", $125.*

| Description | Price |
|---|---|
| **R6143**, 2 blade congress, brown bone, Remington Circle UMC, 3-1/2" | 200 |
| **R6145**, 2 blade congress, pyremite, 3-1/2" | 225 |
| **R6153** bone | 150 |
| **R6155** pyremite | 150 |
| **R6163**, congress, bone, 4" | 500 |
| **R6175**, office knife, pyremite, 3-3/4" | 150 |
| **R6182**, 2 blade, black, SHAD, 3-1/4" | 75 |
| **R6183**, 2 blade, bone, SHAD, 3-1/4" | 100 |
| **R6184**, 2 blade, pearl, SHAD, 3-1/4" | 150 |
| **R6185**, 2 blade, pyremite, SHAD, 3-1/4" | 125 |
| **R6192**, black, 3-3/8" | 100 |
| **R6193**, bone, 3-3/8" | 130 |
| **R6194**, equal end, pearl, 3-3/8" | 175 |
| **R6195**, equal end, brown mottled, 3-1/4" | 140 |
| **R6203**, file blade, bone, 3-1/4" | 150 |
| **R6204**, pearl | 200 |
| **R6205**, pyremite | 150 |
| **R6214**, whittler, pearl, 3-1/4" | 400 |
| **R6215**, pyremite, 3-1/4" | 350 |
| **R6223**, 3 blade whittler, bone, 3-1/4" | 350 |
| **R6224**, 3 blade whittler, pearl | 400 |
| **R6225**, whittler, long pull & regular pull, green-swirl pyremite, 3-1/4" | 300 |
| **R6233**, 3 blade whittler, equal end, bone, 3-1/4" | 400 |
| **R6234**, 3 blade whittler, equal end, pearl, 3-1/4" | 450 |
| **R6235**, 3 blade whittler, pyremite, 3-1/4" | 400 |
| **R6243**, bone, lobster | 125 |
| **R6244**, lobster, pearl, 3" | 125 |
| **R6249**, metal, 3" | 90 |
| **R6255**, pyremite | 100 |
| **R6259**, lobster blade & file, metal | 100 |
| **R6265**, pyremite | 150 |

*R6295, whittler, pyremite, scalloped bolsters, rare, 3-1/4", $800.*

*R6334, whittler, genuine pearl, 3-1/8", $500.*

*R6393, whittler, brown bone, blood groove, 3-3/8", $600.*

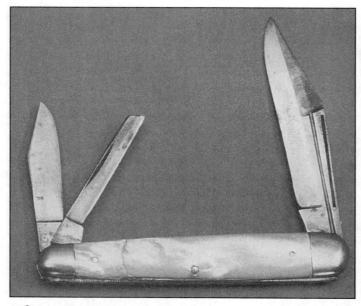

*R6394, whittler, pearl, blood groove, rare, Remington Circle UMC, 3-1/2", $800.*

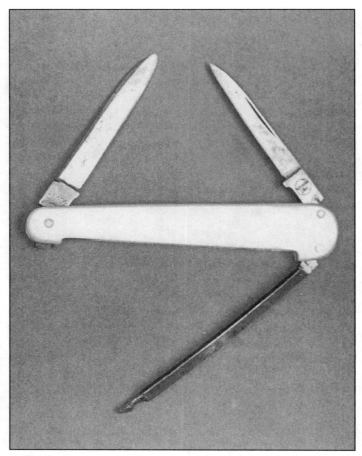

*R6424, sleeveboard/lobster, pearl, 2-3/4", $125.*

*R6434, lobster, pearl, 2-3/4", 150.*

| Description | Price |
|---|---|
| **R6275**, pyremite | 335 |
| **R6285**, pyremite | 335 |
| **R6295**, whittler, pyremite, scalloped bolsters, rare, 3-1/4" | 800 |
| **R6303**, bone | 150 |
| **R6313**, whittler, bone | 225 |
| **R6323**, bone | 240 |
| **R6325**, pyremite | 200 |
| **R6330**, buffalo horn | 250 |
| **R6333**, bone, 3-1/8" | 300 |
| **R6334**, whittler, genuine pearl, 3-1/8" | 350 |
| **R6334**, pearl, 3-1/8" | 350 |
| **R6335**, pyremite, 3-1/8" | 500 |
| **R6340**, whittler, buffalo horn, 3-1/2" | 350 |
| **R6343**, 3 blade whittler, bone, 3-1/2" | 400 |
| **R6344**, 3 blade whittler, pearl, 3-1/2" | 450 |
| **R6345**, 3 blade whittler, pyremite, 3-1/2" | 350 |
| **R6350**, buffalo horn | 200 |
| **R6353**, bone | 250 |
| **R6355G**, pyremite | 250 |
| **R6362**, 2 blade half whittler, black, 3-1/2" | 125 |
| **R6363**, 2 blade half whittler, bone, 3-1/2" | 150 |
| **R6365**, 2 blade half whittler, pyremite, 3-1/2" | 150 |
| **R6390**, whittler, buffalo horn, 3-3/8" | 400 |
| **R6393**, whittler, brown bone, blood groove, 3-3/8" | 600 |
| **R6394**, whittler, pearl, blood groove, Remington, Circle, UMC, rare, 3-1/2" | 800 |
| **R6395**, whittler, pyremite, blood groove, 3-3/8" | 500 |
| **R6400**, buffalo horn | 130 |
| **R6403**, bone | 130 |
| **R6404**, pearl | 200 |
| **R6405**, pyremite | 175 |
| **R6423**, bone | 125 |
| **R6424**, sleeveboard/lobster, pearl, 2-3/4" | 125 |
| **R6429**, metal | 85 |
| **R6433**, lobster, bone | 100 |
| **R6434**, lobster, pearl, 2-3/4" | 15 |
| **R6434**, lobster, pearl, 2-3/4" | 150 |
| **R6439**, lobster, metal, 2-3/4" | 150 |
| **R6443**, 3 blade lobster, bone, 2-11/16" | 125 |
| **R6444**, 3 blade lobster, pearl, 2-11/16" | 150 |
| **R6445**, 3 blade lobster, pyremite, 2-11/16" | 125 |
| **R6448**, 3 blade lobster, cocobolo, 2-11/16" | 100 |
| **R6454**, gunstock whittler, pearl, 3" | 500 |
| **R6454**, gunstock whittler, pearl, 3" | 600 |
| **R6456**, gunstock lobster, genuine stag, shows grooved file, 3" | 600 |
| **R6463**, bone, 3" | 75 |
| **R6464**, pearl, 3" | 100 |
| **R6465**, onyx, 3" | 90 |
| **R6473**, bone | 100 |
| **R6474**, pearl | 125 |

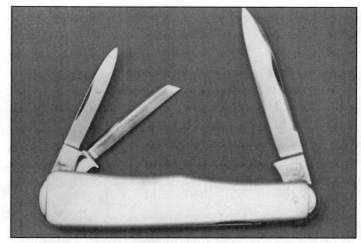

*R6454, gunstock whittler, pearl, 3", 600.*

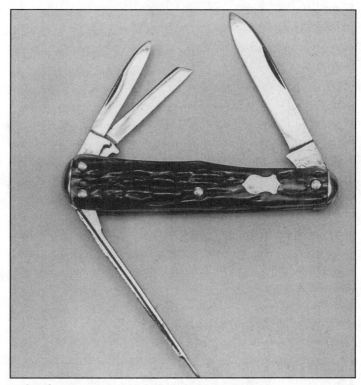

*R6456, gunstock lobster, genuine stag, shows grooved file, 3", $600.*

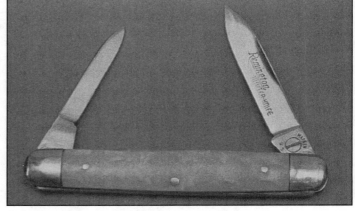

*R6465, onyx, 3", $90.*

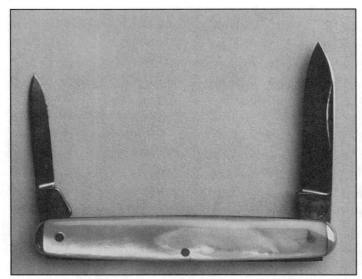

*R6484, genuine pearl, tip bolsters, 3", $200.*

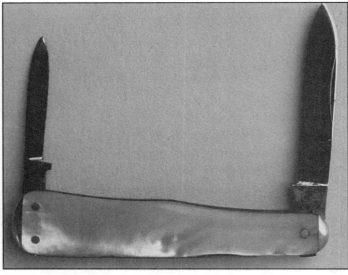

*R6514, gunstock, pearl, 3-1/8", $350.*

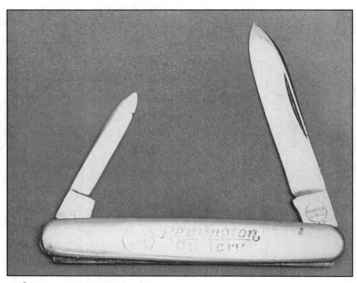

*R6499, all metal, 3", $75.*

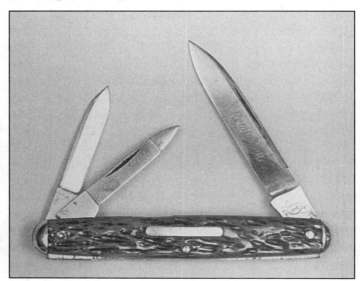

*R6533, whittler, brown bone, 3", $300.*

*R6504, file, pearl, tip bolsters, w/bail, 3", $150.*

*R6553, sleeveboard whittler, bone, 3-3/8", $300*

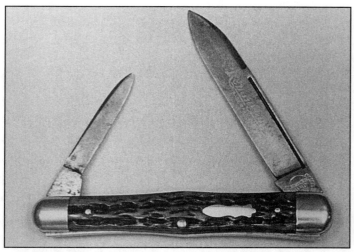

*R6563, swell center, long pull, brown bone, 3-5/8", $150.*

*R6573, sleeveboard, brown bone, tip bolsters, 3-1/2", $125.*

| Description | Price |
|---|---|
| **R6483**, senator pen, bone, tip bolsters, 3" | 125 |
| **R6484**, genuine pearl, tip bolsters, 3" | 200 |
| **R6494**, pearl, 3" | 100 |
| **R6495**, pyremite, 3" | 80 |
| **R6499**, all metal, 3" | 75 |
| **R6504**, file, pearl, tip bolsters, w/bail, 3" | 150 |
| **R6505**, pyremite | 100 |
| **R6514**, gunstock, pearl, 3-1/8" | 350 |
| **R6519**, 3 blade lobster, metal | 125 |
| **R6520**, equal-end whittler, buffalo horn, 3" | 250 |
| **R6524**, equal-end whittler, pearl, 3" | 350 |
| **R6533**, whittler, brown bone, 3" | 300 |
| **R6534**, whittler, pearl, 3" | 350 |
| **R6543**, bone | 200 |
| **R6545**, pyremite | 200 |
| **R6553**, sleeveboard whittler, bone, 3-3/8" | 300 |
| **R6559**, 3 blade lobster, metal | 100 |
| **R6563**, swell center, long pull, brown bone, 3-5/8" | 150 |
| **R6565**, pyremite, 3-5/8" | 150 |
| **R6573**, sleeveboard, brown bone, tip bolsters, 3-1/2" | 125 |
| **R6575**, pyremite | 125 |
| **R6583**, sleeveboard, bone, 3-1/2" | 150 |
| **R6585**, pyremite, 3-1/2" | 125 |
| **R6593**, bone | 135 |
| **R6595**, pyremite | 125 |
| **R6603**, whittler, bone, 3-1/2" | 300 |
| **R6604**, whittler, pearl, 3-1/2" | 400 |
| **R6605**, whittler, pyremite, 3-1/2" | 300 |
| **R6613**, bone | 150 |
| **R6615**, pyremite | 150 |
| **R6623**, bone, 3-1/8" | 200 |
| **R6624**, pearl, aluminum bolsters & liner, 3-1/8" | 225 |

*R6583, sleeveboard, bone, 3-1/2", $150.*

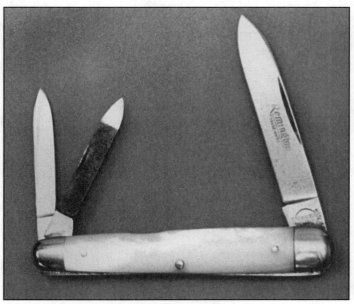

*R6604, whittler, pearl, 3-1/2", $400.*

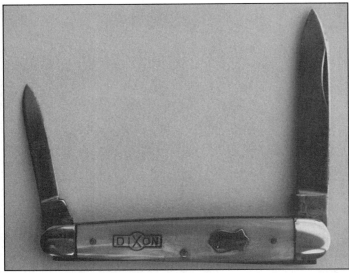

*R6625, advertising, celluloid, aluminum bolsters, 3-1/2", $150.*

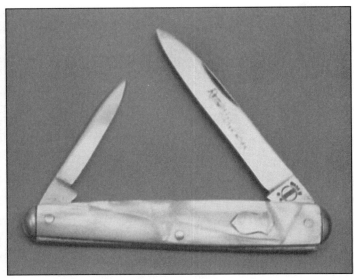

*R6645, sleeveboard, cracked ice, tip bolsters, 3-1/8", $125.*

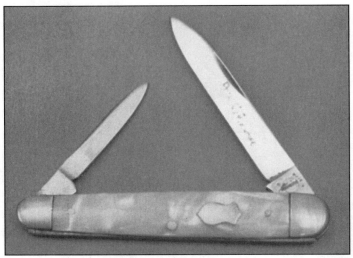

*R6625, sleeveboard, cracked ice, aluminum bolsters & liners, 3-1/8", $200.*

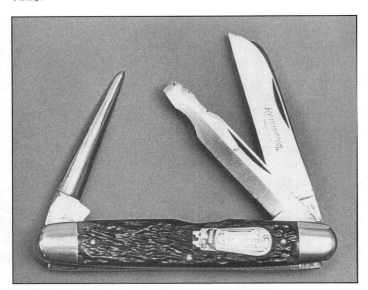

*R6653, whittler, brown bone, 3-1/8", $300.*

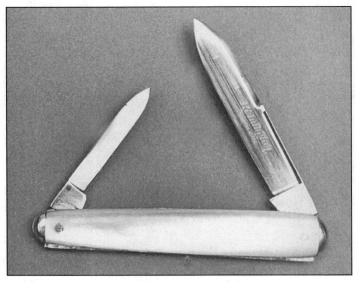

*R6644, sleeveboard, pearl, 3-1/8", $150.*

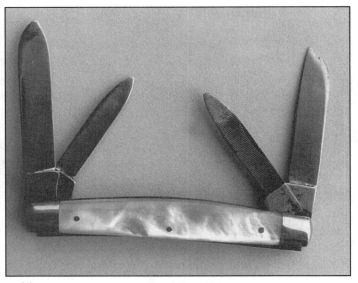

*R6674, congress, pearl, 3-1/8", $500.*

| Description | Price |
|---|---|
| **R6625**, advertising, celluloid, aluminum bolsters, 3-1/2" | 150 |
| **R6625**, sleeveboard, cracked ice, aluminum bolsters & liners, 3-1/8" | 200 |
| **R6633**, bone, 3-1/8" | 150 |
| **R6634**, pearl, 3-1/8" | 175 |
| **R6644**, sleeveboard, pearl, 3-1/8" | 150 |
| **R6645**, sleeveboard, cracked ice, tip bolsters, 3-1/8" | 125 |
| **R6653**, whittler, brown bone, 3-1/8" | 300 |
| **R6654**, whittler, pearl, 3-1/8" | 350 |
| **R6663**, bone | 150 |
| **R6664**, pearl | 200 |
| **R6673**, 4 blade congress, bone, 3-1/8" | 250 |
| **R6674**, congress, pearl, 3-1/8" | 500 |
| **R6683**, bone | 175 |
| **R6693**, congress, brown bone, 3-1/8" | 400 |
| **R6694**, congress, genuine pearl, threaded bolsters, 3-1/8" | 600 |
| **R6695**, pyremite, 3-1/8" | 500 |
| **R6703**, 4 blade, equal end, bone, 3" | 250 |
| **R6704**, congress, equal end, pearl, 3" | 300 |
| **R6705Q**, congress, 4 blade, equal-end, pyremite, 3" | 250 |
| **R6713**, equal end, brown bone, 3" | 250 |
| **R6714**, 4 blade, pearl, tip bolsters, 3" | 300 |
| **R6723**, whittler, brown bone, long pull, 3-1/8" | 300 |
| **R6724**, whittler, pearl, 3-1/8" | 350 |
| **R6725**, whittler, pyremite, 3-1/8" | 300 |
| **R6733**, 2 blade, bone, tip bolsters, 3-1/4" | 125 |
| **R6735**, 2 blade, pyremite, tip bolsters, 3-1/4" | 100 |
| **R6744**, pearl, 3-1/8" | 150 |
| **R6745F**, pyremite, 3-1/8" | 125 |
| **R6754**, pearl | 200 |
| **R6755A**, pyremite | 160 |
| **R6763**, bone | 225 |
| **R6764**, pearl | 275 |
| **R6765A**, pyremite | 150 |
| **R6773**, bone | 235 |
| **R6775**, pyremite | 175 |
| **R6781**, redwood, 3-1/4" | 100 |
| **R6785**, pyremite, 3-3/8" | 125 |
| **R6793**, bone | 125 |
| **R6795**, pyremite | 100 |
| **R6803**, whittler, bone, 3-3/8" | 250 |
| **R6805**, whittler, waterfall, 3-3/8" | 250 |
| **R6816**, whittler, humpback, lockblade, genuine stag, rare, 3-5/8" | 7,500 |
| **R6823**, whittler, humpback, grooved bolsters, 3-5/8" | 1,500 |
| **R6825**, whittler, pyremite, 3-3/8" | 750 |
| **R6834**, whittler, pearl, 3-1/8" | 600 |
| **R6835**, whittler, pyremite, 3-1/8" | 500 |

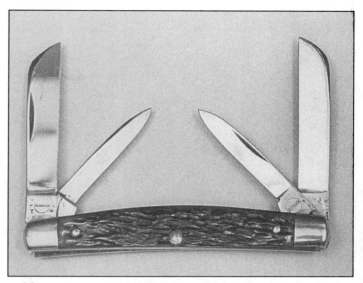

*R6693, congress, brown bone, 3-1/8", $400.*

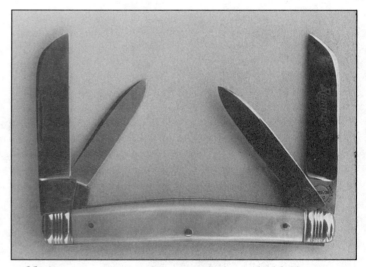

*R6694, congress, genuine pearl, threaded bolsters 3-1/8", $600.*

*R6713, equal end, brown bone, 3", $250.*

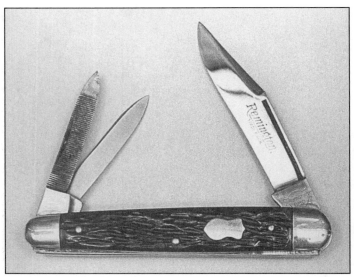

**R6723, whittler, brown bone, long pull, 3-1/8", $300.**

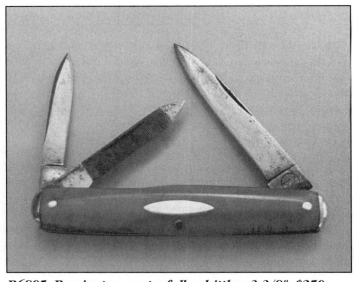

**R6805, Remington, waterfall, whittler, 3-3/8", $250.**

**R6744, pearl, 3-1/8", $150.**

**R6816, whittler, humpback, lockblade, genuine stag, rare, 3-5/8", $7,500.**

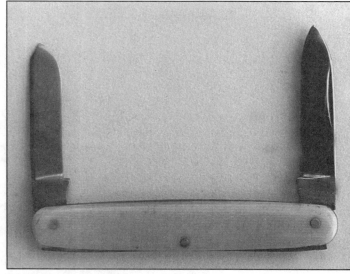

**R6785, pyremite, 3-3/8", $125.**

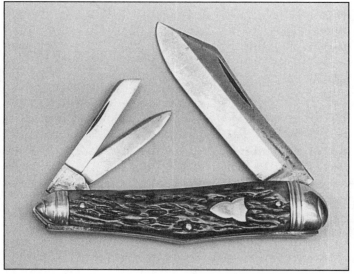

**R6823, humpback whittler, grooved bolsters, 3-5/8", $1,500.**

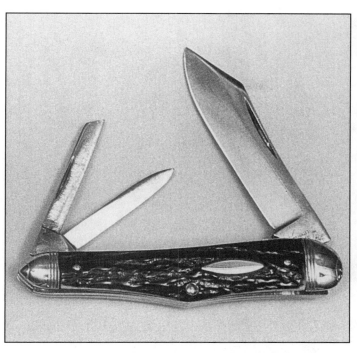

*R6836, whittler, humpback, stag, grooved bolsters, 3-1/8", $1,200.*

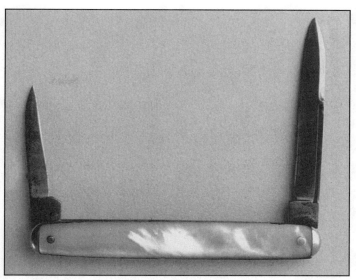

*R6844, pearl, 2-7/8", $125.*

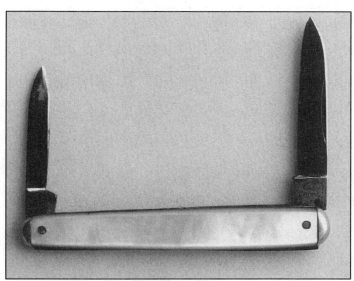

*R6864, pearl, 2-5/8", $125.*

| Description | Price |
|---|---|
| R6836, whittler, humpback, stag, grooved bolsters, 3-1/8" | 1,200 |
| R6843, 2 blade pen, bone, tip bolsters, 2-7/8" | 100 |
| R6844, pearl, 2-7/8" | 125 |
| R6845, pyremite, 2-7/8" | 75 |
| R6854, 2 blade, pearl, SHAD, 2-7/8" | 125 |
| R6859, 2 blade, metal, SHAD, 2-7/8" | 75 |
| R6863, 2 blade sleeveboard, bone, tip bolster, 2-5/8" | 75 |
| R6864, pearl, 2-5/8" | 125 |
| R6865, pyremite, 2-5/8" | 100 |
| R6872, jack, 2 blade, equal-end, tip bolsters, 3-1/8" | 125 |
| R6874, split pearl, 3-1/8" | 250 |
| R6875, pyremite, 3-1/8" | 125 |
| R6883, 2 blade, Wharncliffe blade, bone, 3" | 300 |
| R6885, 2 blade, Wharncliffe blade, pyremite, 3" | 300 |
| R6893, 3 blade, Wharncliffe whittler, bone, 3-1/8" | 450 |
| R6894, 3 blade, Wharncliffe whittler, pearl, 3-1/8" | 500 |
| R6895, 3 blade, Wharncliffe whittler, pyremite, 3-1/8" | 450 |
| R6903, 2 blade, equal end, bone, tip bolsters, 2-1/2" | 100 |

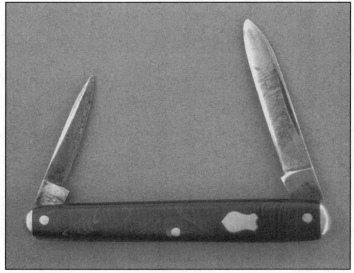

*R6865, pyremite, 2-5/8", $100.*

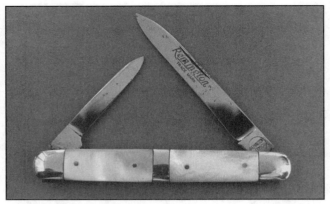
*R6874, split pearl, 3-1/8", $250.*

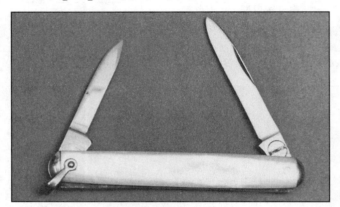
*R6904, pen, pearl, w/bail, 2-1/2", $100.*

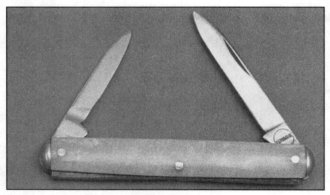
*R6905, pen, onyx, 2-1/2", $90.*

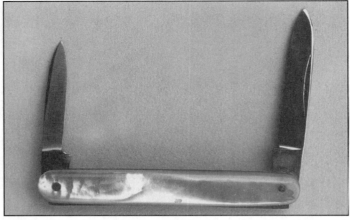
*R6914, pen, pearl, 2-1/2", $125.*

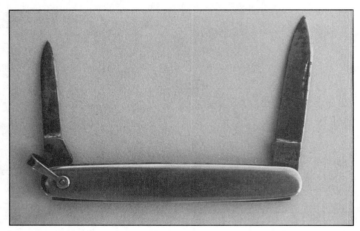
*R6919, NS, bail, 3", $75.*

*R6923, congress, bone, threaded bolsters, 3", $250.*

| Description | Price |
|---|---|
| **R6904**, pen, pearl, w/bail, 2-1/2" | 100 |
| **R6905**, pen, onyx, 2-1/2" | 90 |
| **R6914**, pen, pearl, 2-1/2" | 125 |
| **R6919**, NS, bail, 3" | 75 |
| **R6923**, congress, bone, threaded bolsters, 3" | 250 |
| **R6924**, congress, pearl, grooved bolsters, 3" | 300 |
| **R6925**, congress, imitation ivory, threaded bolsters, 3" | 200 |
| **R6933**, bone | 175 |
| **R6934**, pearl | 225 |
| **R6949**, metal | 75 |
| **R6954**, pearl | 325 |
| **R6956**, genuine stag | 350 |

| Description | Price |
|---|---|
| **R6964**, long slim sleeveboard, pearl | 325 |
| **R6966**, 2 blade, stag, 3-3/4" | 300 |
| **R6973**, bone | 250 |
| **R6974**, pearl | 400 |
| **R6984**, pearl, worked backspring, 3-1/4" | 1,000 |
| **R6993**, bone | 200 |
| **R6994**, pearl | 250 |
| **R6995**, sway-back congress, pyremite | 700 |
| **R7003**, bone | 250 |
| **R7004**, pearl | 300 |
| **R7005**, pyremite | 250 |
| **R7023**, bone, 3-1/4" | 250 |
| **R7026**, genuine stag, 3-1/4" | 300 |

| Description | Price |
|---|---|
| R7034, pearl | 250 |
| R7039/6, metal | 75 |
| R7039/7, metal | 75 |
| R7039/8, metal | 75 |
| R7039/15, metal | 75 |
| R7044, pearl | 125 |
| R7045, pyremite | 100 |
| RG7049/21, metal | 75 |
| RG7049/22, metal | 75 |
| RG7049/23, metal | 75 |
| RG7049/24, metal | 75 |
| RG7054, pearl | 125 |
| RG7059/17, metal | 75 |
| RG7059/18, metal | 75 |
| RG7059/19, metal | 75 |
| RG7059/20, metal | 75 |
| RG7064, pearl | 125 |
| R7069/25, metal | 75 |
| R7069/26, metal | 75 |
| R7069/27, metal | 75 |
| R7069/28, metal | 75 |
| R7073, whittler | 400 |
| R7074, pearl | 150 |
| RG7079/10, metal | 75 |
| RG7079/11, metal | 75 |
| RG7079/12, metal | 75 |
| RG7079/35, metal | 75 |
| RG7079/36, metal | 75 |
| RG7079/37, metal | 75 |
| R7084, pearl | 125 |
| RG7084, gold metal | 200 |
| RG7089/13, metal | 75 |
| RG7089/14, metal | 75 |
| RG7089/15, metal | 75 |
| RG7089/16, metal | 75 |
| RG7089/32, metal | 75 |
| RG7089/33, metal | 75 |
| RG7089/34, metal | 75 |
| R7090, buffalo horn | 100 |
| R7091, redwood | 200 |
| R7094, lobster, 3 blade, pearl, bail | 125 |
| RG7099/1, metal | 100 |
| RG7099/2, metal | 100 |
| RG7099/3, metal | 100 |
| RG7099/4, metal | 100 |
| RG7099/29, metal | 100 |
| RG7099/30, metal | 100 |
| RG7099/31, metal | 100 |
| RT7099, metal | 70 |
| R7103, bone | 100 |
| R7104, pearl | 125 |
| R7114, pearl | 125 |

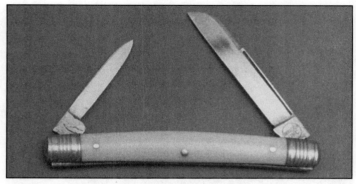

*R6925, congress, imitation ivory, threaded bolsters, 3", $200.*

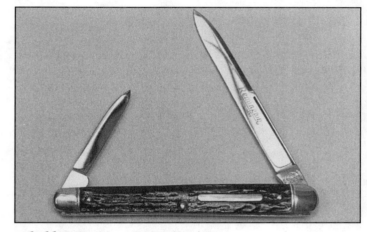

*R6966, 2 blade, stag, 3-3/4", $300.*

| Description | Price |
|---|---|
| R7116, genuine stag | 125 |
| R7124, long pull, genuine pearl, 3-1/4" | 350 |
| R7124, sleeveboard, long pull, pearl, Circle UMN, 3-1/4" | 400 |
| R7126, 4 blade sleeveboard, genuine stag, 3-1/4" | 350 |
| R7134, pearl | 200 |
| R7144, pearl | 250 |
| R7146, genuine stag | 250 |
| R7153, bone | 150 |
| R7163, bone | 135 |
| R7176, genuine stag | 200 |
| R7183, bone | 250 |
| R7196, genuine stag | 250 |
| R7203, bone | 270 |
| R7216, swell center, genuine stag, tip bolsters, 3-1/2" | 400 |
| R7223, 2 blade swell center, bone, 3" | 150 |
| R7224, pearl | 150 |
| R7225, swell center, long pull, green swirl pyremite, 3" | 250 |
| R7233, 2 blade swell center, bone, tip bolsters, 3" | 130 |
| R7234, swell center, pearl, 3" | 250 |
| R7236, 2 blade swell center, genuine stag, tip bolsters, 3" | 200 |

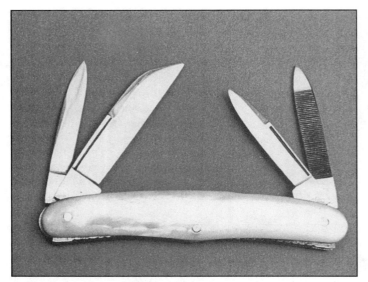

*R6984, pearl, worked backspring, 3-1/4", 1,000.*

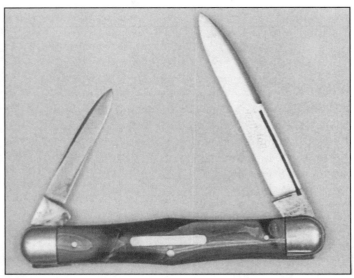

*R7225, swell center, long pull, green swirl pyremite, 3", $250.*

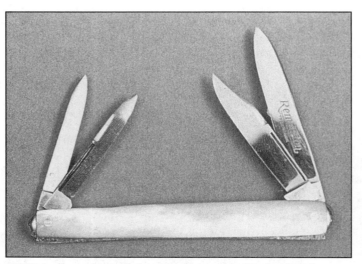

*R7124, sleeveboard, long pull, pearl, Circle UMN, 3-1/4", $400.*

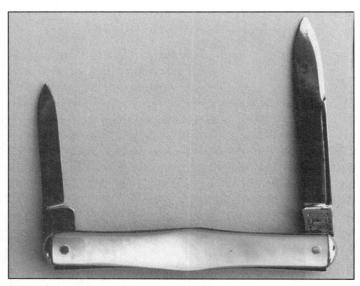

*R7234, pearl, swell center, 3", $250.*

*R7216, swell center, genuine stag, tip bolsters, 3-1/2", $400.*

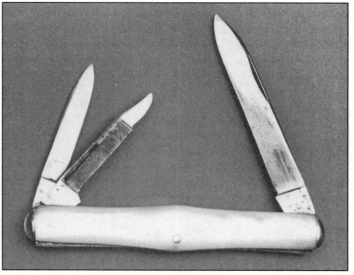

*R7244, swell center whittler, genuine pearl, 3", $400.*

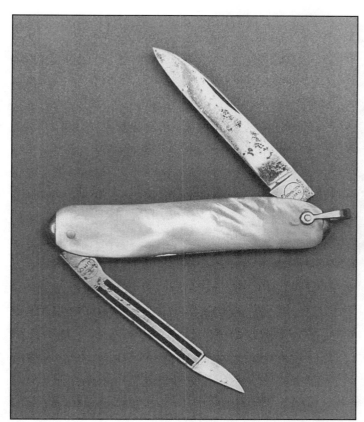

*R7284, lobster, pearl, w/bail, 3", $100.*

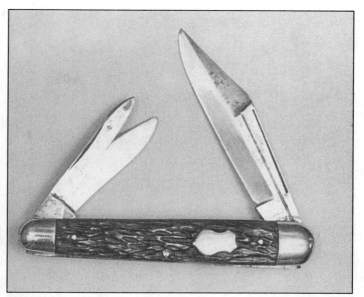

*R7293, whittler, grooved saber blade, long pull, brown bone, 3-3/8", $600.*

| Description | Price |
|---|---|
| R7243, swell-center whittler, bone, 3" | 250 |
| R7244, swell center whittler, genuine pearl, 3" | 400 |
| R7246, swell-center whittler, genuine stag, 3" | 300 |
| R7254, pearl | 125 |
| R7264, pearl | 125 |
| R7274, pearl | 125 |
| R7284, lobster, pearl, w/bail, 3" | 100 |
| R7293, whittler, grooved saber blade, long pull, brown bone, 3-3/8" | 600 |
| R7309, metal | 90 |
| R7319, metal | 75 |
| R7324, pearl | 100 |
| R7329, metal | 50 |
| R7335, pyremite, 3" | 60 |
| R7339, metal, 3" | 60 |
| R7343, corkscrew, brown bone, 3-1/8" | 250 |
| R7344, pearl, 3-1/8" | 225 |
| R7353, whittler, bone, 3-1/8" | 350 |
| R7363, lobster, sleeveboard, scissors, bone, 2-3/8" | 200 |
| R7366, lobster, sleeveboard, genuine stag, 2-3/8" | 250 |
| R7374, lobster, pearl, 2-3/8" | 150 |
| R7375, pyremite, 2-5/8" | 140 |
| R7375, lobster, cracked ice, 2-5/8" | 150 |
| R7385, lobster, 2 blade-file, green pyremite, bail, | |

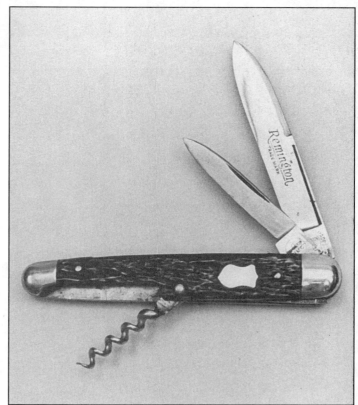

*R7343, corkscrew, brown bone, 3-1/8", $250.*

| Description | Price |
|---|---|
| Remington Circle UMC, 2-5/8" | 150 |
| R7394, pearl, 2-5/8" | 125 |
| R7396, genuine stag, 2-5/8" | 175 |

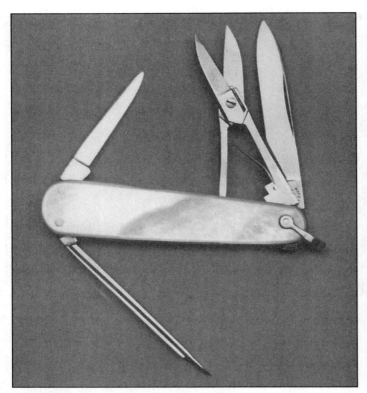

*R7414, scissors, pearl, 3-1/8", $200.*

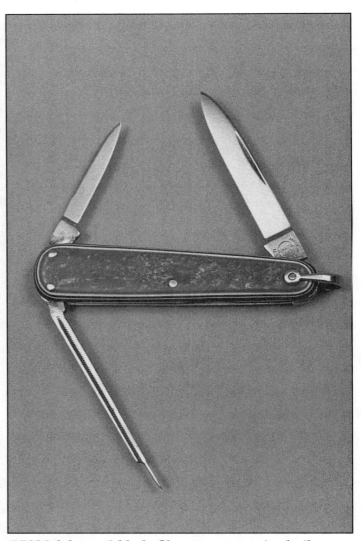

*R7385, lobster, 2 blade-file, green pyremite, bail, Remington Circle UMC, 2-5/8", $150.*

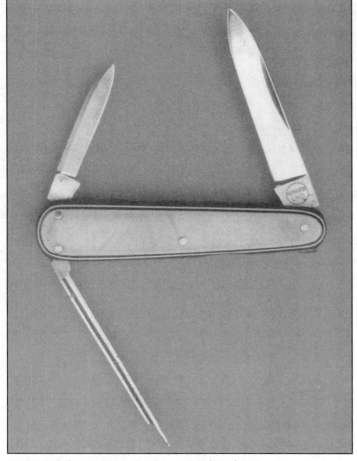

*R7375, lobster, cracked ice, 2-5/8", $150.*

| Description | Price |
|---|---|
| R7403, scissors, bone, 3-3/8" | 250 |
| R7404, pearl, 3-3/8" | 250 |
| R7414, scissors, pearl | 250 |
| R7423, 2 blades, blade etched Pal Fine Cutlery, 3-1/8" | 150 |
| R7425, sleeveboard, onyx, 3-1/8" | 125 |
| R7433, bone | 150 |
| R7443, bone | 125 |
| R7453, bone | 110 |
| R7463, bone | 110 |

*R7394, pearl, 2-5/8", $125.*

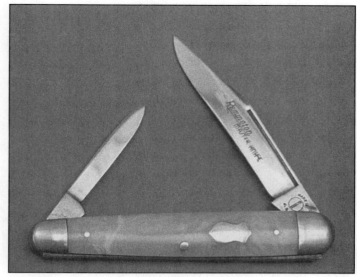

*R7425, sleeveboard, onyx, 3-1/8", $125.*

*R7403, scissors, bone, 3-3/8", $250.*

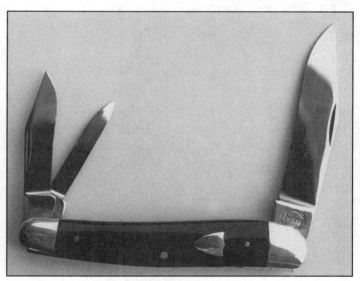

*R7495, pyremite, 3-3/8", $350.*

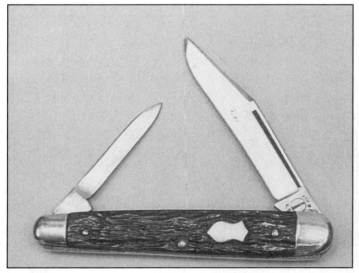

*R7423, 2 blades, blade etched Pal Fine Cutlery, 3-1/8", $150.*

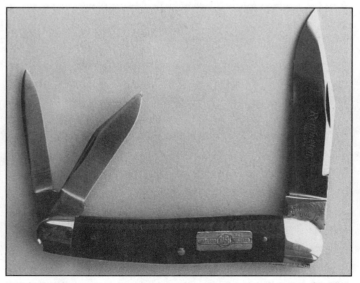

*R7495, pyremite, Isaacson, Nash shield, 3-3/8", $500.*

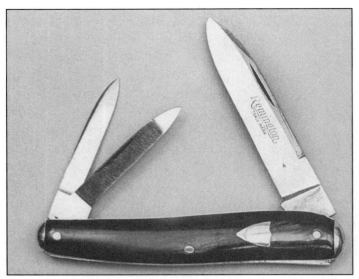

*R7500, whittler, horn, 3-3/8", $350.*

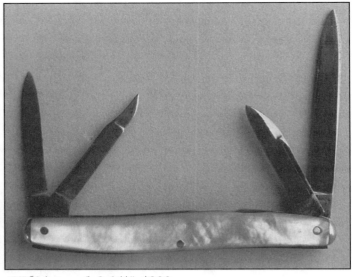

*R7604, pearl, 3-1/4", $300.*

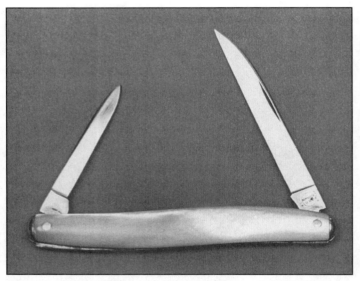

*R7574, Wharncliffe, pearl, tip bolsters, 3-1/4", $200.*

*R7654, whittler, pearl, 3-1/8", $400.*

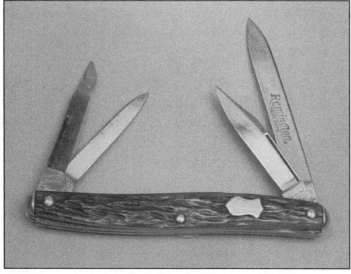

*R7603, serpentine, bone, tip bolsters, 3-1/4", $300.*

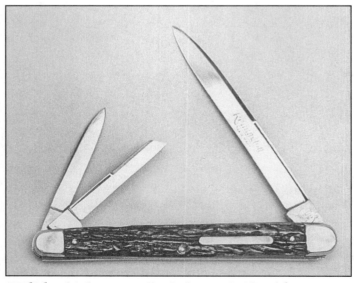

*R7696, whittler, stag, flat bolsters, 3-5/8", $600.*

| Description | Price |
|---|---|
| **R7465**, pyremite | 100 |
| **R7473**, bone | 110 |
| **R7475**, pyremite | 100 |
| **R7483**, bone | 200 |
| **R7485**, pyremite | 200 |
| **R7493**, whittler, bone, 3-3/8" | 350 |
| **R7495**, pyremite, 3-3/8" | 350 |
| **R7495**, pyremite, Isaacson, Nash shield, 3-3/8" | 500 |
| **R7500**, whittler, horn, 3-3/8" | 350 |
| **R7503**, whittler, bone, 3-3/8" | 250 |
| **R7513**, bone | 235 |
| **R7526**, genuine stag | 150 |
| **R7536**, genuine stag | 150 |
| **R7544**, pearl | 125 |
| **R7546**, genuine stag | 150 |
| **R7554**, pearl | 125 |
| **R7564**, 2 blade Wharncliffe, pearl, 3-3/8" | 175 |
| **R7566**, 2 blade Wharncliffe, genuine stag, 3-3/8" | 200 |
| **R7573**, Wharncliffe, bone, tip bolsters | 150 |
| **R7574**, Wharncliffe, pearl, tip bolsters, 3-1/4" | 200 |
| **R7576**, Wharncliffe, genuine stag | 200 |
| **R7584**, whittler, pearl, 3-3/8" | 250 |
| **R7586**, whittler, genuine stag, bar shield 3-3/8" | 250 |
| **R7593**, bone, 3-1/4" | 115 |
| **R7594**, pearl, 3-1/4 | 175 |
| **R7596**, genuine stag, 3-1/4" | 175 |
| **R7603**, serpentine, bone, tip bolsters, 3-1/4" | 300 |
| **R7604**, pearl, 3-1/4" | 300 |
| **R7604**, pearl, 3-1/4" | 300 |
| **R7606**, genuine stag, 3-1/4" | 350 |
| **R7613**, bone | 100 |
| **R7614**, pearl | 125 |
| **R7624**, pearl, 3" | 150 |
| **R7633**, bone, 3-1/8" | 150 |
| **R7643**, bone | 100 |
| **R7645**, pyremite | 100 |
| **R7653**, bone | 175 |
| **R7654**, whittler, pearl, 3-1/8" | 400 |
| **R7663**, whittler, 3 blades, bone, 3" | 225 |
| **R7664**, whittler, 3 blades, bone, pearl, 3" | 250 |
| **R7674**, pearl | 125 |
| **R7683**, bone | 100 |
| **R7684**, pearl | 125 |
| **R7696**, whittler, stag, flat bolsters, 3-5/8" | 600 |
| **R7706**, genuine stag | 200 |
| **R7713**, bone, w/bail, 2-1/2" | 100 |
| **R7725**, pyremite | 100 |
| **R7734**, genuine pearl, 2-3/4" | 200 |

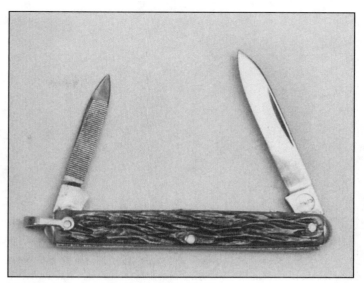

*R7713, bone, w/bail, 2-1/2", $100.*

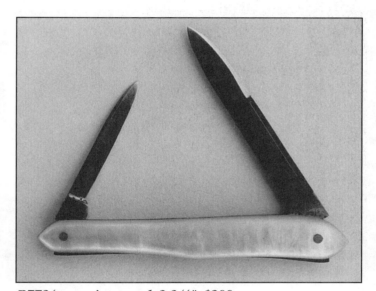

*R7734, genuine pearl, 2-3/4", $200.*

| Description | Price |
|---|---|
| **R7744**, pearl | 125 |
| **R7756**, whittler, pen & clip blade, genuine stag, pinched bolsters, 4-1/2" | 2,000 |
| **R7756**, whittler, genuine stag, 4-1/2" | 2,500 |
| **R7766**, whittler, genuine stag, pinched bolsters, 4-1/2" | 2,000 |
| **R7772**, black, 3-1/8" | 75 |
| **R7773**, bone, 3-1/8 | 75 |
| **R7775**, pyremite, 3-1/8" | 75 |
| **R7783**, bone | 100 |
| **R7785**, pyremite | 125 |
| **R7793**, bone | 100 |

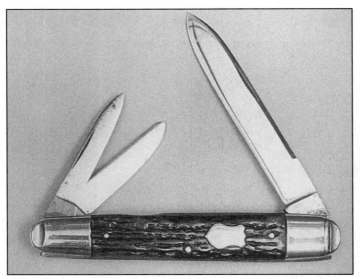

R7766, whittler, genuine stag, pinched bolsters, 4-1/2", $2,000.

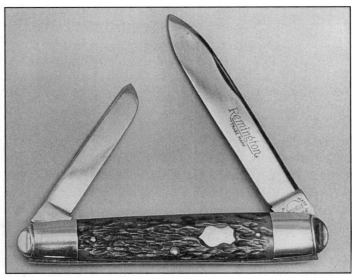

R7833, brown bone, pinched bolsters, 4-1/2", $1,000.

R7803, white pyremite, 3-1/8", $250.

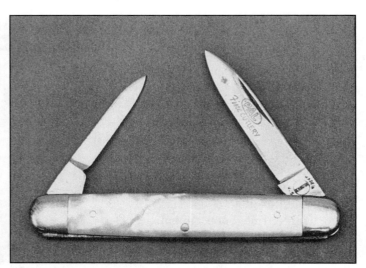

R7854, equal end, pearl, blade etched "Pal Fine Cutlery," 3", $200.

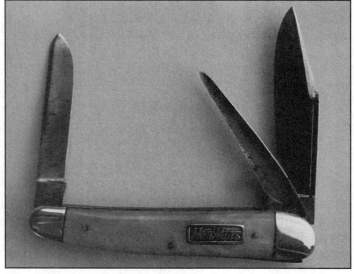

R7825, pyremite, Moor Mans shield, 3-3/8", $200.

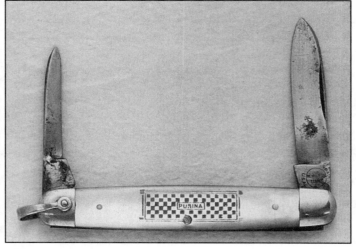

R7854, Purina checkerboard engraved, pearl w/bail, very rare, 3", mint price, $500.

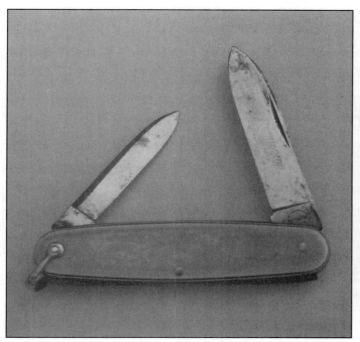

*R7945, pyremite, bail, 2-7/8", $90.*

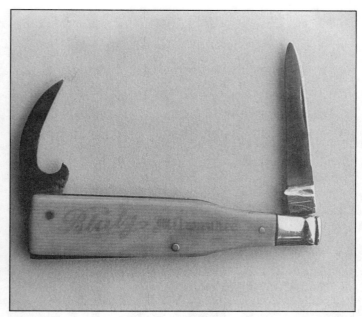

*R7985, bartender knife, imitation ivory, 3-1/8", $350.*

| Description | Price |
|---|---|
| **R7795**, pyremite | 100 |
| **R7803**, white pyremite, 3-1/8" | 250 |
| **R7805**, whittler, pyremite, 3-1/8" | 225 |
| **R7813**, bone, 3-3/8" | 150 |
| **R7814**, pearl, 3-3/8" | 150 |
| **R7825**, pyremite, Moor Mans shield, 3-3/8" | 200 |
| **R7833**, brown bone, pinched bolsters, 4-1/2" | 1,000 |
| **R7853**, bone, 3" | 125 |
| **RC7853**, bone, 3" | 100 |
| **R7854**, equal end, pearl, blade etched "Pal Fine Cutlery," 3" | 200 |
| **R7854**, Purina checkerboard engraved, pearl w/bail, very rare, 3", mint price | 500 |
| **R7857**, ivory, 3" | 100 |
| **R7863**, bone | 100 |
| **R7873**, bone | 100 |
| **R7895**, pyremite | 75 |
| **R7925**, pyremite, 2-13/16" | 75 |
| **R7945**, pyremite, bail, 2-7/8" | 90 |
| **R7985**, bartender, imitation ivory, 3-1/8" | 350 |
| **R7993**, bartender knife, bone, 3-3/8" | 200 |
| **R7995**, bartender, 3 blades, pyremite, Remington Circle UMC, 3-3/8" | 200 |
| **R8004**, pearl, 3" | 175 |
| **R8013**, bone | 75 |
| **R8023**, bone, 3-3/8" | 175 |
| **R8044**, file & scissors, 2-3/4" | 250 |
| **R8053**, switchblade, bone, 3-3/8" | 650 |
| **R8055**, switchblade, imitation onyx, rare, 3-3/8" | 600 |
| **R8059**, bartender, metal, 3-1/2" | 300 |

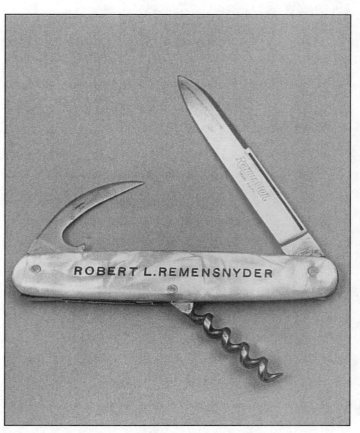

*R7995, bartender, 3 blades, pyremite, Remington Circle UMC, 3-3/8", $200.*

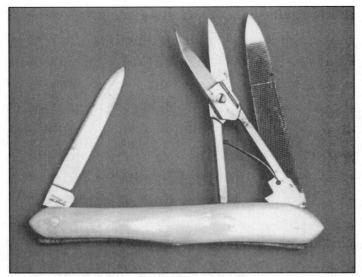

**R8044, file & scissors, 2-3/4", $250.**

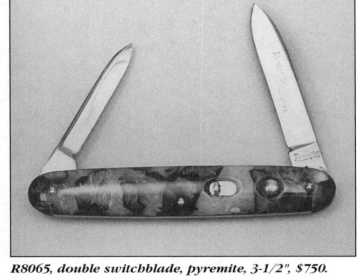

**R8065, double switchblade, pyremite, 3-1/2", $750.**

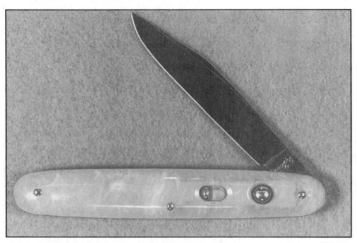

**R8055, switchblade, imitation onyx, rare, 3-3/8", $600.**

**R8623, brown bone, 3-1/8", $100.**

**R8059, bartender, metal, 3-1/2", $300.**

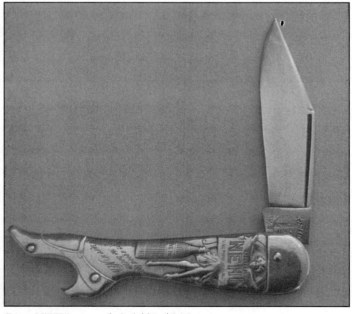

**Leg, NEHI, metal, 3-1/4", $200.**

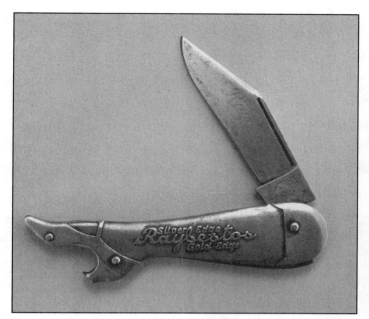

*Leg, Raybestos, metal, 3-1/4", $200.*

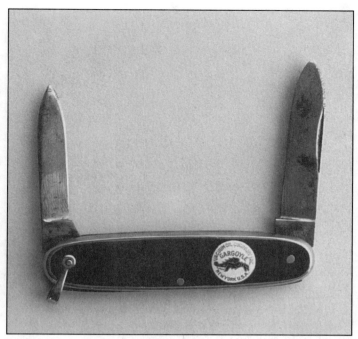

*Unknown, pyremite, gargoyle shield, 2-3/4", $150.*

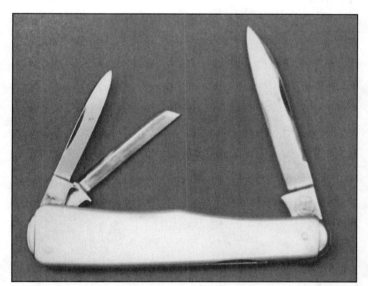

*Unknown, pyremite, 2-1/2", $250.*

| Description | Price |
|---|---|
| **R8065**, double switchblade, pyremite, 3-1/2" | 750 |
| **R8069**, metal sterling | 450 |
| **R8623**, brown bone, 3-1/8" | 100 |
| **R8623**, brown bone, 3-1/8" | 100 |
| **R9003SS**, bone | 150 |
| **Leg**, NEHI, metal, 3-1/4" | 200 |
| **Leg**, Raybestos, metal, 3-1/4" | 200 |
| **Unknown**, pyremite, 2-1/2" | 250 |
| **Unknown**, pyremite, gargoyle shield, 2-3/4" | 150 |
| **Advertising**, (insurance) metal, 1929, (the backside of handle reads: The Franklin Fire, Philadelphia, 1829-1929), 3" | 125 |
| **Pipe knife**, punch, metal, 3-1/8" | 150 |

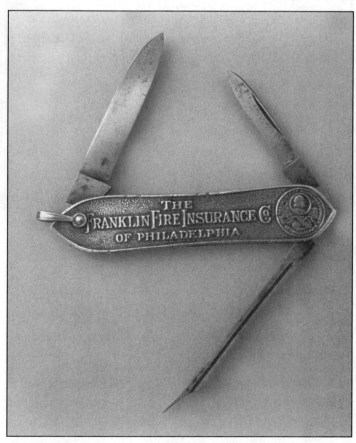

*Advertising, (insurance), metal, 1929, (backside of handle reads: The Franklin Fire, Philadelphia, 1829-1929), 3", $125.*

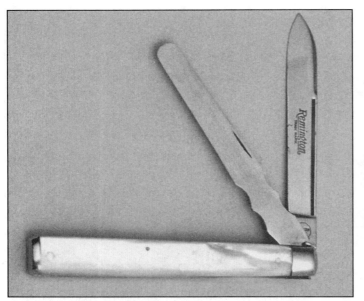

*Unknown, physician's knife, spatula, genuine pearl, Circle UMC, embossed mentholatum, 3-5/8", $1,000.*

*R7854: Only one feature makes this a super rare knife. Note the Purina checkerboard engraved in the pearl. With good eyes or a high-powered glass, you might be able to see Purina spelled out in the center of the checkerboard. There are a lot of Remington Purina red checkerboard knives under clear pyremite handles, but not in pearl. This is indeed a little jewel, $500.*

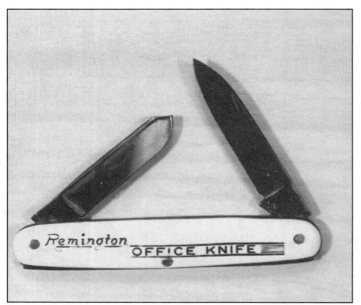

*This Remington office knife is very rare because of one feature: The spear blade is marked Circle Remington, and the spey blade is marked straight line Remington, which makes it a transition knife. I have never seen this marking before, but quite a few transitions are marked Remington Circle UMC and Remington Circle, $150.*

*This is a super rare Camp Fire Girls Remington knife and, in my estimation, should be rated very high in value. The triangular WO HE LO emblem shield stands for Camp Fire Girls and is etched on the master blade. The two-part can opener is marked straight line Remington with Pat. No. 1635649. The two cutting blades are marked Remington Circle UMC. The screwdriver cap lifter blade is not marked. Note that the smaller blade is a very unusual shape. As far as I know, this knife has not been catalogued and does not have a number. The knife is mint and is a real prize in a Remington collection, $1,000.*

*Patriotic Scout, pyremite handle, rare, 3-3/4", $400.*

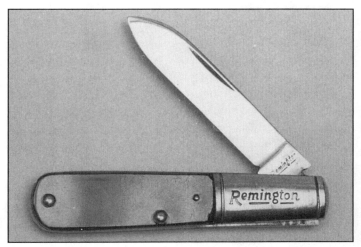

*No number, Barlow, 1 blade, smooth bone, straight lined, 3-3/8", $125.*

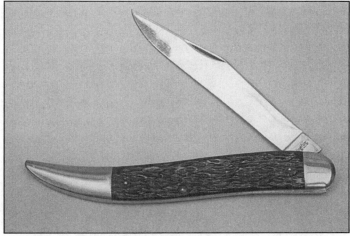

*No number, 1 blade, imitation bone, straight lined, $200.*

| Description | Price |
|---|---|
| **Unknown**, physician's knife, spatula, genuine pearl, Circle UMC, embossed mentholatum, 3-5/8" | **1,000** |
| **Office knife**, transition, spear blade marked Circle Remington, spey blade marked straight line Remington, rare | **150** |
| **R7854**, Purina checkerboard engraved in pearl, very rare | **500** |
| **Camp Fire Girls knife**, triangular WO HE LO shield and etch on master blade, two-part can opener with straight line Remington and Pat. No. 1635649, two cutting blades marked Remington Circle UMC, screwdriver cap lifter blade not marked, very rare | **1,000** |
| **Patriotic Scout**, pyremite handle, rare, 3-3/4" | **400** |
| **No number**, Barlow, 1 blade, smooth bone, straight lined, 3-3/8" | **125** |
| **No number**, 1 blade, imitation bone, straight lined | **200** |
| **R1773**, 2 blades, bone, Hanover Shoe emblem, 3-1/2" | **200** |

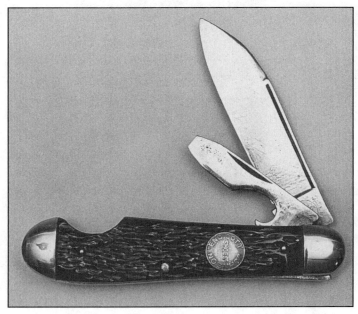

*R1773, 2 blades, bone, Hanover Shoe emblem, 3-1/2", $200.*

*Easy opener, brown bone, chain, 3-1/2", $200.*

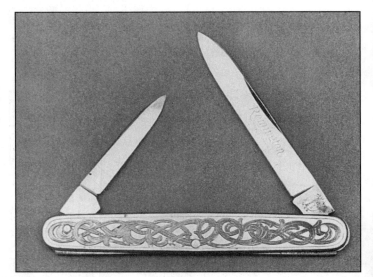
*Pen, metal, 3-1/8", $125.*

*R8243, easy opener, bone, round Endicott Johnson emblem, screwdriver/cap lifter, 3-1/2", $250.*

*Doctor's knife, brown bone, 2 blades, 3-1/2", $800.*

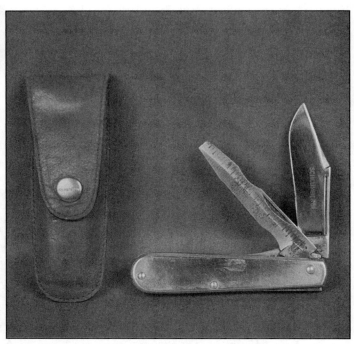
*R43, electrician's knife, aluminum handle, both blades stamped circle Remington, rare, $250.*

Remington 491

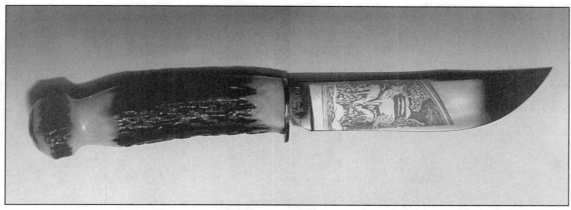
*Stag handle, blade etched w/wildlife scene, $250.*

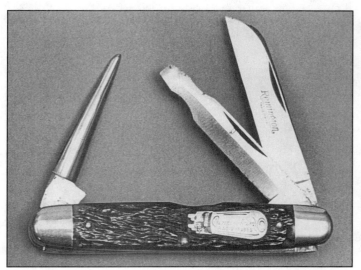
*electrician's blade & punch, Cunningham radio tube, regular pull, brown bone, radio tube shield, $1,000.*

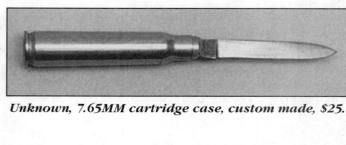
*Unknown, 7.65MM cartridge case, custom made, $25.*

*Knife opener, $25.*

| Description | Price |
| --- | --- |
| **Easy opener**, brown bone, chain, 3-1/2" | 200 |
| **Pen**, metal, 3-1/8" | 125 |
| **R8243**, easy opener, screwdriver/cap lifter, bone, round Endicott Johnson emblem, 3-1/2" | 250 |
| **Doctor's knife**, 2 blades, brown bone, 3-1/2" | 800 |
| **R43**, electrician's knife, aluminum handle, both blades stamped circle Remington, rare | 250 |
| **Stag handle**, blade etched w/wildlife scene | 250 |
| **Unknown**, 7.65MM cartridge case, custom made | 25 |
| **knife opener** | 25 |
| Electrician's blade & punch, Cunningham radio tube, regular pull, brown bone, radio tube shield, | 1,000 |
| **Advertising display knife**, lobster, gold scale, w/bail, 2-3/4" | 200 |

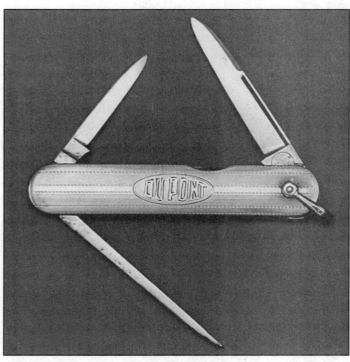
*Advertising display knife, lobster, gold scale, w/bail, 2-3/4", $200.*

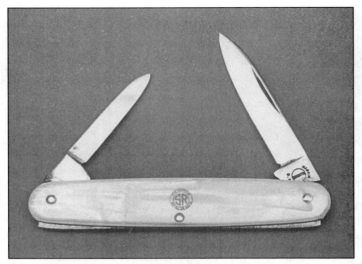

*Pen, imitation pearl, Southern Railroad emblem, 3-1/4", $100.*

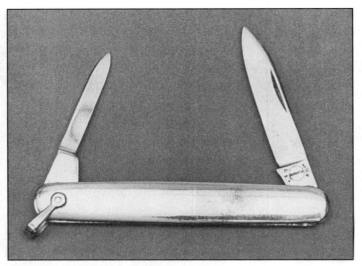

*R6919, all metal, w/bail, 3", $75.*

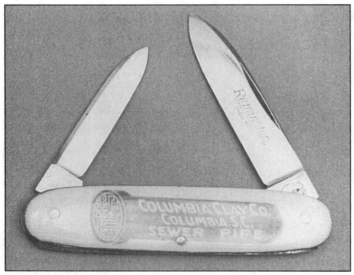

*Advertising, imitation ivory, 2-7/8", $100.*

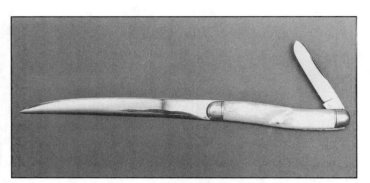

*Letter opener, pearl, 4" knife handle, 9", $350.*

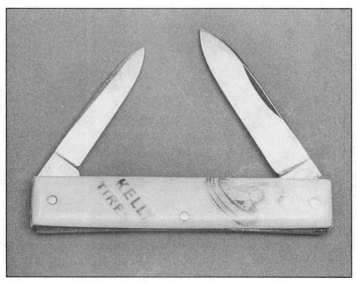

*Advertising, imitation ivory, 2-7/8", $100.*

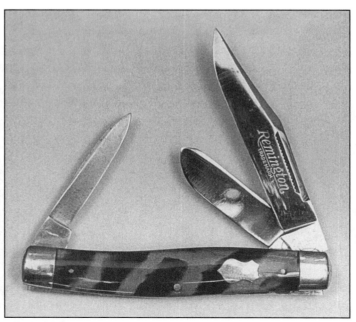

*Long pull, imitation tortoise, 4", $500.*

Remington 493

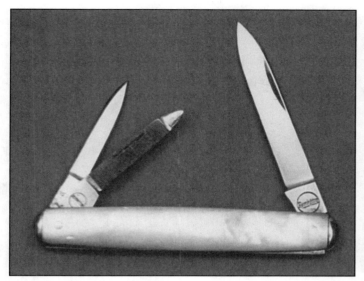

*Whittler, pearl, 3", $300.*

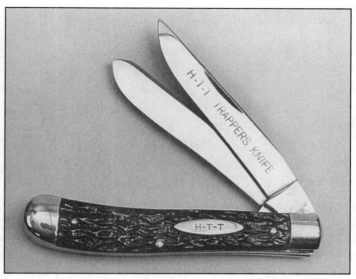

*Trapper HTT, regular pull, brown bone, HTT shield, 3-3/4", $1,500.*

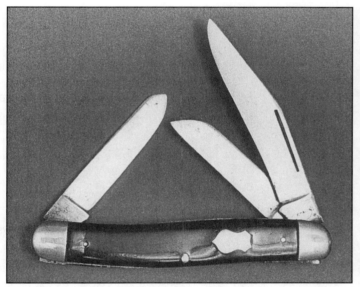

*Stockman, slick black, 4", $350.*

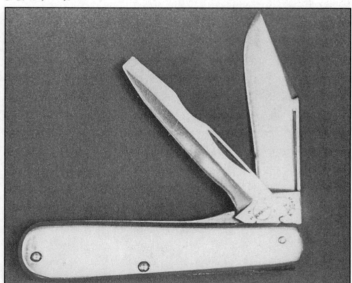

*Electrician's knife, screwdriver blade w/lock, long pull, all metal, 3-1/2", $250.*

| Description | Price |
|---|---|
| **Pen**, imitation pearl, Southern Railroad emblem, 3-1/4" | 100 |
| **Advertising**, imitation ivory, 2-7/8" | 100 |
| **Advertising**, imitation ivory, 2-7/8" | 100 |
| **R6919**, all metal, w/bail, 3" | 75 |
| **Letter opener**, pearl, 4" knife handle, 9" | 350 |
| **Long pull**, imitation tortoise, 4" | 500 |
| **Whittler**, pearl, 3" | 300 |
| **Stockman**, slick black, 4" | 350 |
| **Trapper** HTT, regular pull, brown bone, HTT shield, 3-3/4" | 1,500 |
| **Electrician's knife**, screwdriver blade w/lock, long pull, all metal, 3-1/2" | 250 |
| **Swell center**, imitation pearl, 2-7/8" | 125 |

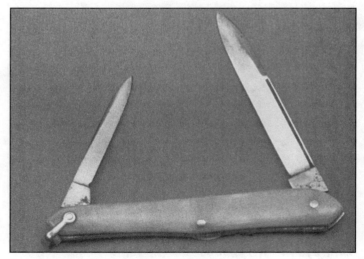

*Swell center, imitation pearl, 2-7/8", $125.*

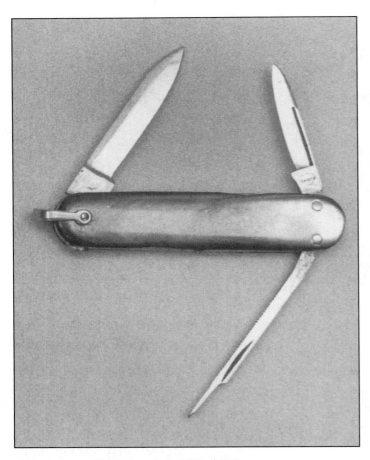

*Lobster, smoked pearl, 2-1/8", $150.*

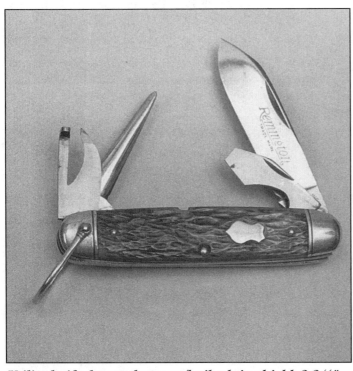

*Utility knife, brown bone, w/bail, plain shield, 3-3/4", $300.*

*Wharncliffe, equal end, round Wayne Feed emblem, 3-1/4", $275.*

*Jack, Rogers bone, straight line, $140.*

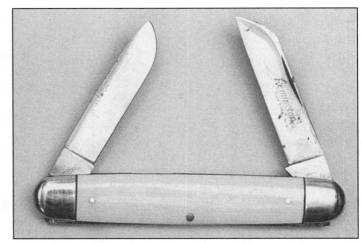

*Florist or drafting knife, imitation ivory, 3-7/8", $150.*

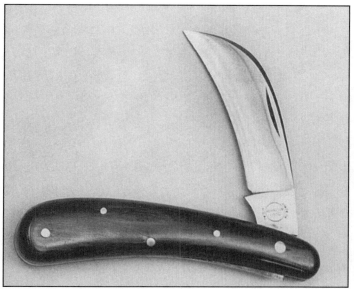
*Hawkbill, rosewood, 4", $150.*

*Jacks*
*Left: brown bone, 4-1/2", $600.*
*Right: brown bone, Pal shield, 4-1/2", $600.*

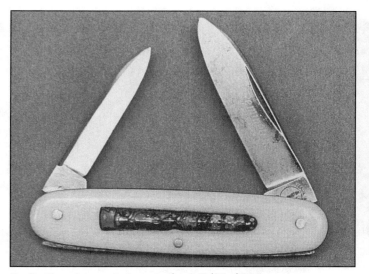
*Imitation ivory, totem pole, 2-7/8", $800.*

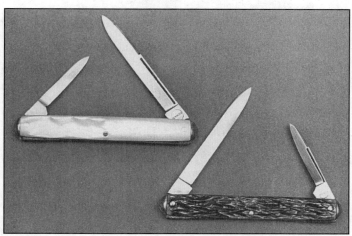
*Salesman's knife showing a different handle for each side, one side pearl, other side bone, 2-7/8", $400.*

| Description | Price |
|---|---|
| **Lobster**, smoked pearl, 2-1/8" | 150 |
| **Utility knife**, brown bone, w/bail, plain shield, 3-3/4" | 300 |
| **Wharncliffe**, equal end, round Wayne Feed emblem, 3-1/4" | 275 |
| **Jack**, Rogers bone, straight line | 140 |
| **Stockman**, red composition | 400 |
| **Florist or drafting knife**, imitation ivory, 3-7/8" | 150 |
| **Hawkbill**, rosewood, 4" | 150 |
| **Imitation ivory**, totem pole, 2-7/8" | 800 |
| **Jack**, brown bone, 4-1/2" | 600 |
| **Jack**, brown bone, Pal shield, 4-1/2" | 600 |
| **Salesman's knife**, with different handle for each side, one side pearl, other side bone, 2-7/8" | 400 |
| **Bartender's knife**, bottle shaped, imitation ivory, 3" | 350 |

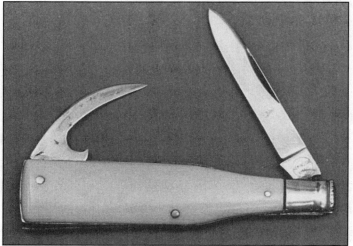
*Bartender's knife, bottle shaped, imitation ivory, 3", $350.*

*Lobster, smoked pearl, bail, 2-5/8", $250.*

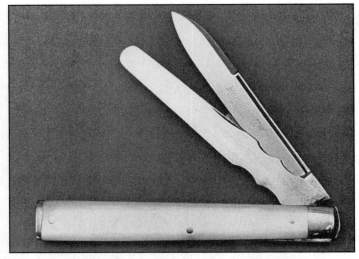

*Doctor's knife, spatula, pearl, 3-1/2", $1,000.*

*Purina advertising knife, checkerboard, 3-3/8", $350.*

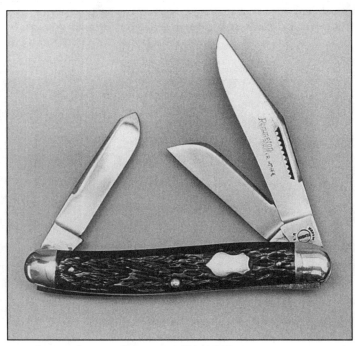

*Stockman, brown bone, 3-3/4", $350.*

*Jack, brown bone, Axton shield, 3-1/2", $500.*

Remington 497

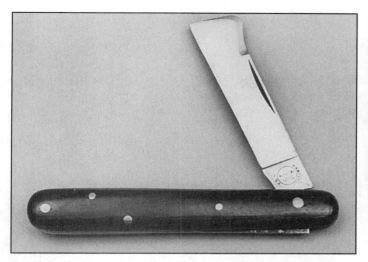

*Horticulture, rosewood scales, 4-1/8", $150.*

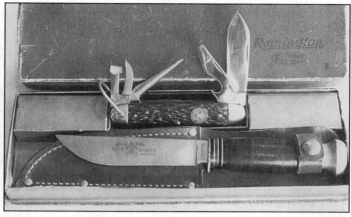

*Boy Scout Set*
*Top: RS3333, Boy Scout pocketknife*
*Bottom: RRH51, Boy Scout sheath knife*
*Mint in original box, $700.*

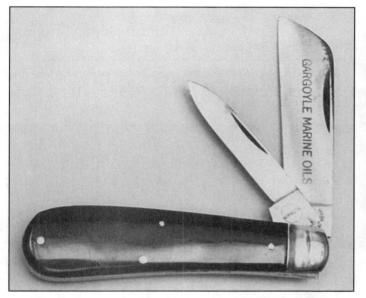

*Half hawkbill, slick black scales, 3-3/4", $150.*

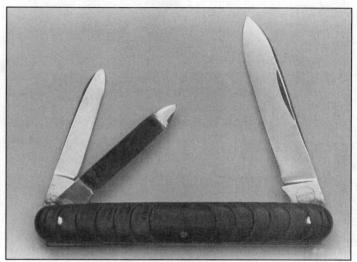

*No number, whittler, 3 blades, black composition, rare scalloped handles, Remington Circle, 3-1/4", $400.*

| Description | Price |
|---|---|
| **Lobster**, smoked pearl, bail, 2-5/8" | 250 |
| **Stockman**, brown bone, 3-3/4" | 350 |
| **Doctor's knife**, spatula, pearl, 3-1/2" | 1,000 |
| **Purina advertising knife**, checkerboard, 3-3/8" | 350 |
| **Jack**, brown bone, Axton shield, 3-1/2" | 500 |
| **Horticulture**, rosewood scales, 4-1/8" | 150 |
| **Half hawkbill**, slick black scales, 3-3/4" | 150 |
| **Boy Scout Set**: RS3333, Boy Scout pocketknife; RH51, Boy Scout sheath knife, mint in original box | 700 |
| **No number**, whittler, 3 blades, black composition, rare scalloped handles, Remington Circle, 3-1/4" | 400 |
| **No number**, two-blade jack, long spey blade, yellow scales w/shield, Remington, Circle UMC, 3-3/8" | 200 |

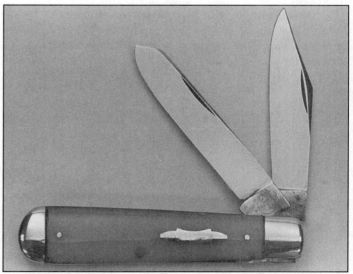

*No number, two-blade jack, long spey blade, yellow scales w/shield, Remington Circle UMC, 3-3/8", $200.*

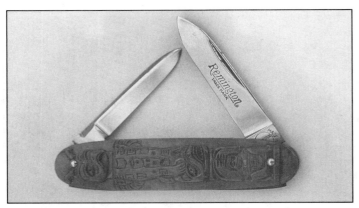

*Totem pole knife, fossilized walrus ivory, rare, $1,000.*

*This Remington Dupont Cutlery counter mat serves well for the R1123 Remington bullet knife. The Remington Model 1875 44-cal. single-action revolver is not out of place, even though it is about 50 years older. The serial number of this revolver 579 was probably made in the first year of production (1875). It is well known that most of the Texas Rangers used the Colt single-action revolver and the Winchester rifle. It is also a well-known fact some of the Rangers used other good brands of handguns and long guns. Therefore, the Ranger badge is not out of place w/ the Remington revolver or the Remington knife. This badge was made from a five peso Mexican coin, and it fits in well with most any gun or knife collection. All are super rare.*

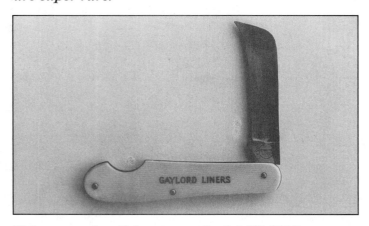

*Unknown, advertising, pyremite, 3-1/2", $125.*

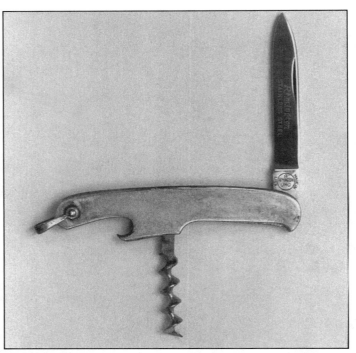

*No number, blade & corkscrew, bottle opener, all metal, bail, stainless, Remington Circle UMC, 3-1/8", $125.*

*Unknown, Purina advertising, 3-3/8", $250.*

| Description | Price |
|---|---|
| **Totem pole knife**, fossilized walrus ivory, rare | 1,000 |
| **No number**, blade & corkscrew, bottle opener, all metal, bail, stainless, Remington Circle UMC, 3-1/8" | 125 |
| **Unknown**, advertising, pyremite, 3-1/2" | 125 |
| **Unknown**, Purina advertising, 3-3/8" | 250 |
| **Unknown**, advertising, lobster, 2-1/4" | 75 |
| **Unknown**, advertising, celluloid, 3-3/8" | 125 |

*Unknown, advertising, lobster, 2-1/4", $75.*

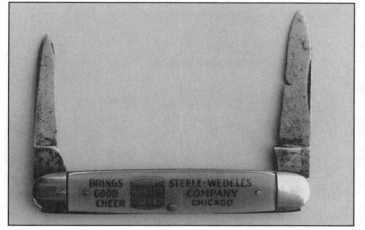

*Unknown, advertising, celluloid, 3-3/8", $125.*

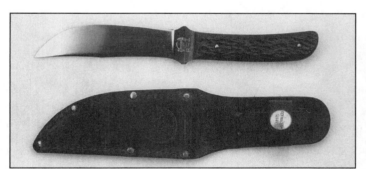

*RH4, blade length 4-1/2", length 7-1/2".*
| VG | Exc | Mint |
|---|---|---|
| $50 | $75 | $125 |

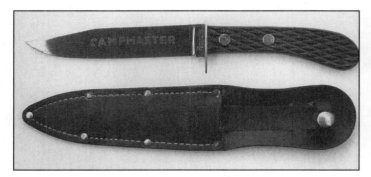

*RH6, blade length 5-1/4", length 9-1/4".*
| VG | Exc | Mint |
|---|---|---|
| $50 | $85 | $125 |

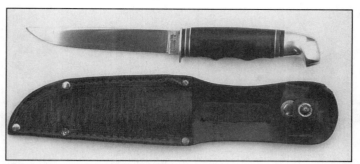

*RH14, blade length 4", length 7-3/4".*
| VG | Exc | Mint |
|---|---|---|
| $75 | $125 | $175 |

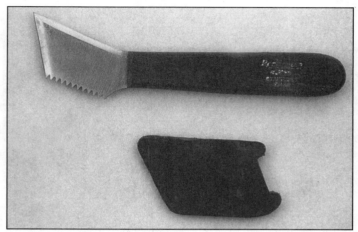

*RH22, blade length 2", length 6-1/4".*
| VG | Exc | Mint |
|---|---|---|
| $75 | $100 | $150 |

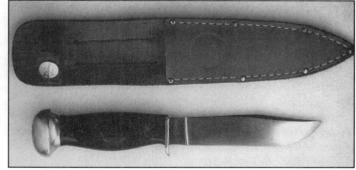

*RH28, blade length 4-1/2", length 8-1/2".*

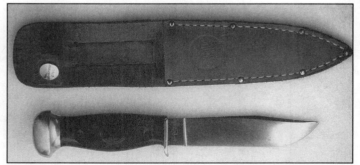

*RH28, blade length 4-1/2", length 8-1/2".*
| VG | Exc | Mint |
|---|---|---|
| $75 | $125 | $200 |

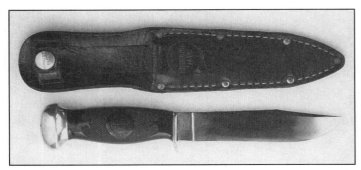

**RH29, blade length 5", length 9".**
| VG | Exc | Mint |
|---|---|---|
| $100 | $150 | $225 |

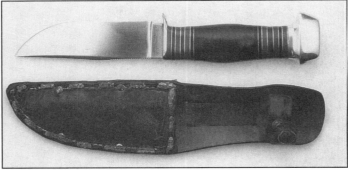

**RH33, blade length 4-1/2", length 9".**
| VG | Exc | Mint |
|---|---|---|
| $150 | $250 | $375 |

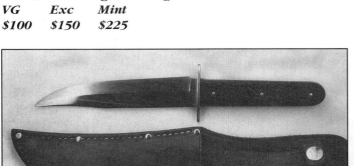

**RH30, blade length 5-3/4", length 10".**
| VG | Exc | Mint |
|---|---|---|
| $225 | $450 | $700 |

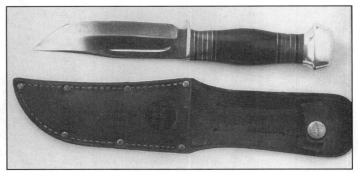

**RH34, blade length 5", length 9-3/8".**
| VG | Exc | Mint |
|---|---|---|
| $100 | $175 | $350 |

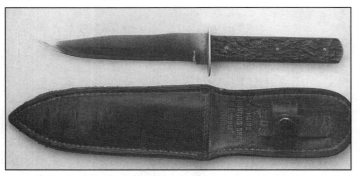

**Remington RH30, made by Dupont (Remington sold out to Dupont). This is a contract knife marked and sold by L. L. Bean, $250.**

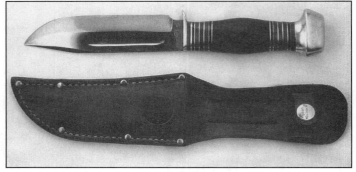

**RH35, blade length 5-1/4", length 9-3/4".**
| VG | Exc | Mint |
|---|---|---|
| $125 | $250 | $400 |

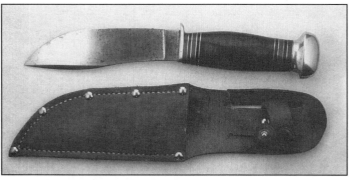

**RH32, blade length 4-1/2", length 8-1/2".**
| VG | Exc | Mint |
|---|---|---|
| $75 | $135 | $200 |

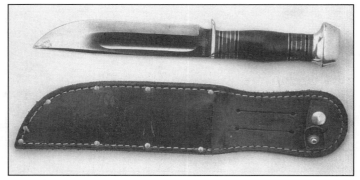

**RH36, blade length 6-1/4", length 10-1/2".**
| VG | Exc | Mint |
|---|---|---|
| $150 | $325 | $500 |

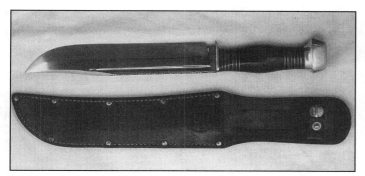

*RH38, blade length 8", length 12-1/2".*
| VG | Exc | Mint |
|---|---|---|
| $500 | $850 | $1,200 |

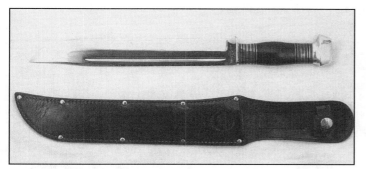

*RH40, blade length 10", length 14-1/2".*
| VG | Exc | Mint |
|---|---|---|
| $1,200 | $1,800 | $2,500 |

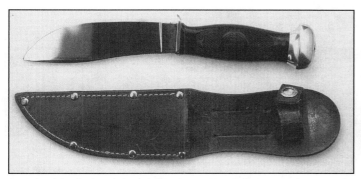

*RH42, blade length 4-1/2", length 8-1/2".*
| VG | Exc | Mint |
|---|---|---|
| $150 | $275 | $400 |

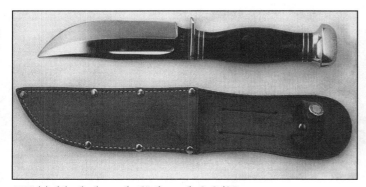

*RH44, blade length 5", length 9-3/8".*
| VG | Exc | Mint |
|---|---|---|
| $400 | $600 | $850 |

*RH45, blade length 5-1/4", length 9-3/4".*
| VG | Exc | Mint |
|---|---|---|
| $100 | $125 | $175 |

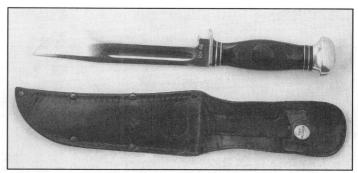

*RH 46, blade length 6-1/4", length 10-1/2".*
| VG | Exc | Mint |
|---|---|---|
| $500 | $750 | $1,000 |

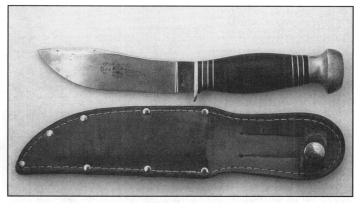

*RH50, blade length 4-1/2", length 8-1/2". Blade etched w/Boy Scout logo.*
| VG | Exc | Mint |
|---|---|---|
| $125 | $200 | $350 |

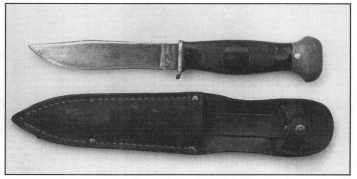

*PAL RH50, rare. This knife is just like RH28, w/black hard rubber handle, $250.*

*RH65, blade length 4-1/2", length 8".*
| VG | Exc | Mint |
|---|---|---|
| $75 | $150 | $200 |

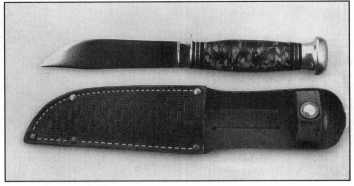

*RH74P, blade length 4", length 8".*
| VG | Exc | Mint |
|---|---|---|
| $75 | $100 | $150 |

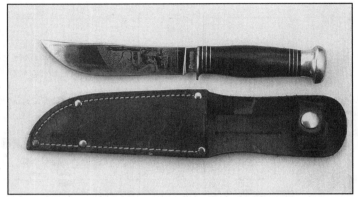

*RH71, blade length 4-1/2", length 8". Blade etched w/ deer scene.*
| VG | Exc | Mint |
|---|---|---|
| $85 | $200 | $250 |

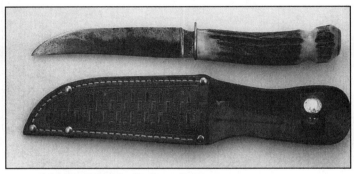

*RH75, blade length 4", length 8".*
| VG | Exc | Mint |
|---|---|---|
| $100 | $150 | $250 |

*RH84, blade length 4", length 8".*
| VG | Exc | Mint |
|---|---|---|
| $100 | $150 | $225 |

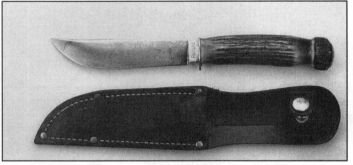

*RH73, blade length 4-1/2", length 8". Blade etched w/ deer scene.*
| VG | Exc | Mint |
|---|---|---|
| $85 | $175 | $300 |

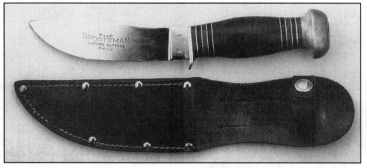

*RH92, blade length 4-1/2", length 8-1/2". Blade chrome plated & etched "The Sportsman Chrome Surface RH92."*
| VG | Exc | Mint |
|---|---|---|
| $150 | $300 | $400 |

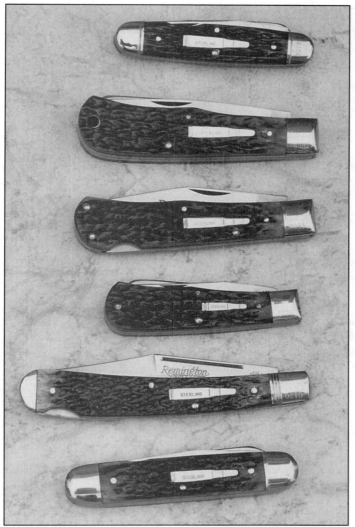

*Silver Bullets: From the top: '88, '89, '90, '91, '92 & '93. Started in 1988-only 5,000 serialized knives produced for each year. Made exclusively for Smoky Mountain. They have genuine bone handles, w/sterling-silver bullet.*

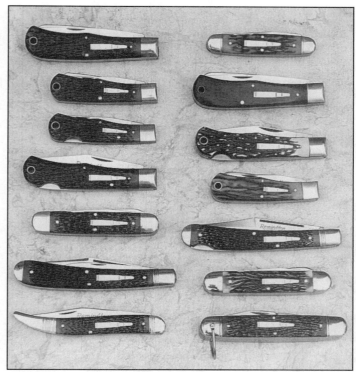

*At left, from the top, are 1982, '83, '84, '84, '85, '86 & '87. At the right, from the top, are 1988, '89, '90, '91, '92, '93 & '94. Started in 1982. All have delron handles, except '89, which is cocobolo wood.*

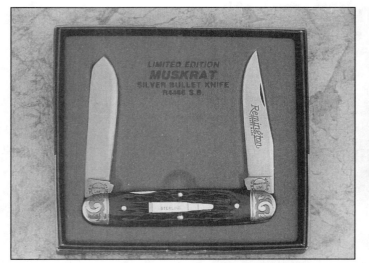

*1988 engraved silver bullet; only 500 produced. Each has bone handles, w/sterling silver bullet.*

*Rare bullet knife, 1920s-'30s vintage bone handles, blades are marked, 1123 bullet appears to be a pistol cartridge instead of the normal 30-cal. rifle cartridge. This could have been a special production for one of the pistol manufacturers? Maybe a lunchbox knife?*

# Remington Year Knives & Posters

This information courtesy of Steve Koonce, Smoky Mountain Knife Works.

## Year Knives

| | |
|---|---|
| 1982-R 1123 Trapper | $625 |
| 1983-R 1173 Baby Bullet | $275 |
| 1984-RI 173L Lockback | $175 |
| 1984-R 1303 Lockback | $225 |
| 1985-R4353 Woodsman | $225 |
| 1986-R 1263 Hunter | $275 |
| 1987-R 1613 Fisherman | $175 |
| 1988-R4466 Muskrat | $125 |
| 1989-R 1128 Trapper | $95 |
| 1990-R1306 Tracker | $45 |
| 1991-R1178 Baby Bullet | $55 |
| 1992-R 1253 Guide Lb | $55 |
| 1993-R4356 Bush Pilot | $65 |
| 1994-R4243 Camp Knife | $65 |

## Year Knife Posters

| | |
|---|---|
| 1982 Poster | $375 |
| 1983 Poster | $1,000 (very rare) |
| 1984 Poster | $250 |
| 1985 Poster | $195 |
| 1986 Poster | $125 |
| 1987 Poster | $125 |
| 1988 Poster | $55 |
| 1989 Poster | $55 |
| 1990 Poster | $30 |
| 1991 Poster | $30 |
| 1992 Poster | $25 |
| 1993 Poster | $25 |
| 1994 Poster | $25 |

## Special Editions

| | |
|---|---|
| 10th Anniv. Bullet | $250 |
| Lost Poster Knife | $250 |

## Silver Bullets

| | |
|---|---|
| R4466SB - 1988 | $225 |
| R1128SB - 1989 | $175 |
| RI306SB - 1990 | $125 |
| R1178SB - 1991 | $125 |
| R1253SB - 1992 | $100 |
| R4256SB - 1993 | $75 |

Only 5,000 made.

## Engraved Silver Bullets

| | |
|---|---|
| R4466SBE - 1988 | $275 |
| R1128SBE - 1989 | $225 |
| R1306SBE - 1990 | $175 |
| R1178SBE - 1991 | $150 |
| R 1253SBE - 1992 | $150 |
| R4256SBE - 1993 | $125 |

Only 5,000 made.